# THE CHANGING CHARACTER OF WAR

THE OXFORD LEVERHULME PROGRAMME ON THE CHANGING CHARACTER OF WAR

The Changing Character of War Programme is an inter-disciplinary research group located at the University of Oxford, and was funded by the Leverhulme Trust between 2003 and 2009.

# THE CHANGING CHARACTER OF WAR

EDITED BY HEW STRACHAN
AND SIBYLLE SCHEIPERS

OXFORD
UNIVERSITY PRESS

# OXFORD
## UNIVERSITY PRESS

Great Clarendon Street, Oxford OX2 6DP

Oxford University Press is a department of the University of Oxford.
It furthers the University's objective of excellence in research, scholarship,
and education by publishing worldwide in

Oxford New York

Auckland Cape Town Dar es Salaam Hong Kong Karachi
Kuala Lumpur Madrid Melbourne Mexico City Nairobi
New Delhi Shanghai Taipei Toronto

With offices in

Argentina Austria Brazil Chile Czech Republic France Greece
Guatemala Hungary Italy Japan Poland Portugal Singapore
South Korea Switzerland Thailand Turkey Ukraine Vietnam

Oxford is a registered trade mark of Oxford University Press
in the UK and in certain other countries

Published in the United States
by Oxford University Press Inc., New York

British Library Cataloguing in Publication Data

Data available

Library of Congress Cataloging in Publication Data

Data available

Typeset by SPI Publisher Services, Pondicherry, India
Printed in Great Britain
on acid-free paper by
MPG Books Group, Bodmin and King's Lynn

ISBN 978-0-19-959673-7

1 3 5 7 9 10 8 6 4 2

# Contents

# List of Contributors

**Tarak Barkawi**
Senior Lecturer in War Studies, Cambridge University

**Mats Berdal**
Professor of Security and Development, King's College London

**Alia Brahimi**
Global Security Research Fellow, London School of Economics and Political Science; and Senior Research Fellow, CCW Programme

**Shane Brighton**
Lecturer in International Politics, Birkbeck College, London

**Michael Broers**
Lecturer in Modern History, Fellow and Tutor at Lady Margaret Hall, Oxford University

**Gerard J. De Groot**
Professor of Modern History, University of St Andrews

**Anne Deighton**
Professor of European International Politics and Fellow of Wolfson College, Oxford University

**Antulio J. Echevarria II**
Director of Research, Strategic Studies Institute, US Army War College, Carlisle, PA

**Azar Gat**
Ezer Weitzman Chair for National Security, Tel Aviv University

**Guy S. Goodwin-Gill**
Senior Research Fellow, All Souls College, Oxford University

**Thomas Hippler**
Lecturer in Politics, University of Lyon; and Senior Research Fellow, CCW Programme

**Bruce Hoffman**
Professor in Security Studies, Georgetown University, Washington, DC

**Stathis N. Kalyvas**
Arnold Wolfers Professor of Political Science and Director of the Program on Order, Conflict, and Violence, Yale University

**Audrey Kurth Cronin**
Professor at the US Naval War College, National Defense University; and
Senior Research Fellow, CCW Programme

**Kimberly Marten**
Professor in the Department of Political Science, Barnard College, Columbia
University, New York, NY

**Patricia Owens**
Senior Lecturer in International Relations, Queen Mary, University of
London; and Senior Research Fellow, CCW Programme

**David Parrott**
Lecturer in Modern History and Fellow of New College, Oxford University

**Sarah Percy**
Lecturer in International Relations and Tutorial Fellow of Merton College,
Oxford University; and Senior Research Fellow, CCW Programme

**William Reno**
Associate Professor in Politics, Northwestern University

**Sir Adam Roberts**
Professor Emeritus in International Relations and Fellow of Balliol College,
Oxford University

**David Rodin**
Co-director, Institute for the Ethics and Law of Armed Conflict; and Senior
Research Fellow, CCW Programme

**Sibylle Scheipers**
Lecturer in International Relations, University of St Andrews; and Senior
Research Fellow, CCW Programme

**Henry Shue**
Professor Emeritus in International Relations and Fellow of Merton College,
Oxford University

**P. W. Singer**
Director of the 21st-Century Defense Initiative, Brookings Institution,
Washington, DC

**Uwe Steinhoff**
Assistant Professor in Politics, University of Hong Kong; and Senior Research
Fellow, CCW Programme

*Hew Strachan*
Chichele Professor of the History of War at the University of Oxford, Fellow of All Souls College; and Director of the Oxford University Programme on the Changing Character of War

*D. J. B. Trim*
Director of the Archives of the Seventh-day Adventist Church, Silver Spring, MD

*Gil-li Vardi*
Assistant Professor in Military History, University of Notre Dame; and Senior Research Fellow, CCW Programme

*Pascal Vennesson*
Professor in Security in Europe, European University Institute, Florence

# Introduction

## The Changing Character of War

*Hew Strachan and Sibylle Scheipers*

In 2003, the Leverhulme Trust invited universities in the United Kingdom to compete for a research grant to run a five-year programme on the Changing Character of War. Oxford won it. The primary debt owed by the editors and contributors to this volume is therefore to the Leverhulme Trustees. *The Changing Character of War* is our attempt to provide a summary of the results produced as a consequence of their generous support of the study of war in the university.

Oxford established its chair in what was then called military history, and since 1946 has been called the history of war, in 1909. A century ago, the Faculty of Modern History fulfilled some of the functions which today would be undertaken by a department of politics or—more exactly—of public policy. The first professor of military history, Spenser Wilkinson, certainly embraced contemporary strategic studies as much as history more narrowly defined and, when the First World War broke out five years later, he and other members of the Faculty produced a series of pamphlets which set out to explain the war's underlying causes to a wider public. Although the expectation that the holder of the chair span both past and present has been a persistent feature in the 100 years of its existence, the subsequent growth in the study of war across several disciplines has now made it impossible for a single academic to be master of the subject in its entirety.

Therefore, a principal attraction of the Changing Character of War project, both to Oxford and, presumably, to the Leverhulme Trust, was the opportunity which it offered of generating truly interdisciplinary study. Although in 2003 Oxford still had only one established post in the study of war, it could claim several scholars with interests in war. Five of them—Guy Goodwin-Gill, David Rodin, Sir Adam Roberts, Henry Shue, and Hew Strachan—put together the proposal which won the grant for the university. Collectively, they represented (in the order of those names) the disciplines of Law, Philosophy, Politics, and History, all of them core subjects in this volume. Over the five years of the Leverhulme funding, each discipline profited from the insights of the others, and the members of the programme found themselves moving towards a common vocabulary, progressively related less to individual disciplines and more to war itself. The programme and this book have therefore already begun to respond to the call sounded by Tarak Barkawi and Shane Brighton in the volume's final chapter. Certainly, the conclusions of the programme have proved even greater than the sum of its parts.

An important reason for this growth in understanding has been the programme's engagement with practitioners, particularly (but not exclusively) through its series of seminars on Campaigning and Generalship organized by one of its Visiting Fellows, Major-General Jonathan Bailey.[1] The fact that British forces were engaged in operations in Iraq and Afghanistan throughout the duration of the programme contributed immeasurably to the realization that the character of war is always changing, to the awareness of fresh ethical and legal pressures on war's conduct, and to the reciprocal relationship between academic and soldier.

When the Leverhulme Trust advertised the Changing Character of War competition, the context was set by the attacks on the United States of 11 September 2001. Some more hyperbolic commentators believed that so radical and so lasting were their effects that they had changed not merely the character of war but even its nature. President George W. Bush's decision to declare a global war on terrorism elevated a means of fighting into an end, and created a set of goals so broad as to suggest that this might be a struggle as persistent and protracted as the Cold War had been. By the time that the Changing Character of War conference convened at St Antony's College, Oxford, in March 2009, a sense of perspective had begun to be restored: the Obama administration was drawing back from the rhetoric of the global war on terror, and cynics were tending to argue that in the aftermath of 9/11, terrorism studies had flourished even more than terrorism itself.

This is not to say that terrorism is not a feature of war today. It is a subject that has directly engaged two members of the Changing Character of War team, Uwe Steinhoff, one of the programme's initial cohort of research associates, who has worked on the ethics of terrorism, and Audrey Kurth Cronin, the programme's director of studies between 2005 and 2008 and the author of a major study of how terrorism ends.[2] Neither of them claims that terrorism has ousted other forms of war and both are well aware that terrorism's antecedents go far back beyond 9/11. Bruce Hoffman, whose reputation as a leading student of terrorism was firmly established before 9/11, uses his chapter to trace the continuities in terrorist identities, but his stress in this volume on similarity across time does not blind him in his other writings to the immediacy or scale of the threat.[3] More explicitly, Cronin, in her chapter, points up the changes in what she calls the motivation, method, mobilization, morphology, and mindset of terrorism, and Azar Gat, in the opening chapter of the book, warns against the academic temptation to reduce the significance of terrorism by too much contextualization.

One of the reasons that the 9/11 attacks resonated so loudly within the academic study of war was that scholars before the attacks were already suggesting that new actors within war were threatening what was presumed to be the state's monopoly in the application of armed force. In 1991, Martin van Creveld argued in *On future war* (US title: *The transformation of war*) that guerrillas, bandits, and terrorists would oust traditional armed forces. Van Creveld was not best served by the timing of the book's appearance, which coincided with a classic interstate war as the armed forces of a US-led coalition waged a campaign of manoeuvre against Saddam Hussein's Iraq. For many, its quick success seemed to be a portent of the future rather than a last hurrah. Led by the United States, and in thrall to it, the armed forces of NATO and of other advanced countries throughout the 1990s followed the trajectory set in the first Gulf War. Much of the intellectual running in the study of war was shaped by operational level thinking, which built on the ideas of manoeuvre and tempo, saw new technologies as confirming the advantages which professional armed forces could bring to such forms of warfare, and developed bodies of self-sustaining thought through concepts like the 'revolution in military affairs', 'network-centric warfare', 'effects-based operations', and 'transformation'.[4] In 2003, Major-General Robert Scales, who had presided over the US Army's 'Army after next project' between 1995 and 1997, published *Yellow Smoke: The future of land warfare for America's military*. His vision of war, unlike van Creveld's, assumed that war 'cannot be divorced from political authority', and that the United States' enemies would continue to have the trappings of statehood, including control over the army and the police.

The 'manoeuvrists' understood war largely in terms of how it would be waged, but their critics—like Martin van Creveld—asked who would do the fighting. They argued that it would not be the apostles of manoeuvre, the state-controlled professional armed forces. In *New and old wars: Organized violence in the global era*, first published in 1999, Mary Kaldor focused on the rise of warlords. Her principal case studies were derived from the Balkans, rather than Africa, the focus of such thinking since decolonization in the 1960s; indeed by redirecting a phenomenon associated with the problems of emerging statehood to Europe, Kaldor was able to argue—as van Creveld had done—that it was one that was growing rather than contracting. For Kaldor, warlords needed war to sustain their income flows, their crime, and their drug-running, as well as their authority. In other words, unlike states, warlords had an interest in the perpetuation of war rather than in its termination.

The contributors to this book, particularly Mats Berdal, are uniformly sceptical about 'new wars', but the title was catchy. Kaldor's use of it was appropriated three years later by Herfried Münkler, when he described how states themselves were abdicating their monopoly of armed force through their use of mercenaries.[5] But he drew a number of crucial distinctions central to the more variegated picture painted by the Changing Character of War programme, and especially by Sarah Percy in her work on the privatization of military force.[6] First was the need for a historical context in understanding what was really new, as opposed to what seemed to be new. The debate about the relationship between mercenaries and states (both weak and strong) was addressed by Machiavelli at the beginning of the sixteenth century, is central to David Parrott's discussion of early modern warfare in this book, remained a vibrant one in Europe until the French Revolution in 1789, and even thereafter. Strategic studies had lost contact with its historical roots. Second, Münkler pointed out that strong states, which employed private military companies to fulfil some of the functions that they would previously have entrusted to their armed forces, did so out of fiscal strength rather than out of weakness. Mercenaries were only problematic for weak states which lacked the monopoly of armed force, and so—like warlords—were symptomatic of a deeper set of structural problems.

Münkler aired some uncomfortable truths, one of them being that aid provided by strong states and by non-governmental organizations to help the victims of war in broken states might actually sustain the conflict. Just as private military companies have a vested interest in the opportunities for profit which armed conflict creates for them, so insurgents and guerrillas are able to feed off the aid and supplies provided to the indigenous victims of war. Refugee camps can be the conduits through which food and medicines can be extracted, willingly or unwillingly, to reach those in the field. Wars develop their own economic lives, and in backward countries war itself can sustain economic activity. In Afghanistan in the first decade of the twenty-first century, the fragmentation of governmental authority enabled the cultivation of poppy for the heroin trade and so generated the profits to feed the war. The US-led coalition, which responded by pumping in aid for construction projects, education, and welfare, in ways and at levels which would have been unimaginable without the war, inadvertently confirmed that war can pay.

The proposition that war might have economic utility was one with which Western liberal orthodoxy has found it hard to come to terms, particularly in the aftermath of two devastating world wars. Conflict constituted disinvestment. But in early modern Europe, war was related both to state growth and, partly as a result, to the emergence of the cash economy. Soldiers were paid, and their supplies and equipment bought, with specie that the state raised through taxation. Monarchs went to war for profit, a motive which held good until the later stages of Napoleon's career; even in 1871 France paid for its defeat at the hands of Prussia with an indemnity.[7]

So unfamiliar had some of these features become to Western conceptions of war that commentators privileged them with a title that suggested both a novelty and a unity that they largely lacked. 'Asymmetric warfare' was a neologism that, although associated with non-state actors, embraced their preferred tactical responses more than it described the groups who adopted those responses. They knew that they would lose a battle against professional armed forces trained for 'manoeuvre warfare', and so they rejected such a confrontation. Instead, they employed methods of fighting that suited their own strengths, rather than those of their opponents, and these tended to be irregular and unconventional. Nothing in this was very new: it was military common sense. But it seemed new to those who assumed that the 'Western way of warfare' not only rested on battle—and particularly bloody battles at that—but was also guaranteed success because it was underpinned by demo-cratic principles.[8]

Central to all these issues were the state and its position in relation to war. Martin van Creveld and Mary Kaldor had both misread Clausewitz, in order to associate his description of war solely with the state.[9] During the Cold War, the state had indeed seemed to be supreme in its monopoly of armed force, not least because the most sophisticated weapons of the day, nuclear missiles, were in the hands solely of certain states. Indeed, they became a way of distinguish-ing those which were great powers from those which were not. The end of the Cold War, not least because it reduced the salience of nuclear deterrence, was far more important in our understanding of the relationship between war and the state than were the 9/11 attacks. It left the United States in triumphant mood, the dominant but democratic force in a unipolar world, thus fulfilling—or so it seemed—its manifest destiny.

In just over a decade, the 9/11 attacks had threatened the assumptions which underpinned this world vision, but they did so less because of the attacks themselves (which for all their awfulness were no more than pinpricks for a great power) and more because of the United States' mismanagement of its response. Unprepared for the shock of 9/11 (despite warnings which in hindsight looked clear enough),[10] it sought to provide a context for what had happened in the suggestion that the state was undergoing some form of existential crisis. Philip Bobbitt argued, in a book whose antecedents predated the 9/11 attacks, but whose publication in 2002 was neatly timed to ride on the hysteria they generated, that the nation state, which 'justified itself as an instrument to serve the welfare of the people (the nation)', was being replaced by the 'market state', which 'exists to maximize the opportunities' of its citizens. Having constructed a questionable edifice on the basis of a selective reading of the past, he then went on in a second book, published in 2008, to relate the rise of terrorism to the specific vulnerabilities of the market state.[11]

Part of the difficulty in 'lumping' events, which is what Bobbitt was doing, is that in pursuing general trends, which by definition can only be evident in hindsight, it fails to allow for contingency or exception. Categorization rides roughshod over difference. The US administration, in identifying 'failed' or 'rogue' states as the principal threats to its security, similarly raised existential questions about the state and its future. The proliferation of states, with almost 200 in the world by the end of the millennium, and with many formed on the basis of neither military strength nor military action, certainly helped more 'weak' states survive. Moreover, the end of the Cold War loosened the pressures that had subsumed them within alliance blocs. But before 1789, the geographical space that is now Germany embraced even more petty states, and the correlation of such weakness with a threat to the international order was no more invariably true then than it is now. This is not to say that the circumstances were and are the same; by the late eighteenth century, nationalism was a driver for the aggregation of states, not least in Germany and Italy, whereas by the early twenty-first century it was more likely to be a source of division and separation. The assumption was that globalization, particularly through the Internet and new forms of real-time communication, was destroying state frontiers and with them national identities. And yet there was something deeply paradoxical in all this. Ethnicity, among Czechs as distinct from Slovaks, Slovenes as distinct from Croats, and even Scots as distinct from English, provided greater national cohesion, so much so that it possessed the potential to create new state entities. The state still remained—provided it was not among the minority of states that had failed to establish a monopoly of armed force—the principal repository of military power.

The sense of crisis had been deepened by the self-serving reading of Clausewitz which identified war solely with the state and saw war exclusively as an instrument of state policy. That was not how Clausewitz defined war; rather, it was how Clausewitz defined war's utility. War itself, he roundly declared at the very beginning of *On war,* is 'a clash of wills'.

This issue—the question of what is war and what is not war—had to be the departure point for the Changing Character of War programme. We could hardly answer the question which we were being asked from the very outset of the programme's existence—is the character of war changing? Or, more precisely, in what ways is the character of war changing?—if we were not sure what war is.

So, the seminar series at the beginning of the calendar year 2004, the first term of the programme's existence, was designed to address the big question of what is war, the better to be able to address the principal, but necessarily second-order, issues. After a series of talks by subject specialists both in areas where the programme lacked research expertise as well as areas in which it possessed it, we agreed on five criteria. First, war involves the use of force, although there can be a state of war in which active hostilities are suspended, and some would argue that the threat of the use of war (as in the Cold War) constitutes war. Fighting is what defines war, a point made by Clausewitz, and echoed in this book by Barkawi and Brighton. Second, war rests on contention.

If one party attacks another, the other must respond for war to occur, or else what will follow will be murder, massacre, or occupation. This reaction means that possibly the most important feature of war is reciprocity: part of the problem with much operational thought in the 1990s was that it had forgotten that the enemy has a vote and that his responses might be 'asymmetrical' or even unpredictable. Third, war assumes a degree of intensity and duration to the fighting: scale matters, and skirmishes and border clashes are not necessarily war. Fourth, those who fight do not do so in a private capacity, and fifth, and consequently, war is fought for some aim beyond fighting itself. Both the last two criteria tend normatively to be associated with states and their policies, but they do not have to be defined in these ways, and wars have been pursued—for example, by Germany and Japan in 1945—beyond the point at which they seem able to deliver worthwhile results.[12]

Having established a degree of consensus, the programme's next task was to identify what within this framework was changing. The historians argued that we could not identify change if we did not have the historical awareness which enabled us to recognize continuity. This is not to say that the historians' role is to stress the lack of change: that would be to misunderstand the real challenges for the historical profession and to condone much that is lazy in strategic thought. If we seek 'lessons from history' and jump from the appearance of continuity to conclude that at bottom nothing changes, we fail to tackle the really difficult task which confronts the student of the past. As the great French medieval economic historian, Marc Bloch, wrote, reflecting on his experience of the two world wars:

> History is, in its essentials, the science of change. It knows and it teaches that it is impossible to find two events that are ever exactly alike, because the conditions from which they spring are never identical. I do not mean to deny that it recognizes certain elements in the evolution of mankind which, though not permanent, are extremely long-lived. But even while it lays this down, it has to admit that the possible number of their combinations is almost infinite. It realizes, properly enough, that successive civilizations show repetitive patterns, and that these resemble one another in their general lines, if not in their details, when the conditions determining them may be said to have a family likeness. It can even try to see into the future, and not always, I think, unsuccessfully. But the lesson it teaches is not that what happened yesterday will necessarily happen to-morrow, or that the past will go on reproducing itself. By examining how and why yesterday differed from the day before, it can reach conclusions which will enable it to foresee how to-morrow will differ from yesterday.[13]

The historians in the programme agreed that the state's role in relation to war was changing but attributed that in part to the fact that states increasingly define themselves in national terms rather than in state terms, while at the same time using multinational institutions—pre-eminently the United

Nations and NATO—to legitimate their actions.[14] The historians therefore tended to interpret war as a collective act engaged in by communities often defined not only in political terms but also in national or ethnic ones.

The philosophers, on the other hand, stressed that a big change had been in the individualization of war. In the just-war tradition, soldiers kill their enemies as part of a collective identity, but in wars governed by international humanitarian law, killing is justified on the basis of a moral responsibility to act against behaviour which defies the norms of humanitarianism. These are the sorts of dilemmas which lie at the heart of David Rodin's chapter. The current convention is that killing carried out by soldiers within a war waged according to the norms of just-war theory is morally justified even if the decision to go to war in the first place is unjust. But can it be? If the war is unjust in the first place, how can those called up to fight it be acting in ethically acceptable ways, even if they respect non-combatant immunity, take prisoners, and so on? And in that case what is the relationship between individual morality, and individual responsibility, and collective action? Al-Qaeda holds the peoples of democratic states responsible for the actions done by their governments in their names. Thomas Hippler's chapter on Giulio Douhet's early thinking on air power shows that a similar logic underpinned the rationales for strategic bombing: that terror attacks on cities would turn a people against its own state in order to terminate the war. Inherent in all this is an idea central to the thought of Carl Schmitt, and explored by Patricia Owens, that man's fundamental identity is political, and that all war is therefore potentially 'existential'. If the law is less an overarching set of absolute and internationally accepted norms than a tool of states which themselves have political goals, then law is simply a creature of the state's interest. Henry Shue's discussion of the United States' readiness to define torture in terms which suit its needs rather than conform to international agreements provides a precise illustration of this point. But in the United Kingdom, and especially as a result of the European Convention of Human Rights, civilian courts have increasingly opted to intervene on behalf of individuals in war-related issues, and so found themselves at odds with the state rather than its servant.

This interaction between the public sphere of war and the private sphere of moral responsibility, and the consequent dialogue between ethics, political philosophy, and law, has proved particularly fruitful for the Changing Character of War programme. After 9/11, moral issues which were deemed to be closed, of which the prohibition on the use of torture was one, were both reopened and specifically challenged by state behaviour. The clear definition of non-combatant status was already a problem for 'total war' in the early twentieth century. Why should a civilian worker in an armaments factory be exempt from aerial attack? But, if he or she was a legitimate target, should not the farmer producing the food which sustained the soldier in battle or the industrial worker in the factory also be treated as a *de facto* combatant? This sort of thinking culminated in 1945 in the attacks on Hiroshima and Nagasaki, seen by G.J. De Groot in his chapter as 'a climactic assertion of the right of a nation to slaughter civilians for purposes of national security'. As Guy Goodwin-Gill argues, the employment of child soldiers, particularly in sub-Saharan Africa—at once both combatants of war and victims of war—foreshadowed some of the problems which have multiplied since 9/11, even if their origins precede it.[15] The suicide bomber who is coerced to attack, or who for other reasons such as age could be exempt from responsibility for his or her actions, shows the fuzziness of the combatant/non-combatant distinction in practice. Certainly, the association of civilian status with the status of non-combatant has proved hard to maintain.

An assumption underpinning the security debate at the turn of the twentieth and twenty-first centuries was that these were both new developments and ones which were somehow worsening: that the world was becoming less secure, not more so. Somehow, the period before 1990 or even 1945 became recast as an era of stable international order, despite two devastating world wars and their attendant horrors. This sort of thinking declared it as axiomatic that at the start of the twentieth century most of those killed in war were soldiers but that at its end 90 per cent were civilians. The fallacy in this generalization, addressed in part in this book by Adam Roberts, rests not just on its identification of civilians with non-combatants; it is also statistically, historically, and culturally ignorant. We have no secure grasp on the numbers of civilians killed in earlier wars, including the First World War. Should such figures include those who died of disease which may have been promoted by war (but there again may not have been)? How should wars outside Europe be treated, particularly those of colonization and decolonization, where warriors were not necessarily able to conform to the definitions of belligerent status propagated by the Geneva conventions, where few were counting the dead, and where economic warfare, for example the destruction of crops and villages, may have resulted in indirect casualties, for example through starvation? And, even if it is still true that more civilians than soldiers die in wars waged today, that does not contradict the point made by Pascal Vennesson's chapter, that wars are fewer and that losses of life in battle are declining. Paradoxically, the proportionate increase in the number of those civilians who died in wars at the end of the twentieth century, if true, may be no more than a reflection on the dramatic decline in overall numbers of war-related deaths.

After the 9/11 attacks, both the United States and the United Kingdom abandoned any norms against preventive war. They conflated the notion of pre-emption, the attack of an opponent whose intention himself to attack is manifest, with the notion of prevention, the attack of a potential enemy who might threaten an attack at some stage in the future.[16] Attacks at a distance, both in geographical space and also in time (in other words, before the threat could be construed as imminent), fostered the idea that such wars were not mandatory but 'discretionary'. Again Western liberal orthodoxy, conditioned to see war as at best an awful necessity, struggled to make sense of so-called 'wars of choice'. Leaders, including President Obama and the British Prime Minister Gordon Brown, who by 2009 argued that the war in Afghanistan was not 'discretionary' but 'necessary', principally in order to forestall terrorist attacks on their own homelands, struggled to persuade their own populations that such was the case.

Public opinion, certainly in European states after the end of the Cold War, seems to believe that interstate war has declined since 1945 and that civil war is increasing. This shows the force of both long- and short-term memories. The shadow of the Second World War, reinforced by the threat of all-out nuclear war in the Cold War, kept alive the belief that true interstate war could only be major war; in reality, interstate war has occurred at about the same frequency ever since 1945, with the exception of the years 1990–2.[17] On the other hand, the incidence of civil war is now declining from a peak, which Stathis Kalyvas in his chapter in this book links to the problems of state formation specifically associated with colonial withdrawal. But these beliefs, that international war is obsolescent and civil war ascendant, affect perceptions of what war is. The first sees war as the final sanction which maintains international order; in this framework, war retains utility. The second suggests the idea of war as chaos: civil war is deemed to be profoundly destructive and unproductive, its role in the formation of strong states, including both the United Kingdom and the United States, strangely forgotten.

The conceptual force of major interstate war and yet its relative absence help explain the attraction to military doctrine writers (not least within NATO) of the idea of a 'spectrum of conflict', where the use of armed force occurs at many points, most of them not involving any formal declaration of war by states. But the 'spectrum of conflict' erodes any clear demarcation between war and peace. Today's ideas of peace are very ambitious, encompassing more than the absence of war, and including the provision of justice and good government, as well as human security more broadly defined. As a result conflict is seen as both pervasive and persistent. Peacekeeping operations in the 1990s, which developed into peace enforcement, and then into counterinsurgency, suggested that both peace, at one end of the spectrum, and general war, at the other, belonged on a continuum.

Those working in the Changing Character of War programme recognized the force of all these ideas—not only the continuity within the spectrum from peace to war but also the fusion of the public and the private in war and the erosion of the distinction between collective action and individual responsibility. But we also realized that their combined effect was to create uncertainty about how to define war below the level of major international war, a phenomenon which today is indeed fortunately so rare that it does not provide an effective method of measurement or of understanding for most Western audiences.

Whatever our disciplinary background, we agreed that change and newness are not the same, and that change can be a reversal back to something which has existed before. We were therefore persuaded of the force of Clausewitz's distinction between the nature of war, which has an essential continuity, even integrity, and the character of individual wars, which vary. History therefore can do more than simply provide background knowledge; it can be a route into understanding these themes. This is not to claim that history, any more than any of the other core disciplines which the programme has embraced, is capable of providing universal explanations of what war is or is not. The programme does not claim to have developed a comprehensive way of looking at war; instead, it has used different disciplines and varying examples to generate sufficient insights which have then coalesced to produce themes and patterns.

Undoubtedly, there are more—both more insights to corroborate our arguments and more patterns which have escaped us entirely. Those working within the Changing Character of War programme, although a reasonably large group by the standards of Oxford research in the Humanities and Social Sciences, and by comparison with most units studying war in the United Kingdom today, have been as conscious of the programme's disciplinary weaknesses as its strengths. Geographically, it has failed to escape as much as it would have liked the conceptions of the West, both of the United States and of Europe. Too much of the study of war is shaped by America's preoccupations; the programme has consciously tried to provide a European balance, but it has failed to do justice to Africa and probably to Asia. Secondly, in seeing change as precipitated overwhelmingly by social and political influences, it has neglected the role of science and technology. Its approach has the virtue (if it is that) of being fashionable: technological supremacy, as manifested in the military power of the United States, was thwarted in Iraq and Afghanistan. But it may also be selective. The conceptual dominance of nuclear weapons in the Cold War, the function of qualitative superiority in conventional warfare in Operation Desert Storm in 1991, and the role of air power in the Kosovo campaign in 1999, all suggest that in downplaying technology the Changing Character of War programme too may be privileging current conflicts as much as did the technological determinism of much military thought in the 1990s.

If that is the case, it has been in good company. The continuing force of Carl von Clausewitz's *On war* derives in large part from the very fact that his understanding of war rests to a remarkably limited extent on the impact of new technologies. His brief history of war, in book VIII, Chapter 3, privileges political change in explaining changes in war's character; in his own lifetime, the French Revolution had so mobilized the resources of the state through its identification with the nation that war had approached a state of wholeness or entirety, which he dubbed 'absolute war'. For him the biggest likely change to war was the impact of a true 'people in arms'. What he did not envisage was that air power would take war into a third dimension, or that the capacity for intelligence collection (if not analysis) would be transformed through electronics.

Because Clausewitz was not sure that all wars in the future would conform to the pattern of the Napoleonic wars, just as wars in the past had not, he used paradox to probe for truth. His book uses dialectics to reveal war's nature more than it uses unequivocal assertion. That too has been the approach of the Changing Character of War programme. Perhaps it suits our academic natures, just as it revealed the tension in Clausewitz between the man of action, the soldier and aspirant field commander, and the reflective product of the Enlightenment. This introduction has already raised some of the debates that have been important in deepening our understanding: that between war and peace, and the problem of defining the latter as well as the former, and particularly whether it includes the mandatory provision of certain irreducible human rights; that between the state and non-state actors, who are in fact not opposites, not least because many non-state actors aspire to statehood and few seem hell-bent on destroying the idea of the state in general as opposed to certain states. There are others, most of them also expressed most dramatically in terms of apparent contradictions and all of them revolving specifically around the state.

The state occupies a specific geographical space; it has a local and regional identity. And yet it interacts internationally. This seems to suggest that a civil war is geographically contained, whereas an interstate war is by definition fought across a state's frontiers. In practice, however, the distinction between civil war and interstate war is not so neat. The wars in Iraq and—even more—in Afghanistan were civil wars between competing factions determined to impose their own systems of governance in their own territories. But they were not just that; they had international repercussions, and they also acquired some of the trappings of interstate war, especially given the intervention in both countries by neighbours from beyond their frontiers and ready to use armed force—from Iran in Iraq's case and from Pakistan in Afghanistan's.

The difficulty of sustaining the distinction between combatants and civilians has already been alluded to, and yet that problem should not surprise us as both derive their identities in most international law from the state. The clearest legitimate combatant is the uniformed soldier of the army of a state. Similarly, civilians are citizens of states, and if they aspire to non-belligerent status do so in part because of their functions within the state, of which they are members and from which they derive certain benefits and obligations in exchange for their civic rights. If we follow Martin van Creveld or Mary Kaldor in doubting the state and its definition, then we may also not be able to define who is a civilian, and we may also struggle to create any presumption of innocence in any group. This is the problem we already confront with child soldiers or suicide bombers.

Whether the actions of the last two groups are legitimate or illegitimate depends not only on a set of presumptions derived from the *ius in bello* tradition, from what is acceptable within the conduct of war, but also from that of *ius ad bellum*, from the justice of the cause in whose name the war is fought. If the child soldier fights for reasons that are legitimate, for example as part of a force resisting occupation by an invading army, then he or she does so under right authority. Some would therefore reverse the line of argument adopted by David Rodin, and argue, exactly as Alia Brahimi shows that they do argue, that the illegitimate use of child soldiers or suicide bombers is in fact offset by the legitimacy of the cause for which they are fighting, and that *ius ad bellum* both feeds into and in this case trumps *ius in bello*.

These are understandably live issues on Jihadi websites, as they were in the Second World War among peoples resisting German occupation—even after their states had surrendered and so in terms of international law had ended the war between themselves and Germany. The dichotomy here is that between accountability and empowerment. Public expectations in regard to the decision to go to war and to the manner of its conduct, voiced through the 'traditional' media, such as opinion polls, the press and broadcasting, and the new media of websites, blogs, and mobile telephones, hold governments and their armed forces to account. So too do courts, domestic and international. Governments, on the other hand, empower their armed forces to use violence and to do so in ways that can be at odds with the norms of peacetime democracies. Al-Qaeda goes further: it holds the people of a democracy to account for the actions carried out in its name by the government which it has elected. In other words, on this reading, the democratic process means that the electorate not only holds its government to account but also empowers it.

Therefore, the essence of a dialectical approach to the study of war may reside less in the pairing of dichotomies and more in their fusion. For Clausewitz, this was part of the interplay between theory and reality; the former sets up alternative propositions, but the latter shows how much they react off each other in practice. Thus, the truism, that reciprocity lies at the heart of war, reasserts itself. For many in the programme, the alternatives posited above are better seen as end points in a continuum, just as they are in the spectrum of conflict.

The challenge that these insights threw up for the programme was how to produce an organization both for its summation conference and for this resulting book which would get to their heart while keeping the papers and chapters to the themes which best reflected the disciplinary expertise of their authors. We resolved this by dividing our work according to five major subject areas:

1. The need for a historical perspective: what has changed?
2. The purpose of war: why go to war?
3. The changing identities of combatants: who fights?
4. The changing identities of non-combatants;
5. The ideas which enable us to understand war.

The discussion that resulted and the chapters in this book produced yet another way—indeed a third way—of conceptualizing the relationship between change and continuity, reflecting the fact that they can often pull in different directions at the same time. It is therefore useful to distinguish between three aspects of change and continuity: their empirical manifestations (what has changed and in what form that change occurred), their conceptual 'fabrications' (how our conceptual approaches to and narratives about war impact on our perceptions of change and continuity), and, lastly, their political implications (how political power and interest influence and are influenced by perceptions of change and continuity in the practice of war).


## THE EMPIRICAL MANIFESTATIONS OF CHANGE AND CONTINUITY

A number of chapters in this book come to the conclusion that the practice of war has changed over the past 500 years. The most striking factual changes in this respect are, first, the unlocking of the close relationship between war and the state and, second, the unlocking of the relationship between war and the nation. However, this change is not to be misunderstood as a sudden dissolution of the 'normal' trinity consisting of war, the state, and the nation, and the dawn of a new, less orderly, and more chaotic era of war. Rather, the interlocking of war and the state was, according to David Parrott, an exceptional case in the history of war that prevailed only for the rather short period from 1750 to 1950. Similarly, the nationalization of war started only with the French Revolutionary and Napoleonic Wars (1792–1815), as Michael Broers reminds us, and, according to Pascal Vennesson, it is currently declining: today's wars are being largely fought 'without the people'.

Importantly, this tendency affects not only conventional interstate war but also intrastate war. It does not result in a replacement of the former with the latter, as many scholars assume. Rather, as Stathis Kalyvas shows, just like interstate war, civil war was, for a certain period of time, characterized by a coincidence of nationalist ideologies (mixed together with Marxist ideas), large-scale mobilization of the population, and the aim to build state(-like) institutions in those areas that were controlled by the insurgents, if only to be able to make effective use of the available resources. Whereas earlier forms of guerrilla warfare within Europe were often motivated by resistance to the nationalization of war (e.g. the French war in the Vendée 1793–6), the insurgencies that accompanied the wave of decolonization after the Second World War often drew upon nationalist ideologies. After the Cold War, however, as Kalyvas notes, the connection between war, nation, and state dissolved with respect to civil wars too: today's civil wars tend to mobilize along the lines of either local or transnational identities. Moreover, they are either too peripheral to pose a serious threat to the state or they engage in terrorist tactics for which state-building activities comparable with those of the nationalist–Marxist insurgencies are not necessary.

As Kimberly Marten argues, today's warlords—unlike those of early modern Europe, who were central actors in the state-building process[18]—are unlikely to engage in state-building activities. Paradoxically, this is mainly a result of the success of the state system: warlords are unlikely to acquire a sufficiently large chunk of territory to be able to turn it into a state of its own. Therefore, it is more profitable for them to continue operating on the margins of one or several states than to create a viable, law-governed polity. This observation should caution us against drawing too dramatic conclusions regarding the dissolution of the trinity of war, the state, and the nation: the unlocking of this close connection does not mean, as many globalization theorists argue, that the state as such becomes decentralized and powerless.

If the change that we are observing is to a certain extent one of retrogression rather than of progress, the interlocking of war, the state, and the nation is an historical anomaly. Instead, we are currently revolving into a phase in which this trinity can no longer be taken for granted as a factual entity, although it retains its analytical value. Closely related to the dissolution of the connection between war and the state is a development in the normative realm, which Stephen Neff has called the rebirth of just-war thinking in the twentieth century.[19] The notion of war as an essential tool of statecraft slowly disappeared after the end of the First World War and with the foundation of the League of Nations. Peace was seen as the norm in international relations. After the Second World War, this tendency was strengthened, as the Charter of the United Nations contained an explicit ban on the aggressive use of force and spelled out in detail the very narrow conditions under which force could be used. Not only did this development help to loosen the connection between war and the state at a normative level, it also had the very practical effect that states came together in multilateral security institutions with the purpose of defending themselves collectively against potential aggressors. However, as Anne Deighton argues in her chapter, these multilateral security institutions did not simply replace the state as a strategic actor. Rather, from the very beginning they suffered from the paradox that they were based on the pro-scription of the aggressive use of force, while at the same time being charged with stopping aggressors, if necessary with military means. This ambivalence about the use of force has always been a characteristic feature of multilateral security institutions, and is likely to account at least in part for their shortfalls.

However, change in the practice of war can also take the form of a pendulum swinging back and forth. This holds in particular in those areas where there is a close connection between certain norms and the conduct of war. One such area is humanitarian intervention. Contrary to the widely held belief that humanitarian intervention is a phenomenon of the post-Cold War era, David Trim shows in his chapter that the use of force on humanitarian grounds has been practised throughout the past 450 years, although not in a consistent way. Rather, the pendulum has swung back and forth between, on the one hand, humanitarian concerns and a greater flexibility in the use of force, and on the other the absolute view of sovereignty and its corollary, non-intervention. In a similar vein, Sibylle Scheipers argues in her chapter that the legal regime governing the treatment of prisoners of war and detainees has oscillated between two paradigms: decisions on protections for captured individuals were either made along the lines of the distinction between regular and irregular fighters, or they depended on the captor's assessment of the legitimacy of the cause for which the captives had fought.[20]

Whether change occurs in the form of a pendulum swinging back and forth or as the dissolution of an historical anomaly, it seems to happen more slowly and incrementally than many scholars assume. Although the end of the Cold War had a deep and lasting impact on the structure of the international system, it did not lead to a sudden paradigm shift in the practice of war. As Mats Berdal argues in his chapter, many of the so-called 'new wars' have strong roots in the Cold War period and the era of colonialism. This applies both to their causes and to the weapons with which they are fought. The technologies of war have in fact changed less dramatically and rapidly than the rhetoric associated with them suggests. In part, this is no more than the reflection of the life cycle of many big-item weapons' systems, including aircraft, warships, tanks, and missiles. The period from research and development, through procurement to deployment and eventual obsolescence, can span half a century. In part, it reflects the fact that certain weapons, including infantry small arms and manned aircraft, have reached a level of perfection which amounts to a steady state, where improvements modify rather than overthrow tactical practice. In this sense, 'the shadow of the past' works as a stabilizer and provides for a certain degree of continuity.

The 'shadow of the past' also plays a role in recent and/or ongoing wars in sub-Saharan Africa. They are frequently subsumed under the category of the so-called 'new wars' that are allegedly no longer fought for political ideas or interests but for identities.[21] Yet, according to Will Reno, the pre-conflict political conditions have a decisive impact on the way in which these wars are fought: 'connected violence' is committed by actors who had privileged access to resources in the pre-war political system. These actors are relatively detached from popular support, and as a result more likely to direct violence against the civilian population. In contrast, 'marginalized violence' is characteristic for actors who held less privileged positions in the pre-war political system. They tend to discriminate more in their use of violence, as they depend to a greater extent on the support of the local population. In such cases, there is a great deal of continuity between the pre-conflict political system and the conduct of war. As a consequence, these wars appear to be deeply political although in a different way from the means–ends relationship that we usually assume operates between war and politics.

In a more general sense, norms and discourses often function as stabilizers in the practice of war. They do not inhibit change and they can themselves become subject to change, but they slow down the processes of transformation and make them more incremental. Alia Brahimi provides good examples for this mechanism in her chapter on religion and war. According to her, just-war arguments and religious claims turned out to be a double-edged sword for both Al-Qaeda and the Bush administration. On the one hand, both drew upon the just-war discourse in order to justify their actions; on the other, by entering into that normative and religious discourse, they made themselves vulnerable to the charge that they used those norms in an incorrect and dishonest way. This shows that norms and normative discourses have a life of their own. While they are liable to adaptation and even reinterpretation, they are also to a certain extent sticky and inert and cannot be manipulated at will.

This is not to say that norms and discourses cannot change, or cannot themselves be a driver for change in the practice of war. On the contrary, as Henry Shue shows, even legalized norms such as the definition of legitimate targets in war or the definition of torture are open to reinterpretation, in particular if a powerful actor such as the United States is pushing for such change. Yet, even a superpower's attempts at driving normative change do not go unchallenged as the current debate about torture shows. The instances of normative change discussed in this book thus indicate that norms and discourses can change. However, such transformations will happen slowly and will be accompanied by fierce battles over the definitional power and ownership of these norms.

## CONCEPTUAL 'FABRICATIONS' OF CHANGE AND CONTINUITY

Much recent scholarship on war has been characterized not only by assertions of change but also of unprecedented 'newness'. Indeed, the explanatory lure of the 'new' is evident in this book: the 'military revolution' of the seventeenth century is cited by Sarah Percy, Tarak Barkawi, and Shane Brighton, all historically aware students of politics, but is now deeply contested by early modern historians, and explicitly discounted by David Parrott. According to Mats Berdal, this assumption of change is often precisely due to a *lack of historical contextualization*. The 'new wars' thesis, in particular, is oblivious to history in that it is based on a stark dichotomy between 'new wars' and 'old wars', with the latter category comprising the ideal typical conventional interstate war fought by states and their regular armies for political aims. Yet, on closer inspection these supposedly 'old' wars are rather new when viewed against the whole history of warfare. This goes back to David Parrott's point about the interlocking of the state and war that happened only about 1750. Moreover, even the period between 1750 and 1950 was by no means exclusively characterized by 'old wars'. First, the 'states make war and war makes states' model only dominated within Europe, whereas war in the colonies or, rather, the European conquest of the colonies took different forms. Second, even within Europe, conventional interstate war did not completely prevail. On the contrary, as Stathis Kalyvas reminds us, the nationalization of war that shortly succeeded the interlocking between war and the state often triggered the emergence of guerrilla movements. And while interstate wars were in fact often fought by regular state armies, the subsequent occupations were likely to meet with resistance from irregular fighters.

In short, the perception of newness is often not so much a matter of empirical change but of our conceptual perspective on war. In particular, much depends on our treatment of history: if the past serves as a mere smokescreen for ideal typical forms of war, whereas today's wars present themselves in a disturbing variety of forms and practices, the chances are that we perceive the present as an era of unprecedented and chaotic newness. In fact, the juxtaposition of 'old' and 'new wars' is the latest example of the tendency in international relations to think in terms of hierarchical dichotomies. As Richard Ashley observed, international relations theory often builds upon conceptual opposites in which one of the concepts serves as the regulative norm and the other as the chaotic and threatening deviation from that norm. Thinking of international relations in terms of dichotomies provides for order and thus 'opposes the realm of reasoned understanding against a realm of anarchical, threatening Otherness'.[22] One could easily substitute Ashley's classical example of domestic sovereignty and international anarchy with the dichotomy between old and new wars. This creates practical problems, however, since the hierarchical dichotomy suggests that the 'new wars' are more chaotic, less restrained, and more ferocious than the ideal type of 'old wars'. Indeed, as Adam Roberts notes, the 'new wars' discourse was partly based upon, and partly fed back into, the myth of a dramatic increase in civilian casualties in post-Cold War armed conflict. In the same vein, Pascal Vennesson's argument that contemporary wars are fought 'without the people' rather than 'amongst the people'[23] suggests that they are actually more restrained than the 'new wars' thesis would suggest.

A slightly different narrative of change is embodied in the idea of *techno-logical progress*, embodied in such conceptions as the 'revolution in military affairs'.[24] While the 'new wars' thesis suggests that change takes place in the form of a dramatic historical rupture, predictions of change that are based on technological transformations are more likely to suggest steady progress culminating in occasional breakthroughs. At first glance, it seems plausible to assume that technological innovations will have an impact on warfare, and, in fact, there are historical examples for such a pattern. For instance, the invention of aviation had a lasting effect on warfare in that it added a third dimension to the battlefield. Strategic thinkers and practitioners clearly per-ceived the ramifications of this innovation, as Thomas Hippler shows in his chapter on the Italian air power strategist Giulio Douhet. While Douhet at first thought that the appearance of aircraft on the battlefield—and, more impor-tantly, behind the frontlines—would render war too costly and therefore almost obsolete, he later came to embrace the idea of strategic bombing. So Douhet, having initially envisaged that air power would effect a much more complete rupture with the past, then incorporated air power's revolutionary effects within an existing framework. After all, the concept of seeking a strategic effect on the opponent's population was not entirely new. It had its roots in both maritime blockade and siege warfare.

Several chapters in this volume confirm this tendency of strategic thinkers and strategy makers to integrate new technologies into established concepts. Gil-li Vardi shows how the German armed forces simply assimilated the technological innovations presented by the mechanization of warfare in the interwar period into their existing operational concepts. As a result, German operational planning in the Second World War was akin to the 'Schlieffen plan on wheels'. In a similar vein, Henry Shue points out that the promise of greater accuracy engendered by precision-guided munitions over the past few decades paradoxically coincided with efforts of the technologically most advanced state, the United States, to broaden the definition of legitimate targets. Peter Singer highlights the potential challenges to war-fighting norms contained in the advent of robotics to the battlefield, and their corollary—the distancing or even removal of the human from the battlefield. The earlier examples of apparently dramatic technological innovation suggest that, while their impact on the practice of war is real, the conceptual level of norms and operational cultures takes precedence over the enabling potential of technology.

However, conceptual narratives are not only suggestive of change and unprecedented newness. Equally, they can turn out to be a trick of the eye that privileges continuity over change. In particular, this applies to the con-cepts of strategic and military culture. As Antulio Echevarria writes in his chapter, 'studies of strategic culture tend to suppress change in favour of continuity; tensions and uncertainties are muted.' In this perspective, strategic behaviour is not so much guided by changing security environments and threats but by enduring cultural features within the military (military culture) or in the security institutions of a state (strategic culture). States and their armed forces thus tend to engage in strategic and operational actions that are largely prescribed by their cultures, in spite of the fact that the threats they face are likely to vary.[25] Theoretical approaches focusing on culture tend to be trapped in some form of conceptual structuralism, in which culture only makes sense if one assumes that inertia and a certain degree of permanence are its main features. Otherwise, 'culture' would disintegrate into the volatile surface of mere 'behaviour'. According to Echevarria, the first step in overcoming this rigid structuralism consists in questioning the assumption of strategic culture as a singular, consistent, and uncontested entity, and in allowing conceptually for a plurality of ways of war. At the same time, plurality means contestation among the proponents of the different ways of war, which in turn enables us to understand strategic culture not as static but as constantly evolving. In this way, strategic culture will no longer allow us to predict the future, but it will become a strong hermeneutical tool to understand both continuity and change in the past and the present practice of war.

## POLITICAL IMPLICATIONS OF CHANGE AND CONTINUITY

As mentioned above, the perception of unprecedented newness is often caused by a lack of historical contextualization. But political concerns can be a powerful motivation privileging the perception of change over that of continuity. Patricia Owens argues in her chapter that one of the Bush administration's most authoritative arguments for undermining the established legal framework of warfare and for strengthening the power of the executive was the recurrent narrative of the 'war on terror' as an entirely new kind of conflict. Although the 'new wars' thesis and the political discourse of 'jihadist' terrorism as an entirely new threat are different in terms of their substantial propositions, they share the assumption of change as a historical rupture from an era of order to a period of chaos and unprecedented newness. Hence, such narratives of factual change possess the potential to produce very real political change, a point reflected in Hew Strachan's chapter, that it is policy above all which presents strategy with the real threat of discontinuity.

But there is more to this narrative of 'jihadist' terrorism as the most important new threat. It is striking that the two chapters on terrorism in this book give differing assessments of change and continuity, depending on which aspects are explored. While Audrey Kurth Cronin writes about global terrorism from the strategic perspective and concludes that the potential for terrorist actors to acquire weapons of mass destruction requires qualitatively new strategic answers, Bruce Hoffman stresses the demographic continuities of terrorism and insurgency. However, both aspects have been neglected in framing the politics of counterterrorism. Policymakers have not come up with a viable strategic answer to the novel threat posed by weapons of mass destruction in the hands of terrorists, nor have they geared counterterrorism measures towards the continuing mechanisms of recruitment. Instead, it seems, they have been trapped in the narrative of 'jihadist' terrorism, a narrative that by its very characteristic of unprecedented and chaotic newness makes it very difficult to find viable political and strategic answers to the phenomenon.

The tone of this volume is critical and corrective, rather than sensationalist and assertive. At that level, it is pragmatic rather than fanciful. It is also more optimistic than pessimistic, as the chapters of, among others, Stathis Kalyvas, Pascal Vennesson, Adam Roberts, and Guy Goodwin-Gill suggest. The story is more one of war's containment than expansion. That is not a position which a collaborative volume could have easily embraced in 1945, and it may say more about our own position in time rather than about the future. This volume reflects the present refracted through the prism of the past, more than it attempts to predict. Its own vulnerability to dramatic change is precisely why it uses a broad range of perspectives, not only of discipline and methodology but also of nationality and region, to give its conclusions greater robustness. We believe that such an approach will give its contents more endurance than many less considered but exaggerated analyses. Nonetheless, in the nature of things (and of war), this book can only ever be a form of stocktaking, an interim rather than a definite statement. All of those working in the Changing Character of War programme have learnt humility, both through the recognition of exceptions to every seeming rule and through the realization that the character of war does indeed change.

This introduction began with an acknowledgement to the Leverhulme Trustees. It needs to end with thanks to those whose administrative contribution to the programme over five years has enabled it to stay on course: Colonel David King, Dr Andrew Fairweather-Tall, Andrew Wasiliweski, Naomi King, and Rosemary Mills. The Department of Politics and International Relations has backed them up, especially Dr Mark Philp and Professor Neil MacFarlane, successively heads of department, Dr Bridget Taylor and Esther Byrom. The programme's first director of studies, Dr Audrey Kurth Cronin, has done much more to make this book possible than her chapter alone suggests. Other academics whose names may not appear on the contents page but who have contributed include Dr Alexandra Gheciu, Dr Rob Johnson, Dr Christian Malis, Dr David Alan Rosenberg, and Dr Noel Sharkey, as have a number of the programme's Visiting Fellows, especially Dr Tom Kristiansen, Carey Schofield, Ben Shephard, and the late Sir Michael Quinlan.

Sir Michael died just before the conference on the Changing Character of War was held, and only days before he was due to speak at the programme's regular seminar on his book, *Thinking about nuclear weapons: principles, problems, prospects*, published, as this book is, in the Changing Character of War series with Oxford University Press. He embodied for many of us the clarity of thought which practice lends to theory: his life and work were, and continue to be, an instructive and salutary example.

## NOTES

1. A volume which embraces this aspect of the Changing Character of War programme is in preparation, under the editorship of Jonathan Bailey, Richard Iron, and Hew Strachan.
2. Audrey Kurth Cronin, *How terrorism ends: Understanding the decline and demise of terrorist campaigns* (Princeton, NJ: Princeton University Press, 2009); Uwe Steinhoff, *On the ethics of war and terrorism* (Oxford: Oxford University Press, 2007).
3. For example, Bruce Hoffman, 'American jihad', *National Interest*, 20 April 2010.
4. The literature on this sort of thinking is massive. Tim Benbow, *The magic bullet? Understanding the revolution in military affairs* (London: Brassey's, 2004), provides a survey; key texts include (from one end of the spectrum to the other) Alvin and Heidi Toffler, *War and anti-war: Survival at the dawn of the 21st century* (London: Little, Brown & Co., 1994), and Donald Rumsfeld, 'Transforming the military', *Foreign Affairs*, 81/3 (2002), 20–32.
5. Herfried Münkler, *Die neuen Kriege* (Reinbek: Rowohlt, 2002); English edition *The new wars* (Cambridge: Polity, 2005).
6. Sarah Percy, *Mercenaries: The history of a norm in international relations* (Oxford: Oxford University Press, 2007).
7. William H. McNeill, *The pursuit of power: Technology, armed force and society since A.D. 1000* (Oxford: Oxford University Press, 1983; first published in the United States in 1982).
8. Victor Davis Hanson, *Why the west has won: Carnage and culture from Salamis to Vietnam* (London: Faber and Faber, 2001); the most sustained of many criticisms of Hanson's argument is John A. Lynn, *Battle: A history of combat and culture from ancient Greece to modern America* (Boulder, CO: Lynne Rienner, 2003).
9. Hew Strachan and Andrea Herberg-Rothe (eds.), *Clausewitz in the 21st century* (Oxford: Oxford University Press, 2007), 7–9, 37, 43, 80, 82, 182.
10. See *The 9/11 Commission Report: The final report of the National Commission on Terrorist Attacks upon the United States* (Washington DC, 2004).
11. The quotation is deliberate in order to show how self-referential Bobbitt's arguments are. It is cited from Bobbitt, *The shield of Achilles: War, peace and the course of history* (New York: Alfred Knopf, 2002), 229, by Bobbitt in *Terror*

*and consent: The wars for the twenty-first century* (London: Penguin, 2008), 44. For a fuller critique of the latter book, see Adam Roberts, 'Limits of a new-age worldview', *Survival*, 51/2 (2009), 183–90.

12. The principal disciplinary driver in identifying these criteria was applied ethics, especially through the work of David Rodin. For a development of these points, see Hew Strachan, 'The changing character of war', a Europaeum lecture delivered at the Graduate Institute of International Relations, Geneva, 9 November 2006, and published by the Europaeum, Oxford, 2007; reprinted in Karl-Erik Haug and Øle-Jørgen Maao (eds.), *What is modern war?* (London: Hurst, 2011).

13. Marc Bloch, *Strange defeat: A statement of evidence written in 1940* (New York: W. W. Norton, 1999), 117f.

14. On this point, see also Janne Haaland Matlary, 'The role of institutions under regional and global power rivalry (the UN, NATO, the EU)', in Norwegian Defence University College and the Norwegian Institute of International Affairs, *The seminar on military power 2009* (Oslo, 2009).

15. See also Guy Goodwin-Gill and Ilene Cohn, *Child soldiers* (Oxford: Oxford University Press, 1994).

16. Henry Shue and David Rodin (eds.), *Preemption: Military action and moral justification* (Oxford: Oxford University Press, 2007).

17. On the role of the United Nations Security Council in the control and prevention of interstate war, see Vaughan Lowe, Adam Roberts, Jennifer Welsh, and Dominik Zaum (eds.), *The United Nations Security Council and war: The evolution of thought and practice since 1945* (Oxford: Oxford University Press, 2008).

18. Charles Tilly, 'War making and state making as organized crime', in Peter B. Evans, Dietrich Rueschemeyer, and Theda Skocpol (eds.), *Bringing the state back in* (Cambridge: Cambridge University Press, 1985), 169–91.

19. Stephen C. Neff, *War and the law of nations: A general history* (Cambridge: Cambridge University Press, 2005), 277.

20. For further research by the Changing Character of War programme in this field, see Sibylle Scheipers (ed.), *Prisoners in war* (Oxford: Oxford University Press, 2010).

21. Kaldor, *New and old wars*; Münkler, *Die neuen Kriege*.

22. Richard K. Ashley, 'Untying the sovereign state: A double reading of the anarchy problematique', *Millennium: Journal of International Studies*, 17/2(1995), 202.

23. Rupert Smith, *The utility of force: The art of war in the modern world* (London: Penguin, 2005).

24. See, among others, Earl H. Tilford, Jr, *The revolution in military affairs: Prospects and cautions* (Carlisle, PA: Strategic Studies Institute, 1995); Eliot A. Cohen, 'A revolution in warfare', *Foreign Affairs*, 75/2 (1996), 37–54; Steven Metz and James Kievit, *Strategy and the revolution in military affairs: From theory to practice* (Carlisle, PA: Strategic Studies Institute, 1995).

25. On strategic culture, see among others Alastair Iain Johnston, 'Thinking about strategic culture', *International Security*, 19/4 (1995), 32–64; Colin Gray, 'Strategic culture as context: the first generation of theory strikes back', *Review of*

*International Studies*, 25/1 (1995), 49–69; on military culture, Isabel V. Hull, *Absolute destruction: Military culture and the practices of war in Imperial Germany* (Ithaca, NY: Cornell University Press, 2005) and Elizabeth Kier, *Imagining war: French and British military doctrine between the wars* (Princeton, NJ: Princeton University Press, 1997).

# PART I

# The Need for a Historical Perspective: What Has Changed?

# 1

# The Changing Character of War

*Azar Gat*

This book, and the Oxford Programme on the Changing Character of War which it sums up, would not have come into being if it were not for a deep and widespread feeling that war has entered a new era, significantly different from what we have known in the past. Such a feeling of transformation in war has occurred every generation or two over the past two centuries—during the French Revolutionary Wars, with industrialization, during the First World War, with mechanization, and with the advent of nuclear weapons. For in the modern age, marked by highly accelerated and sweeping historical change, war has followed suit. Thus, in order to lay out the changes affecting war today, it is necessary to identify the broader historical processes from which these changes arise. Some of these processes in fact go back quite far in time—only to have become more entrenched and prominent today—while others are more recent. I suggest three such broad (and in many ways interrelated) historical processes as a framework for our discussion: modernization, democratization, and technological innovation.

## MODERNIZATION

The occurrence of wars among the world's most developed countries—historically the most destructive type of interstate war, taking place among the most powerful states—has been declining dramatically. This is not a new trend. It has been very marked since the onset of the industrial age. In the century after 1815, wars among the great powers and other economically advanced countries declined in their frequency to about a *third* of what they had been in the eighteenth century, and even less compared with earlier times. The same low frequency continued during the twentieth century, although resource and manpower mobilization in the major wars that did occur, and, hence, wars' intensity and lethality per time unit increased, most notably in the two world wars.[1]

What accounts for this decline in war among developed powers? Many assume that wars have simply become too expensive and lethal, with a trade-off of sorts being created between the intensity and frequency of warfare: fewer larger wars replacing many smaller ones. This hypothesis barely holds, however, because *relative to population and wealth*, wars have not become more lethal and costly than earlier in history.[2] Particularly in nineteenth-century Europe, the frequency of war sharply declined, even though the wars that did occur were far from being devastating, compared with both earlier and later times. No great power war occurred for thirty-nine years after Waterloo—the longest period of peace in European history until then. The ensuing Crimean War (1854–6) was limited, while the Franco-Austrian War (1859) and the Wars of German Unification (1864, 1866, 1870–1) were relatively short and inexpensive. All the same, these wars were followed by another record: forty-three peace-years among the European great powers between 1871 and 1914.

Conversely, in the twentieth century, the mere twenty-one years that separated the two world wars—the most intense and devastating wars in modern European history—do not support an inverse relation between war intensity and frequency either. Obviously, when great power wars did occur, the antagonists were able to throw much greater resources into them. At the same time, however, they proved reluctant to embark on such wars in the first place. The world wars have been followed by a third consecutive record: to date, an absence of war between economically developed countries for more than sixty years. Although this 'Long Peace' is widely attributed to the nuclear factor—a decisive factor to be sure—the trend became evident long before the advent of nuclear weapons. The three longest periods of peace by far in the modern great powers system occurred from 1815 onwards.

Even before the middle of the nineteenth century, thinkers such as Saint-Simon, Comte, John Stuart Mill, and the Manchester school were quick to note the change, realizing that it was caused by the advent of the industrial–technological–commercial revolution, the most profound transformation of human society since the Neolithic adoption of agriculture. The main change to human existence brought about by the evolution was a steep and continuous growth in wealth, a dramatic breakaway from the 'Malthusian trap' that had characterized earlier human history. Earlier increases in productivity had been largely absorbed by population growth, leaving the vast majority of humanity in dire poverty, precariously close to subsistence level. Since the outbreak of the industrial–technological revolution, however, production per capita registered substantial and sustained real growth at an average annual rate of 1.5–2.0 per cent. In the developed countries, per capita production has increased in comparison with pre-industrial times by a factor of 15–30, so far.[3]

This revolutionary change has worked against war in several ways. In the first place, wealth, which is undergoing rapid and continuous growth, no longer constitutes a fundamentally finite quantity as it did earlier, when the main question was how it was to be distributed. Thus, wealth acquisition has progressively shifted away from a zero-sum game, where one participant's gain could only be achieved at others' expense. Secondly (and this is the most widely recognized factor of all), as production has now been intended for sale in the marketplace rather than directly consumed by the family producers themselves as in the pre-industrial economy, economies have no longer been overwhelmingly autarkic and therefore barely affected by one another. They have become increasingly interconnected in an intensifying and spreading network of specialization, scale, and exchange—nationally as well as internationally—the much celebrated 'globalization' of the markets.[4] During industrialization, the European powers' foreign trade increased at twice the rate of their fast-growing GNP (gross national product), so that by the late nineteenth and early twentieth centuries, exports plus imports grew to around half of the GNP in Britain and France, more than a third in Germany, and around a third in Italy (and Japan).[5] In consequence, prosperity abroad became interrelated with one's own, to the extent that foreign devastation potentially depressed the entire system and was thus detrimental to a state's own well-being. This reality, already noted by John Stuart Mill,[6] starkly manifested itself after the First World War, as John Maynard Keynes had anticipated in his criticism of the reparations regime imposed on Germany, *The economic consequences of the peace* (1920). Thirdly, greater economic openness has decreased the likelihood of war by disassociating economic access and opportunity from the confines of political borders and sovereignty. It is no longer necessary to possess a territory politically in order to benefit from it. To conclude, the greater the yields of competitive economic cooperation, the more counterproductive and less attractive conflict becomes. Rather than war becoming more costly, as is widely believed, it is in fact peace that has been growing more profitable.

And yet, in the wake of the two world wars, nineteenth-century optimistic economic pacifism lost its credibility, at least for a while. What were the theory's flaws? Where did the generally valid economic rationale prove deficient? A first clue is provided by the causes of the great powers' wars that disturbed the nineteenth century's relative peacefulness. Apart from the Crimean War (1854–6), these were the War of 1859 that led to Italy's unification, the American Civil War (1861–5), and the Wars of German Unification (1864, 1866, 1870–1). It was above all issues of national unity, national independence, national self-determination, and national identity that constituted the deepest and most inflammable motives for these major wars. The same held true for violent conflict in general throughout Europe.[7] The hotspots of such conflict were nationalist: conquered and partitioned Poland, fragmented and foreign-dominated Italy, disunited Germany, the territories of the future Belgium briefly stitched to Holland, suppressed Ireland, Habsburg-incorporated Hungary, Ottoman-held Balkans, and Alsace-Lorraine, annexed to Germany but retaining their affinity of national sentiment to France. Thus, the rising tide of modern nationalism often overrode the logic of the new economic realities, as it continues to do so today.

Furthermore, the benefits of free trade were not undiluted. As so-called 'national economists', from Alexander Hamilton and Friedrich List, pointed out, nascent industries in newly developing countries needed the protection of tariff barriers in their home markets, at least until they developed sufficiently to be able to compete successfully with the products of more established industrial economies. Following the high point of free trade in the mid-nineteenth century, the United States, Germany, France, Russia, and Japan all adopted strong protectionist policies against British manufacturing during their period of industrial take-off.

Moreover, by the late nineteenth and early twentieth centuries, the great powers expanded their protectionist policies to the undeveloped parts of the world, signalling that the emergent global economy might become partitioned—rather than remaining open for all—with each imperial domain becoming closed to everybody else, as, indeed, they eventually did in the 1930s. A snowball effect ensued, generating a runaway grab for territory. For the territorially confined Germany and Japan, the need to break away into imperial *Lebensraum* or 'co-prosperity sphere' seemed particularly pressing. Here lay the seeds of the two world wars.

Since 1945, the decline of major great power war has deepened further. Nuclear weapons have concentrated the minds of all concerned wonderfully, but no less important have been the institutionalization of free trade and the closely related process of rapid and sustained economic growth throughout the capitalist world. The communist bloc did not participate in the system of free trade, but at least initially it too experienced substantial growth, and, unlike Germany and Japan, it was always sufficiently large and rich in natural resources to maintain an autarky of sorts. With the Soviet collapse and with the integration of the former communist powers into the global capitalist economy, the prospect of a major war within the developed world seems to have become very remote indeed. This is one of the main sources for the feeling that war has been transformed: its geopolitical centre of gravity has shifted radically. The modernized, economically developed parts of the world constitute a 'zone of peace'. War now seems to be confined to the less-developed parts of the globe, the world's 'zone of war', where countries that have so far failed to embrace modernization and its pacifying spin-off effects continue to be engaged in wars among themselves, as well as with developed countries.

While the trend is very real, one wonders if the near disappearance of armed conflict within the developed world is likely to remain as stark as it has been since the collapse of communism. The post-Cold War moment may turn out to be a fleeting one. The probability of major wars within the developed world remains low—because of the factors already mentioned: increasing wealth, economic openness and interdependence, and nuclear deterrence. But the deep sense of change prevailing since 1989 has been based on the far more radical notion that the triumph of capitalism also spelled the irresistible ultimate victory of democracy; and that in an affluent and democratic world, major conflict no longer needs to be feared or seriously prepared for. This notion, however, is fast eroding with the return of capitalist non-democratic great powers that have been absent from the international system since 1945. Above all, there is the formerly communist and fast industrializing authoritarian-capitalist China, whose massive growth represents the greatest change in the global balance of power. Russia, too, is retreating from its post-communist liberalism and assuming an increasingly authoritarian character.

Authoritarian capitalism may be more viable than people tend to assume.[8] The communist great powers failed even though they were potentially larger than the democracies, because their economic systems failed them. By contrast, the capitalist authoritarian/totalitarian powers during the first half of the twentieth century, Germany and Japan, particularly the former, were as efficient economically as, and if anything more successful militarily than, their democratic counterparts. They were defeated in war mainly because they were too small and ultimately succumbed to the exceptional continental size of the United States (in alliance with the communist Soviet Union during the Second World War). However, the new non-democratic powers are *both* large and capitalist. China in particular is the largest player in the international system in terms of population and is showing spectacular economic growth that within a generation or two is likely to make it a true non-democratic superpower.

Although the return of capitalist non-democratic great powers does not necessarily imply open conflict or war, it might indicate that the democratic hegemony since the Soviet Union's collapse could be short-lived and that a universal 'democratic peace' may still be far off. The new capitalist authoritarian powers are deeply integrated into the world economy. They partake of the development-open-trade-capitalist cause of peace, but not of the liberal democratic cause. Thus, it is crucially important that any protectionist turn in the system is avoided so as to prevent a grab for markets and raw materials such as that which followed the disastrous slide into imperial protectionism and conflict during the first part of the twentieth century. Of course, the openness of the world economy does not depend exclusively on the democracies. In time, China itself might become more protectionist, as it grows wealthier, its labour costs rise, and its current competitive edge diminishes.

With the possible exception of the sore Taiwan problem, China is likely to be less restless and revisionist than the territorially confined Germany and

Japan were. Russia, which is still reeling from having lost an empire, may be more problematic. However, as China grows in power, it is likely to become more assertive, flex its muscles, and behave like a superpower, even if it does not become particularly aggressive. The democratic and non-democratic powers may coexist more or less peacefully, albeit warily, side by side, armed because of mutual fear and suspicion, as a result of the so-called 'security dilemma', and against worst-case scenarios. But there is also the prospect of more antagonistic relations, accentuated ideological rivalry, potential and actual conflict, intensified arms races, and even new cold wars, with spheres of influence and opposing coalitions. Although great power relations will probably vary from those that prevailed during any of the great twentieth-century conflicts, as conditions are never quite the same, they may vary less than seemed likely only a short while ago.

One is obliged to refer, if only briefly, to the global economic crisis that erupted in 2007–8. Analogies with the 1930s are inevitable. Having been the world's only superpower and a widely envied model of success during the 1920s, the United States was dealt a crushing blow by the Great Depression. It withdrew inwardly, leaving the scene to fascist and communist totalitarianism that throve on the apparent failure of capitalist democracy. One dare predict that the current economic crisis and its repercussions will not be nearly as catastrophic. Capitalism will be adjusted and amended both domestically and internationally. The United States will need some serious domestic reconstruction, but it will remain the paramount power for a long time, while avoiding isolationism. Hopefully, the world will also resist protectionist pressures. Yet, at the same time, the global allure of state-driven and nationalist capitalist authoritarianism may grow.

## DEMOCRATIZATION

We have seen that developed countries of the industrial–technological era have tended to be far more powerful but less belligerent than premodern states. Yet, liberal and democratic societies have proven inherently more attuned to modernity's pacifying aspects. Although this proposition was long regarded with scepticism, the supporting evidence has become quite overwhelming. Relying on arbitrary coercive force at home, non-liberal and non-democratic countries have found it more natural to use force abroad. By contrast, liberal democratic societies are socialized to peaceful, law-mediated relations at home, and their citizens have grown to prefer and expect that the same norms be applied internationally. Living in increasingly tolerant, less conformist, and argumentative societies, they have grown more receptive to the Other's point of view. Promoting freedom, legal equality, and political participation domestically, liberal democratic powers—though initially in possession of vast empires—have found it increasingly difficult to justify rule over foreign peoples without their consent. And sanctifying life, liberty, and human rights, they have proven to be failures in forceful repression. Furthermore, with the individual's life and pursuit of happiness elevated above group values, sacrifice, let alone self-sacrifice, of life in war has increasingly lost legitimacy in liberal democratic societies. War retains legitimacy only under narrow and narrowing formal and practical conditions, and is generally viewed as extremely abhorrent and undesirable.

The fruits of these deepening trends and sensibilities have been nothing short of miraculous. Their most striking and widely noted manifestation is the inter-democratic peace. International relations scholars have discovered that although modern democracies have been extensively involved in wars with non-democracies, they hardly ever fight among themselves. With growing liberalization, democracy, and economic development, the probability of war between democracies has declined to a vanishing point, where they no longer even fear or see the need to prepare for the possibility of a militarized dispute with one another. A 'positive' peace, based on shared interests, outlook, and ideals, rather than on the balance of power and deterrence, prevails among them. Domestically too, on account of their stronger consensual nature, plurality, tolerance, and, indeed, a greater legitimacy for peaceful secession, advanced liberal democracies have become practically free of civil wars, the most lethal and destructive type of war. At the same time, weak non-democratic countries (and less-developed democracies) continue to fall victim to such internal conflicts, while strong non-democratic countries prevent them through suppression.

The inter-democratic peace is merely the most conspicuous element of a larger whole. Less noted is the fact that liberal democracies tend to exhibit characteristic conflict behaviour that grows increasingly more pronounced the more liberal, democratic, and economically developed they become. Indeed, because the democracies have enjoyed a hegemonic position since the collapse of the Soviet Union, their norms have been codified in increasingly visible international institutions, and their discourse resonates through the international system, even if it does not dominate it. This is a second source of the widespread feeling that war is undergoing a profound change.

As war between great powers has become decreasingly likely and great powers' conflict has receded as well, at least for now, attention is drawn to the democracies' most typical war: limited wars with little-developed non-democratic rivals that are less affected by either of the above-mentioned pacifying trends (and therefore also continue to fight among themselves). Insurgency warfare in particular constitutes an enigma. Insurgencies have been credited for driving the democracies out of their former colonial empires and for frustrating military interventions even where the asymmetry in regular force capability is the starkest. Mighty powers that proved capable of crushing the strongest of opponents fail to defeat the humblest of military rivals in some of the world's poorest and weakest regions. It has been barely noted that, rather than being universal, this difficulty has overwhelmingly been the lot of liberal democratic powers—and encountered precisely because they are liberal and democratic.[9]

Historically, the crushing of an insurgency necessitated ruthless pressure on the civilian population, which liberal democracies have found increasingly unacceptable. Premodern powers, as well as modern authoritarian and totalitarian ones, rarely had a problem with such measures, and overall they have proved quite successful in suppression. Suppression is the *sine quo non* of imperial rule. The British and French empires could sustain themselves at a relatively low cost only so long as the imperial powers felt no scruples about applying ruthless measures—in India, Ireland, Scotland, or Africa. However, as liberalization deepened from the late nineteenth century, the days of formal democratic empires became numbered even while outwardly they were reaching their greatest extent. At the turn of the twentieth century, the British setbacks and eventual compromise settlement in South Africa and withdrawal from Ireland were the signs of things to come for other liberal democratic empires as well.

Non-liberal powers were less involved in imperial wars of suppression precisely because they were so effective in suppression that resistance was not allowed to grow into insurgency. Because modern non-democratic empires were either crushed in great power wars (as with Germany and Japan) or dismantled peacefully when the totalitarian system disintegrated (as with the Soviets), the sample of insurgencies is strongly biased, as it overwhelmingly comprises struggles against liberal democratic powers. Yet, as Sherlock Holmes noted, it is 'the dog that didn't bark' under the totalitarian iron fist that is the most conspicuous.

Sceptics may cite the successful guerrilla waged against Nazi Germany in Yugoslavia and some occupied parts of the Soviet Union. However, there can be little doubt that had Germany won the Second World War and been able to apply more troops to these troublesome spots, its genocidal methods would have prevailed there too. Russia's failure in Afghanistan is another obvious counter-example, but in reality, ruthlessness has always been a *necessary* but not *sufficient* condition for effective suppression. Defeating irregular warfare, carried out by a backward and fanatical rival in a vast, desolate, and sparsely populated country, has always been a difficult undertaking. Afghanistan was the exception, the outlier, rather than the rule in the Soviet system. Chechnya may be more enlightening in this respect. Under Stalin, the Soviet Union felt no scruples about deporting whole populations, including the Chechens, *en masse* from their homeland, a classic technique for the eradication of popular resistance. Indeed, the sequence along the scale of ruthlessness is unmistakable: Soviet methods under Stalin were the most brutal and most effective in curbing resistance, while liberal Russia of the 1990s proved to be the least brutal and least effective, with Putin's authoritarian Russia constituting an intermediate case. The same logic applies to China, whose continued successful suppression of Tibetan and Moslem nationalism is likely to persist so long as China retains its non-democratic regime, albeit with inferior effectiveness compared to Mao's totalitarian standards.

This is not to say that the democracies' conduct has been saintly—far from it. Atrocities, tacitly sanctioned by political and military authorities or carried out unauthorized by the troops, have regularly been committed against both combatants and non-combatants. All the same, strict restrictions on the use of violence against civilians constitute the legal and normative standard for liberal democracies. And although many, probably most, violations of this standard remain unreported, those incidents that have been exposed in open societies with free media are met with public condemnation and judicial procedures. All these developments radically limit the liberal democracies' powers of suppression, judged by historical and comparative standards. That not only a massacre such as that of My Lai but also the terror and intimidation practices at Abu Ghraib now evoke the most resounding outcry is an illustration of the continuous rise in the standards of conduct that liberal democracies apply to themselves.

The above should not be interpreted to mean that democracies *always* lose counter-insurgency wars, while non-democracies *always* win. Democracies can moderately succeed when they are able to isolate the insurgents from the civilian population and when pressed to the wall, but overall they find dealing with insurgencies highly problematic. Weak authoritarian regimes have sometimes failed in counter-insurgency conflicts because of their weakness, but strong authoritarian regimes and especially totalitarian ones rarely fail. Other factors are surely involved in each particular case, but the record is heavily tilted against democracies in such struggles.

Thus, although the military forces and civilian infrastructure of developed democracies' weak rivals are vulnerable to crippling blows in case of war, the weaker party may switch to irregular warfare and take cover within a friendly civilian environment, exploiting the liberal democracies' self-imposed limitations on ruthlessness against civilians. It may thereby frustrate or even deter invasion and occupation. In consequence, the democracies face a paradoxical predicament in many small wars: while sacrificing military capability and even victory for humanitarian considerations, they still face a heightened outcry both at home and abroad concerning alleged atrocities, the killing of civilians, and collateral damage that, while regrettable and partly avoidable, are often trifles by the standards of non-democratic powers; and as they are unable to win under such conditions, their mounting costs and their casualties—though sometimes inconsequential, historically and comparatively—become the cause for national trauma. While this syndrome is stronger in morally disputed wars, such as those taking place in colonial settings, it also exists when the cause is broadly viewed as one of self-defence and even in humanitarian interventions.

There is a catch that lies at the root of affluent liberal democracies' torment in conflict situations. Since wars are abhorred in liberal societies as antithetical to both their interests and values, to their entire way of life and worldview, they are sanctioned only as a last resort—after all other options have failed. Yet in practically no situation does it ever become clear that all alternative policies have indeed been exhausted, and that war has really become unavoidable. A feeling that there may be another way, that there *must* be another way, always lingers on. Errors of omission or commission are ever suspected as being the cause of undesired belligerency. Moreover, it never becomes clear that the democracies come to a conflict with entirely clean hands, morally, because of past or more immediate alleged wrongs; nor indeed can they, given the inevitable gap that always separates ideals from reality.

The democracies' reaction to the Axis challenge during the 1930s amply epitomizes this predilection. Everything was done to avoid military action, even if this meant allowing Germany to regain its power, grow in confidence owing to the democracies' inaction, and cross the point of no return on its road to expansion. The democracies' feelings of guilt for not having treated Germany in good faith after the First World War contributed to their paralysis. As long as the prospect of peaceful accommodation and containment remained—and it hardly ever faded, not even in 1939—there was no way the democracies would have initiated armed confrontation. To be sure, as critics caution, Hitlers are rare and not every crisis is the 1930s. All the same, the 1930s are a standing reminder that the democracies' strong aversion to war, while immensely beneficial overall, can become a grave problem in serious conflict situations.

It is often said that the democracies' inhibitions and self-imposed constraints are a source of moral strength that, when all else fails and war erupts, galvanizes their resolve and helps them gain the upper hand. Although there is truth in this view, it is more than a touch idealized. It largely rests on heroic Second World War images, when in reality the Axis powers fought, if anything, more tenaciously than the democracies, and it was the United States' superior size and strength that decided the issue (in coalition with a supremely tenacious Soviet Union), rescuing the democracies from their potentially fatal initial blunders and setbacks. Moreover, since the Second World War, the pacification of the democracies has advanced much more, on account of growing liberalism and affluence.

This should not be interpreted as a moral–political criticism or call for change. My aim is descriptive. What I am suggesting is that the liberal democracies' attitude to, and conduct in, war is thoroughly imbedded in the democracies' overall make-up and outlook, and is deeply structural. They correspond to the general parameters within which liberal society thinks and works, that might be challenged but not radically altered. There are variations, of course, arising from the particular historical–cultural and geopolitical conditions characterizing the various democracies—the United States, Europe, Japan, India, and other democracies. Yet, for better or for worse, underlying similarities have given rise to a typically 'liberal democratic way' in conflict.

Torn between their threat perceptions on the one hand and their fundamental view of conflict and war as harmful and deeply at variance with the modern world, high quality of life, hope for mutually rewarding international cooperation and peaceful accommodation, humanitarian universalism, and sense of self-guilt on the other, the liberal democracies are likely to find a revival of great power conflicts deeply agonizing. In forming policy in such circumstances, they are likely to adopt patterns of action they recurrently pursued in the twentieth century's great conflicts, successively against Imperial and Nazi Germany, Imperial Japan, and the Soviet Union; that is, they are likely to vacillate between isolationism, appeasement, containment, and cold war—progressing most reluctantly up the ladder if they sense that this cannot be helped, and down whenever deemed possible.[10] In military confrontations with smaller rivals, the democracies will tend to prefer war by proxy, blockade, naval and aerial actions, and limited operations by technologically superior strike forces. Large-scale ground operations, where the risk of messy entanglements is high and casualties might be greater, will tend to be avoided as much as possible. Because of far-reaching global commitments and citizens' unwillingness to enlist in the military, the democracies are likely to continue their shift towards professional forces. However, ever-growing sensitivity decreases liberal democracies' tolerance of casualties among professional troops as well.

Legal and normative constraints on the conduct of war, 'lawfare', are gaining in potency in liberal societies and their international institutional offshoots. An older view of war as a clash between national collectives, mobilized societies, and conflicting communal wills is increasingly giving way to a view of the enemy population as detached from its political leadership and as possessing rights of immunity from collective pressure. These rights are often interpreted as covering not only civilian life but also civilian well-being and dual-function civilian-strategic infrastructures.[11] A demand for greater reliance on non-lethal weapons even against combatants may lie in the future.

I intend no scaremongering or alarmism. The liberal democracies are likely to remain prosperous and powerful. Potential great power conflict need not necessarily materialize most of the time. Mutually beneficial international economic relations may continue to grow. At the same time, however, there are also contravening forces at work. An economically developed liberal democratic world, if it were to materialize, promises to be pacific. But we have not reached that point yet. Future developments are less secure than they were deemed to be in the immediate aftermath of the Cold War. The democracies' special practices and qualms about conflict dominate the discourse on war and accentuate the feeling of change—yet they are far from being shared by all.


## TECHNOLOGICAL INNOVATION

Global developments in technology, and their military applications, constitute a third source for the feeling that war is undergoing change. Major technological transformations have taken place in both the conventional and unconventional realms of warfare. I start with the conventional, where the change is most widely known as the 'revolution in military affairs' (RMA). The problem with this label is that it tells us nothing about the nature of the revolution and, indeed, fails to place the current revolution in the broader context of earlier technology-driven revolutions of the industrial–technological age. For as military theorist J. F. C. Fuller saw, ever since the beginning of that era, the advances in military technology have been closely related to the vastly accelerated pulse of technological development in general.[12]

Fuller identified three such major revolutionary waves of civil–military technological change during the nineteenth and twentieth centuries. In the so-called first industrial revolution, the application of the steam engine to railroads revolutionized the strategic mobility and logistics of armies, while its adoption at sea transformed naval architecture and warfare. To these was added the revolution in information communications, as electric telegraph lines connected armies across countries and naval bases across oceans and between continents in real time. Simultaneously during the nineteenth century, the revolution in metallurgy and machine tools transformed firearms and tactics. Rifling, breech loading, and rapid firing followed each other in quick succession.

From the 1880s, a new revolutionary wave of industrial technology, the so-called second industrial revolution, was beginning to unravel in civilian life, affecting the military field as profoundly as the first industrial revolution had. Chemicals, electric power, and the internal combustion engine dominated that second revolutionary wave. The chemical industry contributed high explosives and chemical warfare, and developments in electricity also had numerous military applications, including radio communication. But it was the internal combustion engine that affected war the most decisively. Lighter and more flexible than the steam engine, the internal combustion engine made possible cross-country mobility, away from railways. The appearance of the tractor and automobile was followed during the First World War by the tank, extending mechanized mobility into the battlefield.

The radio similarly extended real-time information transmission to the battlefield, away from stationary telegraph lines. Simultaneously, the internal combustion engine made possible mechanized air flight, while dual propulsion with the electric engine inaugurated the submarine. All these innovations were pioneered around 1900, made their military debut during the First World War, and matured to dominate warfare completely by the Second World War.

By then, new technological breakthroughs were beginning to make their mark in other sectors, most notably electronics, again revolutionizing both civilian life and war in the so-called third industrial or information revolution. Radar, developed in the late 1930s, deeply affected air, air–land, and sea warfare in the following decades. From around 1970, electro-optic, television, and laser guidance for missile weapon systems began to revolutionize air–land and land battle. Since then, fast improving sensors of all sorts, in combination with electronic computation capacity that more or less doubled every eighteen months, have made the identification, acquisition, and destruction of most hardware targets almost a foregone conclusion, nearly irrespective of range. Showing little signs of levelling off, the electronic revolution is bringing about increasing automation—the electric–robotic warfare that the pioneering Fuller predicted as early as 1928 as the third great wave after mechanization.[13]

The far-reaching effects of the ongoing electronic-information revolution on warfare have been endlessly discussed. The old mechanized-armoured armies of the previous era may not be disappearing, but they have been shrinking in size and transformed to embrace electronic warfare themselves, defensively as well as offensively. The two Gulf wars demonstrated this most strikingly, for the Iraqi side that lacked the new technologies found out to its cost that its numerous old-style formations were as vulnerable as herds of prehistoric mammoths. The gap between developed and less-developed protagonists seems to have widened considerably. And yet, the latter have been adjusting quicker and in ways different from expected. In the first place, less-developed players have been moving to get rid of their heavy formations, adopting instead low-signature troops, weapons, and tactics. (Notably, though, they cannot dispense of their heavy civilian infrastructure that remains highly vulnerable, as Serbia's experience in the Kosovo war demonstrated.) Second, the massive market penetration of new technologies into every aspect of daily life makes them available to less-developed players as well, if not in the form of the most expensive cutting-edge military systems, then as widely available and cheap gadgets. Satellite navigation systems (GPS) that offer precision guidance, computer networks that can be exploited and disrupted, and cellular phones that can be activated from afar are some examples. Indeed, high-tech technologies have both polarized *and* democratized the balance between the more and less advanced sides in war, for the means to generate massive damage with pinpoint accuracy have been trickling down to below the state level, becoming available to non-state actors as well. This trickling-down effect may be even greater in the field of unconventional weapons, to which I now turn.

The mega terror attacks of 11 September 2001 constitute a landmark in history, not so much in their direct and indirect consequences but in demonstrating an ominous potential that had been building for some time and is yet fully to unravel. This is the threat of unconventional terror, employing the so-called weapons of mass destruction (WMD): nuclear, biological, and chemical. In part, the change here is driven by technological innovation but, even more, it is generated by technological proliferation.

Terror is neither entirely new nor as old as many believe it to be.[14] While the assassination of leaders is as old as humanity, terror only emerged from the late nineteenth century, riding on the back of modern technological and social developments: high explosives and later automatic weapons gave individuals and small groups the ability to cause damage disproportionate to their numbers; trains and later cars gave them mobility across countries; telegraph communication and popular newspapers gave their operations national publicity and resonance that vastly magnified the public 'terror' effect of what after all constituted very limited actions.

Again, it has been mainly liberal and old-style authoritarian countries that proved to be the most susceptible to terror. Totalitarian regimes not only policed far more effectively but also denied terror the publicity that was essential for its success. From the 1960s, terror exhibited a new surge as passenger jets offered both much greater global mobility and vulnerable targets, and as television further enhanced the terrorists' public exposure. Yet it is only the prospect of terrorists acquiring and using WMD that has turned terrorism from an irritant and a media-political tool into a serious destructive threat, thereby producing the alarming twist of the new era.

The so-called WMD are an assortment of different technologies with widely diverging potencies. Chemical weapons, pioneered in the First World War, were almost immediately countered by defensive gear, which when available sharply decreased their effectiveness. The potential use of chemical weapons by terrorists is predicated on the element of surprise, catching masses of people unprotected in open urban space. However, the bulk of the chemical agents needed and the problem of disseminating them effectively make chemical weapons the least dangerous of the WMD, with lethality from a highly successful chemical terror attack estimated in the thousands.

Biological weapons pose a threat of a much greater magnitude. The revolutionary breakthroughs achieved during recent decades in the decipherment of the genome, in biotechnology, and in genetic engineering make this field the next big thing in technological development, opening up new horizons in terms of lethality and accessibility. A virulent laboratory-cultivated strain of bacteria or virus, let alone a specially engineered 'superbug' against which no immunization and medication exist,[15] might bring the lethality of biological weapons within the range of nuclear attacks and result in anything between thousands and many millions of fatalities, while being far more easily accessible to terrorists than nuclear weapons.

Still, nuclear weapons constitute a category of their own that sets them apart from all other known weapons. In the absence of effective defence, mutual deterrence is the only protection against them. Yet, precisely here lies the bewildering nature of the new mix which is unconventional terror, because deterrence is infinitely less effective against terrorist groups than it is against states. Not only are such groups more likely to consist of zealots who are willing to sacrifice their lives and may positively desire a general apocalypse; they are also too elusive to offer a clear enough target for retaliation, on which the whole concept of deterrence is based.

The root of the problem is the trickling down to below the state level of the technologies and materials of WMD. The relatively simple technological infrastructure needed to manufacture chemical weapons is now available in some 100 countries.[16] The biotechnological sector in particular constitutes one of the spearheads of today's scientific–commercial revolutionary wave. In the United States alone, the number of scientists authorized to work with biological agents has sharply risen to 15,000, rendering monitoring by government agencies all the more difficult.[17] As markets and communications globalize rapidly, the acquisition of the materials and know-how required for WMD has become both far easier and more difficult to detect and block. Finally, the disintegration of the Soviet Union left in the debris of its advanced military infrastructure unemployed scientists, poorly guarded production facilities, unaccounted-for materials, and, most troubling of all, the weapons themselves. For these reasons, terrorists' ability to buy, steal, rob, and/or manufacture WMD has increased dramatically.

To be sure, the practical difficulties facing terrorist groups aspiring to pursue the unconventional path are still considerable. In the early 1990s, the Aum Shinrikyo cult in Japan was the first non-state group to build production facilities for biological and chemical weapons. It failed in its early attempts to produce potent biological agents, while even its largest chemical attack, in the Tokyo subway in 1995, resulted in only twelve fatalities, mainly because of the low quality of the sarin used and a primitive dissemination mechanism (plastic bags punctured by umbrellas). All the same, the cult was making rapid progress when the police closed in on its facilities: it was in the process of producing more effective spraying mechanisms and 70 tons of sarin, while also building a large biological laboratory.[18] Furthermore, technological capability and accessibility have increased considerably since the 1990s.

Similarly, the anthrax attack in the United States in the wake of 11 September, now attributed to Bruce Ivins, a scientist in the US biological warfare laboratory who committed suicide in 2008, was delivered in envelopes sent through the US postal service, killing only five people. While Ivins seems to have been mentally disturbed and his motives remain unclear, he probably did not want to perpetrate mass death. However, the use of aerosolized anthrax effectively sprayed could result in a disaster of an entirely different order of magnitude. According to a congressional assessment made as early as 1993, a light aircraft flying over Washington DC spraying the city with 100 kilograms of anthrax could fatally injure 3 million people.

Nuclear weapons have not yet been used by terrorists, and, in contrast to chemical and biological agents, fissile material is not within the realm of their production capabilities, at least not in the foreseeable future. All the same, stolen or bought materials can be used by terrorists to create a radioactive bomb, which does not compare with nuclear weapons in terms of destructiveness but can still contaminate entire urban blocs. Furthermore, according to several tests carried out by scientists for the American authorities, a nuclear bomb can be built from parts available in the open market, with the fissile material bought or stolen. Nuclear weapons themselves might be stolen or bought in the black market, and not at a high cost. Abdul Qadeer Khan, the Pakistani nuclear scientist who headed his country's nuclear programme, sold the nuclear secrets to perhaps a dozen countries, reportedly for as little as millions or tens of millions dollars in each case.

For much of history, non-state players, such as tribal and armed gang leaders, often challenged the state successfully. With modernity, the state gained dominance as it effectively came to control the heavy infrastructure that increasingly underlay power. Although state dominance still holds, despite encroachments from various directions, the 'encapsulation' of destructive power in WMD, particularly the nuclear and biological, recreates a situation whereby one no longer has to be big in order to deliver a heavy punch. Scenarios of world-threatening individuals and organizations, previously reserved to fiction of the James Bond genre, suddenly become real. The notion of 'a bomb in the basement', originally coined in relation to states' undeclared development of nuclear weapons, assumes a new and chilling meaning. Indeed, because deterrence based on mutual assured destruction (MAD) does not apply to terrorists, the use of ultimate weapons is *more* likely to come from them than it is from states, even though the latter may possess far greater capability. In contrast to the mindset that has dominated strategic thinking since the onset of the nuclear age, unconventional capability acquired by terrorists is *useable*.

It has been claimed by some in the wake of 11 September that it is wrong to define terror as the enemy, because terror is only a tactic, whereas the enemy is militant Islam. True, radical Islam stands behind most terrorist attacks in today's world, and dealing with it is an intricate and complex problem. Yet even if this problem were overcome, other causes and 'Super-Empowered Angry Men' (as the *New York Times* journalist Thomas Freedman has called them) would always be present and, in contrast to the past, could now make themselves felt in horrendous ways. The Aum Shinrikyo cult, anthrax scientist

Bruce Ivins, and, indeed, the Christian millenarians and extreme right-wing perpetrators of the massive conventional bombings in Oklahoma City (1995) and the Atlanta Olympics (1996) were not Muslim. Thus, unconventional terror *is* the problem.

Indeed, this is a baffling problem, which does not lend itself to easy or clear solutions. The main feasible measure against unconventional terror is a coordinated global crackdown, which includes tightened security measures, tougher controls on the materials and facilities for the production of WMD, and a relentless pursuit of terrorists, including highly controversial foreign interventions. Despite much haggling and conflicts of interest, such concerted action is not wholly utopian, for no state is immune to the threat. International norms and international law are likely to change in response to the new challenges, most notably perhaps with respect to the concept of sovereignty.[19]

The greatest obstacle for the success of a policy of global crackdown is the proliferation of WMD, above all nuclear weapons. A number of scholars have argued that the spread of nuclear weapons actually constitutes a good thing, because it will expand to other regions of the world the same deterrence against war that prevailed between the blocs during the Cold War. However, critics of this view question whether the logic of MAD is full-proof as nuclear weapons reach a growing number of hands in less and less stable parts of the world. Furthermore, critics point out that as undeveloped countries with inferior technological and institutional infrastructures increasingly come to possess nuclear capabilities, the likelihood of an accidental use of nuclear weapons or of a nuclear accident will increase considerably.[20] Finally, with respect to terrorists, the greatest threat of nuclear proliferation into countries with low security standards and high levels of corruption is the much-increased danger of leakage. Not only, as happened in the Pakistani case, might people and organizations with access to nuclear facilities sell or otherwise transfer nuclear materials, expertise, and even weapons to terrorists, with or without the knowledge of their governments, but also states in the less developed and unstable parts of the world are ever in danger of disintegration and anarchy. When state authority collapses and anarchy takes hold, who is to guarantee the country's nuclear arsenal? The collapsed Soviet Union rather than the former nuclear superpower may be the model for future threats.

Thus, defunct states may constitute an even greater problem than militant ones. Weak or 'failed' states simply do not exercise effective control over their territory and cannot be held accountable. In vast and barely approachable tracts of the globe inhabited by fragmented and unruly societies, the ability to monitor and crack down on the activity of terrorist groups is inherently limited. The difficulties of finding a needle in a haystack pale in comparison.

The disproportion between the terrorists' material investment and that required by states to counter them is so great that it is viewed as absurd by some critics. Some have come close to suggesting that the United States should drop its highly expensive countermeasures and take its chances with the prospect of a biological or nuclear terror action which they anyway consider to be remote.[21] Quite apart from the stupendous cost of the wars in Afghanistan and Iraq, the United States spent \$57 billion on bioterrorism defences alone between 2001 and 2008. This included the development and stockpiling of drugs, hospital preparations, and the installation of detection stations along the perimeters of thirty-five major cities—and the effect is still judged to be insufficient in view of the increasing threat.[22]

The normative–legal aspects of the democracies' defensive measures are equally problematic. The expansion of the state's authority in such spheres as the detainment of suspects by means of extraordinary legal procedures, debriefing methods, surveillance of people and communication, and other infringements of privacy is hotly debated and litigated in the liberal democracies. As with the offensive and pre-emptive elements of the 'war on terror', the debate within the democracies assumes a bitterly ideological and righteous character. Indeed, all the above measures are deeply problematic for them. And yet, the threat of unconventional terrorism is real, is here to stay, and offers no easy solutions.


## CONCLUSION

A view from a longer perspective on the apparent transformation of war in today's world reveals a complex causal web, in which the continuation and deepening of older processes blend with the effects of more recent changes that may themselves be partly transitory. In large part, the perception of change derives from the apparent disappearance of great power conflict with the collapse of the Soviet Union and the end of the Cold War. But great power war has been growing increasingly rare since the beginning of the industrial–technological age, becoming even less likely in the nuclear age. At the same time, the return of capitalist non-democratic great powers, above all China and also Russia, may result in the resumption of at least some level of great power tensions and rivalry. Democracies have exhibited unique conflict behaviour from the later part of the nineteenth century. But democracies' inhibitions in using forceful suppression, their low casualty tolerance, and conflict aversion in general have all grown ever deeper the more liberal, democratic, and affluent they have become, and the more they have increased in number and their norms have grown to dominate the global discourse and international institutions. How long this dominance will last is yet to be seen. As with earlier technological revolutions, today's electronic revolution initially magnified the advantage of developed militaries. Yet, some catching up and adjustment by the less developed have ensued. In part, terror has risen on the scale of threats simply because great power conflict has receded, at least for a while. At the same time, although the world has been living with nuclear, biological, and chemical weapons for generations, the continued proliferation of the technologies in question, as well as the revolutionary advances in biotechnology, renders unconventional terror a far more likely prospect.

Proverbially, predictions are just fine as long as they are not applied to the *future*. Much that is unpredicted and unpredictable can and will occur. And yet, people must prepare for the future the best they can, and they can only do so by extrapolating from past experience. The character of war is certainly changing, but our strong perception of change stems from the coming together of several, partly related and partly unrelated, trends that may develop in different directions over time. Indeed, only time will tell.

## NOTES

1. Melvin Small and David Singer, *Resort to arms: International and civil wars, 1816–1980* (Beverly Hills, CA: Sage, 1982), based on their important Correlates of War database, gives no basis for comparison to earlier times and between developed and developing countries. But see Jack Levy, *War in the modern great power system, 1495–1975* (Lexington, KY: University Press of Kentucky, 1983), esp. 112–49, which concentrates on the great powers' wars among themselves, that is, by definition, the major wars by the most advanced states. Also Evan Luard, *War in international society* (London: Tauris, 1986), 53, 67.

2. For more detail, see my *War in human civilization* (Oxford: Oxford University Press, 2006), 524–9, 534f.

3. These are my rough calculations based on the estimated data. The most comprehensive and update estimates are Angus Maddison, *The world economy: A millennial perspective* (Paris: OECD, 2001), 28, 90, 126, 183–6, 264f. See also Paul Bairoch, 'Europe's gross national product: 1800–1975', *Journal of European Economic History*, 5/2 (1976), 301; and Idem., 'International industrialization levels from 1750 to 1980', *Journal of European Economic History*, 11/2 (1982), esp. 275, 284, 286; W. W. Rostow, *The world economy: History & prospect* (Austin, TX: University of Texas, 1978), 4–7, 48f.

4. E.g. Richard Rosecrance, *The rise of the trading state: Commerce and conquest in the modern world* (New York: Basic Books, 1986); also, Stephen Brooks, 'The globalization of production and the changing benefits of conquest', *Journal of Conflict Resolution*, 43/5 (1999), 646–70.

5. Calculated on the basis of the data in B. R. Mitchell, *International historical statistics, Europe 1750–1988* (New York: Stockton, 1992), 553–62; Maddison, *The world economy*, 126f., 184; Simon Kuznets, *Modern economic growth* (New Haven, CT: Yale University Press, 1966), 306f., 312–14.

6. John Stuart Mill, *Principles of political economy* (New York: Kelley, 1961), book III, 582.

7. Cf. Kalevi Holsti, *Peace and war: Armed conflict and international order 1648–198* (Cambridge: Cambridge University Press, 1991), 139–45.

8. Azar Gat, 'The return of authoritarian great powers', *Foreign Affairs*, 86/4 (2007), 59–69; Idem., *Victorious and vulnerable: Why democracy won in the 20th century and how it is still imperiled* (Lanham, MD: Rowman & Littlefield for the Hoover Institution, 2008).

9. See originally: Gil Merom, *How democracies lose small wars: State, society, and the failure of France in Algeria, Israel in Lebanon, and the United States in Vietnam* (New York: Cambridge University Press, 2003). For a greater elaboration of the thesis, and more bibliographical references, see Merom and Gat, 'Why counterinsurgencies fail' in Gat, *Victorious and Vulnerable*, Chapter 7.

10. Gat, *War in human civilization*, 609–18.

11. A full acceptance of such a doctrine wholly negates nuclear deterrence, and there is no known defence against a wholesale nuclear attack other than deterrence through mutual assured destruction (MAD). For a discussion of the irreconcilable moral dilemmas here, see: Michael Walzer, *Just and unjust war* (New York: Basic Books, 1997), Chapter 17.

12. These ideas repeatedly occur in J. F. C. Fuller's voluminous writings; but see esp. his *On future warfare* (London: Praed, 1928); and Idem., *Armament and history* (London: Eyre, 1946).

13. J. F. C. Fuller, *Towards armageddon* (London: Dickson, 1937), 92, 132.

14. See, for example, Walter Laqueur's otherwise excellent, *The new terrorism: Fanaticism and the arms of mass destruction* (New York: Oxford University Press, 1999), 8–12.

15. Philip Cohen, 'A terrifying power', *New Scientist*, 30 January 1999, 10; Rachel Nowak, 'Disaster in the making', *New Scientiest*, 13 January 2001, 4–5; Carina Dennis, 'The bugs of war', *Nature*, 17 May 2001, 232–5.

16. Michael Moodie, 'The chemical weapons threat', in Sidney D. Drell, Abraham D. Sofaer, and George D. Wilson (eds.), *The new terror: Facing the threat of biological and chemical weapons* (Stanford, CA: Stanford University Press for the Hoover Institution, 1999), 19.

17. Spencer Hsu, 'Modest gains against ever-present bioterrorism threat', *Washington Post*, 3 August 2008.

18. David Kaplan, 'Aum Shinrikyo', in Jonathan B. Tucker (ed.), *Toxic terror: Assessing terrorist use of chemical and biological weapons* (Cambridge, MA: MIT Press, 2000), Chapter 12.

19. Graham Allison, *Nuclear terrorism: The ultimate preventable catastrophe* (New York: Times, 2004) is a proposed blueprint for such a strategy. More generally, Philip Bobbitt, *The shield of Achilles: War, peace and the course of history* (London: Allen Lane, 2002); Idem., *Terror and consent: The wars for the twenty-first century* (New York: Knopf, 2008).

20. See, for example, Scott Sagan (against) and Kenneth Waltz (for), *The spread of nuclear weapons* (New York: W. W. Norton, 1999); references to terrorist nuclear threat have been added in the second edition. (2003), 126–30, 159–66. Also, Martin van Creveld, *Nuclear proliferation and the future of conflict* (New York: Free Press, 1993) (for); and a good balanced treatment by Devin Hagertly, *The consequences of nuclear proliferation* (Cambridge, MA: MIT Press, 1998).

21. John Mueller, *Overblown: How politicians and the terrorism industry inflate national security threats and why we believe them* (New York: Free Press, 2006) is a provocative corrective to the threat perception, emphasizing the difficulties of generating unconventional terror, the small number of casualties so far compared to other sources of mortality, and the counter-effectiveness of many of the measures employed. But it is spoiled by the author's one-sided depreciation of the threat and his bizarre suggestions that the United State's involvement in the Second World War and the Cold War was equally unnecessary: the United States should not have gone to war after Pearl Harbor but rather should have stuck to economic sanctions and containment that would have brought down Japan (how, after the latter had conquered east Asia, thereby becoming self-sufficient, is unclear); nor should it have opposed Soviet expansion, because the failed Soviet system was doomed anyhow.

22. Hsu, 'Modest gains'.

# 2

## Had a Distinct Template for a 'Western Way of War' been Established before 1800?

*David Parrott*

According to one well-established historical tradition, the Western way of war came to birth on 17 September 1631. The battle of Breitenfeld, just outside Leipzig, where Gustavus II Adolphus of Sweden with an army of 42,000 Swedes, Saxons, Scots, and other German mercenaries smashed the Catholic-Habsburg army of 32,000 battle-experienced troops, was even at the time regarded as 'no ordinary victory'. It was both a providential reversal of the previous decade of protestant defeats and the first great demonstration of a series of military reforms associated with the Swedish king. These reforms redeployed infantry in smaller, linear formations in which the firepower of muskets could be made more effective, while smaller units in turn permitted more battlefield flexibility and better coordination between infantry, cavalry, and artillery. This transformation of the army on the battlefield was optimized through the introduction of a codified system of military drill, taught via illustrated handbooks and intended to formalize and coordinate infantry musket-firing, unit deployment, and tactical manoeuvres.[1] The mass and brawn of the traditional infantry pike-square of the fifteenth and sixteenth centuries were replaced by the disciplined firepower and tactical brains of the new model armies, where intelligent use of developing technology (muskets and battlefield light artillery) combined with a more responsive, flexible, and better-integrated structure of authority and responsibility down to the level of individual company and non-commissioned officers.[2] The result, and Breitenfeld is cited as key evidence, was the transformation of the battlefield from the scene of indecisive, attritional encounters in which traditional armies had proved unable to break each other's defence in depth. The reformed army now had the military capacity to engage with and annihilate an enemy in a single battle or a short campaign. This in turn opened up new strategic possibilities, whether of ending conflict quickly and decisively on the basis of outright victory or of pursuing political objectives that were more extensive and radical than previous wielders of military force could realistically have envisaged.

An added virtue of this military transformation was that the 'new' programmes of drill and strict discipline were consciously linked back to the ancient world and the military organization of the Roman Republic and Empire. The military reformers were keen to emphasize their debt to Roman prescriptions for discipline and formalized drill, and that this latter could as easily be applied to pikes and muskets as to javelins and short swords. It gave contemporaries and later historians a strong sense of the continuity of a Western military tradition; it established a 'right direction' in military developments and institutions which would prove a powerful force in critiques of alternative organizational or tactical approaches to war.[3]

Contemporaries and posterity were impressed by the military reformation pioneered by Gustavus Adolphus, and variously adopted by what have been deemed forward-looking powers in the seventeenth and eighteenth centuries. However, of itself it would not have been enough to make a case for a distinctive 'Western way of war'. Geoffrey Parker points out the intriguing way in which the warring Japanese territorial rulers, or Daimyo, of the second half of the sixteenth century acquired a handful of muskets from Portuguese traders. They rapidly mass-produced these from the basic model, equipped part of their infantry with them, and—seemingly intuitively—worked out how to maximize their impact in battle through volley-fire and disciplined firing drill.[4] Understanding the potential of military technology and how to integrate that effectively with existing military organization and institutions was no Western prerogative, and grasping these principles evidently did not require an attentive reading of Vegetius. What acted as a decisive transformational factor, taking up these widely disseminated seventeenth-century ideas of military reformation and placing them in a context which might be considered distinctively Western, was the concept of an early modern European 'military revolution'.

The origins of this concept are associated with Michael Roberts and his celebrated lecture, then article, of 1955.[5] Essentially, Roberts recapitulated the traditional argument that a series of early seventeenth-century tactical and organizational innovations transformed the art of war, making it possible to win decisively on the battlefield through the deployment of drilled and disciplined troops. But he combined this with another set of ideas that had been developing since the nineteenth century, namely that the increasing scale, the manpower demands, and the financial burden of war had led both to a transformation of government in early modern European states and to a direct and irreversible involvement of the state in military organization. War and the state were henceforth locked in a symbiotic relationship: only the state could mobilize the financial and human resources and provide the administrative, logistical, and organizational support required for war on a modern scale; on the other side, it was precisely the non-negotiable and immediate demands of waging war which had forced rulers and governments to act to transform the modest administration and the large-scale decentralization of power that were characteristic of the medieval state. What might have been a lengthy process of concession, negotiation, and temporization by rulers in the face of powerful subjects and institutions became the assertion of state power through bureaucracy, uniform and efficient tax systems, the imposition of common legal and administrative processes, and, not the least, the mobilization of military resources.[6]

Such sociological accounts of the rise of state power had typically been unspecific about the precise nature and timing of the military changes that had led to this administrative and governmental transformation. The attraction of Roberts' thesis was that he inserted the missing detail. The military transformation of the early seventeenth century became the 'military revolution' of early modern Europe. As Roberts himself put it, this military revolution 'stands like a great divide separating medieval society from the modern world'.[7] Those tactical and organizational changes that brought victory on the battlefield could lead, by stages through a broadening of strategic aims and the much larger numbers of troops required for their achievement, to a wholesale transformation of every aspect of state and society, the achievement of modernity. Breitenfeld, on this account, really was a world-changing event.

This has been a potent combination: the linkage of military effectiveness to the rise of state power offers a strong case for the distinctiveness of the Western way of war. This distinctiveness lies above all in its apparent capacity to give unstoppable momentum to an upward spiral in the scale and destructive potential of military force from the seventeenth to the twenty-first century. The singularity (or at least rarity) of this deserves attention. Where in other societies, military elites have enjoyed a dominant position—many ancient empires, Byzantium, the mesoamerican military states culminating in the Aztecs, Tokugawa Japan—what started as efficient military systems have tended to atrophy: there is no inevitability that armies or navies will be more powerful, larger, or more effective than those of a century earlier. These were in all cases highly militarized states or empires; but the military elites, who also enjoyed strong political and social influence, often saw military innovation as a threat to their own authority and status; moreover, they saw no advantage or benefit in changing or developing military systems that seemed capable of confronting any immediate challenges to the state. Under the Tokugawa Shogunate in Japan, those muskets which had been manufactured from a few Portuguese examples and deployed with decisive effect on the battlefields of the late sixteenth century were subsequently stored in arsenals and no further attempt was made from the seventeenth century to develop their capabilities and effectiveness.[8] In contrast, what the closely integrated European military–political state system appeared to achieve was to link military organization to dynamic economic and organizational systems, born in an atmosphere of continuous military but also economic competition between states. If the military elites remained a dominant presence in Western societies (though never *the* dominant force), from early on they were significantly more attuned to a military system that had as its principal dynamic a constant concern to increase and develop the scale and effectiveness of power projection and force.[9]

This model of a military–state symbiosis has a powerful influence on claims for subsequent Western military revolutions, which gain their legitimacy through making the same link between military power and a further ratcheting up of the power of the state. The last two decades have seen intensive debate about historical and contemporary instances of radical military transformations. The identifying feature of what might claim to be true 'military revolutions', rather than 'revolutions in military affairs', or still lower in the hierarchy, 'military-technical revolutions', has been precisely the direct symbiosis between technological or organizational innovations in military force and developments in the resource-base and the political and social structures of the state.[10]

There are some convincing elements in this model for the Western way of war. But the view that the West has spawned a single, holistic template, based on the tight integration of military innovation and organization, and its relationship to growing state power and administrative rationalization, deserves further scrutiny.

An obvious starting point is the assumed centrality of military technology and innovation to a Western way of war. It is taken as part of the general template that Western states have proved more inventive in their ability to find technological solutions to military problems, and have been more flexible and adaptable in accommodating this new technology within their military systems. From the seventeenth century onwards, Western military superiority has rested on the ability of states and peoples to stay ahead of the game in developing cutting-edge military technology, both in wars between European powers and in European expansion into the wider world.

However, although study of the military history of the last two centuries has placed at its core the impact of technological change, whether the technology at issue is the breech-loading rifle or nuclear weapons, it is also apparent when looking at cases where there has been a great leap forward in pure military potential and effectiveness, that many transformations have little to do with a single, or even a combination of, technological innovations. Whether or not certain state-systems are more conducive to technological innovation and its deployment, the simple fact is that many war-transforming developments were about organization and resources, not technology. If the French Revolutionary Wars are considered to have precipitated a genuine 'military revolution' in which war, state and society are all in turn radically and permanently transformed, then that is owed for the first time in European history to something akin to the mass mobilization of the citizens and the establishment of the principle of universal military service as the mechanism to raise armies of unparalleled size.[11] There is no technological innovation here: indeed the weapons-systems of the Revolutionary and Napoleonic Wars are distinctive only in their lack of innovation and simply represent a vastly larger scale deployment of the weapons of the mid-eighteenth century.[12]

If this is accepted without much debate for those aspects of the Western way of war which first evolved in the 1790s, it can also encourage a more critical approach to other periods of military history where technological innovation is assumed to be central. Rather awkwardly given its role as the progenitor of the idea of 'military revolution', it is apparent that the first great early modern military transformation had little to do with weapons technology. Although it is assumed that the *raison d'être* of the military changes in this period was the maximization of infantry firepower, throughout this period infantry handguns remained of relatively minor importance with extremely limited killing-power: matchlock arquebuses or heavier muskets were hopelessly inaccurate at anything above a couple of dozen yards; they had an outside range of not much more than 100 yards; they were extraordinarily slow and cumbersome to reload.[13] Stress on the importance of smaller, linear formations and drilling troops in countermarch and salvo, as if these could determine battlefield outcomes, has been misleading, or at least an anachronistic prefiguration of developments which would only begin to come into their own in the later century with the use of flintlocks and ring-bayonets.[14] And even in the armies of Frederick the Great, the precision-drilling of infantry in rapid, synchronized musket fire can easily obscure the fact that the musket represented a virtually static and underdeveloped technology. If firepower did transform the early modern battlefield, this was the result of the proliferation of artillery, from a few dozen cannon on the battlefields of the Thirty Years War to the 100 or more guns mustered by each army for the battles of the War of the Spanish Succession in the early eighteenth century. But the technology of the muzzle-loaded field gun had hardly changed in its essentials from the sixteenth century. It was not until the mid-eighteenth century that anything approaching a 'revolution' in artillery occurred.[15]

The most clear-cut example of radical technological evolution in this period came not on land at all but in the construction of warships. The evolution of the three-masted, ocean-going ship with guns mounted in two or three decks along her flanks was not a single technological innovation: the struggle to balance seaworthiness, speed, firepower, and resilience was lengthy and resulted in a steady series of innovations and experiments until an optimum point was reached around the mid-seventeenth century. Lesser improvements and innovations continued, but the basic patterns of rated warships had been established and would continue largely unchanged until the nineteenth century.[16] Arguably, the contribution of this naval technology to European military power, above all in its assertion outside Europe, was greater than any other military development. Yet naval technology fits awkwardly into traditional ideas of the military–state synthesis which is set at the heart of a full-scale 'military revolution'. The growth of state-power is usually linked to the massive demands of fielding and sustaining armies of hundreds of thousands of troops in protracted wars across Europe. While navies clashed in the course of these wars, neither the military outcomes of these naval campaigns nor the resources required to raise state-navies have been granted the same transformative potential: it was not navies which created the modern state. And if naval technology lay at the heart of European power-projection in the wider world, this was very largely deployed not by states but by the capital and enterprise of subjects, coming together as chartered, shareholder companies. Mercantile activity in the Americas, the Indian Ocean, and the Far East was protected and expanded by warships built, manned, and funded by private enterprise, not, initially, by the state. I will return to this point later.

The emphasis on technological innovation as the key to a Western way of war can be misleading even at a purely tactical–operational level. It has tended to reinforce a narrow, decontextualized approach to the pitched battle as both the test of that technology and a decisive means to achieve military outcomes. Too many identified 'revolutions in military affairs'—from the tactics of Gustavus Adolphus to US army doctrines of 'shock and awe' in the early 2000s—concentrate on developments which may seem to enhance the battle-field capability of armies, without confronting the simple fact that it may still be possible to win a major field battle and yet still end up at a strategic disdvantage at the end of the campaign.[17] The battle of Breitenfeld, with which this chapter began, is a prime candidate for such contextualization. Not only had the defeated Imperialists managed within six weeks to reassemble 60,000 troops from the apparent wreckage of their defeat but reconstituted Imperial armies were to fight the Swedish victors to a standstill in the following year.[18] The main reason why this resurgence was so easily achieved was that Gustavus Adolphus had little choice after the battle but to pursue a course driven by logistical needs that would feed and pay his army but not bring the war any nearer to a conclusion: he chose the comparatively 'soft' occupation of the Rhineland and Bavaria, rather than a drive into the Imperial heartlands of Bohemia and Austria.[19] An appreciation of the logistical dimensions of military operations is the key, here as in many other historical contexts, to an understanding of the significance of victory on the battlefield in this period. If the evolving 'Western way of war' meant the ability to win an apparently decisive tactical success, but without capacity to turn it to operational or strategic benefit, then its limitations are fairly fundamental. One direct consequence of the logistical dimensions of military operations, as contemporaries recognized, was that the most typical form of military engagement throughout these centuries was not the battle but the siege. Complex artillery-resistant fortifications which had been evolving dramatically since the late fifteenth century were confronted by a science of siege warfare which was able to counter many of the advantages brought by new fortifications. However, the challenge of sustaining a large army in a lengthy siege was the single most demanding logistical problem faced by early modern military organization, and failure to keep the besieging army supplied was far more likely to end the siege than the strength of the fortifications.[20]

More general doubts about the extent that technological innovation underpins a Western way of war have been expressed in the last decade, perhaps an inevitable reaction to the fashionable enthusiasm for identifying technologically based 'revolutions in military affairs' during the 1990s. Emphasis has instead been placed on the significance of a distinctive 'culture of combat': the particular character of Western warfare does not lie in an ability to devise, appropriate, and apply new weapons, organization and military thinking, but in a cultural conditioning towards certain types of military behaviour that optimize the impact of these developments.[21] This behaviour would include forbearance under fire, a disciplined subordination to the military requirements of the collectivity, and a powerful sense of group identity and responsibility. As the proponents of these cultural arguments point out, none of these qualities is likely to develop naturally in a warrior society which is conditioned to value individual prowess and feats of arms.[22] At some point, such cultural conditioning had to be created or instilled, and a search for this can of course take us back to the initial early modern military revolution: the science and practice of drill can be regarded as a momentous departure from a traditional warrior culture, a means to impose a powerful, external discipline on troops in order to achieve qualities of self-restraint and collective action.[23] This laid the groundwork of a military superiority which would allow small numbers of Europeans to challenge vastly superior numbers of troops from other cultures, even when these troops had comparable technology, remaining confident that drill and discipline would win the day.

Such an argument is an appealing means to salvage the importance of the first, early modern military revolution, even helping to maintain its significance as a world-transforming event. As part of the general Western template for war, however, it has two obvious problems. Within Europe, it completely fails to explain why drill and exact discipline when applied amongst some troops should produce outstanding military results, and amongst others prove a complete failure. If Scottish mercenaries in Gustavus Adolphus' Swedish army appear to have fallen easily and smoothly into the demands of a drill-based battle discipline, numerous German militias raised by territorial rulers in the early seventeenth century on the promise that drill would transform them into effective soldiers showed no signs of such transformation. French and Italian troops throughout the seventeenth and eighteenth centuries were far more resistant to exactly the same disciplinary prescriptions and practices that turned the Prussian and Russian conscripts into military automatons.[24] This may of course be a good reason to talk of European military cultures, rather than culture: some cultures being more able to trade off warrior individualism for group subordination than others. More challenging is the perceived capacity of non-European cultures to demonstrate equal, if not superior, qualities of forbearance and group discipline, either when drilled by European officers or through a recognition that such collective discipline would optimize the impact of their weaponry. Thus, north Indian Rajput tribesmen, enlisted as sepoys by the British East India Company, demonstrated at least as high a degree of military discipline as their European counterparts; furthermore, they might find themselves fighting other Indian soldiers who had independently been taught the same military skills.[25]

This danger of seeing a European military culture as in some way a unique product of a particular social and political evolution is compounded by the far from straightforward issue of identifying what actually produces military effectiveness in Western, or indeed any other, armies and navies. The introduction of drill and professional standards of discipline seems to offer a neat link with states and societies pushing forward into the modern world of centralized and bureaucratic control, administrative regulation, and individual self-restraint under the rule of law, but it is not an exclusive explanation for the military effectiveness of Western soldiers. If group cohesion is a crucial means by which troops can enhance military performance, then we can draw in military institutions and practices which might be seen as the antithesis of the military innovations of the seventeenth century. One typical example of this would relate to 'small group dynamics', the encouragement of soldiers within a military unit to form themselves into subsidiary, often voluntary, informal groups with an experienced leader and a strong sense of collective bonding. This is vitally important in understanding why units fight effectively, but impossible to establish as the innovation of a particular army. In the European case, we have evidence that the system was formalized in the German mercenary *Landsknecht* regiments of the sixteenth century as the *Rott* of eight to ten men, with its informally elected *Rottmeister*, and in the Spanish *tercios* of the same period, with their system of *camaradas*.[26] There is no mention of any such system in the literature relating to the organization of units under the reformed military discipline, and indeed it might be thought that such an informal structure with its emphasis on the cohesion of the small group would be the antithesis of the demand for drill and discipline applied uniformly across the unit. If the reformed armies positively sought to eliminate what might be seen as a potentially subversive system of lower level authority, mutual support, and reliance, then evidence from other contexts would suggest that it would most likely diminish the military effectiveness of their troops. If, as seems more likely, such systems persisted under the surface of the new drill and discipline, it inevitably dilutes the idea that the Western way of war was linked to a single, distinctive set of military reforms.

All of these qualifications and modifications bring us to the largest and most fundamental assumption about both the character of 'military revolutions' and the distinctiveness of a Western template for war: that the military development of the West rested from the seventeenth century onwards on the symbiosis of military and state power. The growth of centralizing authority, extending its administrative reach over the resources, rights, and actions of subjects, facilitated a military expansion which was itself state controlled and directed. For the two centuries between *circa* 1750 and *circa* 1950, this offers a convincing picture of Western military organization: war and the state do appear to be tightly interlocked. But stepping outside this period, the situation looks very different. Seen across a broader sweep of European history, the maintenance of state-recruited and state-administered military forces is an anomaly. The characteristic pattern of European warfare from the world of the Greek city-states to the *ancien régime* of the eighteenth century, and once again emerging during the half-century down to the present, is military organization deployed on the basis of private contracts, whether these are for the recruitment and maintenance of fighting soldiers, for the provision of military hardware and munitions, or for military support systems. This willingness to place military organization and authority into private hands does not in general mean handing the military over entirely to private military contractors and commanders; more often it is what could be described as varying forms of public–private partnership, in which very substantial elements of private contracting, finance and administration are present in systems which may still retain a core of state-raised or state-maintained troops and/or ships.

The argument that rulers and governments, faced with the mounting costs and burdens of war, would inevitably embark on a course of military and political centralization, and undertake what are assumed to be rational programmes of administrative expansion, concentration of power, and the elimination of legal and political particularism and privilege, rests on a number of unwarranted assumptions about the existing character of authority and control of resources within the early modern state. Traditionally, the establishment of mutually reinforcing systems of military and state power has been presented as a simple act of will on the part of rulers, subsumed under the concept of the 'rise of the absolute state'. Faced with the obvious problems of such personalized explanations ('Louis XIV was a strong king'), more recent historical accounts slip into a fuzzy circularity about exactly how it was that exponentially increased demands for military resources were translated into higher taxes, the reduction of provincial and institutional autonomy, the introduction of conscription, and the militarization of society.[27]

The dilemmas posed for rulers by the increasing scale, expense, and diversity of warfare extended back well before the period of an early modern military revolution. For the European great powers and many secondary states, wars in the century from the 1460s down to the 1560s had been fought not with armies of subjects but on the basis of large-scale contracts with military specialists: Swiss and German pikemen, German and Italian pistol-armed cavalry, light cavalry from eastern Europe. There was nothing new about the hire of mercenaries, typically used as force-enhancers within armies throughout the middle ages. But the scale of contracting with military specialists raised outside the authority of the state grew to an unprecedented level in these decades. In 1558, the main French campaign army of 40,000 troops comprised 70 per cent German and Swiss mercenaries, hired on the basis of cash advances and wage premiums well above levels of native soldiers' pay.[28] This huge commitment to military contracts offered attractive organizational and military benefits to rulers, but it was bought at a massive and inflexible financial cost. And these financial demands fell upon governments whose real access to the resources of their subjects had remained constrained at almost every level from the geographic to the constitutional.[29] By the mid-sixteenth century, an impasse had been reached as successive warring governments toppled into insolvency and debt-rescheduling, so that warfare threatened to grind to a halt amidst unpaid and mutinous troops.[30]

One response to this mid-century military-fiscal crisis might have been the abandonment of dependence on private military contracting and a radical overhaul and rationalization of the state's fiscal and administrative machinery to permit the more effective, economical, and direct control of armies—a 'military revolution', in effect. The actual response was a further ratcheting up of the scale of private military contracting, and the full flowering of the large-scale military enterpriser, a mercenary commander but one prepared to make substantial advances from his own financial resources to recruit, equip, and maintain military force. Lengthier wars and a new willingness by rulers specifically to delegate authority to collect war taxes—'contributions'—directly from territory where the troops were billeted made unprecedented levels of investment in the state's military activity attractive to a range of freelancing military commanders. At its largest, this could result in the establishment of a so-called general contractor, like Albrecht von Wallenstein, who had been prepared to advance huge sums of money from his own resources, from his own financial backers, and from the subcontracted resources of his colonels and other participating officers to raise an army of over 100,000 troops. Or it could be seen in the smaller scale but no less significant and almost universal dependence on enterpriser-colonels, bringing one or several of their privately raised regiments into Swedish, Spanish, French, or other military service at their own expense.[31] With a slight lateral move, it can also encompass the emergence of a commercial–military enterprise like the Dutch East India Company, founded in 1602. Entirely funded by shareholders' capital, the Dutch East India Company invested in state-of-the-art military technology—ships, fortifications, off-the-peg mercenary companies—and paid interest to its shareholders not from the exaction of war taxes but from the profits of trading monopolies—many of which involved the direct sale of 'protection'—from Africa to Indo-China.[32]

This period, which might more justifiably be termed the age of 'military devolution', rather than military revolution, sits uncomfortably with most traditional accounts of the rise of the Western military tradition. Steeped in a rhetoric of hostility to mercenaries and to non-state-controlled military force, historians have usually dismissed the period as an anomalous wrong-turning along the inexorable path to the creation of the state army, one characterized by feeble levels of tactical and operational coherence; self-interested, short-termist commanders and officers; and a conflict—the Thirty Years War—which is taken as a byword for stagnant, futile, and brutalizing warfare. It is assumed to be axiomatic that war fought on the basis of massive delegation of military authority and almost unfettered private enterprise was a disastrous failure. Gustavus Adolphus' death at the battle of Lützen, only fourteen months after Breitenfeld, removed the one figure considered capable of implementing a modern, rational approach to warfare. None of his successors during the remainder of the Thirty Years War could rise to his achievement, but a lesson was learnt through the protracted, destructive futility of the war.[33] After 1648, the rulers of European states set about reforming the military enterpriser out of business and seizing upon the modernizing legacy of Gustavus Adolphus as the model for reformed, state-controlled armies. Starting with the army reforms of the Great Elector of Brandenburg-Prussia, and from the 1660s the army of Louis XIV, there was a general, deliberate move towards the creation and expansion of state-controlled, state-raised, and state-administered armies.

The dismissal of the fighting qualities and military effectiveness of the armies raised by private enterprise has little justification in the light of the actual evidence of their performance. But it does appear that European rulers from the mid-seventeenth century had decided, more or less collectively, that contracting-out the military organization and control of their armies was incompatible with their sovereign status. Yet at the same time as wishing to assert this principle of state control, they and their ministers were aware that military enterprise in the preceding period had allowed the waging of war on an unprecedented scale and duration: it had mobilized the financial and organizational resources of groups of their powerful subjects in a way that could offer these subjects a variety of benefits and attractions from direct participation in war. Without this active and willing participation, rulers would have been faced with a bitter, difficult, and, quite possibly, losing struggle to try to tap the bulk of economic and financial resources concentrated in the hands of their political and social elites.[34]

The result of these two pressures—a ruler wished to be in command of his/her army and navy, but to preserve the mechanisms that could tap the financial resources of the elites—led to the compromises that actually under-pinned the supposedly state-controlled European armies of the later seven-teenth and eighteenth century. If considerably larger, better, and more lavishly equipped armies and navies were to be supported by states whose tax-base might have increased, but to nothing approaching a level sufficient to fund this military expansion, then the financial support of the elites needed to be co-opted. This was done by maintaining formal military proprietorship for the unit officers under a façade of centralized state control. Rulers, anxious to raise and equip large numbers of soldiers, raised the funds for this by continuing to sell rights as officer-stakeholders in the armies. This is quite familiar in the case of German armies of the period, with their constant references to regimental proprietors, or *Obristinhaber*, and later on the 'business of the company', the *Kompaniewirtschaft*.[35] But as two recent studies have demon-strated, the mechanism by which the French army was vastly expanded from the 1660s to the 1690s was a deliberate formalization and institutionalization of venality in military office.[36] Granting colonels of regiments, and later company captains, the opportunity to buy and sell their units under proprie-tary contracts gave them strong incentives to invest capital not just in purchasing the unit in the first place but in being prepared to enhance its capital value by further financial commitments. Private–public partnership stood at the heart of military systems in which, in theory, the state held the power to raise, operate, and break units, and to subject their officers to external discipline. In practice, the tradition of a relatively autonomous officer corps, whose cooperation needed to be bought if the army—or navy—was to be made effective, remained the characteristic of the Western way of war throughout this period.[37]

Regimental and company proprietorship may have stood at the heart of the military system down to the mid-eighteenth century (and in many armies such as the British, well beyond this time), but it should be seen as only one part of a much larger and persistent role for private enterprise in all the ancillary aspects of warfare.[38] Private contractors continued to be used in most circum-stances to ensure munitions and food supply for armies and navies, for the transport of foodstuffs and weapons, contracts for the repair and maintenance of fleets and fortifications. The evidence that the state was encroaching on these areas and seeking to extend its direct authority is slight.

All of this sounds less anomalous when added to what is seen as the great test and the triumphant demonstration of successive European military revo-lutions, the projection of European military power into a wider world. Private shareholder companies were the dynamo of European colonial expansion. It was not states so much as colonial trading companies which brought the new military technology and organization of the West into contact with African, Asian, and American indigenous states and civilizations, above all in the long period of expansion down to 1800. What conditioned a quest for military effectiveness, the economical deployment of greater force through better military technology or organization, was not the 'Western' synthesis of state power and military reform but shareholder capital in search of investment returns.

Such a perspective offers a very different account of the dynamics of Western military expansion, one which seems to challenge the necessity for a direct connection between the growth of state power and the demands of war. Down to the mid-eighteenth century, the response of European rulers to larger scale, more expensive, and more organizationally demanding warfare was not the growth of the state and the establishment of its monopoly over military force but a series of experiments with various forms of military contracting-out, or, ultimately, private–public partnership. That the Western way of war shifted towards direct control by the state of the organization, financing and waging of war in the latter half of the eighteenth century was owed to a particular set of European political and industrial developments which altered both the character and scale of warfare, and demanded a level of military participation and commitment which simply could not be met through adjusting and developing the traditional mechanisms for organizing and waging war.

The link between military revolution, state power, and a particular Western way of war has undoubtedly provided one of the most powerful and tenacious grand theories to explain both European state development and European global expansion and reach. However, it has depended on the acceptance of certain basic premises, whether about the leading role of technological innovation, or about the centrality to Western military success of what may be little more than a particular style of drill-based organization and discipline, of relatively local and particular tactical significance. Above all, the argument places at its core an assumption about the development of state power as an essential concomitant of military power-projection which looks less than convincing in the light of the practical mechanisms for raising and deploying armies and navies in the period before 1750. Such unilinear accounts look unsatisfactory as a depiction of a developing Western way of war in 1650, just as they appear increasingly limited and unsatisfactory today.

## NOTES

1. *The Swedish Discipline* (translated by William Watts) (London, 1632). Notable exponents of the 'innovative drilling by numbers' approach were Jacob de Gheyn, with his much-translated *Exercise of Arms* (1st published 1607; reprinted London, 1986), and the numerous illustrated manuals of Jacobi of Wallhausen: see for example the *Kriegskunst zu Fuß* (Oppenheim, 1615).

2. Michael Roberts, 'Gustav Adolf and the art of war', in Michael Roberts (ed.), *Essays in Swedish history* (London: Weidenfeld and Nicolson, 1967), 56–81; Idem., *Gustavus Adolphus: A history of Sweden*, 1611–32 (London: Longmans, Green & Co., 1958), 169–271.

3. A point frequently made by historians and with varying levels of credulity. See the classic study: Werner Hahlweg, *Die Heeresreform der Oranien und die Antike* (Berlin: Junker und Dünnhaupt, 1941).

4. Geoffrey Parker, *The military revolution. Military innovation and the rise of the West, 1500–1800* (Cambridge: Cambridge University Press, 1996), 140f.

5. Michael Roberts, 'The military revolution, 1560–1660' in Idem., *Essays in Swedish history*, 195–225.

6. Otto Hintze provides the classic argument: *Gesammelte Abhandlungen zur allgemeinen Verfassungsgeschichte*, edited by Gerhard Oestreich (Göttingen: Vandenhoeck und Ruprecht, 1962–1967), see especially: 'Der Commissarius und seine Bedeutung in der allgemeinen Verwaltungsgeschichte; eine vergleichende Studie' (1910), 242–74; 'Machtpolitik und Regierungsverfassung' (1913), 424–56; 'Die Hohenzollern und der Adel' (1914), 30–55.

7. Roberts, *Military revolution*, 195.

8. Noel Perrin, *Giving up the gun: Japan's reversion to the sword* (Boston: D.R. Godine, 1979).

9. Numerous studies have examined aspects of this issue, but see especially William H. McNeill, *The pursuit of power: Technology, armed force and society since A.D. 1000* (Chicago: University of Chicago Press, 1982); Brian M. Downing, *The military revolution and political change: Origins of democracy and autocracy in early modern Europe* (Princeton, NJ: Princeton University Press, 1992); Bruce Porter, *War and the rise of the state: The military foundations of modern politics* (New York: Free Press, 1994).

10. MacGregor Knox and Williamson Murray (eds.), *The dynamics of military revolution 1300–2050* (Cambridge: Cambridge University Press, 2001), 1–14, which identifies five credible candidates for 'military revolution' status in modern Western history.

11. Peter Paret, 'Conscription and the end of the ancien régime in France and Prussia', in Idem., *Understanding war: Essays on Clausewitz and the history of military power* (Princeton, NJ: Princeton University Press, 1993), 53–74.

12. T.C.W. Blanning, *The French Revolutionary Wars, 1787–1802* (London: Arnold, 1996), 1–20, 116–28.

13. Bert S. Hall, *Weapons and warfare in Renaissance Europe: Gunpowder, technology, and tactics* (Baltimore: Johns Hopkins University Press, 1997), 134–56.

14. And even then, see Jürgen Luh, *Kriegskunst in Europa, 1650–1800* (Cologne: Böhlau Verlag, 2004), 129–54, which *inter alia* stresses contemporary evidence that even with eighteenth-century muskets and drill, 250–400 shots were fired in battle for every man killed or wounded (173). Similar scepticism in David Chandler, *The art of war in the age of Marlborough* (London: Batsford, 1976), 114–30.

15. Luh, *Kriegskunst*, 160–73.

16. Jan Glete, *Navies and nations: Warships, navies and state building in Europe and America, 1500–1860* (Stockholm: Almqvist & Wiksell International, 1993), 6–48.

17. Notable here is Colin Gray's argument that an obsession with identifying RMAs in the Western military tradition has had a retrograde and unhelpful effect on our understanding of what underpins military effectiveness: Colin S. Gray, *Strategy for chaos: Revolutions in military affairs and the evidence of history* (London: Frank Cass, 2002).

18. Michael Kaiser, *Politik und Kriegführung: Maximilian von Bayern, Tilly und die Katholische Liga im Dreißigjährigen Krieg* (Münster: Aschendorff, 1999), 466–70: different accounts give the total number of troops reassembled by mid-October at between 40,000 and 70,000.

19. Roberts, *Gustavus Adolphus*, 538–59.

20. Geoffrey Parker, 'The artillery fortress as an engine of European overseas expansion, 1480–1750', in James D. Tracy (ed.), *City walls: The urban enceinte in global perspective* (Cambridge: Cambridge University Press, 2000), 387–93.

21. An altogether less convincing 'cultural' argument seeks to construct a general template for warfare focused upon the supposedly greater ruthlessness and freedom from convention of the West in pursuing its military objectives, based upon the defence of political rights and individual liberty: Victor D. Hanson, *Why the West has won: Carnage and culture from Salamis to Vietnam* (London: Faber and Faber, 2001).

22. John Lynn, *Battle: A history of combat and culture* (Boulder CO: Lynne Rienner, 2003).

23. Dennis E. Showalter, 'Caste, skill and training: The evolution of cohesion in European armies from the middle ages to the sixteenth century', *Journal of Military History* 57/3 (1993), 407–30; William H. McNeill, *Keeping together in time: Dance and drill in human history* (Cambridge, MA: Harvard University Press, 1995).

24. For the failure of militias to develop military effectiveness, see: Winfried Schulze, 'Die deutschen Landesdefensionen im 16. und 17. Jahrhundert', in Johannes Kunisch (ed.), *Staatsverfassung und Heeresverfassung in der europäischen Geschichte der frühen Neuzeit* (Berlin: Duncker & Humblot, 1986), 129–49. On the problems of drilling French infantry, see Blanning, *French Revolutionary Wars*, 17, quoting the comte de Saint Germain in 1757.

25. On Russia and the Ottoman Empire, see: David B. Ralston, *Importing the European Army: The introduction of European military techniques and institutions into the extra-European world, 1600–1914* (Chicago, IL: Chicago University Press, 1990), 13–78. For Maratha soldiers' ability to deploy Western drill and discipline against forces of European-led Sepoys, see Randolf G.S. Cooper, *The Anglo-Maratha campaigns and the contest for India: The struggle for control of the South Asian military economy* (Cambridge: Cambridge University Press, 2003), 287–91.

26. Reinhard Baumann, *Landsknechte: Ihre Geschichte und Kultur vom späten Mittelalter bis zum Dreißigjährigen Krieg* (Munich: Verlag C.H. Beck, 1994), 101: the same system had existed in the Swiss pike-squares of the fifteenth century;

Geoffrey Parker, *The army of Flanders and the Spanish road, 1567–1659* (2nd ed., Cambridge: Cambridge University Press, 2004), 151–2.

27. For a neat example of this circularity, see Berhard Sicken, 'Der Dreißigjährige Krieg als Wendepunkt: Kriegsführung und Heeresstruktur im Übergang zum *miles perpetuus*', in Heinz Duchhardt (ed.), *Der Westfälische Friede. Diplomatie, politische Zäsur, kulturelles Umfeld, Rezeptionsgeschichte* (Munich: Oldenbourg, 1998), 598.

28. James B. Wood, *The king's army. Warfare, soldiers and society during the Wars of religion in France, 1562–1576* (Cambridge: Cambridge University Press, 1996), 38–41.

29. See for example, James B. Collins, *Fiscal limits of absolutism. Direct taxation in early seventeenth-century France* (Berkeley, CA: University of California Press, 1988); Jean Bérenger, 'Fiscalité et économie en Autriche XVIe–XVIIe siècles', in Jean Bouvier, Jean-Claude Perrot (eds.), *États, fiscalités, économies. Actes du cinquième congrès de l'association française des historiens économistes* (Paris: Presses de l'Université de Paris-Sorbonne, 1983), 13–25.

30. As a general overview: Henri Hauser, 'The European financial crisis of 1559', in *Journal of Economic and Business History* 2 (1929–30), 241–55.

31. David Parrott, *The business of war. Military enterprise and military revolution in early modern Europe* (Cambridge: Cambridge University Press, 2011). See the classic study by Fritz Redlich, *The military enterpriser and his work force* (Wiesbaden: F. Steiner, 1964).

32. Niels Steensgard, 'The Dutch East India Company as an institutional innovation', in Maurice Aymard (ed.), *Dutch capitalism and world capitalism* (Cambridge: Cambridge University Press, 1982), 235–57.

33. Roberts, 'Gustav Adolf and the Art of War', 74.

34. The stakes in attempting direct confrontation with recalcitrant local elites were high, as both the Catalan revolt of 1640 and the French *Frondes* of 1648–53 demonstrate.

35. Redlich, *Military enterpriser*, 48–87; Christopher Duffy, *Instruments of war: The Austrian army in the Seven Years' War, Vol. 1* (Rosemont, IL: Emperor's Press, 2000), 151–3.

36. Guy Rowlands, *The dynastic state and the army under Louis XIV. Royal service and private interest, 1661–1701* (Cambridge: Cambridge University Press, 2002), 166–71; Hervé Drévillon, *L'impôt du sang. Le métier des armes sous Louis XIV* (Paris: Éditions Tallandier, 2005), 179–211.

37. For a succinct account of some of these implications, see: Jean Chagniot, 'La rationalisation de l'armée française après 1660', in *Armées et diplomatie dans l'Europe du XVIIe siècle* (Actes du colloque des association des historiens modernistes), (Paris: Presses de l'Université de Paris-Sorbonne, 1991), 97–108.

38. For Britain, see: Alan J. Guy, *Oeconomy and discipline: Officership and administration in the British army, 1714–1763* (Manchester: Manchester University Press, 1985).

# 3

# Changes in War: The French Revolutionary and Napoleonic Wars

*Michael Broers*

The ideological currents that flow around the fighting during the Revolutionary and Napoleonic Wars, together with their sheer length and scale, make it all too easy to see them as harbingers of the new. The most recent manifestation of this is to see in them the dawn of modern 'total war', a view which, itself, draws on rather better established tendencies to accept the political rhetoric of the protagonists at face value.[1] To concentrate on the waging of the wars themselves presents a very different picture, however. The military profile of tactics, armaments, and the conduct of armies in the period 1792–1815 points to quite the opposite of dramatic change. Indeed, the Revolutionary–Napoleonic wars are not the beginning of a new era in European warfare. Rather, they are the end of something; they are the last great wars fought without modern technology, and so the last fought with early modern tactics.

Their precise point in time is essential in grasping this. Napoleonic armies marched or rode into battle; they fought overwhelmingly with muskets and swords; they were still constrained by the seasons, specifically by the cycle of the harvests, at least if their commanders had any sense. Commanders predicated all they did, and all they considered viable, on these basic, seemingly eternal constraints. It is not without significance that the most novel military innovations of period were often almost retrograde, technologically, such as the re-emergence of the lance among the light cavalry or the heavy cavalry charge as a decisive factor in combat. Innovations in conventional warfare were about adapting, refining, and even resurrecting what was already there.

Where the new is truly evident is in the management of war, primarily through the role and character of the state in raising troops and maintaining them on a war footing, but also in the response of what were still, fundamentally, early modern rural, peasant societies to the new state and this unprecedented period of prolonged fighting, most emphatically in the emergence of true guerrilla warfare in much of western Europe. The real changes wrought by the Napoleonic wars were in the art of government; the mobilization of rural Europe was not achieved by new technology but by the honing of a professional bureaucracy, aided by a new police force, the Gendarmerie, and their merger into a potent coercive administrative machine.

Thus, this chapter is divided into two distinct sections, beginning with a survey of how the Revolutionary–Napoleonic wars were waged, followed by an analysis of how they were managed. If so short an essay concentrates overwhelmingly on the Napoleonic, essentially French, armies, to the neglect of their opponents, that is because France set the pace of the wars, and so the military agendas of the era. The Prussian reform movement, the piecemeal—if highly effective—emergence of a mass land army in Britain, the frustrated reforms of the Archduke Charles in Austria were all responses to the galvanizing of France, 'the China of Europe', into life.

## WAGING WAR

The most striking and decisive innovation in the Revolutionary–Napoleonic wars came at their very outset and, indeed, made them possible. This was the unexpected revitalization of France as an aggressive, successful military power. The new, revolutionary regime was able to mobilize huge numbers of men on a hitherto unimaginable scale, beginning in 1791, and more or less, from then onwards. This was primarily a feat of management, a mixture of political will and administrative efficiency that will be discussed later. Its immediate military impact was twofold. First, it provided France with a mass army of over 200,000 men early in the war, at the very point it was readily assumed by all sides—the French revolutionaries included—that the army of monarchy was melting away, and that it would have proved of little effectiveness, even had it not. Instead, Revolutionary France actually brought into being the long cherished goal of the old order, a huge standing army paid for from public funds, if only just, and, conversely, it finally incarnated the worst nightmare of all the other powers, great and small, that of the most populous nation in Europe fully mobilized in the field.

The corollary of the sudden influx of untrained men into the ranks was to coarsen training and reduce battlefield tactics to their essence, if only momentarily. The famous bayonet charges of Valmy and other early battles over 1792–4 became the stuff of both ideological legend and professional derision, and both assessments are not without foundation. The volunteers of 1791 and 1792 had to be trained in great haste, many were poorly armed and unable to cope with the complex field manoeuvres expected of the professional troops of the regular army. The result was the use of the column and the bayonet, where the line proved too new to *les bleus* and the musket too complicated. Columns were easier for raw recruits to grasp as a formation, and easier for them to hold to under fire. They were narrow, compact, and lacking in firepower but easy to manoeuvre and better suited to the bayonet charge than the line.

It did not stay this way for long, however. The new tactics which so inspired and terrified the German poet Goethe at Valmy did not overly worry the allies, nor did they really impress the French themselves. The whole point of mixing the regulars among the new troops was to instil traditional methods in them, and it worked. New recruits learning from veterans became the norm in the armies of the Republic and the Empire henceforth. The real result of mixing the remaining troops of the regular army—*les blancs*—with the new recruits was to perpetuate the battlefield tactics and discipline of the old order. It could hardly have been otherwise, and the practical result of the amalgamation of *blancs* and *bleus* was the mixed use of column and line. Columns were used to advance into positions, lines for the real fighting, which were, as Clausewitz graphically portrayed, about mass musket fire, punctuated by charges by columns.[2] Napoleon often favoured dispersing columns along the line, where he perceived weak points in the enemy's positions. Only towards the end of the wars, from about 1812 onwards, as raw recruits swelled the armies of both sides, did the use of the column become frequent again.[3] Despite the bloody ebb-and-flow of revolutionary politics, the army did its best to get back to the habits of professionalism as soon as possible, at least on the battlefield. The vastly different size of the new forces was what really changed in the 1790s; musket fire was now fundamentally an exercise in saturation and reciprocal exhaustion. Large reserves were now feasible and increasingly central to combat, but weaponry remained unaltered.

The wars of the 1790s were desperate affairs, perhaps the ultimate expression of which was the deliberate French policy of 'living off the land'—that is, of sanctioning plunder by its troops, an undisguised regression to early modern norms. The French Republic, for all its bellicosity, was unprepared for war, and the allies were largely caught unawares and preoccupied by rivalries in the Balkans and Poland. This left little time or money to improve the quality of arms; poor muskets remained a trademark of the French armies from beginning to end, although their artillery, particularly the medium-range field howitzers favoured by Napoleon, did improve in the course of the wars. Experimentation concentrated on organization. The overall trend saw the end of the regiment and the downgrading of the division as fighting units, replaced increasingly by the battalion and brigade, at field level, and by the corps— deliberately predicated on being self-contained in all three arms—at the strategic level. Revolutionary commanders were given fairly free hands in terms of tactics and organization, a result of the political chaos in Paris more than of grand design, and so the 1790s allowed these new structures to evolve ad hoc, and intermittently.

What allowed these experiments to become systematized, and for a coherent military structure finally to re-emerge, was not really Napoleon's seizure of power. He assumed office in direct response to the worst military emergency the Republic had faced since 1793 and could only fight the campaigns of 1799–1800 with the exhausted remnants of the armies of the 1790s. Rather, the respite in the fighting accorded to him by the Treaty of Amiens in 1801, coupled with his abortive attempt to invade Britain, allowed him almost by chance to forge a completely new army in the Channel camps between 1802 and 1805. The corps system finally became the working basis for the army; regular drill—still of *les blancs* trained under the old order or by veterans of the 1790s whom they had trained in their turn—created unprecedented levels of parade-ground discipline, if not always uniform practice; the whole army learned how to swim, giving it singular levels of fitness; the line troops were drilled hard in amphibious embarking and landing, useless on the face of it, but instilling in them habits of teamwork that transferred to combat.[4] The whole combination of factors produced in the Channel camps—the high levels of fitness and morale, the exceptional amounts of drill and high-precision training this time afforded to the ranks, the youthful and ambitious character of the commanders—created a uniquely great army. All this enabled Napoleon to count on success at a tactical level; the Camp de Boulogne was what allowed him to go looking for major engagements in his subsequent campaigns, at least until 1809. These circumstances, at once fortuitous and exploited with such genius, allowed him to negate considerations at campaign or theatre level. As Clausewitz noted, 'Bonaparte could ruthlessly cut through all his enemies' strategic plans in search of battle, because he seldom doubted the battle's outcome'.[5] Put another way, after the experience of the Channel ports, the French could—and did—crush all comers in direct combat.

One arm, more than any other, was galvanized by the unique experience afforded by the Camp de Boulogne, the cavalry. Cavalry were expensive and took a long time to train, but Boulogne turned the French cavalry from something close to a joke into a large, deadly weapon that transformed the Napoleonic battle in two ways. The army of Louis XVI had one regiment of truly heavy cavalry; by 1804, there were thirty dragoon regiments of the line, twelve of *cuirassiers*—the truly heavy units, armed with *sabres* and fully armoured—and two carbine regiments, as the reserve. Napoleon used the dragoons all round the battlefield, to plug holes in the infantry line and support the artillery, but the *cuirassiers* were shock troops, held back until the right moment, and used, literally, to punch holes in the enemy infantry. These tactics had more to do with Hastings than Blenheim, but they could work to perfection, as they came close to doing even at Waterloo. By 1804, the light cavalry comprised ten hussar regiments and twenty-four of light *chasseurs*, but it was put to a very different, if equally effective use: pursuit.[6] Henceforth, few Napoleonic victories were over when the enemy withdrew from the field, as the light cavalry's task was to turn retreat into rout. Indeed, where one mounted arm did its job ruthlessly enough, the other was often almost redundant. The *cuirassiers* so splintered the allied infantry at Austerlitz that they scattered in four directions, so making pursuit unnecessary, whereas at Jena-Auerstadt the Prussians initially managed to extricate a coherent body of troops, with a clear line of retreat outlined for them, only to be harassed into panic and disarray by a well coordinated pursuit by the light cavalry. The conquest of central Europe in 1806–7 handed Napoleon the great stud farms of Prussia and Poland, so allowing the arm to expand in size and quality beyond previous possibilities, and he was so impressed by the Prussian and Austrian lancers he encountered on these campaigns that new lancer regiments were added to the light cavalry. Thus, an ancient weapon returned to the field, as well as primordial tactics. Proof of how important the reemergence of the cavalry was to Napoleonic warfare became clearest when it was no longer there. The French lost almost all their horses in the 1812 Russian campaign and, when Napoleon initially defeated Russian and Prussian forces in the battles of Bautzen and Lützen, in 1813, it was soon apparent that he could no longer follow up set-piece victories. Alexander I of Russia now had the powerful cavalry, and in the years between Jena and 1812 he had also done much, in clandestine manner, to help the Prussians rebuild their mounted units. Napoleon was henceforth deprived of what had so rapidly—and almost unexpectedly—become an essential arm of his forces. He sought, with some success, to rebuild it after 1812; it came too late for the last campaigns of 1813–14 but was sufficiently powerful by the 100 Days almost to turn the tide at Waterloo.

This was what was novel about Napoleonic warfare, but none of it could be described as innovation derived from technology. Muskets still dominated infantry weaponry; rifles were thinly spread and concentrated on specialist light infantry skirmishers and the dragoons. Target practice was, therefore, secondary to drill. The line re-emerged as the essential formation for infantry in the field, supported and interspersed with columns, as the average experience of line units increased. If skirmishers were used more than in earlier conflicts, they were there to protect traditional lines of traditionally armed heavy infantry. If heavy cavalry got a new lease of life, it was to deliver something closer to a mediaeval hammer blow than anything else. Pre-battle manoeuvres reached high levels of premeditated sophistication, but the field, itself, was increasingly dominated by something that can almost be described as crude impact. Only the ever-improving accuracy of field artillery really points the way to the future, but, just as with infantry fire, guns were still not accurate enough to count for much in terms of selective targeting. Mass cannon, pouring down into the enemy prior to first engagement, were still what really did the damage. Discipline did not stretch far beyond the parade ground; unruly, brutal foraging was always the rule for the Napoleonic armies.

The genuinely new aspect of the wars was their scale, and what was entailed in managing it. The *Grande Armée* that left the Channel ports for the Rhine in 1805 numbered 190,000 men—closer to half a million, if its south German allies are counted—while Napoleon poured over 200,000 men into Spain in 1808. The following year, 180,000 men and 550 cannon formed the French army for the 1809 Wagram campaign. A total of 440,000 men and 1,200 pieces of artillery entered Russia in 1812. Battles, not just entire campaign forces, were huge too. Just over 75,000 French troops fought actively at Austerlitz. Roughly the same numbers existed for the campaigns of 1806 and 1807, but over 130,000 troops of the *Grande Armée* fought at Borodino in 1812, of whom over 30,000 became casualties—and over 9,000 of whom were corpses.[7] The Allies kept pace with these escalations, yet it is also worth remarking that probably the best trained, equipped, and led national army by the end of the wars was the Prussian, which was also the smallest. The corps system, with a command structure predicated first and foremost on delegation, proved the most efficient way of coping with this vast new world. Napoleon was fortunate in having so many excellent and, even more, experienced commanders in such big operations, and his failure to delegate to the usual degree in 1812 was, almost certainly, a major part of his undoing. If innovation, as opposed to adaptation, is to be sought in the armies of the Revolutionary–Napoleonic wars, it is found, first and foremost, in the sheer scale of the armies involved and, then, in the command structures needed to manage them. Generals had never really been able to control their troops once combat actually began, but the growth in numbers in the field, and the new complexities of positional manoeuvres prior to engagement, meant that delegation and coordination became more crucial than in the past. However, in the 1812 campaign it was clear that Napoleon was beginning to have serious problems managing an army of so great a size, the logistics and methods of management he had developed so well on a smaller scale now proving inadequate to coping with so many men over so wide a front. These were lessons that were carried into the nineteenth and early twentieth centuries.

## THE MANAGEMENT OF WAR

Little genuinely new actually came out the Revolutionary–Napoleonic wars. Napoleon could still draw genuine insight, as well as inspiration, from Alexander and Caesar, because he, like them, still had to haul himself and his men over the Alps by the same methods, march along roads that were not much better—where they existed—and, given the relatively poor quality of firearms of all sizes, he had to rely on shock troops, like—if not exactly like—his boyhood heroes. The army of the French Revolution resurrected the bayonet, Napoleon the lance.

Nevertheless, there was something very different about the scale of it all. Scale sacrificed training, advanced armaments, and even the whole concept of proper supply, but the vast numbers that led to a coarsening on the one hand denoted the growing sophistication of the state apparatus on the other. A very new, very modern civilian administrative system recruited and mobilized the *Grande Armée* and stood in stark contrast to the almost retrograde bluntness of its fighting capacity and the lawlessness with which it provisioned itself, once set on campaign. How the armies of the period became this huge, and remained so, is a very pertinent question, and it is also, without doubt, the biggest single change in warfare in this period and, arguably, the most significant. To underline this, it might be recalled that the reason Napoleon was swayed to fight on in 1813 and, again, in 1814 was the sure knowledge that 237,000 new conscripts were awaiting him in the depots.[8] He found the same in March 1815. That the near obliteration of the *Grande Armée* in 1812 was almost made good, in quantity if not in quality, was a civilian achievement. It began with the first reforms of the French Revolution.

In 1789, the institutional structures of *ancien régime* government simply collapsed in France. The revolutionaries, however bitter and bloody their political divisions, had a clear, rational answer to filling the void. At a stroke, they abolished feudal, corporate, and provincial privilege on the famous night of 4 August 1789. Individual cases of deprived lords versus under-empowered peasants would drag on in the courts for decades afterwards, but from the point of view of the central government—any central government, right or left, royal, republican, or imperial—this was not what mattered. Rather, the way was now clear to tax all Frenchmen according to their personal wealth; money could now flow unimpeded by either privilege or the administrative mess of fragmented local government. A rational, profitable system of taxation was in place; local government was streamlined and centralized. Manageable, broadly uniform departments replaced the jigsaw of provinces, fiefs, and lopsided government intendancies; population records and statistics were taken out of the hands of the church and made the responsibility of the civil authorities; henceforth, the government would have at its fingertips data on who was married, who was alive or dead, who was what age. Those who, at the time, saw this as interfering and intrusive may have been paranoid in the hopeful, pacific honeymoon years of 1789–91, but they were proved right once war broke out with the rest of Europe in 1792: for the first time in its long history, the French state knew how many people it ruled, how they were distributed across its administrative units—the departments—and who was of conscription age. Taken together, the administrative and institutional reforms of the first years of the French Revolution—of the brief pre-war period—made it possible to tax and conscript the largest population in Europe, should the need arise, and arise it did, as early as the spring of 1792.

This was all purely on paper, in 1792. The new authorities had no real teeth, and they knew it. The new, rational taxes were not collected until about 1792–3, although it seems that the collection of marriage, birth, and death statistics for the new *État civil* had made remarkable progress. France was not, on the face of it, a state prepared for major war in 1792, but the structures were now in place to enable the new regime to make effective use of the institutional reforms of the early years. Ironically, the power vacuum in local government had been created as a result of the refusal of the new regime to use the old royal army, whose loyalty it rightly suspected, to repress rural unrest in 1789–90. To protect themselves, the towns and cities of provincial France set up their own local militias, more or less loyal to the Revolution, and they were soon subsumed under the new, pan-national umbrella as the National Guard, a part-time citizen force seen as a counterweight to the regular army. From its ranks emerged three crucial elements for the management and waging of war in the 1790s: the first, most famous and spectacular, were *les bleus*, over 100,000 volunteers who raced to the defence of France in the months leading up to the declaration of war, followed by 120,000 more in 1792. Most of these men came from local National Guard units and were the only significant volunteer force France produced in the whole of the wars. Second, within *les bleus* were a surprising number of men with considerable military experience who had been asked to take charge of local security during the mass peasant revolts of 1789, men retired from the army for one reason or another who, in 1792, now found themselves recalled to new national colours; they trained their own local units and now merged easily with their old comrades, *les blancs*. *Les bleus* produced several Napoleonic marshals, as the sons of the bourgeoisie learned from local veterans and then were mobilized in 1792–3. Augereau and Oudinot represented the ex-soldier who took over training his local volunteers; Lannes, Bessières, and Suchet—the only marshal created in Spain—were civilians-turned-volunteers in 1792.

However, the most crucial contribution to managing the war was made by *les bleus* who stayed behind in 1792. The early unrest of the Revolution had, broadly, armed and opposed the pro-revolutionary towns against the coun-tryside, but the climate had been one of unease, rather than confrontation. The needs of war changed that. By the winter of 1792–3, the scales had well and truly fallen from the eyes of the revolutionaries. This was nowhere more obvious than in their stark realization that the army of the new regime had now got all the volunteers it was ever going to get. Concomitant with this was their admission that the Revolution had evolved into an almost purely urban phenomenon; the peasantry had lost interest in it, as manifest by the fact that *les bleus* were, overwhelmingly, urban men. Thus, the new republican govern-ment in Paris had no other recourse but mass conscription to continue the war, and the masses were peasants, who would have to be conscripted. The result was open rebellion, most successfully and tenaciously across large swathes of western France, beginning in the Vendée, but replicated on a smaller scale almost everywhere, where the local terrain afforded peasant rebels some protection. From this came one of the most ruthless, cynical, and rational decisions of the new regime, but one that too often goes almost ignored: the National Guards of the larger towns and cities were exempted from conscription and deployed to scour the countryside, to enforce the call-ups, the first of which was the *levée en masse* of February 1793, which sought 350,000 men and was based on the statistics of the *État civil*. The urban National Guard emerged as the force that fought the rampant, inchoate civil war inside France throughout the 1790s. Its most famous and notorious component was the *armées révolutionnaires* of the Terror period, which virtually rampaged across the countryside, spreading ideological hooliganism in the form of church-wrecking, alongside the suppression of revolts sparked by conscription, taxation, and the confiscation of food and other necessities for the war effort.[9] The hard truth was that the revolutionary government had to wage a war on its own people to sustain its war effort, and it did so, with the National Guard as its principal weapon. *Les bleus* carried the bulk of the early fighting in the Vendée and elsewhere and suppressed the urban Federalist revolts of 1793–4. The 'blue islands' of the towns of western France were supported by re-enforcements from the Parisian *armées révolutionnaires*. Above all, their thoroughly thuggish efforts extracted the conscripts, materials, and taxes so vital to the war.

The grandiose demands set by the revolutionary regime, particularly in the Terror period, between the spring of 1793 and the summer of 1794, could not disguise the ad hoc, often anarchic nature of the war government run by the Committee of Public Safety in these months. Authorities at every level over-lapped with each other in their briefs, and Paris often chose to confide requisi-tioning and conscription to local Jacobin clubs, bodies outside state structures. It sent out politically reliable members of the government, the representatives-on-mission, to sprawling jurisdictions with wide but ill-defined powers to oversee the organization of the war effort and quash resistance. It was a brutal mess, yet it worked. The Terror was, above all else, intended to be a war government, and it was overthrown in great part when the wider government in Paris felt its leadership had lost sight of this, by the summer of 1794. The Committee of Public Safety was not the sole preserve of ideologues like Robe-spierre; it also contained a core of 'technocrats' led by Lazare Carnot, who went on to serve Napoleon and earn the sobriquet 'the Organiser of Victory'. Most of the 350,000 men called for in February 1793 were raised, marched off to the front, and became hardened veterans. They were intermittently paid, often badly armed and clothed—but not until the Committee of Public Safety had long gone and been replaced by the more corrupt, less efficient if less brutal,

Directory between 1795 and 1799. As the French armies advanced into the Low Countries, the Rhineland, Switzerland and, above all, Italy, the war began to pay for itself from 1794 onwards, through the ruthless exploitation of the extra-French territories it acquired. However, in the fraught, often desperate years between 1792 and 1794, a war government emerged that laid important foundations and precedents for the successor Napoleonic regimes. There was real method at work, under the revolutionary madness.

The Napoleonic regime continued the ethos of total mobilization developed under the Terror and extended it to every part of Europe brought under its control. It had to. However, even before Napoleon took power late in 1799, the new regime was taking basic steps to regularize conscription. From this fundamental military need, a whole state structure emerged, unprecedented in its efficiency, power, and intrusiveness. In 1798, a future Napoleonic marshal, Jourdan, drafted and saw accepted the law on conscription that came to bear his name. By its terms, each department was assigned a quota of conscripts, based on its eligible male population as known from the *État civil*; it was now officially the duty of the departmental authorities to raise these men, and it was to happen at least three times a year by a ballot, appropriately but without a trace of irony, named the *tirage*—the same word for 'shooting' as for drawing—under official supervision. All Frenchmen were henceforth assigned a 'class', denoting the year they reached 17, and became eligible for conscription. It remains part of popular jargon among French males to this day, it being more common to ask 'What class are you?' than 'When were you born?'.

Napoleon was swift to give the Jourdan law the teeth it needed, for he knew even as he embarked on the campaigns of 1800 that the army of the 1790s was exhausted and undermanned, and that, even in the four years of peace that followed the Treaty of Amiens, it had to be rebuilt. Even more, he knew that the conscription of the peasantry was the only way to do it. Before he could transform them at Boulogne, he had to whip them into the depots. In 1800, Napoleon transformed the structure and character of local government with the creation of the prefects. These centrally appointed civil servants now had sole and executive control of the civil administration of their departments, accountable only to the central government, and they directed the tri-annual conscription levies in person. Three times a year, they toured their entire departments, escorted by the Gendarmerie and national guards, going to the *chef lieu* of every canton, the seat of the justices of the peace, to supervise the *tirage* and the initiation of police operations to catch any eligible man who failed to appear; at the height of big campaigns, and from 1812 onwards as a rule, these tours and levies grew to four per year. This process had many significant offshoots: prefects came to know their departments and local affairs much better than any previous agents of central government, simply because they were obliged by conscription to be 'out-and-about' so frequently; local infrastructure was noted, repairs to roads, bridges, and buildings were discussed and acted upon; the personnel of the lowest rungs of local government became known personally to the prefects. A machinery of local government now grew up in the Napoleonic empire and its satellite states, regular, professional, and reliable, however detested. Its mainspring was the needs of war, but its consequences were wide ranging. In the immediate context of the wars, it came to supply men with stunning regularity; it made the huge armies of these campaigns not just possible but predictable. Napoleon never ran out of armies.

All this was hard won. Conscription was hated and resisted throughout the empire, France included. It perpetuated and extended the unrest of the 1790s to the rest of Europe, and right up to 1814.[10] The 'other war' never let up, and no one had any illusions about it. Peasant communities all over Europe, whose local patois and dialects were incomprehensible to each other, all dubbed conscription 'the blood tax'. To fight them, Napoleon resuscitated the Gendarmerie. The highly sophisticated, refined administrative machinery that ran conscription depended on ruthless, brutal strong-arm tactics to enforce it, and those enforcers were the gendarmes. They assumed the role of the early *bleus*, as the regulated ruthlessness of the empire replaced the anarchic enthusiasm of the revolution. The Gendarmerie stood at the cutting edge of the process of conscription, in a very literal sense. Drawn exclusively from the ranks of veterans, most with more than three years service, mainly ex-*sous officiers*, and over two-thirds French, even in the non-French parts of the Empire, this force was dedicated to policing the countryside and the highways, thus forcing the way for the state into the most remote parts of Europe. It was disseminated in six-man brigades across the countryside, not concentrated in towns and cities, as were the garrisons of line troops. When prefects set about the work of the *levée*, they did it with the Gendarmerie at their backs. Very few restored rulers dismantled this component of the Napoleonic machine after 1814.[11]

Every action has a reaction, and the peasantries subject to Napoleonic hegemony did not go willingly to the colours. The Gendarmerie was armed and drawn from the ranks of the army for a reason; it had to fight literally thousands of tiny engagements with peasant rebels from one end of the empire to the other, in conflicts that never really ceased. Even if some regions were gradually worn down into subservience,[12] the expansion of the empire into new territories always opened a new front, as these areas were, in their turn, subjected to conscription, or just to the aggression of French troops. This produced irregular fighting on a scale never witnessed before and engendered its politicization in many cases. Conventional warfare saw many adaptations and adjustments in its waging in the course of these conflicts, but the 'other war'—the *guerrilla*, not just in Spain but throughout much of Napoleonic Europe and, indeed, in Latin America—witnessed a fundamental metamorphosis from the early modern peasant *jacquerie* into something very different, thus creating a tradition that has outlived all the shifts in conventional warfare attendant on the spiralling pace of technological change that dominates Western history since the mid-nineteenth century. Behind the lines, 'the war of liberation' was born.

## THE POST-WAR WORLD

The Revolutionary–Napoleonic wars present a stunning paradox, representative of the wider contradictions of their age. Just as the iconoclastic, secularist intellectual ideas of the Enlightenment, including its vision of a modern, bureaucratic state, were spread by horse and sail over poor or non-existent roads, and were written by candlelight, so the sophisticated, highly developed state machinery, the meticulous record-keeping and all-pervading presence of prefects and gendarmes, could only produce an army capable of fighting in very primitive ways, by the standards of the next generation.

The creation and mobilization of the Napoleonic armies were a stunning sign of the new age. It represented the most concrete, enduring achievement of the new regime at its most determinedly innovative, but the closer the armies came to the face of battle, the less modern they became. In its major and probably most vital respects in terms of deciding combat, muskets, not rifles, heavy cavalry and massed infantry, not new weaponry, were what turned crucial engagements. They were the rocks upon which battles were won and armies were built. The unrelenting chronology of the wars between 1792 and 1800, and again from 1805 to 1815, meant that soldiers—ranks and non-commissioned officers especially, but many officers as well—learned their profession on active service and so perpetuated many eighteenth-century norms. This was chance, as the new military academies at St Cyr and [Fontainebleau were turning out young men with new ideas, but they were in charge of experienced troops, still rooted in tried and trusted routines.

Even the innovations of the period would have a limited life, however, at least in the original context in which they evolved. Mobility, as it was honed by the Napoleonic armies, was chief among them. Clausewitz emerged from the experience of the Napoleonic wars convinced 'that defence is *the stronger form of waging war*'.[13] He saw his justification in the two great defensive campaigns of the wars that brought down Napoleon: Russia and Spain were the crucial theatres in this, and both were dominated by mediated, prolonged defences, if very different in nature.[14] Indeed, the capacity of the British to supply besieged Portugal by sea in many ways prefigures the way in which railways, while revolutionizing troops' mobility in one sense, would actually facilitate the success of defence on wide fronts, consummated by broad counteroffensives, as in the American Civil War and, indeed, in the First World War.[15] Improved communications would do much to transform the use of the reserve—so well honed by Napoleon as the last of a series of offensive assaults—into the springboard of the counteroffensive, as Clausewitz acutely deduced. However,

Napoleon's reliance on rapid, lightly supported long advances was a phenomenon of his own time, and the product of a pre-mechanized age, not to be widely or axiomatically imitated by his successors. It worked brilliantly, often to devastating effect, at a certain time and in a certain set of circumstances, but it did not represent the future of war. Ironically, if seen in this context, his much admired 1814 campaign in France proved Clausewitz—and his implicit repudiation of Napoleonic offensive mobility—correct. Clausewitz already perceived this in operation at Leipzig in 1813, which saw Napoleon 'twist and turn like a caged animal when the ratio of forces was no longer in his favour'.[16] In all of this, the Revolutionary–Napoleonic wars mark the end of an era, more than a new dawn.

The Napoleonic wars came too soon for the Industrial Revolution, but only just. By mid-century, mobility would be governed less by the need to abandon baggage trains to live off the land, than by the positive contributions of steam travel, by rail and sea; rifles and better artillery would become standard by the 1860s; the role of heavy cavalry would shrink, and the nature of siege warfare would alter substantially. Cavalry charges soon became easier to contain; marksmanship came to take precedence over mass fire; mass fire itself became more deadly, if harder to deliver at close range as artillery improved. This was the almost immediate future, foreshadowed in the Crimean war of the 1850s and finally realized in the American Civil War of the 1860s. At the risk of oversimplification, Lee's was the last Napoleonic army; Grant's the first of the new industrial age. Many important innovations of the period would find their longest applications in the colonial wars of the nineteenth century, against technologically inferior opposition, and in circumstances where light infantry and cavalry, and the need for mobility over difficult terrain, still mattered. The development of better, mass-produced rifles was the really decisive factor in the emergence of light infantrymen and skirmishers as central components of European armies, and this was only on the distant horizon for Napoleonic commanders.

Many of the lessons regarded as fundamental, and readily assumed as being learned from Napoleon's methods of managing the wars of the period, were not absorbed as directly or rapidly as all that, although, in the long run, they emerged as his most lasting, perhaps greatest, achievement. The British dismantled their unique war machine almost immediately, even before Waterloo, while the Austrian emperor, Francis I, steadfastly refused to introduce mass conscription and its attendant military reforms. The continued presence of serfdom in Russia and Prussia, and the effectiveness of the hybrid, only quasi-Napoleonic, ideas of the Prussian reform movement at best buffered the introduction of or, indeed, the need for the introduction of the Napoleonic state machine on which the mass conscription of a free peasantry depended.

The French were forced to dismantle their army, and the Restoration became the age of the *démi-solde*, which was just as well for the restored monarchy. France was exhausted and demoralized in the immediate aftermath of the wars, and the promise of an end to the 'blood tax' bolstered the fragile popularity of Louis XVIII, just as it did the other newly restored rulers of Piedmont-Savoy, Spain and Naples. If the *guerrilla* and the widespread, ever-present, if increasingly ineffective, resistance to conscription won a victory, it was in the promises of the restored rulers to abandon it. Nostalgia for Napoleonic *gloire* within France, and the growing needs of security, coupled with the resurgence of older territorial ambitions among the other Bourbons and the House of Savoy, would return, but not until the 1830s. Initially, armies were regarded as too prone to Napoleonic influences, still too full of those who had served the French, and too infused with the ideology of the new regime, to be trusted by the restored rulers. The Napoleonic system for the management of war arose later in the century, however, and it did so almost comprehensively in western Europe. France, like most of the states most thoroughly imbued with the Napoleonic system of government, retained the essence of its judicial and administrative structures after 1814 and so, when times began to change, the propensity to raise large conscript armies returned. Prussia adapted this, following the abolition of serfdom in 1849 and, as its relationship with the *Mittelstaaten* grew closer in the second half of the century, Napoleonic conscription also resurfaced; Piedmont-Savoy revived it after 1831, and it was extended in undiluted form to the unitary Italian state post-1860. Most ironically of all, it was imposed on Spain early in the 1830s and put to immediate use against the Carlists, along with much else of Napoleonic provenance in the realm of administration. The new nations of Latin America would turn to it, as a blueprint, from the 1820s onwards.

What really changed by 1814, and changed forever, was the scale on which conventional war could be fought. At the face of battle, this made the line more potent, if cruder; it facilitated mass charges to break the deadlock, whether by infantry or heavy cavalry. Mass conscription was what made the reserve possible and, once a fixture, it soon became indispensable to battlefield tactics. This would change as technology advanced, but the kind of leadership needed to control large formations, and the kind of state apparatus needed to recruit mass armies, transcended technical advances. These two elements, mass conscription and the methods needed to command such large armies pioneered by Napoleon—however imperfectly by the end—together with the state machinery needed to harness recalcitrant rural populations, were the most salient contributions of the period to the future of warfare. Accompanying them was the *guerrilla* resistance that mass conscription did so much to provoke, sustain, and transform from crude peasant *jacqueries* into something more menacing, until it too succumbed to newer, unforeseen advances in technology.

## NOTES

1. See especially: David A. Bell, *The first total war: Napoleon's Europe and the birth of warfare as we know it* (Boston, MD: Houghton Mifflin, 2007).
2. Carl von Clausewitz, *On war* (Princeton, NJ: Princeton University Press, 1993) edited and translated by Michael Howard and Peter Paret, 266–8.
3. Rory Muir, *Tactics and the experience of battle in the age of Napoleon* (New Haven, CT: Yale University Press, 1998), 68–76.
4. Jacques Morvan, *Le Soldat impérial* (Paris: Librairie Historique Fabrice Teissèdre, 1904).
5. Clausewitz, *On war*, 462.
6. M. Dugué MacCarthy, 'Cavalerie', *Dictionnaire Napoléon*, edited by Jean Tulard (Paris: Fayard, 1989), 386–8.
7. Figures drawn from David Gates, *The Napoleonic Wars 1803–1815* (London: Arnold, 1997) *passim*.
8. Gates, *Napoleonic Wars*, 231.
9. Richard Cobb, *Les armées révolutionnaires* (Paris: Mouton, 1961–3).
10. Alan Forrest, *Conscripts and deserters: The army and French society during the revolution and empire* (Oxford: Oxford University Press, 1989). Alexander Grab, 'State power and rural resistance in Napoleonic Italy', *European History Quarterly*, 25/1 (1995), 39–70.
11. Clive Emsley, *Gendarmes and the state in nineteenth century Europe* (Oxford: Oxford University Press, 1999).
12. Isser Woloch, *The new regime: Transformations of the French civic order, 1789–1820s* (New York: W.W. Norton, 1994), 380–426.
13. Clausewitz, *On war*, 429. Italics are the author's own.
14. Clausewitz, *On war*, 465, 515.
15. Clausewitz, *On war*, 460.
16. Clausewitz, *On war*, 466.

# 4

## The Change from Within

### *Gil-li Vardi*

What brings about change in the way war is fought? What are the necessary factors, causes, contexts, or combination thereof that allegedly produce transformation in the way armies perceive, think of, prepare for, and fight wars? A vast literature is dedicated to questions of 'revolutions in military affairs' (hereinafter RMA) and military transformation, celebrating some changes as 'revolutionary' while dismissing others as ordinary.[1] The debate focuses mostly on explaining the greater strategic implications of this or that military technology or operational method, as well as on classifying types of revolutions and their respective eras. However, relatively little theoretical consideration has been given to necessary generators of change, and to mapping the conditions without which change—whether intended, incidental, or even undesired—is not likely to take place.

The usual suspects when examining change in the military realm are the great forces of politics (the rise or fall of new political orders, ideologies, or any form of internal political change), economics (radical changes in the macro- or microeconomic systems), and technological advances.[2] It is usually assumed that the dynamics of change are hasty or slow responses to new political, economic, or technological developments and threats (and sometimes all of these combined), which supposedly in and of themselves directly pave the way for change. Such transformations are introduced, and further reinforced, through conscious and continuous renewal of doctrine, training, force employment, or new operational and strategic goals which often appear, or are at least perceived as, unavoidable—by military practitioners and historians alike. As one study put it, 'in a dynamic environment . . . organisations must accept change if they are to survive'.[3]

But can we assume that, simply put, there is a direct, uninterrupted link between 'reality', its demands and impositions on the one hand, and change in how war is fought, on the other?[4] In the case of the First World War and thereafter, did the pressures of political, economic, and technological forces prescribe or predetermine change in the character of war? Let us examine the German army of the interwar era as our example. If we assume that there is a direct link between the reality of war and ensuing military discourse, then we should have witnessed a great change taking place in German military thought and practice between the world wars, followed by evidence of radically new German operational concepts in the opening phases of the Second World War. Indeed, some historians have argued as much. Many others, however, have emphasized the strong, noticeable traditional character of German operational patterns, with no evidential great transformations in the German military frame of mind.[5]

Yet, assuming a direct link between political, economic, and technological changes and military responses to them makes preposterous the suggestion that continuity is the main characteristic of the German army. After all, in 1919 the German army (later the *Reichswehr*) had profoundly lost its identity, arms, might, political sovereign, dignity, and everything it held to be an operational truth. Allegedly, historical reality pulled the rug from beneath German traditional military convictions, outlooks, and practices. But this was not the Germans' interpretation. The army that marched through France in 1940 held pretty much the same truths and convictions as did the army that marched through Belgium in 1914. The only dramatic change was the technology it employed, but this technology served existing doctrinal maxims, rather than dictating new doctrine and conduct.

## MILITARY CULTURE AS A MEDIATOR OF EXTERNAL PRESSURES FOR CHANGE

What can thus explain such persistent military practice in face of a very different and indeed turbulent political, economic, and technological reality? Military organizations, as with individuals or any other organization, act upon and in accordance with fundamental and often hidden assumptions about their craft and its nature, assumptions that mould their understanding of reality and preferences for certain ways of action. More than anything else, these unspoken assumptions determined the German army's world view and created a shared pool of precepts, shaped German military practitioners' thought, prescribed their goals, and rendered self-evident the best ways to achieve them. Prescribing and maintaining habits, moods, sensibilities, and views,[6] German military organizational culture regulated actions by defining what is 'possible', 'desirable', 'appropriate', and 'effective'.[7] It offered a set of guiding assumptions that seemed 'natural' or 'self-evident truths' to Germany's military leadership, truths which repeatedly failed to change and evolve either with time or under the pressure of crises and traumas.[8]

The tenets and axioms of that culture were clear and remained essentially unaltered before, throughout, and after the First World War: extreme warfare, aimed towards the most destructive, and eventually self-destructive, forms of war; extreme risk-taking elevated from the tactical and operational realms into the domain of strategy; the endless pursuit of battles of annihilation that dictated the reduction of strategy to meticulous operational and tactical planning; the trust in German fighting spirit—*Kampfgeist*—and 'qualitative superiority' to overcome the adversary's advantage in materiel and manpower; a ruthlessness that subordinated everything to a self-constructed 'military necessity'; and an exaggerated drive for action.[9] In grand strategy, German military leaders perceived war as the only way to solve political problems and to elevate the nation's— and the army's—prestige, and accordingly placed the army's interests and plans above civilian interests and decision-makers. In terms of operational method, German officers, restricted by geography and economics to envisage short wars, always preferred decisive operations involving movement, in which speed and extreme tactical risk-taking were mutually reinforcing.[10]

The evolution of German military thought did not manage to break the glass walls of these unselfconscious assumptions about war and the best way to wage it. Virtually all prominent German military thinkers in the 1920s saw war as the only way for Germany to re-establish its international status, and backed rearmament efforts regardless of their serious ramifications for German security. The military leadership maintained a deterministic approach to future scenarios, exhibited a strategic short-sightedness that imposed upon all decisions an operational and tactical rather than strategic frame of thought, and wished to subordinate all facets of civilian life to 'military necessity'. *Reichswehr* planning demonstrated extreme risk-taking coupled with the concentration of all forces on a single decisive effort, an approach embodied in the long-held ideal of the battle of annihilation.[11] And despite attempts to come to terms with grave military reality and choices, German military planners demonstrated a shared, rooted, and even conscious pattern of detachment from reality in their assessments of military capabilities, in their strategic and operational planning, and in their projection of future political and strategic possibilities.

Thus, the conservative chief of staff Hans von Seeckt wished to resurrect a traditional war of movement with the aid of new technology that would allow once again great battles of annihilation. The operational concepts and doctrinal manuals produced during his tenure as chief of staff focused on traditional operational principles despite the fact that he headed an army incapable of fighting anything resembling a great battle of annihilation or of employing modern arms in the foreseeable future. The so-called radical Joachim von Stülpnagel, chief of the operations department, called for a national suicidal scorched-earth guerrilla war against France, which chimed with ideas already suggested in 1918 and 1919. General (and later, war minister) Werner von Blomberg tested Stülpnagel's ideas—apparently not too radical for the

*Reichswehr*—in the war games of 1927 and 1928, facilitating their successful ending by predicting imaginary and highly unlikely international intervention in favour of Germany at the decisive moment. In this, he once again demonstrated the limited understanding of the members of this circle of the complexity of the political and diplomatic world, which did not stand awaiting their orders, as they naively and consistently assumed.[12]

As in its pre-war operational studies, the German army's post-war continued focus on tactics and tactical imperatives subjugated strategic conduct to operational and tactical demands, rather than vice versa; that tendency was evident in the studies, plans, and official documents produced by Seeckt and Stülpnagel, as well as in the institutional research conducted by the *Reichsarchiv* and the general staff history branch. Although fully recognizing the totality of the world war as a decisive cause of German failure, the *Reichswehr*'s official–historical analysis still privileged battle narratives, technological issues, and 'strictly military'—that is, non-political—history.[13] The supplementary volume on finance and economics was only published in 1930; it was dedicated to the question of Germany's allegedly inadequate armaments in comparison to those of its enemies, and managed to express two of the army's main arguments about the war—that its launching had been against German interests and therefore Germany was not to be blamed for it; and that the decision to go to war had been solely a civilian one.[14] Both the major operational visions debated in the army and in its official history of the world war indicate that, for the high command, the tactical aspects of the operational level of warfare were, implicitly and explicitly, still the only ones that determined the outcome of wars and, while the general staff had recognized more comprehensive aspects of planning, these were, as always, of a lesser significance.[15]

Likewise, and in accordance with the centrality of traditional operational axioms, the army's official manual of 1921, *Führung und Gefecht der verbundenen Waffen*, still held the infallible flank attack and annihilation battle as the best way to achieve victory, though, as mentioned, the *Reichswehr* could not even come close to realizing such methods. Similar suggestions appeared in proposed manuals in the early 1930s,[16] and were retained in the next field service manual of 1933, the *Heeresdienstvorschrift 300: Truppenführung*. *Truppenführung* offered few, if any, novel ideas, intellectual frameworks, or operational concepts. Its declared purpose was to reconcile traditional perceptions, such as 'decisive' battles of annihilation, with new military technology.[17] *Truppenführung* further accentuated the high traditional value attached to 'decisive' conduct and 'decisive' outcomes, which could be achieved in several ways, some (traditionally) better than others:

> [T]he attack is executed along its base direction by movement, fire and shock. The attack can be launched from a single direction against the enemy front, where the greatest strength usually lies. Normally, however, the attack is directed against

the flank or the rear of the enemy ... a flanking attack is more effective than a frontal attack. The simultaneous attack against both enemy flanks requires great superiority. The envelopment of one or both enemy flanks, reaching deep into his rear, can result in the destruction of the enemy.[18]

The omnipotence of the axiom of annihilation thus remained as central as ever to the evolution of German military thought, campaign planning, and operational patterns. Nothing whatsoever transcended *Vernichtung* as a principle, a guide, a state of mind, and of course a practice.

## TECHNOLOGY

We can thus see that none of the political, economic, or even security pressures of the 1920s managed to force change on the German army. How about technology, then? Could it be the generator of change in the way Germany waged wars, and thus perhaps in the character of war in general? Technology and its application in the military realm call for further analysis, since technological rejuvenation can become, quite simply, a matter of sheer survival for armies. Of course, new technologies cannot guarantee victory, but they all too often demand rapid adaptation of warfare in an attempt to answer the threat they pose. So far, so simple. However, two points should be taken into account when discussing the effects of technological changes on the German army in the 1920s and 1930s, namely its version of mechanized warfare. The first is that the usage and the meaning of technology are always socially constructed.[19] Thus, the German officers' understanding of mechanized warfare and its implications for the modern battlefield was inherently confined to their own world view and mental framework. Similarly, they interpreted other, competing visions of mechanized warfare only in line with their idiosyncratic mindset. Quite naturally, German military leadership understood and perceived any given technological artefact, its significance, and, above all, its appropriate employment, only within the interpretations that their organizational culture fostered.

The second point is that, according to German axioms, technology was always to serve doctrine and not vice versa. In the Prussian and German armies, technology in the form of new weapons and means of communications received careful scrutiny, and—if found useful—rapid introduction into service. The *Reichswehr* and *Wehrmacht* had no inherent aversion to new weapons. On the contrary, the *Wehrmacht*'s 1933 field service manual, *Truppenführung*, reads: 'The conduct of war is subject to continual development. New weapons dictate ever-changing forms. Their appearance must be anticipated and their influence evaluated. They then must be placed into service quickly.'[20] Yet, as mentioned, technological novelties, however demanding and transformative they may seem in retrospect, rarely enforced changes in strategic conduct.[21] In other words, for the Germans, new military technology served existing conceptual structures rather than changed them.[22]

Since the faith in modern technology and in new weapons as the means to implement traditional concepts had been prevalent in the *Reichswehr* since the early 1920s, no conceptual transformation—as expressed in the army's doctrinal documents—and surprisingly little organizational change accompanied the incorporation of the modern weapons that purportedly led to the birth of the new doctrine of '*Blitzkrieg*'. German armour was designed and expected to serve traditional operational goals, namely annihilation, in close cooperation with other fighting arms. Up until 1938, it was, as a rule, to serve the needs of the infantry, which was still seen by most members of the general staff as the most important component of the fighting machine.[23] In a nutshell, the new technology did not alter the *Reichswehr's* and the *Wehrmacht's* self-understanding as a fighting organization in either theory or practice. It was rightly identified as facilitating old concepts, further enhancing ancient operational axioms and long-prized values—speed, combined arms, initiative, and shock—as well as placing within reach the time-honoured operational goals of decisive battle and swift and total *Vernichtung*.

The new technology thus did not induce a radical change in military concepts, in the organization of forces, and in German assumptions about the character of war.[24] While the German army underwent a significant evolution in the course of its experiments with and incorporation of new technology into existing perceptions and an existing organizational culture, technology alone did not prescribe change in its operational thought. Post-1919 German military culture made radical change improbable while disguising conceptual stagnation as renewal and vigorous lesson-learning from the First World War. German military thought and practice throughout and immediately after the First World War exhibited a radicalization of existing patterns, rather than fundamental shifts in strategic and operational concepts and tenets. During the interwar era, German military thought seemingly revolutionized itself, with precepts and doctrine following a supposed outburst of ostensibly new but in reality fundamentally traditional ideas. This stagnation-disguised-as-transformation was made possible by a combination of stubborn organizational culture and a unique historical setting that allowed the elite of the German army to pretend for years that reality and its constraints did not really bind it, and that it was free to recast the past, present, and future as it wished.

To conclude, any 'external' factors such as political, technological, or other pressures—pressures that present challenges of renewal and change to any military organization—are bound to be understood and processed through the internal lenses of organizational culture. These lenses might, in turn, tone these pressures down to bear new, idiosyncratically reassuring meanings that would eventually reaffirm organizational 'truths'. What, therefore, is required in order to change military culture?

## CHANGE

Let us compare the German experience with another example of an army that faced tremendous political and economic transformations in the interwar era. The Red Army emerged as a new military organization following a devastating national defeat, and dramatic and revolutionary change of government, with the ensuing imminent instabilities this change had unleashed. It also faced threatening security challenges and even more threatening economic setbacks. It was, in short, in a predicament very similar to that of the *Reichswehr*.

One important attribute, though, set the Red Army on a completely different course from that of the *Reichswehr*. The Red Army was deeply and consciously committed not only to transform but actually to revolutionize itself, its doctrine, and its practice. Emphasizing the operational manoeuvre and discarding the great battle of annihilation as a central means and rationale for action in the late 1920s, Soviet military thinkers paved the way for a complete renewal of military theory. The deep operations theory that followed, based on mechanized formations aiming for operational shock while using the principle of depth, and skilfully playing between manoeuvre and attrition, fitted well with Soviet Russia's new social, industrial, and ideological aspirations.[25] The conscious commitment to evolve into a well-equipped, mechanized mass proletarian army, the encompassing ideological requirement to start afresh and discard old convictions, and the self-aware attempt to create a new army generated a profound change in the Russian-cum-Soviet way of war, and thus reflected, as well as reinforced, change in the character of war.

The immense, comprehensive political changes of the years 1917–19, and the dramatic economic and technological changes of the 1920s, are by no means directly linked to the military changes they supposedly implied or allegedly begat in Germany and Soviet Russia. Germany's traumatic defeat did not result in a complete break with 'truths' that had failed when tested and tested again to the point of destruction. Such a break is more likely to happen when both outer- and inner-organizational pressures make complete transformation a desirable organizational goal. A mediating factor is required in order to explain the military responses to challenging realities, and military culture, with its dynamics and mechanisms, can explain why and how change took place, or did not occur. An important element in shaping and reshaping the character of war is thus military organizations' shaping and reshaping of their organizational assumptions, and their idiosyncratic links with, and understandings of, 'reality'.

## NOTES

1. Historical analysis of change and continuity in military affairs benefits—or rather, suffers—from a plethora of competing RMA definitions and 'paradigms'. However, most fall into two main categories, which Clifford Rogers has described as 'military revolutions' (MR) and 'revolutions in military affairs' (RMA); a military revolution—a far-reaching strategic, political, and social transformation—results directly from changes initially restricted to the military–technical and operational realms (Clifford J. Rogers, '"Military revolutions" and "revolutions in military affairs"', in Thierry Gongora and Harald von Riekhoff (eds.), *Toward a revolution in military affairs? Defence and security at the dawn of the 21st century* (Westport, CT: Greenwood, 2000), 22–4. Williamson Murray and MacGregor Knox employ similar categories in 'Introduction: Thinking about revolutions in warfare', Idem. (eds.), *The dynamics of military revolution, 1300–2050* (Cambridge: Cambridge University Press, 2001), 6–14. See also Andrew N. Liaropoulos, 'Revolutions in warfare: Theoretical paradigms and historical evidence. The Napoleonic and First World War revolutions in military affairs', *Journal of Military History*, 70/2 (2006), 363–84, proposing as paradigms the 'social wave' (corresponding to MR) and the 'radical transformation' (corresponding to RMA). Some of the most relevant works discussing change, transformation, and revolutions in military thought and practice are: MacGregor Knox and Williamson Murray (eds.), *The dynamics of military revolution, 1300–2050* (Cambridge: Cambridge University Press, 2001); Stephen Biddle, 'The past as prologue: Assessing theories of future warfare', *Security Studies*, 8/1 (1998), 1–74; Eliot A. Cohen, 'A revolution in warfare', *Foreign Affairs*, 75/2 (1996), 37–54; Theo Farrell and Terry Terriff (eds.), *Sources of military change: Culture, politics, technology* (Boulder, CO: Lynne Rienner, 2002); Emily O. Goldman and Leslie C. Eliason (eds.), *The diffusion of military technology and ideas* (Stanford, CA: Stanford University Press, 2003); Andrew F. Krepinevich, 'Cavalry to computer: The pattern of military revolutions', *The National Interest*, 37 (1994), 30–42; John A. Lynn, *Battle: A history of combat and culture* (Boulder, CO: Lynne Rienner, 2003); Idem., 'The evolution of army style in the modern west, 800–2000', *International History Review*, 18/3 (1996), 507–45; William R. Thompson, 'A test of a theory of co-evolution in war: Lengthening the western Eurasian military trajectory', *International History Review*, 28/3 (2006), 473–503.

2. See for instance Williamson Murray and Allan R. Millett, 'Military innovation in the interwar period', in Idem. (eds.), *Military innovation in the interwar period* (Cambridge: Cambridge University Press, 1996), 1–5; Knox and Murray, 'Introduction', 6–11; and Lynn, *Battle*, 331–41.

3. Murray and Millett, 'Military innovation', 5.

4. Lynn, *Battle*, 331–41. While Lynn is aware of cultures as mental structures that can 'change or control reality to fit conception' a process he labels 'reformation', he also claims that through 'recognition', cultures may come to appreciate that conception does not suitably reflect reality, and 'adjust the discourse [of war]'. Lynn does not explain, however, why some realities produce 'reformation' and others 'recognition', but suggests that this difference in outcome might have more to do with cultural needs than with the pressures of reality.

5. For analysis of the issues of tradition, innovation, and revolution in German military thought and practice, see Williamson Murray, 'Armoured warfare: the British, French and German experiences', in Murray and Millett (eds.), *Military innovation*, 17, 38, 40–5; Cohen, 'Revolution in warfare', 46f.; Colin S. Gray, *Modern strategy* (Oxford: Oxford University Press, 1999), 203; Robert M. Citino, *German way of war: From the Thirty Years War to the Third Reich* (Lawrence, KA: University Press of Kansas, 2005), xvi–xvii, 244–56, 267, and idem, *Blitzkrieg to Desert Storm: The evolution of operational warfare* (Lawrence, KA: University of Kansas Press, 2004), 18–28; Karl Heinz Frieser and John T. Greenwood, *The Blitzkrieg legend: The 1940 campaign in the west* (Annapolis, MD: Naval Institute Press, 2005), 329–46, and Biddle, 'The past as prologue', 44–55, 61. Biddle offers an eloquent refutation of claims that a German RMA existed. For Biddle, 'essential continuity' provides the best explanation of the *Wehrmacht*'s initial successes in the Second World War. Biddle, however, does not provide an explanation of the dynamics or mechanisms that maintained continuity in face of technological innovation.

6. Ann Swidler, 'Culture in action: Symbols and strategies', *American Sociological Review*, 51/2 (1986), 273–86. Swidler uses the term 'strategy' to mean a general approach to organizing action.

7. See also Farrell and Terriff, 'The sources of military change', in Idem. (eds.), *The sources of military change*, 7f., who use the term 'cultural norms' instead of 'culture'.

8. Isabel V. Hull, *Absolute destruction: Military culture and the practices of war in imperial Germany* (Ithaca, NY: Cornell University Press, 2005); Idem., 'Military culture, Wilhelm II, and the end of the monarchy in the First World War', in Annika Mombauer and Wilhelm Deist (eds.), *The Kaiser: New research on Wilhelm II's role in imperial Germany* (Cambridge: Cambridge University Press, 2003). For a cultural analysis of French and British interwar strategic thinking, see Elizabeth Kier, *Imagining war: French and British military doctrine between the wars* (Princeton, NJ: Princeton University Press, 1997). Farrell and Terriff, 'Sources of military change', 3–20, discuss culture as a tool for inducing change in military organizations; see also the general summary by Theo Farrell, 'Culture and military power', *Review of International Studies* 24/4 (1998), 407–16; Lynn, *Battle*, offers a different approach and interpretation of 'military culture', and Peter H. Wilson discusses patterns and definitions of various aspects of military culture in 'Defining military culture', *Journal of Military History*, 72/1 (2008), 11–43.

9. Hull, *Absolute destruction*, 93–181; and 'End of the monarchy', 239–45.

10. See Gerhard P. Gross, 'Das Dogma der Beweglichkeit. Überlegungen zur Genese der deutschen Heerestaktik im Zeitalter der Weltkrieg', in Bruno Thoss and Hans-Erich Volkmann (eds.), *Erster Weltkrieg, Zweiter Weltkrieg. Ein Vergleich* (Paderborn: Schöningh, 2002), 143–66; and Citino, *German Way of War*, xiii–xviii. Although Citino does not use the concept of military culture, he does claim that *Bewegungskrieg* in its many manifestations—some of which he argues were revolutionary—was an institutional characteristic of the German army from Frederick the Great onwards, an operational answer to Prussia's

geopolitical weakness. Citino explains in great detail the various manifestations of the 'war of movement' dogma, but does not investigate the institutional dynamics that maintained that form of war, with its unique set of operational requirements, as an institutional axiom. It is also important to note that German military culture had a profound influence on logistical planning. The role of logistics centred on the requirement to assist in creating decisive operational advantages during the initial phases of the campaign or as it culminates in an annihilation battle; however, it also rendered careful planning of protracted fighting inessential, since such fighting was to be avoided (and was often comfortably assumed unlikely).

11. For these characteristics of the Wilhelmine army, see Hull, *Military culture*, 257f.

12. See especially Gil-li Vardi, 'Joachim von Stülpnagel's military thought and planning', *War in History*, 17/2 (2010), 193–216; Wilhelm Deist, 'Rearmament', in Wilhelm Deist et al. (eds.), *Germany and the Second World War*, volume I, *The build-up of German aggression* (Oxford: Oxford University Press, 1990); Idem., 'The road to ideological war: Germany, 1918–1945', in Alvin Bernstein, MacGregor Knox, and Williamson Murray (eds.), *The making of strategy: Rulers, states, and war* (Cambridge: Cambridge University Press, 1994); Michael Geyer, *Aufrüstung oder Sicherheit: Die Reichswehr in der Krise der Machtpolitik 1924–1936* (Wiesbaden: Steiner, 1980), 76–112, 189–228; Idem., 'German strategy in the age of machine warfare, 1914–1945', in Peter Paret (ed.), *Makers of modern strategy: From Machiavelli to the nuclear age* (Oxford: Oxford University Press, 1986), 527–96; and Idem., 'The dynamics of military revisionism in the interwar years: Military politics between rearmament and diplomacy', in Wilhelm Deist (ed.), *The German military in the age of total war* (Leamington Spa: Berg, 1985), 100–51.

13. Markus Pöhlmann, 'Yesterday's battles and future war. The German official military history, 1918–1939', in Roger Chickering and Stig Förster (eds.), *The shadows of total war. Europe, East Asia and the United States, 1919–1939* (Cambridge: Cambridge University Press, 2003), 230–8; see also Idem., *Kriegsgeschichte und Geschichtspolitik: Der Erste Weltkrieg: Die amtliche deutsche Militärgeschichtsschreibung 1914 bis 1965* (Paderborn: Schöningh, 2002).

14. Ibid., 233f.; among the more plausible accounts of the decisive army role in July–August 1914, see especially Annika Mombauer, *Helmuth von Moltke and the origins of the First World War* (New York: Cambridge University Press, 2001); and Idem., 'A reluctant military leader? Helmuth von Moltke and the July crisis of 1914', *War in History*, 6/4 (1999), 417–46.

15. The intensity and centrality of the German high command's interest in tactics reflected and maintained its tactical frame of thought at the expense of strategic planning. Timothy Lupfer points out the marked discrepancy between German tactical flexibility and innovativeness on the one hand and 'flawed' strategic conduct on the other, but he does not attempt to explain it. Timothy T. Lupfer 'Dynamics of doctrine: The changes in German tactical doctrine during the First World War', *Leavenworth Papers* 4 (Fort Leavenworth, KA: Combat Studies Institute, 1981).

16. Richard Schürmann, *Gedanken über Krieg- und Truppenführung*, BA-MA, RH2-2901.

17. See James Corum, Bruce Condell, and David Zabecki's forward and introductory notes, *On the German art of war: Truppenführung* (Boulder, CO: Lynne Rienner, 2001), viii–xiii, 1–12. Corum points out the traditional character of the document as a faithful expression of the 'German way of war', as well as its effective incorporation of new arms into existing concepts. Condell and Zabecki specifically link *Truppenführung* to Seeckt's *FuG* in concepts and even in phrasing: 'entire paragraphs and sections were carried over into *Truppenführung*'.

18. *Truppenführung*, 88.

19. Trevor J. Pinch and Wiebke E. Bijker, 'The social construction of facts and artefacts: Or how the sociology of science and the sociology of technology might benefit each other', in Wiebke E. Bijker, Thomas P. Hughes, and Trevor J. Pinch (eds.), *The social construction of technological systems: New directions in the sociology and history of technology* (Cambridge, MA: MIT Press, 1989), 40–4.

20. *Truppenführung*, 17.

21. In part, because of their frequency; see Howard E. Aldrich and Martin Ruef's analysis of frequent organizational changes (an army's adoption of new weapons constitutes such a change), leading to a short-lived momentum rather than comprehensive organizational transformations: Aldrich and Ruef, *Organisations evolving* (London: Sage, 2006), 138.

22. 'The German army considered new tools of war . . . in the context of their probable contribution to the army's "macro systems" of making war . . . [that is] the legacy of seeking decisive battles to resolve limited wars in stable matrices.' Dennis E. Showalter, 'More than nuts and bolts: Technology and the German army, 1870–1945', *The Historian*, 65/1 (2002), 125; see also Frieser, *Blitzkrieg legend*, 329–31.

23. This is hardly surprising given German traditional emphasis on the infantry as the only force capable of delivering the desired annihilation of enemy forces. For the Wehrmacht's mid-1930s debate on armour build-up, deployment, missions and prioritization in relation to infantry forces, see especially: Beck, 'Erwägungen über die Erhöhung des Angriffskraft des Heeres', 30 December 1935, BA-MA, RH2-1135, 129–43 (see also 174–225); 2. Abteilung (the general staff section dealing with force structure and unit organization), 'Heeresaufbau 1937', January 1936, BA-MA, RH2-1010, 178–80; Beck, 'Ausstattung und Organisation der Panzerverbände', 9 January 1936, BA-MA, RH2-1135, 273–8; Allgemeine Heeresamt (AHA), 'Organisation und Ausstattung der Panzerverbände', 15 January 1936, BA-MA, RH2-1135, 269–72; Beck, 'Organisation und Ausstattung der Panzerverbände', 21 January 1936, BA-MA, RH2-1135, 257–60; AHA, 'Erhöhung der Angriffskraft des Heeres', 22 January 1936, BA-MA, RH2-1135, 115–26; AHA, 'Pz.-Verbände' (production of heavy tanks), 28 January 1936, BA-MA, RH2-1135, 254–6; Heereswaffenamt (Wa A), 'Panzerverbände', BA-MA, RH2-1135, 261–8; 'Panzerverbände', February 1936, BA-MA, RH2-1135, 252f.; Wa A, 'Entwicklung von Pz.Kpf.Wg.', 23 March 1936, BA-MA, RH2-1135, 241–9; 2. Abteilung, 'Vortragsnotizen zur Übersicht der Inspection d. Kraftfahrkampftruppen', 2 June 1936, BA-MA, RH2-1135, 285–8;

2. Abteilung, 'Vortragsnotiz' (tank armament), 13 August 1936, BA-MA, RH2-1135, 23–5.

24. The *character* of war did change between the world wars—as Thomas G. Mahnken has suggested, a combined-arms revolution affected all the leading armies of Europe, as well as the United States, in the course of the 1920s, the 1930s, and—following the stunning initial successes of the *Wehrmacht*—the early 1940s. Thomas G. Mahnken, 'Beyond Blitzkrieg: Allied responses to combined-arms armoured warfare during World War II', in Goldman and Eliason (eds.), *The diffusion of military technology and ideas*, 243–66. Yet that general revolution, widespread and authentic as it was, and induced both by technology and by the lessons of the Great War, neither began nor was 'made' in Germany, despite Germany's starring role from the late 1930s until 1941. Each army transformed itself through struggle within and against its own idiosyncratic organizational culture, doctrine, and constraints. While certainly providing an initial incentive for change, the Wehrmacht did not prescribe a formula for change in the early 1940s—just as it did not innovate by following any such formula prescribed by others in the early to mid-1930s.

25. Mary R. Habeck, *Storm of steel: The development of armour doctrine in Germany and the Soviet Union, 1919–1939* (Ithaca, NY: Cornell University Press, 2003), xv; Azar Gat, *Fascist and liberal visions of war: Fuller, Liddell Hart, Douhet, and other modernists* (Oxford: Oxford University Press, 1998), 116–21; Shimon Naveh, *In pursuit of military excellence: The evolution of operational theory* (London: Routledge, 1997), 175–230. Of course, this is not to say that Soviet military thinkers easily or willingly abided by the 'correct' or 'true' Bolshevik 'interpretations' of military concepts, whatever such interpretations might have meant. Likewise, military innovation certainly did not guarantee Stalin's appreciation of its practitioner; more likely to the contrary, as demonstrated by Michael Tukhachevskii's execution in 1937. However, regardless of Tukhachevskii's ideological preferences and those of his circle, their operational ideas were implemented because they ultimately served the Soviet Government's political, ideological, technological, industrial, and other preferences, limitations, and demands. On the intertwined links between the Red Army's different military schools and their political sponsors and supporters—and the latter's motivation—see Naveh, *In pursuit of military excellence*, 177–81.

# 5

## 'Killing is Easy': The Atomic Bomb and the Temptation of Terror

### Gerard J. DeGroot

'The lesson we should learn from all this,' the atomic physicist Isidor Rabi remarked shortly after the explosion of two atomic bombs in August 1945, '[is] . . . how easy it is to kill people when you turn your mind to it. When you turn the resources of modern science to the problem of killing people, you realize how vulnerable they really are.'[1] While Rabi was referring specifically to advances in the technology of war, he was also painfully aware of the simultaneous collapse of morality that had allowed those technologies to be used.

The atom bomb is rightly seen as a weapon that revolutionized war and diplomacy. Analysis of its impact has, however, been confused by the context in which it emerged, namely the Cold War. It is not entirely clear whether the peaceful stalemate that characterized the period 1945–91 was the consequence of nuclear deterrence or simply a manifestation of older notions of the balance of power. Recently, for instance, John Mueller has argued rather convincingly that the United States and the USSR would have been unlikely to go to war with one another even had the atom bomb not existed.[2] While counterfactuals should perhaps be avoided, Mueller's argument raises intriguing questions about the bomb's actual impact. That impact should become clearer as time passes and distance from the Cold War lengthens. Rather than analysis being dominated by issues characteristic of a bygone era (like counterforce strategy), it could be that, over the longer term, the most important impact of the bomb will seem to be its seminal role in making killing easy. In other words, its true importance might lie in the fact that it represented a final surrender to barbarity—a climactic assertion of the right of a nation to slaughter civilians for purposes of national security.

So how did the world arrive at this terrible terminus? The process arguably began in the Great War, when bombs were first used for the sole purpose of killing civilians. The war was not yet three weeks old when a Zeppelin hit Antwerp, killing six. Raids quickly intensified, with the British enduring the brunt of this menace. Since, however, cumbersome airships were prey to ground-based fire and fighter aircraft, a more effective method of delivering death soon emerged in the form of the Gotha bomber. A glimpse of the future was provided on 20 June 1917, when eighteen tiny coffins were arranged in front of the altar at All Saints Church, Poplar, London. The victims, most of them 5 years old when they died, were killed when a Gotha dropped a single 110-pound bomb on the Upper North Street School.

The war minister, Lord Derby, reassured the British public that the Gotha raids, while tragic, were militarily insignificant since no soldiers had been killed. This was not simply bluster. The argument had some logic at a time when battlefields were still paramount. Since the Germans lacked a bomber force large enough to destroy British civilian morale, the bombs were simply canisters of spite. Nowadays, however, Derby's logic seems rather quaint.

The Gotha raids convinced the Italian General Giulio Douhet that a new type of warfare, dominated by air power, had emerged. 'To have command of the air means to be in a position to wield offensive power so great that it defies human imagination,' he wrote in 1925. 'No longer can areas exist in which life can be lived in safety and tranquillity . . . the battlefield will be limited only by the boundaries of the nations at war, and all of their citizens will become combatants, since all of them will be exposed to the aerial offensives of the enemy. There will be no distinction any longer between soldiers and civilians.'[3] Rather than interpreting Douhet's logic as a calamity to be avoided, nations saw instead a capability to be developed. Civilians first became targets not because it was sensible to kill them but because it was suddenly possible to do so. The British Prime Minister Stanley Baldwin typified the easy acceptance of savagery: in future, he argued in 1932, war would mean that 'You have to kill more women and children more quickly than the enemy if you want to save yourselves.'[4]

International law was hastily formulated to try to close a barn door from which a warhorse had already bolted. Civilized war, it was still argued, should not involve civilians. The 1923 Hague convention prohibited 'aerial bombardment for the purpose of *terrorizing* the civilian population'. (The present participle is noteworthy.) Bombing cities was not, however, absolutely proscribed. Aerial bombing was 'legitimate only when directed at a military objective', which was defined as 'military forces; military works; military establishments or depots; [munitions] factories . . . lines of communication or transportation'.[5] Through that loophole, a bomber could easily fly.

Once the possibility of killing civilians arose, justification was quickly formulated. War, it seemed, had evolved into a contest not between armies but between peoples. As the Great War had demonstrated, success required an efficient system of organizing the productive capacities of the nation. The concepts of 'total war' and the 'home front' emerged. Once the latter was defined, it became a target. Strategists argued that an enemy might be defeated by starving his people—or by killing workers in their beds. Failing that, it might be possible to frighten the enemy population so completely as to destroy their will to persist. Bombs seemed an efficient means of delivering terror.

On 1 September 1939, Franklin Roosevelt expressed concern about aerial bombing in the impending war. He feared that, if bombing went unchecked, 'hundreds of thousands of innocent human beings who have no responsibility for, and who are not even remotely participating in, the hostilities . . . will lose their lives'. He asked combatants 'to affirm [their] determination that [their] armed forces shall in no event, and under no circumstances, undertake the bombardment from the air of civilian populations'.[6] Both Britain and Germany expressed agreement, the latter as it laid waste to Warsaw.

A fine line exists between indiscriminate—or 'terror'—bombing and the 'strategic' variety. Indiscriminate bombing means killing civilians for purposes of attrition—the killing is the object. Strategic bombing, on the other hand, arises from the logic that a nation's industry consists of both its factories *and* its workers. Thus, bombing homes can cripple industry in the same way as bombing plant. Two strategies are delivered by the same means, but one seems morally bankrupt, the other grimly sensible. The difference often comes down to perspective. In the Second World War, General Curtis LeMay justified the saturation bombing of Tokyo by arguing that there were no civilian areas; the city was one giant factory. Because children made fuses, it made sense to kill them.

The British claimed that Luftwaffe raids on London were barbaric. RAF raids on German cities, on the other hand, though much more intense, were presented as legitimate attacks upon the enemy's productive capacity. Air Marshal Arthur Harris, the *eminence grise* of British Bomber Command, also applied biblical logic: he who sows the wind should reap the whirlwind. Evil was defined by the first blow struck; guilt lay in initiative, not response. Thus, to bomb Germany day and night for four years seemed fitting retribution for the comparatively short blitz on Britain. That same logic would eventually characterize the 'war on terror', an asymmetric response to the atrocities of 11 September 2001.

Air strategists assumed that a sufficient number of bombs would break an enemy's spirit. When early raids failed to cause collapse, the tactic was not abandoned but intensified. Evidence that terror bombing did not work was ignored; air strategists convinced themselves that the enemy's breaking point would eventually be reached. This logic led seamlessly to the conclusion that an ideology or regime could be defeated if a sufficient number of its supporters were killed or terrorized. Missing from the analysis was any awareness of the fact that bombing might be counterproductive—terror might convince the wavering to support an otherwise loathsome regime. Though her evidence is admittedly anecdotal, Christabel Bielenberg, an Englishwoman living in Germany during the war, found that support for the Nazis rose after each Allied air raid.[7]

Strategy was adapted to fit capability. People became legitimate targets because bombers were imprecise. While factories were difficult to hit, neighbourhoods were impossible to miss. The vulnerability of their bombers to German defences forced the British to bomb at night, with an inevitable decline in precision. The bombing campaign against Germany therefore evolved into a pattern of the British striking cities indiscriminately at night and the Americans attempting to hit precise military targets by day. Even though they were not entirely successful, Americans took moral pride in the fact that they had not lowered themselves to area bombing. That approach did not, however, work in Japan, where weather conditions made precision bombing virtually impossible. General Henry Arnold, the US Army Air Forces commander, grew increasingly frustrated at his arm's impotence. In desperation, he brought in LeMay, a man who, like Harris, felt no qualms about killing civilians. LeMay decided to bomb Japanese cities with B-29 bombers from low altitude at night. This implied an acceptance that the purpose was to kill people. In line with this strategy, a high proportion of incendiary bombs were dropped, in the interests of setting fire to Japanese houses, built primarily of wood. A morally questionable strategy was justified as preferable to invasion.

Progress in the technology of killing clearly demonstrated the importance of the laboratory to victory. An understanding of that importance inspired the race to harness atomic power. The first breakthroughs in this field indicated that a nuclear bomb constituted a decidedly different weapon from bombs already in existence. The differences were material *and* moral. Stated simply, the yield of an atomic weapon was too large for the pretence of precision to be maintained—its only legitimate target could be a city. That in turn implied that its main purpose was to kill civilians. As early as February 1940, the physicists Otto Frisch and Rudolf Peierls forecast that 'the bomb could probably not be used without killing large numbers of civilians, and this may make it unsuitable as a weapon'. They additionally warned that the radioactivity produced would continue to kill long after the moment of explosion. It was, they concluded, 'a weapon of unparalleled violence, a weapon of mass destruction such as the world had never seen'.[8] Though the moral issues were vexing, power of that magnitude proved alluring.

The Manhattan Project scientists and engineers who developed the atomic bomb thought in terms of a deterrent, not a weapon. The device was, they convinced themselves, the only logical response to the grim possibility that the Germans might develop a bomb of their own. Politicians, however, had difficulty imagining a hugely expensive weapon used only for deterrence. The Secretary of War Henry Stimson insisted that it was always Roosevelt's intention to use the bomb as soon as it became available. 'At no time, from 1941 to 1945, did I ever hear it suggested by the President . . . that atomic energy should not be used in this war . . . on no other ground could the wartime expenditure of so much time and money be justified.'[9] If Stimson's claim is true (and one suspects it is), the president who in 1939 had urged world leaders to avoid the wanton slaughter of civilians was, within a couple of years, fully prepared to use a weapon that had no other realistic purpose than to kill civilians.

When Harry Truman first learned of the bomb a few days after the death of Roosevelt in April 1945, he heartily welcomed this 'almost unbelievable destructive power'. The new president thought that 'the bomb might well put us in a position to dictate our own terms by the end of the war'.[10] In other words, even before the first weapon was tested, Truman was already thinking of its potential as a tool of coercion. It could kill, yes, but it also promised to be a massive version of the pistol displayed prominently on the lawman's gunbelt. That seemed useful to a nation aspiring to be the world's policeman.

The first atomic bomb was tested at the Trinity site near Alamogordo, New Mexico, on 16 July 1945. While most Manhattan Project scientists rejoiced that the war in Japan was essentially over, a few worried about the Faustian deal they had struck. 'This is not a pleasant weapon we have produced,' the metallurgist Cyril Smith remarked, 'A city is henceforth not the place in which to live.'[11] Leo Szilard, the driving force behind the effort to convince Roosevelt to commission the project, now felt deep dismay. 'In 1945, when we ceased worrying about what the Germans would do to us, we began to worry about what the . . . United States might do to other countries.'[12] He feared that using the bomb would weaken the American moral position and make it 'more difficult for us to live up to our responsibility of bringing the unloosened forces of destruction under control'.[13]

While some scientists felt moral torment, politicians saw only a new weapon in need of a role. When the Danish physicist Niels Bohr counselled Churchill against using the new device, the latter replied: 'I cannot see what you are talking about. After all, this new bomb is just going to be bigger than our present bombs. It involves no difference in the principles of war.'[14] Szilard meanwhile sought out James Byrnes, shortly to become Secretary of State, only to find him excited about using the bomb to manipulate the Soviets. 'I was completely flabbergasted by the assumption that rattling the bomb might make Russia more manageable.'[15] Byrnes was not alone in thinking along these lines. Stimson thought that the bomb might provide 'the opportunity to bring the world into a pattern in which the peace of the world and our civilization can be saved'.[16] That delighted Truman, who was pleased that Stimson 'seemed at least as much concerned with the role of the atomic bomb in the shaping of history as in its capacity to shorten this war'.[17]

The extension of Soviet power as a result of the war frightened the Americans. At the Yalta Conference, Roosevelt and Churchill had secured a promise of Soviet participation in the Pacific War by granting Stalin important concessions including the maintenance of communist rule in Outer Mongolia, the lease of Port Arthur, and the annexation of the Kurile Islands. Byrnes privately regretted what seemed a swindle: 'somebody had made an awful mistake in bringing about a situation where Russia was permitted to come out of a war with the power she will have'.[18] To the Truman administration, the bomb offered a magical way to escape the straitjacket of diplomacy. 'We have got to regain the lead and perhaps do it in a pretty rough and realistic way,' Stimson argued on 14 May. Thanks to the bomb, the United States now held all the cards. 'I called it a royal straight flush and we mustn't be a fool about the way we play it.'[19]

Running parallel to the game of atomic poker was the more immediate concern of defeating Japan. Here, the advantages of the bomb seemed self-evident. General Leslie Groves, military head of the Manhattan Project, told Truman on 25 April 1945 that dropping the bomb on Japan would nullify the need for an invasion, and therefore save 1.5 million lives. That figure was plucked from mid-air. No less an authority than General George Marshall had estimated that an invasion might cost 40,000 American lives. But, as Truman saw it, that was 40,000 more than would die if the bomb was used to end the war. No other justification was needed.

Groves was already busy on the logistics. The Interim Committee advised on 31 May that 'we could not concentrate on a civilian area; but . . . we should seek to make a profound psychological impression on as many of the inhabitants as possible . . . the most desirable target would be a vital war plant employing a large number of workers and closely surrounded by workers' houses'.[20] That recommendation straddles the old world and the new. The committee pretend-ed that the bomb would be used on a military target, but widened the definition to accommodate extraordinary power. In other words, the committee had approved terror bombing but called it something else.

Mixed motives were even more clearly apparent in the recommendations of the Target Committee. It drew up four requirements. Firstly, since the effect of the bomb would primarily be blast and, secondarily, fire, the target had to consist of dense, highly flammable construction—namely houses. Secondly, the target should contain a built-up area of at least one square mile, as that would be the area of greatest explosive effect. That implied a city. Thirdly, it should have important strategic and military value, a requirement convenient-ly defined in vague terms. Finally, the target should have escaped earlier bombardment, so as to facilitate measurement of the bomb's effect. That suggested a site of low military importance, since strategically significant places had already been hit. Groves added a final proviso: the target should be a place 'the bombing of which would most adversely affect the will of the Japanese people to continue the war'.[21]

Planners assumed that the atomic bomb would achieve what had previously proved impossible—it would kill with such ruthless efficiency that a resurgence of morale after the raid would be unlikely. The emphasis upon civilian morale is evident in three Target Committee recommendations: (*a*) that aiming points need not be specified, (*b*) that industrial targets need not be given high priority because they were too small and highly dispersed in Japan, and (*c*) that the bomb should be dropped in the centre of a city since bombing on the outskirts (where militarily important facilities were usually concentrated) would waste the bomb's power on sparsely inhabited areas. In other words, talk of military targets was mere window dressing designed to assuage the guilt of those who found terror bombing distasteful. This bothered Stimson, who had difficulty keeping pace with the erosion of morality. Worried that the United States might 'get the reputation for outdoing Hitler in atrocities', he wanted the bomb used exclusively on industrial targets.[22] Marshall shared Stimson's unease, arguing that the bomb should be used on a specifically military target and only after a precise warning. Their wishes, however, were incompatible with the strategic consensus, not to mention with the comprehensive power of the bomb.

News of the Trinity test reached Truman while he was meeting Churchill and Stalin at Potsdam. At that summit, Stalin promised that the Soviets would attack Japan on 15 August. 'I've gotten what I came for,' Truman wrote to his wife. 'We'll end the war a year sooner now, and think of the kids who won't be killed!'[23] Though reassured by Russian promises, he remained confident that the 'Japs will fold up before Russia comes in. I am sure they will when Manhattan appears over their homeland.'[24] That was Truman's dream scenario. Churchill noticed how he was a 'changed man' after hearing news of the Trinity test. 'He told the Russians just where they got on and off and generally bossed the whole meeting.'[25] The prime minister sensed ulterior motives. 'It is quite clear that the United States do not at the present time desire Russian participation in the war against Japan.'[26]

'We have discovered the most terrible bomb in the history of the world,' Truman told his diary. It seemed 'the most terrible thing ever discovered, but it can be made the most useful'. In order to be useful, however, it had to be used. 'I have told ... Stimson to use it so that military objectives and soldiers and sailors are the target and not women and children.'[27] That entry suggests deep confusion on Truman's part about the power of his new weapon. He seems to have been unaware (or perhaps reluctant to accept) that, even if a 'purely military' target could be found, heavy civilian casualties would result.

In view of the way bombing had escalated during the war, using the bomb against Japan was not illogical. There remained, however, a crucial confusion of purpose. On the one hand, the Americans spoke of destroying important military targets; on the other, they confessed to a desire to destroy Japanese morale. Had the former aim been paramount, it seems unlikely that Hiroshima would have been targeted and even less likely that the bomb would have been dropped in the residential centre of the city. Assessment of motives is further muddled by the additional aim of manipulating the Soviets—firstly, preventing their entry into the Pacific War, and, secondly, impressing upon them the unbridled nature of American power. While that aim might not have been predominant, neither was it insignificant. Two important questions hovered in mid-air, never explicitly stated. How many bombs would it take to destroy Japanese morale? Probably just one. How many bombs were necessary to frighten the Soviets? At least two.

As if to underline the terrible nature of total war, the atomic bomb dropped on 6 August 1945 exploded directly above Shima hospital in Hiroshima. Assessments of its impact made no mention of industrial targets destroyed, but instead concentrated on the scale of human tragedy, with estimates hovering around 80,000 dead. As in any instance of bombing, there was no shortage of horror stories associated with the strike. What made the atomic bomb different, however, was the efficiency with which horror was produced.

Truman's thoughts about the bomb were no clearer after the first one was dropped. 'I know that Japan is a terribly cruel and uncivilized nation,' he wrote to Senator Richard Russell on 9 August, 'but I can't bring myself to believe that, because they are beasts, we should ourselves act in the same manner.' He added: 'I certainly regret the necessity of wiping out whole populations because of the "pigheadedness" of the leaders of a nation . . . I am not going to do it unless it is absolutely necessary.'[28] On that same day, the President interrupted a long speech to the American people with two bizarre sentences about Hiroshima: 'The world will note that the first atomic bomb was dropped on Hiroshima, a military base. That was because we wished in this first attack to avoid, insofar as possible, the killing of civilians.'[29] The description of Hiroshima as a military base has continued to perplex historians. Could it be that he did not know that Hiroshima was a city? Or was he simply reluctant to face the reality of atomic power used for purposes of terror?

If, as seems likely, the Hiroshima bomb was intended to destroy the enemy's will, logic suggests that the Japanese should have been given time to digest the atomic message. Doing so was complicated because the communications system was in chaos. The Americans helped realization along by dropping leaflets on Japanese cities. But this took time, and the United States was in a hurry, since the date of the Soviet invasion was rapidly approaching. In any case, in order to demonstrate limitless power (to the Soviets in particular), the Americans had to suggest that they possessed a limitless supply of atomic weapons. One bomb alone would not send that message, but two might. The original intention was for a second strike on 11 August. It is entirely likely that five days of reflection would have caused the Japanese to surrender, especially since they had shown a willingness to accept conditional terms *before* Hiroshima. Since, however, bad weather was forecast from 10 August, the mission was moved forward two days, to 9 August.

On that day, Nagasaki was hit. Perhaps 40,000 were killed instantly; another 30,000 died by the end of the year. On 10 August, the Japanese agreed to surrender, though they refused to accept American demands for the emperor to be deposed. On the assumption that Japanese terms would be rejected, Groves prepared a third strike. Truman was at first inclined to allow Groves to go ahead, but on reflection decided to stop the bombing. According to Henry Wallace, his Commerce Secretary, 'He said the thought of wiping out another 100,000 people was too horrible. He didn't like the idea of killing, as he said, "all those kids".'[30] Truman accepted conditional surrender, in other words, the same terms the Japanese had been prepared to offer before Hiroshima.

Back in America, the news brought profound relief. Polls showed about 85 per cent approval of the bombings, with some enthusiasm for further strikes. Significant reservations were, however, expressed. The left-wing commentator Dwight Macdonald regretted America's 'decline to barbarism' while, on the right, David Lawrence argued that 'Military necessity . . . will never erase from our minds the simple truth that we, of all civilized nations . . . did not hesitate to employ the most destructive weapon of all times indiscriminately against men, women and children.'[31] The prominent clergyman Samuel McCrea Cavert protested to Truman that the 'necessarily indiscriminate' effect of the atomic bomb 'sets [an] extremely dangerous precedent for [the] future of mankind'. Truman replied with characteristic bluntness, reminding Cavert of Pearl Harbor and the Bataan death march. 'When you have to deal with a beast you have to treat him as a beast.'[32]

A year after the bombing, Admiral William Halsey, the Third Fleet commander, publicly argued that the scientists 'had a toy and they wanted to try it out . . . The first atomic bomb was an unnecessary experiment. . . . It was a mistake ever to drop it.'[33] That was fair criticism wrongly targeted, since it was not the scientists, but politicians and soldiers, who had pushed for deployment. That was certainly General Dwight Eisenhower's judgement; he protested that 'the Japanese were ready to surrender and it wasn't necessary to hit them with that awful thing'.[34] The Strategic Bombing Survey (SBS), released in June 1946, similarly concluded that 'certainly prior to 31 December 1945, and in all probability prior to 1 November 1945, Japan would have surrendered even if the atomic bombs had not been dropped, even if Russia had not entered the war, and even if no invasion had been planned or contemplated'.[35] If the authors of the SBS were right, the bombs shortened the war by at most a few months. In this light, Hiroshima seems unnecessary, perhaps even wanton. Nagasaki, on the other hand, seems an atrocity. With typical acuity, Szilard proposed a scenario in which Germany beat the Americans to the bomb, dropped two of them, but still managed to lose the war. 'Can anyone doubt that we would then have defined the dropping of atomic bombs on cities as a war crime, and that we would have sentenced the Germans who were guilty of this crime to death at Nuremberg and hanged them?' Telford Taylor, the chief prosecutor at Nuremberg, confessed that he had 'never heard a plausible justification of Nagasaki'. To him, it seemed a war crime.[36]

Truman repeated a standard refrain: 'Dropping the bombs ended the war [and] saved lives.' As for alleged ulterior motives, he insisted that 'My objective was . . . a military blow to create a military surrender . . . That is all I had in mind.'[37] As the years passed, the number of lives supposedly saved remained monumental. 'I knew what I was doing when I stopped the war that would have killed a half million youngsters on both sides if those bombs had not been dropped,' Truman wrote in 1963. 'I have no regrets and, under the same circumstances, I would do it again.'[38] Like Truman, most Americans took solace in the assumption that, while their power was ruthless, their cause was just. As the *Chicago Tribune* put it: 'Being merciless, [we] were merciful.' A cartoon showed a dove flying over Japan, an atom bomb in its beak.[39]

Stalin saw things differently. 'Hiroshima has shaken the world,' he remarked. 'The balance has been destroyed.' His foreign secretary Vyacheslav Molotov felt that the bombings 'were, of course, not against Japan, but against the Soviet Union'. He thought Truman was essentially saying 'see, remember what we have. You don't have the atomic bomb, but we do'.[40] Alexander Werth, the *Sunday Times* correspondent in Moscow, recalled that Hiroshima and Nagasaki 'had an acutely depressing effect on everybody. It was clearly realized that this was a New Fact in the world's power politics, that the bomb constituted a threat to Russia, and some Russian pessimists . . . dismally remarked that Russia's desperately hard victory over Germany was now "as good as wasted".'[41]

Stalin understood that the atomic bomb was a weapon of terror from which the Americans would extract maximum advantage. That strategy was apparent when foreign ministers met in London in early September 1945 to discuss the post-war settlement. Before the conference, Stimson expressed unease that Byrnes '[has] the bomb in his hip pocket, so to speak, as a great weapon to get through the thing'.[42] With remarkable synchronicity, during the conference Byrnes sneered at Molotov: 'You don't know southerners. We carry our artillery in our pocket. If you don't . . . get down to work, I'm going to pull an atomic bomb out of my hip pocket and let you have it.'[43] Molotov, under strict instructions from Stalin not to show fear, simply chuckled. A short time later, he warned the United States that 'there can be no large-scale technological secrets that can remain the property of any one country . . . therefore the discovery of atomic energy must not encourage . . . enthusiasm for using this discovery in a foreign-policy power game'.[44] In other words, bombs would breed bombs.

Byrnes subsequently concluded that the Soviets were 'stubborn, obstinate, and they don't scare'.[45] Rather than abandoning the terror tactic, however, the Americans decided to intensify it through a bold demonstration of their might. In July 1946, two tests of atomic weapons were carried out in Bikini Atoll, with hundreds of foreign observers invited along for the show. The official explanation held that the tests were designed to amass data about the new weapon. Cynics, however, suspected that the real purpose was swagger. Several members of Congress openly condemned the tests, and disgruntled scientists criticized the government for flexing its nuclear muscles at a particularly sensitive time. Even Byrnes complained that Bikini rendered negotiation with the Soviets much more complicated.

The American decision to explode the bombs among surplus ships in the atoll badly backfired because deep water masked the weapon's true power. That, however, did not prevent the Soviets from expressing annoyance at the Americans' manipulative tactics. 'The atomic bomb at Bikini . . . explode[d] something more important than a couple of out-of-date warships,' a Soviet observer complained. 'It fundamentally undermined the belief in the seriousness of American talk about atomic disarmament.'[46] Had they been sufficiently perceptive, the Americans might have learned a valuable lesson about using fear to coerce. Stalin correctly calculated that the United States did not have enough bombs to destroy the Soviet Union. 'They cannot decide the outcome of a war,' he argued. 'Atomic bombs are quite insufficient for that.'[47] American intimidation simply encouraged greater Soviet intransigence, with Stalin even more determined to join the nuclear club.[48] As Stanley Baldwin recognized well before the advent of nuclear weapons: 'Fear is a very dangerous thing. It is quite true that it may act as a deterrent in people's minds against war, but it is much more likely to act to make them want to increase armaments to protect them against the terrors that they know may be launched against them.'[49]

The Americans were struggling to come to terms with the new world that had dawned. On 30 June 1947, the Joint Chiefs of Staff evaluation board for Operation Crossroads directed its attention to the bomb's potential, both as a threat and as a tool. Its report, entitled *The Evaluation of the Atomic Bomb as a Military Weapon*, foretold the way the United States would wield power in the post-war world. To the authors of that report, the bomb was, quite simply, a 'threat to mankind' which had fundamentally altered conventional standards of risk assessment.[50] Huge advantage seemed to lie in striking first with nuclear weapons. This implied:

a consequential revision of our traditional attitudes toward what constitutes acts of aggression . . . Our policy of national defense must provide for the employment of every practical means to prevent surprise attack. Offensive measures will be the only generally effective means of defense, and the United States must be prepared to employ them before a potential enemy can inflict significant damage upon us.[51]

In the past, American military power had been deployed in response to actual attacks. But since a single attack could now kill 100,000 people in seconds, it seemed prudent to be more proactive. 'It is necessary that, while adhering . . . to our historic policy of non-aggression, we revise past definitions of what constitutes aggression.' The duty of the military would henceforth be 'to defend the country against imminent or incipient atomic weapon attack'.[52] The mere manufacture of nuclear weapons by another power, or even the procurement of fissile materials, seemed grounds for action.[53] In line with this thinking, Groves advocated pre-emptive nuclear strikes against any hostile power about to develop a nuclear capacity. In time, the logic of pre-emption would be extended towards other threats, not specifically nuclear ones. In other words, the rationale that justified the 2003 attack on Iraq was first explicitly expressed in 1947.

With obscene understatement, the Crossroads report concluded that 'From a military viewpoint, the atomic bomb's ability to kill human beings or to impair, through injury, their ability to make war is of paramount importance.'[54] In other words, the bomb implied acceptance of the notion that civilian populations were now legitimate targets. To this end, the Bikini tests provided guidance on maximizing savagery:

> TEST BAKER gave evidence that the detonation of a bomb in a body of water contiguous to a city would vastly enhance its radiation effects by the creation of a base surge whose mist, contaminated with fission products, and dispersed by wind over great areas, would have not only an immediately lethal effect, but would establish a long term hazard through the contamination of structures by the deposition of radioactive particles.[55]

The advantage of radiation, the report suggested, was not just that it killed but also that it demoralized those it did not immediately kill. Analysts cast a cold eye on the implied opportunities:

> multiple disaster . . . would befall a modern city, blasted by one or more atomic bombs and enveloped by radioactive mists. Of the survivors in contaminated areas, some would be doomed to die of radiation sickness in hours, some in days, and others in years. But, these areas, irregular in size and shape, as wind and topography might form them, would have no visible boundaries. No survivor could be certain he was not among the doomed and so, added to every terror of the moment, thousands would be stricken with a fear of death and the uncertainty of the time of its arrival.[56]

The bomb's effect would quickly spread to areas not immediately affected by blast or heat. Panic would extend inexorably outwards on a tide of shattered refugees. 'Thousands, perhaps millions . . . would rush from the city in panic, breaking down remaining transportation facilities, congesting highways, and creating in their flight new hazards to life.' These fugitives would expand the chaos; their 'contaminated clothing and any goods they carried could establish in others the fear of dangerous radioactivity, thus creating a unique psychological hazard'.[57]

Throughout the report, strategic possibilities were discussed with respect not only to the threats Americans might face but also to the opportunities they might exploit. It is not entirely clear, for instance, whether the following paragraph sought to expose a danger or to explore an option:

> It cannot be assumed that in a future war, a participant, with a range of choice, will rely altogether upon a single weapon of mass destruction. Driven by the necessity of overwhelming his adversary, lest he himself be overwhelmed, a combatant might well choose to compound the horror of an atomic bomb attack with the simultaneous delivery of pathogenic agents which would insure that frightened fugitives would spread, not only their panic, but epidemic disease as well.[58]

In a massive nuclear attack, the report concluded, 'of primary military concern will be the bomb's potentiality to break the will of nations and of peoples by the stimulation of man's primordial fears, those of the unknown, the invisible, the mysterious'.[59]

The Crossroads report reveals, in striking fashion, the easy acceptance of a level of barbarity that would have been considered abhorrent only a few years earlier. Strategists dispensed with the attempt to justify civilian casualties with reference to military necessity; killing kids was no longer accident but object. Those who criticized this descent into savagery were dismissed as naïve or un-American (Szilard and Oppenheimer were early additions to the FBI's list of suspected subversives). The need to prepare for this new type of warfare, including the stockpiling of chemical and biological weapons, was justified by the assumption that evil enemies were already doing so. That need to pre-empt had originally been the driving force behind the building of the atomic bomb, and would continue to fuel the relentless proliferation of armaments in the post-war period. Moral qualms were smothered under a blanket assumption that desperate measures were necessary to defend American ideals.

When opportunities for setting a moral example occasionally arose, the United States chose instead cold, hard scepticism. A case in point was the decision to develop the hydrogen bomb, or 'Super'. On 30 October 1949, the General Advisory Committee (GAC), chaired by Oppenheimer, expressed unanimous opposition to the thermonuclear bomb for the simple reason that it had no purpose other than to kill civilians. 'It is clear,' the GAC argued, 'that ... it is not a weapon which can be used exclusively for the destruction of material installations of military or semi-military purposes. Its use therefore carries much further than the atomic bomb itself the policy of exterminating civilian populations.'[60] The GAC argued that the hydrogen bomb had no strategic utility since the Soviet Union had only two cities— Moscow and Leningrad—of sufficient size to justify such a large bomb. In other words, everything the Super could achieve could be done more effectively by smaller and cheaper atomic weapons.

The GAC argued, with considerable logic, that weapons were being developed not because they made strategic sense but simply because of their unbridled capacity to kill. Enrico Fermi and Isidor Rabi voiced the fiercest outrage, arguing that 'by its very nature', the Super 'cannot be confined to a military objective but becomes a weapon . . . of genocide'. For that reason, it 'cannot be justified on any ethical ground. . . . Its use would put the United States in a bad moral position relative to the peoples of the world'.[61] The other committee members agreed that the United States stood on the banks of a moral Rubicon:

> Let it be clearly realized that this is a super weapon; it is in a totally different category from an atomic bomb . . . reasonable people the world over would realize that the existence of a weapon of this type whose power of destruction is essentially unlimited represents a threat to the future of the human race which is intolerable. Thus we believe that the psychological effect of the weapon in our hands would be adverse to our interest.[62]

The GAC thought that the weapon offered an opportunity to reject escalation of the arms race—to provide 'by example some limitations on the totality of war and thus of limiting the fear and arousing the hopes of mankind'.[63] Rabi and Fermi thought that the president should 'tell the American public, and the world, that we think it wrong on fundamental ethical principles to initiate a program of development'.[64] An American refusal might, they believed, kick-start arms control negotiations by setting an important moral example. The gesture seemed worth the risk because the weapon itself carried no strategic advantage. For that suggestion, Rabi and Fermi were dismissed as hopelessly naïve.

Truman's decision to develop the Super was based on very simple logic: the weapon—no matter how horrific it might be—should be built not because it was necessary but because it was possible. That brought a blistering rebuke from the eminent nuclear physicist Hans Bethe:

> The usual argument . . . is that we are fighting against a country which denies all the human values we cherish and that any weapon, however terrible, must be used to prevent that country and its creed from dominating the world. It is argued that it would be better for us to lose our lives than our liberty; and this I personally agree with. But I believe that . . . we would lose far more than our lives in a war fought with hydrogen bombs, that we would in fact lose all our liberties and human values at the same time, and so thoroughly that we would not recover them for an unforeseeably long time.
>
> We believe in peace based on mutual trust. Shall we achieve it by using hydrogen bombs? Shall we convince the Russians of the value of the individual by killing millions of them? If we fight a war and we win it with H-bombs, what history will remember is *not* the ideals we were fighting for but the method we used to accomplish them. Those methods will be compared to the warfare of Genghis Khan, who ruthlessly killed every last inhabitant of Persia.[65]

These criticisms were shouted into a vacuum. For most Americans, the logic of bigness was inescapable. In an atmosphere of virulent anti-Communism, an open debate about military power could not thrive.

The Cold War had a way of vaporizing subtlety. The simple logic of the playground usually prevailed. At the time, developing the hydrogen bomb made perfect sense, since naked power seemed all-important. Twenty years after the end of the Cold War, however, it is possible to separate atomic rationale from the weapons themselves and, in the process, recognize the momentous nature of decisions made. While the atom bomb was never again used in anger after 1945, Hiroshima and Nagasaki are nevertheless important as a surrender to the temptation of terror. The striking feature of the period 1945–9 is the number of times the United States, when offered an opportunity to step back from the brink, chose instead to enhance its capacity for terror. American assumption of virtue provided redemption for what once seemed barbaric.

On 1 March 1955, Churchill remarked on the 'sublime irony' that, in the Cold War, 'safety will be the sturdy child of terror, and survival the twin brother of annihilation'.[66] Churchill was talking about the balance of terror which, thanks to atomic weapons, seemed the best guarantee of peace and security. In time, however, the faith in terror encouraged an uninhibited and unilateral deployment of it as an instrument of state policy. In this sense, Hiroshima and Nagasaki confirmed a new way of war in which it had become perfectly acceptable to slaughter innocent civilians for purposes of national security. Running parallel to that belief was the supposition that America was justified to attack pre-emptively if a threat was perceived. Strategic planners took solace in the assumption that evil rested with the first sin, never with the response to it. The implications of those beliefs, barely discussed at the time, are painfully evident today. Bethe's protest quoted above seems agonizingly relevant to the twenty-first century. 'Shall we convince the Russians of the value of the individual by killing millions of them?' he had asked. For Russians, substitute Vietnamese, Iraqis, or Afghans. 'What history will remember is *not* the ideals we were fighting for but the method we used to accomplish them.'[67] At the time, it seemed that Bethe was writing about hydrogen bombs. In fact, he had something more fundamental in mind.

## NOTES

1. Richard Rhodes, *The making of the atom bomb* (Harmondsworth: Penguin, 1986), 779.
2. See John Mueller, *Atomic obsession* (New York: Oxford University Press, 2010), 29–54.

3. Giulio Douhet, *The command of the air* (New York: Arno Press, 1942), 8–10.

4. *Hansard*, 10 November 1932.

5. 'The Hague rules of air warfare', World War I document archive, http://wwi.lib. byu.edu/index.php/The_Hague_Rules_of_Air_Warfare

6. Appeal of Franklin Roosevelt, 1 September 1939, http://www.dannen.com/decision/int-law.html#E

7. See Christabel Bielenberg, *The past is myself* (London: Corgi Books, 1988).

8. Rhodes, 336.

9. Henry Stimson, 'The decision to use the atomic bomb', *Harper's Magazine* (February 1947), 98.

10. Rhodes, *Atom bomb*, 618.

11. C. S. Smith to Lieutenant Taylor, 25 July 1945, http://nuclearfiles.org/menu/key-issues/nuclear-weapons/history/pre-cold-war/manhattan-project/trinity/eyewitness-cyril-smith_1945-07-16.htm

12. Robert Jungk, *Brighter than a thousand suns* (Harmondsworth: Pelican, 1978).

13. Chicago Metallurgical Laboratory, 'A petition to the President of the United States', 17 July 1945, http://www.nuclearfiles.org/menu/key-issues/ethics/issues/scientific/petition-chicago-metallurgical-laboratory.htm

14. Rhodes, *Atom bomb*, 530.

15. Ibid., 638.

16. Henry Stimson to Harry Truman, 25 April 1945, http://nuclearfiles.org/menu/library/correspondence/stimson-henry/corr_stimson_1945-04-25.htm

17. Harry Truman, *Memoirs by Harry S Truman, Vol. 1: Years of decision* (New York: Doubleday, 1955), 87.

18. Joseph Gerson, *Empire and the bomb* (London: Pluto Press, 2007), 52.

19. Gar Alperovitz, *The decision to use the atomic bomb* (New York: Vintage Books, 1995), 143f.

20. Notes of the Interim Committee, 31 May 1945, Harry S. Truman Library, http://www.trumanlibrary.org/whistlestop/study_collections/bomb/large/documents/fulltext.php?fulltextid=7

21. Rhodes, *Atom bomb*, 627.

22. Ibid., 650.

23. Robert L. Messer, 'New evidence on Truman's decision', *Bulletin of the Atomic Scientists* (August 1985), 54.

24. Truman Diary, 18 July 1945, Truman Library, http://www.trumanlibrary.org/whistlestop/study_collections/bomb/large/documents/fulltext.php?fulltextid=15

25. Stimson Diary, 22 July 1945 (reel 9); Henry Lewis Stimson Papers, Yale University Library.

26. Paul Baker (ed.), *The atomic bomb: The great decision* (New York: Holt, Rinehart, and Winston, 1968), 61.

27. Truman Diary, 24 July 1945, Truman Library, http://www.trumanlibrary.org/whistlestop/study_collections/bomb/large/documents/fulltext.php?fulltextid=15

28. Barton J. Bernstein, 'Understanding the atomic bomb and the Japanese surrender: Missed opportunities, little-known near disasters, and modern memory', *Diplomatic History*, 19/2 (1995), 267f.

29. New York Times, 10 August 1945.
30. Rhodes, *Atom bomb*, 742f.
31. Robert Jay Lifton and Greg Mitchell, *Hiroshima in America: A half century of denial* (New York: Avon Books, 1995), 37.
32. Alperovitz, *The Decision*, 563.
33. Ibid., 445.
34. *Newsweek*, 11 November 1963.
35. United States Strategic Bombing Survey, 1 July 1946, 26, http://www.anesi.com/ussbs01.htm#jstetw
36. *US News and World Report*, 15 August 1960, 68–71.
37. Robert H. Ferrell (ed.), *Harry S. Truman and the bomb* (Worland, WY: High Plains Publishing Company, 1996), 109f.
38. Harry S. Truman to Irv Kupcinet, 5 August 1963, Truman Library, http://www.trumanlibrary.org/whistlestop/study_collections/bomb/large/documents/index.php?documentdate=1963-08-05&documentid=74&studycollectionid=abomb&pagenumber=1
39. *Chicago Tribune*, 11 August 1945.
40. David Holloway, *Stalin and the bomb* (New Haven: Yale University Press, 1994), 132, 164.
41. Alexander Werth, *Russia at War* (London: Barrie and Rockliff), 925.
42. Holloway, *Stalin and the bomb*, 156.
43. Gregg Herken, *The winning weapon* (Princeton, NJ: Princeton University Press, 1988), 48.
44. Holloway, *Stalin and the bomb*, 157.
45. Mueller, *Atomic obsession*, 47.
46. Lloyd J. Graybar, 'The 1946 atomic bomb tests: Atomic diplomacy or bureaucratic infighting?', *Journal of American History*, 72/4 (1986), 902.
47. Holloway, *Stalin and the bomb*, 171.
48. Ibid.
49. Mueller, *Atomic obsession*, 27.
50. 'The evaluation of the atomic bomb as a military weapon: The final report of the Joints Chiefs of Staff evaluation board for Operation Crossroads', 30 June 1947 (hereafter), http://www.nuclearfiles.org/menu/key-issues/nuclear-weapons/issues/testing/crossroads-final-report_1947-06-30.htm, 10.
51. Ibid., 11.
52. Ibid., 29.
53. Herken, *The winning weapon*, 218.
54. 'The evaluation of the atomic bomb as a military weapon', 21.
55. Ibid., 34.
56. Ibid.
57. Ibid., 34f.
58. Ibid., 35.
59. Ibid., 36.
60. 'General Advisory Committee report', 30 October 1949', *Atomic Archive*, http://www.atomicarchive.com/Docs/Hydrogen/GACReport.shtml
61. Ibid.
62. Ibid.

63. Ibid.
64. Ibid.
65. Hans Bethe, 'The hydrogen bomb', *Bulletin of the Atomic Scientists* (April 1950), 102.
66. *Hansard*, 1 March 1955.
67. Bethe, 'The hydrogen bomb', 102.

# 6

# The 'New Wars' Thesis Revisited

*Mats Berdal*

It is difficult to pinpoint when precisely the notion of 'new wars' and the basic idea underlying it—that contemporary wars display features that are qualitatively different from 'old' or 'Clausewitzian' wars—acquired the kind of popular currency and matter-of-fact status which it enjoys in many quarters today. Mary Kaldor's *New and old wars*, first published in 1999, certainly played a key role in fleshing out the notion itself and in popularizing it for a wider audience.[1] It remains the boldest and most unequivocal statement of the argument.[2] According to Kaldor, 'new wars' developed 'during the 1980s and 1990s...especially in Africa and Eastern Europe', and their emergence had 'to be understood in the context of the process known as globalization'.[3] The evidence of newness was to be found in the war aims of belligerents, in the 'mode' or 'methods of warfare', and in the manner that the wars were now being financed and sustained.[4]

While Kaldor's book has attracted particular attention, the general proposition that 'some sort of historic rupture'[5] in the character of war took place in the late twentieth century is a theme that runs through a number of works from the early post-Cold War years. Writing in 1993, Martin van Creveld saw a '*new* form of armed conflict developing' that would be the 'domain of much smaller, less powerful, and in many ways more primitive political entities similar to those existing before 1648'.[6] Future conflict, he suggested, would resemble premodern, non-Trinitarian forms of warfare, aimless and increasingly devoid of any meaningful distinction between combatants and non-combatants.[7] This theme of a 'new medievalism' was picked up and popularized by Robert Kaplan whose coverage of war in West Africa in the early 1990s also led him to conclude that 'a new kind of war' was emerging.[8] In *Civil Wars*, Hans Magnus Enzensberger drew attention to what he saw as the new and distinguishing feature of modern civil wars: the 'absence of conviction'.[9] Others again, notably Herfried Münkler, have derived newness from the 'simultaneous coincidence' of different features, none of which on its own is entirely novel, including the privatization of war and the increasingly irregular and 'colourful mix of combatants' involved.[10]

It is evident from these isolated examples that differences of emphasis and even some genuine disagreements exist among authors on particular issues. Indeed, there is no consistent body of thought regarding the essential features of 'new wars' and this explains in part why the term itself is now used with such abandon, as a catch-all phrase covering any armed conflict after 1990. For all this, the basic proposition nonetheless remains: contemporary wars are 'substantively distinct'[11] from older patterns of armed conflict and, as such, 'the "new war" argument does reflect a new reality'.[12]

It is with this proposition that this chapter is concerned. There are two related aspects to this general proposition that will be considered. The first concerns the idea of a historical disjunction between 'old' and 'new' wars and the accompanying argument that the emergence of 'new wars' is connected to *two* fundamental processes of change. Chief among them is the process of globalization in the late twentieth century. The second driver of change, though emphasis on this factor varies greatly and is generally more confused, is the end of the Cold War.[13]

The second aspect concerns the actual features of the 'new wars' as identified by Kaldor, and the way in which 'they differ from earlier wars in terms of their goals, the methods of warfare and how they are financed'.[14] The most interesting of these, and therefore deserving of more detailed treatment, relates to the economic underpinnings of contemporary intra-state armed conflicts. Of special interest is the evidence suggesting that belligerents have increasingly been able to sustain military activity by raising funds and purchasing weapons through the mechanisms of a more open and deregulated international economy, by exploiting diaspora connections to conflict, by forming symbiotic links to organized crime, and by diverting humanitarian aid intended for vulnerable, war-affected populations.

## ARGUMENT IN BRIEF

The 'new wars' thesis has done much to stimulate debate about the character of war in the modern age. In doing so, it has helped draw attention to aspects of intra-state armed conflicts that appear relatively more important now than they did in the recent past. Chief among these is the rise in 'combatant self-financing' made possible, in part, by the opportunities provided by a more globalized international economy. These opportunities have enabled belligerents in some wars not only to keep going but also to develop a vested economic interest in continued conflict, something which in turn has affected the duration, intensity, and dynamics of the conflict.[15] It is one thing, however, to stimulate debate. As an analytical category, the notion of 'new wars' does more, in the end, to obscure than to illuminate. This is not only because there are historical precedents for what today is sometimes identified as 'new';

establishing this fact alone is easy enough. More serious is the persistent tendency to abstract contemporary armed conflicts from their specific historical and cultural context, to make sweeping generalizations across a wide variety of cases and, above all, to undervalue the continuous influence of the past on present patterns of war and violent conflict.

## 'NEW WARS' AND HISTORY

The essentially static and ahistorical character of the 'new wars' thesis is one of its most striking and problematic features. The fact that this has already received much attention does not make it any less important; it remains a fundamental criticism.[16] This is because it is not an isolated issue that can be addressed and then set aside. Neglect of historical context suffuses the thesis as a whole and is ultimately what renders more specific claims to novelty—say, the increasingly criminal character of war or the deliberate targeting of civilians—that much harder to sustain. The issue is not, therefore, merely one of demonstrating that features of 'new wars' have historical precedents, though this in itself is not unimportant. The problems run deeper, involving a failure both to place individual wars in their historical context and to take proper account of the many insights offered by the history of warfare itself.

The literature on 'new wars', concerned as it is with establishing broad trends, covers a wide variety of different armed conflicts. While this is required to extrapolate distinctive features of these wars as a category, the attendant risk is that in moving from case to case, the historical and cultural specificity of each is lost. Nowhere perhaps are the dangers of this more evident than in the case of Africa; a continent whose wars over the past twenty years have figured prominently in the 'new wars' literature. And yet, as Dominique Jacquin-Berdal has shown, the very notion of 'new wars' is 'deeply unhelpful' when it comes to understanding post-Cold War patterns of violence and conflict on the continent. This is the case whether one is looking at the Horn, Central, or West Africa.[17]

This is true, to start, in a purely chronological sense: many of Africa's so-called 'new wars' have distinctly old roots, reaching back in time well before the passing of the Cold War.[18] An obvious case in point is Angola, where fighting began with the anti-colonial struggle against Portuguese rule in the early 1960s, continued after formal independence in 1975, and ended only with the death of Jonas Savimbi in 2002; a period of nearly forty years, punctuated by occasional ceasefires and abortive peace processes. The Angolan example is also of interest, however, for a second and more substantive reason. The long-drawn-out war in Angola, as with 'many of Africa's current generation [of armed conflicts] are directly linked to (or are actual continuations of) struggles which occurred around the time of independence'.[19] This very fact 'means that to understand how these wars became possible, we certainly need to ask questions about the organization of power and authority during colonial times'.[20] This of course applies not only to African countries but also to other regions identified as sites of 'new wars'. In one of these—the Transcaucasian region—the wars that erupted in the 1990s were connected not only in an immediate sense to the end of empire but also to the legacy of Stalin's ruthless deportations and ethnic-cleansing policies in the region during and after the Second World War. Thus, the legacies of colonial rule, including the effects of what were often ill-prepared and bloody processes of decolonization, are critical to an understanding of the violent struggles that, in many cases, erupted within newly independent states and often persisted, even if in a mutated form, into the contemporary era.

Then there is the Cold War itself, a period whose links to contemporary armed conflict are often strangely ignored by writers and policymakers, many of whom undervalue its 'intimate, unfinished relationship with the world it left behind'.[21] At a basic *material* level, the persistence of older and the eruption of new armed conflicts—in Africa and elsewhere—are often linked to Cold War legacies and to processes set in motion during the global confrontation between East and West. These include, *inter alia*, the large stocks of surplus weapons built up during the Cold War that became available as the competitive engagement of the superpowers in the Third World wound down; the selling off in the 1990s by former Warsaw Pact countries of non-NATO standard equipment 'at a discount . . . much of it going to Africa';[22] the creation of semi-official and secret arms pipelines that have continued to fuel war in the aftermath of the Cold War; the privatization of Cold War security services and intelligence outfits, some of whose members have found new work as 'conflict entrepreneurs' and 'violence specialists' on the African continent and elsewhere.[23]

Another, arguably more critical, Cold War connection to 'new wars' concerns the *nature* of the regimes that patrons were prepared to prop up in the interests of their own political and ideological struggle. Questions of political and economic governance, let alone human rights, were usually strictly subordinated to those interests and the accompanying search for Cold War allies. One consequence of this was to allow for the 'development of a militarized politics'[24] within many client states, which in turn set the stage for renewed violence at a later date. A particularly striking example of this is the 'Mobutuist system of institutional theft and corruption',[25] the longevity and slow death of which provide an essential backdrop to the two Congo wars that began in 1996 and 1998. Although the New War features of these wars have received much attention— notably their economic dimensions (discussed below)—they still cannot be separated from the tensions and fault lines whose roots lie deep in the precolonial, colonial, as well as the Cold War and postcolonial history of the region.[26]

At the same time, armed conflict in the post-Cold War era cannot be viewed as *merely* the result, or continuation, of Cold War politics. For one, there are examples of regions that have seen almost continuous conflict since the early 1990s—notably West Africa—where direct Cold War competition played a comparatively minor role in stoking conflict. What those conflicts suggest though, as Paul Richards has shown, is that developments since the end of the Cold War can only be fully grasped in light of 'local political culture' and local history.[27] Indeed, the wars in West Africa in the 1990s can only be properly understood against the background of the *'longue durée* of West African history', including the precolonial relations and the sociopolitical imbalances that have long existed between coastal-based elites and peoples of the interior, as well as the central importance of religion to the peoples of the region.[28]

One of the principal difficulties with the 'new wars' thesis as elaborated by Mary Kaldor lies in the juxtaposition of 'newness' against what is supposedly a distinctive 'Clausewitzian' era of warfare. Kaldor appears to accept that the 'classification of types of wars does not represent hard and fast distinctions' and, elsewhere, talks of 'prevailing perceptions of war drawn from an earlier era'. Yet, the subsequent analysis remains firmly predicated on the assumption that 'new wars' can be usefully contrasted with those of a historically distinctive era. Not only is the notion of such an era itself problematic but it excludes from view historical experiences *within* the period itself that offer a rich source of insight and comparison with contemporary wars.[29] In particular, it pays little attention to the wars of Western imperial conquest; of colonial rule and pacification; and of decolonization in the nineteenth and twentieth centuries. The dividing line between each of these three phases is naturally blurred. Still, even a cursory look at the patterns of warfare in each calls into question claims central to the 'new wars' thesis.

One of these for example is the 'growth of para-state and private players'[30] and, more generally, the 'privatization' of war. In fact, private economic interests, private capital, and actors all played key roles as drivers and sources of military activity in the period of colonial conquest and expansion. In the early modern period, the financing requirements of expanding armies, coupled to state weakness administratively and fiscally, gave the private military entrepreneur a vital role during war.[31] But public–private partnerships were also very much a motor force behind the growth of territorial empire in the nineteenth century. And with respect to the period of colonial rule, conditions of warfare were often a permanent feature of life at the 'violent edge of empire'.[32] Here, warfare differed sharply from the stylized notion of Clausewitzian war, though it often differed much less from the mode of warfare supposedly distinctive to 'new wars'.

## METHODS AND MODE OF WARFARE

Proponents of the 'new wars' thesis have all emphasized the 'intense savagery'[33] of 'new wars' and the central and unprecedented role of 'extreme and conspicuous atrocity'[34] in them. According to Münkler, 'force is mainly directed not against the enemy's armed force but the civilian population'.[35] Kaldor echoes these views, identifying, as a distinguishing feature of 'new wars', the calculated use of atrocities.[36] 'Systematic murder of those with a different label', 'ethnic cleansing', and 'rendering an area uninhabitable', all of which 'were considered to be undesirable and illegitimate side-effects of old war have become central to the mode of fighting in the new wars'.[37]

The many atrocities and horrors that have accompanied the wars of the post-Cold War era are well documented. The attempt, however, to assert newness on the grounds that civilians are now the main object of war and that atrocities are a feature that, in their intensity and widespread use, is peculiar to 'new wars' is, perhaps, the least convincing of all the claims underpinning the 'new wars' thesis. Indeed, the idea that the deliberate targeting of civilians is a peculiar feature of the late twentieth century and that evidence for this is to be found in a reversal of the ratio of combatant to civilian deaths—from 8:1 at the beginning of the twentieth century to 1:8 in the 1990s[38]—is one of those assertions that, having been stated often enough, appears to have become an axiomatic truth. The ratio arrived at depends entirely on the choice of wars examined, on the definition of battle or 'war-related' deaths, and on whether the many 'spheres of civilian suffering' in war, to borrow Hugo Slim's apt formulation, are included in calculations.[39] Even then, precise figures—ones that would allow for definite trends to be identified—are hard to acquire, and those that exist do not necessarily support the claims of the 'new war' thesis, something which, interestingly, the case of Bosnia-Herzegovina between 1992 and 1995—'the archetypical example, the paradigm of the new type of warfare'[40]—illustrates.

Until 2007, when a new Sarajevo-based research institute published its findings, the most widely cited figures for the number of people killed in Bosnia ranged between 250,000 and 300,000.[41] According to the Research and Documentation Centre Sarajevo (RCD)—now widely considered to be providing the most accurate figures on account of the more rigorous method-ology involved in collecting data—the total number of people killed in Bosnia between 1991 and 1995 is just below 100,000.[42] While this discrepancy is itself striking, of particular interest in the context of the 'new wars' thesis is what the RCD found to be the ratio of soldiers to civilians killed during the war. Out of 97,207 listed as killed (80,545) and missing (16,662), 57,523 are soldiers and 39,684 civilians, that is, just over 40 per cent of those killed in the war were civilians. These figures are still staggering, though they do raise obvious questions about the widely cited ratio of 8:1 civilian to military deaths at the end of the twentieth century.[43]

In meticulous and horrifying detail, the RCD has also documented the cruelties of the Bosnian war: the suffering of civilians at the hands of marauding and predatory bands of ethnic militias, widespread sexual violence, local massacres, and indiscriminate bombardment of urban areas in the service of the 'policy of ethnic cleansing'.[44] Such acts are not, however, distinctive to a new era of warfare. The suggestion that it is sits oddly—to put it mildly—with the 'barbarization of warfare' in the twentieth century, a carefully documented process linked by historians to the fighting on the Eastern front and in the Pacific theatre in the Second World War in particular.[45]

As indicated above, the notion that civilian targeting and suffering were previously deemed 'undesirable side effects' of war is also at odds with 'the darker underside of the colonial story'.[46] In the 1840s, General Thomas-Robert Bugeaud, serving as both military commander and governor general in Algeria, embarked on a campaign of 'pacification' that 'created precedents and generated principles that would characterise and influence colonial warfare in Africa ever after'.[47] A distinguishing feature of that campaign was its 'calculated ferocity', reflected in Bugeaud's 'adaptation of the time-honoured Arab practice of the *razzia*'.[48] In the words of Vandervort:

> ... whereas traditional *razzias* had been a means of obtaining booty or demonstrating and enemy's vulnerability, the French variant of the practice bordered on total war. Bugeaud's flying columns seized Arab flocks and herds, destroyed crops and orchards, looted granaries, and burned villages. Arab peoples who did not succumb to this kind of persuasion and accept French rule could expect a war of extermination. This was not a theoretical proposition.[49]

The 'unnatural violence of the total war waged against the indigenous population by the *Armée d'Afrique*' in Algeria was not, of course, confined to the 'Bugeaud era'.[50] It set a pattern for subsequent campaigns of pacification and imperial control; following the revolt of 1871, at Sétif and Guelma in 1945, and later during the war of independence in the 1950s and early 1960s.[51] Nor, of course, was the readiness to use exemplary force, deliberately targeting civilians and their means of sustenance, a peculiar feature of French colonial policy. One of the many virtues of Piers Brendon's *The decline and fall of the British Empire* is precisely to show what 'pacification' at the hands of colonial forces often meant in practice. Thus, in Iraq in 1920, General Aylmer Haldane's men 'burned villages, destroyed crops, slaughtered livestock, killed some 9,000 people and executed ringleaders without trial'.[52] The brutality and atrocities that accompanied Belgian and Portuguese empire-building and colonial pacification certainly did not stand back from that of other metropolitan powers.[53] Nor, as Lothar von Trotha's notorious *Vernichtungsbefehl* and infamous campaign against the Herero in South West Africa in 1904 made clear, was extermination more than just a 'theoretical proposition' only for the French.[54] As for the United States, its conquest of the Philippines between

1899 and 1902 was notable for its 'cruelty' and 'aggressive pacification' and for the extraordinarily skewed ratio of civilian to military deaths. An estimated 200,000 civilians died between 1898 and 1902. By contrast, the number of Americans and Filipinos killed in combat, according to US figures, was just over 4,000 and 16,000 respectively.[55]

All of these examples reinforce Hugo Slim's grim but inescapable conclusion that the killing of civilians 'has always been with us' and, moreover, 'is not the cultural preserve of particularly barbaric polities'.[56] Not only that, but since 'a main purpose of much civilian killing is to use war as an opportunity to reorder society by brutally transforming its social and political demography ... extermination has been part of most wars ancient and modern'.[57]

## GOALS OF WARFARE

According to Kaldor, the goals of belligerents in 'new wars' differ from 'the geo-political or ideological goals of earlier wars'.[58] They are no longer about 'ideas' but are instead 'about identity politics'. It is unclear exactly what this means. War has always played a critical part in shaping and cementing identities. It is true that many of the wars of the post-Cold War era have been 'fought by groupings of people, banded together by a notion of common belonging which is itself contingent on hostility to other, similar, groupings [and] in that sense, war has become an agent of identity'.[59] But this is itself hardly new, nor does it shed any light on how and why the goals of belligerents in 'new wars' differ from the goals pursued by combatants in the past. That 'the new identity politics is about the claim to power on the basis of labels' does not clarify matters, unless one simply accepts that 'new wars' are *all* about gaining 'power' without enquiring into the range and complex of reasons *why* someone may want 'power'.[60]

It would seem that the emphasis on identity politics is instead meant to convey *two* aspects of 'new wars'. First, unscrupulous leaders and political elites have sought to mobilize followers by stirring hatred, playing upon fear, and encouraging violence, all in order to suit their own narrow and demagogic purposes. To this end, markers of identity—religion, language, appeal to a common history, ethnicity, clan affiliation—have been used, manipulated, even 'constructed', to foment war and violence. That this has been the case is indisputable.

This is sometimes, though it does not in fact follow, linked to the second aspect alluded to above: that 'new wars' are no longer about 'ideas'.[61] Enzensberger puts the argument in extreme form: 'what give today's civil wars a new and terrifying slant is the fact that they are waged without stakes on either side, that they are wars about nothing at all.'[62] Van Creveld in *The transformation of warfare* appears to be saying something similar: war is 'very often not a means to an end but an end in itself' and is best thought of as a 'form of sport' rather than a 'continuation of policy' animated by ideas.[63] This is a tempting line; it is also, in the end, unconvincing. One may not like the ideas that have inspired belligerents in contemporary wars, finding them 'retrograde', 'backward looking', and cynically held for devious and instrumental purposes. And indeed, many of them are justly considered deeply offensive to our liberal conscience. But as ideas, they may still be genuinely held and play a powerful role in motivating people towards violence. Even when armed movements have been associated with extreme violence against civilians, such as the Revolutionary United Front in Sierra Leone in the 1990s, elements of 'ideology', rooted in a deep and genuine sense of grievance, have been found to play an important role in mobilizing recruits and followers, especially in the early and formative years of the movement.[64] The Taliban, whose social programme is, quite literally, 'backward looking' and contrary to any notion of common humanity, is similarly held together, in part, by the 'strong ideological commitment of their "cadres"'.[65]

Insistence on the view that ideas no longer matter also tends to carry with it another implication: it leads naturally to a neglect of other forces and factors— especially *religion* and *nationalism* but also to the importance in many societies and cultural settings of notions of honour and prestige—without which the sources and dynamics of so-called 'new wars' cannot be properly understood. It is much too easy to dismiss these kinds of elements as being 'invented' or merely 'instrumental'.[66]

The wider point here is perhaps best illustrated with a concrete example, again from the war in Bosnia. In May 1994, a commission of experts looking into the military structure, tactics, and strategy of the warring factions in Bosnia concluded that 'most paramilitary units sustained themselves through looting, thefts, ransoms and trafficking in contraband'.[67] To journalists, peacekeepers, and NGOs on the ground, these findings did not come as a surprise as they could hardly have failed to notice that patterns of fighting and military confrontation *locally* often had more to do with the criminal and economic agendas of paramilitary units than with the ideological convictions and fantasies of nationalist politicians and elites (hence the many instances of collusion among enemies across ethnic lines throughout the war). Yet, those convictions played a crucial role in providing the framework and impetus for the cleansing policies and atrocities that took place. And they were not held simply for instrumental purposes, as an excuse for plunder or the consolidation of power. There is, for example, no reason to believe that Franjo Tudjman and his closest nationalist allies were not deeply committed to the *idea* of Greater Croatia, however repugnant the convictions on which that *idea* was based.[68] Nor is there any doubt that this idea in turn provided powerful encouragement for the activities of the Bosnian Croat (HVO) forces in central

Bosnia, including those who saw it as a licence to plunder and terrorize local non-Croat communities.


## THE ECONOMIC UNDERPINNINGS OF 'NEW WARS': FINANCING AND SUSTAINING ARMED CONFLICT

Several writers on 'new wars' have identified the process of globalization as a driving force behind the new forms of organized violence in the late twentieth century. The term itself, however, remains notoriously imprecise and there is much truth in Weinstein's observation that 'pundits argue about its consequences because they make up its meaning to suit their needs'.[69] One of the major difficulties with 'new wars' writing has been precisely the tendency to adopt an exceedingly broad definition of the phenomenon: as the 'intensification of global interconnectedness—political, economic, military, and cultural—and the changing character of political authority'.[70] A narrower definition of globalization that focuses strictly on its economic dimensions—the opening of markets, the deregulation of industries and services, and the impact of new information technologies on trading and cross-border flows of capital—does permit more precise questions to be asked and these have indeed yielded valuable findings in relation to contemporary intra-state conflict. But even the effects of economic globalization, as a growing number of qualitative case studies have shown, are far from uniform and connections to violent conflict are neither as simple nor as direct as the 'new wars' literature suggests.

Leaving aside the issue of definition for the moment, the deeper problem with globalization as a motor force for change lies—just as it does with the term 'new war' itself—in its 'totalizing pretensions' and the deeply distorting effect which this has on any effort to understand individual cases and specific mechanisms at work.[71] To understand those, as Frederick Cooper has remarked, we need 'concepts that are less sweeping, more precise . . . which seek to analyze change with historical specificity rather than in terms of a vaguely defined and unattainable end-point'.[72] This is all the more important in light of work done on civil wars over the past ten years; work that has emphasized the need to pay much closer attention than has traditionally been the case to the 'micro-foundations of war', that is, to the role of 'local—village, town, community—and personal dynamics' in the generation and perpetuation of violence.[73]

The most valuable contribution of the 'new wars' thesis lies in the attention that it has drawn to changes in the economic underpinnings of intra-state wars, including the way that warring parties—whether 'rebels', 'insurgents', or government forces—have adapted their strategies to a new 'globalized' economic environment. Qualitative case studies from post-Cold War conflicts have clearly shown that belligerents have successfully *financed* and sustained fighting in the absence of Cold War patronage, and that they have done so through a combination of strategies. Three of these merit special attention, all of them having been identified by writers on 'new wars' as critical to modern war economies.

First, by making use of 'local–global networks'[74] and tapping into global processes of exchange, warring parties have proved increasingly adept at realizing local resources and assets under their control, notably natural resources of various kinds. Second, belligerents have raised funds from global diasporas. Finally, humanitarian aid intended for the victims of war has been diverted, taxed, and manipulated to support the aims of warring factions. Closely linked to all three of these, the line between 'crime' and 'war' has become increasingly blurred as the latter has come to provide 'legitimation for various criminal forms of private aggrandizement', which in turn are the 'necessary sources of revenue in order to sustain the war'.[75] Taken together, these changes in the economic underpinnings of intra-state conflict, so the argument runs, have increased the salience of economic agendas in war and have influenced both the patterns and longevity of fighting.

There is clearly evidence to support this argument. In terms of the rise of combatant self-financing, the most widely cited and best-documented example is provided by the post-Cold War history of UNITA in Angola.[76] When war resumed in late 1998, following the collapse of yet another peace process, Jonas Savimbi was able to field a more formidable military force than at anytime in the long history of the movement. Significantly, he was able to do so in spite of the withdrawal of external support following his decision to return to war in 1992 and the subsequent imposition of Security Council sanctions against his movement. Other examples include Sierra Leone, Liberia, DRC, and Cambodia, all places where warring factions have successfully realized local resources under their control. This has been possible in part, as Mark Duffield has noted, because 'market deregulation has deepened all forms of parallel and transborder trade and allowed warring parties to forge local–global networks and shadow economies as a means of asset realization and self-provisioning'.[77]

An important example of this, first highlighted by the UN's investigation into sanctions busting against UNITA in the 1990s, is provided by the effects of the deregulation of the international air transport industry. As Wood and Peleman observed in the late 1990s, the process of deregulation created 'new market realities'[78] that were shrewdly exploited by UNITA, as well as by numerous other actors especially on the African continent, notably in Liberia, the DRC, Somalia, Sierra Leone, and Sudan.[79] Specifically, cross-border mergers, leasing, chartering, franchising, and offshore registration of airlines, companies, and crews, as well as the use of flags or registers of convenience have all made it much more 'difficult to monitor the airspace and freighting industry'.[80] As a result, air cargo carriers have been able to increase significantly the volume of illicit transfers, especially of small arms and light weapons, to zones of conflict and, in many cases, have also assisted in the extraction of natural resources from zones controlled by belligerents. Indeed, according to one recent and comprehensive survey, the 'war economies which prevailed or continue in Angola, Colombia, the DRC, Liberia, Sierra Leone, Somalia and Sudan . . . are [all] inextricably linked to and facilitated by air transport actors'.[81] Critical to those war economies have been local middlemen and transnational organized criminal networks, drawn in part from the privatized intelligence and security networks of the Cold War era.[82] And their involvement helps explain the criminalization and transnational dimensions of many conflicts as combatants eager to convert 'captured assets into revenues and war material' do so 'through often overlapping business, criminal, and diaspora networks'.[83]

For all this, the *relative* importance of global economic processes in sustaining armed conflict is easily exaggerated and it is clear that the importance attributed to globalization by some writers on 'new wars' does not fairly reflect the mixed and partly contradictory record presented by a growing number of qualitative case studies. With respect to combatant self-financing, three considerations in particular need to be borne in mind.

First, while self-financing is indeed a feature of many post-Cold War conflicts, the view that conflict economies simply transitioned from 'patronage to self-financing' after the Cold War is too simplistic.[84] Even in the case of UNITA, Cold War patronage was only *one* part of a long-standing strategy of self-reliance and 'much of the UNITA's insurgency [was] largely sustainable from inside Angola'.[85] More generally, the exploitation of natural resources by guerrillas and insurgents to finance a conflict, the subject of an increasingly voluminous literature on post-Cold War conflict, also took place during the Cold War.[86] The aforementioned example of the effects of the deregulation of the international airline industry also needs qualification. Certainly, global deregulation made it easier, especially in the 1990s, for networks of subcontractors and front companies to locate arms and other commodities and bring them to customers. Since then, however, evidence suggests that regulation, notably by the EU, has had some impact on the activities of airlines operating in and out of war zones. The overall problem posed by poorly regulated air cargo carriers in the illicit flow of arms and goods, however, has not diminished, though, crucially, this fact has less to do with the effects of further deregulation or 'globalization' than it has with the role played by certain key states in facilitating the operations of carriers. According to Griffiths and Bromley, 'states such as Belarus, Russia and Ukraine . . . provide commercially inexpensive refuelling, repair, or service nodes from which air cargo carriers may legitimately base themselves—and they are doing so in ever increasing numbers'.[87]

Second, many of the conflicts that have been referred to as 'new wars' remain, in terms of their prosecution, low-cost and low-technology affairs that rely first and foremost on access to ground transportation, small arms, and a reliable supply of ammunition. Meeting these requirements has rarely proved an insurmountable obstacle for warring parties, not least because of the surplus in small arms that circulate within regions of conflict but also because of the decentralized nature and the many actors and middlemen involved in small arms manufacture and distribution. In other words, access to global networks may be useful but is rarely critical to sustaining the war effort. The claim that 'external assistance is crucial'[88] simply does not fit the reality of a number of supposedly 'new wars'.

There is a further consideration here. It has been argued that a key aspect of globalization—the information revolution and the diffusion of relatively cheap and accessible communication technologies—has given non-state actors an effective force multiplier. The actual evidence for this is mixed and does not lend itself to categorical conclusions. Certainly, where insurgents have faced technologically superior opponents—as the case of the Taliban in Afghanistan since 2002—traditional methods of command and control have been relied upon to nullify the technological edge enjoyed by opponents.[89] Elsewhere, the ability to absorb new technologies on the battlefield appears limited, one reason being that even easily accessible and low-cost technology requires a basic infrastructure in order to be used effectively, and in war-ravaged countries that infrastructure is often lacking or too unreliable.

Third, and most critically, while economic interest and opportunities have in many cases resulted in the 'economization' of conflict—that is, the rapid mutation of war aims from more overt security and political objectives to ones driven primarily by economic agendas and predation—the deeper sources of any given conflict, its dynamics, and the aim of belligerents still cannot be abstracted from what will always be a distinctive historical and cultural context. Thus, even the 'local–global networks and shadow economies, found to underpin modern war economies are not simply the recent product of globalization. On closer inspection, such war economies turn out to be embedded within informal regional networks of a social, military, and economic kind, all with deep historical roots.[90] Such cross-border linkages among peoples and groups across formal frontiers—making use of long-standing trade and commercial networks, often based on bonds of kinship, and taking advantage of the lack of effective state control over the periphery— qualify claims to the newness of wars in important ways.[91] This is most obviously the case in relation to violent and conflict-ridden 'borderlands', prominent examples of which include the border regions of Afghanistan; the Ferghana valley in Tajikistan, Uzbekistan, and Kyrgyzstan; the Presevo valley in southern Serbia and the territory along the Kosovo-Macedonian border; and the Kivu region in DRC bordering Rwanda, Burundi, and Uganda. These are all areas that have witnessed violence and war during the post-Cold War era; indeed, the last of these has been a site of almost continuous conflict since the mid-1990s. The case of the DRC is of special interest in part because it represents an extreme case of the economization of war.[92] And yet, as with other conflicts where economic agendas have played an important part in sustaining violence, at its core are still socio-economic grievances, issues of power and identity, political ambitions, and security concerns. Some of these are directly traceable to the genocide in 1994 in Rwanda and its aftermath, which saw an influx into eastern Congo of *génocidaires*, extremist Hutu militia members, and soldiers of the former Rwandan Armed Forces (FAR) who had been directly involved in the genocide. Others involve deep-seated historical tensions over access to land, citizenship, and ethnicity.[93] One is not, in other words, dealing with a simple resource war or an entirely new breed of organized violence, and the attempt to 'make sense' of the conflagration, as Prunier has argued, demands multiple 'layers of explanation'.[94]

Writings on 'new wars' have stressed the importance to military groups of two further sources of income: funding from diaspora communities, either through remittances or 'direct assistance'; and the diversion or 'taxing' of humanitarian aid to support military activities and objectives.[95] Reliance on these 'new' sources stems, it is argued, from the need to compensate for the decline in foreign assistance and support. And what makes it possible to tap into these sources is the emergence—as discussed above and itself a feature of 'new wars'—of 'a new type of globalized informal economy…in which external flows, especially humanitarian assistance and remittances from abroad, are integrated into a local economy based on asset transfer and extra-legal trading'.[96]

In fact, the violence-generating role ascribed to diasporas and wartime humanitarian aid in writings on 'new wars' is—as more detailed studies have shown—much too unqualified and one-sided. Again, the question is not whether diaspora networks or relief aid have ever played a 'regressive' role in individual conflicts. There certainly are many examples of diaspora communities making a contribution through remittances to warring parties in war zones. Similarly, there are numerous examples of humanitarian aid having been diverted, taxed, and stolen by warring factions. What is of interest, however, is the volume of support, its significance relative to other sources, and, above all, whether or not they have significantly affected the patterns and dynamics of war.

There is nothing *inherently* conflict-generating about the role of diaspora and migrant remittances in relation to armed conflict.[97] Qualitative case studies make it clear that the impact of diaspora and migrant remittances on conflict is highly context-specific: it can fuel conflict but it can also mitigate violence by acting as a socio-economic safety net that discourages predation on vulnerable populations. Either way, as Kenneth Bush stresses, analysis of impact on conflict has 'to focus on specific diasporic subgroups rather than undifferentiated and artificially homogenized constructs of "diaspora-writ-large"'.[98] Thus, the elaborate and sophisticated global support structure set up by the Liberation Tigers of Tamil Eelam (LTTE) undoubtedly provided it with vital economic support from Tamil communities around the world, allowing it 'to pursue a more direct and high-intensity campaign against the Sri Lanka state security forces'.[99] Even so, it is worth noting that the catastrophic reversal of LTTE's fortunes on the battlefield in 2008 and 2009 is only partly attributable to the loss of diaspora support and income. While that income has declined since 2004, other factors—above all, the defection in March 2004 of Vinayagamoorthy Muralitharan (alias 'Karuna'), representing Tamils in eastern Sri Lanka—were, arguably, more significant to the LTTE. Another critical factor in the success of Sri Lankan army against the LTTE in 2009 appears to have been the military and diplomatic support provided by China.[100] But more importantly in terms of the overall argument made here, the case of the LTTE in Sri Lanka does not permit wider conclusions to be drawn about the role of diaspora income in fuelling 'new wars'. The LTTE's overseas support structure and the role played by the diaspora in generating funds, building political support, and procuring arms is 'unrivalled by any other insurgent organization worldwide'.[101] In most other cases, diaspora remittances perform legitimate and, indeed, vital humanitarian functions. Moreover, during conflict, the role of diaspora communities and income may evolve in response to changes in political context. Thus, the Dayton Accord, which in 1995 brought the war in Bosnia to an end, also changed the role played by diaspora income in the simmering conflict in Kosovo. According to Alexandros Yannis: 'As long as remittances were controlled by Rugova's Kosovo Republic, they appear to have played a conflict-averting role in underwriting badly needed social welfare services, thereby enhancing the attractiveness of Rugova's non-violent approach to independence. Once captured by the Kosovo Liberation Army, however, remittance flows helped finance the armed struggle.'[102]

What then of the claim that *humanitarian aid* has played an increasingly important part in sustaining 'new wars'? A number of studies of the relationship between war, famine, and aid in Sudan in the latter half of the 1980s certainly appeared to support this view, showing plainly how international relief aid could be captured, manipulated, and used for political and military purposes. They also showed how donor countries could be drawn into the complex political economy of a conflict and in some cases end up, in spite of their best intentions, fuelling violence and local predation.[103] Of special importance in this regard were the assessments of Operation Lifeline Sudan (OLS), a large-scale multi-agency humanitarian assistance operation whose creation in April 1989 enshrined and sought to apply the principle of 'humanitarian access' in wartime.[104] The application of that principle, however, proved inherently problematic with both sides in the war manipulating relief and foreign aid to their own advantage. The tendency for this to happen, especially in cases where humanitarian relief efforts are not complemented by a political strategy aimed at ending violence, is a feature of several post-Cold War conflicts. The 'new wars' thesis, however, goes further by stressing that aid, UN agencies, and humanitarian NGOs have become an integral or 'fixed part' of war economies and that relief aid in 'new wars' is often an essential source of income for belligerents.[105] There are two considerations here.

First, the 1990s saw a significant increase in 'emergencies per year evoking a concerted international response' and a corresponding increase in 'food aid going to relief during emergencies' as opposed to more traditional development aid.[106] This increase quite naturally enhanced the scope for manipulation and drew international attention to the complex policy dilemmas—moral as well as practical—presented by the wartime delivery of humanitarian aid. In the mid-1990s, these dilemmas were exposed most starkly in the refugee crisis that built up in eastern Congo, then Zaire, in the aftermath of the Rwandan genocide. Following the influx of refugees into Zaire, it soon became apparent that the refugee camps maintained and supported with international aid were not only fully controlled by Hutu militias, *génocidaires*, and former members of the Rwandan army that had arrived in the wake of the genocide but were also being used as bases from which to regroup and launch attacks into Rwanda.[107] A few years earlier, in Somalia, the siphoning off and control of relief aid by warring factions amidst appalling civilian misery had similarly drawn international attention to the issue.

Both cases, however, only illustrated—albeit in extreme form—a familiar problem: namely that 'in the midst of war conflict-related aid will inevitably form part of the political equation'.[108] The fact that aid to refugees and needy populations has ended up supporting military activity—whether as an unintended consequence of war or as part of calculated policy by unscrupulous leaders—is plainly not a phenomenon of the post-Cold War era. Many of the issues posed by humanitarian relief in wartime were evident during the Biafran war from 1967 to 1970; a war seen by some as having been needlessly prolonged by international relief efforts and one where the blockage of aid into Biafra by Nigeria's military government was employed as a weapon of war. In the late 1970s and 1980s, aid and refugee camps along Thailand's border with Cambodia served as sanctuaries and support bases for Cambodian guerrilla groups (including the Khmer Rouge) fighting the Vietnamese occupation of Cambodia. Similarly, in the 1980s, aid was channelled through refugee camps in Pakistan in support of Mujahedeen fighters in Afghanistan while *Contra* rebels, encouraged and supported by the United States, operated out of UNHCR-assisted camps in Honduras.[109]

The second consideration concerns the impact of aid on the course of wars. While the case of Sudan demonstrates that it can, in the right circumstances, play a critical role, the picture varies greatly across cases. One reason for this, as Stewart and Samman note, is simply that 'the economy of a country at war is more complex and *sui generis* even than a typical developing country in normal times', and any generalization about the impact of aid in wartime is therefore fraught with difficulty.[110] There are certainly many examples of diversion, theft, and extortion of relief aid in post-Cold War conflict, including in those that have been treated as 'new wars'. Its impact on the duration and dynamics of conflict, however, appears to have been exaggerated and based too heavily on anecdotal evidence from a limited number of cases. Stressing this very point, David Shearer has argued that, even in the case of Somalia where he served as head of Save the Children Fund in 1991–2, there was 'little observable correlation between amounts of aid and levels of violence', and that, overall, 'relief aid appears to have had little impact on the course of civil wars'.[111] This conclusion is supported by more recent studies of post-Cold War conflict in which the role of humanitarian aid has long been assumed to have played a significant role, including, again, the war in Bosnia-Herzegovina where, according to Silvia Lauzzana, 'relief aid per se did not have a substantial impact on either the course or duration of the war'.[112]

Writings on 'new wars' have nearly all stressed the extent to which the spheres of 'crime' and 'war' have become increasingly blurred, contributing to the emergence of war economies whose economic foundations are criminalized, predatory, and increasingly transnational in character.[113] And there is no doubt that in several zones of post-Cold War conflict—notably the Balkans, West and Central Africa, and Haiti—armed conflict has been powerfully shaped by criminal elements, networks, and agendas.[114] Indeed, in some of these cases, the 'point of war' has been less about 'winning' than it has been about providing cover for 'actions that in peacetime would be punishable as crimes'.[115] In such circumstances, patterns of fighting and the behaviour of warring parties on the ground have assumed their own distinctive, sometimes almost quasi-ritualistic, character. This also helps explain why in many intra-state conflicts, supposed enemies have tended to form local understandings in order to reap economic or criminal benefits from a state of war.[116] Where belligerents have engaged in cooperative behaviour of this kind, they have eschewed costly fighting and drawn-out battles. Such local alliances have frequently cut across ethnic, communal, and other ascriptive ties: Serbs, Croats, and Bosniac forces during the war in 1992–5; Serbs and Albanians in Kosovo since 1999; Khmer Rouge soldiers, Cambodian government officials, and Thai military between 1994 and 1997; the MPLA 'business elites' and UNITA commanders in Angola throughout the 1990s; and between different militias in eastern Congo since 1999. In all these cases, economic and criminal incentives resulted in 'politically perverse but economically rational alliances'.[117]

While the object of collaboration has often been personal enrichment and greed, the salience of criminal agendas also reflects a more basic consideration: the need to find new ways of financing continued war in the absence of reliable systems of revenue collection and logistics support. This need has been especially acute where external patrons have withdrawn support, leaving criminal actors with a key role in ensuring that critical supplies, especially fuel and arms, are available to warring parties. Even where belligerents have had direct access to natural resources through physical control of territory, criminal actors and networks have remained vital to ensure the realization of local assets and access to international markets. The growth and increased sophistication of some transnational organized groups have facilitated that process. Where wartime alliances have been forged between organized crime and belligerents, they have proved difficult to dismantle after the formal end of hostilities, and this has contributed to the breakdown—rightly observed in the 'new wars' literature—of the distinction between war and peace, conflict and post-conflict.

While the role of criminal networks and groups thus merits serious attention, in terms of the 'new war' thesis, three important qualifications still need to be made. The first, again, concerns historical context and the question of whether there is something 'substantively distinct' in the role played by criminal agendas and players in contemporary wars. Certainly, the 'relationship of war to crime' is well established by historians.[118] Nor, arguably, is the role of crime as a factor contributing to a breakdown of the distinction between war and peace quite as novel as is sometimes implied, especially if one adopts a local- or micro-level perspective of conflict. Thus, in their account of the turmoil and 'forgotten wars' that engulfed much of the 'great crescent' from Bengal to Singapore following the defeat of Japan in the Second World War, Bayly and Harper observe of the situation in Malaya in 1945 that 'the distinction between patriotism and criminality was merely one of perspective'.[119] That observation also captures the reality of many contemporary conflicts, with the history and evolution of the KLA in Kosovo offering one striking example. In the Po valley in Italy, the end of the Second World War was also followed by a 'formidable crime wave' that involved 'hundreds of summary executions, as well as thousands of assaults, lynchings, abductions, robberies and beatings' and which, within the so-called 'Triangle of Death', lasted for three years.[120] Finally, in cases where crime and criminal organizations have played a central role in recent conflicts, most notably in the Balkans, that role is itself far from historically unprecedented. As Robert Hislope has noted, specifically challenging the 'new wars' line on this point, the 'intertwined problems of proliferating paramilitaries, organized-crime structures, and nationalist politicians' have a very long history in the Balkans, and that history is deeply relevant to the understanding of more recent developments.[121]

The second qualification relates to the fact that in much of the literature, the terms 'criminal activity' and 'organized crime' are typically employed in a way that reflects the language and categories of classical law-enforcement. This, however, does pose conceptual problems when analysing the role of crime in some intra-state conflicts, including those that have been labelled as 'new wars'. The reality is that in war-torn societies characterized by extreme levels of socio-economic dislocation, persistent insecurity, and the collapse of entitlements, what would in normal circumstances be classified as criminal activities may well be impossible to distinguish from coping strategies and daily struggles for survival. As for the notion of organized crime, it fails to capture 'the complex interpenetration of the legitimate and the illegitimate, the state and crime, that is part of the lived experience of many populations in weak states and conflict-affected areas'.[122] In such circumstances, where shadow economies may be critical to sustaining basic livelihoods and where crime may even enjoy a measure of 'local legitimacy' through provision of protection and basic services, key assumptions on which the definition of organized crime in international legal documents rests become problematic.[123] Thus, while the 'new wars' literature is right to identify the importance of organized crime in many contemporary conflicts, its emphasis on *only* the 'regressive' and predatory aspects of the phenomenon (much like its treatment of diasporas and the role of aid in conflict) is too simplistic, and, ultimately, provides a poor basis for meaningful and effective policy intervention by the international community.

The final qualification relates specifically to Bosnia-Herzegovina, Kaldor's 'paradigm of the new type of warfare'. The growth of organized crime in south-eastern Europe in the 1990s and its role in the Bosnian war are not in dispute. As a phenomenon, it was, however, directly linked to a combination of two historically contingent factors: the imposition of a comprehensive sanctions regime on former Yugoslavia and the collapse of neighbouring communist regimes resulting in the purging and privatization of communist-era security services, notably in Bulgaria and Romania.[124] In other words, the sanctions regime created unique business opportunities for organized crime just as ex-Warsaw Pact countries sought to purge and reform their security services.[125] This may have been a historically unique confluence of factors and it has been argued that the grip of organized crime in south-eastern Europe, though still significant, has begun to loosen.

## CONCLUSION

By advancing arguments in bold, sometimes crude, fashion, advocates of the 'new wars' thesis have done much to spur discussion about the changing character of war after the Cold War. The 'thesis' itself has served a heuristically important purpose by sharpening debate and stimulating qualitative and more historically informed research into contemporary intra-state conflict. More than that, it has helped draw attention to the ways in which the economic foundations of *some* civil wars have changed in response to new geostrategic realities, even though—as argued above—some of the key claims advanced regarding the effects of globalization, the conflict-generating potential of diasporas and humanitarian aid, and the criminal character of modern wars require both qualification and context. This reflects a larger weakness: in the end, the claims advanced are too sweeping, failing to capture key elements of continuity as well as discontinuity in the character of war.

## NOTES

1. Mary Kaldor, *New and old wars: Organized violence in the global era* (Cambridge: Polity Press, 1999). A second edition appeared in 2006 and includes a new chapter on 'The "new war" in Iraq'. The author wishes to thank James Cockayne, Antonio Giustozzi, Peter Wilson, Achim Wennman, and David Ucko for helpful comments on an earlier draft of this chapter.
2. Partly for this reason, this chapter will refer to it rather more than to some of the other contributions to the 'new wars' thesis. Unless otherwise stated, references are to the second edition of the book.
3. Kaldor, *New and old wars* (1st edition), 1, 3.
4. Ibid., 6.
5. Stephen Ellis, 'The old roots of Africa's new wars', *Internationale Politik und Gesellschaft*, 2 (2003), 30.
6. Martin van Creveld, *Nuclear proliferation and the future of conflict* (New York: The Free Press, 1993), 126.
7. For a fuller exposition of the argument, see *The transformation of war* (New York: The Free Press, 1991).
8. Robert D. Kaplan, 'The coming anarchy', *Atlantic Monthly*, February 1994, 72.
9. Hans Magnus Enzensberger, *Civil war* (London: Granta Books, 1994), 19.
10. Herfried Münkler, 'What is really new about new war', in John Olsen (ed.), *On new wars* (Oslo: IFS, 2007).
11. Mary Kaldor and Robin Luckham, 'Global transformations and new conflicts', in Susan Willett (ed.), *Structural conflict in the new global disorder*, IDS Bulletin, 32/2 (2001), 49.
12. Kaldor, *New and old wars*, 3.
13. There is little precision in the literature about just when 'new wars' are supposed to have crystallized, though as one review of the literature makes clear, 'it is fair to say that the post-Cold War period is seen as *the* moment when "new wars" became the prevalent mode of conflict'. Dominique Jacquin-Berdal, 'How new are Africa's new wars? A historical sketch', April 2005, unpublished paper.
14. Kaldor, *New and old wars*, 7.
15. Karen Ballentine, 'Introduction', in Karen Ballentine and Jake Sherman (eds.), *The political economy of armed conflict: Beyond greed and grievance* (Boulder, CO: Lynne Rienner, 2003).

16. See Edward Newman, 'The "new wars" debate: A historical perspective is needed', *Security Dialogue*, 35/2 (2004), 173–89.

17. Jacquin-Berdal, 'How new are Africa's "new wars"?', 2.

18. Ellis, 'The old roots of Africa's new wars', 33.

19. Ibid.

20. Ibid.

21. Tony Judt, 'Whose story is it? The Cold War in retrospect' in Tony Judt (ed.), *Reappraisals* (London: Vintage Books, 2008), 379.

22. 'Report of panel of experts on violations of Security Council sanctions against UNITA', S/2000/203, 10 March 2000, paragraph 39.

23. Mats Berdal, *Disarmament and demobilisation after civil wars*, Adelphi Paper no. 303, Institute for Strategic Studies (Oxford: Oxford University Press, 1996), 18–20. The notion of 'specialists in violence' is taken from Charles Tilly, *The politics of collective violence* (Cambridge: Cambridge University Press, 2003).

24. Ellis, 'The old roots of Africa's new wars', 32.

25. Georges Nzongola-Ntalaja, *The Congo from Leopold to Kabila* (London: Zed Books, 2002), 154–6.

26. See Gérard Prunier, *Africa's world war* (Oxford: Oxford University Press, 2009).

27. Paul Richards, 'Rebellion in Liberia and Sierra Leone: A crisis of youth?', in Oliver Furley (ed.), *Conflict in Africa* (London: I.B. Tauris, 1995), 134.

28. Stephen Ellis, 'Liberia's warlord insurgency' in Christopher Clapham (ed.), *African guerrillas* (Oxford: James Currey, 1998), 169. For the Liberian civil war, see also Morten Bøås, 'The Liberian Civil War: New war/old war?', *Global Society*, 19/1 (2005). For the importance of religion, see Stephen Ellis, *The mask of anarchy: The destruction of Liberia and the religious dimension of an African civil war* (London: Hurst & Company, 1999).

29. This holds true even if one leaves aside, as I do here, non-Western ways and traditions of warfare.

30. Herfried Münkler, *The new wars* (Cambridge: Polity Press, 2005), 16.

31. Frank Tallett, *War and society in early modern Europe, 1495–1715* (London: Routledge, 1992), 77; and Geoffrey Parker, *The military revolution: Military innovation and the rise of the West, 1500–1800* (Cambridge: Cambridge University Press, 1988), 64–8.

32. R. Brian Ferguson and Neil L. Whitehead (eds.), *War in the tribal zone: Expanding states and indigenous warfare* (Santa Fe, NM: School of American Research Press, 1992).

33. Kaplan, 'The coming anarchy', 72.

34. Kaldor, *New and old wars*, 105.

35. Münkler, *The new wars*, 14.

36. Mary Kaldor and Basker Vashee, *Restructuring the global military sector—Volume 1: New wars* (London: Pinter, 1997), 16.

37. Kaldor, *New and old wars*, 105f.

38. Ibid., 9.

39. Hugo Slim, *Killing civilians: Method, madness and morality in war* (London: Hurst & Co., 2008), 39.

40. Kaldor, *New and old wars*, 33.

41. See Richard Holbrooke, *To end a war* (New York: Random House, 1998), xv; Kaldor, *New and old wars*, 33.

42. See Research and Documentation Centre Sarajevo, http://www.idc.org.ba/ prezentacija/rezultati_istrazivanja.htm. I am grateful to Merima Zupcevic for drawing my attention to the work and findings of the RCD.

43. For a critical discussion of the issues and problems involved in arriving at reliable figures for civilian casualties, see Adam Roberts, '"Nine out of ten war victims are civilians": A critique', *Survival*, 52/3 (2010).

44. 'Final report of the UN commission of experts established pursuant to UNSC Resolution 780', May 1994, 17.

45. See George Kassimeris (ed.), *The barbarisation of warfare* (London: Hurst, 2006); and John Dower, *War without mercy: Race and power in the Pacific war* (New York: Pantheon Books, 1986).

46. Christopher Bayly and Tim Harper, *Forgotten wars—The end of Britain's Asian empire* (London: Penguin Books, 2007), 550.

47. Bruce Vandervort, *Wars of imperial conquest in Africa 1830–1914* (London: UCL Press, 1998), 63.

48. Ibid., 68f.

49. Ibid., 68.

50. Ibid., 69.

51. Alistair Horne, *A savage war of peace: Algeria 1954–62* (London: Papermac/ Macmillan, 1996), 23–8.

52. Piers Brendon, *The decline and fall of the British Empire, 1718–1997* (London: Vintage Books, 2008), 318.

53. For the Portuguese response to revolts in Angola in the early 1960s, see Anthony Clayton, *Frontiersmen: Warfare in Africa since 1950* (London: UCL Press, 1999), 37–9.

54. Thomas Pakenham, *The scramble for Africa* (London: Abacus, 1991), 609–15.

55. Max Boot, *The savage wars of peace: Small wars and the rise of American power* (New York: Basic Books, 2003), 115–25.

56. Slim, *Killing civilians*, 3.

57. Ibid., 41. For ancient examples, see the Melian Dialogue in Thucydides's *History of the Peloponnesian War* and Euripedes' *The Trojan women*.

58. Kaldor, *New and old wars*, 7.

59. Philip Windsor, 'Strategic thinking after the Cold War', in Mats Berdal (ed.), *Studies in international relations—Essays by Philip Windsor* (Brighton: Sussex Academic Press, June 2002), 149.

60. Kaldor, *New and old wars*, 7.

61. 'The politics of identity can be contrasted with the politics of ideas.' The former are 'fragmentative, backward-looking and exclusive'; the latter about 'forward-looking projects'. Kaldor, *New and old wars*, 81.

62. Enzensberger, *Civil war*, 30.

63. Martin van Creveld, 'The transformation of war revisited', in Robert J. Bunker (ed.), *Non-state threats and future wars* (London: Frank Cass, 2003), 13.

64. See David Keen, *Conflict and collusion in Sierra Leone* (Oxford: James Currey, 2005), 39–47.

65. Antonio Giustozzi, *Koran, Kalashnikov and laptop: The neo-Taliban insurgency in Afghanistan* (London: Hurst, 2007), 84.

66. Even the unmitigated horrors of the Rwandan genocide of 1994 cannot be grasped without some reference to the 'evolution of a genocidal ideology' in which religious ideas, 'biblical narratives, and symbols' played an essential part. See Martin Kimani, *Genocide as revelation: Religion, race and the 1994 Rwandan genocide*, Ph.D. Dissertation, King's College London, 2010.

67. 'Final report of the UN commission of experts established pursuant to Security Council Resolution 780 (1992)', May 1994, paragraph 80.

68. See Warren Zimmermann, *Origins of a catastrophe* (New York: Random House, 1996), ix, 72–4.

69. Michael Weinstein (ed.), *Globalisation: What's new?* (New York: Colombia University Press, 2005), 1.

70. Kaldor, *New and old wars*, 4.

71. Frederick Cooper, 'What is the concept of globalization good for? An African historian's perspective', *African Affairs*, 100/399 (2001), 193.

72. Ibid., 192.

73. Susan Woodward, 'Do the root causes of civil war matter?', *Journal of Intervention and Statebuilding*, 1/2 (2007), 156.

74. Mark Duffield, *Global governance and the new wars: The merging of security and development* (London: Zed books, 2001), 14.

75. Kaldor, *New and old wars*, 116f.

76. Jakkie Cilliers and Christian Dietrich (eds.), *Angola's war economy: The role of oil and diamonds* (Pretoria: Institute for Security Studies, 2000); 'Report of panel of experts on violations of sanctions against UNITA', S/2000/203, 10 March 2000; Charles Cater, *Corporations, resources and war: Angola 1992–2002*, D.Phil. Dissertation, Oxford University, 2008.

77. Duffield, *Global governance and the new wars*, 14.

78. Brian Wood and Johan Peleman, *The arms fixers* (Oslo: PRIO Report 3/99, 1999), 15.

79. Mats Berdal, 'How "new" are "new wars"?', *Global Governance*, 9/3 (2003), 495; 'Report of panel of experts pursuant to UNSC 1343', S/2001/1015, 26 October 2001; 'Report of panel of experts on Somalia pursuant to UNSC 1474', S/2003/1045, 4 November 2003, 24–6; and Hugh Griffiths and Mark Bromley, *Air transport and destabilising commodity flows*, SIPRI Policy Paper 24, May 2009, 13–18.

80. Wood and Peleman, *The arms fixers*, 14–15.

81. Griffiths and Bromley, *Air transport and destabilising commodity flows*, 13.

82. 'Report of panel of experts on violations of Security Council sanctions against UNITA', 17–19. See also 'Flying anything to anybody', *The Economist*, 20 December 2008, 72.

83. Ballentine and Sherman (eds.), *The political economy of armed conflict*, 2.

84. Achim Wennmann, *Conflict financing and the recurrence of intra-state conflict*, Ph.D. Dissertation, University of Geneva, 2007, 85–8.

85. See Jakkie Potgieter, 'UNITA's support structures', in Cilliers and Dietrich (eds.), *Angola's war economy*, 271.

86. See Wennmann, *Conflict financing*, 85. The use of private and front companies in conflict zones is not of course a post-Cold War phenomenon, though often they worked more closely with security and intelligence outfits and to their agendas during the Cold War. See Larry Devlin, *Chief of station, Congo— A memoir of 1960–67* (New York: Public Affairs Books, 2007).

87. Griffiths and Bromley, *Air transport and destabilising commodity flows*, 5.

88. Kaldor, *New and old wars*, 109.

89. See Antonio Giustozzi, 'Novelty is in the eyes of the beholder: Understanding the Taliban in Afghanistan', in Caroline Holmqvist-Jonsäter and Christopher Coker (eds.), *The character of war in the 21st century: Paradoxes, contradictions and continuities* (London: Routledge, 2009).

90. Michael Pugh, Neil Cooper, and Jonathan Goodhand, *War economies in a regional context* (Boulder, CO: Lynne Rienner, 2003).

91. See Frederick Cooper, 'Networks, moral discourse, and history', in Thomas Callaghy, R. Kassimir, and R. Latham (eds.), *Intervention and transnationalism in Africa: Global–local networks of power* (Cambridge: Cambridge University Press, 2001).

92. Stephen Jackson, 'Making a killing: Criminality and coping in the Kivu war economy', *African Review of Political Economy*, 29/93–4 (2002), 528.

93. Timothy Raeymaekers, *The power of protection: Governance and transborder trade on the Congo-Ugandan frontier*, Ph.D. Dissertation, University of Ghent, 2006, 95–104.

94. Prunier, *Africa's world war*, xxxii.

95. Kaldor, *New and old wars*, 109–13; Münkler, *The new wars*, 87–90.

96. Kaldor, *New and old wars*, 110.

97. Writing in 2001, Paul Collier listed 'large diasporas' as one of four 'significant and powerful predictors of civil war', while Kaldor termed them 'regressive globalizers'. Paul Collier, 'The economic causes of civil conflict and their implications for policy', in *Turbulent peace: The challenges of managing international conflict* (Washington, DC: USIP, 2001), 61, 155; and Kaldor, quoted in Mandy Turner, 'Three discourses on diasporas and peacebuilding', in Michael Pugh, Neil Cooper, and Mandy Turner (eds.), *Critical perspectives on war-transformed economies* (Basingstoke: Palgrave, 2008), 177.

98. Kenneth Bush, 'Diaspora engagement in peacebuilding: Empirical and theoretical challenges', in Pugh, Cooper, and Turner (eds.), *Critical perspectives*, 195.

99. Rohan Gunaratna, 'Sri Lanka: Feeding the Tamil Tigers', in Ballentine and Sherman (eds.), *The political economy of armed conflict*, 209.

100. M. Mayilvaganan, 'Is it the endgame for the LTTE?', *Strategic Analysis*, 33/1 (2009), 25–39; Joe Leahy, 'Tigers' harsh taming', *Financial Times*, 16/17 May 2009, 10.

101. C. Christine Fair, 'Diaspora involvement in insurgencies: Insights from the Khalistan and Tamil Eelam movements', *Nationalism and Ethnic Politics*, 11 (2005), 140.

102. Alexandros Yannis, 'Kosovo: The political economy of conflict and peace building', in Ballentine and Sherman (eds.), *The political economy of armed conflict*, 175.

103. David Keen, *The benefits of famine* (Princeton: Princeton University Press, 1994).

104. Ataul Karim, Mark Duffield et al., *OLS: Operations Lifeline Sudan: A Review* (Birmingham: University of Birmingham, 1996).

105. Münkler, *The new wars*, 87.

106. Frances Stewart and Emma Samman, 'Food aid during civil war', in Frances Stewart, Valpy Fitzgerald et al. (eds.), *War and underdevelopment* (Oxford: Oxford University Press, 2000), 170.

107. Joint evaluation of emergency assistance to Rwanda, March 1996, Study I, Chapter 5, www.reliefweb.int/library/nordic/book1/pb020.html

108. Stewart and Samman, 'Food aid during civil war', 202.

109. Sarah Kenyon Lischer, *Dangerous sanctuaries: Refugee camps, civil war, and the dilemmas of humanitarian aid* (Ithaca, NY: Cornell University Press, 2005), 3.

110. Stewart and Samman, 'Food aid during civil war', 200.

111. David Shearer, 'Aiding or abetting? Humanitarian aid and its economic role in civil war', in Berdal and Malone (eds.), *Greed and grievance*, 189–203.

112. Silvia Lauzzana, *Does relief aid prolong wars? Explaining the interaction between humanitarian assistance and conflict during the war in Bosnia-Herzegovina, 1992–1995*, Ph.D. Dissertation, Cambridge University, 2005, 274.

113. Münkler, *The new wars*, 15; Kaldor, 'Introduction', in Kaldor and Vashee (eds.), *Restructuring the global military sector*, 19.

114. See Peter Andreas (ed.), *Transnational crime and conflict in the Balkans, problems of post-Communism*, May–June 2004; Antonio L. Mazzitelli, 'Transnational organised crime in West Africa', *International Affairs*, 83/6 (2007), 1071–90.

115. Keen, *Economic functions of violence*, 12.

116. One internal UN assessment about the situation in parts of Eastern Congo by 2008, for example, highlighted the 'remarkable symbiosis between the vested interests of seemingly opposing factions'. 'Natural resource economy in North Kivu', MONUC, JMAC-HR Team, ND.

117. Jackson, 'Making a killing', 527.

118. Julius R. Ruff, *Violence in early modern Europe, 1500–1800* (Cambridge: Cambridge University Press, 2001), 223.

119. Christopher Bayly and Tim Harper, *Forgotten wars* (London: Penguin Books, 2007), 45.

120. David Stafford, *Endgame 1945* (London: Abacus, 2008), 420.

121. Robert Hislope, 'Crime and honor in a weak state', in *Problems of Post-Communism*, May–June 2004, 18–24.

122. James Cockayne and Daniel Pfister, 'Peace operations and organised crime', GCSP/IPI Report, 2008, 7.

123. See James Cockayne and Adam Lupel, 'Introduction', *International Peacekeeping*, 16/1 (2009), 4–19.

124. For more detailed discussion, see: Mats Berdal, *Building peace after war*, Adelphi Book, Institute for International and Strategic Studies (Abingdon: Routledge, 2009), 61–71.

125. For the relationship between the Yugoslav wars and the rise of region-wide criminal networks, see: Marko Hajdinjak, *Smuggling in southeast Europe: The Yugoslav wars and the development of regional criminal networks in the Balkans* (Sofia: CSD, 2002).

# 7

# What is Really Changing?
# Change and Continuity
# in Global Terrorism*

*Audrey Kurth Cronin*

Fortunately, the ahistorical and amnesiac approach to global terrorism that prevailed in the post-9/11 era is being replaced by a more sophisticated understanding of both continuity and change. In the wake of the attacks of 11 September 2001, most pundits argued that al-Qaeda was unprecedented. Observers labelled Islamist groups the 'new terrorism' and rejected comparisons to historical predecessors, which they claimed reflected different aims, organizational structures, ideologies, types of attacks, potential lethality, and goals, and were fundamentally discontinuous with al-Qaeda.[1] After the break-up of the Soviet Union, the intersection of a virulent religious ideology with vastly expanded access to weapons of mass destruction (WMD) offered a new international environment that seemed uniquely favourable for catastrophic terrorism. The attacks of 11 September seemed to confirm the looming threat, offering proof to many Americans that terrorism had transitioned from a peripheral nuisance to a core threat. Critics also believed that the twentieth-century study of terrorism had been too heavily biased towards Europe, with the lessons of 1970s postcolonial and leftist groups drawing disproportionate resources and attention. If that was the 'old terrorism', then it was obviously irrelevant: al-Qaeda was hardly the IRA with long beards or the Red Brigades with suicide belts. In short, this was an 'existential threat' that required fresh new thinking and a total jettisoning of the old.

Many in the West thus confused actors and means, concluding that because the range of weapons had expanded to include greater terrorist access to potential so-called 'weapons of mass destruction', especially by Islamist groups, there was similar discontinuity in the evolution of terrorist actors themselves.[2] And this was not merely an American attitude; some European observers likewise saw in the Islamist threat a novel challenge unrelated to any predecessors.[3]

For once, history, especially the history of al-Qaeda's predecessors, was truly irrelevant—or so the argument went. Especially in the United States, well-entrenched habits of mind (not to mention resources and expertise) began to cast the international terrorist threat into Manichean, Cold War strategic frameworks, as if the potential for WMD use in itself shifted the paradigm into the realm of nuclear theology and away from the need for an in-depth understanding of those who might or might not use them—and why. An intellectual dichotomy between 'old' and 'new' terrorism thus became entrenched, accompanied by a glossing over of what exactly this new-style enemy 'al-Qaeda' was.

So with a deep intolerance for complexity, many in the United States substituted another kind of historical precedent for a nuanced understanding of terrorism and terrorist campaigns, as if al-Qaeda were the new 'Communist international'—looming and undifferentiated, alike and equally threatening in all aspects. Our policies were sometimes based upon a vague dread of this movement, with al-Qaeda associates from Morocco to Indonesia considered to be equally novel and threatening. Yet, some of the groups associated with al-Qaeda were all-too-familiar in the history of terrorism, having more in common with nationalist predecessors than with the so-called 'new' Islamist terrorist groups. Some al-Qaeda-associated groups have narratives of xenophobia and anti-colonialism, as well as other motivations that have been well known in earlier eras. Yet, we rarely knew enough about local history and cultures to develop the differentiated responses that were required, or to discern the complex characteristics of al-Qaeda that made it both normal and novel.

This was a mistake that we are now hastening to correct. Like most things, al-Qaeda is a complex mix of new and old. It is new, because of its hybrid structure (of central core, nebula, and indigenous volunteers), its radicalization and recruitment methods, and its means of communication. No previous terrorist organization has exhibited quite the elasticity, staying power, and deep global reach of al-Qaeda, with its fluid operational style based not just on a central command but also on a common mission statement and brilliant media campaign, facilitated by the means of globalization. It is old, because it employs classic techniques of popular mobilization and a networked structure that echoes Greek resistance to the Ottoman Empire, the anarchist movement of the late nineteenth century, and, not coincidentally, the Egyptian Muslim Brotherhood from which it arises. It draws upon both inspiration and kinship. Some al-Qaeda-associated groups have narratives of nationalism and anti-colonialism, as well as other motivations that were well-known in earlier eras. It also suffers many of the typical challenges that terrorist groups have experienced, and all of the classic vulnerabilities of an illicit network, including the infighting and factionalization of the FLQ, the Second of June Movement and the Japanese Red Army; the loss of operational control of the Ulster

Volunteer Force and the Weather Underground; and the targeting errors of the Real IRA, ETA, and the Red Brigades.

Yet there is a lot more going on now in the broader evolution of global terrorism than merely the innovations of al-Qaeda. One way to analyse this period of change and continuity is to broaden our focus beyond arguments about al-Qaeda's nature, towards a deeper understanding of the historical, social, and political context within which it has appeared. What is new and will be most enduring is the evolving nature of the international environment in which groups such as al-Qaeda are appearing. Like war, terrorism reflects the context within which it occurs, as well as the kinds of states against which it is arrayed. It has aspects that both endure and evolve as a result. While states are still the strongest and most important actors in this realm, non-state actors are gaining relative advantages. The goal is to understand the broader historical setting for both.

So the question to be addressed here is: What is new, relevant, and enduring about the changing strategic environment in which al-Qaeda and other terrorist groups operate? And how will that context affect the evolving threat of global terrorism overall?

## LOOKING BEYOND AL-QAEDA: FIVE CHANGES

There are five broad developments shaping twenty-first-century terrorism, specifically changes in 'motivation', 'method', 'mobilization', 'morphology', and 'mindset'. This quintet will have staying power long beyond the demise of al-Qaeda, affecting future campaigns and the significance of the threat that arises from them. These five are not revolutionary breaks but important shifts in nature or degree appearing within a broader realm of historical continuity. While terrorism is typically a peripheral concern, particularly compared with war, these five together could make the tactic a key to the future stability or instability of the international system.

### Motivation

The first new development is the explosive intersection of radical Islamism and anti-Americanism.[4] Religiously motivated terrorism was not the dominant paradigm in the twentieth century—though the phenomenon reaches back, of course, to premodern behaviour dating at least to the first century.

(Indeed, in the earliest terrorist attacks, religion was the *only* motivation considered creditable.)[5] But in the modern context, the role of a particular brand of extreme Salafism, as interpreted by al-Qaeda's Osama bin Laden and Ayman Zawahiri, combined with the re-targeting of some violence away from local Arab regimes towards the 'far enemy', especially the United States and its Western allies, is a new historical development that will need to be reckoned with for some time.[6]

Radical Islamism is a fringe element of Islam, and it should not be confused with a mainstream ideology. The tenets of this movement are ill-contrived, nihilistic, unauthoritative, and lacking in any shred of hopeful vision for the future of the Muslim world. In their pronouncements, bin Laden and Zawahiri have tried to act as if they were leaders of an emerging pseudo-state, addressing the Muslim community (the *umma*) as if it belonged to them—a hollow fantasy that is further perpetuated by the West's tendency to hyperbolize its rhetoric in return. Al-Qaeda represents a powerful Salafist ideology, but its extreme anti-modern fundamentalism is adhered to by only a minority of Sunnis, and is hated by most Shi'ites and Sufis. This is unquestionably a complex movement packed with discord about what it stands for and what it aspires to be. Nevertheless, the broader historical effects of this peripheral cult, and the US response to it, are neither marginal nor temporary.

Political Islam was born in opposition to Western ideological concepts, especially in the Arab world. Early Islamist movements, such as the Muslim Brotherhood, developed primarily as a response to British colonialism in Egypt and to all forms of foreign domination of the Islamic world.[7] Sometimes Islamism was used as a kind of safety valve in the twentieth century, where it was seen as a more palatable alternative to Arab nationalism and Communism. Political Islam was consciously courted by the United States to counter Communism in Pakistan (with the funding of the mujahideen against the Soviet invasion of Afghanistan) and in Indonesia (with Indonesian Islamist parties checking the advance of the Indonesian Communist Party in 1965–70), for example.[8] The redirection of radical Islamist violence from local regimes (the near enemy) to the United States and its allies (the far enemy) was a response to perceived Western domination combined with a violent rejoinder to the spread of political, cultural, and economic influence that accompanies unprecedented forces of globalization.[9]

The NEW element is the changed perception of the United States and its role as a lightning rod. Political Islam is again reacting to outside forces, and the main focus is the United States and its allies (especially Britain). Admittedly, the resentment derives in part from the dominant position of the United

States as a world power and the ubiquitous reach of American politics, economics, and culture; but that explanation is insufficient to explain either the degree of the shift or its timing. Groups are driven both by the 'pull' of opportunistic Islamist ideology and by the 'push' of deeper and broader levels of popular anger against the United States and its influence. This will be hard to reverse.

Extensive polls of Muslim public opinion completed in 2007 by the Gallup organization indicate that ambivalence towards the United States results not from an adverse reaction to its values and culture but from the belief that America is interested in domination, intervention, and occupation.[10] This is not to argue that the al-Qaeda movement is about to gather steam: it is not. Thus far bin Laden has been better at exploiting issues of opportunity (including global warming, events in Gaza, and the war in Iraq), than he has at bringing large numbers of Muslims to his cause. But al-Qaeda's loss is not the United States' gain. Despite the noble intention of spreading democracy, US policies in the Muslim world, especially the American invasion of Iraq and a perceived unwillingness to resolve the Israeli–Palestinian conflict, are seen as hostile to all Muslims. Most of the victims of al-Qaeda attacks are Muslims; but often the United States is blamed.[11]

The United States has gradually assumed a new position in the Muslim world and it remains to be seen whether this trend will—or can—be halted. Earlier in the twentieth century, there was a strong tradition of US support (moral, political, and sometimes financial) for anti-colonial forces in Muslim majority countries such as Algeria, Indonesia, Morocco, Tunisia, Malaysia, Egypt, and Sudan. Americans had been seen as supporters of indigenous movements, distinct from the British, French, Dutch, and Spanish, whose colonial empires dissolved (often violently) in the twentieth century. Whatever American intentions, a new image of the United States as the latest hostile foreign force to be repelled will be difficult to revise—especially among young populations.

Not unrelated, the degree of anti-Americanism throughout the Muslim world has been unprecedented, increasing steadily since 2002 in most Muslim countries in the Middle East and Asia. Indeed, the 2007 Pew Global Attitudes Project characterizes the US image in most parts of the Muslim world as 'abysmal'.[12] Sadly, anti-Americanism was strongest among countries that had been US allies, including Turkey (in 2007, those who held favourable views of the United States dropped to 9 per cent, lower than ever), Pakistan (2007 favourable views dropped to 15 per cent), and Morocco (in 2007, only 15 per cent of those polled had favourable views of the United States). Success in Iraq and Afghanistan will help improve the US position; so will the determined efforts of the Obama administration to reach out to the so-called 'Muslim World'.[13] But the United States' primary image has shifted in the last sixty years from anti-colonial sympathizer and role model for self-determination in the Middle East and Asia, to perceived neocolonial power. Thus, beyond al-Qaeda, the potent intersection of Islamism and anti-Americanism is a driver of conflict, and this is the first aspect that, in combination at least, is new.

## Method

The second development is the widespread exploitation by global terrorist groups of pre-existing local insurgencies and wars, and the blurring of many potent methods of non-state conflict in relation to the state.

Terrorism, insurgency, and war are all terms that describe the use of force by or against the modern nation-state as it emerged and was consolidated during the nineteenth and twentieth centuries. They have meaning today in reference to the organizational and intellectual structures of that kind of state, especially its legal and strategic communities. But the early twenty-first century is another period of transition—not towards the dissolution of the state itself and its replacement by non-state actors, a false and ahistorical dichotomy drawn by short-sighted pundits. Instead, in keeping with a long-standing pattern, today's familiar nation-state is evolving to become a range of other types of states. For good or ill, we are witnessing the natural evolution of the nineteenth-century European-style nation-state towards new, more flexible structures better suited to the challenges of the global, information-based context of the twenty-first century, with virtual communities overshadowing parliaments, international corporations displacing government bureaucracies, and private contractors supporting—even supplanting—national armies.

How states and non-state actors use force is naturally evolving as well, dragging our descriptive concepts along behind them. Terrorism continues to embody certain core ideas, including a fundamentally political nature, the surprise use of symbolic violence against seemingly random targets, and the targeting of civilians. But there are crucial areas of ambiguity as well. These hazy aspects are not the result of our inability to be intellectually rigorous, or our hypocrisy or deceit in describing the violence—though terrorism is, admittedly, designed to be a matter of perception and always has been. They are more a reflection of our limitations in understanding the changes underway for nation-states in many different regions of the world, and how they use force.

The concepts of terrorism and insurgency overlap, and admittedly always have. Local insurgencies often used terrorism to further their aims; indeed, there has rarely been an insurgency that has completely avoided killing civilians. The difference now is that the dynamic is in the other direction: global terrorist groups including al-Qaeda and its successors are *using local insurgencies* and their causes to gain adherents, hone their skills, and further their aims. This shift will have staying power.

Al-Qaeda has opportunistically drawn in a wide range of causes that arose in the era of decolonization within its broad tent. For example, the movement has co-opted the vision pursued by Kashmiri, Chechen, Uighur, Indonesian, Filipino, and Palestinian Muslims towards degrees of association with an Islamist agenda. We also saw an attempt to do this in the Iraq war, with al-Qaeda in Iraq—a group that did not exist before 9/11. And now we are observing the movement of foreign fighters from Iraq and the Federally Administered Tribal Areas of Pakistan into Afghanistan to join with local forces, and to fight US and NATO forces there. Al-Qaeda consciously presents itself as the supporter of the underdog, and its model will be mimicked by successors as the century unfolds because it is having some success.

In this respect, it is counterproductive to speak of the al-Qaeda movement itself as a global insurgency. Calling it an insurgency only serves al-Qaeda's interests, as the group (like many terrorist groups) aspires to such a status and enjoys the enhanced standing that the label imparts. It bestows legitimacy on the group, puts the United States and its allies in a dichotomous strategic framework with respect to local struggles, emphasizes territorial control, sometimes forces them to defend regimes that they may not like, and again places them firmly in the role of neocolonial power. Most of the historical examples currently plumbed for lessons about the tactics of counter-insurgency—such as the French in Algeria and the United States in Vietnam—are stories of short-term tactical success and long-term strategic failure. Against the will of a determined populace, the *status quo* foreign power has usually lost, especially in the long run. To the extent that terrorist groups such as al-Qaeda continue to position themselves as supporters of local movements, they will turn attention away from their nefarious tactics and gain staying power in the twenty-first century, a development that must be vigorously resisted.

## Mobilization

The third characteristic of this new era is the one that gets all the attention: the development of globalized means of communication affecting the means and ends of terrorist violence. Today's global terrorism both reacts against the modernization that globalization brings, and also uses the avenues of globalization to carry out its attacks more widely and more effectively.

As in most aspects of twenty-first-century life, the means of communication for terrorist violence have evolved. Information technologies such as the Internet, mobile phones, instant messaging, and even Twitter have extended the global reach of many groups. These tools have led to enhanced efficiency in many terrorist-related activities, including administrative tasks, coordination of operations, recruitment of potential members, communication among adherents, and the attraction of sympathizers. In recruitment and fundraising, for example, the Internet has become a vital tool for perpetuating terrorist groups, both openly and clandestinely. Many of them employ elaborate list serves, collect money from witting or unwitting donors, and distribute savvy political messages to a broad audience online. Groups as diverse as Aum Shinrikyo, Israel's Kahane Chai, the Popular Front for the Liberation of Palestine, the Kurdistan Worker's Party, and Peru's Shining Path maintain user-friendly websites. Al-Qaeda uses a wide range of imagery in its websites to reach back to key events described in the Quran, impart a kind of divine character to their messages, and attract young people to a distortedly heroic view of the path of Islam.[14] Terrorist groups also use the Web for research, data mining, instruction manuals, chat rooms, and sharing of information about successful attacks.

Globalization has enabled terrorist organizations to reach across international borders, in the same way (and often through the same channels) that commerce and business interests are linked. The dropping of barriers through the North American Free Trade Area and the European Union, for example, has facilitated the smooth flow of many things, good and bad. This has allowed terrorist organizations as diverse as Hezbollah, al-Qaeda, and the Egyptian al-Gama'at al-Islamiyya to move about freely and establish cells around the world. Movement across borders can obviously enable terrorists to carry out attacks and evade capture, but it also complicates prosecution of operatives if they are apprehended, with a complex maze of extradition laws varying greatly from state to state. The increased permeability of the international system has enhanced the ability of non-state terrorist organizations to collect intelligence (not to mention evade it): states are not the only actors interested in collecting, disseminating, and/or acting on clandestine information. In a sense, then, terrorism is in some respects becoming like any other international enterprise, and some terrorist organizations like fledgling pseudo-states.[15]

The innumerable ways that innovative communications are affecting human interactions naturally affect non-state actors as well. Terrorist organizations often go to areas of opportunity, so as to operate in conditions that are most conducive to success, and increasing connectivity facilitates their physical mobility. While connections between groups have always been common, sharing safe houses, techniques, and sometimes resources, for example, they are now cooperating with each other in more fluid and temporary ways, operating together for short periods of time rather than in the formalized organizations that existed in the 1970s and 1980s, the peak of state-sponsored terrorism. The 1993 World Trade Center bombers gathered in New York in an ad hoc way, only for the one attack, for example. Indeed, with global connectivity, this 'ad hockery' is becoming more widespread, making the gathering of traditional intelligence much more difficult. Globalized communications have also facilitated the development of home-grown networks that have developed ties primarily through the Internet—or have used the Internet to consolidate ties first developed in the local mosque or gym.

All of these channels enhance the contagion effect that has long been observed in terrorism. When they have learned about them, groups have always copied each others' successful techniques, especially related to bombings, and also kidnappings and hijackings.[16] But because of information flows, this copycat factor has accelerated. In particular, the twenty-first century has seen a dramatic increase in the spread of suicide attacks, a tactical evolution that is not likely to reverse itself. More groups are using suicide tactics, for a wider range of purposes and with more types of operatives within the group. Suicide attacks are well known in Hezbollah and among Palestinian groups, but they have also been extensively employed by the LTTE, Chechen groups, Kashmiri separatist groups, PKK (Turkey), and al-Qaeda, among others. They have appeared regularly in Iraq and now also in Afghanistan, used not only by al-Qaeda-associated groups but also increasingly by factions of the so-called Taliban and other indigenous groups.[17] Suicide attacks are clearly a globally spreading phenomenon, facilitated by globalized Internet connections and video clips that exaggerate their effectiveness and lionize their so-called martyrs.[18]

A glimmer of optimism in an otherwise depressing picture is the difficulty of staying on top of developments in communication, a challenge that may be more difficult for terrorist groups on the run than it is for governments that are trying to defeat them. While it has been a remarkable innovator, al-Qaeda is about a generation behind now in its use of the Web. The central leadership still wants to control the message, and to use sites that carefully represent its orthodoxy. In particular, al-Qaeda's second-in-command, Egyptian Ayman al-Zawahiri, recently elicited questions online. His response to almost 2000 of them was slow, old fashioned, and controlled, demonstrating an anachronistic attitude to a burgeoning conversation now happening largely without him on the Web. Zawahiri is certainly not 'tweeting' with his youthful contacts, and many are leaving him behind. Examples of other groups that are innovating more quickly and more effectively include Aleph, Israel's Kahane Chai, the Popular Front for the Liberation of Palestine, Hizbollah, and the Tamil Tigers (at least until recently). Future groups will be even better at communications than al-Qaeda is. Waves of international terrorism throughout history have often been connected to powerful new ideological paradigms and changes in communication,[19] and that continues to be the case in the twenty-first century.

## Morphology

A fourth and integrally related development in the changing character of terrorism is an evolution in the structure of political violence, in particular the emergence of more robust networks of terrorist groups combining with *other types* of non-state actors. This is not to overstate the novelty of the phenomenon: highly dispersed, networked organizations are by no means unprecedented, and we have already described the closer ties developing between terrorist groups. But the phenomenon is evolving wider, deeper, and faster in a globalized world that at least until recently has been awash with money.

Global terrorism has achieved a level of sophistication in developing cross-border links and extensive global networks that, even in a global downturn, will not be reversed. Al-Qaeda's use of a global network is well known and well established: Abu Musab al-Suri (alias Mustafa Setmariam Nasar), thought to be a chief strategist for al-Qaeda, beginning in 2000 put forth a formula for transforming al-Qaeda from a hierarchical organization to a decentralized movement strategy. This plan seems to have been put into place following the routing of al-Qaeda from Afghanistan in 2002.[20] There are many recent examples, including the Praline case in the United Kingdom, which appears to be an indigenous, dispersed plot facilitated by the Internet.[21] Members were recruited online, and there was contact with operatives in Pakistan, but not apparently initiative or direction from there. Another example is the case of Bilal Abdullah, the British Iraqi doctor who plotted to blow up central London and Glasgow International Airport, who seems to have been a totally self-motivated individual, without external direction.[22] (He was convicted in 2008.) These international networks are more complex, proliferate, disparate, and hearty than those of the twentieth century.

Beyond the increasing sophistication of terrorist networks, however, is their convergence into other kinds of threats, including piracy, terrorism, insurgency, guerrilla warfare, narcoterrorism, and criminal networks. Criminal activities in which al-Qaeda has been directly or indirectly implicated include drug trafficking, people smuggling, extortion, kidnapping, and murder.[23] Organizations are sharing organizational and operational characteristics, combining in ways that used to be avoided by altruistic politically motivated groups seeking to avoid the taint of criminality.

This is most easily seen in the blurring of terrorism and criminal behaviour. Terrorist groups, whose assets are comparatively small compared with organized criminal groups, are especially difficult to track, using everything from direct currency transport (by couriers) to reliance on traditional banking, Islamic banking, money changers, and informal exchange mechanisms including the hawala, hundi, and black market peso exchange. Numerous groups engage in intellectual property crime to fund their activities—the selling of pirated CDs and DVDs plays a role in funding the activities of Lashkar-e-Taiba, for example. Criminal fraud is also very common: Irhabi007, the online hacker who was crucial to the UK Praline plot, had funded his activities using stolen credit card numbers. But much of the activity involves complex intersections between terrorist organizations and criminal networks. According to Interpol, for example, Hezbollah has used the profits from counterfeit goods manufactured in Europe, sold in South America, and then remitted to Lebanese criminal groups, who then transfer profits back to Hezbollah. The PIRA (Provisional Irish Republican Army) has cooperated with the Colombian narcoterrorist group the FARC (Fuerzas Armadas Revolucionarias de Colombia). The connection between poppy-growing in Afghanistan and the financing of al-Qaeda is well known. There are many other examples.

These threats are blending together in our studies of war and conflict because they are blending together in the real world.[24] The blurring of distinctions between criminal organizations and terrorist groups makes traditional state sanctions against terrorist organizations (such as the State Sponsors of Terrorism and Foreign Terrorist Organization lists in the United States) increasingly anachronistic and toothless.[25] In short, the morphology of global terrorism is evolving in new directions that are leaving our twentieth-century semantic distinctions and bureaucratic structures in the dust.

## Mindset

Finally, the fifth new development is the unfortunate clash of twentieth-century Western strategic thinking and twenty-first-century proliferation—in other words, the potential for future catastrophic terrorism combined with an appalling absence of government planning, that reflects in-depth knowledge of the strategies of terrorism. There is too little understanding of evolving terrorist thinking, and too much reliance upon outdated, state-centric strategic models that are becoming increasingly anachronistic and even dangerous.

Many have written about the dangers of proliferation to terrorist groups, and in the wake of the A.Q. Khan network, no one can doubt the dangers of the threat of proliferation of WMD to (or by) non-state actors. Catastrophic terrorism can also be accomplished using conventional means (as we know from the attacks of 9/11). It is worth noting that we are currently in the midst of two conventional wars that were set off by a major terrorist attack. The classic strategies of leverage, notably the nineteenth century's use of terrorist attacks for provocation of state action, are more dangerous than ever before.[26]

Western strategic thinking is ill-suited to respond effectively to major attacks by non-state actors in the twenty-first century. Many have focused on the hazards of WMD proliferation to terrorist or criminal groups. But the threat goes well beyond the potential for al-Qaeda (or its successors) to use a nuclear device or even to launch another major conventional attack. The most dangerous repercussion of another major attack would not be the direct casualties (as tragic as they would be) but the likelihood of a massive, indiscriminate, and ill-targeted state response by a wounded power such as the United States, Russia, Israel, India, Pakistan, or China. Yet, policymakers are stuck in state-centric strategic thinking that leaves them vulnerable to exactly this outcome.

A major risk of future global instability lies in the grey area between states and non-state actors, and the potentially explosive results of their continued interaction. Yet, policymakers consistently misread the strategies of terrorism and expect state-like behaviour. This leaves them open to potentially counterproductive and destabilizing responses that are far more dangerous than the original attack. Terrorists often aim to draw states into hasty and imprudent actions that are self-defeating, ineffective, or relinquish power— sometimes even where the effort is suicidal. Now there is a serious risk that these formerly peripheral actors may gain access to nuclear weapons, giving them the destructive power of states and making it vital to improve our understanding of the patterns and pitfalls in confronting them. Our lag in serious strategic planning and thinking is an important development that may increase terrorist motivations for such an attack and make its probability greater than it needs to be.


## CONCLUSION

These five changes in 'motivation', 'method', 'mobilization', 'morphology', and 'mindset' highlight the need to reconsider the strategic implications of global terrorism in the twenty-first century. For policymakers, the important question is not 'when will the next attack be?' but 'what will we do after that?'.

The wisest course of action as we move further into the twenty-first century is to avoid heightening anxiety about the threat of terrorism and stop trying to convince people that we can eliminate the risks. The most dangerous aspect of any terrorist campaign lies in its intersection with the nation-state, especially the potential that terrorist attacks by al-Qaeda or another group will set off a cascade of state actions that results in systemic conventional war. (India/Pakistan, and the Israel/Palestine territories immediately come to mind.) It is in the grey area between states and non-state actors, and the potentially explosive results of their continued interaction, where the real threat of global terrorism in the twenty-first century lies.

So, even though the threat of terrorism pales in comparison to the spectre of major conventional war, as a result of these five developments in the political, social, economic, and historical context for conflict, the question of the changing character of global terrorism will be central to the changing character of war. Innovative Western thinkers must develop an updated strategic canon that moves beyond the state-centric nuclear theology and game theoretical models that prevailed in the twentieth century, and deals more seriously with the intersection of powerful weapons, non-state actors, and strategies of leverage against the state—especially the question of what major powers should do in the wake of the next serious terrorist attack.

## NOTES

1. Authors who held this view include: Daniel Benjamin and Steven Simon, *The age of sacred terror: Radical Islam's war against America* (New York: Random House, 2003) and *The next attack: The failure of the war on terror and a strategy for getting it right* (New York: Owl Books, 2006); Walter Laqueur, *The new terrorism: Fanaticism and the arms of mass destruction* (New York: Oxford University Press, 1999); Ian O. Lesser et al., *Countering the new terrorism* (Santa Monica, CA: RAND, 1999); L. Paul Bremer, 'A new strategy for the new face of terrorism', *The National Interest* (November 2001), 23–30; and Andrew Tan and Kumar Ramakrishna (eds.), *The new terrorism: Anatomy, trends and counter-strategies* (Singapore: Times Academic Press, 2002). For an excellent analysis of the concept, see Martha Crenshaw, 'The American debate over "new" vs. "old" terrorism', unpublished draft paper presented at the 2007 American Political Science Association conference. The 'new terrorism' was introduced as a concept at the end of the millennium but gained widespread purchase after 9/11.

2. Actually, terrorist groups have shown interest in chemical, biological, and nuclear weapons for decades. But their access was potentially increased by the end of the Soviet Union.

3. See the text of a lecture by Anthony Giddens, delivered at the London School of Economics, 10 November 2004, 'The future of world society: The new terrorism' available at Columbia International Affairs Online (CIAO); and Farhad Khosrokhavar also refers to 'new' terrorism in *Les Nouveaux Martyrs d'Allah* (Paris: Flammarion, 2003). Crenshaw, 'The American debate'.

4. Olivier Roy would argue that it is anti-Westernization; however, I would argue that the focus on the United States has become increasingly dominant, especially since 2003. Olivier Roy, *Globalized Islam: The search for a new ummah* (New York: Columbia University Press, 2004), 6.

5. David Rapoport, 'Fear and Trembling: Terror in Three Religious Traditions', *American Political Science Review*, 78/3 (1984), 658–77.

6. On this subject, see Fawaz Gerges, *The far enemy* (Cambridge, UK: Cambridge University Press, 2005).

7. See, for example, Richard P. Mitchell, *The society of the Muslim Brothers* (Oxford: Oxford University Press, 1969; 2nd edition, 1993); and Gilles Kepel, *The prophet and the pharaoh: Muslim extremism in Egypt* (London: Al Saqi Books, 1985).

8. Ahmed-Noor, 'Political Flux in a Nonpolar World', Chapter 1 of *Global strategic assessment*, INSS, 2009. It was also an organic response to secular autocratic regimes, as in Syria, Iraq, and Iran—at least until the 1979 Iranian Shia revolution demonstrated the perils of this approach.

9. See Audrey Kurth Cronin, 'Behind the curve: Globalization and international terrorism', *International Security*, 27/3 (2002/3), 30–58.

10. John L Esposito and Dalia Mogahed, *Who speaks for Islam? What a billion Muslims really think* [based on Gallup's world poll—the largest study of its kind] (New York: Gallup, 2007), especially 65–98, 140–2.

11. Audrey Kurth Cronin, *Ending terrorism: Lessons for defeating al-Qaeda*, Adelphi Paper no. 394, International Institute for Strategic Studies (London: Routledge, 2008), especially 66–70.

12. 'Global unease with major world powers: 47-nation Pew global attitudes survey', *The Pew global attitudes project*, 27 June 2007, Chapter 1; 'Views of the US and American foreign policy', 3, http://pewglobal.org/reports/pdf/256.pdf. The report does point out that in some places opinion of the United States has risen above spring 2003 levels. In the wake of start of the war in Iraq, favourable opinion of the United States in Jordan and the Palestinian territories was 1 per cent and less than 1 per cent, respectively, compared to 20 and 13 per cent in June 2007.

13. Most important among these efforts was US President Barak Obama's speech at Cairo University, 'A new beginning', 4 June 2009, http://www.whitehouse.gov/the_press_office/Remarks-by-the-President-at-Cairo-University-6-04-09/

14. For the best analysis (in English) of this use of imagery, see Combating Terrorism Center at West Point, *The Islamic imagery project: Visual motifs in jihadi internet propaganda*, March 2006, http://ctc.usma.edu/imagery/imagery_pdf.asp

15. Some of the information from this section is drawn from my 'Behind the Curve'.

16. See Manus I. Midlarsky, Martha Crenshaw, and Fumihiko Yoshida, 'Why violence spreads: The contagion of international terrorism', *International Studies Quarterly*, 24/2 (1980), 262–98.

17. See Christine Fair (ed.), *Suicide attacks in Afghanistan, 2001–2007*, prepared for the United Nations Assistance Mission to Afghanistan (UNAMA), 2007.

18. This is a particularly worrisome development, as groups that use suicide attacks are much harder to defeat, especially if they must be reconciled with other populations living side-by-side. For evidence and a much more detailed explanation, see Chapter 3 of my *How terrorism ends: Understanding the demise and decline of terrorist campaigns* (Princeton, NJ: Princeton University Press, 2009).

19. David Rapoport argues that two critical factors in what he calls 'waves' of terrorism are communications and transportation patterns, on the one hand, and shifts in doctrine or culture, on the other. See David C. Rapoport, 'The four waves of modern terrorism', in Audrey Kurth Cronin and James M. Lude (eds.), *Attacking terrorism: Elements of a grand strategy* (Washington, DC: Georgetown University Press, 2004), 48–9.

20. Al-Suri's real name is Mustafa Setmariam Nasar, and is sometimes called Setmariam for short. The videotapes were recovered from Afghanistan in 2006, dated August 2000. See the 'Introduction'; and Paul Cruickshank and Mohannad Hage Ali, 'Abu Musab Al Suri: Architect of the new Al Qaeda', *Studies in Conflict and Terrorism*, 30/1 (2007), 1–14.

21. Rafaello Pantucci, 'Operation Praline: The realization of Al-Suri's Nizam, la Tanzim?' *Perspectives on Terrorism*, Vol. II, Issue 12 (2008); accessed at http://www.terrorismanalysts.com/pt/.

22. Dominic Casciani, 'Iraqi Doctor's Road to Radicalism', BBC News, 16 December 2008; accessed at http://news.bbc.co.uk/2/hi/uk_news/7784799.stm.

23. '20th annual regional conference' opening remarks by Ronald K. Noble, INTERPOL Secretary General, Viña del Mar, Chile, 1 April 2009, http://www.interpol.int/Public/ICPO/speeches/2009/20090401SG_ARC20.asp

24. See, for example,Thomas M. Sanderson, 'Transnational terror and organized crime: Blurring the lines', *SAIS Review*, XXIV/1 (2004), 49–61.

25. For more information about the Foreign Terrorist Organization list, see my *The FTO list and Congress: Sanctioning designated foreign terrorist organizations*, CRS Report for Congress #RL32120, 21 October 2003, http://www.fas.org/irpcrs/RL32120.pdf

26. I have written much more about the strategies of terrorism in *Ending terrorism: Lessons for defeating al-Qaeda*.

\* The opinions expressed in this chapter are the author's alone and do not necessarily represent those of the National War College, the National Defense University, or any other US government agency.

# PART II

# The Purpose of War: Why Go to War?

# 8

## Humanitarian Intervention

### D. J. B. Trim

This chapter examines the role of concern about 'crimes against humanity' or 'mass atrocity crimes' in motivating states to make war.[1] Military operations resulting from such concerns are typically known as 'humanitarian intervention' (although in some interventions, the use of military force is threatened and prepared for, but not ultimately required). Interventions can be defined by their site, subject, and object. A military humanitarian intervention, firstly, is (or is intended to be) carried out in a foreign state; secondly, it is a coercive action, either aimed at that state's government or imposed on it and reluctantly accepted by it; and thirdly, the intervention's objective is, at least nominally and to some extent really, to prevent, halt, and/or 'to forestall . . . reoccurrence' of large-scale mortality, 'egregious abuse', or other 'widespread suffering' caused by the action of the *de facto* authorities in that state.[2] Because humanitarian intervention involves the threat or use of foreign military force, it can be distinguished from wider 'humanitarian action' or humanitarian aid.[3]

For many scholars, accustomed to understanding war as an instrument of national interest, humanitarian intervention is a recent innovation: it appears, in fact, to be a perfect example of the changing character of war. It is widely assumed by academics, practitioners, and politicians that the practice of intervention is a recent development, with concern for 'mass atrocities' a genuine factor in policymaking only since the genocides of the Second World War, if not since the end of the Cold War, and that the very term 'humanitarian intervention' is a neologism of the early 1990s.[4]

This chapter shows that in fact the *terminology* of 'humanitarian intervention' dates not from the 1990s but from the mid- and late nineteenth century; and it argues that the *concept* of using military force to protect oppressed people groups from 'egregious abuse' is at least 450 years older—that its origins lie in interventions by early-modern princes against tyrants and perpetrators of massacres. Such interventions, to protect people groups from regimes that arbitrarily and forcibly deprived them of established privileges and liberties, murdered those who resisted, and thus (to use the language of early-modern Christendom) ruled tyrannically, comprise the precedent out of which developed the practice of interventions avowedly to protect human rights (in modern terminology). That they would so develop was far from inevitable, but it is the case that the series of developments that would eventually lead to the modern concept of 'humanitarian intervention' began in the sixteenth century; a change in the character of war-making in the post-Reformation era triggered further changes in attitudes about why wars ought to be waged. This, then, is a story of change—of frequent change throughout the last four-and-a-half centuries, of change both backwards and forwards, of movement and reaction, rather than of permanent transformation.

The remainder of this chapter first examines the early-modern precedents, in theory and practice; it then considers the treaties of Westphalia (1648) and argues that they did not establish a norm of non-intervention, based on modern concepts of state sovereignty; before examining humanitarian intervention in the nineteenth century and the early twentieth century, including the advent of the term 'humanitarian intervention' into the jargon of statesmen and lawyers. It then surveys both the concept of intervention and actual interventions from the League of Nations to the present day. Finally, a concluding section attempts to relate the particular story of this chapter to the wider themes of the book.

The practice of intervention in early-modern Europe owed a great deal to concepts previously adumbrated in medieval Christendom: by St Augustine, on just war, and by St Thomas Aquinas, on just war, government, and, especially, tyranny.[5] The theories advanced by Aquinas were significant, but it was only in the sixteenth century that they were first put into practice. This was no coincidence. European encounters with new lands and cultures during the 'age of discovery' naturally generated new reflection on sovereignty and on how Christian states fitted into the world. Even more important were the effects of the Protestant Reformation. Previously, persecuted people groups were heretics. Princes retained, 'even in the bitterest . . . quarrels, a sense of solidarity in one Catholic faith'; they had no interest in aiding heretics, whose beliefs invited God's judgement on those who allowed them to flourish. By fracturing 'the unity of Christendom', the Reformation created confessionally opposed polities, whose elites and rulers had a natural sympathy for the persecuted, and whose theology might impel them to aid co-religionists. For the first time, princes or republics were disposed to take the side of religious dissidents; and to both the dissidents and their foreign sympathizers, their persecutors naturally seemed tyrannical.[6] Thus, in post-Reformation Europe, concerns about bad government, tyranny, and abuses of power were among both the underlying motivations for warring states and the official justifications given for their recourse to war.

Furthermore, the interventions of this period are very significant. Tyranny and atrocity have been regarded as illegitimate, and as legitimate reasons for resistance of rulers by the ruled, throughout history and across the globe. However, in early-modern Christendom, the right to resist abusive authority went beyond the internal relations of a polity and became a factor in international relations, exactly as concepts of the nation-state and international system were beginning to form. Because Europe rose to global dominance, what emerged as normative there became normative across much of the globe. The significance of early-modern practice thus extends beyond the period and beyond Europe.

England intervened in the French wars of religion several times during the 1560s, 1570s, and 1580s, and in the revolt of the Netherlands from 1585 until 1604; some states of the Holy Roman Empire also joined in interventions in France. In the case of France, Queen Elizabeth I and her government and the German princes were moved by the suffering (and, in modern terms, literally genocidal killing) of a religious minority: the Huguenots (as French Protestants were known).[7] They faced persecution of uneven rigour for almost forty years after 1558, suffering particularly appalling massacres in 1572. The St Bartholomew's massacre in Paris, in which some 3,000 Huguenots were killed without any kind of judicial proceedings, was only the first in a series of a dozen emulatory massacres in provincial cities, in which deaths totalled another 4,000–7,000.[8] In the case of the Netherlands, the Elizabethan government regarded the Spanish government as tyrannous and oppressive, of both Protestants and Roman Catholics. In internal memoranda, Elizabeth's counsellors explicitly termed the Spanish government a 'tyranny', and when England went openly to war with Spain in 1585, Elizabeth drew attention to the fact that, 'howso ever in the beginning of these cruell persecutions, the pretence thereof was for maintenance of the Romish religion, yet they spared not to deprive very many Catholiques . . . of their franchises and priviledges'.[9] Meanwhile, under Philip II and Philip III, Spain three times attempted to invade England in the ten years 1588–97, and sent an expeditionary force to Ireland in 1601, largely because of English opposition in the Netherlands, but partly because of 'the brutal and cruel yoke' of persecution imposed on Catholics—a minority in England, the majority in Ireland—which, as Philip II's counsellors argued, violated England's own 'ancient laws'.[10]

Perhaps most notably, in the mid-1650s, Oliver Cromwell, Lord Protector of the British republic, mobilized commercial, diplomatic, and naval power to bludgeon Savoy into halting persecution of the Vaudois (or Waldenses). Cromwell earlier, in 1649, had been guilty of initiating one of the first forced migrations, driving large portions of the Catholic population of Ireland from the best agricultural land to make way for Protestant settlers from Britain. However, he was concerned to halt or ameliorate persecution of religious minorities, both in England and abroad. When the Vaudois suffered a series of massacres in the spring of 1655, British action compelled the Duke of Savoy to halt the confessional-ethnic cleansing of his state.[11] Aiding the Vaudois did little or nothing to aid the British republic's security, geopolitical position, or strategic interests. The Vaudois were too weak to be useful future allies in any renewed war of religion; British commerce with Savoy was of minimal importance; and the region was strategically unimportant for Cromwell's foreign policy objectives, which focused on the Low Countries and the West Indies. Cromwell's 'laying aside [of] all other Reasons of State' to aid the Vaudois (as one of his diplomats described it) stemmed from his own and his ministers' desire to conduct foreign policy (as they averred) with 'regard . . . to the honest Maximes of Humane Policy', and from their genuine concern and horror at 'the inhuman murther of the Vaudois'.[12]

In each case, from Elizabeth I to Philip II to Oliver Cromwell, confessional interests were hugely important in the decision to undertake interventions. It is notable that victims of tyranny, atrocity, or abusive government were always described in terms of their confessional identity, not of their humanity, except in the case of Cromwell. This explains why all the governments in question, including Cromwell's, persecuted and oppressed minorities in their own states. Yet historically it has not been unusual for those who avow principles to make (to them, obvious) exceptions in the way they are applied. It is important that early-modern interventions were not simply justified as support for fellow believers; they were also, or sometimes were instead, justified in terms of stopping unnecessary suffering—of striking down tyranny. This conceptual expansion was a hugely important precedent, opening up the possibility of acting on behalf of people who were not co-religionists. It is, moreover, important to note that justifications were not merely theoretical; they went hand in hand with action, and drew on a common ideology, which underpinned state praxis.

Among diplomats, jurists, and philosophers (and in this age of the Renaissance, the same man was often all three), there was a developing discourse that there was a right to 'defend' neighbouring peoples from 'tyrannical and oppressive laws against the innocent'; war could rightfully be made on rulers guilty of 'tyranny and oppression'.[13] In the first half of the sixteenth century, the Spanish theorists who argued for this right restricted its application to the 'barbarian' indigenous inhabitants of the New World. While they argued that it could only be applied in the case of actual infliction of harm to 'other men', rather than of offences against Christian morality, and that there was no right to 'eject [native American rulers] from their dominions . . . at whim', still, if 'no other method of ensuring safety' existed than what today would be called 'regime change', then they held that it was justified.[14] In the latter half of the sixteenth century, however, the right to act against tyranny and oppression was extended to Christian princes and characterized as a duty. Military intervention was to be undertaken only in exceptional circumstances: a tyrant was not 'a less than good prince, but the worst'; and commentators warned against making the protection of people from tyranny a 'pretext [to] invade foreign borders, or seize the jurisdiction of another'.[15] However, in the case of a 'tyrant afflicting his own people, any king throwing downe the props and stayes of his common wealth', or a regime 'violently' breaking the bounds 'of piety and justice', foreigners could legitimately take corrective military action.[16] In those cases, 'an other prince may justly and lawfully exceede his owne limittes' to restore good government. Furthermore, at least in England, it was argued that another prince not only might act—he ought to act. 'If a prince use tyrannie towards his people, we *ought to ayde*', and the 'princes in these dayes ought to imitiate' the 'worthy Examples' of past princes who 'resisted the tyrants, and defended the people'.[17] In early-modern English, 'ought' was used to express 'duty or obligation', especially 'moral obligation'.[18] Thus, sixteenth- and seventeenth-century English commentators were arguing, in effect, for an 'obligation to aid', prefiguring the twenty-first-century concept of a 'responsibility to protect'.[19]

The early-modern era thus saw a combination of repeated action, along with a set of principles on which action was based. It witnessed the emergence of a norm in the law of nations that where law and good governance were absent, and tyranny flourished, other princes could legitimately interfere, or intervene, to restore them.

The development of this norm was interrupted, but far from destroyed, by the peace treaties of Westphalia in 1648, which ended the Thirty Years War and, more broadly, are usually held to have established the modern concept of state sovereignty and hence the modern international system. The 'norm of non-intervention' is typically portrayed as one of the essential principles of the new order, without which it could not have succeeded.[20]

Yet Westphalia was much less of a watershed with regard to intervention than is often assumed. The peace treaties included guarantees of freedom of conscience for some religious minorities, for which certain powers stood as guarantors: thus, Sweden was the Westphalian guarantor of the rights of Protestants within the Empire. Such provisions continued to be built into treaties made subsequent to 1648. By the terms of the Treaty of Oliva (1660), Sweden and Brandenburg-Prussia guaranteed the rights of Protestants in Polish Prussia, and Britain was added as a guarantor power a few years later.[21] In 1704, Great Britain and the Dutch Republic made a treaty of alliance with Victor Amadeus of Savoy conditional on his conceding to the Vaudois the 'entire and inviolable observance' of their religion, and the two maritime powers guaranteed the Waldenses religious liberty by the same treaty.[22]

Thus, even after 1648, the sovereignty of some rulers was not absolute in some parts of their territories, and some princes had both a right and an obligation to concern themselves in other princes' affairs. They took these obligations seriously. In 1719–20, Britain explored the possibility of 'becom[ing] a guarantor power of the Westphalian agreement', so as to have a basis for halting oppression of Protestants in Heidelberg; and in 1724, Prussia, as guarantor power, mobilized troops to force the Polish government to protect Protestants in Thorn from Catholic violence.[23] For nearly eight decades after 1648, the supposed Westphalian system did not provide for absolute sovereignty, and earlier models of sovereignty continued to be influential into the late eighteenth century. In 1774, Russia became guarantor of the rights of the Ottoman Empire's Greek Orthodox subjects by the treaty of Kutchuk-Kainardji; in the 1790s, a military intervention in France was urged by the Anglo-Irish statesman Edmund Burke on the grounds that the revolutionaries constituted a 'positively Vicious and abusive Government', guilty of 'the most atrocious and bloody tyranny'.[24]

In sum, it is a myth that Westphalia established modern state sovereignty and hence a norm of non-intervention. As recent scholarship emphasizes, within academia it is 'a constitutive foundation myth' for scholars of international relations. It was also, however, a myth that began to develop within a few decades; indeed, by the late eighteenth century, there was an increasing attachment among European statesmen to the norm of non-intervention, which they believed had been established in 1648.[25] By 1815, when the Congress of Vienna redrew the map of Europe after the Napoleonic Wars and consciously sought to restore tranquility, the Westphalian reality had largely been forgotten. The Vienna settlement did innovatively and specifically grant a right to use force in another state's affairs—indeed, all the Continental great powers committed themselves to acting 'in the affairs of other states in a systematic way' to an extent unmatched for nearly 100 years.[26] However, this was intended to maintain governments struggling against populist movements, rather than to compel governments to cease abusive practices. Force would be used, not against a regime or in the face of its opposition (or resentful submission), but rather to sustain it; thus, what was provided for at Vienna was not truly intervention, much less humanitarian intervention.

By the 1820s, then, the Westphalian myth was powerful and predominant, and the so-called Concert of Europe had as its purpose preservation of the status quo—not only between nations (avoiding war) but also within them, suppressing republican or popular reformist movements. Yet, despite this, the trend of the nineteenth century was actually to be towards privileging moral factors in international relations, over the (supposedly) Westphalian principle of non-intervention. Although the founders of the *concert européen* were conservative, they also identified it as a 'guardian of civilization' and expressed hopes it would foster moral policymaking.[27] As a result, and as a result too of the rise of 'liberal' values in western Europe, the Concert actually became an informal mechanism for taking collective action in response to treatment of people groups that 'shocked the conscience of mankind'.[28] The grounds for intervention moved away from tyranny, instead emphasizing first liberty and liberalism, then civilization, then humanity. The great liberal thinker John Stuart Mill argued in 1859 that 'intervention' (his term) to halt 'severities repugnant to humanity' had been 'practised during the present generation with such general approval that its legitimacy [had] passed into a maxim of... international law'.[29]

The nineteenth century, as Gary Bass points out, in fact became the great century of intervention.[30] The great powers made multiple interventions in the Ottoman Empire, sending warships and troops to carry out 'civilizing missions', to restore law and order, and to prevent anti-Jewish and anti-Christian violence. Naval forces were deployed to Greece in the 1820s, to compel Ottoman recognition of Greek independence; although Russia could and did present itself as acting as treaty guarantor of the rights of Greek Christians, Britain and France only had as their justification the moral outrage felt in their nations at Ottoman atrocities.[31] The great powers sent naval forces and agreed to the despatch of a French expeditionary corps to Lebanon and Syria in the 1860s; British reservations were overcome partly by *Realpolitik* considerations, and partly by public demands, generated by stories of massacres of Christians in Lebanon and Damascus, that Britain, like France, govern its foreign policy by *'principes d'humanité'.*[32] The third Russo-Turkish War in 1877 was motivated partly by Russian anger at atrocities allegedly committed by the Ottoman authorities after risings in Bosnia, Bulgaria, and Herzegovina in 1877, and by ongoing persecution of Christian Armenians. In 1905, with the sanction of all the great powers, Austrian warships and troops attacked and captured strategically vital islands in the Aegean, thereby forcing the Ottoman government to put into action a Russian and Austrian plan for reform in Macedonia, implemented by officials from the European powers, and supported by local troops trained and commanded by European officers and non-commissioned officers.[33]

Geopolitical considerations were factors in the decisions to undertake all these interventions, but so were concerns for what became known as 'humanity rights' and then 'human rights'.[34] Furthermore, it was not only the Ottomans against whom interventions were undertaken. In the 1820s and 1830s, Britain used the power of the Royal Navy to end the West African slave trade, acting despite the absence of international treaties authorizing them to do so. They blockaded West Africa, searched and seized the ships of numerous European countries, and made landings to attack particularly important slaving posts on the African coast.[35] In the 1880s and 1890s, in eastern Africa and the Middle East, British military and naval force was deployed against the slave trade in East Africa. While use of force increased Britain's empire, the force was focused against slave trading, rather than on securing coaling stations or commercial concessions. It was, moreover, often carried out *against* the wishes of the imperial government, which did not necessarily wish to prioritize moral factors over geopolitical ones, but had its hand forced by zealous anti-slavers on the ground in Africa and by an increasing public demand, fed by missionary activism and newspaper reports of the horrors of slavery, that imperial policy *should* take notice of humanitarian concerns.[36] In 1898–9, the United States of America invaded Cuba, in a war that undoubtedly was partly motivated by naked imperialism, but which could never have been waged had not some American politicians and many influential Americans fervently agreed with President William McKinley, that freeing the Cubans from Spain was a means to advance 'civilization' and 'the interest of humanity', so that the war with Spain was a 'war for humanity'.[37]

The very term 'humanitarian intervention' was coined in the nineteenth century by scholars of the new academic discipline of international law, precisely because of the frequency of intervention. To a marked extent in Britain, France, and the United States, and to some extent in Germany, Austria, and Italy, a 'humanitarian public' had emerged. Keenly interested in the fate of oppressed people groups (albeit admittedly especially if they were Christian or Jewish, or 'primitive' peoples who could be converted to Christianity), it both consumed and helped to produce numerous printed reports, in books, pamphlets, magazines, and newspapers, of atrocities, mass murder, and brutality. The humanitarian public could be manipulated by propaganda and polemic, as happened to some extent in the 1890s in the build-up to the Spanish–American War and the Ashanti Wars (discussed below); however, it could also impel the governments of democratic states to action, as with British participation in the intervention in Lebanon in 1860–1 and action against the slave trade in East Africa in the 1890s; and its support could embolden even non-democratic governments, as happened in France in the 1860s.

Nevertheless, among some liberal thinkers, intervention became clearly associated with imperialism. As well as 'liberating' Cuba, the United States annexed the Philippines and Puerto Rico, outraging many supporters of the 'war for humanity' against Spain.[38] France, Austria, and Russia used interventions in the Ottoman Empire to leverage concessions in the Middle East, Balkans, and Caucasus. And unquestionably at times, the British government used the public enthusiasm for spreading civilized values as cover for acquisitive wars (just as the US government used the Cuban struggle for freedom to expand the American empire). In contrast to the anti-slave trade campaigns in East Africa, the third and fourth Ashanti Wars (1895–6, 1900) were undertaken to secure the British imperial position in West Africa and British control over goldfields; press reports before and after the war of a newly crowned king's acts of cruelty and barbarism in this case only provided a pretence for purely imperialist action.[39] By the start of the First World War, there were many authorities on international jurisprudence who 'recognized the lawfulness' of intervention *d'humanité*, but many others who denied it.[40] Yet, in terms of state practice, humanitarian intervention was a norm, with consistent action underpinned by a relatively clear ideology that was influential at both the popular and elite levels.

The history of interventions to maintain or impose civilized government before the First World War, and the obvious potential a right of intervention created for renewed conflict, was an important reason why the Covenant of the League of Nations did not provide for a specific right of intervention on humanitarian grounds.[41] When this was followed up by the renunciation of 'war as an instrument of national policy' by many of the world's leading nations in the Kellogg–Briand Pact (1928), and then in 1945 by the ratification of the United Nations Charter, it seemed that the era of armed humanitarian intervention finally was over. The UN Charter clearly mandates that nation-states must 'refrain from the threat or use of force against the territorial integrity or political independence of any state'. It even restricts the right of the United Nations, much less any individual nation-state, to intervene in 'matters which are essentially within the domestic jurisdiction of any state'.[42] The result was an 'emphatic embrace' of the 'principle of non-intervention'. Yet, interventions *were* carried out in the forty-five years from the agreement of the Charter to the end of the Cold War; if 'the UN almost routinely condemned them', several had humanitarian motivations or at least official rationales.[43]

The maintenance or restoration of law and order (of civilized government, in fact, though that language was not used) and the termination of violence and human rights abuses were part of the rationale for US interventions in the Dominican Republic in 1965 and Grenada in 1983. However, the official justifications to the Organization of American States and other international organizations characterized the interventions as defensive and 'anti-subversive or anti-revolutionary', arguing that Communist action necessitated 'American counter-intervention to uphold the principle of non-intervention'.[44] Indeed, the US government in the Cold War era appealed much more often 'to norms of peace and security' than to 'human justice', when justifying 'interventions to the world at large'.[45] Nevertheless, the US ambassador to the UN asserted that the American and Belgian use of force in the Congo in 1964 was a 'humanitarian mission'.[46] Then in 1971 India's government explicitly drew on nineteenth- and early twentieth-century precedents to justify its invasion of East Pakistan, which halted what is widely regarded as genocide against the people of what is now Bangladesh. In contrast, however, Vietnam's intervention in Cambodia in 1978–9, which ended probably the worst genocide since the Second World War, drew on Western concepts of what was and was not legitimate as a cause of war, rather than on long-standing indigenous concepts of tyranny as immoral; Vietnamese officials argued that intervention was justifiable because it was an act of self-defence and one prominent Vietnamese ideologue declared it 'in harmony with the principles of [ . . . ] the United Nations Charter'.[47] The Tanzanian intervention in Uganda, in 1978–9, which toppled the murderous government of Idi Amin, was likewise explained to the world as an act of self-defence, though the Tanzanian government seems to have been motivated by genuine outrage at Amin's brutal regime, as well as fears for national security.[48]

The end of the Cold War produced a brief period of consensus in the UN Security Council, during which humanitarian military action stood a good chance of receiving Security Council sanction. It also, for reasons that are unclear, produced a series of appalling humanitarian crises, making traditional arguments for non-intervention difficult to maintain.[49] Military action was taken by the United States and the Western powers with Security Council approval in northern Iraq in 1991; by the Economic Community of West African States in Liberia in 1992; by the United States and the UN in Somalia in 1992–3 and Haiti in 1994–5; by Nigeria, Ghana, and the United Kingdom in Sierra Leone in 1998; by Australia and the UN in East Timor in 1999; and by NATO in Kosovo in 1999. All of these were both justified in communiqués to the media, and regarded, at least to some extent, by the governments that intervened, as humanitarian interventions. In contrast, while a desire to remove Saddam Hussein's brutal government seems to have been a motivating factor for the Anglo-American invasion of Iraq in 2003 for some members of the Bush and Blair governments, for others it clearly was not, and it certainly was not the chief rationale advanced for the invasion, which rather was Iraq's alleged possession of weapons of mass destruction.

Since 1990, in sum, intervention on humanitarian grounds has become common state practice, although it is not universally accepted as an absolute right in international law. Praxis has been undergirded by theory, and by public pressure. The humanitarian public that emerged in the nineteenth century is still alive and even more aware and active in the 1990s and 2000s. Although it also is still susceptible to manipulation, in democratic states it has helped to create a near-consensus that, regardless of stipulations about sovereignty in international jurisprudence, sometimes 'use of force [is] the only means of ending atrocities on a massive scale'.[50] The normative status of intervention is now widely accepted, by both academics and practitioners, including both proponents and sceptics of its legitimacy,[51] and 'the emerging norm' that a right of 'military intervention [exists] as a last resort' was explicitly endorsed in 2004 in the report of the UN's 'High-Level Panel on Threats, Challenges and Change'.[52]

The history of the significance of humanitarian considerations in decisions to conduct military operations is an excellent example of the changing character of war, because that significance changed regularly over the last 450 years. From the sixteenth century, when the fragmenting of Christendom was triggered by the Reformation, creating governments that were ideologically in sympathy with oppressed people groups in other polities, until the early eighteenth century, it was widely (albeit by no means universally) accepted that sovereignty was not absolute—that there were certain behaviours, or at least certain circumstances (including some mandated by international instruments), which legitimately allowed intervention in a state's internal affairs by other states, or even called for intervention: the 'obligation of aid'. From 1648, this position on sovereignty existed in tension with (and was gradually eroded by) a different theoretical view of sovereignty, associated with the Treaties of Westphalia; yet for eighty or so years, in practice a right of intervention *in certain circumstances* was still permitted. In the second half of the eighteenth century, the absolute view of sovereignty held sway—that is, that state sovereignty was impermeable, allowing *no* legitimate interference or intervention, regardless of how a ruler or regime treated those they ruled; and this view was predominant for the first decade after the Congress of Vienna.

From the late 1820s until *circa* 1920, however, the pendulum swung back the other way. Indeed, by the 1870s, many statesmen and international lawyers were certain that a right of humanitarian intervention (as they termed it) did exist—though again, only in certain circumstances. This view existed, as in the century after Westphalia, in tension with other more absolute concepts of sovereignty, but certainly, in terms of what was practised, a norm of humanitarian intervention indubitably existed, and was increasingly favoured in international law. The Covenant of the League of Nations saw a shift away from the legitimacy of intervention, a shift apparently made definitive by the Charter of the United Nations in 1945, which inaugurated a forty-five-year period when a norm of non-intervention obtained. The last fifteen to twenty years have witnessed the re-emergence of a norm of humanitarian intervention. It is, however, as much debated as in the century after Westphalia and the century after Vienna.

The history of humanitarian intervention is important in and of itself, for there is little doubt that the question of how to prevent mass atrocities will continue to be a live issue in the international community. But it also has particular relevance when considering the degree of change in the character of war.

There is often an implicit assumption that, even if change is not inevitable, once it occurs, it *keeps* occurring: that progress is linear. Yet, while this chapter has told a story of change in the character of war, it casts doubt on whiggish or transhistorical understandings of military change. The history of humanitarian influences on war-making is not only historically contingent, it is also (to borrow the terminology of fluid dynamics) turbulent, as well as laminar, characterized 'by recirculation, eddies, and apparent randomness',[53] and it is not linear. Yet, nor is it cyclical, for, while the pendulum has swung, to a greater or lesser extent, between accepting and rejecting moral or humanitarian purposes for war, the concepts involved have evolved, so that, while the pendulum seems to have swung, or the wheel to have turned, actually it has not always been returning to the same position. To be sure, developments in the concept of state sovereignty seem to have been somewhat cyclical—even the recent concept of a 'responsibility to protect' is somewhat akin to the sixteenth-century 'obligation to aid' against tyranny. However, there were significant shifts over the 500-year period discussed in this chapter: in the people groups who were thought to deserve interventionist protection; in the rationale for protecting them; and in the rhetoric used both at home and abroad to justify the use of force to protect foreign peoples. All of these changed.

The concept of people deserving protection evolved: from confessional co-religionists, to all fellow Christians, to all human beings. The concept of what was illegitimate evolved: starting with 'tyranny' and religious persecution, it then encompassed slavery (which had been a staple of civilized commerce) and 'uncivilized' governance; then focused on war crimes, before expanding to crimes 'against humanity'. The concept of what international society ought to support and maintain evolved, too: from Christendom, to liberty, liberalism, and civilization, then ultimately to universal human rights. Thus, even while what we might term the moralist position on war was being alternatively sustained and undermined, legitimated and delegitimated, the nature of the moralist position was changing. But at particular moments, such as 1945 and *circa* 1990–5, radical change occurred. Thus, when it comes to morality and humanity as motivations for war, change sometimes was revolutionary as well as evolutionary.

In conclusion, then, states have often waged war for ethical and humanitarian reasons. The purpose of war has, over the centuries, included—and on the whole has *increasingly* included—overturning rampant tyranny and preventing mass atrocity. But while the international community increasingly favours the norm of humanitarian intervention, history suggests that this trend can be reversed. To understand where the norm came from and how it might fall into disfavour, historical contextualization is essential. To extrapolate from the particular case of humanitarian intervention to the general question of assessing whether the character of war is changing, disproportionate attention to recent and present changes may blind us not only to why they came about but also to how they might be undone.

## NOTES

1. The author thanks Brendan Simms, Adam Roberts, Kimberly Marten, Thomas Hippler, and Tarak Barkawi for insightful criticisms and suggestions.

   For the latter term, Gareth J. Evans, *The responsibility to protect: Ending mass atrocity crimes once and for all* (Washington, DC: Brookings Institution Press, 2008).

2. R. John Vincent, *Nonintervention and international order* (Princeton, NJ: Princeton University Press, 1974), 13; Adam Roberts, *Humanitarian action in war*, Adelphi Paper 305 (Oxford: Oxford University Press, 1996), 19; Eric Heinze, *Waging humanitarian war: The ethics, law, and politics of humanitarian intervention* (Albany: State

University of New York Press, 2009), 7; Davide Rodogno, 'The European powers' intervention in Ottoman Lebanon and Syria in 1860–61', in Brendan Simms and David J. B. Trim (eds.), *Humanitarian intervention—A history* (Cambridge: Cambridge University Press, 2011), Chapter 7.

3. Howard Adelman, 'The ethics of humanitarian intervention: The case of the Kurdish refugees', *Public Affairs Quarterly*, 6/1 (1992), 62;Heinze, *Waging Humanitarian War*, 8.

4. For example, Tony Blair, 'New generation draws the line', *Newsweek*, 133/16 (19 April 1999), 37; 'Doctrine of the international community', speech to the Economic Club of Chicago, 22 April 1999, at http://www.number10.gov.uk/ Page1297; Evans, *Responsibility to Protect*, 13–16; Michael Ignatieff, *Empire lite: Nation-building in Bosnia, Kosovo and Afghanistan* (London: Vintage, 2003), 57. Most recent works on humanitarian intervention only consider the second half of the twentieth century or focus totally on the 1990s and early 2000s.

5. See, for example, Richard Tuck, *The rights of war and peace: Political thought and the international order from Grotius to Kant* (Oxford: Oxford University Press, 1999), 55–7, 68–9; Heinze, *Waging humanitarian war*, 2. A study by the present author of Aquinas's writings and the use made of them by sixteenth-century commentators will appear in David J. B. Trim et al. (eds.), *Opposing tyranny and persecution in early modern Europe* (Woodbridge: Boydell, forthcoming).

6. Garrett Mattingly, *Renaissance diplomacy* (London: Jonathan Cape, 1955), 18–19; Tuck, *The rights of war and peace*, 28–30.

7. David J. B. Trim, '"If a prince use tyrannie towards his people": Interventions on behalf of foreign civilian populations in early-modern Europe', in Simms and Trim (eds.), *Humanitarian intervention*, Chapter 2.

8. Menna Prestwich, 'Calvinism in France 1555–1629', in Idem. (ed.), *International Calvinism 1541–1715* (Oxford: Clarendon Press, 1985), 91–2; Arlette Jouanna, *La France du XVIᵉ siècle 1483–1598*, 2nd ed. (Paris: Presses Universitaires de France, 1997), 471–3.

9. Quoted in Trim, 'Interventions in early-modern Europe'.

10. Quoted in A. J. Loomie, 'Philip II's armada proclamation of 1597', *Recusant History*, 12 (1974), 216, 221.

11. Randolphe Vigne, '"Avenge, o Lord, thy slaughtered saints": Cromwell's intervention on behalf of the Vaudois', *Proceedings of the Huguenot Society of Great Britain*, 24 (1983–8), 10–25.

12. Samuel Morland, *The history of the evangelical churches of the valleys of piemont*, (1658), A2v, A3r; Thomas Birch (ed.), *A collection of the state papers of John Thurloe* (London: 1742), IV, 18. See Trim, 'Interventions in early-modern Europe'.

13. Francisco de Vitoria, 'On the American Indians', 3.5, in Anthony Pagden and Jeremy Lawrence (eds.), *Political writings* (Cambridge: Cambridge University Press, 1991), 287–8.

14. See de Vitoria, Ibid., and 'On dietary laws', 1.4–6 and 'On the law of war', 1.3, *Political writings*, 224–6, 303; Domingo de Soto, quoted in Tuck, *The rights of peace and war*, 75.

15. 'Stephanus Junius Brutus', *Vindiciae, contra tyranos* [1579], ed. and trans. George Garnett (Cambridge: Cambridge University Press, 1994), 155, 183.

16. *A short apologie for christian souldiours* [pt 4 of *Vindiciae contra tyrannos*] (London, 1588), sigs. B6r-v; *Vindiciae*, trans. Garnett, 183; Theodore Beza, 'On the right of magistrates', in Julian H. Franklin (ed. and trans.), *Constitutionalism and resistance in the sixteenth century: Three treatises by Hotman, Beza, and Mornay* (New York: Pegasus, 1969), 130.

17. *A short apologie for christian souldiours*, sigs. B6v-B7r (emphasis supplied); anon. (trans.), *Vindiciae, contra tyranos* (London: 1689), 163 (cf. 127, discussing how a tyrant 'ought' to be resisted).

18. *Oxford English Dictionary* (2nd ed.), *s.v.* 'ought', *v.*, II, 6, 7a.

19. *The responsibility to protect: Report of the International Commission on Intervention and State Sovereignty* (Ottawa: International Development Research Centre, 2001); see, for example, Evans, *Responsibility to protect*; Richard H. Cooper and Juliette V. Kohler (eds.), *Responsibility to protect: The global moral compact for the 21st Century* (New York: Macmillan, 2009).

20. For example, Kalevi J. Holsti, *Peace and war: Armed conflicts and international order 1648–1989* (Cambridge: Cambridge University Press, 1991), 35; J. Bryan Hehir 'Intervention: From theories to cases', *Ethics & International Affairs*, 9 (1995), 2, 4; Paul Hirst, *War and power in the 21st century: The state, military conflict and the international system* (Cambridge: Polity, 2001), 57.

21. Andrew Thompson, 'The protestant interest and the history of humanitarian intervention, *c.*1685–*c.*1750', in Simms and Trim (eds.), *Humanitarian intervention*, Chapter 3.

22. Randolphe Vigne, 'Richard Hill and the saving of liberty of conscience for the Vaudois', in Richard Bonney and David J. B. Trim (eds.), *The development of pluralism in modern Britain and France* (Oxford and Bern: Peter Lang, 2007), 163.

23. Thompson, 'Protestant interest'.

24. J. A. S. Grenville, *Europe reshaped 1848–1878*, 2nd ed. (Oxford: Blackwell, 2000), 171; Brendan Simms, '"A false principle in the law of nations". State sovereignty, [German] liberty, and intervention in the age of Westphalia and Burke', in Simms and Trim (eds.), *Humanitarian intervention*, Chapter 4.

25. Benno Teschke, *The myth of 1648: Class, geopolitics, and the making of modern international relations* (London & New York: Verso, 2003), 3 *et passim*; cf. Stéphane Beaulac, *The power of language in the making of international law* (Leiden: Martinus Nijhoff, 2004), 70 *et passim*. See also Stephen Krasner, 'Rethinking the sovereign state model', *Review of International Studies*, 27/1 (2001), 17–42; Simms, 'State sovereignty, liberty, and intervention'.

26. J. P. A. Bew, '"From an umpire to a competitor": Castlereagh, Canning and the issue of international intervention in the wake of the Napoleonic Wars', in Simms and Trim (eds.), *Humanitarian intervention*, Chapter 5.

27. For example, Matthias Schulz, 'Did norms matter in nineteenth-century international relations?', in Holger Afflerbach and David Stevenson (eds.), *An improbable war: The outbreak of World War I, and European political culture before 1914* (New York & Oxford: Berghahn), 43–60, esp. 45–7.

28. Quoted in Richard B. Lillich, 'Forcible self-help under international law', *Naval War College Review*, 22/6 (1970), 61; cf. R. John Vincent, 'Grotius, human rights, and intervention', in Hedley Bull, Benedict Kingsbury, and Adam Roberts (eds.),

*Hugo Grotius and international relations* (Oxford: Oxford University Press, 1990), 255.

29. Quoted in Bew, 'Castlereagh, Canning and international intervention'.
30. Gary J. Bass, *Freedom's battle: The origins of humanitarian intervention* (New York: Alfred Knopf, 2008).
31. Natalino Ronzitti, *Rescuing nationals abroad through military coercion and intervention on grounds of humanity* (Dordrecht: Martinus Nijhoff, 1985), 90; Bass, *Freedom's battle*, 49ff; Bew, 'Castlereagh, Canning and international intervention'.
32. Quoted in Rodogno, 'European intervention in Lebanon and Syria'.
33. Bass, *Freedom's battle*; Matthias Schulz, 'The guarantees of humanity: The concert of Europe and the origins of the Russo-Ottoman War of 1877'; and Davide Rodogno, 'The European powers' intervention in Macedonia, 1903–1908', in Simms and Trim (eds.), *Humanitarian intervention*, Chapters 8–9.
34. Even scholars sceptical about the extent to which these interventions were humanitarian concede this point: see Thomas Franck and Nigel S. Rodley, 'After Bangladesh: The law of humanitarian intervention by military force', *American Journal of International Law*, 67 (1973), 280–3; J. A. Joyce, *The new politics of human rights* (London & Basingstoke: Macmillan, 1978), 21–3; cf. François Rigaux, '"Humanitarian" intervention: The Near East from Gladstone to Rambouillet', paper read at the International School on Disarmament and Research on Conflicts, 15th Winter Course (Andalo, 2002): http://www.isodarco.it/courses/andalo02/paper/andalo02-rigaux1.html
35. Maeve Ryan, 'The price of legitimacy in humanitarian intervention: Britain, the European powers and the abolition of the West African slave trade, 1807–1867', in Simms and Trim (eds.), *Humanitarian intervention*, Chapter 10.
36. William Mulligan, 'British anti-slave trade and anti-slavery policy in East Africa, Arabia, and Turkey in the late nineteenth century', in Simms and Trim (eds.), *Humanitarian intervention*, Chapter 11.
37. Quoted in Mike Sewell, 'American intervention in Cuba, 1898–99', in Simms and Trim (eds.), *Humanitarian intervention*, Chapter 13.
38. Sewell, 'American Intervention in Cuba'.
39. *Encyclopedia of nineteenth-century land warfare* (New York: W. W. Norton & Co., 2001), 57; Jan Nederveen Pieterse, *White on black: Images of Africa and blacks in western popular culture* (New Haven, CT & London: Yale University Press, 1992), 80, 82.
40. Ronzitti, *Rescuing nationals abroad*, 89.
41. Joyce, *New politics*, 23.
42. Charter of the United Nations, arts. 2(4), 2(7).
43. S. Neil MacFarlane, *Intervention in contemporary world politics*, Adelphi Paper 350 (Oxford: Oxford University Press, 2002), 19; Adam Roberts, 'Humanitarian war: Military intervention and human rights', *International Affairs*, 69 (1993), 433.
44. Hedley Bull, *The anarchical society: A study of order in world politics* [1977], 3rd ed. (New York: Columbia University Press, 2002), 210–11; Anthony Payne, Paul Sutton, and Tony Thorndike, *Grenada: Revolution and invasion* (Sydney: Croom Helm, 1984), 207.

45. Bull, *The anarchical society*, 212.
46. Quoted in Franck and Rodley, 'After Bangladesh', 288.
47. Quoted in Sophie Quinn-Judge, 'Fraternal aid, self-defense, or self-interest? Vietnam's intervention in Cambodia (1978–1989)', in Simms and Trim (eds.), *Humanitarian intervention*, Chapter 15.
48. On humanitarian crises and interventions, 1945–90, see esp. Nicholas J. Wheeler, *Saving strangers: Humanitarian intervention in international society* (Oxford: Oxford University Press, 2000); see also Samantha Power, 'A problem from hell': *America and the age of genocide* (New York: Basic Books, 2002); Patricia Marchak, *No easy fix: Global responses to internal wars and crimes against humanity* (Montreal & Kingston: McGill-Queen's University Press, 2008).
49. See Roberts, 'Humanitarian war', esp. 433–6.
50. Wheeler, *Saving strangers*, 295.
51. For example, Gareth Evans, address to Community Legal Centres and Lawyers for Human Rights, Sydney, 28 August 2007, text at http://www.crisisgroup.org/home/index.cfm?id=5036&l=1; MacFarlane, *Intervention in contemporary world politics*, 19.
52. *A more secure world: Our shared responsibility* (New York: United Nations Department of Public Information, 2004), 66 (pt 3, para. 203).
53. http://en.wikipedia.org/wiki/Fluid_dynamics

# 9

# Democracy and War in the Strategic Thought of Giulio Douhet

*Thomas Hippler*

## INTRODUCTION

From the point of view of the fashionable theory of democratic peace, war and democracy seem to be irreconcilable concepts.[1] Although the theory of 'democratic peace' has been widely discussed in recent years, one facet of the issue has rarely been addressed: both concepts—democracy and peace—intrinsically link descriptive and normative aspects, and both are values in the Nietzschean sense. Moreover, as political values, democracy and peace have acquired the status of a 'historical a priori' in our understanding of politics. This might seem today to be self-evident. But from a historical perspective it is clearly a situated assumption: not all societies have considered democracy and peace to be fundamental values, even in very recent times. Arguably only since the end of the Second World War have democracy and war definitely consolidated their status, and even today peace and democracy are challenged by terrorist movements all over the world. The purpose of this chapter is to suggest some links between two different sorts of historical change: on the one hand, the development of the aircraft was primarily a technological change that had implications in the strategic realm; on the other, this technological change was inseparable from a normative change. This normative change can be understood as a clash between the traditional norm of non-combatant immunity and that of democracy as a growing value in international affairs. It permitted the bombing of cities to be seen as a legitimate option in modern war. This chapter is thus a contribution to the genealogy of the democratic peace theory.

During the European Enlightenment, the link between democracy (or rather republicanism) and peace was constructed on the basis of two developments: first, the ancient definitions of peace with respect to order and justice, which are religiously grounded, lost their impact with the religious reforms and, second, the consolidation of modern territorial states helped define war as a state activity. This conjunction led to the Enlightenment ideas of republicanism and peace, which present themselves as intrinsically secular but have nevertheless a visible religious subtext. It should also be remembered that the civic republican tradition, to which the democratic tradition is clearly a successor, certainly could have a pacifistic stance but did not necessarily do so; on the contrary, it was explicitly bellicose in many cases.[2] As such, it explicitly praised war and the experience of combat as a necessary means to forge civic coherence. Moreover, until the twentieth century, a strong counter-revolutionary tradition argued that democracy led inevitably to despotism, conflict, and finally to (civil) war: if democracy stems from revolution, that is, violent uprising against constituted authority, the idea that democracy should lead to peace seems obviously to be flawed. What is at issue here are questions of definition, of the origin of democracy, and of its relation to liberalism.

The problematic link between democracy and war involved two facets: an active and a passive side. First, the massive active involvement of the people in the nation's war effort was contemporary with the French Revolution and thus with one of the essential historic turning points towards the development of a democratic statecraft. Since the time of classical republicanism, military service has been conceived of as a civic duty and an expression of political and civic rights. If we accept Max Weber's definition of the state as the monopoly of legitimate violence,[3] this link between military service and citizenship becomes clear: the basic component of the state, that is, the monopoly of legitimate violence, is exercised by the sovereign people. Republican political theory has thus been constantly keen to construct a link between military service and political liberty.[4] Compulsory conscription, on the other hand, implies another aspect that is difficult to reconcile with democratic citizenship, since life in barracks and the relation of command to obedience clearly involve facets that are in flagrant contradiction with the values of a liberal-democratic polity. Conscription 'incorporates some of a liberal-democratic society's most precious values and some values utterly repugnant to it'.[5] While doing military service some of the conscript's fundamental rights are restricted; military education aims at developing a respect for authority and hierarchical subordination through an institutionalized social discipline.[6] This active involvement of the population in the war effort, however, had a counterpart. While becoming an essential actor of war, the population also becomes one of its principal targets. From the principal actor of war, *le peuple* became its main victim. This paper will insist on this second facet of the link between democracy and war but the overall question obviously remains: how are these two facets connected?

The civic and civil participation of the population in the war effort of the nation state is intimately linked to the democratization of war and, as such, it has been a step towards total war. Military historian Stig Förster uses four criteria to define total war: total goals, total methods, total mobilization, and total control. The civil population is implicated twice over in total war as both actors and victims.[7] However, a fifth element should be added to Förster's list. Ludendorff, who is one of the fathers of the concept of total war, insisted in the very first chapter of his book *Der totale Krieg* that total war had a higher 'ethical value' than a limited war.[8] The justification of a war, in other words, becomes independent of the classical criteria of *in bello* limitations with regard to the means employed. On the contrary, the existential goal of the war not only dismisses all limitations on warfare but even becomes the decisive criterion for the justice of war. For advocates of total war like Ludendorff, a total war is *ipso facto* a just war: it is just because it is total and total because it is just.

Undeniably, the classical idea of limited just war, which respects the distinction between combatants and the civil population, has been seriously at odds with the emergence of popular mass armies since the French Revolution. During the era of absolute monarchies the case was clear: war was fought between sovereigns and their agents, while the remainder of the population enjoyed non-combatant immunity.[9] But since armies have become popular and national, the belligerent parties can no longer be seen as the agents of the sovereign. The national army of a popular state is nothing other than the will of the sovereign people.[10] There is a relation between the totality of war and something that can be labelled popular sovereignty, and that relationship comes very close to the concept of democracy.

In line with this thinking, the German air-power historian Horst Boog stated that the British doctrine of morale bombing was indebted to the 'democratic' concept of all power stemming from the people.[11] If the strategic goal of morale bombing is—according to Trenchard's words—'to induce the enemy government, by popular pressure, to sue for peace',[12] it is not clear whether this is because one supposes that the government will be sympathetic to the population's wishes, or whether it will react out of fear of a revolution, or if it will have been removed from power by revolution. And the air-power strategists presumably were not clear about this either. The idea was just that a properly 'influenced' public opinion would bring about the political decision to sue for peace. The conceptual problem seems to be that we lack a useful descriptive tool that allows us to conceive of the different forms by which the people are politically integrated, whether we are speaking of parliamentary, democratic, revolutionary, totalitarian, or other forms of political integration.

## DEMOCRACY, WAR, AND GUILIO DOUHET'S AIR POWER THEORY

This chapter follows the link between the changing character of war during the early twentieth century and the growing importance of democracy as a political value during the same period with a focus that may seem surprising:

the development of the strategic doctrines of Giulio Douhet. Douhet's strategic concepts address some of the key questions posed by the advent of mechanized mass warfare in the era of the First World War. The concomitant evolutions in our political and normative perceptions remain highly topical today, in particular in regard to the relationship between war, the nation, and democracy. Douhet is best known as the first comprehensive strategist of airpower as well as its ruthless apologist. His book *The command of the air*[13] had a considerable audience and was devoured by airpower enthusiasts virtually all over the world. As the first person to have developed a coherent doctrine of strategic airpower, Douhet has been a constant reference in all subsequent efforts to think about strategic bombing. However, his life and thought have received remarkably little scholarly attention. Apart from a few articles in English, the only serious study is Azar Gat's recent *Fascist and liberal visions of war*, which dedicates a chapter to 'The sources of Douhetism'.[14] However, Gat's reading of Douhet as an inherently fascist writer misses the point: Douhet's political commitment on the side of Italian fascism is not sufficient to explain the strategic options he came to advocate. The real problem is the fact that Douhet, in his early writings about air power, adopted a viewpoint that seems to be radically opposed to anything that later came to be identified as 'Douhetism', that is, the ruthless bombing, with explosives, incendiary ammunition, and gas, of the urban populations and industrial centres of the enemy nation.

Little known is the fact that Douhet started his career as an airpower thinker with a strictly pacifistic outlook. Douhet's writings of 1910 and 1911 are very explicit in this respect. Douhet declared categorically that 'we must not even consider action against defenceless cities. It would be an act of such barbarism that the conscience of the entire civilised world would revolt, and it would cause more damage to those who committed the act than to those who suffered it.'[15] But there is more: Douhet declared himself to be in favour of an international convention to outlaw air warfare. It was the right moment to do so, since military aviation was in the early stages of its creation: 'Is it necessary to fight in the air as well? No. The land and the sea offer a sufficiently ample field for our wretched rivalries. . . . It is simply a matter of maintaining the "status quo," agreeing with one another to keep the air neutral by preventing the use of aircraft in war through an international agreement.'[16]

In 1910–11, when Douhet published his first articles on air warfare under the title *Le possibilità dell'aeronavigazione* (*Possibilities of air navigation*), aviation was undergoing rapid technological development and was thus of potential use to the military. Douhet used these articles to deplore the fact that there was no coherent military doctrine for these new developments.[17] What Douhet essentially did in these articles was to apply Mahan's theories to the newly conquered field of the air in order to provide concepts for the military employment of aircraft. These early articles constantly compared the new air strategy, yet to be developed, to naval strategy. The command of the air is thus the primary objective for air forces and a necessary prerequisite for all secondary actions in the same way in which Mahan conceived of the command of the sea. In just the same way in which Mahan's doctrine of naval warfare stemmed from his conception of sea power, Douhet's doctrine of air warfare was the direct consequence of the axiom of *dominio dell'aria* (command of the air): in order to gain the control of the air it was necessary first to defeat the enemy air fleet. This, however, could only be done within the specific element in which the new devices operated, that is, in the air. As a consequence, Douhet was one of the first to insist on the importance of the war *in* the air, and he was furiously opposed to ideas that would advocate the war *from* the air. Since 'no bombardment has ever proved decisive except against cowardly people', 'the dropping of bombs on a city from a dirigible would be a useless and savage act'. More precisely, since the shelling of open cities would be useless, it would also be barbarism:

> The killing of a couple of hundred citizens and the ruin of a few hovels cannot influence the outcome of a modern war, and so the act is useless. If the war is then lost, damages for the bombardment will have to be paid, so the act is doubly useless, and all evil which is done uselessly is savage, even if in times of war and with the consent of the Hague [Convention].

Accordingly 'the conscience of mankind in my century shows me that there are methods which cannot be honestly used even in war'.[18] In his lectures at the Popular University of Turin in 1914–15 on the art of war, which he published in 1915, Douhet expanded similar views. In the chapter on aeronautics, he stated that 'naturally the offensive action of aeroplanes must not be directed against cities but should be aimed against the entire enemy army and its rear.[19] One can find similar claims in Douhet's writings until the spring of 1915.

On 3 July 1915, however, he wrote a memorandum from Edolo, arguing for the construction of a fleet of heavy bombing planes. He began his text with a reference to two significant influences: H.G. Wells' idea of building an offensive air fleet and the incursion of a German plane over France. A couple of months later, on 20 November 1915, another memorandum was even more categorical. He now declared himself openly in favour of strategic bombing against urban centres.[20] How did Douhet move so quickly from one opinion to its exact opposite?

## THE NATIONALIZATION OF WAR

Perhaps the most important theme in this respect, and the one on which Douhet insisted on several occasions, is the nationalization of war. Modern wars were no longer fought any more between enemy armies, but between enemy nations. Armies were but the manifestations of national forces.

This principle had a whole series of consequences. Military strength was understood as no more than the product of the underlying and more fundamental strength of a nation.[21] But what was the strength of a nation? In Douhet's thinking the force of nations had two facets: industrial power, and political, social, and moral coherence.

This association between the economy and more narrowly political elements is obviously problematical and leads directly to some core issues in the political theory of liberalism as elaborated since the eighteenth century. More particularly, it bears resemblance to the meaning of the nation as expressed in Adam Smith's *The wealth of nations*, or to Sieyès's definition of the third estate as 'the nation', since both thinkers closely linked the economic sphere to some underlying form of social coherence. When the concept came to be assimilated to a common ethnic descent at the turn of the eighteenth and nineteenth centuries, this meaning of 'nation' was partially replaced by derivative concepts like Adam Ferguson's 'civil society' or Hegel's *bürgerliche Gesellschaft*. At the same time, however, military thinkers like Douhet also clearly adopted a 'nationalistic' or even racial outlook, with which the concept of nation had come to be assimilated during the nineteenth century.[22] Douhet's use of the concept of the nation was thus highly problematical, and he made no efforts to clarify its different meanings or otherwise to define what might link this 'nationalistic' understanding to the realm of the economy.

There are, however, a few indications concerning the nature of the 'national bond' in the sense of 'civil society'. For example, he declared, as early as 7 August 1914, that Germany and Austria–Hungary had made a fundamental mistake in not sufficiently taking into account the national character of the war.[23] Douhet's view that the Germany of 1914 was insufficiently 'nationalistic' clearly seems to presuppose a peculiar concept of the nation. And at this point another meaning of the word national clearly comes into play. Douhet was a military commentator who fully understood the importance of 'public opinion' in modern warfare: 'public opinion is the great check which imposes itself even on the most unstoppable demands of war; one of the greatest errors of Germany is that of refusing to accept this fact'.[24] It is, however, at this point that normative and descriptive claims seem to get intermingled.

In all his public comments in the opening months of the First World War, it is obvious that Douhet had clear-cut sympathies for the Entente (even if he explicitly denied any partisanship and described himself as an impartial observer[25]), and he constantly tried to justify this position, adopting the Western powers' collective image of themselves. In particular, this image conveys the idea of a fight for 'civilization'.

Douhet clearly hesitated between a concept of the nation as an entity whose unity has to be produced and reproduced by governmental action, and one of the nation as a 'civil society' that spontaneously produces consent and social coherence. Public discussion and free forms of consent that might derive from this were considered to be a more certain ground for national integration but, at the same time, discussion implied divergences of opinion that might also undermine the national unity that is critical for success in a national war. The nation, in other words, was conceived of as simultaneously a source of unity and of social destabilization. And this is precisely why the nation was not only the principal actor in a modern war but also its principal target: 'an army can be beaten, a capital seized, but a people cannot be destroyed while it still has faith and hope... [This war] will end with exhaustion, tiredness, with the rebellion of the people against a state of prolonged pain and excessive anguish.'[26] The 'hope and faith' of a people thus became factors which heavily influenced the outcome of a war and so it was necessary to enhance the moral resistance of the population by any means. Only these positive moral energies could possibly delay the inevitable social breakdown caused by either exhaustion or revolution. Hence the objective was to hold on longer than the enemy.

These considerations are the basis for Douhet's discussion of bombing raids carried out by the German navy on British coastal towns in late 1914. According to Douhet's analysis, the objective of the German high command was to carry out a 'moral counteroffensive'. These kinds of attacks—that bear some resemblance to the strategic outlook of the French *Jeune École*[27]—were obviously the opposite of the Mahanian strategic outlook to which Douhet unreservedly subscribed in these years: 'The chief objective of naval warfare is to defeat the enemy fleet; all the rest is secondary.'[28] But Douhet not only condemned these seaborne attacks as a strategic error that put at risk German ships: there were at least two other points where he criticized the Germans. Most importantly and most strikingly when compared with the positions he was to adopt a couple of years later, Douhet denied that missions which targeted the morale of the civil population could have any effect. On the contrary, 'England will feel the lash of these attacks and will stand tall beneath the blow.... Results will thus be negative [for Germany] with regards to England.' The only possible positive outcome for the Germans might be with regard to 'the moral effect produced domestically with respect to German national sentiment'.[29] Bombing raids on defenceless enemy towns, in other words, were but a 'public relations' campaign whose target was the attackers' own home front. As for the effect on public opinion within the enemy country, the effect was more likely to strengthen morale than to weaken it and to create a sentiment of solidarity with the victims and of hatred against the perpetrators. Public opinion had thus become a very important factor in modern national warfare, but it was not always easy to manipulate.

However, public opinion was not confined to national boundaries. Douhet revived the Enlightenment idea of a 'European civil society', with its own international mechanisms of public opinion. He did so by criticizing the 'Manifesto of the Ninety-Three', produced in September 1914 by a group of German scientists, scholars, and artists who expressed their support for the military actions carried out by German troops, and who denied that the military had committed atrocities against the civil population in Belgium. In an article entitled *La cultura* and published on 6 October 1914 in the *Gazzetta del popolo*, Douhet replied to these German intellectuals that 'the civil nations collectively make up public opinion, which sees with its own eyes and judges with its own mentality; they make a kind of public which judges more with sentiment than with cold logic'.[30]

Public opinion was thus intrinsically transnational, and this existing public opinion condemns the Germans' methods. Interestingly, however, Douhet had to add that this 'public'—which was also a sort of international 'court', invested with the actual power to decide what was just and unjust—judged more by sentiment than by logic. Should this not have induced him publicly to rectify the international public's judgement? However, this was not what he did: 'It is not only useless but dangerous to provoke unusual hostility within the enemy [nation], filling its mind with hatred; it is not only useless but dangerous to challenge public opinion and make oneself disliked by the whole world; and in war, one must damage the enemy, not oneself.'[31] Douhet actually criticized the Germans for committing a strategic error in underestimating the importance of international public opinion. He thus appeared to advocate a purely instrumental relationship with public opinion, according to which it is a factor to be taken into account, to be manipulated if necessary, or to be obeyed in other cases. However, Douhet does not seem to credit this international public opinion with any normative value per se: the normative implications of public opinion merited being taken into account since public opinion was a factor to be taken into account, but this did not necessarily mean that these normative claims were justified as such.

However, in other articles from the same period, Douhet seems to adhere to different positions in this respect. For instance in an article entitled *La più barbara guerra?* (The most barbarous war?) published on 20 August 1914, in which he talked once more about the German methods of conducting the war, Douhet wrote: 'The politics of strength are not always the best policy; for nations as for individuals it is not enough to be feared, one must also be loved. As well as fists, man has both a heart and a mind.... Violent and unjust action provokes a reaction which is the more violent for being right.'[32]

What we see here is an evident shift in meaning: from what was perceived as preferable by the hearts and minds of some, Douhet proceeds directly to what was just and unjust as such. The qualifications of just and unjust, in other words, no longer denoted a certain way of perception which had to be reckoned with, but acquired a normative value per se. This was an important shift, which Douhet introduced somewhat surreptitiously. But there was more. Surprisingly for a professional army officer, Douhet held the view that war as such is unnatural. He exposed this view in a quite straightforward way at the beginning of his lectures on the art of war, which he gave at the Popular University in Turin in

1914–15.[33] War was depicted as abnormal and as being in contrast with the distinctive feature of human life, which is to live peacefully in society. Moreover, war was depicted as being in contrast to humanity as such, even 'deforming the face of humankind'. It represented, so to speak, the radical evil in human nature, something in humankind that contradicted its very essence. It is also interesting to note that Douhet depicted this contradiction of humanity to itself as the result of its unfinished history, since humankind 'still has a long way to go in its development' and so human society is not yet perfect. This description seemed to presuppose the idea of a normal course to human history, which has yet to attain its true end.

But how was the end of this teleological process conceptualized? It is quite obvious that Douhet made use of what theorists of International Relations call the 'domestic analogy', that is, the analogy between the establishment of a political power in the domestic realm and the domain of international relations.[34] In the realm of international relations, humanity was at a lower stage than it was in the domestic realm: in the latter, there was a society with its laws and sanctions, and these coercive means had effectively succeeded in creating a sense of brotherhood among humans. Unfortunately, these means were lacking in the international realm and this was why nations were opposed to each other in their character, interests, and aspirations. It was, therefore, a sacred duty of humankind to work towards the improvement of humankind and—which was the same—of human society.

How was this to be achieved? The answer is unsurprising given the general framework of Douhet's reasoning. His positions can actually be labelled 'pacifist' not only at a metaphorical level but in the precise meaning of a particular strand of political thought. Peace, according to this political tradition, could only be guarded if supranational institutions were created and invested with the necessary power to coerce troublemakers on the international scene. Douhet developed this idea at some length in one of his last articles in the *Gazzetta del popolo* in March 1915, entitled *Incursione in Utopia* (Incursion to utopia): 'It is therefore necessary to introduce in the international setting the sanctions and the means of applying them which are already found within national boundaries'.[35] On the national level, no individual was allowed to administer justice on his own and this was what should be established at the international level too.


## DEMOCRACY, STRATEGIC BOMBING, AND THE CRIMINALIZATION OF WAR

The term 'justice' thus reappeared—however, not in a morally substantial sense, but in the sense of jurisdiction. No nation should be allowed to stand up for itself, just as citizens are not allowed to make their own justice. International justice should be delegated to the competence of an international court that would be able to decide upon disputed cases on the basis of an international Magna Carta:

> All nations should agree to respect both the Magna Carta and the sentences of the International Tribunal; this would require, naturally, the creation of a kind of international Gendarmerie to enforce such measures. This international gendarmerie would come to replace the current armies and navies.... The international tribunal should be staffed by the most illustrious men of all nations, and each nation would have a number of votes equal to that of its inhabitants since all men are equal in the world: and the deliberations of the sentences issued by this supreme Tribunal should be carried out, if necessary, through military means.... The coexistence of nations would lose its condition as an anarchic relationship and be replaced by civil cohabitation. There would be no more abuse of power or overbearing action, no more brutal use of force to suppress every right; no more war, just occasional brawls between police and wrongdoers.[36]

Douhet thus argued for the abolition of war by the establishment of an international power that would have armed forces at its disposal in order to be able to impose its decisions by force if necessary. He acknowledged quite straightforwardly that this settlement would transform war—that is a relationship between states—into some form of police action. This establishment of an international power would also transform the anarchic state of international affairs into civilized forms of commonwealth. It would transform the brutal use of force in war into a rightful use of force in police actions. At the same time, however, this international power and this international police force would radically transform the image of the enemy. In a traditional image of war—that can, broadly speaking, be dated to apply between the peace treaties of Westphalia in 1648 and the First World War—the enemy was considered as just if he fulfilled two characteristics: he had to be a legitimate power (the legitimacy *ad bellum*) and had to respect the fundamental laws *in bello*. Given these conditions the enemy was to be defeated but not to be subdued. He was considered precisely as an enemy and not as a criminal.

This characteristic of the enemy radically changed around the time of the First World War, and Douhet was indeed one of the thinkers in whom this transformation can be observed. The establishment of the international police force he advocated would transform the image of the enemy inasmuch as the latter was explicitly correlated with a criminal. War would no longer be a struggle between equally respectable adversaries, but would consist only of police actions against wrongdoers. The image of war, in other words, would become asymmetrical. Interestingly, however, this asymmetry of war was first and foremost a moral asymmetry, rather than an asymmetry in the realms of tactics or strategy.[37] The enemy was actively excluded from the symmetrical realm of norms and reduced to a mere criminal who should be dealt with by police forces.

It is striking that Douhet used here a whole series of key concepts of Enlightenment thought: civilized nations as a name given to European Christendom, public opinion, and public, civil commonwealth, and international courts. However, Douhet left somewhat implicit another key concept, that of justice. The attribute of justice is traditionally employed in order to distinguish a legitimate power to which obedience is due, from a usurpation that should be resisted. In this sense, the attribute of justice is integral to and part of the very definition of peace, inasmuch as it distinguishes true peace from mere oppression, that is from a situation in which the forces of resistance are just held down. Augustine thus defined peace as 'tranquillity of order', while order was defined as the 'disposition of beings according to their place'.[38] Peace was thus defined in relation to the concepts of order and of justice. This is why Augustine distinguished 'just peace' from 'unjust peace': the latter designated a region of reality that does not correspond to the norms of the just order in general. Aquinas was even more explicit in affirming that only a peace that corresponded to the norms of justice merited the name of true peace, to be distinguished from 'apparent peace'.[39] Obviously, this attribute of justice was another name for the Christian character of peace, and 'true peace' only applied within the *Res publica Christiana*. Accordingly, the Reformation had radically transformed the conceptual framework of peace, since the meaning of notions such as justice and Christendom was no longer unequivocal.[40] The development of absolutist states in Europe with their effective capacity to monopolize violence and thus to put an end to the religious civil wars was a further step in this direction: from now on, state power tended to be defined without reference to the attribute of justice. What mattered was the capacity to assure material security, and this end was achieved through the monopolization of the means of violence and the setting up of systems of jurisdiction. Citizens were thus deprived of the means of making justice for themselves, and given in return the possibility of obtaining justice through law courts. However, during the Enlightenment, the reference to justice reappeared in the discourses on peace, but on a different level from before.[41] Within the framework of medieval political theology, justice was conceived of as emanating from God. In modern discourses justice appears on the contrary as an eminently human characteristic. Justice now signifies institutional and political frameworks, which are fully human.

In Douhet's reasoning, the attribute of justice reappeared in his distinction between different forms of social discipline.[42] It is, in other words, inherent in different forms of government and distinguishes—to use Kant's famous definition—forms in which human beings are counted as such, as against others in which they are mere instruments in the hands of others. According to Kant's concept, such a state would be a republic[43] and there were arguably elements of such republicanism in Douhet too. This became clear in his idea of the citizen's individual responsibility for a political decision, according to a concept that was to be labelled popular sovereignty.

In the articles on the first months of the First World War published in the *Gazzetta del popolo*, Douhet still held the traditional Jominian viewpoint that the only objective of military operations was the organized forces of the adversary. However, in contrast to earlier statements, in an article published on 8 September 1914 he significantly qualified this assertion: 'It is now a fundamental rule of war that the chief objective of an army must be the adversary's army; any other objectives cannot be other than of secondary importance.'[44] Interestingly, he did not affirm that civil populations were to be immune; he just stated that the main objective was the organized forces and the remainder was of secondary importance. The following day, however, on 9 September 1914, he discussed, in another article entitled *Militarismo*, the statement made by a high-ranking British official according to which 'the present war is a war of liberty against German imperial militarism'. Douhet justified this assertion, with reference to the domestic analogy once again:

> The man who arms himself to violate the rights of another commits a criminal action: just as criminal is the nation which arms itself in order to impose its will on the nations among which it lives. Militarism, so conceived, is a barbarous and incivil thing, which drags people backwards through the centuries; it is repugnant to an advanced man and . . . revolts every feeling of balance and justice. In today's civil society man has no further need to use force and violence in order to live and progress.[45]

If there was no need any more to use force in international affairs, there was accordingly no justification for it either. However, when advocating the establishment of some kind of international association according to models that would later give rise to the League of Nations, Douhet used the argument that the existence of such an international court with its own means of coercion would render superfluous the need of nations to defend their own rights by force. In other words, he seemed to presuppose the actual existence of the kind of international association he was advocating. The ambivalence actually lay in the fact that some mechanisms of international integration were said already to be in existence, without, however, possessing a proper institutional form.[46] Humankind was thus said to have become effectively united by mechanisms of cultural and economic integration, and by the improvement of the means of transportation. Among the latter, Douhet explicitly cited the development of aircraft as a means that contributed to peace and civilization. As a result, frontiers between the different countries were but an anachronism that would soon disappear in favour of a world state.

But there was more. His article *Militarismo* went on: 'Against this militarism, synonymous with international banditry, not only should the world rise up in protest but also the population of the country which has created it: no one should be complicit in a criminal act.'[47] The Central Powers were accused of militarism, which Douhet defined as 'international banditry'. He explicitly criminalized the latter and considered it a misdemeanour against which the whole world should stand up. More than criminalization, this argument involved moral annihilation. In conformity with the enlightened universalism that informed Douhet's whole discourse, this pinnacle also applied to the citizens of the enemy nation individually: each person who did not stand up against his or her own government and its war effort was individually guilty. Obviously, this whole argument would be inconceivable if it were not set within a conceptual framework of popular sovereignty: citizens could only be held individually responsible for the actions taken by their governments if they were effectively able to influence their political decisions and it seems to be clear that Douhet indeed adhered to such a vision.[48] Taken together these theoretical elements—the pacifistic claims for the establishment of an international power that should have armed forces at its disposal, the reference to justice and lawfulness in the international realm, the allegation of moral asymmetry, and the assumption of popular sovereignty—seem utterly to contradict any interpretation of Douhet in terms of his fascist commitment only. On the contrary and quite paradoxically, his position seems to have endorsed some key elements of democratic pacifism. All these arguments converged logically in a proposal Douhet made in a paper written in November 1917 with the title *Sottomarini ed aeroplani* (Submarines and aeroplanes). After having explained that aeroplanes would soon have the capacity to destroy any large city in a single night, he concluded that this would produce 'an intolerable state, a total absence of security', and thus 'the absolute necessity of finding an effective means to render war impossible, since it is impossible that humankind should have to remain always threatened by such a nightmare'.[49] As a solution to this task of abolishing war, Douhet repeated his proposal for an international court, which would represent 'a true international parliament, a real Parliament of all Humankind, which could quickly take truly humane action'. However, this parliament of humanity would have no practical value if it had no means of coercion at its disposal. And in 1917, Douhet suggested that the necessary international gendarmerie could consist of—an international air force. It is at this point that the early pacifistic Douhet touched the later ruthless Douhet. And both shared the assumption that strikes from the air were justified. This international air force would be capable of carrying out 'punitive expeditions' against any country that might violate the international order.[50] A legacy of this idea can be found in article 45 of the UN Charter, which states that 'in order to enable the United Nations to take urgent military measures, Members shall hold immediately available national air-force contingents for combined international enforcement action'.[51]

It is precisely in this sense that Douhet's 'democratic pacifism' also contained some of the theory's most dangerous shortcomings. In particular, this specific kind of pacifism allowed him morally to disavow not only the political system of the enemy but also to hold responsible each individual citizen for the mischief of those in power. It was obviously a small step from denying the legitimacy of the enemy to justifying an actual attack on them. Douhet's strategic concepts thus contained much more than a simple advocacy of ruthless strategic bombing. The evolution of his thought clearly showed that he made use of the concept of democracy in order to deconstruct earlier norms of legitimacy, in particular non-combatant immunity. And it is precisely in this sense that Douhet is arguably still highly topical: while 'Douhetism' is largely disavowed today, the conceptual ground on which Douhetism came to be legitimized enjoys a higher prestige than ever before.

## NOTES

1. I would like to thank Hew Strachan and Adam Roberts for their valuable comments on earlier versions of this chapter. Many thanks also to Vanda Wilcox who translated the quotations by Douhet into English. This chapter contains arguments that are further developed in a forthcoming book on Douhet within the context of the strategic debates in Italy during the first third of the twentieth century.
2. R. Claire Snyder, *Citizen-soldiers and manly warriors: Military service and gender in the civic republic tradition* (Lanham, MD: Rowman & Littlefield, 1999).
3. Max Weber, *Economy and society: An outline of interpretative sociology* (New York: Bedminster Press, 1968), 56, 65.
4. Quentin Skinner, *The foundations of modern political thought*, volume I: *The Renaissance* (Cambridge: Cambridge University Press, 1978), 76f., 129–31, 150f., 173–5.
5. Eliot A. Cohen, *Citizens and soldiers: The dilemmas of military service* (Ithaca, NY: Cornell University Press, 1985), 35.
6. This was the starting point of my *Citizens, soldiers, and national armies: Military service in France and Germany, 1789–1830* (London: Routledge, 2007).
7. Stig Förster, 'Das Zeitalter des totalen Krieges, 1861–1945. Konzeptuelle Überlegungen für einen historischen Strukturvergleich', *Mittelweg 36*, 8/6 (1999), 12–29.
8. Erich Ludendorff, *Der totale Krieg* (Remscheid: Deutscher Militär Verlag, 1988), 6.
9. Martin van Creveld, *The transformation of war* (New York: Free Press, 1991), 41.
10. Hippler, *Citizens, soldiers, and national armies*.
11. Horst Boog, 'Der strategische Bombenkrieg. Luftwaffe, Royal Air Force und US Army Air Force im Vergleich bis 1945', *Militärgeschichte*, 2/2 (1992), 26.
12. Hugh Trenchard, Memorandum for the record [1923], Trenchard Papers, RAF Hendon, England, File CII/19/1, cited in Philip Meilinger, 'Trenchard, Slesssor, and

Royal Air Force Doctrine before World War II', in Idem. (ed.), *The paths of heaven: The evolution of air power theory* (Alabama: Air University Press, 1997), 52f.

13. Two Italian editions were published during Douhet's lifetime, the first in 1921 and an augmented second edition in 1926. The best Italian edition is Giulio Douhet, *Il dominio dell'aria e altri scritti*, edited by Luciano Bozzo (Rome: Aeronautica Militare – Ufficio Storico, 2002). The English edition, Giulio Douhet, *The command of the air*, translated by Dino Ferrari (Washington, DC: Air Force History and Museums Program, 1998), can also be found at http://www.airforcehistory.hq. af.mil/Publications/Annotations/douhetcommand.htm. However, the translation is not satisfactory, since it tries to amend Douhet's text, adding 'explanations' and sometimes omitting passages without informing the reader.

14. Azar Gat, *A history of military thought from the Enlightenment to the Cold War* (Oxford: Oxford University Press, 2001).

15. Giulio Douhet, 'Le possibilità dell'aereonavigazione', *Rivista militare italiana* 7 (1910): 1303–19, reprinted in Douhet, *Scritti 1901–1915*, edited by Andrea Curami and Giorgio Rochat (Rome: Ufficio Storico Stato Maggiore dell'Aeronautica, 1993), 102.

16. Giulio Douhet, 'La limitazione degli armamenti navali e la costituzione delle flotte aeree', *Il giornale d'Italia* (20 August 1910), reprinted in Douhet, *Scritti 1901–1915*, 106.

17. Douhet, 'Le possibilità dell'aereonavigazione', 96.

18. Giulio Douhet, 'Quasi per fatto personale', *La Preparazione*, 8–9 July 1911, reprinted in Douhet, *Scritti 1901–1915*, 206–7.

19. Giulio Douhet, *L'arte della guerra, Raccolta di sei confereze tenute all'Università Popolare Torino 1914–15* (Turin: S. Lattes & C., 1915), 133f.

20. 'Impressioni e vedute del colonnello cav. Giulio Douhet sull'aviazione militare italiana'. The text is published as an appendix to Antonio Pelliccia's *Nessuno è profeta in patria: Riflessioni sulla dottrina del Dominio dell'Aria* (Genoa and Rome: SIAG, 1981), 105–13.

21. See Giulio Douhet, 'La forza della nazione', *La Gazzetta del popolo*, 24 February 1915, reprinted in Douhet, *Scritti 1901–1915*, 477–8.

22. Giulio Douhet, 'La grande guerra', *La Gazzetta del popolo*, 7 August 1914, reprinted in Ibid., 326. See also the article 'Lotta di razze', *La Gazzetta del popolo*, 26 August 1914, reprinted in Ibid., 337f.

23. In *La grande guerra* (326), Douhet argues that the German and Austrian way of waging war is 'too narrowly strategical', which meant that the Central Powers did not sufficiently take into account the fact that war occurred between nations and no longer between armies.

24. Giulio Douhet, 'La vana minaccia', *Gazzetta del popolo*, 25 February 1915, reprinted in Douhet, *Scritti 1901–1915*, 479.

25. Giulio Douhet, 'Germanofobia?', *Gazzetta del Popolo*, 2 February 1915, reprinted in Ibid., 463–5.

26. Giulio Douhet, 'La grande guerra', 326.

27. On the strategic thinking of the *Jeune École*, Theodore Ropp, *The development of a modern navy: French naval policy 1871–1904* (Annapolis, MD: Naval Institute Press, 1987), in particular chapters 10 and 15.

28. Giulio Douhet, 'Controffensiva morale', *Gazzetta del popolo*, 16 December 1914, reprinted in Douhet, *Scritti 1901–1915*, 433.

29. Ibid.

30. Giulio Douhet, 'La cultura', *Gazzetta del popolo*, 6 October 1914, reprinted in Ibid., 384.

31. Ibid., 385.

32. Giulio Douhet, 'La più barbara guerra?', *Gazzetta del popolo*, 20 August 1914, reprinted in Ibid., 331f.

33. Giulio Douhet, *L'arte della guerra*, 4f.

34. On the 'domestic analogy', see Chiara Bottici, *Uomini e stati: percorsi di un'analogia* (Pisa: ETS, 2004).

35. Giulio Douhet, Incursione in Utopia, *Gazzetta del Popolo*, 5 March 1915, reprinted in Douhet, *Scritti 1901–191*, 491.

36. Ibid., 492.

37. On the problem of moral asymmetry, see David Rodin and Henry Shue (eds.), *Just and unjust warriors: The moral and legal status of soldiers* (Oxford: Oxford University Press, 2008).

38. 'pax omnium rerum tranquillitas ordinis. Ordo est parium dispariumque rerum sua cuique loca tribuens dispositio', Augustine, *City of God*, 13.

39. 'Si enim concordet com alio non spontanea volutate, sed quasi coactus timore alicuius mali imminentis, talis concordia non est vera pax.' Aquinas, *Summa theologiae*, 2,2, qu. 29, article 2.

40. See article 'Friede' by Wilhelm Janssen in Otto Brunner, Werner Conze and Reinhart Koselleck (eds.), *Historische Grundbegriffe: Historisches Lexikon zur politisch-sozialen Sprache in Deutschland*, volume II (Stuttgart: Cotta, 1975), 543–91.

41. See Reinhart Koselleck, *Critique and crisis: Enlightenment and the pathogenesis of modern society* (Oxford: Berg, 1988); and Thomas Hippler, 'La "paix perpétuelle" et l'Europe dans le discours des Lumières', *European Review of History – Revue Européenne d'Histoire*, 9/2 (2000), 167–82.

42. See Giulio Douhet, 'Disciplina', *La gazzetta del popolo*, 19 September 1914, reprinted in Douhet, *Scritti 1901–1915*, 369.

43. Immanuel Kant, *Political Writings*, edited by Hans Reiss (Cambridge: Cambridge Univerisity Press, 1991), 94f. and 99.

44. Giulio Douhet, 'Non disprezzare l'avversario', *Gazzetta del popolo*, 8 September 1914, reprinted in Douhet, *Scritti 1901–1915*, 354f.

45. Giulio Douhet, 'Militarismo', *Gazzetta del popolo*, 9 September 1914, reprinted in Ibid., 357.

46. Giulio Douhet, 'Il perché', *Gazetta del popolo*, 18 October 1914, reprinted in Ibid., 391.

47. Douhet, 'Militarismo', 358.

48. Another example of a quite straightforward expression of the doctrine of popular sovereignty in this series of articles is the following: 'The Central Powers lost the war at the Battle of the Marne.... After this battle the supreme interest of Germany should have led its government to seek peace, because from that moment onwards peace has grown ever more costly.' Douhet, 'La locomotiva ed il rullo', *Gazzetta del popolo*, 20 March 1915, reprinted in Douhet, *Scritti*

*1901–1915*, 497f. According to this viewpoint, the decision whether or not to sue for peace depends ultimately on the population and the pressure it is able to exercise upon the government.

49. Giulio Douhet, 'Sottomarini ed aeroplani', in Douhet, *Scritti inediti*, edited by Antonio Monti (Firenze: Scuola di Guerra Aerea, 1951), 169.
50. Ibid., 170f.
51. Thanks to Adam Roberts, who drew my attention to this article of the Charter. On the idea of setting up an international air force as gendarmerie of the League of Nations, see Roger Beaumont, *Right backed by might: The international air force concept* (Westport and London: Praeger, 2001).

# 10

## Religion in the War on Terror

### *Alia Brahimi*

This is a war which, like previous wars, is reviving the Crusades. Richard the Lionheart, Barbarossa from Germany, and Louis from France—the case is similar today, when they all immediately went forward the day Bush lifted the cross. The Crusader nations went forward.

Osama bin Laden, 21 October 2001

The basic proposition for our adversaries—and we ought to take a minute and focus on it—they . . . want to re-create the old caliphate that stretched from Spain all the way around to Southeast Asia.

Richard Cheney, 10 September 2006

### INTRODUCTION

The historical record testifies to the moral dangers of intermingling God and war. The combination evokes the barbarism of the Crusades, the ruthless Islamic wars of conquest, and the campaigns of extermination against the non-Jewish tribes of Transjordan. As wars are fought for religious causes, enemies are demonized, restraint is abandoned, war is total, and the stakes become zero-sum. Yet, it is important to remember that out of the religious precepts of the Christian, Islamic, and Jewish civilizations, the traditions of just warfare sprang forth, connecting the justness of war to moral imperatives concerning the human race.[1] Indeed, the just war is defined against pacifism on one end of the spectrum, and holy war on the other.

Although the Western just war tradition has been significantly secularized in recent times, as moral philosophy and international law have engaged with its central tenets, it is worth bearing in mind that the just war idea was introduced by St Augustine, who invoked the Biblical values of peace, justice, and the protection of innocents, and it owed its continuation to such theologians as Aquinas, Gratian, Suarez, Vitoria, and Ramsey, among others. In Islam, even as the early wars of expansion were taking place with a perceived divine mandate, specific Quranic injunctions combined with the faith's humanistic dimensions to give rise to a series of restrictions on *jihad*, with the classical jurists arguing for a legal obligation to respect the rights of non-Muslims in war, civilians and combatants alike. In the Torah, the seminal passage in Deuteronomy which calls for a war of extermination against the non-Jewish inhabitants of Palestine simultaneously sets forth a catalogue of restraints for 'normal' warfare which formed an important basis for Jewish thinking on the laws of war. The legacy of religion and war, then, is not only the holy war but also the just war.

Moreover, in the west, as in Islamic and Jewish contexts, religious leaders and thinkers continue to play central roles in reaffirming restraint in war. Just as Muslim scholars invoke the *sharia* to condemn '*jihadi*' terrorism and the Chief Rabbis of Israel raise their voices against militant Judaism of the type which gave rise to the 1994 Hebron massacre, so church leaders have been at the forefront in denouncing the barbarism of the Lord's Resistance Army in Africa. Religion, then, can serve to limit war just as it can broaden war and make it more zealous.

Given the historical and conceptual enormity of the topic, religion and war, it is incumbent upon this chapter to drastically narrow its scope. It will take as its focus the role of religion in the 'war on terror' and, in turn, limit its attention to the just cause for resorting to war. With al-Qaeda's attacks upon the United States on 9/11 and the Bush administration's subsequent invasion of Iraq, the world was confronted by a situation in which both sides claimed to be acting in self-defence. This phenomenon will be explained with the following argument: each side employed an expansive conception of self-defence that was ultimately informed by broadly religious factors. In justifying the invasion of Iraq, George W. Bush repeatedly appealed to an overarching moral cause, involving 'good' versus 'evil' and the bestowing of 'freedom's blessings' upon an oppressed people, which became the dominant justification for the US adventure in the absence of proof of weapons of mass destruction (WMD) and of Baathist links with al-Qaeda. This heavily value-laden formulation of just cause represented a shift away from the established understanding of self-defence as responding to an (actual or imminent) act of aggression. Similarly, Osama bin Laden's case for a defensive war against the United States was ultimately reliant upon religious difference to establish the prior occurrence of an American act of aggression.

This paper additionally seeks to suggest that while religion was used, on both sides, in service of an expansive and more permissive conceptualization of just cause for war, so too was religion mobilized in opposition to such expansionism, as religious figures in the west and in Islam re-articulated the proper, and more limited, boundaries of the legitimate right of self-defence.

The backlash against Bush and bin Laden's attempts at change (or rather, reversion to long-ago discredited views of just cause) is unsurprising. Those who attempt change, for a mainstream audience at least, must invoke and operate within a pre-existing normative framework. As Quentin Skinner pointed out, 'an ideologist changes one part of an ideology by holding another part fast; by appealing to and so reinforcing convention'.[2] Yet convention is jealously guarded, and those who seek to tweak it and simultaneously speak for it will be challenged with its full weight.

This chapter will first examine the Bush administration's just cause for the invasion of Iraq and then turn to al-Qaeda's attacks against America on 9/11.

## THE BUSH ADMINISTRATION AND THE IRAQ WAR

'Goddamn, what the fuck are they talking about?'[3] Such was the reaction of General Tommy Franks, the Commander in Chief of United States Central Command, to the Bush administration's request for a detailed war plan for Iraq. Indeed, the announcement of Iraq as a choice of target in the 'war on terror' was met with scepticism and incredulity worldwide. But for the Bush administration, the Iraq war was an 'essential step' in its 'war on terror', which had been initiated after al-Qaeda attacked the United States on 11 September 2001.

The just cause of the war on terror was double-pronged: it involved safe-guarding national security as well as a value-laden contest between ways of life. It was both 'the security challenge and the moral mission of our time'.[4] Indeed, Bush was clear that 'we fight not to impose our will but to defend ourselves and extend the blessings of freedom'.[5] This 'defend and extend' justification was manifested in the Iraq war with reference to three phenomena. These three phenomena, in turn, underpinned the case for a pre-emptive attack on Iraq.

In the first place, the allegation that Saddam Hussein was illegally stock-piling WMD was pivotal to justifications for the war along the conventional lines of self-defence. The existence of WMD allowed for the depiction of the war's objective as 'the end of terrible threats to the civilised world'.[6] The Bush administration put forward a sophisticated case that rendered the Iraqi stock-pile both knowable and unknowable simultaneously. Among other things, detailed catalogues of lethal materials were listed, allusions were made to a range of deadly diseases, references were made to jets with modified aerial fuel tanks, and five different methods of enriching uranium for a nuclear bomb were mentioned.[7] That Iraq was actively developing such dangerous programmes was said to be beyond doubt (by Cheney on 27 August 2002, by Powell on 5 February 2003, and by Bush on 17 March 2003). Yet this certainty was coupled with a subtle case for the inherent mysteriousness of the stockpile. The Baathist regime was alleged to be 'moving'[8] its arsenal, 'tunnel[ling] underground',[9] and generally 'housecleaning'[10] in order to evade UN inspectors. The secretive, impenetrable nature of the regime was also offered up as a reason for the intangibility of the illicit weapons programme, and it was argued that 'the first time we can be completely certain he has nuclear weapons is when, God forbid, he uses one' (Bush, 12 September 2002). This tacit admission that complete certainty had not yet been attained jars with the 'no doubt' claims that hurried the path to war. But this seeming contradiction appears to have worked well in both heightening the perception of danger and lessening the burden of proof.

Secondly, a connection between Saddam Hussein and the perpetrators of the 9/11 attacks was established in three ways. In the first place, Iraq was said to be a material 'ally of al-Qaeda'.[11] It was repeatedly charged that there existed a 'sinister nexus between Iraq and the al-Qaeda terrorist network',[12] that Saddam had 'an established relationship with al-Qaeda',[13] and that 'the passing of Saddam Hussein will deprive terrorist networks of a wealthy patron that pays for terrorist training'.[14] Dick Cheney was particularly vocal on this issue, insisting that Saddam had supplied al-Qaeda with training in biological and chemical weaponry.[15] Second, there was an implied ideological affinity. According to Bush, there is such a thing as an 'ideology of terror',[16] and it was suggested that the Baath party and the al-Qaeda network shared it: 'our principles and security are challenged today by outlaw groups and regimes that accept no law of morality and have no limit on their violent ambitions'.[17] As a result, rogue regimes and their terrorist 'allies' constituted an 'axis of evil'. Finally, it was suggested that Saddam and his cronies were themselves 'terrorists'. The administration often referred to 'the terror regime in Iraq',[18] which evoked a tacit affiliation between the way in which a dictator 'terrorizes' his own population and the very different phenomenon of international terrorism. Rumsfeld exemplified this well when he spoke of 'the tyranny of terrorism'.[19] Wolfowitz too took to describing Iraq's alleged WMD stockpile as 'weapons of mass terror' and 'an arsenal of terror'.[20] Indeed, Bush was remarkably candid about this obfuscation when he explained to the Australian Prime Minister, John Howard, that 'every speech I give I remind them of the atrocities of the [Iraqi] regime just to make the point that they acted like terrorists'.[21]

The third strand of the Bush administration's case for war against Iraq was the nature of the regime. Saddam Hussein's dictatorship and sometime appalling human rights record were used to accentuate his 'evil'. He was dubbed 'a student of Stalin'[22] and UN reports were invoked to chronicle his grave human rights abuses. Iraq as a target was consistent with the ideological objectives of the war on terror, which involved extending freedom's 'blessings'. In the absence of ongoing or imminent mass slaughter—which could trigger a right of 'humanitarian intervention' possibly sanctioned under Chapter VII of the UN Charter—Saddam's 'police state' and the climate of political repression in Iraq were crucial to the ideological packaging of the US invasion. The war was said to transcend power politics and national interest: 'America's cause is right and just: liberty for an oppressed people and security for the American people.'[23]

We have broken down the Bush administration's presentation of just cause into the three factors of WMD, the al-Qaeda connection, and the nature of the Iraqi regime. In the absence of proof of WMD and/or a connection between Saddam Hussein and al-Qaeda, the third feature of the just cause was increasingly pointed to as the dominant justification for the US-led invasion. As early as September 2003, Bush admitted that Saddam Hussein was not linked to the 9/11 attacks,[24] and by the time of the State of the Union Address in 2005 the usual references to Iraq's alleged WMD capacity were dropped, with significant efforts devoted to lauding Iraqi elections. In his final speech as president, Bush summarized the venture in Iraq as the transformation 'from a brutal dictatorship to an Arab democracy'.[25] This remains an uncomfortable development for the British, who had originally treated regime change in Iraq as epiphenomenal—an unintended but positive outcome of disarming Iraq.[26] For the Bush administration, on the other hand, it formed a markedly more robust part of a case for war which subtly moved beyond established understandings of self-defence.

Warring to install democracy was, and continues to be, treated with moral scepticism. Such an enterprise shifts away from the more restrictive understanding of just cause as limited to self-defence and draws upon the larger conception of the just war as the preservation and protection of value—for St Augustine and, more recently, Paul Ramsey, fundamental to the just war was the protection of innocents. Such a moral goal is said to be universalizable. For the Bush administration, and 'neo-conservatives' more generally, the 'cause of liberty' is depicted as an equally fundamental moral goal: 'we serve the cause of liberty, and that is always and everywhere a cause worth serving'.[27] Buttressing this claim is the belief that 'the values we call Western are indeed universal'.[28] However, the ideals of 'liberty' and 'freedom' as realized by liberal-democratic political systems are not as obviously basic as the protection of innocent life and other core just war values, which have prompted and shaped the norm of humanitarian intervention. The 'freedom' to which Bush so often appeals can conceivably be realized in a number of varying ways. Bin Laden himself has offered such an argument, declaring that al-Qaeda fights 'because we are free men who cannot acquiesce in injustice'.[29] But the legitimacy of Bush's value-laden agenda was merely assumed—he did not offer a full account of why 'freedom' in the form of *democratization* might be as obvious a just cause for war as protecting the inalienable right to life threatened by such occurrences as aggressive war or genocide. Certainly, many would maintain that 'democracy' itself is not a universal human right.[30]

However, in frequently describing liberty as 'God's gift', Bush himself implied that religion was a part of the picture. He emphasized—indeed, campaigned heavily upon—his personal religiosity, and he was widely believed to have become a 'born again' Christian at the age of 40. Thus, when five days after 9/11 he referred to the war on terror as a 'Crusade',[31] commentators began to conjecture that Bush's faith would shape his administration's response to the attacks (foremost among these was bin Laden himself, who noted that 'Bush has said in his own words "crusade attack". The odd thing about this is that he has taken the words right out of our mouth'[32]). A few weeks later, it was reported that Bush and UK Prime Minister Tony Blair had prayed together at a meeting during which the invasion of Iraq was agreed. Shortly before the war, Bush confirmed to the journalist Bob Woodward that, instead of tapping the expertise of his father, former president George H. W. Bush, who had fought the 1991 Gulf War against Saddam Hussein, he sought the counsel of God: 'You know, he is the wrong father to appeal to in terms of strength. There is a higher father I appeal to.'[33] Likewise, at a prayer meeting on the eve of war he explained his conviction that America could not fail because 'behind all of life and all of history, there's a dedication and purpose, set by the hand of a just and faithful God'.[34] The theory that Bush was motivated by a religious agenda—which, at best, would amount to paternalism and, at worst, to some form of Crusade—was given renewed momentum when, four months into the Iraq war, it was alleged that Bush admitted to a delegation of Palestinians that God had told him, 'George, go and end the tyranny in Iraq.'[35]

Whether religion played a causal role in the decision to go to war with Iraq or not, it seems likely that Bush's faith supported an expansive understanding of just cause that was heavily value-laden, Manichean even: 'the choice here is stark and simple: The Bible says "I have set before you life and death; therefore choose life"'.[36] Indeed, though members of the Bush administration took great care to maintain that theirs was not a war against Islam, the ideological motif of the war on terror—a narrative about 'good versus evil'—had decidedly religious overtones: 'We are in a conflict between good and evil and America will call evil by its name.'[37] By postulating the existence of an 'axis of evil' and deeming that 'evil is real and it must be opposed',[38] Bush's stark, biblical terminology evoked a moral battle between the forces of darkness and light. A graphic choice was presented between 'a world at peace and a world of chaos'.[39] 'Freedom and fear' were 'at war'—'they have always been'—but the president was confident that 'God is not neutral between them'.[40] Like 'the terrorists', the Baathist regime was said to be evil. Upon describing Saddam's torture chambers, Bush reasoned that 'if this is not evil, then evil has no meaning'.[41]

The classic expression of the just cause involved one or more of three conditions: defence against an armed attack, recovery of something wrongly taken, or the punishment of evildoers. In justifying this last condition, Aquinas quoted Romans 13:4: '[the soldier] beareth not the sword in vain, for he is God's minister, an avenger to execute wrath upon him that doth evil'.[42] However, the condition worried the likes of Suarez and Vitoria and, in their efforts to counter holy war thinking and stamp out the Crusade, they maintained that 'a war was just only if waged to correct some perfectly definite wrong'.[43] The idea was to insist upon a conception of just cause objective and precise enough to be adjudicated in a law court, which evolved into the twentieth century push to limit all justified war to defence against aggression. The two remaining conditions have been subsumed under the predominating right of self-defence, such that it is wrongly seized territory which is recovered and aggression which is punished. The Bush administration's statements, on the other hand, appeared to revive the classical version of punishing evildoers and, in turn, implied that military action could serve the will of God.

Thus, Bush's expansive interpretation of just cause involved the mobilization of values such as 'freedom' and 'democracy' as part of a Manichean worldview. This conception challenged the prevailing understanding of just cause which limited war to responding to a specific act of aggression, that is, a more objectively determinable *casus belli*. Of course, Bush tried to make this case with the WMD argument and the postulation of a Saddam-al-Qaeda axis, but both claims were doubted before the war and disproved after it. This left the administration with its value-laden agenda of democratization and fighting evil, which many had conjectured was both steeped in religion and the primary driver of the war all along: ' . . . you got to understand, this decision is not like all of a sudden there's a threat to Kuwait. And boom. This is part of a larger obligation that came to be on September the 11th, 2001. This is part of a large and a different kind of war.'[44]

The role of religion was not confined to the ideological packaging of the just cause, however. Lee Marsden has argued that certain sectors of 'the Christian Right' in America saw the Iraq war as an unmissable opportunity to evangelize in the region. Glenn Miller, for example, upheld that the purpose of the war was to break the stranglehold of 'the lying and masquerading Islamic Allah, the demon prince',[45] and by 2004 there were thirty evangelistic missions operating in Iraq. Evangelical Christians also gained ground in the highest levels of the military—for example, General Jerry Boykin, who was in charge of the manhunt for Saddam and bin Laden, believed that Satan was trying to 'destroy us as a Christian Army'—and they also wielded greater influence in the Pentagon, where they were actively proselytizing. Moreover, evangelists took over 50 per cent of the military chaplaincy posts. While this development is in no way objectionable in itself, it becomes relevant because, as Marsden bluntly puts it, 'the combination of intense patriotism, American exceptionalism and born-again Christianity is hardly conducive to cultural sensitivity and respect for faiths which [soldiers] are taught to regard as inferior, false or satanic'.[46]

Indeed, one of most controversial elements of the Bush administration's conduct in the 'war on terror', its detention policy at Guantanamo Bay, suggested that some form of demonization was at work. The images which emerged from the detention facility, of manacled men kept indefinitely in cages on the presumption that they were guilty of terrorism, corroborated this impression. Further, it was reported that Islamic practices were both mocked and weaponized, with allegations ranging from forced nudity[47] to flushing the Koran down the toilet[48] to smearing detainees with the menstrual blood of prostitutes during interrogation[49] to the words 'Fuck Islam' scrawled above the latrines.[50] I have argued elsewhere[51] that the abrogation of the Geneva Convention protections was ultimately justified with reference to the virtues of the Bush administration's overarching just cause. However, the just war's two regimes of justice are supposed to apply separately, as a bulwark against the demonization of the enemy characteristic of holy wars. In any case, the Geneva Conventions were deemed to be applicable in Iraq, yet the horrendous photographs documenting abuse at Abu Ghraib prison—including naked prisoners handcuffed and piled into a human pyramid, along with allegations of brutal beatings, rape, torture, sodomy, and homicide[52]—can be viewed as indicators that the enemy had been systematically demonized.

However, if religious factors underpinned the Iraq war and other controversial policies in the war on terror, they also played an enormous part in the denunciation of those policies. A series of important Christian voices, including that of the Papacy, joined the (more secular) legal and political opposition to the invasion of Iraq. One commentator described 'an ocean of faith-based opposition to the Bush-Cheney-Rumsfeld plans for war on Iraq'.[53] Some religious proponents of the war notwithstanding,[54] the just war tradition was cited by religious leaders, time and time again, against the invasion. Just as the criteria of right authority, right intention, goal of peace, proportionality, last resort, and reasonable hope of success were invoked to cast doubt on the legitimacy of an invasion of Iraq, *jus in bello* principles were appealed to in order to undermine the Bush administration's conduct during the invasion and its detention policy at Guantanamo Bay. Most significantly for our purposes, a great many religious commentators and church leaders made clear that the Bush administration did not possess a just cause for war in Iraq—scepticism was consistently registered with regard to intelligence about WMD and Saddam's connection with al-Qaeda, and Bush's appeal to the doctrine of pre-emption was repeatedly rejected. On the whole, the notion that the threat from Saddam Hussein was imminent enough to legitimize a defensive war was shunned. The US Conference of Catholic Bishops concluded that 'based on the facts that are known to us, we continue to find it difficult to justify the resort to war against Iraq, lacking clear and adequate evidence of an imminent attack of a grave nature',[55] and Bush's own United Methodist Church wrote to the White House urging 'extreme caution in launching an unprovoked attack'.[56] While the New Zealand Council of Churches 'state[d] unequivocally: pre-emptive war is not a just war',[57] the Federation of Swiss Protestant Churches made clear that it did 'not consider the imminent threat to be of the required precondition to start a preventive war'.[58]

John C. Ford wrote in 1945 that 'the practically unanimous view of American Catholicism, including that of the hierarchy, is that we are fighting a just war at present'.[59] By contrast, in 2003, the National Catholic Weekly concluded that 'with the exception of some Southern Baptist leaders and mega-church pastors, nearly all US churches are opposing war with Iraq'.[60] In the end, even religious readers of the just war tradition reaffirmed the more modern and limited conception of the just cause as self-defence against aggression, despite Bush's appeal to a larger moral cause and his quasi-Biblical assertion that 'good' was confronting 'evil'. A collection of Filipino bishops went so far as to turn Bush's Manichean narrative on its head: 'those who speak of *war* speak evil, and those who advocate aggression promote wickedness and impiety'.[61] In this way, just as religion was used in the service of an expansive reading of the just war tradition, so it was mobilized to contract it.


## AL-QAEDA'S WAR AGAINST THE UNITED STATES AND ITS ALLIES

Osama bin Laden is all too often depicted as a fundamentalist and a Salafist attempting to revive the expansionary *jihad* of the classical era. However, whatever his ultimate ambitions, his statements explaining the case for war against America are thoroughly modern—that is, they rely for the most part on the idea of resisting unprovoked aggression. Indeed, bin Laden is quite clear that 'he who commences hostilities is the unjust one'.[62] Under pressure from an Al-Jazeera journalist, he wondered: 'what is wrong with resisting those who attack you? All religious communities have such a principle, for example these Buddhists, both the North Koreans and the Vietnamese who fought America. This is a legal right... this is reassurance that we are fighting for the sake of God.'[63] Thus, al-Qaeda's leaders persistently fashion their case for war using the language of self-defence.

Bin Laden maintained that 'we ourselves are the victims of murders and massacres. We are only defending ourselves against the United States'.[64] In a letter addressed to the American public he stated plainly that 'as for the question why are we fighting and opposing you, the answer is very simple: because you attacked us and continue to attack us'.[65] Similarly, Zawahiri gave a message to the American people in the run-up to the 2004 US Presidential elections: 'Elect whoever you want, Bush, Kerry or Satan himself. We don't care. We only care about purifying our country of the aggressors and resisting anyone who attacks us.'[66]

At various junctures, al-Qaeda's ideologists have recognized that this strategy is most in tune with Muslim opinion. In a 2005 letter to Abu Musab al-Zarqawi, in which the zealous Jordanian was asked to desist from his campaign of savagery in Iraq, Zawahiri cautioned that 'the Muslims masses—for many reasons, and this is not the place to discuss it—do not rally except against an outside occupying enemy, especially if that enemy is firstly Jewish and secondly American. . . . The sectarian factor is secondary in importance to outside aggression.'[67] More recently, Abu Hazam al-Salafi has penned a pamphlet complaining that the very same Islamic scholars who are willing to support Hamas' resistance in Gaza are foremost among those issuing *fatwas* against al-Qaeda's *jihad*.[68]

Al-Qaeda's leaders also emphasized that their 'defensive *jihad* against the American enemy'[69] was perfectly in line with Islamic teaching. Zawahiri explained that 'resistance is a duty imposed by the *sharia*'[70] and bin Laden stressed that 'the highest priority after faith is to repel the invading enemy'.[71] He was careful to underline that his command to 'kill the Americans and their allies—civilian and military' is 'in accordance with the word of God Almighty: fight the idolaters at any time if they first fight you'.[72] Indeed, bin Laden compared members of the American administration directly to the Mongols,[73] who ran roughshod over the Islamic empire in the thirteenth century, and made a cross-traditional appeal to the Hitler case, exclaiming suddenly in an interview: 'did not the Europeans resist the German occupation in World War Two'?[74]

In this way, the notion of merely *responding* to the use of armed force ('reacting in kind'[75]) serves to define al-Qaeda's just cause very narrowly. With this argument, bin Laden invoked the principle of reciprocity. He stated clearly that 'the road to safety begins with the cessations of hostilities and reciprocal treatment is a part of justice'.[76] That is, because the United States is 'attacking' the Muslims, the Muslims have a right to respond: 'it is well known that every action has a reaction. If the American presence continues, and that is an action, then it is natural for reactions to continue against this presence.'[77] This appeal to reciprocity allowed bin Laden to emphasize that al-Qaeda were not the aggressors, because 'what is happening in occupied Palestine, and what happened on September 11 and March 11 are your goods returned to you. It is well known that security is a vital necessity for every human being. We will not let you monopolise it for yourselves.'[78] Contained within this argument, therefore, are the conditions for the cessation of hostilities—to wit, stop attacking us and we will stop attacking you. Bin Laden observes that 'whichever state does not encroach upon our security thereby ensures its own'.[79] The resort to war is a paradigmatic case of self-defence, 'a very simple equation that any American child could understand: live and let others live'.[80]

However, given that America had not launched any invasion of bin Laden's country before 11 September, be it Saudi Arabia, Sudan, or Afghanistan, the theory of bin Laden's defensive war did not sit easily with the reality of the international situation. As a result, it was incumbent upon bin Laden to qualify 'aggression' in two critical ways.

Firstly, he employed an expansive conception of the territorial entity that was being defended against attack. To that end, he drew upon the universalism of the Islamic message to demarcate the relevant unit: the global community of Muslims. Bin Laden told the International Conference of Deobandis in April 2001 that 'I write these lines to you at a time when every single inch of our *umma*'s body is being stabbed by a spear, struck by a sword, or pierced by an arrow'.[81] The attacks on 9/11 were depicted as 'merely a response to the continuous injustices inflicted upon our sons in Palestine, Iraq, Somalia, Southern Sudan, and places like Kashmir'.[82] Indeed, bin Laden's list is sprawling. In his 'Declaration of *Jihad*' against America in 1996, he makes the point that Muslim blood is regarded as cheap by referring to a series of 'massacres' in Lebanon, Tajikistan, Burma, Kashmir, Assam, the Philippines, Fatani, Ogaden, Somalia, Eritrea, Chechnya, and Bosnia-Herzegovina. In 2001, he reiterates that 'every day, from east to west, our *umma* of 1200 million Muslims is being slaughtered in Palestine, in Iraq,[83] in Somalia, Western Sudan, Kashmir, the Philippines, Bosnia, Chechnya, and Assam'.[84] Thus, in attempting to construct his just cause as narrow (that is to say, defence against aggression), bin Laden falls back on broader ideas about religious difference. In conceptualizing the 'self' that has been attacked, bin Laden employs a religious demarcation: the entire Islamic *umma*.

Secondly, bin Laden must resort to religious idioms when defining the US's aggressive actions. His main bone of contention is with 'the invasion by the American and western Crusader forces of the Arabian peninsula and Saudi Arabia, the home of the noble Ka'ba'.[85] He speaks repeatedly of 'this barefaced occupation',[86] but, since US troops were not occupying Saudi Arabia and instead kept a military presence there on the invitation of the regime, he must explain their aggression religiously: 'the Noble sanctuary is attacked and the direction of prayer for 1200 million Muslims is attacked'.[87] Thus, the US 'attack' is ultimately figurative, for 'the sacred symbols have been looted'[88] and the Holy territories are 'defiled'[89] as American troops roam the lands which are 'the cornerstone of the Islamic world, place of revelation, source of the Prophetic mission and home of the Noble Ka'ba'.[90]

The 'occupation' of Saudi Arabia is not limited, however, to the Christian military presence in the lands of Islam. Though he favours religious imagery, bin Laden also refers to the United States' support for the Saudi monarchy and its regional policies: 'America has occupied the holiest parts of the Islamic lands, the Arabian peninsula, plundering its wealth, dictating to its leaders, humiliating its people, terrorising its neighbours and turning its bases there into a spearhead with which to fight the neighbouring Muslims'.[91] Further, it has been considered that bin Laden must additionally cite a slew of other 'Islamic' causes to bolster his claim of outright aggression. The most cogent of bin Laden's examples is the case of Palestine, where his argument is again imbued with religious terminology. He frequently speaks of striving to 'liberate the al-Aqsa mosque'[92] and makes reference to America 'helping Israel build new settlements in the point of departure for our Prophet's midnight journey to the seven heavens'.[93] In fact, because of the Israeli–Palestinian conflict, and the US' support for Israel, bin Laden can posit the existence of a 'Zionist-Crusader alliance'[94] and 'a neo-Crusader-Jewish campaign'.[95]

The weakness of bin Laden's argument is crudely apparent when he lists the aforementioned massacres in the 'Declaration of *Jihad*' and must conclude, with a relatively anti-climactic flourish, that the United States 'has prevented the dispossessed from arming themselves'. In order to gloss over the fact that no flagrant aggression has been committed (arguably, at least, until the 2003 invasion of Iraq), he resorts to rhetorical flourishes that emphasize the religiosity of the Americans: 'the evident Crusader hatred in this campaign against Islam';[96] 'the Crusader hordes that have spread like locusts';[97] 'the Romans [that] have gathered under the banner of the cross to fight the nation of beloved Mohammad'.[98]

Bin Laden sought to maintain that it was the enemy, the 'global Crusader', that was inherently and ineluctably aggressive:

> Bush admitted that there can only be two kinds of people.... So the world today is split into two parts, as Bush said 'either you are with us or you are with terrorism'. Either you are with the Crusade or you are with Islam. Bush's image today is of him being in the front of the line, yelling and carrying the big cross.[99]

Suleiman Abu Ghaith echoed this when he observed 'they have announced explicitly that this is a Crusader war so the banner is clear and henceforth there is only the trench of faith or the trench of unbelief.[100] Bin Laden was insistent that America 'carries the unspeakable Crusader hatred for Islam'[101]—thus, 'this third world war was started by the Crusader-Zionist coalition against the Islamic nation'.[102] Because the United States instigated a religious war against the Muslims, they are obliged to defend themselves.

His confessed hatred for Americans, Jews, and Christians notwithstanding, bin Laden wanted to maintain that his was a straightforward defensive war against a Crusading enemy that any reasonable external observer would regard as justified. However, we have seen that religious difference played an important role in bin Laden's case for war in ways more complex than simply pointing to a Christian invader. In the end, he enlisted religious criteria to demarcate the 'self' that was being attacked as well as the actions which constituted an invasion. This broadened the scope of 'aggression' and thus 'self-defence'. Prior to the war on Iraq in 2003, bin Laden had little to work with in suggesting that the United States had launched an unprovoked assault. By throwing together a host of international injustices framed in Islamic terms, bin Laden avoided having to pin down any single act of aggression and could instead claim that there was an overall war against Islam.

Unfortunately for bin Laden, a series of other Muslims did not agree that any such campaign had been started by the United States. The 9/11 attacks were passionately denounced by Muslim leaders, intellectuals, and religious figures, who invoked the Islamic *jihad* tradition to dispute al-Qaeda's proper authority to declare *jihad*, its claim of last resort, the prospects for the jihad's success, and, perhaps most vociferously, to register their horror at the mass targeting of civilians. The just cause, too, was repeatedly rejected—bin Laden's argument that the United States had already launched an attack was shunned and the hijackers were regarded as the aggressors.

To Yusuf al-Qaradawi's mind, bin Laden was 'the aggressor'.[103] A well-known advocate of suicide bombing in the Palestinian territories, Qaradawi drew a firm distinction, commenting that 'the difference is huge. What happens in Palestine is self-defence. But in 9/11 they were not fighting an invasion.'[104] The Palestinian Islamist group Hamas similarly undercut the linchpin of bin Laden's case by distancing itself from al-Qaeda, and the Grand Mufti of Jerusalem indicated that bombings were not acceptable outside Israel.[105] In Egypt, the Grand Imam of al-Azhar, Mohammad Tantawi, described 9/11 as 'an abominable aggression'. He stated that the attacks were 'an inhuman crime that no religion, law, or sound mind approves, because they constitute an aggression against male and female and Muslim and Christian civilians who have nothing to do with wars'.[106] Egyptian Mufti Nasr Farid Wasel declared that 'Islam and Muslims do not approve of the September 11 aggression on the United States',[107] and a group of Arab NGOs also referred to the assaults on New York and Washington as an 'aggressive attack against American civilians'.[108] A statement released by the Lebanese Shia group Hizballah similarly deemed the perpetrators to have 'committed aggression and terrorism',[109] while Saudi Arabia's leading Wahabi cleric decreed that 'those who kill non-Muslims with whom Muslims have treaties will never see paradise'.[110]

In the days after 9/11, two hugely influential clerics associated with both Sunni and Shia radicalism each suggested bin Laden might be 'tried by an Islamic court consisting of Muslim *ulema*' for the war he waged upon America.[111] Thus, bin Laden's arguments for self-defence ultimately relied upon ideas of religious warfare that were unacceptably broad to the minds of others within the Islamic tradition. Though artful, the expansive conceptualizations of 'self' and 'attack' did not amount to a convincing case for the resort to war, and a host of Muslim leaders asserted anew the more modern and limited conception of the just cause as defence in the face of aggression. Of course, this re-establishment of the legitimacy of defensive war became highly problematic for the Bush administration as it launched the first strike against Iraq in 2003.

## CONCLUSION

Each side in the 'war on terror' denounced the other for waging a war of religion, yet they themselves invoked religious factors in making their cases for allegedly defensive wars. This chapter has also sought to demonstrate, albeit briefly, that religion was as much relevant to the narrowing as to the widening of the just cause; to reasserting the limits of the right of self-defence as to attempts to define that right more broadly. In terms of the larger theme of this volume, religion was, in a sense, indeterminate: it was as important to the proponents of continuity as it was to the pioneers of change.

Although not explored here, it is worth mentioning that both the Bush administration and al-Qaeda's larger agendas have been depicted as doomed to failure. That is, 'reasonable hope of success', the prudential just war criterion, common to both the West and Islam, has been deployed against Bush and bin Laden. Such diverse figures as Paddy Ashdown, Shirin Ebadi, and Professor Eric Hobsbawm continue to maintain that any attempt to export democracy through the barrel of a gun will not succeed. At the same time, a series of prominent and *radical* Muslims—among them the *jihadi* ideologist Sayyed Imam Al-Sharif, the puritanical Saudi preacher Sheikh Salman ibn Fahd Al-Odah, and Zarqawi's former mentor Abu Muhammad Al-Maqdisi—have condemned al-Qaeda's *jihad* for its unrealistic goals and its ultimate wastefulness. The salience of these inherently pragmatic arguments suggests, albeit tentatively, that reckless, ideologically driven warfare will continue to lose its legitimacy.

## NOTES

1. Father Claude Selis, 'Conditions for the just war in a time of new conflicts', in Wim Smit (ed.), *Just War and Terrorism: The end of the just war concept?* (Leuven: Peeters, 2005), 82.
2. James Tully, 'The pen is a mighty sword: Quentin Skinner's analysis of politics', in James Tully (ed.), *Meaning and context: Quentin Skinner and his critics* (Princeton, NJ: Princeton University Press, 1988), 14.
3. Quoted in Bob Woodward, *Plan of attack* (New York: Simon & Schuster, 2004), 8.
4. Condoleezza Rice, 'Remarks to veterans of foreign wars', 25 August 2003. Unless otherwise indicated, all citations of Bush administration speeches refer to transcripts available online at http://georgewbush-whitehouse.archives.gov/
5. 'President's remarks to the nation', 11 September 2002.
6. George W. Bush, 'State of the Union', 28 January 2003.
7. See, for example, Colin Powell, 'Remarks to the United Nations Security Council', 5 February 2003.
8. Ibid.

9. Donald Rumsfeld, 'Remarks to FORTUNE Global Forum', 11 November 2002. Unless otherwise noted, references to remarks made by the staff of the Department of Defense were accessed at http://www.defenselink.mil/speeches/archive.html

10. Powell, 'Remarks to the UNSC', 5 February 2002.

11. 'President remarks on National Day of Prayer', 1 May 2003.

12. Powell, 'Remarks to the UNSC', 5 February 2003.

13. Richard Cheney, 'Remarks to the Heritage Foundation', 10 October 2003.

14. Bush, 'President discusses the future of Iraq', 26 February 2003.

15. On 'Meet the Press', 14 September 2003, transcript at: http://msnbc.msn.com/id/3080244/default.htm

16. 'President addresses the nation in prime time press conference', 13 April 2004.

17. Bush, 'Remarks to the United Nations General Assembly', 12 September 2002.

18. 'Remarks by the president at Florida rally', 20 March 2004.

19. Rumsfeld, 'July 4 Message to the Troops', 4 July 2003.

20. Paul Wolfowitz, 'Building the bridge to a better future', 6 December 2002.

21. Quoted in Woodward, *Plan of attack*, 407.

22. 'President Bush outlines Iraqi threat', 7 October 2002.

23. 'President discusses future of Iraq', 26 February 2003.

24. 'Bush rejects Saddam 9/11 link', *BBC News*, 18 September 2003.

25. 'George W. Bush's final speech', *Daily Telegraph*, 16 January 2009.

26. See Christine Gray, *International law and the use of force* (Oxford: Oxford University Press, 2004), 192.

27. Bush, 'President addresses the nation', 13 April 2004.

28. Wolfowitz, 'Building a better world: One path from crisis to opportunity', 5 September 2002.

29. Videotape address to the American people, 29 October 29, 2004.

30. King Fahd, of Saudi Arabia, for example: 'the democratic system that is predominant in the world is not a suitable system for the peoples of our region.... We cannot import the methods used by people in other countries and apply them to our people'. See Ann Elizabeth Mayer, *Islam and human rights: Tradition and politics* (Boulder: Westview Press, 1999), 45.

31. Talking to reporters on the White House lawn on 16 September 2001, Bush veered off script and stated that 'this Crusade, this war on terrorism is going to take a while'.

32. Interview with Taysir Alluni, 21 October 2001.

33. Woodward, *Plan of attack*, 421.

34. 'President Bush addresses the 51st annual prayer breakfast', 6 February 2003.

35. 'George Bush: 'God told me to end the tyranny in Iraq', *Guardian*, 7 October 2005.

36. 'President Bush calls for new Palestinian leadership', 24 June 2002.

37. 'President Bush delivers graduation speech at West Point', 1 June 2002.

38. Bush, 'State of the Union', 29 January 2002.

39. Bush, 'State of the Union', 28 January 2003.

40. 'Address to a joint session of Congress and the American people', 20 September 2001.

41. 'State of the Union', 28 January 2003.
42. Thomas Aquinas, *Summa Theologica*, vol. 2 (Westminster, Md: Christian Classics, 1981), 1360.
43. Barry Paskins and Michael Dockrill, *The ethics of war* (London: Duckworth, 1979), 215.
44. In Woodward, *Plan of attack*, 421.
45. See *The Prophetic fall of the Islamic regime* (Lake Mary, FL: Creation House, 2002).
46. Lee Marsden, 'God, war and Iraq', presented at the BISA conference, Exeter University, 16 December 2008.
47. Leaked ICRC report cited in 'Red Cross cites "inhumane" treatment at Guantanamo', *Washington Post*, 1 December 2004, A10.
48. From 'Is torture a good idea?', an investigation by Clive Stafford Smith for *Channel 4*, aired 28 February 2005.
49. Mamdouh Habib in 'Fresh Guantanamo torture claims', *BBC News*, 13 February 2005.
50. See Moazzam Begg, *Enemy combatant: A British Muslim's journey to Guantanamo and back* (London: Free Press, 2006), 158.
51. Alia Brahimi, *Jihad and just war in the war on terror* (Oxford: Oxford University Press, 2010).
52. See Karen J. Greenberg and Joshua L. Dratel (eds.), *The torture papers: The road to Abu Ghraib* (New York: Cambridge University Press, 2005).
53. David Earle Anderson, 'Not a just or moral war', *Sojourners Magazine*, 32/1 (2003), 26.
54. Rev. Richard Land and Rev. Jerry Falwell, for example.
55. Cardinal Roger M. Mahoney, 'Statement on the possibility of a war with Iraq', 13 November 2002, available at http://www.usccb.org/sdwp/peace/mahony.htm
56. Bill Broadway, 'Evangelicals' voices speak softly about Iraq', *Washington Post*, 5 January 2003, B9.
57. 'New Zealand church leaders joint statement on the threat of war against Iraq', 10 September 2002, at http://www.dunedinmethodist.org.nz/just/ldrs.html
58. Federation of Swiss Protestant Churches, 'No preventive war against Iraq', 23 January 2003, at http://www.warc.ch/dcw/iraq/08.html
59. John C. Ford, 'The morality of obliteration bombing', *Theological Studies*, 5/3 (1944), 267.
60. 'Editorial: God or country?' *America: The National Catholic Weekly*, 188/11 (2003).
61. Bishops of the United Church of Christ in the Philippines, 'Cry out for peace, say no to war', 31 January 2003, at http://www.warc.ch/dcw/iraq/01.html
62. Address to the peoples of Europe, broadcast on *Al-Jazeera* and *Al-Arabiyya*, 15 April 2004, reprinted in Bruce Lawrence, *Messages to the world: The statements of Osama Bin Laden* (London: Verso, 2005), 234. Unless otherwise indicated, all page numbers in citations of bin Laden's statements will refer to this compilation.
63. Interview with *Al-Jazeera*, December 1998.
64. Interview with Hamid Mir, 12 November 2001, 141.
65. Letter to the Americans, 6 October 2002, 162.

66. Videotape message, 29 November 2004, reprinted in Laura Mansfield, *In his own words: A translation of the writings of Dr Ayman Al-Zawahiri* (Old Tappan, NJ: TLG Publications, 2006), 236.

67. Letter from Zawahiri to Zarqawi, 11 October 2005, reprinted in Mansfield, *In his own words*, 259.

68. In *Bazugh Al-Fajr Bil-Muhajir Al-Ashr*. See 'Jihadist booklet: Islamic scholars apply double standard', *MEMRI: Special Dispatch No. 2235*, 9 February 2009.

69. Audiotape address to the people of Iraq, 11 February 2003, 181.

70. Zawahiri, *Knights under the prophet's banner* (autobiography, 2001), reprinted in Mansfield, *In his own words*, 128.

71. Interview with *Nida'ul Islam*, November 1996, 42.

72. World Islamic Front *fatwa*, 23 February 1998, 61.

73. He stated that Dick Cheney and Colin Powell had 'reaped more murder and destruction in Baghdad than Haluga the Tartar'. See audiotape address, 12 November 2002, 174.

74. Interview with Robert Fisk, 'Why we reject the West', *Independent*, 10 July 1996, 14.

75. Address to the peoples of Europe, 234.

76. Audiotape address, 12 November 2002, 173.

77. Interview with Peter Arnett (*CNN*), March 1997, 52.

78. Address to the peoples of Europe, 234.

79. Videotape address of 29 October 2004, 244.

80. Interview with Mir, 141.

81. Audiotape address to the International Conference of Deobandis, 9 April 2001, 96.

82. Statement of 26 December 2001, 148.

83. Bin Laden is referring to the sanctions regime levied by the UN against Iraq during the 1990s. UNICEF estimated that this led to the preventable deaths of 500,000 Iraqi children denied access to food and basic medicines.

84. Statement of 26 December 2001, 153.

85. Address to the scholars of Arabia, c.1995/1996, 16.

86. Interview with *Al-Jazeera*, December 1998, 68.

87. Ibid.

88. Interview with John Miller (*ABC Television*), May 1998, text available online at http://www.pbs.org/wgbh/pages/frontline/shows/binladen/who/interview.html

89. Bin Laden, 'To the Islamic umma, on the first anniversary of the new American crusader war', 11 September 2002, http://www.jihadunspun.com/articles/10152002-To.The.Islamic.Ummah/

90. Declaration of *Jihad*, 23 August 1996, 25.

91. World Islamic Front *fatwa*, 23 February 1998, 60.

92. World Islamic Front *fatwa*, 61.

93. Interview with Miller.

94. Statement of 14 February 2003, 191.

95. Statement faxed to *Al-Jazeera*, 24 September 2001, 101.

96. Letter delivered to *Al-Jazeera*, 3 November 2001, 135.

97. World Islamic Front *fatwa*, 23 February 1998, 59.

98. Videotape Message to the people of Iraq, 19 October 2003, 210.

99. Interview with Taysir Alluni, 21 October 2001, 121.

100. 'Under the shadow of spears', June 2002, at http://www.outtherenews.com/
     modules.php?op=modload&name=News&file=article&sid=55
101. Statement of 26 December 2001, 146.
102. 'Osama bin Laden to the Iraqi People', *MEMRI: Special Dispatch Series*, No. 837,
     27 December 2004.
103. 'Sheikh Yusuf Al-Qaradawi Condemns Attacks Against Civilians: Forbidden in
     Islam', 13 September 2001, online at http://www.islamonline.net/English/News/
     2001-09/12/article25.shtml
104. In Madeleine Bunting, 'Friendly fire', *Guardian*, 29 October 2005.
105. Ikrema Sabri in 'Muslims disagree on when jihad OK', *Seattle Times*, 17 Septem-
     ber 2001, A8.
106. Quoted in 'Islam for international anti-terror campaign', *Al-Akhbar*, 8 Novem-
     ber 2001.
107. 'Egyptian mufti does not approve 11 September attacks against US', *Middle East
     News Agency*, 26 October 2001.
108. 'Arab NGOs condemn attacks on US, Palestinians, Iraq', *Middle East News
     Agency*, 13 September 2001.
109. 'Divisions evident in Islamic Mideast, N. Africa', *CNN*, 24 September 2001.
110. Roula Khalaf, 'Saudi rulers seek to counter calls for jihad', *Financial Times*,
     26 October 2001, 2.
111. Sheikh Qaradawi in Volkhard Windfuhr and Bernhard Zand, 'God has
     disappeared', *Der Spiegel*, 26 September 2005. For Ayatollah Fadlallah's
     argument that 'anyone committing this kind of thing must be . . . punished
     for it by an Islamic court', see Adel S. Elias, 'Bin Laden is a legend', *Der
     Spiegel*, 15 October 2001.

# 11

## The Changing Character of Civil Wars, 1800–2009

*Stathis N. Kalyvas*

With few exceptions, the recent and prominent quantitative study of intra-state conflict has been biased towards the post-1945 period.[1] There is an additional way, however, in which history has been ignored and it has less to do with the chronological scope of current research and more with the conceptual implications of this chronological truncation. By treating civil wars as fundamentally homogeneous across time and space, researchers have failed to examine the evolution and transformation of civil wars over time. This neglect is related to their 'on-the-ground' characteristics and, perhaps more importantly, to the ways in which they have been understood and conceptualized—by both actors and observers. This twin historical myopia has produced a striking outcome: the domination of the empirical and conceptual association of insurgency, civil war, and revolution. It is, after all, common to refer to civil war and insurgency interchangeably. This association is often understood as a universal constant when, in fact, it is historically contingent.

This essay provides a corrective to the largely ahistorical character of current research. By adopting a broader chronological perspective, and surveying civil wars in both the nineteenth and twentieth centuries, it traces the evolution of civil wars over time—both empirically and intellectually. It examines the broad outlines of their military characteristics ('how they were fought on the ground'), as well as the way in which they have been described and understood by observers and participants alike. It argues that the way in which civil wars were fought is closely related to how they were understood and conceptualized.

Two key insights emerge. First, it is possible to discern three broad historical periods corresponding to three general types of civil wars. Civil wars were primarily conventional wars in the nineteenth century and the first half of the twentieth century; they were primarily irregular wars or insurgencies during the post-Second World War period; and they have become primarily a mix of conventional and 'low-tech' symmetric wars in the post-Cold War period.

In a different formulation, irregular war prior to the Second World War, and especially during the nineteenth century, *was not* primarily associated with civil war. Instead, it was a major feature of wars of imperial and colonial conquest, pitting modern armies against native resistance. In other words, the association between civil war and irregular war is a product of the Second World War—and, especially, the Cold War.

Second, the association of civil war and revolution is a twentieth-century phenomenon. Before the twentieth century, revolution was conceptualized primarily as mass urban uprising. This was a process that required the participation of urban dwellers and industrial workers rather than peasants. Insofar as a revolution took the form of civil war, its primary association was with conventional rather than irregular war. In contrast, irregular war was spurned by revolutionary theorists and activists alike—until Mao Zedong. Marx, Engels, Lenin, and Trotsky, among others, all thought that guerrilla warfare was a lesser form of armed struggle unfit for real revolutionaries and the working class.

In short, civil wars have undergone a remarkable and so far little studied process of transformation over the past two centuries; in turn, this transformation has informed the general understanding and study of civil war. Thus, historicizing civil wars demonstrates that key assumptions about the character of civil wars are variable rather than constant; they need to be problematized and explored empirically rather than assumed.

Having first provided some key definitions, the chapter then supplies a short review of the changing character of intra-state wars since the beginning of the nineteenth century. It then shows how this transformation is related to the parallel process of intellectually and conceptually understanding civil wars. The concept of warfare or 'technology of rebellion'[2] operates as a convenient proxy for a number of key features, including the organization, ideology, resources, and violence that characterize particular conflicts.

## DEFINITIONS

Civil war can be defined minimally as 'armed combat within the boundaries of a recognized sovereign entity between parties subject to a common authority at the outset of the hostilities'.[3] The intuition behind this definition is best captured by Charles Tilly's description of a revolutionary situation as entailing mutually exclusive claims to authority which produce a situation of *divided* or *dual sovereignty*.[4] Although internal (or intra-state) war is perhaps a more precise term, civil war is more familiar. Following this definition, armed resistance against military occupation following successful invasions, wars of secession, and wars of decolonization can be considered to be civil wars. An observable implication is that the rival parties in these conflicts tend to recruit from among the same local population. 'The American Revolution was a civil war', Shy reminds us, because 'in proportion to population, almost as many Americans were engaged in fighting other Americans during the Revolution as did so during the Civil War'.[5] In contrast, wars of conquest, including imperial and colonial conquest, come closer to the ideal type of the interstate war. When the targeted territory lacks internationally recognized state sovereignty or a modern state apparatus, the boundary between inter- and intra-state war gets blurred. The initial armed clash, following the invasion, can be thought of as the equivalent of an interstate war, whereas armed conflict that erupts after this territory has been conquered can be thought of as approximating civil war.

Very much like civil war, the concept of revolution has been used in a multiplicity of ways. This essay adopts the intuition of revolution as a process producing radical political change. From this perspective, civil wars that only bring about a change of political personnel do not qualify as a revolution, whereas successful revolutions generally avoid the descent into civil war.

Civil wars have been fought in a variety of ways. There are three basic types of warfare or 'technologies of rebellion', all of which are offered as ideal types given the fluidity that tends to characterize these conflicts: conventional, irregular, and symmetric non-conventional warfare.[6]

Beginning with the first type, it is worth stressing that many civil wars have been fought conventionally. This is a term that refers to direct military engagement either across well-defined front lines or via the clash of armed columns; a common form of engagement in that context is the large, set-piece battle between opposing armies arranged in battle formations. Conventional civil wars include such well-known cases as the American Civil War (1861–5), the Russian Civil War (1917–23), the Finnish Civil War (1918), and the Spanish Civil War (1936–9)—but also more recent conflicts such as the Biafra conflict in Nigeria (1967–70), the Abkhazian war in Georgia (1992–4), the war over Nagorno Karabach in Azerbaijan (1991–4), and the Croatian and Bosnian wars in the former Yugoslavia (1992–5).

In contrast to conventional wars, which imply a shared sense of symmetry between the rival sides, irregular or guerrilla warfare is an expression of asymmetry between states and rebels: though rebels have the military capacity to challenge the state, they lack the capacity to confront it in a direct and frontal way. This type of warfare is characterized by indirect and low-level engagement, often dominated by ambush and raid. The rebels eschew direct engagement with the more powerful military of the state and rely on harassment and stealth. Irregular civil wars include the Peninsular War in Spain (1807–14) which introduced the term 'guerrilla' to the lexicon of warfare; the Filipino insurgency against the United States (1898–1902); several resistance wars against German and Japanese occupation during the Second World War, in places such as Greece, Yugoslavia, China, or the Philippines; anti-colonial wars, such as the War of Algerian Independence (1954–62), the Rhodesian War of Independence (1966–79), and the wars in Angola (1961–75), Mozambique (1962–75), and Guinea Bissau (1962–74) against the Portuguese; secessionist wars like the Kurdish rebellion in Iraq (1980–8), various insurgencies in India (e.g. Assam, 1966–86) and Pakistan (e.g. Baluchistan, 1973–7); leftist insurgencies against right-wing governments (e.g. El Salvador, 1979–92; Peru, 1980–96; and more recently Nepal, 1996–2006); and, vice-versa, right-wing insurgencies against leftist governments (RENAMO in Mozambique, 1976–92; Contras in Nicaragua, 1981–8). 'Insurgency' is a term sometimes used to signify any type of rebellion. This chapter takes it to be synonymous with 'irregular' or 'guerrilla war'. From this perspective, insurgencies constitute a subset rather than a synonym of civil wars.[7]

Lastly, some civil wars do not fit into the irregular war/conventional war dichotomy: they diverge from irregular wars in that they lack the asymmetry between state and rebels which characterizes these conflicts. When states are unable (or, in a few cases, unwilling) credibly and systematically to deploy an organized military against ill-equipped insurgents, the two sides are matched at a low level of military capacity. This mutual weakness produces a type of warfare that is often compared with premodern warfare. Such 'symmetric, non-conventional wars' emerge in contexts of extreme state weakness and include examples such as civil wars in Lebanon (1975–90), Somalia (1991–ongoing), Congo-Brazzaville (1993–7), and the Central African Republic (1996–7).

To summarize, the examination of civil wars from the angle of warfare allows us to observe systematic heterogeneity in terms of the warfare that characterizes them. In turn, this type of disaggregation captures important differences between civil wars and makes possible an overview of the transformation of civil wars over time.[8]

Armed with these definitions, this chapter now turns to the record of armed conflicts during the nineteenth and twentieth centuries and identifies the main patterns, relying primarily on the list of conflicts produced by the Correlates of War project (COW).[9]

## THE NINETEENTH CENTURY

It is possible to discern three broad types of conflicts that were not clear interstate wars, during the nineteenth century. The largest category was composed of secessionist wars taking place within empires; more often than not these were fought by conventional means. The second category comprised a smaller number of conflicts where the objective was control of the centre; most of these conflicts took the form of urban insurrection; and they were understood as revolutions rather than civil wars, since they did not involve large-scale fighting between organized armed actors. A few, however, took the form of rural, irregular wars. Lastly, a large number of wars that were characterized by irregular warfare took place in the context of wars of imperial expansion and settlement. These conflicts were often perceived as wars; yet the term 'inter-state' made little sense as one side was usually made up of 'primitive' natives lacking the trappings of modern sovereign states. Indeed, only the first category of conflicts, secessionist wars taking place within empires, fits the definition of civil wars provided above.

The 'national revolutions' or 'wars of independence' in the Americas stand out, in terms of both their magnitude and geopolitical importance. Beginning, just before the close of the eighteenth century, with the American War of Independence (1775–83), these conflicts spread to Central and South America from 1808 to 1829, thus leading to the nearly total dismantling of the British and Spanish colonial empires in the American continent and the creation of a large number of new states. These wars include the Argentine War of Independence (1810–8), the Mexican War of Independence (1810–21), the Venezuelan War of Independence (1811–23), and the Chilean War of Independence (1810–26), among others. Although these are conflicts that a contemporary analyst would characterize as secessionist civil wars, it would be incorrect to follow a common conflation and also describe them as ethnic. These wars were fought largely among European settlers and their descendants; although both colonial and independentist armies recruited among the indigenous population, its role was generally subordinate.[10] A common characteristic among these wars was that they were waged primarily in a conventional fashion between regular armies that fought pitched battles— although episodes of irregular warfare also took place. In fact, their outcome was often decided by decisive battles. For example, the battle of Carabobo (24 June 1821) led to the independence of Venezuela and the battle of Boyacá (7 August 1819) was a key step in the independence of Colombia. Following independence, the new American states experienced a number of civil wars: a few were secessionist (the most important being the American Civil War 1861–5) but most were concerned with the control of the centre.

Besides the Spanish and British colonial empires, the Ottoman empire was also engaged in a flurry of local wars that can be described as secessionist or autonomist. These include the Greek War of Independence (1821–8), the First Syrian War (1831–2), the Bosnian revolt (1841), the war of Wallachian independence (1848–51), and the successive Cretan insurrections (1866–8, 1888–9, and 1896–7), among many others. Clearly influenced by the ideas of the French Revolution, the Greek War of Independence was a watershed for south-eastern Europe: unlike previous 'traditional' rebellions that remained local and demanded autonomy, the Greek uprising became the first Ottoman rebellion to include an explicit demand for a the formation of a new nation-state—and hence a war that could be characterized as both secessionist and ethnic.[11] Unlike the American wars, most of the wars that took place in the context of the Ottoman empires were fought via either traditional irregular warfare or a mix of irregular and conventional warfare.

In contrast, civil wars fought for the control of the centre were much less frequent during the nineteenth century. Some were primarily conventional wars, such as Spain's Carlist Wars (1833–9, 1846–9, and 1872–6). Most, however, took the form of urban insurrection and were called 'revolutions'. These include the various uprisings across Europe in 1848 and, most notably, the 1871 Paris Commune, which towers above most urban uprisings in terms of fatalities.

If secessionist civil wars were primarily fought conventionally and civil wars for the control of the centre took the form of urban uprisings, was there any space for irregular war? It turns out that the great majority of irregular wars during the nineteenth century were *not* civil wars. Sometimes referred to as 'small wars', these conflicts featured irregular warfare which was used primarily by native people (unsuccessfully) resisting settler encroachment and colonial conquest. Thus, many of the wars in which the Russian empire was involved during the nineteenth century were wars of imperial conquest or incorporation, including conflicts such as the Russo-Georgian War (1816–25), the Russo-Circassian wars (1829–40), and the Murid War (1830–59). Likewise, the westward expansion of the United States brought it into conflict with native populations, leading to the many Indian wars fought during that time. Similar wars were also fought in South America. As for the relentless expansion of European powers in Africa and Asia, it generated a large number of conflicts against native peoples. Examples include the British–Zulu wars (1879 and 1906), the Boer wars (1880–1 and 1899–1902), the French wars in Senegal (1890–1), Madagascar (1883–5 and 1894–5), Indo-china (1858–63 and 1885–96), and the war against the United States in the Philippines (1898–1902). Native peoples resisting imperial invasions fought using primarily guerrilla techniques, although this term can be a misnomer since many of these conflicts were, in fact, unsophisticated and misguided attempts by lightly armed natives to fight more or less frontally against numerically inferior but militarily superior European forces—a decision that often resulted in mass slaughter. It is hardly surprising therefore, that irregular warfare became associated in the mind of many observers with primitive warfare and, more generally, with 'primitive' or 'uncivilized' peoples. In short, this was a type of warfare that was widely perceived as representing the past, not the future.

There is an interesting, important, and limited exception to the association of irregular war with primitive warfare: in some cases, irregular war was used in 'advanced' European societies against foreign invading troops—sometimes in the context of a civil war and sometimes in the context of an interstate war, but following the defeat of a state's regular army. The royalist uprisings against the French Revolution that took place in the west of France, known as the *Chouannerie* (1794–1800), the Spanish war against Napoleon that gave the world the term 'guerrilla' (1808–14), and the Tyrolean rebellion against French–Bavarian forces (1809) were all instances of a type of warfare which, though rural and conservative in character, was understood by several thinkers as being potentially path-breaking in modernizing the ancient practice of irregular war into the more sophisticated *partisan war*. From this perspective, partisan war called for the mobilization of a nation's population into a rebel group facing an invading or occupying army behind frontlines. The ideological foundation of this war (nationalism) and the mass character of this mobilization were the two elements of modernization. It was Carl von Clausewitz, in particular, who elaborated the idea of 'people's war in civilized Europe'. In book VI of *On war*, he argued that communal defence based on spontaneous popular resistance using indirect fighting techniques could be an important military factor, as long as it was auxiliary to a regular army. This was a bold claim since organized mass popular resistance remained a very limited phenomenon during the nineteenth century.

In sum, an overview of the patterns of conflict during the nineteenth century suggests that civil war, irregular war, and revolution were distinct phenomena—conceptually as well as empirically: civil wars were mostly fought conventionally, revolutions mostly took the form of urban uprisings, and irregular wars mostly characterized 'primitive' resistance to imperial or colonial expansion.

## THE FIRST HALF OF THE TWENTIETH CENTURY

In many ways, the first half of the twentieth century was one of continuity: the patterns that characterized the nineteenth century continued to dominate, with a couple of key differences. First, irregular warfare was used in some colonies in an infrequent and futile effort to reverse colonial rule. Second, civil war returned to Europe, in the form of large-scale conventional war.

Several rebellions took place in the colonies acquired during the previous period. However, the method of fighting, as well as the outcome, did not diverge. Yet, because these rebellions took place within territories that were now part of European colonial empires, these conflicts can be described as civil wars. Thus, Germany faced the Hottentot uprising (1903–8) and the

Maji–Maji revolt (1905–7), France the Moroccan uprising of 1916–17, Italy the Sanusi rebellion in Libya (1920–31), and so on.

The main area of differentiation between the two periods is the return of civil war to Europe, primarily in the form of major wars that reflected big ideological cleavages and were fought primarily in a conventional way. The Russian Revolution and Civil War (1917–21), the German Revolution (1918–19), the Finnish Civil War (1918), and of course the Spanish Civil War (1936–9) are the most notable cases. Obviously, the first three cases are directly linked to the First World War, a factor that explains the degree of militarization and the type of fighting. Major non-European civil wars during the same period include the Mexican revolution (1910–20) and the Chinese Civil War which began in 1927 as a complex, multifaceted conflict involving several warlord armies, of which the Communists were initially only a minor one. Lastly, the Irish War of Independence (1919–21) stands apart as a secessionist war that was fought using a combination of urban terrorism and insurgency tactics.

Overall, a central element of the civil wars that took place during the first half of the twentieth century is the centrality of the left–right cleavage, super-imposed on some form of Marxist ideology, along with the use of conventional (as opposed to irregular) warfare. Indeed, guerrilla war remained a form of combat selected by native people fighting colonial encroachment on a local basis and without a broader political and ideological vision. In fact, irregular war continued to be seen as a primitive type of war unworthy of 'civilized peoples'—a form of warfare that advanced nations and great powers were able to deal with successfully.[12] This view was not only advanced by arrogant colonizers; it was also shared by Marxist revolutionaries for whom the revolution could only take the form of a mass, working-class, urban uprising. For example, in his 1906 attempt to rethink guerrilla warfare, Lenin recognized that 'guerrilla warfare brings the class-conscious proletarians into close association with the degraded, drunken riff-raff'.[13]

## THE SECOND HALF OF THE TWENTIETH CENTURY

Civil war underwent a massive structural change during and after the Second World War. This change can be traced to three fundamental developments. The first one can be located in the Chinese Civil War. Mao Zedong came to the realization that guerrilla warfare could be an important instrument for revolutionaries, especially when urban insurrection and conventional warfare were unavailable. Just as importantly, he was also able to theorize (and later popularize) his experience and turn it into a doctrine of guerrilla war. The success of the Chinese Communists against the Japanese occupation and their victory over their Nationalist foes in 1949 provided the Maoist doctrine of 'revolutionary people's war' with immense prestige and instant credibility.

The second development was the realization that the combination of revolutionary Marxism and nationalism in the context of Axis occupations during the Second World War could give rise to robust guerrilla movements while extending the influence of Communist parties beyond their restricted working-class basis. Put otherwise, the transformation of Communist parties into catch-all organizations with a strong peasant basis could be achieved through guerrilla war rather than either simple electoralism or mass mobilization and urban protest. The experience of Yugoslavia, Greece, China, or Vietnam, among others, was seen as validating this point. The reason why Communists turned out to be such successful users of irregular warfare lay in their knowledge of clandestine activity, the power vacuum and social dislocation brought about by war and occupation, and the 'popular front' strategy of interwar communism which created the illusion of a vast social and political coalition.

The third development was the Cuban Revolution in 1958–9. The ability of a small band of guerrilla fighters, led by idealistic young men such as Fidel Castro and Ernesto Che Guevara, to topple a corrupt autocracy despite its links with the United States and to implement large-scale social change in a peripheral postcolonial nation proved to be a source of global inspiration and demonstrated that guerrilla warfare was not simply an instrument for revolution but *the* instrument for revolution par excellence.

These three factors, along with the provision of extensive material support to many rebel organizations across the world by the USSR, China, Cuba, and their allies, turned irregular war into the dominant type of warfare in the post-Second World War period. Guerrilla warfare accounted for 66 per cent of all civil wars fought between 1944 and 1990, with conventional wars far behind (27 per cent).[14] In other words, it was only during this period that civil wars became associated with guerrilla wars fought in the name of revolution.

When examining the irregular wars of this period, it is easy to see that a large number of conflicts, including many of the most important ones, were fought by rebels that claimed some degree of allegiance to Marxist ideology. These conflicts include the Greek Civil War (1946–9); the Viet Minh insurgency against the French in Vietnam (1946–54); the Malayan insurgency (1950–60); the Vietnam War (1959–75); the Cambodian War (1970–5); the People's Liberation Front (JVP) insurgency in Sri Lanka (1987–9); the independence wars in Angola (1961–75), Mozambique (1962–75), Guinea Bissau (1962–74), and Rhodesia (1966–79); and the insurgencies in Venezuela (1963–5), Nicaragua (1978–9), Peru (1980–99), Guatemala (1970–1 and 1978–84), El Salvador (1979–92), and Colombia (1964–present)—among others. An additional feature of many of these conflicts was that rebels were able successfully to mix Marxist ideology with nationalism; the so-called 'national liberation movements' provided an opportunity for the successful expansion of these movements' appeal. In contrast, Marxist ideology had very little to do with the conventional civil wars fought during that period.

The power of Marxist-infused guerrilla doctrine was such that it influenced the strategic thinking of its adversaries. Indeed, the anti-Marxist insurgencies of the 1970s and 1980s were often launched by former Marxist insurgents (e.g. Jonas Savimbi in Angola and Edén Pastora in Nicaragua). In his description of these insurgencies, an author remarks that 'some of the most successful anticommunist insurgents today have been influenced by Communist insurgent strategies'; he also speaks of 'the paradox of Communist methods being used against Communist regimes', and refers to 'the deep appeal of Leninism, particularly in its Third World incarnations'.[15]

In short, the link between civil war, guerrilla war, and revolution, which made them interchangeable terms for many observers and participants, was forged during the Cold War. It is worth, therefore, examining exactly how traditional guerrilla warfare was transformed into a people's war and how it came to dominate civil wars.

The starting point is to recognize that although traditional guerrilla war and modern insurgency share common elements, they also diverge in many ways. Traditional guerrilla warfare was generally understood as a purely military form of fighting which used classic 'hit and run' tactics and was employed by indigenous groups in situations where a conventional army either had been defeated or had never existed. Rarely did its primarily unsophisticated practitioners display any wider comprehension of the potential of irregular models of conflict in the way that became commonplace after 1945, when guerrilla warfare became 'revolutionary' and was termed 'insurgency'.[16] In fact, this period coincides with a remarkable reversal in the outcomes of irregular wars: whereas in general before the Second World War, states, 'strong actors', and 'great powers' routinely defeated irregular armies, this pattern reversed itself following the Second World War, with insurgents increasingly more likely to force a 'draw' or defeat their stronger foes.[17] To distinguish traditional guerrilla techniques from the highly politicized version of irregular warfare that was perfected by leftist rebels during the Cold War period, the latter are designated as 'robust insurgencies'.

Kalyvas and Balcells identify three channels through which traditional guerrilla warfare turned into revolutionary people's war:[18] material support, beliefs, and organizational doctrine.

First, whereas traditional guerrilla warfare depended on the mobilization of local resources with the occasional support of a neighbouring state, the robust insurgencies of the Cold War period benefited from extensive and multifaceted superpower support. It is common knowledge that a central aim of Soviet foreign policy was to train and motivate, directly or through surrogates, budding insurgents throughout the developing world. The Soviet Union provided weapons and training to leftist insurgencies immediately following the start of the Cold War (the initial beneficiaries included the Chinese and Greek Communists) and turned the Third World into a foreign policy priority from the early 1950s. Once China turned communist, it entered the fray as well, while various surrogates (most notably Cuba, Libya, and the Palestinian Liberation Organization) played an important role in both training and support. Indeed, material assistance exploded after the mid-1950s. At the same time, the concept of 'proxy wars' is a poor description of Soviet policy, as it only stresses the mechanical infusion of material resources into rebel movements; often, it even implies a purely instrumental relationship between opportunistic rebels who pretended to believe in socialism in order to receive Soviet weapons. Although opportunism was certainly present, it did not exhaust the range of motivations; and although material support typically included weapons, it extended to multiple forms of assistance, training, and in many cases the provision of on-the-ground advisers. Most importantly, assistance and support were channelled through transnational social movements. Thousands of radical activists built supra-regional and even global contacts and networks while training in Soviet-funded military camps and universities, the most famous of which was the 'Patrice Lumumba Friendship University' in Moscow. The centrality of social movements helps differentiate robust insurgency from traditional guerrilla warfare. Whereas the latter was based on the mobilization of primarily conservative, local sentiments and/or local patronage tribal and kin networks, the former mobilized transnational revolutionary networks; these would link-up with traditional rural networks but assume the leadership. This is a point stressed by Carl Schmitt who distinguished between two ideal types of irregular fighters: the traditional 'defensive-autochthonous defenders of home' and the 'aggressive international revolutionary activist'. Modern revolutionary guerrilla war, he argued, reached its fullest expression when it connected these two.[19]

The second mechanism is related to beliefs—particularly the beliefs of middle-level cadres who constituted the critical link between rebel leaders and masses on the ground. After all, the Cold War was also an ideological competition on a global level, whose cognitive frames and ideologies 'aroused passionate ideological commitments among combatants, both domestically and internationally'.[20] Beliefs mattered in three ways. First, as ideas about radical change: the perception that a credible counter-hegemonic model of political and social organization was available and attainable captured the imagination of millions. The specific ideas, as well the labels used, varied but usually included concepts such as national liberation, decolonization, developmentalism, 'third-worldism', and Marxism. Second, beliefs were important as a source of individual, and therefore collective, motivation: they mobilized the energy of many 'first movers' who were willing to invest tremendous effort, to incur significant risk, and to suffer enormous deprivation for the cause of revolution. Lastly, beliefs mattered as perceptions about the feasibility of radical change via armed struggle: subordinate or weak actors could success-fully take on stronger actors if they learned exactly how to deploy the technol-ogy of robust insurgency. Radical change became a matter of training which, in turn, required the right doctrine.

The last component of robust insurgency was organizational doctrine. The equation of revolutionary theory with the organizational principles of irreg-ular war was an important innovation whose global breakthrough came with the Cuban revolution 'which put the guerrilla strategy on the world's front pages'.[21] Writing in 1973, Wolin remarked how 'the military mode of thinking has all but supplanted the political mode in revolutionary circles. Whenever one turns . . . one finds sophisticated discussions of tactic, fire-power, guerrilla warfare, and combat techniques'.[22] The writings of Mao Zedong, Che Guevara, Régis Debray, and Amilcar Cabral, among others, were widely disseminated and read by thousands of activists and sympathi-zers in the developing world, especially among the educated urban youth. They all pointed to the possibility of global, radical political change that would begin in the periphery and take the form of a revolution waged via guerrilla warfare. The examples of China, Cuba, and Vietnam suggested that, despite occasional setbacks, guerrilla warfare was both a feasible and suc-cessful path to political and social change. Leftist guerrilla movements made it a point to invite hundreds of journalists and activists from across the world, thus socializing them in the ways of armed struggle.

Despite its emphasis on action, irregular war was never a simple military tactic, akin to insurgent 'special forces' storming their way to power. Instead, rebel entrepreneurs learned that the key to success lay in the patient formation of a highly structured political organization, typically a party, in control of a disciplined armed wing. The objective was to acquire and govern territory. On the one hand, organization guaranteed discipline in the absence of which rebels could never hope to withstand, even more defeat, the state's military superiority. On the other hand, territory constituted a key resource for armed struggle. Effective administration and mass mobilization in liberated areas were essential foundations for the development of armed struggle under conditions of military inferiority. This amounted to revolutionary state-build-ing, which was absent in traditional guerrilla warfare.[23]

To summarize, during the Cold War a convergence of material support, beliefs, and organizational principles turned robust insurgency into a credible and effective technology of rebellion—one that was reflected in the equation of civil war, guerrilla warfare, and revolution. Beliefs were sustained and repro-duced by examples of successful irregular wars that were based on these organizational principles; in turn, both the dissemination of beliefs and the implementation of organizational principles required training, assistance, and weapons. Although it was possible for each of these factors to operate alone (some leftist insurgencies were able to emerge and even succeed in the absence of external support, while some rightist insurgencies relied more on external support and less on beliefs), the combination of all three was critical at the aggregate level and explains the transformation of civil war in the second half of the twentieth century.


## THE DAWN OF THE TWENTY-FIRST CENTURY

Since the connection between civil war, guerrilla war, and revolution was a product of the Cold War, it follows that its end should have brought significant alterations in the character of civil war, by disconnecting it from both guerrilla warfare and revolution. Indeed, the empirical evidence suggests a secular decline of irregular warfare.

The end of the Cold War was welcomed by optimists as a blessing that would bring global openness, democracy, and peace. At the same time, pessimists warned of a coming global anarchy, an era of ethnic conflict and instability. As we near the twentieth anniversary of the end of the Cold War, it is worth taking stock of the consequences of this momentous event for violent conflict. The first thing to note is that civil war spiked immediately after the end of the Cold War. Observers and analysts alike were initially swayed by this initial spike. Many thought that end of the Cold War spelled a 'coming anarchy', through the eruption of 'new wars' which 'shattered the dreams of the post-Cold War'.[24] Following this wave of doomsday predictions, and after the rate of civil war onsets had returned to its Cold War average, many researchers concluded that 'the prevalence of civil war in the 1990s was *not* due to the end of the Cold War and associated changes in the international system'.[25] More recently, however, the observation of a declining trend in civil wars has produced renewed sensitivity about the end of the Cold War—and rightly so.[26] For example, researchers associated with the Human Security Centre have characterized this decline as an 'extraordinary and counterintuitive improvement in global security'. They note that by 2003 there were 40 per cent fewer conflicts compared to 1992, and that the deadliest conflicts (those with 1,000 or more battle-deaths) had fallen by some 80 per cent. They also added that the end of the Cold War was the single most critical factor in this decline and identified international intervention as the key mechanism: because the two superpowers ended their interest in 'proxy wars' in the developing world, the United Nations, along with other international agencies, donor governments, and non-governmental organizations, was free to play a new global security role that entailed active diplomacy, peacekeeping, and peacemaking, thus preventing new conflicts from taking place and brokering peace agreements to end those that had already erupted.[27]

How about the transformation of civil war? As mentioned above, the 'new war' thesis was based on the expectation that civil wars were likely to become less ideological and more disorganized, a prediction that was challenged on both conceptual and empirical grounds.[28] The fact that there is no stark contrast between 'new' and 'old' wars, however, does not mean that the end of the Cold War had no effect on warfare. In fact, an examination of aggregate patterns confirms that the character of civil war has changed once more—and in a rather dramatic way.

The empirical evidence suggests that following the end of the Cold War (and up to 2004), civil wars underwent yet another remarkable change. The link between revolution, guerrilla war, and civil war, which by the late 1980s appeared natural to most observers, ceased to reflect reality. Now, conventional wars became dominant (48 per cent of all cases), with symmetric non-conventional wars (low-tech wars) matching irregular wars at 26 per cent.[29] The conventional wars of the post-Cold War period include the Yugoslav wars in Croatia and Bosnia (1991–2) and several post-Soviet wars, including conflicts in Transnistria (1992), Tajikistan (1992–7), Georgia (1988–93), and Azerbaijan (1991–4). In contrast, symmetric non-conventional wars characterize primarily sub-Saharan Africa and include conflicts such as Liberia (1989–96 and 1999–2003), Somalia (1991–), Sierra Leone (1991–2002), and Congo-Brazzaville (1997–9). What explains this massive transformation?

The end of the Cold War was a tremendous blow for both states and rebels which lost superpower support. The blow was particularly painful for revolutionary rebels. By depriving them of plentiful superpower support, by destroying the belief that social change could come out of the barrel of a gun, and by undermining the transnational networks that sustained them, the end of the Cold War selected, so to speak, these rebels out of history. Now, relatively weak states that had been previously vulnerable to irregular war could easily deter low-quality rebels. In contrast, the weakest states, deprived of any superpower support, became much more exposed to rebels—but to opportunistic rather than revolutionary ones. In short, the end of the Cold War divorced civil war from both irregular war and revolution. In a way, Collier was not necessarily wrong when he described all rebels as greedy looters rather than justice seekers; he just had in mind a subset of civil wars that happened to be particularly visible in sub-Saharan Africa during the post-Cold War era.[30] His error was to generalize what was, once more, a historically and geographically confined phenomenon.

## THE FUTURE OF CIVIL WAR

Civil wars have experienced considerable transformations during the past two centuries. These transformations reflect evolving geopolitical and ideological dynamics; in turn, they have shaped the way scholars and actors have thought about civil war. The relation between civil war and revolution has been historically variable. These two concepts were not associated until the beginning of the twentieth century and especially the advent of the Russian Revolution and Civil War. The Second World War connected both civil war and revolution with guerrilla warfare, and the Cold War consolidated this connection which is still present in our mental map. Lastly, the end of the Cold War led to the divorce of civil war from both irregular war and revolution. Civil war is now associated with conventional and symmetric non-conventional forms of fighting and appears to have lost its revolutionary ambitions. In a different formulation, the ways of revolution are no longer expressed by civil war. In short, this historical overview has revealed significant transformations both in terms of how civil wars have been fought on the ground and in terms of how they have been conceptualized by scholars and participants. What are the implications of these transformations for the future?

This analysis suggests that robust insurgency may belong to the historical past. Like its revolutionary predecessor in history, the mass urban insurrection modelled after the French Revolution, robust insurgency was historically dependent on an international context characterized by bipolarity and global ideological competition. Future civil wars are less likely to be irregular wars fought in the name of revolutionary change.

This does not mean that irregular war will disappear. An examination of the irregular civil wars of the post-Cold War era suggests that they are likely to come in two major types. The first type consists of minor, peripheral wars, akin to what Fearon calls 'sons of the soil' insurgencies (e.g. Aceh in Indonesia or Southern Thailand);[31] these peripheral ethnic insurgencies signal a return of traditional guerrilla warfare in the place of robust insurgency; they do not threaten power at the centre and can be contained or resolved without major international repercussions. The second type of irregular war consists of insurgencies that display a radical Islamist outlook (e.g. Egypt, Algeria, Iraq, Chechnya, Afghanistan, Pakistan). These wars tend to cluster in the Middle East–North Africa region. Because of the US involvement in Iraq and Afghanistan, these irregular wars have justifiably received considerable attention; in turn, this has contributed to a perception that insurgency is a transhistorical phenomenon.

The first point worth emphasizing is that, despite their importance, radical Islamist insurgencies are not representative of the broader conflict trends.[32] The second point is that radical Islam is today the only global revolutionary movement. Viewed from this angle, it is not surprising that it has tried to resurrect robust insurgency. Radical Islam combines, uniquely so far in the post-Cold War era, a transnational social movement (along with the obligatory training camps), revolutionary beliefs both in the sense of a global counter-hegemonic ideology and the willingness to take up arms in order to implement it, and an organizational doctrine of revolutionary guerrilla warfare formulated by Abu Mus'ab al-Suri, the Che Guevara of jihad. His magnum opus, *The Global Islamic Resistance Call*, has widened the appeal of jihadism to new audiences, 'especially among young, well-educated Westernised Muslims who seem to be motivated more by a mixture of leftist radicalism and militant pan-Islamic nationalism than by religiosity'.[33]

However, of the three elements that marked the ascendancy of robust insurgency during the Cold War, jihadism still lacks the support of a powerful external sponsor. The result has been a wave of military defeats, which has forced the strategists of radical Islam, including Al-Suri, to recommend a shift away from insurgency and towards transnational urban terrorism.[34] This shift suggests an intriguing analogy between the strategy of radical Islam and that of European anarchists at the end of the twentieth century and European radical leftists in the 1970s: terrorism—an analogy that would confirm the divorce between civil war and revolution. In addition, and insofar as it is possible to extrapolate from past experience, terrorist campaigns have had little success.

From a policy perspective, this analysis suggests that if the decline of civil wars proves lasting, and if it is indeed due to the secular decline of irregular wars, we have reasons to be optimistic. Unlike irregular wars, rebels in both conventional and symmetric non-conventional wars are easier to defeat, or at least contain, by a well-organized international force. These conflicts are no guerrilla quagmires and the rebels lack the capacity of putting up a serious, long-term resistance. The worst outcome is the persistence of lingering, low-intensity conflicts in the peripheries of weak states as opposed to higher intensity wars of attrition that threaten power at the centre. This is not to minimize this type of instability, but it is one that is much easier to manage than the irregular civil wars of the Cold War through an emphasis on state-building skills and long-term investment in institution-building and economic development.

Lastly, this analysis holds an important implication about the way we study civil wars. Analysts are always tempted to generalize from the cases they know best and from the historical context that surrounds them. Hence, it was natural for analysts of the Cold War period to equate civil war with guerrilla war and revolution. Likewise, it is natural for development economists in the post-Cold War era to equate civil war with low-tech opportunistic wars fought in sub-Saharan Africa. It is precisely because this tendency comes so naturally that we should be very wary of it. This essay constitutes a move in that direction.

## NOTES

1. Exceptions include Ivan Arreguin-Toft, 'How the weak win wars: A theory of asymmetric conflict', *International Security*, 26/1 (2001), 93–128; Jason Lyall and Isaiah Wilson, 'Rage against the machines: Explaining outcomes in counter-insurgency wars', *International Organization*, 63/1 (2009), 67–106; and Andreas Wimmer and Brian Min, 'From empire to nation-states: Explaining wars in the modern world', *American Sociological Review*, 71/6 (2006), 867–97. The first two, however, focus on insurgencies rather than civil wars, while the third's focus is on all wars, both interstate and intrastate ones.

2. Stathis N. Kalyvas and Laia Balcells, 'International system and technologies of rebellion: How the end of the Cold War shaped internal conflict', *American Political Science Review*, 104/3 (2010), 415–29.

3. Stathis N. Kalyvas, *The logic of violence in civil war* (New York: Cambridge University Press, 2006).

4. Charles Tilly, *From mobilization to revolution* (New York: McGraw-Hill, 1978), 191.

5. John Shy, *A people numerous and armed: Reflections on the military struggle for American independence* (Oxford: Oxford University Press, 1976), 183.

6. Stathis N. Kalyvas, 'Warfare in civil wars', in Isabel Duyvesteyn and Jan Angstrom (eds.), *Rethinking the nature of war* (Abingdon: Frank Cass, 2005), 88–108.

7. Wars against occupiers are considered civil wars following the definition of civil wars as internal or domestic wars; see Kalyvas, *The logic of violence in civil war*.

8. Stathis N. Kalyvas, ' "New" and "old" civil wars: A valid distinction?' *World Politics*, 54/1 (2001), 99–118.

9. My intention here is to provide a rough overview of the main trends rather than a systematic one. For a systematic analysis focusing on the 1944–2004 period, see Kalyvas and Balcells, 'International system and technologies of rebellion'.

10. Christon I. Archer (ed.), *The wars of independence in Spanish America* (Wilmington, DE: SR Books, 2000); Michael P. Costeloe, *Response to revolution: Imperial Spain and the Spanish American revolutions, 1810–1840* (Cambridge: Cambridge University Press, 1986); Jorge I. Domínguez, *Insurrection or loyalty: The breakdown of the Spanish American empire* (Cambridge, MA: Harvard University Press, 1980).

11. The term 'ethnic' is interpreted broadly to include religious cleavages. The Italian peninsula also experienced a number of internal conflicts which, in conjunction with an interstate war, led to the Italian unification in 1871.

12. Arreguin-Toft, 'How the weak win wars'; Lyall and Wilson, 'Rage against the machines'.

13. Vladimir Ilyich Lenin, 'Guerrilla warfare', in *Lenin: Collected works*, vol. 11 (Moscow: Progress Publishers, 1965), 216.

14. Kalyvas and Balcells, 'International system and technologies of rebellion'.

15. Michael Radu, 'Introduction', in Radu (ed.), *The new insurgencies: Anti-communist guerrillas in the Third World* (New Brunswick, NJ: Transaction Publishers, 1990), 14.

16. I. F. W. Beckett, *Modern insurgencies and counter-insurgencies: Guerrillas and their opponents since 1750* (London: Routledge, 2001), viii.

17. Arreguin-Toft, 'How the weak win wars'; Lyall and Wilson, 'Rage against the machines'.
18. Kalyvas and Balcells, 'International system and technologies of rebellion'.
19. Carl Schmitt, *Theory of the Partisan*, translated by G. L. Ulmen (New York: Telos Press, 2007).
20. Ann Hironaka, *Neverending wars: The international community, weak states, and the perpetuation of civil war* (Cambridge, MA: Harvard University Press, 2005), 123.
21. Eric Hobsbawm, *The age of the extremes. A history of the world, 1914–1991* (New York: Vintage, 1996), 438.
22. Sheldon Wolin, 'The politics of the study of revolution' *Comparative Politics*, 5/3 (1973), 354.
23. Kalyvas, *The logic of violence in civil war*.
24. Herfried Münkler, *The new wars* (Cambridge: Polity Press, 2005.); Robert D. Kaplan, *The coming anarchy: Shattering the dreams of the post Cold War* (New York: Random House, 2000); Mary Kaldor, *New and old wars: Organized violence in a global era* (Stanford, CA: Stanford University Press, 1999). See also Mats Berdal's chapter in this volume for a discussion of the 'new wars' thesis.
25. James D. Fearon and David D. Laitin, 'Ethnicity, insurgency, and civil war', *American Political Science Review*, 97/1 (2003), 77–8.
26. Chirstopher Cramer, *Violence in developing countries: War, memory* (Bloomington, ID: Indiana University Press, 2007), 53.
27. Human Security Centre, *The human security report. War and peace in the 21st century* (2005); http://www.humansecurityreport.info/
28. Kalyvas, '"New" and "old" civil wars'.
29. Kalyvas and Balcells, 'International system and technologies of rebellion'.
30. Paul V. Collier, *The bottom billion: Why the poorest countries are failing and what can be done about it* (Oxford: Oxford University Press, 2007).
31. James Fearon, 'Why do some civil wars last so much longer than others?' *Journal of Peace Research*, 41/3 (2004), 275–302.
32. Kalyvas and Balcells, 'International system and technologies of rebellion'.
33. Brynjar Lia, *Architect of global jihad: The life of Al Qaeda strategist Abu Mus'ab al-Suri* (New York: Columbia University Press, 2008), 27.
34. Ibid.

# 12

## Crime versus War

*William Reno*

It is commonplace to refer to recent conflicts, particularly in Africa as 'new wars' that 'involve a blurring of the distinctions between war (usually defined as violence between states or organized political groups for political motives), organized crime (violence undertaken by privately organized groups for private purposes, usually financial gain), and large-scale violations of human rights'.[1] Regardless of whether scholars accept this notion of interrelated war and crime, it has become an integral element of global policy. The Special Court for Sierra Leone reflects this analysis of the relationship between war and crime in its indictment of former Liberian president Charles Taylor. The court asserted that Taylor conducted a criminal conspiracy, a 'common plan ... to gain access to the mineral wealth of Sierra Leone, in particular diamonds, to destabilise the Government of Sierra Leone in order to facilitate access to such mineral wealth and to install a government in Sierra Leone that would be well disposed toward, and supportive of, the accused's interests and objectives in Liberia and the region'.[2]

No sensible person would dispute that wars in West Africa and elsewhere have been violent and disruptive affairs that have involved massive violations of human rights. The argument in this essay is that the concept of criminality as applied to contemporary wars is flawed. This concept mistakenly implies that economic transactions that increase people's personal incomes and assert control over other people's commercial exchanges in wartime are equally dysfunctional and disruptive to public order and are not legitimate in most people's eyes. Yet some of the criminals referred to below do things other than commit crimes. Many of those who are charged with enforcing laws are engaged in pursuits other than law enforcement. In many of these 'new wars', statehood may refer to a condition marked by the absence of effective state institutions. Some states may be run by rulers who are not interested in pursuing an interest of state and who devise laws precisely so that they can violate them. When such states 'fail', this often signals that the people who are supposed to be running these states are engaged in some other political project. Moreover, members of the international community are inconsistent in their decisions about with which 'criminals' or 'states' they will work and against which they will apply sanctions or even fight.

This contention in the labelling of violence as 'crime' and 'war' extends beyond Africa's shores. Communities in places like Afghanistan and Iraq might reasonably prefer the authority of local strongmen who are able to protect them to the central government that they view as violent, corrupt, and incompetent. Each side's protectors are 'criminals' to the other side in struggles that most would agree amount to wars.

Terms such as 'crime' are usually defined in ways that reflect the position of the state, and now also the norms associated with global society and international law. But where the position of the 'state' is called into question and where international actors behave tactically or strategically in contradiction to norms or international law, the definition of 'crime' undergoes constant revision. This blurring of boundaries between public and private behaviour complicates efforts to define stable concepts of deviant or normal behaviour. By this metric, defining 'war' also depends upon the position of the observer. In the first two months of 2009, more than 1,000 Mexicans were killed in association with 'armed engagements'[3] involving drug traffickers and Mexico's army; it would not be unreasonable to call this a 'war'. Political expediency or partisanship might dictate calling it 'crime' rather than 'war', as foreign diplomats and politicians remain reluctant to deter investors and tourists that are vital to the country's economic stability. Like 'crime', 'war' depends on where one stands.


## A DIFFERENT APPROACH

A more important distinction lies in whether violence is used to plunder or to protect people, and under what conditions these strategies of violence change. The state-centric vocabulary of 'crime' and 'war' has limited use in examining and explaining causes of different patterns of violence. This is particularly true in contexts where bureaucratic state institutions and other methods of centralized control have collapsed and armed groups compete for power. 'Crime' is a particular strategy of violence that is associated with distinctive approaches to the recruitment and organization of fighters and the pursuit of goals that undermine the interests of communities from the perspective of non-combatants. Local non-combatants may view behaviour as 'crime' if other people's uses of violence make them less secure and undercut other public goods. Armed groups that plunder local people's possessions or kidnap them to force them to join the fight usually mark uses of violence that do not recognize the rights or interests of other people.

The same armed group that is a plundering 'criminal' organization in local people's eyes may be a state in the eyes of international actors. As late as 2000, UN Secretary General Kofi Annan thanked Liberia's President Charles Taylor for his help in negotiating the release of UN peacekeepers taken hostage.[4] Shortly thereafter, a UN investigating team concluded that Sierra Leone's rebels were financing their campaign of violence through the trafficking of diamonds to Liberia in violation of UN Security Council resolutions, a trade 'that cannot be conducted without the permission and the involvement of Liberian government officials at the highest level'.[5] By 2000, it was unclear in international diplomacy whether Liberia's sovereign leader should be treated as a 'criminal'. Taylor's status was a matter of contention in domestic politics too. In 1997, Taylor threatened Liberia's population with further harm if they did not elect him in an internationally monitored poll. His strategic use of violence gave him a 75 per cent landslide vote and international recognition as the leader of a sovereign state.[6]

Uses of violence that provide security to non-combatants might be appreciated in local opinion as protection. The decision of the Special Court in Sierra Leone to indict the head of the Civil Defense Forces (CDF) for war crimes prompted protestors to argue that 'Chief Hinga Norman stayed to confront the rebels and renegade soldiers... without his contribution and tenacity, the rebels would not have come to the peace table and would have still been in the city, killing and maiming at will'.[7] Though responsible for numerous violations of human rights, the CDF battled government soldiers and Revolutionary United Front (RUF) fighters who had joined forces in 'Operation No Living Thing' conducted against the population of the capital in 1999. Over one week this coalition killed about 250 policemen and targeted law offices and other institutions of public order.[8] Even as the indictment was made public, the militia's second-in-command offered to help stem incursions of Liberian fighters, reflecting the opinions of many that the CDF was better able to protect the country than was the government army.[9]

These examples of the shifting application of the label 'crime' illustrate the value of focusing on explaining why armed groups choose to protect or to plunder surrounding populations. In this approach, 'violence is a means, not an end; a resource, not the final product'.[10] Violence can be used in different ways vis-à-vis non-combatants. An armed group can use violence to attract collaborators or to kidnap 'recruits'. An armed group that is engaged in violence in illicit commerce to get resources can provide services to some or all people in areas that they control, or they can exploit or exclude these people. Different strategies of violence can appear among groups that contend with one another to grab the trappings of sovereignty of a collapsed state. Protectors and plunderers alike fight for wealth and power, but they do so in distinctly different ways.

The causes of these different uses of violence lie in the patterns of pre-conflict regime politics. This essay looks particularly at how political actors have used violence to assert their authority in this earlier period as formal bureaucratic agencies of the state were collapsing, and at how these experiences have shaped political actors' uses of violence once competition for power has grown fiercer. Closer scrutiny of pre-conflict uses of violence also shows the positions of various community 'power associations' such as kinship groups, religious organizations, and businesses. It connects the interests of these political actors and the constraints that they impose on each other with the personal interests and motivations of individuals.

In some respects, this analysis resembles Charles Tilly's explanation for the differences in rulers' strategies for asserting their authority and for how these differences produced a variety of state-building trajectories. Tilly examined the interactions of 'wielders of coercion' with 'manipulators of capital' and the extent to which the interests and authority of each limited or extended the possibilities of action available to political actors.[11] The argument here also focuses on who sets the terms for the uses of violence and on the degrees of autonomy that different users of violence have to pursue their own interests. Extremes of plunder are associated with the specific pre-conflict political strategies of some sub-Saharan African regimes and the operations of the political economies of the patronage-based political systems that they created. These political strategies have included violent forms of clandestine commerce and other rent-seeking activities that enjoyed the support of key state officials. Though these officials and their associates have benefited from the prerogatives of sovereign statehood, in the more extreme cases their authority has not been based upon conventional notions of legitimacy or imposed through bureaucratic administration. Instead, they have manipulated markets, especially in natural resources and cross-border trade, to control other people's access to economic opportunities to enhance their power. This strategy of imposing authority has rested upon monopolizing control over access to formal and informal economic activities in order to limit the autonomy of all other social groups, not just opposition political parties or interest groups in the capital.

The argument then focuses on what happens when these pre-conflict state regime political strategies fail. This is the critical point at which competing armed groups emerge as the primary political actors. They now have to make choices about how to use violence in competition with their peers but without the constraint of their presidential patron. But they still confront the parameters that their involvement in local politics in the earlier period has put on their choices.

The evidence below points to two general propositions about how pre-conflict political economies of patronage affect strategies of violence. First, regions that have been most closely connected to pre-conflict capital-based patronage networks are most likely to host plunderers. The prior organization of the political economy of patronage-based authority allowed those who later became armed group commanders more autonomy from local authorities and community norms in their quests to gather resources and fighters. These commanders already have well-developed personal connections to outside sources of income, weapons, and recruits as part of their role in supporting the pre-conflict regime's ruling clique. This kind of potential or actual violence is called *connected violence* by virtue of these actors' transitions from privileged regime insiders to competitors for resources and power as the authority of these regimes has crumbled.

The second proposition is that the violent contenders for power who have been most marginal to pre-conflict networks have to deal more intensely with other local authorities, including customary religious leaders, local guarantors of commercial contracts, and others outside the formal framework of state administration, before widespread fighting broke out. These relationships usually signalled the dependence of these political actors on local authorities either to protect them from interference from the capital, including help with recruiting and arming local supporters, or to shield them from detection if they exploited clandestine commercial opportunities without the consent of the regime or even if they were suspicious of the reliability of their deals with their patrons in the capital. Then, during wider conflicts, these relationships constrain how political actors can mobilize fighters and regulate the uses of violence among the surrounding population. This context generates *marginalized violence* insofar as those who wield violence have experience in developing their own networks and capabilities independently of the pre-conflict regime as a result of their more peripheral positions in the initial political constellation.

These categories of violence are not mutually exclusive. Many of the cases considered below have involved struggles between different kinds of armed groups over the same geographical and social terrain and have engaged the same communities. This comparative approach explains how these different kinds of armed groups come into being when states collapse, and traces how and why some of these political actors change the ways in which they use violence. It refrains from making judgements about what is 'crime' or 'war' and focuses instead on the circumstances that shape how people use violence when states collapse. It also provides testable hypotheses. For example, are there regime insiders who come to use protective violence in ways that apply to people who are not their immediate ethnic kinsmen? Are there regime outsiders who resort to plunder, and what happens to them? This approach also provides a framework for considering if (and how) political actors move from one use of violence to another. These considerations are integral to this approach and, for the purposes of this essay's more narrow focus on comparing categories of violence, the sections that follow raise them as avenues for further research.

## CONNECTED VIOLENCE

Many of those who lead armed groups where state regimes have lost the capacity to maintain order in sub-Saharan Africa are immediately recognizable figures from pre-conflict political networks. Those who remain and survive to contend for power usually do so through translating their insider personal and business connections that came with their privileged political status into resources to fight competitors and to increase their own wealth and power. This is not to say that leaders of armed groups in this context are devoid of societal legitimacy. Instead, their legitimacy is derived from their capacities as patrons to provide for and to protect members of their groups (such as families, clans, and ethnic communities), much as it was in pre-conflict politics.

Regimes have depended upon these networks as instruments to assert their authority as state institutions collapsed. While some of these networks undergo substantial changes in membership and organization, they play a major role in shaping how political actors use violence in conflicts that accompany the collapse of regimes. Politicians who have enjoyed quasi-official access to illicit commercial activities, for example, discover that they can continue exploiting opportunities for their own benefit as a regime collapses. Previously, they had to use their positions and a portion of their material proceeds to support the regime's political interests.

Seemingly divisive local uses of violence play a large role in maintaining the authority of such regimes. Some local strongmen hire young men to attack their political opponents. More important, however, is the tendency for this process of militarizing supporters to absorb armed ideologues and others who use violence in the pursuit of their own political programmes. Thus, while violent political factional battles in Nigeria at the regional or local level diminish the capacities of state institutions to administer, this kind of struggle maintains the authority of the capital as a referee of these conflicts. Even more critical is the impact of this activity on local armed groups that become tools in these political battles. Affiliation with a well-placed politician serves as one of the few reliable sources of upward mobility in wealth and status, regardless of the political ideas and aspirations of individual members of these armed groups.

This dynamic of incorporation reshuffles the hierarchy of interests for individual fighters. While they recognize the rottenness of the political order of which they are now a part, should they ignore the immediate gains in terms of much needed resources and protection for themselves and for their families? The engagement in local factional struggles also pits armed groups against one another, preventing alliances around political ideas as they serve their local political bosses. This situation commonly agitates individuals with political agendas who lament the interference of politicians. 'We want the government to relocate us to a camp so that we can use regimental system to maintain discipline', said a leader of a Nigerian vigilante group, as he complained that his rank-and-file welcomed the opportunity to loot local businesses as part of their 'payment' for fighting the factional battles of a local state governor.[12]

This political context privileges fighters' short-term interests and is hostile to any group that attempts to organize itself in direct opposition to political actors who are engaged in local-level factional struggles that usually provide better weapons more quickly to those who are willing to compromise. Although the quick movers are subservient to the agendas of their political patrons, they are largely spared the difficult tasks of cultivating the support of local communities in return for resources and recruits. This situation seems to bear out Weinstein's argument that 'rebel groups that emerge in environments rich in natural resources or with the support of an outside patron tend to commit higher levels of indiscriminate violence' in the sense of being more likely to plunder non-combatants.[13] The argument here acknowledges some of the basic truths about the lure of rent-seeking opportunities, but it recognizes what Weinstein calls 'low commitment' individuals as a consequence of a particular kind of political environment. Such 'low commitment' individuals also may harbour 'high commitment' political ideas and can act upon them in different contexts. Here, political context is the engine that drives the explanation for the different uses of violence. It creates 'low commitment' individuals. The plentitude of 'high commitment' individuals in anti-colonial and anti-apartheid liberation struggles in past decades shows that political organization rather than patronage or resources alone can account for this difference.

Another key observation of this approach is that the collapse of patronage-based regimes leaves in their wake numerous strongmen who dominate the political scene, despite their dependence on their ties to the capital that has left them with little capacity to command substantial support beyond their kinsmen or home town. Their old positions, which intentionally left them with serious limits on their power, now translate into a lack of durable administrative or other linkages to communities in order to extract the resources needed to finance fighters. They survive in large part because regimes' political strategies of fragmenting authority outside the 'official' hierarchy of patronage have beaten down organizational alternatives. Strongmen who maintain and adapt parts of the surviving pre-conflict political networks continue to flatten this political terrain, fragmenting, attacking, and selectively co-opting potential rivals and intimidating the rest. This legacy of patronage-based rule and the conflicts surrounding its splintering seriously weaken 'civil society', even when many individuals may continue to act out of a sense of community solidarity or commitment to particular political ideas.

The ironic power of collapsing 'weak' states appears in the marginalization of what initially appear to be formidable mass-based political movements at the start of conflicts. Étienne Tshisekedi in the early 1990s dominated Congo-Zaire's political transition. After his release from prison for criticizing President Mobutu's corrupt rule, he founded *l'Union pour la démocratie et le progrès social*. Popular support for the political opposition and foreign pressure forced Mobutu to accept multiparty competition. Mobutu then helped his clients organize 'opposition parties' to fragment this new political terrain and overshadow popular opposition movements, with over 200 parties registered by 1991 and more than 380 by 1993.[14] The democratic opposition, despite broad support, failed to figure significantly in the fighting that started in 1996. Likewise, the leaders of Liberia's civilian democratic political movement, one of the strongest on the continent in the mid-1980s, appear as footnotes in the histories of state collapse and conflict there after 1989. Even deeply rooted local social organizations failed to shield regime critics. Prior to the outbreak of widespread fighting in late 1989, politicians' positions in 'secret societies', including ones that were officially illegal, and in other quasi-religious institutions turned these community associations into avenues of upward mobility, provided that one adhered to the regime's rules of politics.[15] Zimbabwe in the 1990s hosted some of Africa's most vigorous associational life, heir to two anti-colonial insurgencies that fought for power to 1980. After 2000, the effectiveness of these organizations diminished in proportion to the collapse of Zimbabwe's bureaucratic state institutions and the growth of President Mugabe's patronage networks in the legal and illicit economies and in nearly every other sphere of social endeavour.

The poor showing of 'people power' in Africa's collapsing states and among some of the continent's most politicized populations shows how violence reflects patterns of political contestation and control that are distinctive to this regime type. The tactics and strategies of political actors in this context shape relations between armed groups and non-combatants. This organization of violence creates incentives for followers and ultimately determines the organization of armed groups. The process is compatible with the simultaneous presence of individuals or groups, such as democratic oppositions, that are not able to organize effectively. Moreover, the structure of competition can force highly politicized individuals to act on what they consider to be inferior motives. Where networks associated with an unpopular strongman dominate opportunities for upward mobility or even protection, a politically inspired individual may associate with the local oppressor that he hates. The Nigerian rapper Obiwon-Onyinye sings of this dilemma in his *Streetz of Lagos*: 'Livin everyday on the streets of Lagos, I walk in the valley of the shadow of death', and advises that '419 [advance fee fraud associated with political figures in league with criminals] is the richest road to you'.[16] Under different circumstances, the same person could be advised to take up arms to fight 'the system', but poverty and insecurity are more immediate problems that can be solved by participating in the system that the recruit might personally detest.

Nigerian sociologist Peter Ekeh describes a 'dual morality' that grows out of a pragmatic decision to act as a sycophant in public so as to grab wealth and power for oneself and one's family, while behaving in a morally upright manner in the context of one's own immediate community.[17] Co-option is a powerful tool of political control as it creates suspicions among observers that all critics are potentially tainted. For example, the cabinet of Nigeria's violent and corrupt Abacha regime (1994–8) included the former leader of the Movement for National Reform. As an expert on press law, he was a noted expert on press freedoms,[18] and his appointment as Attorney General made him the chief prosecutor of a government that suppressed press freedoms. The political value to the president of this appointment lay in showing people that he had the power to divert even his most ardent critics, even if the critic later disavowed this association.

'Fake NGOs' contribute to the fragmentation of the political terrain, the impoverishment of public discussion of political ideas, and the extension of patronage networks. In one example, Angola's President Eduardo dos Santos founded the 'private' Eduardo dos Santos Foundation to provide services to the poor. In actual fact, this organization crowded out organizations that were not connected to this political network and forced poor people to seek an accommodation with the regime's interests.[19] 'Anti-corruption' campaigns disrupt other avenues of autonomous organizing. Nigeria's Failed Bank (Recovery of Debts) Decree No. 18 of 1994 was billed as an effort to root out 'criminality' in the banking industry. The insolvency of new banks, most organized as finance for local government contracts to distribute to supporters, provided the justification for the announcement. But the real targets were solvent commercial banks. Union Bank, founded in 1917, came under scrutiny. 'We were too independent and did not come to Abuja to seek contracts, patronage, approvals, and whatever from the Presidency . . . there was a need to destroy private wealth', noted one banker.[20]

These networks emerge in conflict as organizing poles for armed groups, an intensification of the connected violence that characterized the strategies of authority in the pre-conflict regimes. As regimes fragment, some insiders organize armed groups to hold onto these instruments of control and wealth. The centres of gravity of these conflicts are those networks that outside observers consider illicit, an evaluation that local non-combatants do not necessarily share. Thus, a map of connected violence traces the pre-conflict political strategies of control.

## MAPPING CONNECTED VIOLENCE

The fragmentation of Cote d'Ivoire's political networks and the outbreak of large-scale fighting in 2002 illustrate the evolution of regime networks. Laurent Gbagbo, elected president of the country in a contentious poll in 2000, was a major figure in a violent competition of political networks. Like counterparts elsewhere, he was an old regime insider even if he claimed status as a regime critic. As leader of the semi-clandestine *Front populaire ivoirien* (FPI) in 1982, after returning from exile he ran as an opposition candidate in the 1990 multiparty election that followed international pressure for reform. Winning just 18 per cent of the vote, Gbagbo accepted the presidential offer of a cabinet position. Others followed Gbagbo on this political path of upward mobility, such that in the 1990s educators headed at least thirty of the forty opposition parties.

Gbagbo's political value to his president lay in his role as boss of student militias and his appeal as an opposition figure. He had used his position as a professor of history and dean at the Université de Cocody-Abidjan to mobilize student protests. His FPI thus had close links to the student group, *Fédération estudiantine et scolaire de Côte d'Ivoire* (FESCI). FESCI connections gave Gbagbo ties to most of the armed group leaders that emerged in 2002 and before, including future *Forces Nouvelles* organizers. The *Forces Nouvelles* head, Guillaume Soro, was a FESCI leader in the 1990s. Gbagbo's wartime ally, Charles Blé Gouldé, target of 2006 UN sanctions for his leadership of the violent *Congrès Panafricain des jeunes patriots*, succeeded Soro as FESCI head. FESCI also provided an early base for Eugène Djué, the head of the pro-Gbagbo *Union pour la Libération Totale de la Côte d'Ivoire*. The student organization provided these and other 'student activists' with connections to clandestine economic activities as they organized protection rackets and other operations when they were not fighting pre-war election campaigns.[21]

The focus of fighting in Côte d'Ivoire often involved struggles to control patronage networks, including the now-'privatized' agricultural marketing firms that were the main source of wealth in the agricultural economy. Leaders who emerged out of the old regime were in the best positions to define other people's uses of violence. They could use their connections and control over resources to co-opt local grievances. Such strategic flexibility appears in Gbagbo's own background. Having spent part of his career as a historian who praised the accomplishment of the cultures in the north of the country, he developed much of his popular appeal as a politician and an anti-northern xenophobe, mobilizing 'non-state' fighters in old student politics networks and supporting them through exploiting old patronage links.[22] This dominant network of politician-educators was able to use this position to manipulate and amplify existing local tensions over land tenure, economic recession, and numerous other complaints.[23]

Patterns of conflict in Sierra Leone in the 1990s also reflected the contours of pre-conflict patronage networks. That country's politics exhibited a more intensive destruction of formal state institutions and rule though patronage networks than occurred in Côte d'Ivoire, and instead revolved around control over diamonds and the proceeds of their sale in international markets. At independence in 1961, the Sierra Leone People's Party leaders sought the support of local chiefs in mining areas. These chiefs, responsible for local administration and the courts, also had the legal right to grant licences to mine diamonds on their land. Some of these chiefs welcomed migrants into their chiefdoms whom they could recruit as muscle for politicians.

An election, coup, and counter-coup in 1967–8 brought the opposition All People's Congress to power in the capital. The new president quickly began to encourage smuggling and even 'crime' such as the theft in 1969 from the largest foreign mining company of one month's production of diamonds, allegedly in collusion with the president and his Lebanese business partner.[24] The 'nationalization' of the foreign company's operation and the 'privatization' of smaller scale mining put more of these resources into the hands of the regime's political network. Much of this quasi-official 'criminal' trade in diamonds flowed through Liberia. From at least the 1950s, Liberia's use of the US dollar as its official currency made it an attractive partner in this trade, since it gave participants access to a hard currency. It also intertwined political networks in the two countries, a development that shaped the fighting in the 1990s. It was only with UN Security Council Resolution 1306 of 2000 that this mode of politics was criminalized and labelled in the popular media as 'blood diamonds'.

Thus, when fighting broke out in 1991 in eastern Sierra Leone, there were two kinds of incipient conflict. One possibility was that the citizens of the country, angered by the extreme corruption of their rulers, would fight to support a new vision of politics. Observers report that this was an appealing option to many and that some took steps to do just that.[25] What they were really joining was an ongoing struggle within Sierra Leone and in Liberia to control existing political networks attached to the two countries' most lucrative sources of income. It is alleged that the RUF fighters who crossed the border from Liberia to fight a 'civil war' were really mostly Liberian fighters attached to Charles Taylor's National Patriotic Front of Liberia (NPFL).[26] Taylor had made earlier bids to rise in Liberia's political establishment, returning to the country in 1980 at the behest of President William Tolbert after spending time in the United States as a student activist. After Tolbert was murdered in a coup in 1980, Taylor ingratiated himself with President Samuel K. Doe and was appointed the head of a procurement agency, with ample opportunities for graft. He then associated himself with Thomas Quiwonkpa, who was killed in a 1985 coup attempt. After Quiwonkpa's death, Taylor set out to organize his own invasion to fight his way to the presidency. Many of

Taylor's adversaries on the field of battle in the 1990s included other former government officials.

Many Sierra Leoneans saw the RUF invasion in reality as part of Taylor's struggle to control the diamond trade that had been an integral part of the Liberian and Sierra Leonean political systems. Although the RUF controlled Sierra Leone's main diamond mining areas only briefly in 1992 and again for four months in 1995 before a more sustained period of control from 1997, the RUF's association with Taylor and the RUF leadership's own wishes to take over the system of authority that the pre-conflict regime had built shaped how the RUF used violence. Whether the RUF was fighting in resource-rich or resource-poor areas, efforts to map uses of violence in this conflict show that RUF fighters committed the bulk of atrocities against non-combatants in gross terms and in terms of intensity.[27]

RUF and NPFL fighters and their leaders were banking on a strategy in which they would take over the same networks that sustained the corrupt governments that they fought. The odd decision of US diplomats mediating the 1999 Lomé peace agreement between the RUF and the Sierra Leone government to agree to appoint the RUF leader as Chairman of the Commission for the Management of Strategic Mineral Resources highlights the contingency of the 'criminal' label as applied to these uses of violence.

Closer examination of fighting in Sierra Leone, Nigeria, Côte d'Ivoire, and in all of the other cases of fragmenting patronage shows how already-powerful political actors choreograph the ways in which others join in conflict. This legacy of patronage politics and the conjunction of intensified struggles to control its networks incorporates diverse 'causes of conflict' into patterns of violence that rely upon plunder that the international community now labels as 'criminal' and that divide and isolate people who act on ideological and programmatic motivations. The next section explores the context in which uses of violence more often avoid plunder, a pattern of behaviour that requires a different set of mediating factors.

## MARGINALIZED VIOLENCE

Communities where local strongmen were forced into more marginal positions in pre-conflict political networks tend to be able to assert more control over the discipline of fighters, the goals of armed group leaders, and thus over their uses of violence. The consequence is that leaders of armed groups have to put more effort into negotiating with local authority figures to get the resources that they need to fight, whether 'blood diamonds' or some other resource, which are traded in the same illicit international channels that their better connected adversaries use. This 'marginalized violence', which became the basis for the CDF in Sierra Leone, tends to contribute to the protection of core communities, the mobilization of supporters among non-combatants, and even concerted efforts to provide services to these communities. Such uses of violence may be seen as legitimate on the part of local non-combatants, regardless of whether state officials or foreign diplomats apply the 'criminal' label to this violence.

Militias of the CDF also fought in and controlled areas in Sierra Leone where alluvial diamonds are mined. But, according to data collected after the conflict, the CDF was less likely to commit violence against at least certain categories of non-combatants. The highest proportion of documented CDF violations concerned abductions, and not the forced displacement that characterized the highest proportion of RUF and government forces' violations. CDF fighters also accounted for 1.5 per cent of amputations of non-combatants' limbs (a particular feature of this conflict). Moreover, the ratio of CDF violations against children occurred at a ratio of one for every 11.83 adult victims, compared with a ratio of one for every 3.89 violations against adults for the RUF and one for every 4.56 violations against adults for a major breakaway faction of the national army.[28] These patterns suggest that CDF fighters were more discriminating in their targets. Since they enjoyed significant support and were also constrained by popularly accepted local notables within many of the communities where they operated, they could rely upon local information to target people accurately. This proposition finds support in the observation that CDF fighters shifted their tactical uses of violence, usually resulting in more attacks on non-combatants when they joined other groups or left their home area.[29]

Local strongmen and politicians from the region needed to resort to these local societal authorities' capacities to mobilize and discipline young men to fight before widespread conflict began in 1991. The roots of their dependence on local intermediaries lay in the election and coups of 1967–8 that put an opposition party in power. Previously, politicians from this region were poised to benefit from direct control over the state. But they ended up as the suspect junior partners in the old opposition party's increasingly pervasive patronage network, headed by leaders who mistrusted their protests of allegiance. They needed help from these other local notables who could use their standing in communities to protect what benefits they got from politics, including their personal gains in 'illicit' commerce. The prospect of lower standing in the capital-based political network otherwise left these politicians vulnerable to predation from better connected rivals and to more frequent targeting in bogus anti-corruption investigations to please foreign donors and creditors.

The different context for the use of violence appeared in 1982, when an associate of the president tried to rig an election in what was now an opposition stronghold. Local politicians who were the targets of this outsider meddling joined with local people who were angry about government corruption and officially sponsored violence. Some of the local politicians helped to set up militias to fight in what was known as the Ndorgboryosoi rebellion, named after the forest spirits who protect people from enemies, and so began a process which built ties between politicians and the local authorities upon whom politicians relied for mutual protection. These militias fought state security forces for the next year and were defeated when the army joined the fight in 1983.[30] Some of the militia members rushed to join the RUF in 1991, believing that they could gain revenge against their government. But the RUF's goals and its use of violence against non-combatants drove most of these people away. Context again mattered, showing how the RUF's leaders rejected opportunities to mobilize local fighters that conceivably could have made the RUF into a much more powerful and successful fighting force. But that would also have required a different political strategy on the part of the RUF's leaders.

This pattern of control over the use of violence appears in other areas of political marginalization in patronage-based regimes. The leaders of the Somali National Movement (SNM) initially sought protection from Ethiopia's President Mengistu to overthrow the Siad Barre regime in Somalia. But when Mengistu forced the SNM out of Ethiopia and into the line of attack from Barre's forces as part of a peace settlement, the SNM's leadership had to rely on local elders to help them acquire resources and to protect them. They found this less difficult than did other political actors. Many politicians in northern Somalia—the core area of SNM support—already shared the liability of having come from the area that supported the regime that Barre overthrew in 1969, so they did not attract the president's trust. As a consequence, they were more vulnerable to politically motivated investigations of their activities in illicit markets before the collapse of Somalia's central government in 1991. Moreover, Barre reserved for more reliable political associates the most lucrative opportunities associated with 'official' smuggling, foreign financed agricultural projects, and foreign aid rip-offs.

The pre-conflict vulnerability of these politicians led them to turn to local elders to help protect illicit transactions. As in Sierra Leone, these local authorities required that their politician partners take into account the interests of local communities. In return, local clan and religious authorities recruited fighters and helped politicians to buy weapons. The same authorities could use this control to frustrate attempts by armed group leaders to plunder communities so as to become rich or to go to the capital to fight for power. In 1994, a local strongman tried to use his old ties as a former chief of police in the capital to organize a fighting force to capture the northern port and the only local international airport, both valuable sources of income. This breakaway armed group leader wanted to fight his way into the capital to gain power and to recover the properties that he received while he served the old regime. Local elders warned young men that their families would face vendettas if they continued to support the breakaway faction and to misuse violence against non-combatants. Their threat trumped the strongman's promises of material gain, which included handing out car keys to recruits with promises that they could redeem them for cars in the capital.[31]

This comparison shows how political actors in sub-Saharan Africa's recent conflicts use violence in different ways. The key determining factor is the nature of the political struggle prior to the outbreak of widespread conflict. People who participate in these conflicts apply labels such as 'crime' and 'war' with reference to these interests. Such distinctions resemble the changes that Tilly maps in instances where leaders of armed groups have to bargain with other groups and to take account of their interests in the pursuit of their own ambitions.[32] But as noted at the outset of this essay, most international diplomatic discourse does not reflect these distinctions. There is an exception to this generalization that is significant for those who use violence in ways that protect communities. Those who may be labelled as 'criminal' for their violations of the human rights of others may derive some advantage if they associate what they do with an appeal to the practice of counter-insurgency. This is a significant development that has the potential to chip away at global practices that identify 'criminal' activity from a state-centric perspective.

## A NEW DEAL FOR MARGINALIZED VIOLENCE?

External intervention in sub-Saharan African wars focuses on strengthening states, although more immediate concerns often turn to discovering what groups are able to control populations and are willing to associate with the intervention forces. 'State-building', with all of its expensive plans to expand government services and with the problems of dealing with corrupt and inefficient indigenous administrations, increases the strategic value of these local-level organizations. Control over fighters and a capacity to protect at least some populations can render these armed groups more effective instruments of governance than national governments that lack the capacity or political will to rule in this fashion.

Peter Penfold, Britain's High Commissioner to Sierra Leone from 1997 to 2000, recognized this distinction in his views of the CDF and other armed groups, including elements of the national army. He stated that 'the CDF made significant contributions towards the restoration of the democratic government, and, although I do not dispute that some members of the CDF may have committed some terrible deeds—fighting fire with fire—I do not believe that they were part of an orchestrated and deliberate policy, in contrast to the RUF'.[33] Penfold played a role in arrangements to help arm the CDF in violation of a UN embargo. The CDF leader, however, was later charged with war crimes before the Special Court for Sierra Leone.

It is not surprising that international actors violate their own principles about working with non-state authorities when trying to build up state authorities. This kind of brokerage, or direct engagement with existing local authorities, mobilizes local people at the lowest political and financial cost possible to the external actors while also eliminating undesirable groups. It differs from a law enforcement approach to 'crime' and from earlier versions of counter-insurgency strategy in that it does not rely upon boosting state bureaucratic capacities to provide services to lure people into supporting it. It also does not rely as heavily on the deployment of expensive and risky operations to go after 'criminals' in order to disrupt their networks. Instead, '[t]he aim is to displace the enemy network rather than just disrupt it. It builds networks of trust with individuals in the at-risk society, and then extends these networks into the community, gradually displacing the extremists.'[34] The relative autonomy of networks in the marginalized violence context is the kind of social resource that fits well with this kind of counter-insurgency strategy. The conjunction of interests of local and external actors is likely to play a significant role in shaping the changing character of warfare in the context of collapsing states.

In more general terms, a pragmatic approach makes explicit political judgements about what is 'crime' and what is 'war' in the pursuit of efficient and low-cost alternatives to continued violence. Many local actors make distinctions on explicitly political grounds too. Ex-combatants try to present themselves as victims of war or as gallant fighters while resisting the label of collaborators in crime. Some non-combatants seek justice through labelling the violence of others as crimes, while other non-combatants prefer the label of war out of fear that prosecutions will reignite fighting. These points, and the examples earlier in this essay, demonstrate how crime and war are not simply stable outcomes of particular processes as Kaldor and other proponents of the 'new wars' thesis propose. Instead, these distinctions are highly political and are apt to change from one context to another and among actors within a single context.

Such political contingency can expose even pragmatic external actors to manipulation. Southern Somalia's Alliance for the Restoration of Peace and Counter-Terrorism, an alliance of Mogadishu politicians and businessmen active in 2005–6, artfully played on US security concerns and managed to extract some payments. Moreover, there is a risk that external resources replace the hard bargaining with local power holders that characterize those who use violence to protect non-combatants. In any event, if this strategy of counter-insurgency becomes more widespread, it may mark a shift in the 'crime' versus 'war' calculus that brings international actors more in line with the political judgements and strategies of local actors in the context of so-called failed states in Africa where patronage-based regimes have collapsed.

## NOTES

1. Mary Kaldor, *New wars and old wars: Organized violence in a global era* (Stanford: Stanford University Press, 2001), 2.
2. Special Court for Sierra Leone, 'The Prosecutor against Charles Ghankay Taylor...' Case No. SCSL-2003-01-I (amended indictment), 16 March 2006, 10.
3. This is the term used in US Department of State, 'Travel alert: Mexico', 20 February 2009, http://travel.state.gov/travel/cis_pa_tw/pa/pa_3028.html
4. *Fourth report of the Secretary-General on the United Nations Mission in Sierra Leone* (New York: UN Security Council, 19 May 2000), para. 67.
5. United Nations Security Council, Report of the panel of experts appointed pursuant to UN Security Council Resolution 1306 (2000), Paragraph 19 in relation to Sierra Leone (New York: UN, 20 December 2000), para. 2.
6. David Harris, 'From "warlord" to "democratic" president: How Charles Taylor won the 1997 Liberian elections', *Journal of Modern African Studies*, 37/3 (1997), 431–55.
7. Augustine Beecher, 'A tale of two betrayals', *Standard Times* [Freetown], 27 May 2003, 3.
8. Commonwealth Human Rights Initiative, *In pursuit of justice: A report on the judiciary in Sierra Leone* (Freetown: CHRI, 2002), 28.
9. International Crisis Group, *Sierra Leone: The state of security and governance* (Freetown: ICG, 5 September 2003), 13.
10. Diego Gambetta, *Sicilian mafia* (Cambridge, MA: Harvard University Press, 1993), 2.
11. Charles Tilly, *Coercion, capital, and European states, AD 990–1992* (Oxford: Blackwell, 1992), 14–16.
12. Anayochukwu Agbo, 'Bakassi versus MASSOB', *Tell* [Lagos], 26 November 2001, 63.
13. Jeremy Weinstein, *Inside rebellion: The politics of insurgent violence* (New York: Cambridge University Press, 2007), 7.
14. Kgulu Ngoy-Kangoy, *La transition démocratique au Zaire* (Kinshasa: Université de Kinshasa, 1995), Annexe, 27–54.
15. Stephen Ellis, *Mask of anarchy: The destruction of Liberia and the religious dimension of an African civil war* (New York: New York University Press, 1999), 220–80.
16. http://www.youtube.com/watch?v=cFr-tyqSpM4&feature=related
17. Peter Ekeh, 'Social anthropology and two contrasting uses of tribalism in Africa', *Comparative Studies in Society and History*, 32/4 (1990), 660.
18. Olu Onagoruwa, *Press freedom in crisis: A study of the Amakiri case* (Ibadan: Sketch Publishing Company, 1986). He explains his decision to join Abacha's government in his *Rebel in General Abacha's government* (Lagos: Inspired Communication, 2006).
19. Christine Messiant, 'The Eduardo dos Santos Foundation: Or, how Angola's regime is taking over civil society', *African Affairs*, 100/399 (2001), 287–309.
20. Kayode Matthew, 'How Abacha's family ruined us', *Vanguard* [Lagos], 30 November 2000, 4.

21. Yakube Konate, 'Les enfants de la balle: de la FESCI aux mouvements des patriots', *Politique Africaine*, 89 (2003), 49–70.

22. For example, Laurent Gbagbo, *Soundjata: le Lion du Manding* (Abidjan: Ceda, 1979).

23. Mike McGovern, *Making war in Côte d'Ivoire* (London: Hurst Publishers, 2009).

24. Ian Smillie, Lansana Gberie, and Ralph Hazleton, *Heart of the matter: Sierra Leone diamonds and human security* (Ottawa: Partnership Africa Canada, 2000), 42.

25. For example, Ibrahim Abdullah, 'Bush path to destruction: The origin and character of the Revolutionary United Front (RUF/SL)', *Africa Development*, 22/3 & 4 (1997), 45–76.

26. Truth and Reconciliation Commission, *Final report of the Truth and Reconciliation Commission* (Freetown: TRC, 2004), vol. 3B, 61.

27. L. Alison Smith, Catherine Gambette, and Thomas Longley, *Conflict mapping in Sierra Leone: Violations of international humanitarian law from 1991 to 2002* (Freetown: No Peace Without Justice, 2004).

28. Richard Conibere et al., *Statistical Appendix to the report of the Truth Commission and Reconciliation Commission of Sierra Leone* (Palo Alto, CA: Benetech, 2004), forced displacements on page 24, amputations on page 29, child to adult ratios on page 19.

29. Danny Hoffman, 'The civilian target in Sierra Leone and Liberia: Political power, military strategy, and humanitarian intervention', American Political Science Association annual meeting, Philadelphia, PA, 2003, 5.

30. The history of this period can be found in Alpha Lavalie, 'The SLPP in opposition', *Sierra Leone Studies at Birmingham* (Birmingham: Centre for West African Studies, University of Birmingham, 1984). Lavalie was a History lecturer at Fourah bay College who went on to form the predecessor to the CDF before he was killed in 1993.

31. Interview, Hargeisa, 22 June 2006.

32. Charles Tilly, 'War making and state making as organized crime', Peter Evans, Dietrich Rueschemeyer, and Theda Skocpol (eds.), *Bringing the state back in* (New York: Cambridge University Press, 1985), 169–91.

33. Lansana Gberie, 'An interview with Peter Penfold', *African Affairs*, 104/414 (2005), 122.

34. David Kilcullen, *The accidental guerrilla: Fighting small wars in the midst of a big one* (New York: Oxford University Press, 2009), 260.

# PART III

# The Changing Identities of Combatants: Who Fights?

# 13

## War without the People

*Pascal Vennesson*

### INTRODUCTION: WARFARE IN THE AGE
### OF THE VANISHING PEOPLE

Between 1989 and 2009, the number of major armed conflicts declined significantly. Interstate wars and civil wars have been lower in number across the period and, despite their brutality, these conflicts have killed fewer people compared with major conventional wars.[1] The wars of these twenty years were predominantly low-intensity conflicts, usually taking place in the developing world and involving relatively small, ill-trained, lightly armed forces that avoided major military engagements but frequently targeted civilians. Moreover, in the wars involving US-led coalitions against weaker opponents, like the Gulf War (1990–1), Kosovo (1999), and the ongoing conflicts in Iraq and Afghanistan, the military asymmetry was such that the battle phase was over quickly and with relatively few combat deaths. The available evidence also indicates a decline in global battle-deaths, military and civilian, during the second half of the twentieth century.[2]

Why is it that wars at the beginning of the twenty-first century have been comparatively more limited and restrained? Taking as a starting point the key Clausewitzian insight that the conduct of war is shaped in part by the domestic societal and political make-up of polities, this chapter explores the idea that the wars and strategies of the last twenty years, from 1989 until 2009, have been affected by the overall decline in popular participation in politics. The diminished role of the people has affected some key aspects of warfare, like the size, composition, and characteristics of armies, as well as war aims and theories of war. This decline in direct popular participation has been widespread in both democratic and non-democratic regimes although to different degrees and in different ways in each case, and it has affected non-state movements and groups as well. The changing role of the people in politics and in war might help to uncover at least one important source of the changing characteristics of war. The argument is not that this diminished role of the people and its consequences for war is new: in fact, under different forms it has already happened in the history of politics and warfare, as indicated by Clausewitz's own account of the practices of the eighteenth century before the French Revolution. Still, this decreased popular participation, new or not, is affecting today's wars.

The exploration of the relations between war, military institutions, and the social and political order is part of a longstanding research tradition at least since Aristotle. It was, for example, the intellectual inspiration of Hans Delbrück as he explored the relation between the organization of the nation, tactics, and strategy and developed 'the history of the art of war within the framework of political history'.[3] In order to grasp the transformations in the conduct and theory of war, we need to take a close look at domestic sociopolitical characteristics, particularly the evolution of societies and politics and their interrelations with warfare.[4]

The chapter's focus is on the people—conceived in the political sense as a group of persons who govern themselves in a single political unit—and on what Clausewitz called the 'political conditions' ('*politische Verhältnisse*') affecting their involvement in warfare.[5] The variation in level and type of popular participation has significant consequences for warfare, particularly the definition of who fights—the proportion of militarily utilized individuals in the total population[6]—and, given their particular social and educational backgrounds and political motivations, how they do so. The people's implication in war also matters because it can shape the society's capacity for war production, the popular support for the war effort, and the belligerent societies' capacity to resist the ordeal of conflict. Finally, the people's participation also brings to the fore the characteristics and intensity of combatants' motives and their consequences.

Since it touches upon the domestic political organizations of societies, their political regimes, and the characteristics of war, the issue is controversial. On the one hand, democratic theorists underline that the rise of democracy has been associated with periods 'when military organization and technology have required that large numbers of combatants be drawn from the general population'.[7] On the other hand, some scholars and policymakers have raised concern about the direct involvement of the people in war. For example, Hoffman Nickerson called the mass army—the barbarous 'armed horde'—a curse to mankind that should be abolished.[8] Nickerson's main argument, partially inspired by the French historian Hippolyte Taine, was that democratic ideas have come to dominate politics as the mass army has come to dominate war and that their conjunction had created 'barbarism', especially in long wars.[9] The danger that political and military passions override reason in warfare, warned German historian Gerhard Ritter, was growing 'ever greater and more sinister as war more and more assumes popular and mass character'.[10]

This chapter makes two arguments. First, Clausewitz's theory of war, particularly his argument about the influence of the social and political structures of polities on warfare, and his thoughts on the people provide a fruitful way to conceptualize the ways in which changing domestic political conditions might affect the character of war at the beginning of the twenty-first century. Moreover, my focus on the people brings to the fore the fact that Clausewitz's argument is not only about politics and policy but also about polity—a point which adds an intriguing layer of relation between them. Second, the relative weakening of the people's political participation (whatever its causes) has contributed to the changing character of war between 1989 and 2009, making it *comparatively* more limited and restrained.[11]

## THE PEOPLE AND THE CHANGING CHARACTER OF WAR: CLAUSEWITZ'S IDEAS

Clausewitz was, after Guibert, one of the first significant strategic thinkers to explore the ways in which the socio-political characteristics of societies might affect wars and the ways in which they are waged.[12] As Daniel Moran has noted, he lived in what Tocqueville called 'democratic times', characterized by the forceful entry of the people into politics and into war.[13] And, like Tocqueville, he was personally ambivalent about the political capacity of ordinary citizens and the consequences of the spread of constitutional government. He was not in favour of the growing popular involvement in politics and war, and he repeatedly emphasized that it was not so much the spontaneous revolutionary enthusiasm which improved France's military power but the ways in which Napoleon shaped it. Still, for better or, in Clausewitz's view, often for worse, the people had become a political force and their influence on the conduct of war was such that no political or military leader could afford to neglect them. His ideas provide us with two elements. First, *On war* suggests a way to conceptualize the influence of socio-political characteristics on the conduct of war. Second, the treatise gives us a relevant reference point to explore the question of the people's involvement in warfare. The sharp contrast between the intense popular involvement of the French Revolution and the current withdrawal of the people is a stimulating starting point to highlight the influence of changing political conditions on warfare.

In Clausewitz's theory of war, domestic socio-political characteristics play an important role. While he does not focus on the prior question of where these societal and political changes come from, he takes their consequences for war seriously.[14] How does he conceptualize these domestic political factors, especially what he called *Volk*, meaning 'nation' and 'people' as well as the 'political conditions' which may lead to the involvement of the population as a whole? When Clausewitz examined the people he referred to the social and political orders, the socio-political characteristics of societies. While these are related to the political regime, he distinguished the people from the government or the executive branch, the controlling agent in war. These socio-political transformations are also distinct from, but have implications for, military organizations and generalship. Finally, the effects of socio-political transformations are not limited to one country: they are diffused in the international system. The French Revolution had an impact on the internal conditions of every state.[15]

In order to balance ends and means, strategists have to consider a bewildering array of factors. Clausewitz suggested that to get a better grasp of these factors, they should consider 'the nature of states and societies as they are determined by their times and prevailing conditions'.[16] For him, 'war and its forms result from ideas, emotions and conditions prevailing at the time'.[17] Different polities—which he identified as semi-barbarous Tartars, republics of antiquity, feudal lords and ruling cities of the Middle Ages, eighteenth-century kings, and the rulers and peoples of the nineteenth century—'all conducted war in their own particular way, using different methods and pursuing different aims'.[18] In his brief look at the history of these changing polities and prevailing conditions, Clausewitz mentioned their degrees of state cohesion, their political regimes, and the role of exceptional leaders ('new Alexanders'). Regarding the people and the military, he emphasized the size of the army, the inclusion or exclusion of the mass of the people in the military, and the interests of the people in what was at stake in the conflict (is the war a concern for the people?):

> The Tartar people and army had been one; in the republics of antiquity and during the Middle Ages the people (if we confine the concept to those who had the rights of citizens) had still played a prominent part; but in the circumstances of the eighteenth century the people's part had been extinguished. The only influence the people continued to exert on war was an indirect one – through its general virtues or shortcomings.[19]

And Clausewitz added: 'War thus became solely the concern of the government to the extent that governments parted company with their people and behaved as if they were themselves the state. Their means of waging war came to consist of the money in their coffers and of such idle vagabonds as they could lay their hands on either at home or abroad.'[20]

He drew a sharp contrast with the French Revolution, based on the changing role of the people. In the eighteenth century, the role of the people was limited ('simply that of an instrument') while governments could act alone. 'At the onset of the nineteenth century, peoples themselves were in the scale on either side.'[21] The revolution and its quest for a greater social and political equality was for him a key element of the changing character of war. 'Sudden-ly', he explained in book 8, 'war again became the business of the people—a people of thirty millions, all of whom considered themselves to be citizens'.[22] A stupendous change in the character of societies and government came to shape warfare. With the French Revolution, 'the people became a participant in war; instead of governments and armies as heretofore, the full weight of the nation was thrown into the balance'.[23] As a consequence of the people's direct participation, 'the war of today's time is a war of all against all. The king does not wage war against the king, the army not against another [army], but one people against another [people], and king and army are part of the people.'[24]

Depending on the relative involvement of the people—and on policy-makers' perceptions of these social and political conditions—political and social structures can impose or remove restraints on the conduct of war.[25] These socio-political conditions can favour the trend towards absolute war, or they can contribute to the limitation of warfare. Involving the people in politics and war favours war's escalation. Why is it that 'war, untrammelled by any conventional restraints, had broken loose in all its elemental fury'?[26] Clausewitz responds: 'This was due to the people's new share in these great affairs of state; and their participation, in turn, resulted partly from the impact that the Revolution had on the internal conditions of every state and partly from the danger that France posed to everyone.'[27] As Christopher Daase explains, on the offensive, the *levée en masse* and national enthusiasm could be used to conquer foreign countries, while, on the defensive, the people's war could help to protect the national homeland.[28] Stanislav Andreski also noted that the extension of military service 'is conducive to greater ferocity in war'.[29]

How does the degree of people's participation impose or remove restraints on the conduct of war? The people can affect the two main factors of power identified by Clausewitz: the magnitude of means (particularly the number of soldiers) and the strength of will.[30] He associated 'mainly' (*mehr*)—but not uniquely or exclusively—the people with the first element of his most famous trinity, 'violence, hatred and enmity, which are to be regarded as a blind natural force'.[31] For him, the people is in general on the side of the passions. The 'heart and temper of a nation' can alter the conduct of war since it can make an enormous contribution 'to the sum total of its politics, war potential, and fighting strength'.[32] Moral forces can help create a numerous and power-ful army.[33] More generally, thanks to the contribution of popular passions to the war effort, the political conditions created by the French Revolution put into action new means, new forces, and gave to warfare a new energy.[34]

It is important to recognize, however, that passions, particularly popular passion, are only one element of the trinity that can affect the conduct of war. Both the play of chance and probability as well as the instrument of policy subject to reason have the potential to transform warfare. Furthermore, each aspect affects the others and the trinity interacts with the trinity of the other belligerent. If, as Hew Strachan notes, trinities clash, then it is the interaction between trinities which ultimately helps to account for the transformations of wars.[35]

Since social and political conditions can have a significant impact on warfare, policymakers must assess the character and abilities of the opposing government and people and do the same with their own.[36] However, Clausewitz acknowledged that this task is challenging: policymakers do not always perceive or understand socio-political characteristics and changes.[37] Decision-makers can make political errors and, like Prussia's rulers in Clausewitz's time, cling to the belief that the social and political situation has not actually changed. They might neglect social and political conditions altogether and prefer to focus on military factors like armaments or tactics. They might also misunderstand social and political characteristics and their military implications. In short, misperceptions of socio-political conditions, and particularly of the changing participation of the people, are no less influential than in other aspects of strategy.

Military professionals sometimes see popular influence as problematic and undesirable. For example, in 1911, General Jean Colin explained that military leaders should be concerned not only by governments' interference but by the people's interference as well.[38] Driven by passions, popular intervention might force unwanted battles and also shameful capitulations. Consequently, Colin argued, political authorities should calm or even repress popular movements. Before 1914, both the German and the French general staffs were concerned that general mobilization would trigger major social unrest, a danger that they saw as an additional incentive to try to keep the war short.[39] They worried about what they saw as an alarming fragility of societies. More recently, despite the lack of evidence, and despite some evidence to the contrary in the United States, the belief in the general public's casualty aversion has been, and remains, widespread among policymakers and journalists.[40] In 2002–3, Saddam Hussein and the senior Iraqi leadership remained convinced that the United States was unwilling to undertake any action that could result in even very small numbers of American casualties which they thought would prove politically unsustainable.[41]

## THE VANISHING PEOPLE: POLITICAL CONDITIONS AT THE BEGINNING OF THE TWENTY-FIRST CENTURY

What has been the overall place and role of the people in politics in different political systems, both democratic and non-democratic, since 1989? Assessing the changing characteristics of socio-political systems is a challenging task and political scientists and sociologists often disagree. Their assessments are partially dependent on assumptions and premises about democracy and political participation. And yet, despite difficulties in measurement and interpretation, despite the variety of approaches and perspectives (some egalitarian and others elitist), a remarkable consensus has been reached on the evolution of political participation these last twenty years, especially among democracies (even if disagreements persist about the causes and potential remedies). Scholars have been pointing to a trend towards 'disaffected', 'diminished', 'stealth', 'abstentionist', or even 'post-' democracy.[42] Politics at the beginning of the twenty-first century is characterized by the diminishing role of the people, and not just in the west.[43]

One key aspect of democracy is the rule by the many.[44] Democracy implies the possibility for the mass of ordinary citizens to participate actively in the discussion, the organization, and the agenda-making of public life. The capacity of citizens to participate in their polity takes, in particular, the forms of the right to vote, to create and join organizations, and to receive accurate information. In short, government and politics are not the affair of small groups of elite decision-makers alone, and corporate elites are politically constrained to accept certain limitations on their capacity to use their power. This emphasis on the role of the people implies that electoral participation is not the only type of mass participation; that lobbying activities (especially business lobbies), while legitimate, might undermine the people's will; and that a polity which does not interfere with the capitalist economy might undermine the citizens' well-being.[45]

Colin Crouch argues that in established democracies, politics is now shaped by a different configuration of actors and power relations. The global firm has become a prominent political actor, the working class has been declining steadily, and a new political class of advisors and business lobbyists is playing an increasing role in government.[46] The forms of democracy remain in place, but a system of governance has been rising in which the people as such play a diminished role, while the reality of power is more controlled by elites. This political situation generates several significant consequences. Citizens are increasingly disillusioned by politics and have low expectations of politicians' achievements. The mass of ordinary people is less active than powerful minority interests in making the political system work for them. At the same time, political elites have acquired a greater sophistication in managing and manipulating popular demands, notably through top-down communication campaigns to persuade citizens.[47] The advertising industry model of communication has become dominant and mass political communication more fully resembles advertisement: short messages, words and images, instead of arguments. Citizens are less likely to vote or to join political parties, and these rare participants are more often passive and manipulated.[48] Societies are also more fragmented. Politics are shaped in private by interaction between elected governments and elites closed to business interests.

Critics of the disaffected democracy thesis usually argue that involvement in voluntary associations can compensate for the decline of political parties and reinforce citizenship. However, the existing empirical evidence raises doubts about this possibility: people join groups that are homogeneous, not heterogeneous; civic participation does not lead to, and may turn people away from, political participation; and not all groups promote democratic values.[49] The consequences of these transformations are particularly striking concerning warfare, for which the control of the democratic process is traditionally more challenging.[50]

In sum, there has been a weakening of the direct political involvement of ordinary citizens. The people might remain politically significant for policy-makers but more indirectly as public opinion measured by opinion polls, as 'reflected' in parliaments, as journalists perceived as the people's spokespersons or as civil society. Different factors have contributed to this trend: the rise of the global firm as a significant political actor, the growing dominance of business lobbies, the perceived competence of the private sector to run public service activities, the decline of the occupations that powered the rise of popular political participation, and the existence of a fragmented and more passive population which finds it more challenging to generate organizations to articulate its demands, as well as the related transformation of political parties.

The reaction of the American people to the 9/11 attacks is a good illustration of this changing place and role of the people and its implication for war.[51] It was a direct attack on American soil. Almost immediately, President Bush qualified the attack as an act of war and launched the war on terror. Following the attacks, in an outpouring of solidarity and patriotism suddenly 'we' mattered more than 'me'.[52] However, as Theda Skocpol showed, the shift in popular attitudes did not translate into a direct involvement of the citizenry in war.[53] First, US government authorities have not been eager to engage in mass mobilization. Instead, in accordance with a liberal ideology which proclaims self-interested behaviour as a social duty, President Bush urged Americans to take more aeroplane trips and to go shopping to stimulate the economy. The private, consumption-oriented, road was seen as the surest and perhaps the only way in which the individual could make a contribution to the war effort. Furthermore, there were fewer channels to enable people to act together and to connect face-to-face activities in local communities with national projects.[54] The initial characteristics of the war—a limited intervention by a few hundred Central Intelligence Agency officers and US Special Forces soldiers, together with massive air support and 15,000 Afghan fighters, in Afghanistan and the creation and strengthening of homeland security—seemed to entail different requirements for the people. But, as Skocpol notes, it is also true that the conflict occurred 'in a changed public world in which political authorities and non-profit organizations rely on professional management and media messages rather than on organized popular participation'.[55]

The diminished role of the people in politics is confined neither to the Western world nor to established democracies. In many developing countries, situations of governance without government, where the context is fragile and the people are alienated, are frequent.[56] In addition, there is evidence that terrorist networks, unlike the liberation movements of the past, are not relying on a territorially and politically defined people that they seek to mobilize and transform into direct participants in war.[57] In sum, politics and government are less shaped by an active involvement of the people.

If true, following Clausewitz's insights, what does the diminished political participation of the people imply for warfare? First, the people as such should be less direct participants in war. They could, however, continue to play an indirect role, as both insurgents and counterinsurgencies target hearts and minds, locally and globally. This type of warfare would be compatible with the fact that public opinion and the media might be perceived by policymakers as an important centre of gravity. The people could also remain, to different degrees, affected by warfare, although war might be divorced from the interests of the people. Second, military forces would be smaller in numbers. Third, only a fraction of the war potential could be, and would be, mobilized and there would be less pressure to escalate. Fourth, the emotional element in warfare would be kept to a minimum. Overall, wars should be more restricted than during periods of stronger popular involvement.[58]

## VANISHING PEOPLE AND LIMITED WARFARE IN THE EARLY TWENTY-FIRST CENTURY

What are the major characteristics of the armed conflicts fought between 1989 and 2009?[59] Overall, the main characteristics of warfare these last twenty years broadly fit Clausewitzian expectations: in an era of diminished direct popular involvement, warfare appears more limited in terms of means and ends. However, this might not hold for specific armed conflicts in which the people might remain comparatively more involved and in which the characteristics of warfare might therefore continue to be closer to Clausewitz's description of revolutionary warfare.

While the argument of Clausewitz outlined above is about the character of wars, not their causes or frequency, it is important to emphasize that the evolution of the character of war is taking place in a context in which the number of major armed conflicts has declined since 1990 and that the number of interstate conflicts has been declining as well. For example, in the sixteen-year period 1990–2005, four of the fifty-seven active conflicts were fought between states: Eritrea–Ethiopia (1998–2000), India–Pakistan (1990–2 and 1996–2003), Iraq–Kuwait (1991), and Iraq versus the United States and its allies (2003). Furthermore, while the number of civil wars in the world increased from two in 1946 to twenty-five in 1991, there has been a significant decline since then, even if their number has been slowly rising again since 2006.[60]

Significantly, in assessing the changing character of war, the evolution of battle-deaths—which is different from war-related deaths—helps to assess changes in the scope and nature of military operations. While data collection is more difficult than for other indicators, the available work points to a decline in global battle-deaths, military and civilian, during the second half of the twentieth century.[61] The battle-death rate in the 1990s was only one-third that of the 1970s.[62] In 1950, there were more than 38,000 battlefield deaths per conflict; in 2002, there were 600.[63] Between 2004 and 2007, violent deaths in non-conflict settings (66 per cent) and indirect deaths in armed conflicts (27 per cent) comprised a much larger proportion of armed violence than the number of people dying violently in contemporary wars (7 per cent).[64]

The wars of these last twenty years have been predominantly low-intensity conflicts, usually taking place in the developing world. Relatively small, ill-trained, lightly armed forces avoid major military engagements but frequently target civilians. The 2005 *Human security report* notes that, despite their brutality, these conflicts 'kill relatively few people compared with major conventional wars'.[65] In addition, some conflicts involved US-led coalitions against weaker opponents, like the Gulf War (1990–1), Kosovo (1999), and the ongoing conflicts in Iraq and Afghanistan.[66] In these wars, the military asymmetry is such that the battle phase is over quickly and 'with relatively few combat deaths compared with the major wars of the Cold War period'.[67] Other conflicts are also fought between militias, rival guerrilla groups, clans, warlords, or organized communal groups without the involvement of a government. While data on these non-state armed conflicts have only been collected since 2005, the available evidence shows that they are also significantly less deadly than state-based conflicts, and that they tend to be relatively short in duration.[68] Finally, since 1990, and despite the genocide in Rwanda and the Srebrenica massacre, the number of mass killings of civilians has been declining as well.[69]

In these wars, who fights and how? In the west, military forces are smaller and professional, since there are fewer mass armies based on conscription. The percentage of national populations serving in the armed forces has declined across Europe.[70] In 2007, two EU member states, Cyprus and Greece, maintained armed forces comprising more than 0.8 per cent of the population and three, Bulgaria, Denmark, and Finland, had forces comprising between 0.5 and 0.79 per cent of the population. The armed forces of twenty-two out of twenty-seven member states account for less than 0.5 per cent of their populations.[71] While in 1995, five European countries—Belgium, Ireland, Luxembourg, Malta, and the United Kingdom—had all-volunteer forces, in 2007, sixteen do. In some cases, as during the initial phase of the campaign in Afghanistan, special forces units, even smaller and more highly trained, played the most significant role in combat. At times, these special forces conduct covert operations without the local governments' authorization and with only limited parliamentary oversight. However, when military organizations are engaged in counter-insurgency, peacekeeping, and stability operations, numbers become important again.[72] In the United States and other countries peace operations have required the involvement of the National Guard or similar units on a large scale.

In developing countries, direct popular involvement in warfare has also been declining, and this has affected the forces and their support. For example, throughout the 1990s, the war in Sierra Leone was not the product of any national or popular mobilization, shaped by the ideologues and reformers who led many of Africa's armed struggles. Unemployed and violent youth were interested in looting, not in defending citizens, and the Revolutionary United Front (RUF) remained deeply unpopular.[73] More generally, child soldiers, while not a new phenomenon, are an important characteristic of the forces involved in wars today. Peter Singer has emphasized that they are present in 75 per cent of armed conflicts. Child soldiers can use light weapons and reach a certain operational effectiveness. Children appear to be cheap and expendable recruits. As Peter Singer notes, the 'otherwise unpopular armies and rebel groups have been able to field far greater forces than they would otherwise, through strategies of abduction or indoctrination'.[74] Finally, private military firms made a remarkable comeback, reflecting the trend to privatize public assets, and their influence has been significant in both developed and developing countries.[75] Overall, some key characteristics of today's wars are linked to the changing and ambivalent role of the people.[76] Political leaders in the west, seemingly less constrained by the people, can deploy force more often but, deprived of a genuine popular involvement and commitment, face difficulty in committing major resources to the war effort. However, these forces are engaged in 'war amongst the people' and fight for the people's hearts and minds and, similarly, insurgents target, directly or indirectly, peoples and societies in the west.

The kind of limited warfare fought for limited objectives with limited means and with comparatively fewer casualties which characterized the period 1989–2009 bears some resemblance with warfare during the eighteenth century before the French Revolution.[77] Dynastic rulers could not draw on the full human resources of their countries. As Robert Palmer notes, the ties between sovereign and subject were bureaucratic, administrative, and fiscal, and the *ancien régime* government in wartime interfered as little as possible with civilian life. The 'good people' obeyed the laws, paid their taxes, and were loyal to their rulers: there was neither need for a people with their own identity nor a sense of obligation to participate, or support, the war effort.[78] The peoples of the dynastic states felt little sense of participation in the issues of war. The soldiers enlisted for long terms, and as Palmer argues, they 'fought as a business for a living, . . . were thought incapable of higher sentiments, and [their] strongest attachment was usually a kind of naïve pride in their regiments'.[79] The *ancien régime* governments took increasingly good care of the welfare of their soldiers, quartered them in barracks, and provided them with medical services. These professional armies were expensive and battles represented a tremendous risk. As Clausewitz emphasized when he described eighteenth-century warfare, commanders had to use their armies cautiously: 'If the army was pulverized, [the commander] could not raise another, and behind the army there was nothing.'[80] These limits and restrictions resonate with the conduct of war between 1989 and 2009.


## CONCLUSION

In closing, we can highlight two main conclusions. First, the main argument derived from Clausewitz that the people's changing involvement in politics can impose or remove restraints on the conduct of war proves stimulating and useful in exploring the transformation of the character of war at the beginning of the twenty-first century. Second, while more detailed and more differentiated empirical assessments are surely needed, as a first-cut the main characteristics of warfare these last twenty years broadly fit the Clausewitzian hypothesis: in an era of diminished direct popular involvement, warfare appears comparatively more limited in terms of means and ends. While the decline in popular participation is worrisome for democracy, it may to a certain extent have limited wars and their destructive effects these last twenty years.

The point of this chapter is to open a potentially fruitful line of enquiry on the changing character of war, not to provide definitive answers. First, what might be true of the evolution of warfare as a social and political phenomenon over twenty years might not be true of a specific conflict. For example, there is evidence that the people continue to play at least some role in the Israeli–Palestinian conflict. Moreover, the people might also play a much greater role in countries like Iran and particularly China, which could have implications for warfare. Second, the lesser involvement of the people in politics might come to an end. For example, the economic crisis might considerably weaken the global firm and lead to a new role for states and people. Third, missing from this Clausewitz-inspired framework is the role of technology in the changing character of war or, more precisely, the relations between socio-political dynamics and technology. Fourth, if the participation of the people can affect warfare, the opposite is just as relevant: warfare affects the people and can forge its identity. Finally, some prominent strategists, like General Sir Rupert Smith, have argued that wars today are fought 'amongst the people', a case which seems to contradict the notion of a vanishing people. One of the reasons for the tactical and operational challenges and difficulties facing the forces deployed in such conflicts might arise precisely because these wars 'amongst the people' are taking place in an era in which the meaning and political significance of the people have been changing considerably. If so, then some past experiences of counter-insurgency—those in which the role of the people was limited on both sides—might be more useful than others.

## NOTES

1. *Human Security Report 2005*; Andrew Mack, 'Global political violence: Explaining the post-Cold War decline', *Coping with Crisis Working Paper Series* (New York: International Peace Academy, 2007); Geneva Declaration, *Global burden of armed violence* (Geneva: Geneva Declaration Secretariat, 2008). See also Nils Petter Gleditsch et al., 'Armed conflict 1946–2001: A new dataset', *Journal of Peace Research*, 39/5 (2002), 615–37; Lotta Harbom and Peter Wallensteen, 'Armed conflict, 1989–2006', *Journal of Peace Research*, 44/5 (2007), 623–34.

2. Bethany Lacina and Nils Petter Gleditsch, 'Monitoring trends in global combat: A new dataset of battle deaths', *European Journal of Population* 21/1 (2005), 145–66; Bethany Lacina, Nils Petter Gleditsch, and Bruce Russett, 'The declining risk of death in battle', *International Studies Quarterly* 50/3 (2006), 673–80.

3. Hans Delbrück, *The dawn of modern warfare: History of the art of war, volume IV* (Lincoln: University of Nebraska Press, 1990 [1920]), x; Michael Howard, *War in European history* (Oxford: Oxford University Press, 1976). See also Piero Del Negro, *Guerra ed eserciti da Macchiavelli a Napoleone* (Roma: Editori Laterza, 2001), 139–45.

4. Raymond Aron, *La société industrielle et la guerre* (Paris: Plon, 1959); J.F.C. Fuller, *The conduct of war, 1789–1961* (New York: Da Capo Press, 1992 [1961]); Michael Howard, 'The forgotten dimensions of strategy', *Foreign Affairs* 57 (1978–9), 975–86; Martin Shaw, *Post-military society: Militarism, demilitarization and war at the end of the twentieth century* (Philadelphia: Temple University Press, 1991); Eric Desmons, *Mourir pour la patrie?* (Paris: Presses universitaires de France-Béhémoth, 2001).

5. Giovanni Sartori, *The theory of democracy revisited* (Chatham, NJ: Chatham House Publishers, 1987), 21–38.

6. Stanislav Andreski, *Military organization and society* (London: Routledge, 1968), 33.
7. Robert A. Dahl, *Democracy and its critics* (New Haven, CT: Yale University Press, 1989), 245.
8. Hoffman Nickerson, *The armed horde, 1793–1939: A study of the rise, survival and decline of the mass army* (New York: G. P. Putnam's Sons, 1942), xvii.
9. Nickerson, *The armed horde*, 14, 16.
10. Gerhard Ritter, *The sword and the sceptre: The problem of the military in Germany, Volume I: The Prussian tradition, 1740–1890* (Coral Gables, FL: University of Miami Press, 1969), 68. See also Gerhard Ritter, *Frederick the Great* (Berkeley, CA: University of California Press, 1968), 131–2, 141–2; David Kaiser, *Politics and war: European conflict from Philip II to Hitler* (Cambridge, MA: Harvard University Press, 1990), 418.
11. For related but distinct arguments, see: Michael Desch, 'War and strong states, peace and weak States?' *International Organization*, 50/2 (1996), 237–68; Miguel Angel Centeno, 'Limited war and limited states', in Diane E. Davis and Anthony W. Pereira (eds.), *Irregular armed forces and their role in politics and state formation* (Cambridge: Cambridge University Press, 2003), 82–95. On the consequences of social structure for the composition and effectiveness of armies, see Kenneth M. Pollack, *Arabs at war: Military effectiveness, 1948–1991* (Lincoln: University of Nebraska Press, 2002).
12. Michael Howard, 'The forgotten dimensions of strategy', 977. Guibert anticipated the challenges and dilemmas resulting from the people's participation in politics and war: Comte de Guibert, *Stratégique* (Paris: L'Herne-Classiques de la stratégie, 1977); Lucien Poirier, *Les voix de la stratégie: Généalogie de la stratégie militaire: Guibert, Jomini* (Paris: Fayard, 1985), 277–80, 285–302.
13. Daniel Moran, 'Introduction', in Carl von Clausewitz (edited and translated by Peter Paret and Daniel Moran), *Historical and political writings* (Princeton, NJ: Princeton University Press, 1992), 235.
14. Peter Paret, *Understanding war: Essays on Clausewitz and the history of military power* (Princeton, NJ: Princeton University Press, 1992), 167–77; Hew Strachan, *Clausewitz's On War: A biography* (New York: Grove Press, 2007), 160–90. See also: Thomas Hippler, *Citizens, soldiers and national armies: military service in France and Germany, 1789–1830* (London: Routledge, 2008).
15. Clausewitz, *On war*, edited and translated by Michael Howard and Peter Paret (Princeton, NJ: Princeton University Press, 1984) 593; Carl von Clausewitz, 'Agitation', in Clausewitz, *Historical and political writings*, 335–68.
16. Clausewitz, *On war*, 586.
17. Ibid., 580.
18. Ibid., 586.
19. Ibid., 589.
20. Ibid.
21. Ibid., 583.
22. Ibid., 592.
23. Ibid.

24. Clausewitz, *Schriften*, I, 750 quoted by Christopher Daase, 'Clausewitz and small wars', in Hew Strachan and Andreas Herberg-Rothe (eds.), *Clausewitz in the twenty-first century* (Oxford: Oxford University Press, 2007), 192–3.
25. Strachan, *Clausewitz's On War*, 169, 171f.
26. Clausewitz, *On War*, 593.
27. Ibid.
28. Daase, 'Clausewitz and small wars', 192.
29. Stanislav Andreski, *Military organization and society* (London: Routledge, 1968), 117f.
30. Clausewitz, *On war*, 195; Hans Rothfels, 'Clausewitz', in: Edward Mead Earle (ed.), *Makers of modern strategy. Military thought from Machiavelli to Hitler* (Princeton, NJ: Princeton University Press, 1948), 96.
31. Clausewitz, *On war*, 89. Christopher Bassford, 'The primacy of policy and the "trinity" in Clausewitz's mature thought', in Strachan and Herberg-Rothe (eds.), *Clausewitz in the twenty-first century*, 74–90.
32. Clausewitz, *On war*, 3, 17, 220.
33. On the link between moral factors and Clausewitz's theory of friction: Ulrike Kleemeier, 'Moral forces in war', in Strachan and Herberg-Rothe (eds.), *Clausewitz in the twenty-first century*, 107–21.
34. Clausewitz, *On war*, 610.
35. Strachan, *Clausewitz's On War*, 179.
36. Clausewitz, *On war*, 586.
37. Clausewitz, *On war*, 583f., 609.
38. Général Colin, *Les transformations de la guerre* (Paris: Economica-Bibliothèque stratégique, 1989), 242f. For another type of uneasiness vis-à-vis popular involvement: Stig Förster, 'Facing "people's war": Moltke the elder and German military options after 1871', *Journal of Strategic Studies* 10 (1978), 209–30.
39. Hew Strachan, *The First World War. Volume I: To arms* (Oxford: Oxford University Press, 2001), 1010f.
40. Philip P. Everts, *Democracy and military force* (London: Palgrave, 2002), 181; Christopher Gelpi, Peter D. Feaver, and Jason Reifler, *Paying the human costs of war* (Princeton, NJ: Princeton University Press), 2009.
41. Kevin M. Woods et al., *Iraqi perspectives project. A view of operation Iraqi Freedom from Saddam's senior leadership* (Washington: Joint Center for Operational Analysis, 2006), 30. For similar misperceptions, *The 9/11 commission report. Final report of the national commission on terrorist attacks upon the United States* (New York: W.W. Norton, 2004), 48.
42. S. J. Pharr and Robert D. Putnam (eds.), *Disaffected democracies: What's troubling the trilateral countries?* (Princeton, NJ: Princeton University Press, 2000); Robert D. Putnam, *Bowling alone: The collapse and revival of American community* (New York: Simon and Schuster, 2000); John R. Hibbing and Elizabeth Theiss-Morse, *Stealth democracy. American's belief about how government should work* (Cambridge: Cambridge University Press, 2002), 129–59; Theda Skocpol, *Diminished democracy: From membership to management in American civic life* (Norman: University of Oklahoma Press, 2003); Céline Braconnier and Jean-Yves Dormagen, *La démocratie de l'abstention. Aux origines de la*

*démobilisation électorale en milieu populaire* (Paris: Gallimard-Folio-Actuel, 2007); Colin Crouch, *Post-democracy* (London: Polity, 2004); Guy Hermet, 'Un régime à pluralisme limité? A propos de la gouvernance démocratique', *Revue Française de Science Politique*, 54/1 (2004), 159–78. About the evolving characteristics of societies' political involvement: Amitai Etzioni, *The active society. A theory of societal and political processes* (New York: Free Press, 1968).

43. This formulation is inspired by, Thomas E. Patterson, *The vanishing voter. Public involvement in an age of uncertainty* (New York: Vintage, 2003).

44. Carole Pateman, *Participation and democratic theory* (Cambridge: Cambridge University Press, 1970); Albert Hirschman, *Shifting involvements. Private interest and public action* (Princeton, NJ: Princeton University Press, 1982); Benjamin Barber, *Strong democracy. Participatory politics for a new age* (Berkeley, CA: University of California Press, 2003); Pippa Norris, *Democratic phoenix: Reinventing political activism* (Cambridge: Cambridge University Press, 2002).

45. Charles E. Lindblom, *Politics and markets* (New York: Basic Books, 1977); Robert A. Dahl, *A preface to economic democracy* (Berkeley, CA: University of California Press, 1985).

46. Colin Crouch, *Post-democracy* (London: Polity, 2004). See also Susan Strange, *The retreat of the state. The diffusion of power in the world economy* (Cambridge: Cambridge University Press, 1996).

47. Crouch, *Post-democracy*, 19f.

48. Philippe C. Schmitter et al., *The future of democracy in Europe. Trends, analyses and reforms* (Strasbourg: Council of Europe Publishing, 2004), 22f., 38f.; Crouch, *Post-democracy*, 21.

49. Elizabeth Theiss-Morse and John R. Hibbing, 'Citizenship and civic engagement', *Annual Review of Political Science*, 8 (2005), 227–49.

50. Robert Dahl, *Controlling nuclear weapons. Democracy versus guardianship* (Syracuse: Syracuse University Press, 1985); Sheldon S. Wolin, *The presence of the past. Essays on the state and the constitution* (Baltimore, MD: Johns Hopkins University Press, 1989), 180–207.

51. On the changing views and practices vis-à-vis war in Europe, James J. Sheehan, *Where have the soldiers gone? The transformation of modern Europe* (Boston, MA: Houghton Mifflin Company, 2008).

52. Stanley B. Greenberg, '"We"—not "me": Public opinion and the return of government', *The American Prospect*, 17 December 2001, 25–7.

53. Theda Skocpol, 'Will 9/11 and the war on terror revitalize American civic Democracy?' *PS. Political Science and Politics*, 35/3 (2002), 537–40; Idem., *Diminished democracy*.

54. Skocpol, 'Will 9/11 and the war on terror revitalize American civic democracy?', 538f.

55. Ibid., 540.

56. Ken Menkhaus, 'Governance without government in Somalia: Spoilers, state building, and the politics of coping', *International Security*, 31/3 (2006–7), 74–106.

57. Bernard Rougier, *Le Jihad au quotidien* (Paris: Presses universitaires de France, 2004), 244–7.

58. Martin Shaw, *The new western way of war* (London: Polity Press, 2005).

59. In what follows, I use the compilation of data on armed conflicts by the Uppsala Conflict Data Program (UCDP) of the Department of Peace and Conflict Research, Uppsala University, and by the International Peace Research Institute, Oslo (PRIO). The USDP defines a major armed conflict as 'a contested incompatibility concerning government or territory over which the use of armed force between the military forces of two parties, of which at least one is the government of a state, has resulted in at least 1000 battle-related deaths in a single calendar year'. See: *SIPRI Yearbook* 2006, 2007, 2008. I also use the *Human Security Report 2005* and the *Human Security Brief 2006*. For a discussion of these data sets and the best way to assess armed conflicts, see: Michael Brzoska, 'Collective violence beyond the standard definition of armed conflict', in: *SIPRI Yearbook 2007: Armaments, disarmament and international security* (Oxford: Oxford University Press, 2007), 94–106. See also Pierre Hassner and Roland Marchal (eds.), *Guerres et sociétés. Etat et violence après la Guerre Froide* (Paris: Karthala-Recherches Internationales, 2003); Jeremy Black, *War since 1990* (London: The Social Affairs Unit, 2009).

60. *Human Security Report 2005*, 150f.; Mack, 'Global Political Violence'. See also: Gleditsch et al., 'Armed conflict 1946–2001'; Harbom and Wallensteen, 'Armed conflict, 1989–2006'.

61. Lacina and Gleditsch, 'Monitoring trends in global combat'; Lacina, Gleditsch, and Russett, 'The declining risk of death in battle'; Bethany Lacina, 'Explaining the severity of civil wars', *Journal of Conflict Resolution*, 50/2 (2006), 276–89. For a critique of these results: Ziad Obermeyer, C. J. L. Murray, and Emanuela Gakidou, 'Fifty years of violent war deaths from Vietnam to Bosnia: Analysis of data from the word health survey programme', *British Medical Journal* 336 (2008) and the rejoinder: Michael Spagat, Andrew Mack, Tara Cooper, and Joakim Kreutz, 'Estimating war deaths: An arena of contestation', *Journal of Conflict Resolution*, 53/6 (2009), 934–50.

62. *Human Security Report 2005*, 29.

63. Ibid., 31.

64. Geneva Declaration, *Global burden of armed violence* (Geneva: Geneva Declaration Secretariat, 2008), 2.

65. *Human Security Report 2005*, 34.

66. Ibid.

67. Ibid.

68. *Human Security Brief 2006*, 9.

69. Barbara Harff, 'No lessons learned from the Holocaust? Assessing risks of genocide and political mass murder since 1955', *American Political Science Review* 93/1 (2003), 57–73; *Human Security Report 2005*, 40–2; *Human Security Brief 2006*, 11–17. See also: Kristine Eck and Lisa Hultman, 'One-sided violence against civilians in war: Insights from new fatality data', *Journal of Peace Research*, 44/2 (2007), 233–46.

70. Charles C. Moskos et al., *The postmodern military* (Oxford: Oxford University Press, 2000); Anthony Forster, *Armed forces and society in Europe* (Basingstoke: Palgrave-Macmillan, 2006), 253–70.

71. Bastian Giegerich, *European military crisis management: Connecting ambition and reality*, Adelphi Paper No. 397 (London: Routledge, 2008), 35–7.
72. Michael O'Hanlon and Peter W. Singer, 'The humanitarian transformation: Expanding the global intervention capacity', *Survival* 46/1 (2004), 77–100.
73. William Reno, 'The changing nature of warfare and the absence of state-building in West Africa', in Davis and Pereira (eds.), *Irregular Armed Forces*, 322–45; Lansana Gberie, *A dirty war in West Africa: The RUF and the destruction of Sierra Leone* (London: Hurst, 2005). See also Thandika Mkandawire, 'The terrible toll of post-colonial "rebel movements" in Africa: Towards an explanation of the violence against the peasantry', *Journal of Modern African Studies*, 40/2 (2002), 181–208; Isabelle Duyvesteyn, *Clausewitz and African war. Politics and strategy in Liberia and Somalia* (London: Frank Cass, 2005), 53–74; Jeremy M. Weinstein, *Inside rebellion. The politics of insurgent violence* (Cambridge: Cambridge University Press, 2007).
74. Quoted in: *Human Security Report 2005*, 35.
75. Deborah D. Avant, *The market for force. The consequences of privatizing security* (Cambridge: Cambridge University Press, 2005), 1–9, 16–30, 81–142; *Human Security Report 2005*, 37–9.
76. Hew Strachan, *The changing character of war*, Europaeum lecture delivered at the Graduate Institute of International Relations, Geneva, 9 November 2006 (Oxford: Europaeum, 2007), 20–3; General Rupert Smith, *The utility of force. The art of war in the modern world* (New York: Alfred A. Knopf, 2007).
77. Ritter, *Frederick the Great*, 129–48; Robert R. Palmer, 'Frederick the Great, Guibert, Bülow: From dynastic to national war', in Peter Paret (ed.), *Makers of modern strategy from Machiavelli to the nuclear age* (Princeton, NJ: Princeton University Press, 1986), 91–119; Hew Strachan, *European armies and the conduct of war* (London: Routledge, 2006), 8–22. The historiography of the period is naturally richer and more complex than this sketch implies. See in particular: André Corvisier, *Armées et sociétés en Europe de 1494 à 1789* (Paris: Presses universitaires de France, 1976); M. S. Anderson, *War and society in Europe of the old regime, 1618–1789* (Leicester: Leicester University Press, 1988); André Corvisier and Jean Delmas (eds.), *Histoire militaire de la France. 2. De 1715 à 1781* (Paris: Presses universitaires de France, 1992); Jean Chagniot, *Guerre et société à l'époque moderne* (Paris: Presses universitaires de France-Nouvelle Clio, 2001).
78. Robert R. Palmer, Frederick the Great, Guibert, Bülow', 91–3.
79. Ibid.
80. Clausewitz, *On war*, 590.

# 14

---

# The Changing Character of Private Force

*Sarah Percy*

Mercenaries have been dubbed the world's second oldest profession.[1] They have fought alongside soldiers for, perhaps, as long as there have been wars. Given this long history, what conclusions can we draw about private fighters on today's battlefields? To what extent are mercenaries in Africa or private security companies fighting in Iraq like Italian *condottieri* or the mercenary bands of the Hundred Years War? These questions are broad, and of course it is difficult to make useful comparisons over long periods of history and across many different places. But the *concept* of a mercenary has been largely the same over this long period. The idea that a mercenary is a soldier who fights outside the authoritative control of an actor deemed to be in possession of the legitimate use of force (the church, a prince, the state) and for personal financial gain has held true at least since the early middle ages.[2] This continuity means that it is possible to ask some questions about the history of private force that will allow us to consider how its use has evolved and what the mercenaries of the past reveal about their descendants today. To provide an analysis of continuity and change in private force, this chapter will answer four questions. First, who are the private fighters? Second, who hires private fighters? Third, why hire them? Fourth, what concerns about the use of private force have been raised over time?

## WHAT IS PRIVATE FORCE?

Private force, or private fighters, are soldiers who are usually external to the conflict in which they are employed (they have no direct attachment stemming from ideology, nationality, religion, or other motivating factors) and fight instead for private, usually financial, gain. This chapter will use the term 'private force' to cover all fighters working for private financial gain, alongside the term mercenary, for two reasons. First, the term more accurately covers a wide historical range than does the term 'mercenary'. It is not clear whether or not today's private security companies are mercenaries[3]—and they certainly prefer to avoid the term[4]—but it is clear that they are private fighters. Second, there is considerable debate over what constitutes a mercenary in the first place. While there is general agreement that mercenaries are financially motivated fighters employed by a state other than their own,[5] this definition fails to work during periods where mercenaries were commonly recognized actors (like the Hundred Years War). There are obvious logical problems with relying on motivation as a defining characteristic of mercenaries and other private fighters. It is difficult to discern a fighter's true motivation, and of course some private fighters may have profound ideological motivations and some regular soldiers may be purely motivated by financial gain.[6] That said, deviating entirely from this definition would also leave behind the common-sense and commonly accepted view of what private fighters are and do.[7]

## WHO HIRES PRIVATE FIGHTERS?

If private fighters have existed for as long as there have been wars, it is worth considering which actors have employed them, and under what circumstances they have been employed. Private force has swung like a pendulum between two poles: self-employed private fighters, able to fight for a range of employers (including purely for themselves), and private force as a tightly organized state-based trade.

From about the 1100s, and until the seventeenth century, private fighters could be employed by anyone with power and money. Mercenaries were hired both regionally (by the local lord) and nationally (by the king) to fight, and were usually individual entrepreneurs who organized themselves loosely into bands. These bands would hire themselves out to the highest bidder, often under the authority of a captain. When they failed to find gainful employ, they often worked for themselves, extorting from local villages or pillaging. During the Hundred Years War, mercenaries fluctuated between 'official' work and the more dangerous self-employed type, and gained a reputation for cruelty and greed.[8] Unemployed mercenaries posed major problems for public safety and public order. The medieval chronicler Walter Map, writing in the twelfth century, described 'bands of many thousands . . . armed cap-à-pie with leather, iron, clubs, and swords, lay monasteries, villages, and towns in ashes . . . saying with all their heart, "There is no God"'.[9]

The Italian mercenary system, which began with an influx of mercenaries seeking work during the pause in hostilities of the Hundred Years War after the peace of 1360, worked along the same lines. Mercenaries would work for city states, in which case they were relatively controlled, and also would revert to essentially criminal behaviour when they were not, either because of the seasonal nature of war or because of truces. When mercenaries were unemployed, during peacetime and truces, they wreaked havoc.[10] One of the primary sources of money was the payment of protection money, which modern eyes would recognize as 'mafia-style extortion'.[11] The amount of 'purely wanton damage the mercenaries committed before moving on... depended largely on what inducement they were offered'.[12] The extent of the extortion was substantial. The mercenary captain Sir John Hawkwood extorted from Siena in a few days an amount five times the biannual salary of two of the most important Sienese city officials,[13] and the depredations of mercenaries almost certainly hastened Siena's decline in power from a 'position rivalling Florence in the fourteenth century to provincial backwater by 1400'.[14] The power to hire mercenaries was rarely associated with the power to control mercenaries once they were hired.

By the end of seventeenth century, this system of roving and entrepreneurial mercenary bands had been replaced by a highly controlled, state-based, and state-organized trade in mercenary force. Mercenaries in Europe were gradually brought under state control as the state became strong enough to control them. In France, the *compagnies d'ordonnance*, a prototype standing army created by Charles VII in 1435, was created in part to deal with the depredations of uncontrolled mercenaries,[15] and marked the end of mercenary bands operating in France. The French continued to hire Swiss mercenaries, but on the basis of a long-term contract that was essentially a treaty between the two states with provisions for the exchange of troops. In Italy, the leading *condottiere*, or mercenary captains, were gradually hired by city states on increasingly permanent contracts and required to be citizens of these states. By the seventeenth century, only the still weak and relatively decentralized German states still had mercenary captains acting as entrepreneurs under their own power, of whom the military enterpriser Albrecht von Wallenstein was the most famous and successful. Wallenstein managed to become a hugely rich prince in his own right, controlling vast territories.[16] With his murder in 1634, the age of the entrepreneurial mercenary also died.

By the seventeenth century, states could, and did, continue to hire mercenaries from other states on the basis of complex contracts. One type of arrangement was the subsidy, whereby an army was paid either directly for its service during a war or its reserves were paid during peacetime to ensure their availability if war broke out.[17] The main suppliers between the seventeenth and nineteenth centuries were usually the small and more poorly organized states of Europe (the German principalities; Russia).[18]

By the seventeenth century, then, *states* became the only players that hired mercenaries (or indeed, sold them).[19] Bringing the mercenary trade under state control is thus an important step in the evolution of the monopolization of force within the sovereign state. Mercenaries were now hired by actors with power, money, and legitimacy: the right to use force and the power to control that force.

Mercenaries largely disappeared from the world stage from the 1860s until the 1960s.[20] When they reappeared, it was in a fairly recognizable entrepreneurial form. The wars associated with decolonization in Africa seemed to present fruitful opportunities for making fast money.[21] The relative weakness of many of the new African governments meant that when they hired mercenaries, they found it difficult to control them. Mercenaries shifted between fighting for states (or putative states) and fighting purely for themselves, organizing coups or otherwise pursuing their own interests.

In Congo, Angola, and Nigeria, parties to civil wars hired Western mercenaries, who even advertised in the British media for recruits. Katanga, the province of Congo that attempted to secede in 1960, hired Western mercenaries to assist it, beginning eight years of mercenary involvement in the country. In Angola, in the mid-1970s, the National Liberation Front of Angola (FNLA) hired Western mercenaries to assist in its fight against the Popular Movement for the Liberation of Angola (MPLA); twelve of these mercenaries were captured and later tried. The Biafrans hired foreign mercenaries to assist in their fight against Nigeria, including an idealistic Swedish count with anti-Nazi credentials who flew missions for the rebels.[22] Notably, few of these mercenary interventions had much impact on the conflict.

Mercenaries were not just employed by states or those groups wishing to seize state power. They also acted, as their forebears did, in purely entrepreneurial fashion. The mercenaries' last hurrah in the Congo was an attempt by the mercenaries themselves to topple Mobutu Sese Seko; they managed to capture the city of Bukavu and came close to ending Mobutu's rule.[23] They were successful for a short period before finally being defeated by the central Congolese government. Mercenaries also led coups in Benin,[24] the Seychelles, and the Comoros Islands.[25] Mercenary involvement was relatively high in the 1970s and became more sporadic in the 1980s.

Individual mercenaries are still a recognized problem in Africa, although not on the same scale. Mobutu, despite his chequered relations with mercenaries in the past, hired white mercenaries to assist him in the last days of his rule, in 1996. The so-called White Legion[26] was even allegedly organized by some of the same figures involved in the Congo thirty years previously, but failed against the rebels.[27] The United Nations has more recently identified individual mercenaries moving from conflict to conflict in West Africa as a significant threat to peace and stability.[28] Most recently, the mercenary Simon Mann attempted the so-called Wonga Coup in Equatorial Guinea, a plan to overthrow the government and take advantage of the country's oil revenues. Mann's band of mercenaries closely resembles the entrepreneurial bands of the past.[29]

By the early 1990s, however, a new form of private force had largely super-seded the old-style mercenaries of the decolonization period. The private military company (PMC) Executive Outcomes, created in the early 1990s, quickly made a name for itself with interventions first in Angola, and second, and more famous-ly, in Sierra Leone where the company had considerable success when hired by the state to regain territory from the Rebel United Front (RUF), success which continued until their contract was terminated under international pressure. Executive Outcomes' departure was quickly followed by the collapse of the government and a resurgence in hostilities. A second company, Sandline, reached the headlines for its work (ultimately abandoned) for the Papua New Guinea government and for the (still) beleaguered government of Sierra Leone. Both companies attempted to avoid the mercenary label by insisting they would only work for legitimate causes and only fight for states.[30]

PMCs also became involved in training local militaries. The American com-panies DynCorp and MPRI pursued major training contracts in, respectively, Croatia and Angola.[31] This type of contract arguably allows governments—in this case the United States—to intervene in conflicts that are otherwise politically out of bounds. American-based companies are not allowed to take on this type of contract without Congressional approval.[32]

Despite all the attention they received, Executive Outcomes and Sandline were short-lived companies and had closed their doors by the end of the 1990s. There was simply no market for the controversial, combat-oriented services the companies provided.[33] The idea of the business was sensible: it seems obvious that weak states in need of military assistance but unable to provide it themselves would be keen customers of such companies. Indeed, in the 1990s, the government of Sierra Leone argued compellingly that it ought not to be criticized for its decision to employ Executive Outcomes given the very limited assistance it had received from the international community and the problems it faced in fighting the civil war.[34]

International disapproval of PMCs, often closely associating them with mercenaries, was powerful. Executive Outcomes went out of business in January 1999, because of a shrinking client base and its unsavoury mercenary image.[35] British[36] and South African[37] pressure may have contributed to the company's demise. Sandline, which appears to have been a sister company to Executive Outcomes, was arguably created to avoid the problems the latter had with public perception,[38] but Sandline closed its doors in 2004.

Private force did not disappear from the world stage. Rather, it appeared in a more tightly controlled form more beneficial to militarily powerful states in the system. Companies such as Aegis, ArmorGroup, and Blackwater (now Xe), often called private security companies (PSCs), offer a wide range of services that stop short of the open combat provision of Executive Outcomes and Sandline. The latter largely worked for clients of their choice. PSCs, by contrast, either have to go through a formal process of approval to work for another state (as they do in the United States) or an informal one (the UK government has intervened to prevent PSCs from taking particular contracts).[39] More interestingly still, PSCs tend to work either almost exclusively for their own government, as is the case with most American PSCs, or for their own government and close allies, as is the case with British PSCs. The private military trade today is essentially a state-to-state trade involving private actors who retain a profit motive. As in the pre-nineteenth-century period, mercenaries from the 1960s until today moved from relatively uncontrolled entrepreneurs to a tightly controlled form working almost exclusively for states.

It is important to note that the idea that as states became more centralized and powerful, it became possible for them to abandon mercenary use is not a causal argument: if it were, we would expect the most strongly centralized states in the system to bring mercenaries under control first, and the weakly centralized last. The Italian city states were able to bring mercenaries under control without centralization, which did not occur until the nineteenth century; likewise, the German-speaking component states of the Holy Roman Empire stopped the progress of military entrepreneurs like Wallenstein without centralization. Other important factors were at work in this transformation, including normative pressures.[40] But it is nonetheless important to note that state strength seems to be part of the story: states wanted to control mercenaries and largely did when they were strong enough to do so.

Moreover, weak states may appear to need mercenaries the most, as they are the least able to field their own forces. However, since Executive Outcomes and Sandline disbanded in the late 1990s, the use of private force has been almost entirely the province of the strongest military states in the international system—the United States and the United Kingdom—albeit operating in some of the weakest military states (Iraq and Afghanistan). The successful use of private force may require high degrees of military power to prevent private fighters from challenging regular forces.

The contemporary covert market for private force is small, controversial, and poorly developed. While it is possible for groups of mercenaries to engage in illegal behaviour like the organization of coups, as the Equatorial Guinea coup attempt of 2004 demonstrates, it does not seem easy for illegitimate actors to hire mercenaries on a scale larger than a small band. In fact, recent history suggests it may be largely impossible.

## WHO ARE THE PRIVATE FIGHTERS?

If states have been the primary employers of private force, whom do they employ? What forms has private force taken, where does it come from, and what does this indicate about the nature of war more broadly?

The form of organization of private fighters seems to have varied little over the centuries. Private fighting is a deeply individual phenomenon, relying on individual skills and experience. When private fighters organize themselves into bands, as they did in the thirteenth and fourteenth centuries, these organizations are loose and impermanent. The leaders of mercenary bands, such as Sir John Hawkwood, Bob Denard and Mike Hoare in Africa, and Simon Mann, gain fame rather than the band itself.

Today's private military industry similarly relies on the marketing of individual skills sold to buyers as a collective group. But to refer to companies such as Aegis and Xe (Blackwater), or even Sandline and Executive Outcomes, as private armies is a misnomer. PSCs rarely have permanent frontline staff. Rather, the industry is composed of those on relatively short-term contracts. Many employees will only take on one or two contracts and then retire; others will take contract after contract for different companies. Not only do employees change employers regularly, there is evidence that they also move from the legitimate end of the industry (working for PSCs) to working as mercenaries in covert operations.[41] Indeed, PSCs form what could be called a Rolodex industry: companies rely on their contacts to recruit particular people for particular contracts. State armies, as they are currently conceived, could simply never operate in this manner.

Private fighters over the course of history seem to share similar origins. In the pre-nineteenth-century period, private fighters tended to come from poor states; from poorly centralized states; from states with recent experience of war; or via colonial relationships.

Poor states have been a viable recruiting ground for mercenaries both as individuals and as units. The Swiss mercenary industry began as young Swiss men were unable to find other types of work; so rampant was recruitment that the Swiss states placed it under various controls by the late fourteenth century.[42] Irish and Scottish mercenaries often fought in the armies of continental Europe during times of poor economic opportunity.[43]

After the trade in mercenaries became state-based, small, peripheral states made up significant portions of their revenue through the sale of units to fight in foreign wars. Larger states, particularly the German principalities such as Hessen-Kassel found this useful because 'the demand for troops was frequent, but intermittent. Even the strongest states were financially unable to keep permanently under arms as many troops as were needed in war. It was easier to pay retainers to the German princes, who were willing to keep soldiers ready "on call," as it were, for their paymasters.'[44]

Poorly centralized states were likewise hotbeds for mercenary recruitment. After the trade in mercenaries changed to its state-to-state form, European states could be loosely divided into three categories: those with centralized militaries strong enough to prevent foreigners from recruiting on their soil; those with centralized militaries designed for the export market, and so both able and keen to prevent ad hoc mercenary recruitment; and those too weak to prevent foreign recruiters from setting up shop.

British efforts to recruit mercenaries during the American Revolution and the Crimean War offer an interesting picture of the origins of private fighters. To fight the Americans, the British were able to recruit from Hessen-Kassel, Brunswick, and Waldeck with relative ease. Attempts to recruit from Catherine the Great's Russia failed, apparently because of the interference of Frederick of Prussia, and hiring the Dutch Scotch brigade did not work as the Dutch did not allow the brigade to fight outside Europe.[45] Mercenaries came from states with an interest in selling them, and they only sold their soldiers in situations that were politically acceptable. Even so, we can see from this example that the trade in mercenaries was restricted largely to peripheral European powers, in some cases the tiniest principalities in Europe.

By the time the Crimean War broke out, Britain's recruitment efforts abroad were circumscribed by a post-Napoleonic distaste for the mercenary trade. Most states no longer wanted their nationals to fight for foreign powers.[46] Only within the peripheral and weak states of Germany, Italy, and Switzerland, without sufficient authority to close tightly the door on foreign enlistment, was even the attempt at recruiting possible.[47] Troops were eventually recruited from Sardinia, and more problematically from the German states, where Prussia remained strongly opposed to the recruitment and the British operated under the watchful eye of the police.[48] Spectacularly unsuccessful attempts were made elsewhere, including one in the United States which caused a serious diplomatic incident.[49]

It is important to note here that state *centralization* cannot be taken as a factor on its own. Britain was heavily centralized and tightly organized; and although it had a strong navy, it had notorious difficulties with its army, including a poor recruitment system and long-standing opposition to the existence of a standing army. Britain avoided becoming a recruitment ground for mercenaries because it was effectively administered, well-organized, and prosperous enough for non-mercenary jobs to be easily obtainable.

States with recent experience of war were another fertile source of mercenaries. Sometimes this was not because of any active effort made to 'recruit'— rather, mercenaries merely spilled from conflict to conflict, often seeking financial opportunities. The mercenaries involved in the Italian *condottieri* system that arrived in Italy during the pause in hostilities in the middle of the Hundred Years War are a good example.

Foreign officers with recent, and often extensive, experience of conflict were desirable properties in the pre- and post-Napoleonic market for war. Scharnhorst, one of the leading lights of Prussian military reform after the Napoleonic Wars, was from Hanover and served in Saxony before ultimately serving in Prussia.[50] General Yorck, a Prussian, served in the Dutch army and gained expertise from his international adventures which greatly added to his cachet.[51] Gneisenau, another Prussian, had fought in Canada.[52] Baron Rotten-berg, also Prussian, was a crucial element of Wellington's army.[53] The French minister of war, Narbonne, attempted to enlist the Duke of Brunswick during the wars following the French Revolution, a bold plan considering the German duke had just led the allied army against the French.[54]

The final major source of mercenary recruitment has been colonial relation-ships. However, these foreign soldiers cannot properly be considered mercen-aries, as they often form a permanent part of an army, or, while foreign, were considered nonetheless to share the same aims as national soldiers because of the imperial relationship. The most obvious examples are the Gurkhas and Indian sepoys, who formed permanent parts of the British army. The recent debate over whether or not to grant Gurkhas citizenship in the United Kingdom in exchange for military service highlights the degree to which Gurkhas, while foreign, are not deemed to be mercenaries.


## WHY HIRE PRIVATE FORCE?

In pre-nineteenth-century Europe, those requiring the services of an army often hired private force because mercenaries were not just experienced professionals, they had specific experience of techniques and weaponry that regular soldiers did not.[55] Mercenaries could travel from European army to European army bringing with them the latest means of warfighting. For example, mercenaries helped spread the techniques associated with fighting with pikes pioneered by the Swiss.[56]

In the early days of the state, however, the decision to hire private force was not really a decision at all. A combination of several factors meant that pre-nineteenth-century states relied on private force out of necessity rather than choice. First, as Charles Tilly has persuasively argued, significant centralized administration, particularly the ability to raise taxes, is essential to developing a standing army. Before the state develops in this way, its mechanisms for paying and keeping soldiers are insufficiently developed. It is perhaps less an issue of cost than an issue of the ability to pay—once states were organized enough to mobilize financial resources more efficiently, they could pay for more efficient armies.

For example, the use of mercenaries in medieval armies was essential because the mechanisms for raising an army were inefficient. The feudal system, whereby subjects owed military obligations to their lords or kings, meant that in theory there was a large pool of soldiers. However, raising soldiers in this way was inefficient. Long campaigns were stymied by short periods of service,[57] a function of feudal obligations. English knights were only required to serve forty days a year, and wanted to avoid service abroad.[58] It was often more practical to hire an army at the theatre of war than to transport it overseas.[59] Feudal vassals were not professional soldiers and did not have the same skills or experience. Mercenaries, by contrast, could be bought easily and were experienced soldiers.

Even after the mercenary business became a state-to-state trade, and the threat of rapacious entrepreneurial mercenaries receded, states faced significant recruitment difficulties that were eased by hiring private force. Continental European states, despite coercive techniques to conscript soldiers, had to do deal with rural populations that would flee rather than be recruited, as in Prussia, with a consequent negative effect on the rural economy.[60] However, moral distaste for using mercenaries lingered throughout this period, and, accordingly, European states largely abandoned mercenaries as they became sufficiently centralized so as to allow the development of a standing army.

Britain represents a notable exception to this phenomenon, and persisted with the use of mercenaries despite being perhaps the most centralized and effectively administered state in Europe. Even though mercenaries might menace the countryside in the periods when they were not formally employed, they were not the same as having a permanent group of armed and trained men who might challenge state (or kingly) authority. The British dislike of standing armies had its roots in the Civil War, both because the crown had control of the army and then the Protectorate's government through the system of major-generals were associated with the denial of civil liberties.[61] The Bill of Rights, passed after the Glorious Revolution, stated 'that the raising or keeping of a standing army within the kingdom in the time of peace, unless it be with the consent of Parliament, is against law'.[62] In the United States, a shared suspicion of standing armies was combined with suspicion of the very idea of professionalized military service, explaining the lengthy reliance on a purely volunteer militia in the American Revolution.[63]

The reasons for states to hire private force today provide interesting counterpoints to the reasons states hired private force in the past. Cost, specialist skills, recruitment, and centralization all play roles in the contemporary trade in private force, but in ways that both resemble and differ greatly from the historical pattern.

States today argue that they hire private force for cost reasons. The wave of privatization that swept government across all areas in the 1980s did not leave the military unaffected. Using trained soldiers to perform support tasks like laundry or kitchen help was a misallocation of resources. Governments began to privatize certain logistical functions on a large scale (although the United States has relied on private logistical support in some areas since the Vietnam War).[64] The argument is, as it is across all areas of government, that the state achieves huge savings by relying on private provision.

However, even government organizations, such as the Governmental Administration Organization (GAO) in the United States, point out that the cost savings achieved by privatizing military functions may be outweighed by poor contract administration.[65] More effectively administered contracts might increase savings, but of course more effective contract administration (especially when the contracts to be administered are often in places such as Iraq and Afghanistan) will be more expensive.

PSCs such as ArmorGroup, operating in Afghanistan, have been accused of wasteful practices, of poor communication skills, dangerously understaffing their projects, and hazing and humiliation.[66] The company has also been accused of fraudulent hiring practices violating the terms of their contract.[67]

Even if the system of contract administration and the observation of contract fulfilment could be improved, it is still unclear whether private security presents any real cost savings for governments. The economic efficiency argument relating to PSCs runs like this: governments get highly trained personnel, without necessarily having to provide this training, and without all the ancillary costs (food, uniform, medical support, pensions). But, of course, many PSC employees are retired military personnel whose training was paid for by the government in the first place. Critics argue that in privatizing very particular tasks, such as training services or logistical support, the military is losing the capacity to do these things internally.[68] Moreover, battlefield commanders have argued compellingly that, in Iraq, their work has been undermined by PSCs.[69] If this is true, then the savings PSCs bring may be vastly outweighed by the costs they create.

Finally, situations like that of ArmorGroup in Afghanistan and incidents like the Blackwater shootings in a Baghdad market in September 2007 demonstrate that the private security industry requires better regulation and oversight. Even the industry's representative bodies, including the British Association of Private Security Companies (BAPSC) and the Washington-based International Peace Operations Association (IPOA), argue further oversight is necessary. However, to be truly effective this regulation must come at a cost. The British government released proposals in the spring of 2009 arguing that the best system of regulation was industry-led (relying on organizations such as the BAPSC) with an international component, hopefully to be funded by PSCs themselves.[70] The only cost-effective solution, the British government essentially argues, is to pass the buck to the companies themselves. Whether or not the companies are willing to pay and whether or not this type of regulation is sufficiently robust are questions that remain to be answered.

In the United States, Congress has taken the lead in attempting to improve industry oversight. It has set up a variety of measures, from extending the application of the Uniform Code of Military Justice (UCMJ) to PSCs to attempting to improve contract competition and oversight. American oversight is more robust partly because the US government relies much more substantially on contractors in general, and because the US military itself relies on contractors, putting them in more dangerous situations.[71] In both countries, more effective regulation will at the very least impose additional costs. If the military were used to perform the tasks of PSCs, the regular system of military scrutiny and justice would apply, and impose no further costs.

PSCs may be important to contemporary states for more complex reasons than any perceived gains in economic efficiency. As in the pre-nineteenth-century period, using private force eases recruitment difficulties. The American military has had significant recruitment problems in recent years, even (controversially) lowering the required IQ for personnel in order to bring in greater numbers.[72] It has been estimated that the United States, at the height of its military presence in Iraq, was using between 30,000 and 50,000 contractors.[73] America's ability to engage militarily would be vastly affected by the need to recruit tens of thousands more regular soldiers.

The use of PSCs, accordingly, can allow governments to pursue courses of action that would be difficult to sell to the public or the international community should they rely on regular personnel, thereby increasing their foreign policy manoeuvrability. Iraq provides the most striking example. The presence of so many PSC personnel allowed the United States to pursue and sustain an extremely unpopular war in Iraq. Just as contractor numbers in Iraq are high, so too are contractor casualties. The GAO points out that it is extremely difficult to assess contractor casualties, because reporting mechanisms are still inadequate.[74] Even so, it is estimated that, as of autumn 2009, 1,442 contractors had died in Iraq and 246 in Afghanistan.[75] Public pressure to leave Iraq, or change the course of the intervention, could conceivably have been even greater in the absence of PSC support.

Private force can open up foreign policy options to states in other ways. The American company DynCorp was able to provide significant assistance (in the form of training) to the Croatian army during the war in Yugoslavia, assistance that would have been politically impossible for the United States to provide directly.[76]

While this assistance was provided without much public fanfare, it was not covert. Interestingly, governments do not seem to have used private force to accomplish covert foreign policy goals, such as coups or assassinations. The most notable exception was the Wonga Coup in Equatorial Guinea. Although the mercenaries involved had had previous links with PSCs, they were working of their own accord rather than for any company. The Spanish government has been accused of involvement in coup but the evidence is not conclusive.[77] As the industry tries to distance itself from its mercenary roots, it is consciously limiting itself to legitimate contracts (even if individual former employees, as in Equatorial Guinea, get involved in coup attempts). In any case, coups, particularly those either directed or influenced by external forces, are increasingly rare in the post-Cold War environment.

While historically states relied on private force because they were too weakly centralized to have standing armies, in the contemporary context the *most* centralized and militarily powerful states are most reliant on PSCs. There are a number of potential explanations for this phenomenon. First, only states such as the United States, and to a lesser extent the United Kingdom, are involved in expeditionary military action on a scale large enough to require contractor support in the first place. Second, very large military powers can outsource force to the private sector without much concern over whether or not doing so creates the potential for coups or instability. The rest of the military is large enough, and sophisticated enough in technology, to act as a deterrent to any potentially 'rogue' contractors. The same is unlikely to be true for less militarily sophisticated states.

## CONCERNS ABOUT PRIVATE FORCE

While the use of private force has been common throughout history, disapproval of mercenaries in their various forms and private fighters of all types has been similarly common. Interestingly, these concerns follow certain common threads. Concerns about private force can be grouped loosely into three categories: tyranny; fighting for money rather than for a cause; and, later on, the image of the state in the international community.

A criticism commonly levelled at mercenaries and their successors is that they make it easier for states to use force, and therefore easier for states to become tyrannical. A citizen army restrains the state by making it more difficult for the state to engage in war, and specifically more difficult for the state to use the armed forces to quash rebellion among its citizens. Hiring mercenaries disrupts this relationship, because the state will be far less restrained by public opinion in the decision to fight wars if the soldiers are foreign, and in case of rebellion will not need to worry about sympathy preventing soldiers from crushing citizens from the same community. Moreover, the citizen's military duty to the state is a moral one, and mercenaries weaken the community's moral fibre by performing the citizen's duty.

The origins of this objection can be traced at least as far back as Machiavelli and his contemporaries. Machiavelli argued that the citizen owed a special, and irreplaceable, duty to the state. He writes that 'the republic is the common good; the citizen, directing all his actions toward that good, may be said to dedicate his life to the republic; the patriot warrior dedicates his death'.[78] Machiavelli's concerns about mercenary use revolve around a deep-seated feeling that native sons *should* fight for the republic, to ensure its health and success at war. The republic drew strength from the military service of its citizens. Hiring foreigners to fight thus diminished the strength of the republic.[79]

Concerns that the use of foreign troops would lead to tyranny were shared during the French Enlightenment. Rousseau argued that the relationship between the citizen and the republic was especially virtuous, and that citizens would take the greatest care to look after the interest of the common good. A polity relying upon mercenaries is a polity in danger. Its citizens, 'no longer considering themselves interested in the common cause, would cease to be the defenders of the homeland'. Leaders will prefer mercenaries to free men 'if only to use the former at a suitable time and place to subjugate the latter more effectively'.[80] Mercenaries pose a grave threat to the liberty of the people, because they do not care for the common good; they submit to the orders of the leadership of the republic, rather than thinking of the needs of the polity itself. Mercenaries in Rome,

> whose value could be determined on the basis of the price at which they sold themselves, were proud of their debasement, held in contempt the laws by which they were protected, as well as their comrades whose bread they ate, and believed it an honour to be Caesar's satellites rather than Rome's defenders. And given as they were to blind obedience, their task was to have their swords raised against their fellow citizens, ready to slaughter them all at the first signal. It would not be difficult to show that this was one of the principal causes of the ruin of the Roman Empire.[81]

Americans during the Revolution also took the position that the use of mercenaries led to tyranny. Indeed, the revolutionaries believed that Britain's use of German mercenaries indicated its decline into despotism, and demonstrated its moral bankruptcy. The Declaration of Independence declared of King George III's use of mercenaries:

> He is, at this time, transporting large armies of foreign Mercenaries, to compleat the works of death, desolation and tyranny, already begun with circumstances of cruelty and perfidy scarcely paralleled in the most barbarous ages and totally unworthy the Head [sic] of a civilized nation.[82]

The intense debate on the British decision to send mercenaries to fight in the Crimean War drew the same links between the use of mercenaries and tyranny. One MP argued that 'the fact was, that wherever mercenaries were introduced there were found to be corrupt governments—there civil and religious liberty were crushed, and universal national demonisation prevailed'.[83]

Just as mercenaries made it easier for the state to go to war and to repress its people in the past, private military and private security companies might make it easier for modern states to fight war and also reduce democratic control over war.[84] This argument finds echoes in theories of the democratic peace, which argue that public opinion can exert a strong effect on making a state more reluctant to go to war, particularly if too many soldiers are killed or if soldiers' lives are placed in harm's way. As Kant argues, 'if the consent of the citizens is required in order to decide that war should be declared . . . nothing is more natural than that they would be very cautious in commencing such a poor game, decreeing for themselves all the calamities of war'.[85] One objection to the private military industry is that it removes or lessens the restraints of public opinion, because the public will not notice or will be less worried about the deaths of private fighters than they would be about the killings of soldiers.[86] The use of PMCs might lead to a reduction of democracy in states which hire these companies by diminishing democratic oversight of decisions to go to war.

The private military industry has been criticized because of the idea that fighting for financial gain is morally problematic. During the late eighteenth and early nineteenth centuries, this criticism gained strength with a growing sense that fighting for national ideals was the only appropriate motivation for war. The French Revolution and its philosophy made the use of mercenaries untenable on moral grounds.[87] The 'new ideology looked down on men who served for money, calling them hirelings and mercenaries. Soldiering was only respectable when it was done voluntarily by citizens from love of their country, under which circumstances it became morally admirable.'[88]

During the British debates on the decision to send mercenaries to the Crimea,[89] Richard Cobden summed up the prevailing belief that a mercenary cannot be moral because of his motivation in the House of Commons:

> . . . it is assumed that men fight for a cause, that they are actuated by a love of home, devotion to the country, or attachment to a Sovereign; these are the sentiments that are considered to hallow the pursuit of arms. But what motives have these men whom you endeavour to hire out of the back slums of the towns of Germany? They can have no pretensions to fighting from any moral motive whatever; *they are deprived of every ground upon which you can justify war*, and, as they want the motives which I have described, there is just the difference between them and an ordinary soldier fighting for his country that there is between a hero and a cut-throat.[90]

By the 1970s and through until today, states seeking to control mercenaries have done so on the basis that what has made them problematic has been the fact that they were motivated to fight by 'hard cash'.[91] The British government Green Paper, drawn up in response to the actions of the PMC Sandline in Sierra Leone, remained concerned that an inappropriate motivation made mercenaries morally problematic and unable to support the state in the same way as a citizen army. The Green Paper argued that in modern society 'there is a natural repugnance towards those who kill (or help kill) for money'.[92] Enrique Bernales Ballesteros, the former UN Special Rapporteur on mercenaries, has stated that modern private military companies are not really different from their mercenary predecessors. He argues that although 'the manner and the nature of the activity in which mercenaries participate may change, that does not change the mercenary status of those who take part in illicit acts, offering and selling their professional skills for pay, well knowing that it is not for a noble cause, but to kill and destroy outside any licit or ethically permissible context'.[93]

It will be interesting to see the impact of using private force on states in the modern period. In the nineteenth century, the need to use private force became associated with state weakness. When Britain was debating the use of mercenaries in Parliament during the Crimean War, many of the main arguments against using private force relied on the fact that in so doing Britain could not seriously consider herself a great power. Even in the 1980s, Krasner argued that there are very few specifically strategic arguments against state use of mercenaries, and it is otherwise hard to explain in strategic terms why states do not use mercenaries more frequently.[94]

Curiously, in the modern context, the ability to use private force might have become a *marker* of great power status. If states require a high degree of centralization and power to use modern private force effectively, then it follows that the ability to use these forces may come to signal strength. However, a common propaganda criticism of American forces in Iraq is that they have had to rely so heavily on hired fighters, and therefore the American government must lack the power to field its own soldiers. Just as the British were embarrassed in the Crimean War by having to rely on 'hirelings', attempts are made to embarrass the Americans on the same grounds today.

## CONCLUSION

Just as there is a relationship between the centralization of state powers and the development of standing armies, so there are links between the decision to abandon private force and the development of democracy. Scholars have only recently begun to examine the relationship between democracy and private force,[95] which may be more significant both for theories of international relations and for policy.

In the nineteenth century, the great shift away from mercenary use required, in part, new understandings of the relationship between the citizen and the state.[96] Once individual citizens were perceived to have a duty to the state (through military service or conscription), states in turn granted citizens further rights in exchange. Once 'citizens' replaced 'soldiers', it was consequently harder to justify the use of mercenaries alongside them on the battlefield. In France, the Revolutionary Wars rested on a profoundly changed concept of citizenship that could not comfortably coexist with the presence of mercenaries. In Prussia, the government was forced to make both military and political reforms after its defeats at Auerstadt and Jena. Interestingly, its reforms were not just military but also political. There was a conscious move towards providing citizens with more rights in exchange for military service.[97] While the move to democracy proper was a long way off in both these cases, they nonetheless hint at the potential importance of citizen service for the model of military organization that still prevails in the west and in many other states.[98]

The privatization of force also prompts questions that are strongly reminiscent of, if not directly related to, democratic peace theory. The argument that the use of mercenaries disrupts the proper relationship between citizenship and state, and thus might lead to tyranny, has obvious echoes for democratic peace theory. States are able to fight unpopular wars because they can rely on PSCs; citizens may care less about the deaths of PSC employees and consequently become more detached from wars. Deborah Avant has begun to test whether or not the proposition that public opinion cares less about the loss of a private fighter than a state soldier; her preliminary results suggest that this is not so. The public opinion aspect of theories of democratic peace is widely regarded as weak. Public opinion does not always constrain states in war, so it is worth exploring whether or not it does so in the case of private force.[99] If there is a relationship between democracy and a citizen army, then this relationship may well be disrupted by the large-scale use of private force.

Second, those who argue that the use of private force is a neutral development in the history of war would do well to remember the normative concerns regularly levelled at private fighters throughout history. Just as many forms of military technology and tactics are criticized for moral reasons, even if their use is common, it would be a mistake to regard the private use of force as morally neutral. Even if moral objections to private force are irrational, they are commonly held.

Third, and related, is the point that the relationship between the state, its regular army, and its private fighters is a complicated one. The period in which states have relied solely on their own nationals as soldiers has been comparatively short. It may be that the armies of the late nineteenth and early twentieth centuries were an aberration, and that increasing reliance on private force is a return to a more normal state of affairs. This kind of argument overlooks an obvious riposte: that the road along which the national standing army evolved is a long and complex one intimately tied together with the development of the state. A shift to the broader use of private force might also unravel the benefits of this long, slow evolution. At the very least, it behoves states interested in using private force to consider when and why states stopped using mercenaries the first time around.

## NOTES

1. Samuel E. Finer, 'The second oldest trade', *The New Society*, 15 July 1976. I would like to thank the Leverhulme Trust for providing postdoctoral support that allowed me to conduct some of the research in this article, colleagues in the Changing Character of War Programme for stimulating discussions about private force, and Josiah Kaplan for providing excellent research assistance for this chapter.

2. Sarah Percy, *Mercenaries: The history of a norm in international relations* (Oxford: Oxford University Press, 2007).

3. Sarah Percy, *Regulating the private security industry*, Adelphi Paper 384 (London: Routledge and the International Institute of Strategic Studies, 2006), 14.

4. Sarah Percy, 'The United Nations Security Council and the use of private force', in Vaughan Lowe et al. (eds.), *The United Nations Security Council and war* (Oxford: Oxford University Press, 2008), 638.

5. Percy, *Mercenaries*, 52.

6. For more discussions of these definitional issues, see Ibid., chapter 2.

7. The chapter will mainly cover private fighters in the Western tradition of war, as the concept 'mercenary' derives from a particularly European tradition of warfare. An analysis of mercenaries outside the Western tradition of war, and operating outside Europe, is clearly an area for future research. See Patricia Owens, 'Distinctions, distinctions: "Public" and "private" force', *International Affairs*, 84/5 (2008), 977–90; for a discussion of some of the difficulties of focusing only on European war in this context.

8. Michael Prestwich, *Armies and warfare in the middle ages: The English experience* (New Haven, CT: Yale University Press, 1996), 152. See also André Corvisier, *Armies and societies in Europe, 1494–1789* (Bloomington, ID: Indiana University Press, 1979), 10; and Richard W. Kaeuper, *War, justice and public order: England and France in the later middle ages* (Oxford: Clarendon Press, 1988), 1.

9. Walter Map, *De Nugis Curialium*, translated by M.R. James, C.N.J. Brooke, and R.A.B. Mynors (Oxford: Clarendon Press, 1983), 19.

10. Michael Edward Mallett, *Mercenaries and their masters: Warfare in Renaissance Italy* (London: Bodley Head, 1974), 27.

11. Lawrin Armstrong, 'Enemies of God, pity and mercy', *Canadian Journal of History*, 35/2 (2000), 293.

12. Geoffrey Trease, *The condottieri: Soldiers of fortune* (London: Thames and Hudson, 1970), 36.

13. William Caferro, 'Mercenaries and military expenditure: The cost of undeclared warfare in XIVth century Siena', *Journal of European Economic History*, 23/2 (1994), 221.

14. Armstrong, 'Enemies of God', 294.

15. Michael Edward Mallett, 'Mercenaries', in Maurice Keen (ed.), *Medieval warfare* (Oxford: Oxford University Press, 1999), 216.

16. Ronald Asch, *The Thirty Years War: The Holy Roman Empire and Europe, 1618–1648* (New York: St Martin's Press, 1997), 160.

17. Rodney Atwood, *The Hessians: Mercenaries from Hessen-Kassel in the American Revolution* (Cambridge: Cambridge University Press, 1980), 22.
18. For a longer discussion of the pre-nineteenth-century changes in the mercenary business, see Percy, *Mercenaries*, chapters 4 and 5.
19. Atwood argues that there were very few individual 'enterprisers' or individuals engaged in recruiting and running their own units after Wallenstein; he points out that one such enterpriser (even then operating under contract from the British), in 1775, encapsulates the problems faced by such individuals: he was unable to make the business financially viable when competing with princes. Atwood, *The Hessians*, 10.
20. The significance of this lengthy disappearance is discussed later.
21. Indeed, the author Frederick Forsyth's book sets out a blueprint for how a mercenary-led coup could be a financial boon for the mercenaries involved and their investors. Frederick Forsyth, *The Dogs of War* (Arrow, 1996 [1974]). It has been argued that Forsyth was plausibly involved in planning and financing a real coup attempt based on his research in the early 1970s. Adam Roberts, *The Wonga Coup* (London: Profile Books, 2006).
22. Count Carl Gustaf von Rosen. See John de St Jorre, *The Nigerian Civil War* (London: Hodder and Stoughton, 1972) for details.
23. Anthony Mockler, *The mercenaries* (London: Macdonald, 1969).
24. Anthony Mockler, *Hired guns and coups d'etat* (Oxford: Hunter Mackay, 2006); Percy, *Mercenaries*.
25. Repeatedly. The mercenary Bob Denard's last attempt of many was in 1995, when he was 66. He was ultimately tried and convicted in France for his role in the coup but died before he could serve his sentence.
26. Sean Boyne, 'The White Legion: Mercenaries in Zaire', *Jane's Intelligence Review*, 9/6 (1997), 278–81.
27. Peter W. Singer, *Corporate warriors: The rise of the privatized military industry* (Ithaca, NY: Cornell University Press, 2003), 44.
28. Percy, 'The UN Security Council', 635.
29. See Roberts, *The Wonga Coup*, for a detailed explanation.
30. David Shearer, *Private armies and military intervention*, Adelphi Paper 318 (Oxford: International Institute of Strategic Studies, 1998), 18; Peter W. Singer, 'War, profits and the vacuum of law: Privatized military firms and international law', *Colombia Journal of Transnational Law*, 42/2 (2004), 532; Juan Carlos Zarate, 'The emergence of a new dog of war: Private international security companies, international law, and the new world disorder', *Stanford Journal of International Law*, 34 (1998), 124.
31. See below for a more detailed discussion of training contracts.
32. The approval comes from a process known as ITAR (International Trade in Arms Regulation). See Percy, *Regulating the private security industry*.
33. Percy, *Mercenaries*, 229.
34. Ibid.
35. David Shearer, 'Private military forces and the challenges for the future', *Cambridge Review of International Affairs*, 13/1 (1999), 82.

36. Jürgen Brauer, 'An economic perspective on mercenaries, military companies and the privatization of force', *Cambridge Review of International Affairs*, 13/1 (1999), 130.

37. Herbert M. Howe, 'Private security forces and African stability: The case of Executive Outcomes', *Journal of Modern African Studies*, 36/2 (1998), 327.

38. Khareen Pech, 'Executive Outcomes: A corporate conquest', in Jakkie Cilliers and Peggy Mason (eds.), *Peace, profit or plunder? The privatization of security in war-torn African societies* (Johannesburg: Institute for Security Studies, 1999), 93.

39. The UK government intervened to prevent the company Northbridge Security Services from taking a combat-oriented contract to assist the state of Côte d'Ivoire, and the UN Security Council also urged all parties to avoid the recruitment of foreign mercenaries in a resolution. See Percy, *Mercenaries*, 229.

40. Percy, *Mercenaries*.

41. Ibid.

42. Ibid., 84.

43. I. Ross Bartlett, 'Scottish mercenaries in Europe 1570–1640: A study in attitudes and policies', *Scottish Tradition*, 13 (1984–5), 15–24.

44. Atwood, *The Hessians*, 8.

45. Attempts to recruit from Russia and to recruit the Dutch Scotch brigade failed. Interestingly, the British were interested in Russia because they believed a lack of language skills would mean that Russian soldiers were less likely to desert. Atwood, *The Hessians*, 24.

46. The reasons for this shift are outlined at length in Percy, *Mercenaries*, chapter 5. Other discussions can be found in Janice E. Thomson, *Mercenaries, pirates, and sovereigns: State-building and extraterritorial violence in early modern Europe* (Princeton, NJ: Princeton University Press, 1994); and Deborah Avant, *The market for force: The consequences of privatizing security* (Cambridge: Cambridge University Press, 2005).

47. C.C. Bayley, *Mercenaries for the Crimea: The German, Swiss and Italian legions in British service, 1854–1856* (London: McGill-Queen's University Press, 1977), 79.

48. Ibid., 69, 76, 84. French also points out that British recruiting in the German states was illegal. David French, *The British way in warfare 1688–2000* (London: Unwin Hyman, 1990), 130. The Prussian police were interested because a soldier could not serve for the British unless he had completed his term of service for his home state; British zeal meant that recruiters were not always careful about the letter of the law.

49. Bayley, *Mercenaries for the Crimea*, 88, 91, Edward Dumbauld, 'Neutrality laws of the United States', *The American Journal of International Law*, 31/2 (1937), 259.

50. Martin Kitchen, *A military history of Germany from the eighteenth century to the present day* (London: Weidenfeld and Nicolson, 1975), 37.

51. Peter Paret, *Yorck and the era of Prussian reform 1807–1815* (Princeton, NJ: Princeton University Press, 1966), 48–51.

52. T.N. Dupuy, *A genius for war* (London: Macdonald and Jane's, 1977), 21; Paret, *Yorck and the era of Prussian reform*, 43.

53. Paret, *Yorck*, 205.

54. T.C.W. Blanning, *The French Revolutionary Wars 1787–1802* (London: Arnold, 1996), 63.

55. Geoffrey Hindley, *Medieval warfare* (London: Wayland Publishers, 1971), 82.
56. Mockler, *Mercenaries*, 95–6.
57. Kaeuper, *War, justice and Public Order*, 18.
58. Mallett, 'Mercenaries', 213; Mockler, *Mercenaries*, 26; Richard A. Preston and Sydney F. Wise, *Men in arms: A history of warfare and its interrelationships with western society* (New York: Holt, Rinehart and Wilson, 1979), 80.
59. C. Warren Hollister, *The military organization of Norman England* (Oxford: Clarendon Press, 1965), 177.
60. Kitchen, *A military history of Germany*, 7–8.
61. Lois G. Schwoerer, *'No standing armies!' The antiarmy ideology in seventeenth century England* (Baltimore, MD: Johns Hopkins University Press, 1974).
62. Text of the Bill of Rights available at http://www.britannia.com/history/docs/rights.html.
63. Percy, *Mercenaries*, 127.
64. Christopher Kinsey, *Corporate soldiers and international security: The rise of private security companies* (London: Routledge, 2006).
65. 'Interagency contracting: Problems with DOD's and Interior's orders to support military operations, report to Congressional Committees No. GAO05201'. GAO (April 2005), 3–4. Available at http://www.gao.gov/new.items/d05201.pdf
66. Ginger Thompson, 'Official says contractor in Kabul may be ousted', *New York Times*, 14 September 2009. Also see the reports produced by the Project on Government Oversight: http://www.pogo.org/pogo-files/letters/contract-oversight/co-gp-20090901.html#10
67. Spencer Ackerman, 'Whistleblowers unveil more ArmorGroup allegations', *Washington Independent*, 9 September 2009. (Ackerman).
68. Deborah Avant, 'The implications of marketized security', *Perspectives on Politics*, 4/3 (2006), 133.
69. See Steve Fainaru, 'Warnings unheeded on guards in Iraq', *Washington Post*, 24 December 2007, for representative views.
70. http://www.fco.gov.uk/resources/en/pdf/4103709/5476465/5550005/pms-public-consultation
71. As of 2009, only the Foreign and Commonwealth Office (FCO) in the United Kingdom has used contractors, mainly for embassy protection.
72. Fred Kaplan, 'Dumb and dumber: The US army lowers recruitment standards . . . again', *Slate* 2008, http://www.slate.com/id/2182752
73. Jeremy Scahill, *Blackwater: The rise of the world's most powerful mercenary army* (New York: Nation Books, 2007) puts the number even higher, at 80,000; however, his critics argue that this figure must include a large number of purely logistical contractors.
74. http://www.gao.gov/new.items/d101.pdf
75. The Department of Labor keeps track of contractor casualties as part of the Defence Base Act. These numbers are available at http://209.85.229.132/search?q=cache:p5PRk6HHGa0J:www.dol.gov/esa/owcp/dlhwc/dbaallnation.htm+http://www.dol.gov/esa/owcp/dlhwc/dbaallnation.htm&cd=1&hl=en&ct=clnk&gl=uk&client=firefox-a. As noted above, however, these figures are likely to be incomplete.
76. Avant, 'The implications of marketized security', 104.

77. Roberts, *The Wonga Coup*.

78. J.G.A. Pocock, *The Machiavellian moment: Florentine thought and the Atlantic republican tradition* (Princeton, NJ: Princeton University Press, 1975), 201.

79. Mallett, *Mercenaries and their masters*, 133, 97.

80. Jean-Jacques Rousseau, 'A discourse on political economy', in *Jean-Jacques Rousseau: The basic political writings*, edited by Denis Diderot (Indianapolis, ID: Hackett Publishing Company, [1755] 1987), 131.

81. Ibid.

82. Declaration of Independence. Text available at: http://www.law.indiana.edu/ uslawdocs/declaration.html

83. Mr Laing. Hansard, *Parliamentary debates*, vol. CXXXVI (London and Basingstoke: Cornelius Buck, 1854–7), column 853.

84. A similar argument can be found in Avant, *Market for force*, 155–6.

85. Immanuel Kant, *Perpetual peace and other essays*, translated by Ted Humphrey (Indianapolis, ID: Hackett Publishing Company, [1795] 1983), 113.

86. This restraint is of course merely a restraint and cannot end war. Michael Doyle, 'Kant, liberal legacies and foreign affairs', *Philosophy and Public Affairs*, 2/3–4 (1983), 230.

87. Alan Forrest, '*La patrie en danger*: The French Revolution and the first *levée en masse*', in Daniel Moran and Arthur Waldron (eds.), *The people in arms: Military myth and national mobilization since the French Revolution* (Cambridge: Cambridge University Press, 2003), 9. There were twenty-three regiments of foreigners in the French army in 1789. Peter Paret, *Understanding war: Essays on Clausewitz and the history of military power* (Princeton, NJ: Princeton University Press, 1992), 54.

88. Geoffrey Best, *War and society in revolutionary Europe* (Leicester: Leicester University Press, 1982), 77.

89. The mercenaries were ultimately recruited but the war ended before they were sent to the Crimea. Bayley, *Mercenaries for the Crimea*.

90. Hansard (1854–57), *Parliamentary debates*, CXXXVI (London and Basingstoke: Cornelius Buck), column 688 (emphasis added).

91. *Conference Diplomatique de Droit Humanitaire*. Doc *CDDH/236/*Rev.1 at para. 99.

92. House of Commons Foreign Affairs Committee, 'Private military companies: Options for regulation', (London: Stationery Office, 2002), 18.

93. UN Document E/CN.4/2002/20, 16.

94. Stephen D. Krasner, 'Sovereignty: An institutional perspective', in James A. Caporaso (ed.), *The elusive state: International and comparative perspectives* (Newbury Park, CA: Sage, 1989), 91–2.

95. Deborah Avant and Lee Sigelman, 'What does private security in Iraq mean for democracy at home?' (Irvine, CA: UCLA 2008), http://www.international.ucla. edu/cms/files/PrivateSecurityandDemocracy.pdf; Sarah Percy, 'Morality and regulation', in Simon Chesterman and Chia Lehnhardt (eds.), *From mercenaries to market: The rise and regulation of the private military industry* (Oxford: Oxford University Press, 2007), 11–28.

96. Percy, *Mercenaries*, chapters 4 and 5.

97. Ibid., chapter 5, for a discussion of the French and Prussian cases.

98. Another problem here is Britain's status as an outlier, outlined above. The relationship between Britain's development of conscription and the growth of democracy is far less clear. See Hew Strachan, 'Liberalism and conscription, 1789–1919' in Hew Strachan (ed.), *The British army, manpower and society into the twenty-first century* (London: Frank Cass, 2000), 3–15.

99. Avant and Sigelman, 'What does private security in Iraq mean for democracy at home?'

# 15

## Who Fights?—A Comparative Demographic Depiction of Terrorists and Insurgents in the Twentieth and Twenty-First Centuries

*Bruce Hoffman*

Terrorism and insurgency have always been individual avocations. The reasons why someone picks up a gun or throws a bomb represent an ineluctably personal choice born variously of grievance and frustration; religious piety or the desire for systemic socio-economic change; and irredentist conviction or commitment to revolution. Joining an organization in pursuit of these aims is meant to give collective meaning and equally importantly cumulative power to this commitment. The forces that impel individuals to become terrorists and insurgents are thus timeless. Indeed, a broad, though impressionistic and arguably idiosyncratic, comparison of today's terrorists and insurgents with their predecessors shows that only very little has changed in the demographics, socio-economic backgrounds, education, and recruitment, that have always driven men and women into these realms of political violence.

### A YOUNG MAN'S—AND A YOUNG WOMAN'S—GAME

'Revolution is a young man's game,'[1] the late J. Bowyer Bell wrote more than a decade ago. His reflection, based on some forty years spent studying 'active and recent undergrounds' applied to the pre-eminent terrorist and insurgent groups of Bell's era: the young Jewish men and women who challenged Britain's rule in Palestine in the 1940s; their Muslim Algerian counterparts who a decade later undermined France's continued possession of Algeria; the Palestinian *fedayeen* of the 1960s and 1970s who both transformed the nature and conduct of terrorism and insurgency and ushered in the modern era of global political violence in which we are still enmeshed; the teenagers in Northern

Ireland who graduated from throwing stones and Molotov cocktails at British soldiers to the ranks of the Provisional Irish Republican Army (PIRA); and the radical students—the 'generation of 1968'—who manned the barricades in Paris, Berlin, Milan, and elsewhere and subsequently formed such iconic, if mostly forgotten, leftist terrorist groups as West Germany's Red Army Faction (RAF), Italy's Red Brigades, and America's Weather Underground.

Indeed, Eliahu Hakim and Eliahu Bet-Zouri, the two Jewish terrorists who in 1944 assassinated Lord Moyne, the British Minister Resident for the Middle East, were 20 and 23 years of age, respectively.[2] Zohra Drif was only 22 when on a Sunday afternoon in 1957 she left a bomb in an Algiers milk bar packed with *pied noir* beach-goers and their wives and children. Her comrade-in-arms, Ali La Pointe, the FLN (*Front de Libération Nationale*) assassin *extra-ordinare*, was 26 when he spearheaded the battle of Algiers.[3] The famed Palestinian terrorist Leila Khaled was 25 years old when she hijacked her first passenger aircraft[4] and helped revolutionize terrorism by transforming it into the global phenomenon it remains today. Bobby Sands, who starved himself to death at the age of 27 in Northern Ireland's Maze Prison in 1981, had joined the PIRA nearly a decade before when he was 18.[5] Petra Schelm was 19 years old when she left Germany for Jordan to train in a camp run by the Popular Front for the Liberation of Palestine (PFLP)[6]—the same group to which Khaled belonged. Another member of the RAF's first generation, Astrid Proll, joined the group when she was only 19 and later exulted in the breathless manner of a teenager how, 'You must understand that then the most fantastic thing in the world was not to be a rock star, but a revolutionary.'[7] Finally, Susana Ronconi, a key figure in Italy's Red Brigades, was 23 when she joined.[8]

Hence, as Walter Laqueur, one of the most prolific historians and analysts of terrorism, notes, the 'only feature common to all terrorist movements' historically has been that 'their members have been young...and that hardly requires explanation'.[9] Nearly a century ago, for instance, the average age of Irish Republican Army (IRA) volunteers in County Cork between 1917 and 1923 was 24.6 years old.[10] It is no different today. The average age of the nineteen 11 September hijackers, for instance, was 24.2 years; while that of Palestinian suicide bombers is 21.[11] Most Hezbollah fighters similarly were in their late 'teens or early 20s when they died'.[12] According to the 'Sinjar Records', the documents pertaining to some 700 Sunni foreign fighters who joined the insurgency in Iraq, prosecuted by al-Qaeda in Iraq (aQI) between August 2006 and August 2007, show that their average age was between 24 and 25 years: with the oldest volunteer aged 54 and the youngest just 15.[13] The average age of the Taliban cadre fighting in Afghanistan today is between 20 and 25 years of age,[14] while that of recruits to the current generation of al-Qaeda is reported to be about 25 years old.[15]

Indeed, some of the more infamous contemporary individual jihadi terrorists fall squarely into this age group. Although Ahmed Omar Saeed Sheikh was 29 when he kidnapped and executed *Wall Street Journal* reporter Daniel Pearl in 2002, he first attained notoriety nearly a decade earlier when in 1994, at age 21, he orchestrated the abduction of three British backpackers and their American companion in India.[16] Mohammed Bouyeri was 24 when he murdered the Dutch filmmaker Theo van Gogh;[17] and Omar Khyam, the British Muslim who headed the 'Operation Crevice' cell was the same age[18] when he stockpiled some 600 kilograms (1,300 pounds) of ammonium nitrate fertilizer as part of a plot to bomb a London night-club and shopping mall in 2003.[19] Asif Hanif and Omar Khan Sharif, Britain's first suicide bombers, were 21 and 27, respectively, when they attacked a popular Tel Aviv bar in 2003.[20] A would-be suicide bomber from Chechnya, Zarema Muzhakhoeva, was 23 years old when she carried a bomb into Moscow's Mon Café[21] and Abdallah al-Ajimi, a released Guantanamo detainee who subsequently perished in a suicide attack on an Iraqi army base outside Mosul in March 2008, was 22 years old when he left his native Kuwait in 2001 for Afghanistan to join the Taliban.[22] Ajmal Amir Kasab, the 'baby-faced killer'[23] responsible for the bloody assault on Mumbai's Chhatrapati Shivaji Terminus rail station as part of the series of attacks that convulsed the city on 26 November 2008 was 21 years old at the time.[24]

The leadership of terrorist and insurgency groups also crystallizes historically and today at a remarkably consistent point in a fighter's life: most often in one's late 20s and early 30s. The average age of IRA officers fighting in County Cork during the 1910s and 1920s, for instance, was 27.3.[25] Yitzhak Shamir was 29 when, as one of three commanders of the Jewish terrorist group Lehi (the Hebrew acronym for 'Freedom Fighters for Israel'), he dispatched Hakim and Bet-Zouri on their mission to assassinate Lord Moyne.[26] His counterpart, Menachem Begin, was 30 when the previous year he had assumed command of a rival group, the *Irgun Zvai Le'umi* (Hebrew: 'National Military Organization'), and his deputy, Ya'acov Meridor, was the same age.[27] Saadi Yacef was 29 years old when he directed FLN operations in the battle of Algiers[28]—a role he reprised on screen a decade later as the star (and co-producer) of the eponymous film.[29] Yasir Arafat was 28 when he founded *al-Fatah* in 1957[30] and by the time he turned 40 in 1969 he had acceded to the pinnacle of the Palestine Liberation Organization as its chairman.[31] Gerry Adams was appointed the chief of staff of the PIRA's Northern Command in 1977 when he was 29 years old and just 35 when he was elected president of Sinn Féin in 1983.[32] Andreas Baader and Gudrun Ensslin, the co-founders and co-leaders of the RAF, were 29 and 32 years old, respectively, in 1972 when they were captured by the West German police at the height of the movement's terrorist campaign.[33] Renato Curcio was also 29 when he co-founded the Red Brigades, with his girlfriend, Margherita Cagol, who was 25 years old, in 1970.[34]

Similarly, the two most important Taliban leaders in Pakistan, the late Baitullah Mehsud, the commander of Tehrik-i-Taliban Pakistan and alleged mastermind of Benazir Bhutto's 2008 assassination, and Maulana Fazlullah, who is described as the 'most powerful Taliban commander' in the Northwest Frontier Province's Swat Valley,[35] were or are both in their early 30s.[36] Their Afghan counterparts are also about the same age.[37] And, Osama bin Laden was age 27 when he first arrived in Pakistan in 1984 to establish himself as a patron and supporter of *mujahideen* ('holy warriors') fighting the Red Army in Afghanistan.[38] He was 30 when he led his Arab Afghan fighters in the legendary battle fought at Jaji in 1987 and was 32 when his 'military incompetence' contributed to their defeat two years later in the failed siege of Jalalabad. As Laqueur observed in his 1976 book *Guerrilla*: 'Most guerrilla leaders were in their late twenties or early thirties when they launched their campaigns, old enough to impose their authority uniting the experience of age and the activity of youth, and capable of withstanding the exertions of guerrilla warfare.'[39]

## SOCIO-ECONOMIC STATUS AND EDUCATION

The ages of terrorists and insurgents have remained remarkably constant over time, but what about their socio-economic backgrounds and levels of education? These factors have long figured prominently in explanations for the eruption of both terrorism and insurgency.[40] But in the aftermath of the 11 September 2001 attacks, the debate over the 'root causes' of both these violent phenomena acquired both new relevance and greater urgency. A succession of global leaders seemed to fasten on poverty, illiteracy, and lack of education as the sources of worldwide terrorism and insurgency.[41] 'We fight against poverty because hope is an answer to terror . . .', President George W. Bush, for example, declared before the United Nations Financing for Development Conference in March 2002. 'We will challenge the poverty and hopelessness and lack of education and failed governments that too often allow conditions that terrorists can seize and try to turn to their advantage.'[42] His statement was but one of a plethora of similar panaceas repeatedly provided in the wake of 11 September. World figures as diverse as Prime Minister Tony Blair, Pope John Paul II, Malaysia's Prime Minister Mahathir Mohamad, Jordan's Prime Minister Ali Abul Ragheb, and the Philippine's President Gloria Macapagal-Arroyo, as well as Nobel Peace Prize laureates Elie Wiesel, Desmond Tutu, the Dalai Lama, Kim Dae-jung, and Oscar Arias Sanchez identified these same 'root causes'. More than seven years later, such arguments are still heard. In February 2009, Pakistan's Prime Minister Yusuf Raza Gilani attempted to rally support for his government's controversial truce with Taliban fighters in the Swat Valley by claiming that, since illiteracy is the source of terrorism and insurgency, greater peace and stability in the region would now enable Islamabad to improve education there and thereby eliminate political violence.[43]

Both the historical and contemporary empirical evidence fail to support such sweeping claims. According to Laqueur, none of the forty-nine countries that the United Nations designates as the least developed in the world are plagued by terrorism. The often posited causal connection between terrorism and insurgency with poverty, Laqueur believes, is explained by Western guilt, the legacy of imperialism, and a well-intentioned, but misguided, assumption that 'it might be relatively easy to remedy this state of affairs by offering much greater support to the poor countries, to have a redivision of wealth, by providing employment and thus restoring hope'.[44]

To a large extent, those historically attracted to terrorism and insurgency have in fact tended to be reasonably well, if not highly, educated; financially comfortable and, in some cases, quite well off; and often gainfully employed.[45] Peter Hart found that IRA Volunteers in west Cork *circa* 1920 were 'more likely to have jobs, trades, and an education than was typical of their peers'.[46] Menachem Begin, for instance, received his law degree from Warsaw University in 1935.[47] David Raziel, one of his predecessors as the Irgun's commander, was the son of an elementary school teacher and himself studied mathematics and philosophy at Jerusalem's Hebrew University.[48] A fellow Hebrew University student was Avraham Stern, the founder and first leader of Lehi (which the British in fact called the 'Stern Gang').[49] Fluent both in Greek and Latin, Stern majored in classics; was a protégé of the university's first chancellor and later president, Rabbi Judah Magnes, and won a prestigious scholarship to study in Florence, Italy.[50]

Yasir Arafat was employed by the Kuwaiti public works department as an engineer when he founded al-Fatah, having graduated from Cairo's Fouad the First University (now Cairo University).[51] George Habash, the son of a wealthy grain merchant, received his medical degree from the American University in Beirut,[52] as did his close friend and collaborator Wadi Haddad, the mastermind of the PFLP's most spectacular aircraft hijackings (including the 1976 hijacking of an Air France aeroplane en route to Entebbe, Uganda).[53] Leila Khaled was herself also the product of a comparatively well-off, middle-class family.[54] While it is certainly true that the rank-and-file Palestinian *fedayeen* were likely to be from far less comfortable socio-economic backgrounds, it is nonetheless clear that the Palestinian movement's leadership did not conform to the stereotype of the poor, uneducated, jobless fighter much like their terrorist and insurgent counterparts today.

Indeed, if anything, the distinction between leader and foot soldier is now even less demarcated than it once was. As Laqueur explains, for terrorists to survive, much less thrive, in today's globalized, technologically savvy, and interconnected world, they have to 'be educated, have some technical competence and be able to move without attracting attention in alien societies. In brief, such a person will have to have an education that cannot be found among the poor in Pakistani or Egyptian villages or Palestinian refugee camps, only among relatively well-off town folk.'[55] This was precisely the conclusion reached by Peter Bergen and Swati Pandey in their study of madrassas (Islamic schools) and the lack of education as putative terrorist incubators. Using a database of some seventy-nine jihadis who were responsible for the five most serious terrorist incidents between 1993 and 2005, they found that 54 per cent of the perpetrators either attended university or had obtained a university degree. The terrorists they studied 'thus appear, on average, to be as well educated as many Americans'—given that 52 per cent of Americans have attended university.[56] They further note that two-thirds of the twenty-five terrorists involved in the planning and hijacking of the four aircraft on 11 September 2001 had attended university[57] and that two of the seventy-nine had earned PhD degrees while two others were enrolled in doctoral programmes. Finally, they observed that the most popular subjects amongst those who attended university were engineering followed by medicine.[58] 'While madrassas may breed fundamentalists who have learned to recite the Koran in Arabic by rote', Bergen and Pandey concluded, 'such schools do not teach the technical or linguistic skills necessary to be an effective terrorist' in today's world.[59]

The popularity of medicine as a terrorist and insurgent vocation is, of course, not new. In addition to the aforementioned Drs Habash and Haddad, Ernesto 'Che' Guevera was a medical doctor with specialization in the treatment of allergies.[60] Ayman al-Zawahiri, al-Qaeda's chief strategist and bin Laden's deputy, is a trained surgeon.[61] Orlando Bosch, who was active in the militant Miami, Florida-based anti-Castro movement and was charged with the in-flight bombing of a Cubana Airlines flight in 1976 that killed seventy-three persons, practised as a paediatrician.[62] Perhaps the best-known terrorists with medical degrees in recent years were among the eight persons arrested in Britain following the botched attempt to bomb a nightclub in central London and the dramatic, but largely ineffectual, attack on Glasgow's International Airport in June 2007.[63] Six were either doctors or medical students; the seventh person was employed as a technician in a hospital laboratory; and the eighth member of the conspiracy was neither a medical doctor nor in health care, but instead had earned a doctorate in design and technology.[64]

By all accounts, the terrorist cell's leader, British-born Dr Bilal Abdullah, came from a comfortable, indeed privileged, background. His family was well known and his father was a prominent doctor in Iraq, where Bilal was raised. His mother and sisters have degrees in pharmacy and his brother is a medical doctor too.[65] In the annals of terrorism this profile is hardly unusual. The RAF's Astrid Proll drove a Mercedes,[66] as did Shahzad Tanweer, one of the four July 2005 London suicide bombers.[67] Renato Curcio, co-founder of the Red Brigades, came from a rich family. Although his partner and co-founder, Margherita Cagol, was from a 'more conventional middle-class background, her father was a factory owner and her mother a trained pharmacist'.[68] Before she joined the RAF,

Silke Maier-Witt's father had sent her to an exclusive private school and supported her 'lifestyle of a rich young student' while at university.[69] Her comrades, though from less wealthy backgrounds, were nonetheless from comfortable middle-class ones. Horst Mahler's father, for example, was a dentist, Andreas Baader's a historian, and Gudrun Ensslin's a pastor.[70] Little needs to be said about the socio-economic strata of the American university and graduate students who in the 1960s joined the radical political movement, Students for a Democratic Society (SDS), before gravitating to the anti-establishment terrorism of the Weather Underground group. Many of its most prominent leaders—including Bill Ayers, Bernadine Dohrn, Kathy Boudin, Diana Oughton, David Gilbert, and Susan Stern—were all the progeny of wealthy, well-connected families (utility company presidents, bankers, toy manufacturers, and lawyers), while most of the others were of families anchored solidly in the middle class (e.g. Jane Alpert).[71]

The same may be said of their radical Muslim counterparts in Britain today. The father of Shahzad Tanweer, the aforementioned July 2005 suicide bomber, was a prominent local businessman and, indeed, the archetype of the successful, hardworking immigrant owning a string of commercial interests as diverse as a slaughterhouse, a convenience store, and fish-and-chip shops. Tanweer was a graduate of Leeds Metropolitan University where he obtained a degree in sports science.[72] The cell's ringleader, Mohammad Siddique Khan, who was aged 30 at the time of the bombings, had a business studies degree from the same university, and was gainfully employed as a community worker. Although the third, and youngest member of the cell, Hasib Hussain, had an undistinguished academic record, and never completed his college course in business studies, according to the official Parliamentary inquiry's report of the attacks, his family's socio-economic background, like that of Tanweer and Khan, 'was not poor by the standards of the area'.[73]

The previously cited Omar Khyam, the mastermind behind a 2004 bombing plot in London that Scotland Yard code-named 'Operation Crevice', was the son of a wealthy businessman and grew up in a comfortable, upper-middle-class environment.[74] Ahmed Omar Saeed Sheikh also enjoyed a very similar upbringing and attended an exclusive and expensive private school. He was later admitted to the world-renowned London School of Economics (LSE), where he studied applied mathematics, statistical theory, economics, and social psychology. Described as 'handsome, tall and muscular, very bright and charming', his parents expected he would be knighted some day and not languishing in prison awaiting execution.[75] Omar Khan Sharif who, with a fellow British Muslim named Asif Hanif, staged a suicide bomb attack on a Tel Aviv seaside bar in 2003 also studied mathematics at a similarly prestigious British university—King's College, London.[76] As Ed Hussain, the former British Islamic extremist, recounts in his memoir, 'Interestingly, neither Asif Hanif nor Omar Sharif Khan came from an unemployed, disenchanted inner-city Muslim community; both had middle-class backgrounds.'[77] Similarly, Abdullah Ahmed Ali, the then 27 years old, who was one of the ringleaders of the August 2006 plot to bomb simultaneously US and Canadian passenger airliners departing from London's Heathrow Airport, hardly conformed to the stereotype of the wild-eyed, fanatical, homicidal suicide bomber. A husband and father of a 2-year-old son, Ali held a bachelor of science degree in computer systems engineering from a respectable British university. For all intents and purposes, he appeared to be a solidly middle-class product of a successful first-generation immigrant family.[78]

Perhaps the seminal scholarly work to debunk the conventional wisdom that links poverty and lack of education to terrorism and insurgency is the 2003 article by Princeton economist Alan B. Krueger and his Australian colleague Jitka Malecková. Surveying American white supremacists, members of the Israeli Jewish (right-wing) underground, Hezbollah fighters, and Palestinian suicide bombers, and using a variety of data and different methodological approaches, they concluded that not only is there little evidence for this causality but in fact persons with higher incomes and more education are more, not less, likely to join terrorist and insurgent groups.[79] In the case of the Israeli Jewish underground, they found that 'These Israeli extremists were disproportionately well-educated and in high-paying occupations. The list includes teachers, writers, university students, geographers, engineers, entrepreneurs, a combat pilot, a chemist and a computer programmer.'[80] For Hezbollah, they determined that fewer of its members came from impoverished backgrounds compared with the general Lebanese population (28 per cent versus 33 per cent). They also noted that the movement's ranks included more persons who had attended secondary school than most Lebanese.[81] Krueger and Malecková determined that Palestinian suicide bombers were also 'less likely to come from impoverished families and are much more likely to have completed high school and attended college than the general Palestinian population'.[82]

This counter-intuitive conclusion about Palestinian suicide bombers (given the immense poverty and deprivation that continues to define the Palestinian people's existence) is well supported by additional, compelling evidence gathered by Nasra Hassan, a United Nations aid worker based in Gaza, who has studied extensively the tendency of Palestinian youth to embrace terrorist martyrdom. Writing in *The New Yorker* magazine shortly after the 11 September attacks, she tellingly observed that none of the nearly 250 suicide bombers and would-be suicide bombers she interviewed between 1996 and 1999

> conformed to the typical profile of the suicidal personality. None of them were uneducated, desperately poor, simple minded, or depressed. Many were middle class and, unless they were fugitives, held paying jobs. More than half of them

were refugees from what is now Israel. *Two were the sons of millionaires* [my emphasis]. They all seemed to be entirely normal members of their families.[83]

Similarly, according to Ronni Shaked, the Israeli journalist and former Shabak (Israel Security Agency or Shin-Bet) intelligence officer and expert on The Palestinian Islamic Resistance Movement, best known by its acronym, Hamas, 'All leaders of Hamas are university graduates, some with MA degrees.... It is not a movement of poor, miserable people, but the highly educated who are using poverty to make the periphery of the movement more powerful.'[84]

It would of course be wrong to conclude that terrorists and insurgent movements are populated exclusively by the financially comfortable and educated. Indeed, an inevitable, if not timeless, bifurcation generally occurs across all terrorist and insurgent movements whereby the top leadership and mid-level command strata are populated by the educated (or relatively well-educated) and financially well-off, while the majority of foot soldiers are less educated and often from far more modest socio-economic backgrounds. A rule of thumb is that the larger the movement, the more diverse its members' socio-economic and educational backgrounds. In this respect, because insurgent organizations by definition are larger than terrorist groups, they will have broader memberships.[85] For example, while the founder and leader of Sendero Luminoso ('the Shining Path'), Abimel Guzman, was a professor of philosophy, the vast majority of Senderistas were poor and uneducated.[86] Similarly, while the leadership and first generation of the Kurdish Workers Party (PKK) comprised mostly an elite group of middle-class, university-educated intellectuals, their efforts to mobilize the Kurdish population inevitably brought into the PKK's ranks recruits from the lowest economic stratum of the Kurdish minority community.[87] According to one account, the PKK's foot-soldiers were a representation of 'the uprooted, half-educated village, and small-town youth who knew what it felt like to be oppressed, and who wanted action, not ideological sophistication'.[88] A similar pattern can be seen in PIRA recruiting.[89] It was the traditional 'working-class Catholic strongholds' of urban enclaves such as Belfast and Londonderry and rural communities like Counties Armagh, Down, and Tyrone, where the movement drew its recruits.[90]

Even if aQI recruiters preferred Saudis and Kuwaitis because, according to a Syrian who oversaw their infiltration into Iraq, citizens of those two countries came 'with enough money to support themselves and their Iraqi brothers', considerably less well-off Syrians, Jordanians, Egyptians, Libyans, Yemenis, Algerians, Moroccans, and Tunisians were also actively recruited.[91] Among Iraqis who joined aQI, economic, rather than ideological, motivations predominated. Major Matt Alexander, the US Air Force interrogator who obtained the intelligence that led to the killing of aQI's founder and commander, Abu Musab al-Zarqawi, and personally conducted more than 300 interrogations of Iraqi fighters and supervised those of over 1,000 others, concluded that economic necessity and fear of Shi'a reprisal and not fervent religious belief, much less the establishment of the Caliphate, was behind the decision of the 'average Sunni' fighting for aQI.[92] His view is borne out by a US military survey of Iraqi detainees. The majority were 'young, poorly educated men without jobs who accepted money from al-Qaida in Iraq to serve as lookouts, or to build or plant roadside bombs'.[93]

The same can be said of recruits to the Afghan Taliban. Lack of education and the paucity of employment opportunities alongside the grinding poverty endemic to the country's southern provinces provide a significant attraction for young men with few other options but to join the Taliban. Flush with money from narcotics trafficking, the Taliban thus offers an income and elevation in status that would otherwise be unobtainable to these young men.[94] As the US Navy commander of a Provincial Reconstruction Team (PRT) in Asadabad, Nuristan told me during a visit to Afghanistan in March 2008,

> Illiteracy is very high. The majority of young males here are very impressionable. They are told their country is being conquered and Islam destroyed, women are being violated. . . . It is a very compelling message to the un-educated. And then there is the economic component to marriages, where cash or goats is the dowry. Marriage is therefore also a compelling factor in joining the Taliban, in order to have a dowry.[95]

The socio-economic diversity evident in large insurgent movements like the PKK, aQI, and the Taliban can also be present in small, tightly knit terrorist cells as well. While three of the four members of the cell responsible for the suicide bombings of London transportation targets on 7 July 2005 came from the same small community of Pakistan immigrants outside Leeds and were essentially all products of the same middle-class or upper-middle-class backgrounds (albeit atypical of that area), the fourth bomber, Jermaine Lindsay, was not. The Jamaican-born Lindsay, a convert to Islam, was from a broken home and appears to have grown up without either the benefit of a good education or in comfortable financial circumstances. He left school while a teenager and, although intermittently employed as a carpet fitter, allegedly earned his living as a petty criminal.[96] Two other British Muslims who turned to terrorism—Richard Reid and Andrew Rowe—were both also converts, were also from Jamaica, and were also secondary school dropouts.[97] Both Reid, the infamous al-Qaeda shoe-bomber, who attempted to blow up an American Airlines flight in December 2001 whilst en route from Paris to Miami, and Rowe, another al-Qaeda operative implicated in the 2003 plot to attack Heathrow airport, had served time in British prisons.[98] As ex-convicts from broken homes, they were arguably the antithesis of the pampered LSE student Omar Saeed Sheikh or his equally well-off counterparts like Omar Khyam and Shazad Tanweer.

Assad Ali Sarwar, another of the 2006 airline bombing plotters, conforms perhaps more closely to the popular stereotype of the suicide bomber than his better-educated, wealthier peers. He was a loser with little ambition and few prospects and thus prime cannon-fodder for a terrorist movement looking for someone who himself is looking for some purpose or meaning in his life. Sarwar was an unemployed university dropout (from Brunel University) who, though nearly 30, still lived with his parents at their home in High Wycombe, Buckinghamshire. But rather than a pliable bit-player in the plot, Sarwar was one of its lynchpins. It was he who was assigned both to gather information on potential targets and to obtain all the ingredients required to fabricate the homemade explosives to be used to destroy the passenger aircraft.[99]

The Singapore-based Jemaah Islamiya terrorists who in 2001 plotted a series of attacks on American, British, Israeli, Australian, and Singaporean targets on al-Qaeda's behalf were similarly a mixed bag of the well-off and well-educated along with those at the socio-economic margins of society. They included businessmen and engineers with university-level degrees as well as taxi drivers and janitors. What they did have in common—like their British counterparts—was a profoundly deep devotion to their Muslim faith alongside an all-consuming hatred of the non-Muslim countries in which they lived.[100]


## RECRUITMENT AND SOCIAL NETWORKS

In recent years, considerable attention has focused on the importance of social networks as the principal source of recruits for both terrorist and insurgent organizations. Recruitment, it is argued, occurs as a result less of a 'top-down'-directed process than of 'bottom-up' joining. That is, persons gravitate to these violent movements not in response to active organizational efforts but are instead drawn into them by friends, relatives, neighbours, co-workers, and others who are already members.[101] Hence, ideological affinity and commitment to the cause have less to do with mobilization than pre-existing social ties. Donatella Della Porta reached this same conclusion in her study of Italy's Red Brigades during the 1970s. She found that two-thirds of recruits had at least one friend already in the movement and of that number 74 per cent knew two or more people who had previously joined.[102]

In the case of the foreign fighters recruited to aQI, this phenomenon has also been widely observed. Although about a third of volunteers cited 'brothers'— that is, organized, local jihadi organizations (e.g. 'top-down' recruitment)—as the initial or primary contact that drew them to the insurgency in Iraq, half claimed that friends, relatives, neighbours, co-workers, or schoolmates played the most important role in their decision to fight in Iraq.[103] Reuven Paz, who has also extensively studied this phenomenon, similarly concludes that personal networks played a salient role in the recruitment of foreign fighters by aQI. He found that friendship circles and especially close family relations played a salient role in recruitment. In at least ten of the cases he examined, pairs of Saudi brothers, for instance, together volunteered to fight in Iraq and were subsequently martyred.[104] Indeed, '[w]ithout these preexisting networks', Mohammed Hafez argues in his authoritative study of suicide bombers in Iraq, 'jihadists could not have mobilized so many volunteers'.[105]

The Jemaah Islamiya organization in Indonesia similarly attracted recruits on the basis of pre-existing social relationships whether from worship at the same mosque, attendance at the same madrassa, membership of a religious study group, or family relations.[106] Family ties, moreover, also accounted for membership of the various Islamic separatist movements active in the Philippines.[107] Among the most prominent fighters were the three Janjalani brothers (Khadaffy, Abdurajak, and Hector).[108] A cousin stands accused of that country's deadliest terrorist attack: the 2004 bomb explosion that sank a large Filipino passenger ferryboat, killing 116 passengers.[109] And, the Afghan Taliban, of course, is both largely populated and led by 'Kandaharis'— the Pashtun friends and relatives of Mullah Omar's Durrani Pashtun tribe from the southern provinces of Kandahar, Helmand, and Oruzgan.[110]

In addition to these 'friends and family' social network pathways, there is often also a group phenomenon process behind recruitment. In other words, a group of individuals previously connected in some manner—whether sports club, social organization, school, or religious worship group—decide collectively to join a terrorist or insurgent movement. Marc Sageman, for instance, points to the eight postgraduate students who were friends, attended the same Hamburg mosque, and all decided to join al-Qaeda. They then made good on that commitment by traveling in two groups to Afghanistan for this purpose.[111] The same process has been noted in connection with aQI's recruitment of foreign volunteers for the insurgency in Iraq. Paz discovered that 'many of the Arabs killed in Iraq, especially the Saudis, went to Iraq in groups, consisting mainly of friends'.[112] According to Hafez, pre-existing networks of Saudi youths, including the members of an entire soccer team, were recruited.[113] Ami Pedahzur points to a similar phenomenon in Palestine where seven players from the same Hebron soccer team became suicide bombers.[114] This is by no means a new development. In *The I.R.A. and its enemies*, Hart notes how in County Cork during the late 1910s and early 1920s, soccer and Gaelic hurling teams were an 'important source of recruits.... It was a small leap from playing together to marching or drilling together.'[115]

Indeed, each of the aforementioned social network pathways to terrorism and insurgency is clearly evident in the history of Irish Republicanism.[116] Family ties, especially from the mother's side, have long played a singularly important role in recruitment. 'In so far as children learned their nationalism at home', Hart observes of the 1920s IRA, 'it was most likely to be their mothers who taught it to them. It is probably for this reason that so many I.R.A. men have specified their mothers, or their mothers' families, as their primary domestic influence.'[117] A Royal Ulster Constabulary Special Branch detective, who was himself a Catholic, made precisely the same point fifty years later. 'If a mother is from a strong Republican background children are much more likely to become involved' in the PIRA. These ties are further cemented outside the family by participation in Republican youth groups such as the Fianna na Eieran ('Warriors of Ireland') run by the PIRA for boys 11–16 years old.[118]

## CONCLUSION

The 11 September 2001 attacks triggered considerable debate over the advent of a new type of terrorism for a new century. Religious imperatives and theological justifications combined with suicide tactics were said to have ushered in a new era of terrorist violence—even bloodier and more destructive than before.[119] Other scholars pushed back against this notion, pointing to significant continuities in terrorism that were neither terribly new nor, in their view, especially consequential.[120] My position has long been that the nature and character of terrorism had changed as early as two decades ago because of the appearance of new adversaries who had emerged with very different rationales and motivations to challenge the conventional wisdom on terrorists and terrorism. Indeed, the attacks on 11 September clearly validated that conclusion. Nonetheless, these enormous and important changes notwithstanding, the discussion presented in this chapter has shed light on several key aspects of terrorism and insurgency that have remained remarkably constant over time—despite or regardless of these other seminal upheavals.

The ages of persons joining and fighting in terrorist and insurgent movements, for instance, is almost completely unchanged. This has important policy implications for counterterrorism and counter-insurgency public diplomacy and information operations. Efforts employing traditional media (e.g. newspapers, television, and radio) may be irrelevant to Internet-savvy young people who rely on electronic and digital media for their information. Further, this discussion has also underscored how arguments that poverty, lack of development, and stagnant economies are 'root causes' of terrorism and insurgency are challenged by the socio-economic backgrounds and educational levels of many past and contemporary terrorists and insurgents—and especially their leaders. This is not to suggest that eliminating poverty, raising standards of living and education, and creating more employment opportunities may not contribute to reductions in the levels of both terrorism and insurgency by potentially draining the pool of would-be recruits. However, these measures in and of themselves cannot and will not on their own end terrorism and insurgency. Finally, the social networking pathways that lead to terrorism and insurgency have stayed the same for a hundred years or more. All these continuities point to the fact that both terrorism and insurgency are timeless phenomena that cannot be forcibly eradicated, decisively defeated in conventional military terms, or simplistically solved. Recognition of their intractability and appreciation of their complexities are thus essential first steps in managing these two particular forms of conflict.

## NOTES

1. J. Bowyer Bell, *The dynamics of the armed struggle* (London and Portland, OR: Frank Cass, 1998), viii.
2. Gerold Frank, *The deed* (New York: Simon and Schuster, 1963), 171; and Yitzhak Shamir, *Summing up: An autobiography* (London: Weidenfeld & Nicholson, 1994), 52–3.
3. Alistair Horne, *A savage war of peace: Algeria 1954–1962* (Harmondsworth: Penguin, 1977), 185–7. Both Drif and La Pointe's exploits were subsequently immortalized in the landmark 1966 Gillo Pontecorvo film that chronicled this crucial episode in Algeria's war of independence. See, *The Battle of Algiers*, The Criterion Collection, 2004.
4. Leila Khaled, *My people shall live: The autobiography of a revolutionary* (London: Hodder and Stoughton, 1973), 21; and Edmund L. Andrews and John Kifner, 'George Habash, Palestinian terrorism tacticians, dies at 82', *New York Times*, 27 January 2008.
5. Padraig O'Malley, *Biting at the grave: The Irish hunger strikes and the politics of despair* (Boston: Beacon Press, 1990), 44.
6. Jillian Becker, *Hitler's children: The story of the Baader-Meinhof gang* (London: Granada, 1978), 220.
7. Quoted in Eileen MacDonald, *Shoot the women first* (New York: Random House, 1991), 210.
8. Alison Jamieson, 'Mafiosi and terrorists: Italian women in violent organizations', *SAIS Review*, 20/2 (2000), 54.
9. Walter Laqueur, *Terrorism* (London: Weidenfeld and Nicolson, 1977), 120.
10. Peter Hart, *The I.R.A. and its enemies: Violence and community in Cork 1916–1923* (Oxford: Clarendon Press, 1999), 171.
11. Efraim Benmelech and Claude Berrebi, 'Human capital and the productivity of suicide bombers', *Journal of Economic Perspectives*, 21/3 (2007), 224, 230. Ariel Merari, an Israeli terrorism expert, has compiled a database of seventy-four Lebanese and Palestinian terrorists of whom the average age is 22. See Jodi Wilgoren, 'After the attacks: The hijackers: A terrorist profile emerges that confounds the experts', *New York Times*, 15 September 2001.

12. Alan B. Krueger and Jitka Malecková, 'Education, poverty and terrorism: Is there a causal connection?' *Journal of Economic Perspectives*, 17/4, (2003), 131–3.

13. Joseph Felter and Brian Fishman, *Al-Qa'ida's foreign fighters in Iraq: A first look at the Sinjar records* (West Point, NY: US Military Academy, Combating Terrorism Center, 2007), 16.

14. Antonio Giustozzi, *Koran, Kalashnikov, and laptop: The Neo-Taliban insurgency in Afghanistan* (New York: Columbia University Press, 2008), 38.

15. Marc Sageman, *Leaderless Jihad: Terror networks in the twenty-first century* (Philadelphia: University of Pennsylvania Press, 2008), 58.

16. Ibid., 3; and Bernard-Henri Lévy, *Who killed Daniel Pearl?* (Hoboken, NJ: Melville House Publishing, 2003), 84.

17. Ian Buruma, *Murder in Amsterdam: Liberal Europe, Islam and the limits of tolerance* (New York: Penguin, 2006), 2.

18. Assaf Moghadam, *The globalization of martyrdom: Al Qaeda, Salafi jihad, and the diffusion of suicide attacks* (Baltimore, MD: Johns Hopkins, 2008), 218.

19. The average age of the six plotters in Khyam's cell was 27. Channel 4 News, 'The fertilizer bomb plot', 30 April 2007.

20. BBC News, 'Bomb Britons appear on Hamas tape', *BBC Home*, 8 March 2004.

21. Ami Pedahzur, *Suicide terrorism* (Cambridge: Polity, 2005), 120.

22. Rajiv Chandrasekaran, 'From captive to suicide bomber', *Washington Post*, 22 February 2009.

23. Rhys Blakely, 'Mumbai police to use truth serum on "baby-faced" terrorist Azan Amir Kasab', *The Times* (London), 3 December 2008.

24. Emily Wax, 'Surviving gunman in Mumbai attack is formally charged,' *Washington Post*, 26 February 2009.

25. Hart, *The I.R.A. and its enemies*, 171.

26. Shamir, *Summing up*, 51–2.

27. US National Archives and Record Service RG 226 OSS Report XL 18461, 'Biographical Information—Menachem Begin', 11 September 1945; Harry Hurwitz, *Menachem Begin* (Jerusalem: Jewish Herald Press, 1977), 12–13; and Sasson Sofer, *Begin: An anatomy of leadership* (Oxford: Blackwell, 1988), 57–62.

28. Horne, *A savage war of peace*, 183f.

29. *The Battle of Algiers*, The Criterion Collection, 2004.

30. Alan Hart, *Arafat: A political biography* (London: Sidgwick & Jackson, 1984), 45, 100.

31. John K. Cooley, *Green March, Black September: The story of the Palestinian Arabs* (London: Frank Cass, 1973), 103; and William B. Quandt 'Political and military dimensions of contemporary Palestinian nationalism', in William B. Quandt, Fuad Jabber, and Ann Mosley Lesch (eds.), *The politics of Palestinian nationalism* (Berkeley, CA: University of California Press, 1973), 58.

32. David Sharrock and Mark Devenport, *Man of war, man of peace? The unauthorised biography of Gerry Adams* (London: Macmillan, 1997), 21, 152, 212f.; and Sinn Féin: *Profile of Gerry Adams, president of Sinn Féin*, 1 September 1997.

33. Becker, *Hitler's children*, 80, 90, 283–6.

34. Alison Jamieson, *The heart attacked: Terrorism and conflict in the Italian state* (London and New York: Marion Boyars, 1989), 70–3.

35. Jane Perlez and Ismail Khan, 'Taliban truce seems in flux in Pakistan', *New York Times*, 2 February 2009.

36. 'In the face of chaos', *The Economist*, 21 February 2009, 28.

37. Giustozzi, *Koran, Kalashnikov, and laptop*, 38.

38. Peter Bergen, *The Osama Bin Laden I know: An oral history of Al Qaeda's leader* (New York: Free Press, 2006), 2, 49–53, 87–92. See also, Steve Coll, *The Bin Ladens: An Arabian family in the American century* (New York: Penguin, 2008), 302.

39. Walter Laqueur, *Guerrilla* (Boston and Toronto: Little, Brown, 1976), 396.

40. See Ibid.; Idem, *The age of terrorism* (Boston and Toronto: Little, Brown, 1987), 7; Idem, *The new terrorism: Fanaticism and the arms of mass destruction* (New York and Oxford: Oxford University Press, 1999), 8; and Claude Berrebi, 'Evidence about the link between education, poverty and terrorism among Palestinians', 2003, 5–7.

41. See, for instance, Scott Atran, 'Who wants to be a martyr?', *New York Times*, 5 May 2003; BBC News, 'Poverty "fuelling terrorism"', *bbc.co.uk*, 22 March 2002; and Nicholas D. Kristof, 'Behind the terrorists', *New York Times*, 7 May 2002.

42. Online Newshour, 'President Bush's speech at the United Nations Financing for Development conference', Monterrey, Mexico, 22 March 2002, PBS.org, http://www.pbs.org/newshour/updates/march02/bush_3-22.html

43. Saadia Khalid, 'Illiteracy root cause of terrorism, extremism: PM', *The International News*, 21 February 2009.

44. Walter Laqueur, *No end to war: Terrorism in the twenty-first century* (New York and London: Continuum, 2003), 18.

45. Ibid. See also, Laqueur, *Guerilla*, 396.

46. Hart, *The I.R.A. and its enemies*, 131, 155.

47. Frank Gervasi, *The life and times of Menachem Begin: Rebel to statesman* (New York: G.P. Putnam's Sons, 1979), 88; and Eitan Haber, *Menachem Begin: The legend and the man* (New York: Delacorte, 1978), 37.

48. Professor Yehuda Lapidot, 'David Raziel', *Jewish Virtual Library*, http://www.jewishvirtuallibrary.org/jsource/biography/Raziel.html

49. Shamir, *Summing up*, 32.

50. Kati Marton, *A death in Jerusalem* (New York: Pantheon, 1994), 49.

51. Hart, *Arafat*, 61, 106.

52. Anders and Kifner, 'George Habash'.

53. 'Palestinian biography: Wadi Haddad', *Palestine History.com*, http://www.palestinehistory.com/biography/palestine/palbio53.htm.

54. Laqueur, *No end to war*, 16.

55. Ibid., 17.

56. The 1993 World Trade Center bombing; the 1998 bombings of the US embassies in Kenya and Tanzania; the 11 September 2001 attacks; the 2002 Bali, Indonesia nightclub bombings; and the 2005 bombings of London transport targets. See Peter Bergen and Swati Pandey, 'The Madrassa scapegoat', *The Washington Quarterly*, 29/2 (2006), 117f.

57. Peter Bergen and Swati Pandey, 'The Madrassa myth', *New York Times*, 14 June 2005.

58. Bergen and Pandey, 'The Madrassa scapegoat', 118. These findings dovetail with those of Sageman. See *Leaderless jihad*, 58f.; and *Understanding terror networks* (Philadelphia: University of Pennsylvania Press, 2004), 74–8.

59. Bergen and Pandey, 'The Madrassa myth'.
60. Jon Lee Anderson, *Che Guevara: A revolutionary life* (Chatham, Kent: Mackays, 1997), 96f.
61. Lawrence Wright, *The looming tower: Al-Qaeda and the road to 9/11* (New York: Knopf, 2006), 42.
62. Warren Hinckle and William Turner, *The fish is red: The story of the secret war against Castro* (New York: Harper & Row, 1981), 201.
63. Duncan Campbell et al., 'Mastermind based abroad suspected of guiding plot', *The Guardian*, 4 July 2007; and Kevin Sullivan and Karla Adam, 'Terrorism threat level in Britain is lowered', *Washington Post*, 5 July 2007.
64. Dr Mohammed Asha, age 26; Dr Mohammed Haneef, age 27 (cousin of Khafeel Ahmed); Dr Sabeel Ahmed, 26; wife of Asha; and two unidentified trainee MDs ages 28 and 25; and Khafeel Ahmed, PhD, age 27. It was Abduallah and Khafeel Ahmed, the brother of Sabeel, who crashed a Jeep Cherokee into Glasgow airport. BBC News, 'Bomb plot: Arrests and releases', *bbc.co.uk*, 5 October 2007, http://news.bbc.co.uk/2/hi/uk_news/6264230.stm. See also, Serge F. Kovaleski and Alan Cowell, 'London bombers sped to Glasgow, authorities say', *New York Times*, 6 July 2007; Karla Adam and Kevin Sullivan, 'Glasgow suspect angered by Iraq war, relative says', *Washington Post*, 6 July 2007; Victoria Burnett and Alissa J. Rubin, 'Doctor accused in Glasgow attack described as loner angry about the Iraq war', *New York Times*, 5 July 2007; and Raymond Bonner, Jane Perlez, and Eric Schmitt, 'British inquiry of failed plots points to Iraq's Qaeda group', *New York Times*, 14 December 2007.
65. Quoted in Adam and Kevin Sullivan, 'Glasgow suspect'.
66. Becker, *Hitler's children*, 121.
67. Craig Whitlock, 'Trail from London to Leeds yields portraits of 3 bombers: Identities revealed, but motives still a mystery', *Washington Post*, 15 July 2005.
68. Jamieson, *The heart attacked*, 70f.
69. Peter Taylor, *States of terror: Democracy and political violence* (London: Penguin, 1993), 112f., 117.
70. Becker, *Hitler's children*, 37, 80, 90.
71. Todd Gitlin, *Sixties: Years of hope, days of rage* (New York: Bantam, 1973), 385; Paige Whaley Eager, *From freedom fighters to terrorists: Women and political violence* (Aldershot: Ashgate, 2008), 45–53; and Julie Stephens, *Anti-disciplinary protest: Sixties radicalism and postmodernism* (Cambridge: Cambridge University Press, 1998), 91f. See also the memorable first-hand accounts by Jane Alpert, *Growing up underground* (New York: William Morrow, 1981); and Susan Stern, *With the weathermen: The personal journey of a revolutionary woman* (Garden City, NY: Doubleday, 1975).
72. Intelligence and Security Committee, *Report into the London terrorist attacks on 7 July 2005: Presented to parliament by the Prime Minister by command of Her Majesty*, Cmd 6785, May 2006, 13f. See also, Paul Stokes and Nick Britten, 'The cricket-loving terrorist whose father runs the local chip shop', *Daily Telegraph*, 14 July 2005; and Ian Herbert, Arifa Akbar, and Shahzad Tanweer: 'I cannot begin to explain this. He was proud to be British', *Independent*, 14 July 2005.

73. Intelligence and Security Committee, *Report into the London terrorist attacks on 7 July 2005*, 13f.
74. Moghadam, *The globalization of martyrdom*, 218.
75. Sageman, *Leaderless jihad*, 3–7.
76. Shiv Malik, 'NS Profile—Omar Sharif', *New Statesman*, 24 April 2006, http://www.newstatesman.com/200604240017
77. Ed Husain, *The Islamist: Why I joined radical Islam in Britain, what I saw inside and why I left* (London: Penguin, 2007), 263f. Husain also observes that among his radical circle, '[a]ll the students were at top universities in London': including the LSE, SOAS (the School of Oriental and African Studies), King's College, or Imperial College. See Ibid., 132.
78. Sean O'Neill, 'The eight in the dock: The men who appeared at Woolwich Crown Court over a six-month period in the liquid bomb trial which finished yesterday', *TimesOnline*, 9 September 2008, http://143.252.148.161/tol/news/uk/crime/article4707712.ece
79. Krueger and Malecková, 'Education, poverty and terrorism', 119–44.
80. Ibid., 137.
81. Ibid., 131–3.
82. Ibid., 135. See also Claude Berrebi, 'Evidence about the link between education, poverty and terrorism among Palestinians', unpublished manuscript, http://www.irs.princeton.edu/pubs/pdfs/477.pdf
83. Nasra Hassan, 'An arsenal of believers: Talking to the "human bombs"', *New Yorker*, 19 November 2001, 38.
84. Interview with the author, Jerusalem, Israel, 17 December 2002.
85. See Central Intelligence Agency, *Guide to the analysis of insurgency* (Washington, DC: US Government Printing Office, no date), 2; and Bruce Hoffman, *Inside terrorism* (New York: Columbia University Press, 2006), 35f.
86. Laqueur, *No end to war*, 17.
87. Paul J. White, *Primitive rebels or revolutionary modernizers? The Kurdish national movement in Turkey* (London: Zed Books, 2001), 155f.
88. Martin van Bruinessen, *Kurdish ethno-nationalism versus nation-building states* (Istanbul: Isis Press, 2000), 235.
89. Laqueur, *No end to war*, 15.
90. Tim Pat Coogan, *The IRA: A history* (Niwot, CO: Roberts Rhinehart, 1993), 283. See also, J. Bowyer Bell, *IRA tactics and targets: An analysis of tactical aspects of the armed struggle 1969–1989* (Dublin: Poolbeg, 1990), 15; and Ed Moloney, *A secret history of the IRA* (New York: Penguin, 2002), 43.
91. Quoted in Mohammed Hafez, *Suicide bombers in Iraq: The strategy and ideology of martyrdom* (Washington, DC: USIP Press, 2007), 174f. See also, Felter and Fishman, *Al-Qa'ida's foreign fighters in Iraq*, 7f.; and Reuven Paz, 'Arab volunteers killed in Iraq: An analysis', *PRISM*, 3/1 (2005), 5.
92. Alexander interrogated over 300 detainees himself and supervised the interrogations of some 1,000 others. Matthew Alexander with John R. Bruning, *How to break a terrorist: The US interrogators who used brains, not brutality to take down the deadliest man in Iraq* (New York: Free Press, 2008), 124, 219f.

93. Tom Bowman, 'U.S. offers training, pay as it frees Iraqi detainees', *Morning Edition, NPR News*, 16 May 2008, http://www.npr.org/templates/story/story.php?storyId=90506939

94. Giustozzi, *Koran, Kalashnikov, and laptop*, 40. See also, Nasreen Ghufran, 'Afghanistan in 2007; A bleeding wound', *Asian Survey*, 48/1, 155, 163.

95. Interview, Provincial Reconstruction Team (PRT) commander of A.O. Saber, in Asadabad, Nuristan, Afghanistan, 8 March 2008.

96. Intelligence and Security Committee, *Report into the London terrorist attacks on 7 July 2005*, 17f.; Lisette Alvarez, 'New Muslim at 15, terror suspect at 19', *New York Times*, 18 July 2005; Anne-Marie Bradley, 'Bomber was Huddersfield drug dealer', *Huddersfield Daily Examiner*, 8 August 2005; and Alison Pargeter, *The new frontiers of jihad: Radical Islam in Europe* (Philadelphia: University of Pennsylvania Press, 2008), 175f.

97. Pargeter, *The new frontiers of jihad*, 175f.

98. See Olga Craig and Charles Laurence, Rajeev Syal, and Daniel Foggo, 'What drove a boy from Bromley to become a suicide bomber?', *Sunday Telegraph*, 30 December 2001; Paul Harris, Nick Paton Walsh, and Burhan Wazir, 'The making of a terrorist: How a petty thief turned into a human timebomb', *Guardian*, 30 December 2001; and David Leppard, 'Al-Qaeda's Heathrow jet plot revealed', *Sunday Times*, 9 October 2005.

99. Peter Walker and Vikram Dodd, 'Video tirades that sealed case against liquid bomb plotters', *Guardian*, 9 September 2008.

100. Briefings presented to the author by the Ministry of Home Affairs, Singapore, June 2002 and September 2003. See also, Ministry of Home Affairs, *White paper: The Jemaah Islamiyah arrests and the threat of terrorism*, Cmd. 2 of 2003, presented to parliament by command of the President of the Republic of Singapore, 7 January 2003, 15.

101. Sageman, *Leaderless jihad*, 86f; and Idem, *Understanding terror networks*, 103–13.

102. Cited in Hafez, *Suicide bombers in Iraq*, 22.

103. Brian Fishman (ed.), *Bombers, bank accounts, & bleedout: Al-Qa'ida's road in and out of Iraq* (West Point, NY: Combating Terrorism Center, 2008), 45f.

104. Paz, 'Arab volunteers killed in Iraq', 5.

105. Hafez, *Suicide bombers in Iraq*, 23.

106. Noor Huda Ismail, 'The role of kinship in Indonesia's Jemaah Islamiya', *Terrorism Monitor*, 4/11, Jamestown Foundation, Washington, DC, 2 June 2006, http://www.jamestown.org/single/?no_cache=1&tx_ttnews%5Btt_news%5D=791

107. See Anthony Davis, 'Resilient Abu Sayyaf resists military pressure', *Jane's Intelligence Review*, 1 September 2003; and 'Philippines terrorism: The role of militant Islamic converts', *ICG*, 19 December 2005.

108. Zachary Abuza, *Bali-Terrorism: The return of Abu Sayyaf* (Carlisle, PA: U.S. Army War College Strategic Studies Institute, September 2005), 7.

109. 'Super ferry 14 bombing solved, says Arroyo', *Asian Journal* (Los Angeles), 25–27 June 2008.

110. Ahmed Rashid, *Taliban: Militant Islam, oil and fundamentalism in Central Asia* (New Haven, CT: Yale University Press, 2001), 35. See also, Richard H. Schultz, Jr and Andrea J. Dew, *Insurgents, terrorists, and militias: The warriors of contemporary combat* (New York: Columbia University Press, 2006), 51.

111. Sageman, *Leaderless jihad*, 86f.; and Idem, *Understanding terror networks*, 110, 113.

112. Paz, 'Arab volunteers killed in Iraq', 5.

113. Hafez, *Suicide bombers in Iraq*, 177.

114. Pedahzur, *Suicide terrorism*, 121.

115. Hart, *The I.R.A. and its enemies*, 210.

116. Moloney, *A secret history of the IRA*, 40–3, 80. See also, Richard English, *Armed struggle: The history of the IRA* (New York: Oxford University Press, 2004), 3–41; and Peter Hart, 'The social structure of the Irish Republican Army, 1916–1923', *The Historical Journal*, 42 (1999), 207–31.

117. Hart, *The I.R.A. and its enemies*, 175.

118. Interview, 'N' Division, Royal Ulster Constabulary, Londonderry, January 1992.

119. See the first generation of work that presented this argument: Bruce Hoffman, *'Holy terror': The implications of terrorism motivated by a religious imperative* (Santa Monica, CA: RAND Corporation, P-7834, June 1993), subsequently published as '"Holy terror": The implications of terrorism motivated by a religious imperative', *Studies in Conflict and Terrorism*, 18/4 (1995); Idem, 'Holy terror: An act of divine duty', *The World Today*, 52/3 (1996); Idem, 'Old madness, new methods: Revival of religious terrorism begs for broader U.S. Policy', *RAND Review*, 22/2 (1998); Mark Juergensmeyer, *The new cold war? Religious nationalism confronts the secular state* (Berkeley and Los Angeles, CA: University of California Press, 1993); Idem, 'The worldwide rise of religious nationalism', *Journal of International Affairs*, 50/1 (1996); Idem, 'Terror mandated by God', *Terrorism and Political Violence*, 9/2 (1997); Idem, *Terror in the mind of God* (Berkeley and Los Angeles, CA: University of California Press, 2000); Walter Laqueur, 'Postmodern terrorism', *Foreign Affairs*, 75/5 (1996); and Ian O. Lesser et al., *Countering the new terrorism* (Santa Monica, CA: RAND Corporation MR-989-AF, 1999). The more recent works include: Daniel Benjamin and Steven Simon, *The age of sacred terror: Radical Islam's war against America* (New York: Random House, 2003); Nadine Gurr and Benjamin Cole, *The new face of terrorism: Threats from weapons of mass destruction* (London: I.B. Tauris, 2002); and Matthew J. Morgan, 'The origins of the new terrorism', *Parameters*, 34/1 (2004), 29–43.

120. See, among other works, Martha Crenshaw, 'The debate over "new" vs. "old" terrorism', in Ibrahim Karawan et al. (eds.), *Values and violence: Intangible aspects of terrorism* (Rotterdam: Springer, 2008), 117–36; Isabelle Duyvesteyn, 'How new is the new terrorism?', *Studies in Conflict & Terrorism*, 27/5 (2007), 439–54; and David Tucker, 'What's new about the new terrorism and how dangerous is it?' *Terrorism and Political Violence*, 14/3 (2001), 1–14.

# 16

## Warlords

*Kimberly Marten*

The term 'warlord' is used in popular parlance to refer to everything from demonic figures in computer fantasy games[1] to Winston Churchill.[2] Similarly, scholars over the past decade have created a variety of different (and often incompatible) definitions for the term 'warlord', and different schemes for separating 'warlords' from other categories of non-state violent actors.[3] The lack of congruence in the use of the term has meant that there is little coherence in the resulting research, and little commonality in the policy recommendations put forward; people are using the same label to study different phenomena.

This chapter aims to define the term 'warlord' in a way that is both analytically useful for social scientists interested in the changing character of warfare and broadly consistent with how the word has been used by historians and other scholars who have focused on warlords in older political systems, ranging from medieval Europe to Republican-era China. The chapter will also discuss historical continuities and changes in the effects of warlordism on state-building. The vague concept of warlordism is often associated with 'state failure', another poorly defined term.[4] What this chapter argues is that warlords today are neither state builders nor state destroyers. They are instead state parasites and hence creatures of the state system, who thrive along the margins of existing states in the aftermath of violent conflict.

Warlordism is not a new phenomenon; state weakness in today's world has simply made warlords more prominent actors than they were during most of the twentieth century. After providing a generalizable definition of the term, this chapter will defend the utility of the 'warlord' label against its detractors, and then explain, using the component pieces of the definition, why attempts to integrate warlords into state structures today will probably doom those states to instability and underdevelopment. It will conclude by using the definition to understand what must be done in order for warlordism to be overcome by those who wish to build strong states in its place.

## DEFINING THE TERM

'Warlords' are individuals who control small slices of territory, in defiance of genuine state sovereignty, through a combination of patronage and force.[5] ('Warlord' should be considered gender-neutral.[6]) 'Sovereignty' is defined here in Weberian terms, as the ability of modern states to enforce legal writ over the entire territory that is recognized as theirs under international law.[7] Warlords today arise in situations where state institutions are too weak to control all of the territory where states supposedly have jurisdiction. In the era before modern states emerged, the informal system of warlord rule can be seen as a competitor to the abstract, bureaucratic rule of state systems; but today warlords often feed off weak states, using corrupt state actors or poorly controlled state assets for their own ends.

'Patronage' is the ability of an individual to control the distribution of resources, both to immediate supporters and to the local population, without legal or other abstract (such as traditional customs-based) oversight.[8] This patronage is often supported by tacit bargains with official state actors, who are either bribed or intimidated into accepting the warlord's lawbreaking. These bargains between warlords and states are based on personal ties, rather than being legally binding or subject to abstract state enforcement. Relationships are informal and conditioned upon constant renegotiation. A warlord who holds an official governor appointment may enforce state security mandates one day, and turn around and steal from the state the next.[9]

'Force' refers to the warlord's personal command of a loyal militia. The threat or use of force is necessary to defend the resources of the territory and its patronage network from competitors or intruders, including state authorities, who might otherwise threaten its functioning. While Antonio Giustozzi believes that warlords must therefore exercise what he calls 'military legitimacy', by demonstrating their battle prowess at regular intervals in order to retain their followers' respect,[10] there is no particular logical reason why a militia force must be used in order to be respected. If the warlord retains tight discipline while providing generous resources for his militia members, the combination of their loyalty to him and the threat of their employment as necessary can keep competitors at bay. Warlord territories can therefore be relatively peaceful and stable, as the warlord provides protection to the surrounding community. A similar situation can be seen in urban territory controlled by organized crime groups, so that petty criminals are deterred from operating in particular neighbourhoods.[11]

Both patronage and force can be controlled by an individual much more easily when their geographical scope is limited, and warlords who overreach tend to be defeated. It is only the exceptional warlord, such as Charles Taylor of Liberia, who manages to extend patronage over a sufficiently vast territory to become a head of state. Indeed, when warlords become heads of state, they should no longer be classified as 'warlords', if the analytic utility of the term is to be preserved.[12] (They can be called 'former warlords' instead.) Leaders of sovereign states are not necessarily any more 'legitimate' than warlords, and can certainly be as (or even more) corrupt and brutal. In the current world order, nonetheless, sovereign states and their leaders are accorded a set of recognition rights (such as seats in international forums and access to international aid) and limiting devices (such as enforceable treaties and international media attention) that change both their incentive structures and the levers available to their partners and adversaries. Dealing with warlords is not the same thing as dealing with the rulers of autocratic states. In addition, as will be discussed later in this article, modern bureaucratic states with enforceable property rights and abstract succession laws can support large-scale trade and investment in a way that warlords cannot. Warlords exercise personal, not bureaucratic, rule.

While some authors writing about new ways of warfare have included brutality, predation, or greed in their definitions of warlordism,[13] this does not accord with the classic way in which the term was used by scholars writing before the 1990s. Some warlords in Republican-era China were relatively enlightened, and established public health and education programmes on their territories.[14] Indeed, evidence from Afghanistan, Somalia, and elsewhere indicates that wise warlords today, as in the past, will attempt to cement their territorial control over patronage and force by building local legitimacy.[15] They want their followers to see them (and may very well see themselves) as benign and benevolent leaders. To accomplish this goal they may exercise charisma, or the ability to stir emotions and to seem especially gifted or anointed and irreplaceable as a leader. They may use and manipulate clan ties to build a sense of trust and obligation among a network of followers. They may distribute public goods, such as security, infrastructure, and social assistance, to the local population in a show of magnanimity. By creating a sense of loyalty and indebtedness among their followers, warlords avoid constant economic outbidding by rivals, as well as the need to battle a restive population which would otherwise resent warlord control.

Warlords may follow, and may force local populations to follow, strongly held religious or ideological belief systems. They may operate with allies under the banners of nationalism, jihad, or communism. They may have the ultimate dream of ruling a state or the entire globe. Yet whatever ideas warlords may champion, their behaviour is defined by the fact that they employ the threat or use of force when necessary to retain personal control over the political economy of a sub-state slice of territory. Their patronage networks are the fundamental basis for their power, and those networks control resources that are specific to a particular location, including everything from state borders to diamond mines or poppy fields.

This focus on territorial, personal patronage distinguishes warlords from other violent non-state actors. Keeping the definition limited in this way facilitates analytic comparison across cases, and prevents the term from becoming so vague that it is meaningless. For example, some 'drug lords' are warlords and some are not. The type of 'drug lord' who depends on links with farmers in a particular poppy- or coca-growing area or with specific refining labs, or who uses a network of truckers to cover an assigned territory, is a warlord; the patronage network is defined by location. In contrast, a drug lord who manages diffuse international gangs by cell phone from prison, with no particular geographical home base, is not a warlord, however violent the gangs may be and however entwined they are with state corruption. In other words, the presence or absence of the narcotics trade in any one case is incidental to that individual's role as a warlord. Warlords are *not* roving bandits who pillage and plunder and then move on; they are instead what Mancur Olson calls 'stationary bandits', who use a particular territory to try to grow rich.[16]

Furthermore, whatever ideas they may have, warlords are *not* primarily rebels who seek to replace one form of state rule with another abstract and shared system of governance. Warlordism as a concept should remain separate from secessionism. While rebel groups may become predatory as their grievances are replaced by greed over time, and while warlords may be ideological, the behaviour of warlords is centred on retaining their own patronage networks and territorial control, not on losing themselves to revolution.[17]

It should be noted nonetheless that this definition says little about the tactics warlords choose. Warlords may be brutal, cruel, and greedy, or measured, fair, and generous, as long as the actions they take are geared towards forceful personal control of a sub-state territorial patronage system.

## DEFENDING THE TERM

Some analysts may be tempted to substitute the word 'spoiler' for warlord. A 'spoiler' is an actor whose goal is to interrupt or undermine peace negotiations, ceasefires, or treaties.[18] But many warlords are not spoilers. Warlords usually get their start during wartime or periods of civil unrest, by providing some form of protection in return for their ability to run a racket.[19] Yet active warfare inhibits many forms of commerce and the full range of possible patronage activities. Warfare also threatens the well-being of warlord militias, who must then spend their energy in combat, rather than simply in deterring or threatening competitors. Warlords often function best during the unstable peace which follows war or state disintegration, when commerce is not interrupted by constant large-scale fighting, but uncertainty and distrust continue to disrupt the functioning of an impersonal modern government and economy.[20] Their militias demonstrate that they are prepared to go to war if necessary, but their patronage system provides an incentive for local stabilization.

Some analysts dislike the term 'warlord' on principle. For example, Keith Stanski sees it as an orientalist label loaded with political bias, left over from the era of British imperialism. He argues that it tars non-Western actors as the 'other' and thereby undercuts the likelihood of achieving real peace or state reintegration.[21] The meaning of words changes with time and across contexts, however, and there is no universal or abstract reason why a word used one way during the British empire or in today's popular press cannot have rigorous analytical utility when used by scholars. In fact, the term as defined here came into wide use in the early twentieth century when actors in Republican-era China used it to describe themselves.[22] It was used before the 1990s by prominent sociologists, political scientists, and anthropologists, including Max Weber,[23] Lucian Pye,[24] and Akbar Ahmed,[25] and thus has conceptual heft that is not limited by time or place. Giustozzi notes that historians now use it regularly when describing both the fall of the Roman empire and medieval Europe and Japan.[26]

In fact, the term describes a generalizable and well-defined situation that occurs across history and around the globe, wherever state weakness is found. It can be applied even to organized crime bosses or inner-city gang leaders in otherwise strong states like the United States, in geographical areas where the police and other state institutions are either bought off or unwilling to venture.[27] Despite the negative connotations that Stanski finds, the word choice itself has value: a warlord is one who obtains 'landlord' or 'feudal lord' status (i.e. the ability to exercise patronage across a particular geographical space) through control of a violent personal militia that can wreak havoc on the peace. The individual is a 'lord by threat of war', and using some other label to describe the situation will not change the underlying incentive structures involved. It is those incentive structures, not the label, that truly undermine stable peace and state integration.

## THE CONSEQUENCES OF WARLORDISM

Warlord rule is inherently unstable and insecure, and less capable of generating lasting economic development than is the rule of modern, rule-based, bureaucratic states. The reasons for this are fivefold.

First, warlord rule is by definition personal, and hence dependent upon the fortunes and whims of particular individuals. When warlords die or are assassinated, power balances can shift suddenly and unpredictably.[28] When bargains with outside actors (such as states or other warlords) are informal, they can easily be revoked as conditions change, leaving warlord territories vulnerable to upheaval.[29] Such conditions make long-term investment in future gains (by merchants, land-owners, students, and politicians) very risky. For this reason, most local actors will therefore focus on short-term gains in warlord territory, rather than long-term investment. Capital flight (including the 'human capital' flight of emigration, by those who can afford it) will be common.

Second, this focus on the short-term means that reputation matters less, because individuals do not expect to be dealing in the same way with the same clients for very long. As a result, wise actors are more tempted to engage in economic predation than they would be in a stable system.[30] It is not merely that warlord-governed territory lacks reliable *legal* protection against unscrupulous actors; it is that the uncertainty of the long-term environment encourages amoral behaviour.

Third, patchworks of warlord rule increase the transaction costs of long-distance trade. Functional states have consistent customs and tax laws across large territorial spaces, but traders dealing with warlords face constant renegotiation of informal contracts across small spaces. This situation inhibited the growth of economies of scale in medieval Europe, especially for merchants trading in relatively low-value but high-volume or bulky products (such as grain or cloth) that are expensive to protect in transit.[31] As a result, such merchants preferred to settle in powerful kingdoms that spanned large territories, contributing to the growth of modern states.[32] In the past decade, merchants dealing in one such product—cattle—in Somalia have had their trade routes disrupted by warlord rule, and have been some of the most active advocates of peace negotiations to restore the Somali state.[33]

Fourth, warlords do not brook economic competitors on their territories. They tend to shut out small businesses and independent entrepreneurs, with economies dominated by their closed and connected networks instead. Sometimes they do this through intimidation;[34] at other times it requires only that the price of bribes, for example for border-crossings, becomes so high that only the wealthy few can afford them.[35] This means that their territories lack the engines for innovation and growth that are found in stable states with open trading systems.

Finally, warlords in today's world get much of their revenue by breaking the laws of the sovereign states that surround their small territories. Warlords pay their patronage networks through smuggling, customs-tax stealing, drug-running, and gun-running. They thrive when their territories are inside or next to weak and corrupt states that lack good oversight of government activities and strong police enforcement. This means that warlords are unlikely to evolve readily into politicians or businessmen who operate according to state laws; it is simply too profitable for them instead to use their resources to flout state consolidation. Charles Tilly and Mancur Olson both imply that modern states evolved out of medieval warlord societies. Tilly argues that state-making kings were simply the warlords who operated the largest and most successful protection rackets, and Olson argues that 'stationary bandits' gathered more revenue by encouraging (rather than pillaging) the economic activities of the surrounding populations.[36] But today, warlords control only small spaces within or between states; they are not starting from scratch. There is little ungoverned territory to conquer, and few warlords control a space diverse enough to create a functioning state economy.

This explains why the existence of warlords today is a condition incompatible with *successful* statehood, even though warlords may take on elected or ministerial or military command positions in the states where their territories are located. Warlords have strong incentives to trade the political favours that their territorial control permits (such as relative stability, access to borders, or votes) for above-market profits for their own patronage networks. Hence the more they are integrated into states, the more they are likely to hollow out those states from within, stealing from the state to support themselves and acting as parasites rather than state builders.

Examples of this abound across time and space. In the early twentieth century, Chiang Kai-shek integrated Chinese warlords units into his Nationalist Army and appointed warlords to various ministerial positions in his government in Nanking. This simply encouraged political fragmentation, corruption, and inefficiency, as the warlords used their new state-provided resources to replicate the patterns of their old fiefdoms.[37] Giustozzi finds similar results from the attempt to integrate warlords into Afghanistan's post-war polity and economy. Afghan warlords have created regional monopolies or oligopolies in key economic sectors, using intimidation to drive out competitors and further enmeshing state institutions into the illegal narcotics trade.[38] The local economy can surge as a result, but not in a way that furthers state-building or long-term stability and growth. The province of Ajara in post-Soviet Georgia also witnessed the entrenchment of a 'mafia'-like economy under the rule of Aslan Abashidze. Abashidze served in the national parliament and gained the blessing of President Eduard Shevardnadze, even as he robbed the Georgian state of all its customs revenues from the Turkish border and bankrupted the country's Black Sea merchant fleet.[39]

Vadim Volkov argues that when states are weak, organized criminal gangs—a term that can logically be extended to include warlord patronage networks—can contribute to stability by providing contract enforcement and due-diligence intelligence-sharing in what would otherwise be an anarchic environment.[40] This allows some legitimate businesses to function, even if they are limited in their activities and scope. Yet the general wealth of society languishes in the absence of enforceable laws, and few would argue that the residents of warlord territories are better off than the residents of stable states.

## OVERTHROWING WARLORDISM?

Human behaviour is variable. It is always possible that an individual warlord will give up income-generating illegal opportunities and become an honest democrat, risking electoral defeat and the resulting destruction of his or her patronage network. In a related vein, it is always possible that a warlord tired of combat may let his or her militia atrophy. It is always possible that a coalition of warlords may form a binding pact to limit their own predatory behaviour, thereby founding a new federal state. Yet the incentive structure surrounding warlords suggests that these outcomes are unlikely unless a warlord is beaten down by a stronger power; there is too much to be gained by an ambitious individual who continues to use force and patronage to take advantage of state weakness. There also seems to be little historical precedent for such possibilities.

Instead historically, the combination of economic grievance and ideological mobilization has sometimes compelled local interest groups to rise up against warlordism. This occurred in both medieval Europe and Republican-era China, fostering state development in the former case when merchants supported kings, and Maoist revolution in the latter when everyone from farmers to students sought an alternative to warlord rule.[41] Sometimes, too, the appearance of a new state leader has energized a weak state so much that it musters the resources and will to work with local groups to cow a warlord into submission. This happened in 2004 in Georgia, following the Rose Revolution, when President Mikheil Saakashvili forced Aslan Abashidze from Ajara, negotiating with Abashidze's Russian patrons to spirit him out of the country and with his domestic clients to restore Tbilisi's sovereignty.[42]

This latter case, however, suggests an additional factor that can entrench warlords today: their cross-border patronage links can become entangled with realist state-to-state power politics. William Reno, in his classic study of warlord politics, notes that warlords are adept at manipulating external actors to garner profits for themselves.[43] But this relationship is a two-way street, and the availability of external actor support can help determine whether or not warlords will endure in their efforts to thwart state control. In post-Soviet Georgia, Saakashvili succeeded in negotiating with Russia for the unseating of Abashidze, but appears not to have succeeded in a later case, that of Emzar Kvitsiani in the Kodori Gorge, who also turned to Russia for support. Saakashvili appeared initially in 2006 to have succeeded in driving Kvitsiani out, and re-establishing Georgian control over the territory. Yet in the August 2008 war, Kodori Gorge fell to Abkhazian rebels supported by Russia, and there are rumours that members of Kvitsiani's network may have been restored.[44] The problem was not that Moscow valued Kvitsiani so highly, but instead that it was unwilling to relinquish the buffer zone protecting Abkhazia from Georgia proper.[45]

This means that we need to rethink our conceptualization of the term 'ungoverned territories', where warlords often rule, to focus on the role that foreign state actors play in sustaining ungovernability. Whether or not warlords will effectively disrupt state-building processes in areas of the world such as Afghanistan, Somalia, or Iraq may depend on the availability of external state patrons to back individual warlords and their internal patronage networks. In the end, the environment of the 'new wars' may still depend on old balance of power considerations. The re-emergence of warlords has often been aided by states, and should not be assumed to signal the decline of state power in war-making or system-building.

Throughout history there is continuity in the structural conditions—the absence or weakness of functioning states—that lead to warlordism. What may appear on the surface to be a post-Cold War reversal to premodern times is probably more a reflection of the weakness and artificiality of the states that were created as empires collapsed throughout the twentieth century. There has indeed been a major change in the operations of warlords since medieval times, but this change did not coincide with the end of the Cold War. Instead this change occurred when the sovereign state system became dominant throughout the globe, particularly in the postcolonial era: warlords now often thrive because they are supported by corrupt or ambitious state actors whose territories surround the warlord's fiefdom. This limits the territorial scope of warlord control, but simultaneously expands the damage warlords can do by connecting them to regional and global drug, crime, and violence networks.

## NOTES

1. The author is grateful for suggestions received from Sibylle Scheipers; for comments received at 'The Changing Character of War' conference, Oxford University, March 2009; as well as for discussions with Ken Menkhaus, Dipaly Mukhopodhyay, Will Reno, Keith Stanski, and Susan Woodward at the International Studies Association Annual Convention in New York City, February 2009. See the Wikipedia description of the popular 'Warlords' computer game series, http://en.wikipedia.org/wiki/Warlords_(game_series).

2. Carlo D'este, *Warlord: A life of Winston Churchill at war, 1874–1945* (New York: Harper, 2008).

3. Prominent examples include William Reno, *Warlord politics and African states* (Boulder, CO: Lynne Rienner, 1998); Reno, 'Mafiya troubles, warlord crises', in Mark R. Beissinger and Crawford Young (eds.), *Beyond state crisis? Postcolonial Africa and post-Soviet Eurasia in comparative perspective* (Baltimore, MD: Johns Hopkins University Press, 2002), 105–27; Susan L. Woodward, 'Failed states: Warlordism and "tribal" warfare', *Naval War College Review*, 52/2 (1999), 55–68; John MacKinlay, 'Defining warlords', in Tom Woodhouse and Oliver Ramsbotham (eds.), *Peacekeeping and conflict resolution* (London: Frank Cass, 2000), 48–62; Paul Jackson, 'Warlords as alternative forms of governance', *Small Wars and Insurgencies*, 14/2 (2003), 131–50; Gordon Peake, 'From warlords to peacelords?', *Journal of International Affairs*, 56/2 (2003), 181–91; Sasha Lezhnev, *Crafting peace: Strategies to deal with warlords in collapsing states* (Lanham, MD: Lexington Books, 2005); Antonio Giustozzi, 'The debate on warlordism: The importance of military legitimacy', Discussion Paper 13 (London: London School of Economics Crisis States Development Research Centre, 2005); and Giustozzi, *Empires of mud: Wars and warlords in Afghanistan* (New York: Columbia University Press, 2009).

4. Kimberly Marten, 'Failing states and conflict', in the *International studies encyclopedia* (Hoboken, NJ: Wiley-Blackwell, 2010).

5. This definition grows out of Kimberly Marten, 'Warlordism in comparative perspective', *International Security*, 31/3 (2006/7), 41–73, and also appears in Marten, 'The danger of tribal militias in Afghanistan: Learning from the British Empire', *Journal of International Affairs* (Columbia University School of International and Public Affairs), 63/1 (2009), 157–74.

6. A recent prominent example of a female warlord is Bibi Aysha (whose nom de guerre is Kaftar) of Baghlan province in Afghanistan. See Tom Coghlan, 'Fearless female warlord now has UN in her sights', 18 February 2006, www.telegraph.co.uk; and Matt Dupee, 'Taliban "shadow" governor slain; female warlord surrenders', *Long War Journal*, 11 July 2008, www.longwar-journal.org

7. Sometimes analysts look only at one sentence from Max Weber's definition of modern statehood, namely 'that community which (successfully) lays claim to the *monopoly of legitimate physical violence* within a certain territory', and neglect that Weber adds that rule in the modern state is legitimated 'by virtue of belief in the validity of legal *statute* and the appropriate... juridical "competence" founded on rationally devised rules'. Weber, 'The profession and vocation of politics', in Peter Lassman and Ronald Speirs (eds.), *Weber: Political writings* (New York: Cambridge University Press, 1994), 310–12, emphasis in original.

8. This reflects Weber's discussion of legitimate authority in the 'charismatic' type of domination structure, in contrast to both bureaucratic modern states and traditional authority structures; and in fact Weber uses the term warlord here. Max Weber, *Economy and society: An outline of interpretive sociology*, vol. 1, edited by Guenther Roth and Claus Wittich (Berkeley, CA: University of California Press, 1978), 241–5.

9. For examples, see Mary Backus Rankin, 'State and society in Early Republican Politics, 1912–18', *China Quarterly*, 150 (1997), 270; Antonio Giustozzi, 'War and peace economies of Afghanistan's strongmen', *International Peacekeeping*, 14/1 (2007), 75–89; and on Emzar Kvitsiani of the Kodori Gorge in Abkhazia, Mikheil Saakashvili, 'Georgian president promises to crush rebel militia leader', interview on Imedi TV (Tbilisi), 24 July 2006, as reported by the BBC News Worldwide Monitoring News Service.

10. Giustozzi, *Empires of mud*; Idem., 'The debate on warlordism'.

11. Selwyn Raab, *Five families: The rise, decline, and resurgence of America's most powerful mafia empires* (New York: St Martin's, 2006), x.

12. Reno, *Warlord politics*, uses the term 'warlord' to apply to state leaders.

13. This is true for Reno, *Warlord politics*; Idem., 'Mafiya troubles'; MacKinlay, 'Defining warlords'; Peake, 'From warlords to peacelords?'; Lezhnev, *Crafting peace*; and Giustozzi, 'The debate on warlordism'. Mary Kaldor, *New and old wars: Organized violence in a global era* (Stanford: Stanford University Press, 2007), does not use the term 'warlord', but her definition of 'new wars' argues that the non-state actors who fight them will be predatory in a way that differs from the insurgents of old.

14. James E. Sheridan, *China in disintegration: The Republican era in Chinese history, 1912–1949* (New York: Free Press, 1975).

15. Giustozzi, 'War and peace economies of Afghanistan's strongmen', argues that what he calls 'warlords' can evolve into what he calls 'strongmen' over time, with the distinction being based on the degree of social legitimacy exercised. Also see Jackson, 'Warlords as alternative forms of governance'; and Ken Menkhaus, 'Local security systems in Somali East Africa', in Louise Andersen, Bjørn Møller, and Finn Stepputat (eds.), *Fragile states and insecure people? Violence, security, and statehood in the twenty-first century* (New York: Palgrave/Macmillan, 2007), 67–97.

16. Mancur Olson, 'Dictatorship, democracy, and development', *American Political Science Review*, 87/3 (1993), 567–76.

17. Leonard Wantchekon calls predatory rebel factions 'warlords', in 'The paradox of "warlord" democracy: A theoretical investigation', *American Political Science Review*, 98/1 (2004), 17–33.

18. The classic definition is provided by Stephen Stedman, 'Spoiler problems in peace processes', *International Security*, 22/2 (1997), 5–53.

19. For examples, see Charles King, 'The benefits of ethnic war: Understanding Eurasia's unrecognized states', *World Politics*, 53/4 (2001), 524–52; and Peter Andreas, *Blue helmets and black markets: The business of survival in the siege of Sarajevo* (New York: Cornell University Press, 2008).

20. For an example of this, see Kimberly Marten, 'Dislodging warlords: Cases from post-Soviet Georgia', paper prepared for delivery at the 50th Annual Convention of the International Studies Association, New York, February 2009.

21. Keith Stanski, '"So these folks are aggressive": An orientalist reading of "Afghan warlords"', *Security Dialogue*, 40/1 (2009), 73–94; and Idem., 'A discursive critique of the "warlord" concept', paper prepared for delivery at the 50th Annual Convention of the International Studies Association, New York, February 2009.

22. MacKinlay, 'Defining warlords', 50–5.

23. Weber uses the term 'warlord' to describe a typical charismatic relationship. Weber, *Economy and Society*, 241–5.

24. Lucian W. Pye, *Warlord politics: Conflict and coalition in the modernization of Republican China* (New York: Praeger, 1971).

25. Akbar S. Ahmed, *Social and economic change in the tribal areas, 1972–1976* (New York: Oxford University Press, 1977), 22.

26. Giustozzi, 'Debate on Warlordism', 1–2.

27. For an example that fits the definition perfectly with reference to a single housing project on Chicago's south side, see Sudhir Venkatesh, *Gang leader for a day: A rogue sociologist takes to the streets* (New York: Penguin, 2008).

28. James E. Sheridan notes that this was prevalent in Republican-era China; Sheridan, *China in disintegration: The Republican era in Chinese history, 1912–1949* (New York: Free Press, 1975), 12–16.

29. A recent example of this occurred in the Afghan province of Herat after Ismail Khan was appointed to a ministerial position in Kabul. Giustozzi, 'War and peace economies of Afghanistan's strongmen', 84.

30. Olson, 'Dictatorship, democracy, and development'.

31. Hendrik Spruyt, *The sovereign state and its competitors* (PrincetonNJ: Princeton University Press, 1994).

32. Joseph R. Strayer, *On the medieval origins of the modern state* (Princeton, NJ: Princeton University Press, 1970); Perry Anderson, *Lineages of the absolutist state* (New York: Verso, 1974); and Gianfranco Poggi, *The development of the modern state: A sociological introduction* (Stanford: Stanford University Press, 1978).

33. Peter D. Little, *Somalia: Economy without state* (Bloomington, IN: Indiana University Press, 2003).

34. Giustozzi, 'War and peace economies of Afghanistan's strongmen'.

35. Mathijs Pelkmans, *Defending the border: Identity, religion, and modernity in the Republic of Georgia* (Ithaca, NY: Cornell University Press, 2006), 180–93.

36. Charles Tilly, 'Reflections on the history of European state-making', in Idem. (ed.), *The formation of national states in Western Europe* (Princeton, NJ: Princeton University Press, 1975), 3–83; Idem., 'War making and state making as organized crime', in Peter B. Evans, Dietrich Rueschemeyer, and Theda Skocpol (eds.), *Bringing the state back in* (New York: Cambridge University Press, 1985), 169–91; and Olson, 'Dictatorship, democracy, and development'.

37. Lloyd E. Eastman, 'Nationalist China during the Nanking decade, 1927–1937', in Lloyd E. Eastman et al. (eds.), *The nationalist era in China, 1927–1949* (New York: Cambridge University Press, 1991), 8–11; Ramon H. Myers, 'The Chinese state during the Republican era', in David Shambaugh (ed.), *The modern Chinese state* (New York: Cambridge University Press, 2000), 42–72.

38. Giustozzi, 'War and peace economies of Afghanistan's strongmen'.

39. 'Adzhar leader incriminated in Georgian merchant fleet scandal', Radio Free Europe/Radio Liberty *Newsline*, 4 August 1999; International Crisis Group, 'Saakashvili's Ajara success: Repeatable elsewhere in Georgia?' ICG Europe Briefing, Tbilisi/Brussels, 18 August 2004; Mathijs Pelkmans, *Defending the*

*border: Identity, religion, and modernity in the Republic of Georgia* (Ithaca, NY: Cornell University Press, 2006).

40. Vadim Volkov, 'Who is strong when the state is weak? Violent entrepreneurship in Russia's emerging markets', in Beissinger and Young, *Beyond state crisis?*, 81–104; Idem., *Violent entreprenuers: The use of force in the making of Russian capitalism* (Ithaca, NY: Cornell University Press, 2002).

41. Marten, 'Warlordism in comparative perspective'.

42. Kimberly Marten, 'Warlords, sovereignty and state failure: Lessons from post-Soviet Georgia', Working Paper 12 (Saltzman Institute of War and Peace Studies, Columbia University, November 2009), http://www.columbia.edu/cu/siwps/publications.htm

43. Reno, *Warlord politics*.

44. 'Local warlord's ally appointed head of Abkhazia's Kodori Gorge—Georgian TV', Rustavi-2 TV, 3 September 2008, as reported by BBC Worldwide Monitoring. It is unclear what really happened here, since the officially appointed new head of the Kodori Gorge is an ethnic Abkhaz, Sergey Jonua, not the Georgian ally of Kvitsiani, Zaza Gurchiani, originally reported by Georgian state officials.

45. Marten, 'Warlords, sovereignty and state failure: Lessons from post-Soviet Georgia'.

# 17

# The European Union, Multilateralism, and the Use of Force

*Anne Deighton*

## INTRODUCTION

Since the end of the Cold War, European governments have become more willing to deploy military capabilities for voluntary operations in the name of the EU, NATO, the UN, and the international community. Such operations have taken place in former Yugoslavia, and also in Africa and off the African coast.[1] EU governments insist that actions that involve the use of force for voluntary operations are an essential and legitimate way of upholding international norms of behaviour for a peaceful, just, and well-functioning international system. This has not been a one-dimensional shift for the EU however, as member states and the Commission have also sought to balance military operations by developing external policies that include civilian peacekeeping, social and economic reforms, and the rule of law alongside the delivery of military security. This has been accompanied by a reinvention of the word security, which has expanded exponentially. NATO, most of whose members are also member states in the EU, has also given itself new military security tasks since the end of the Cold War, adding these out-of-area voluntary security operations to its defence brief. Last, the UN, too, has become increasingly engaged in militarily based operations across the world, often working with both the EU and NATO: all three organizations inevitably have to continue to re-negotiate their relationships with each other. 'Effective multilateralism' is the optimistic term that is often given to this post-Cold War activity.

Why did EU member states start to act in this way after the end of the Cold War? At first sight this can be explained in terms of objectively assessable new threats which had to be tackled somehow, and which are now being addressed sensibly and more cheaply through collective, rather than individual, state action. The changing nature of the international system has meant that traditional, interstate wars have largely had their day, the argument goes, and new violence and insecurity oblige Western states to look at new ways of managing disorder. So it could be said that, because of external factors, international policing in its broadest sense has had to expand exponentially under the umbrella-titles of peacekeeping, peace enforcement, conflict and post-conflict management, and that the EU is part of this process.[2]

A second way of understanding these changes is through an exploration of changing institutional politics. In this interpretation, the institutional competition and cooperation that shape the management of the international system have been played out in the context of a variety of security challenges, some of which are not in fact as new as is sometimes suggested. Developments within the EU can also be interpreted as a greater preparedness to deploy military force as a means of integrating the EU itself by becoming more effective and visible on the international stage, and thus 'building Europe'. These two rather different approaches are not incompatible, and they have been interacting with each other since 1989.

Why did the EU develop its own Security and Defence Policy after 1998, taking the significant step of creating new institutions and procedures which allow it to act collectively with military instruments, and thereby breaking through a 'glass ceiling' which defined it as a purely civilian entity? It created enormous institutional rivalries when the EU and NATO found themselves competing for space (and money) in the same security terrain, especially over the former Yugoslavia. The uncertainties about how security issues should be approached have dominated the twenty years since the end of the Cold War, and have been made more difficult by this institutional competition. Why were EU member states not prepared to allow the UN to take on this policing role, and instead empowered themselves through the EU and NATO? As we shall see, the previous century had already seen efforts within the League of Nations and then the UN itself to fill this security space. Yet, after the Cold War, the ambitious global security project driven by an invigorated UN institution has not yet taken very firm root.

There is one other element of paradox, and this relates to public sentiment. In a media-dominated world, the desire to 'do something' and intervene militarily over European borders and across the globe to solve humanitarian disasters, state failures, civil wars, and grossly illegal political activity has been a powerful sentiment. Real-time television reporting and the Internet have meant that it is virtually impossible for disasters and gross political behaviour to be concealed (although attempts are made by perpetrators to do just this). Public opinion is at once outraged by injustices, yet at the same time Western political debate appears increasingly to de-legitimize the use of war as an instrument of policy. The use of force for the purposes of individual statecraft is viewed very differently than it has been in the past, or, as Janne Matlary puts it, the institution of war has become largely unacceptable in the West.[3] This has of course long been the case with regard to nuclear weaponry, but now the making of war, and the effects of fighting not only upon professional soldiers and their families but also upon those who get drawn in to military conflict—as 'collateral damage', refugees, innocents—is increasingly criticized. The heroic war ethic is disappearing fast. One of the paradoxical consequences of this is the tension between the normative impulses that drive concern about injustice and malpractice and the sense of unacceptability of war as a form of statecraft. The extent to which wrongs can be remedied and justice sustained without the use of force—with all the unintended consequences that this may bring—is at the very heart of contemporary normative and security policy tensions in the international system. In developing its Common Security and Defence Policy (CSDP), the EU has shifted its ground from civilian politics to becoming an actor with tools that extend to the military spectrum, and this is the fundamental change that this chapter explores.[4]

It will first briefly look at how European states reacted to mechanisms proposed in the League of Nations and the United Nations (UN) charters to deal collectively, using force if necessary, with breaches of charter norms. It will then explain how the EU as a multilateral institution has developed since the end of the Cold War. Until fifteen years ago it eschewed the use of collective force, and was even anxious about the prospect of a common foreign policy that extended beyond trade. It has now acquired tools to allow it to undertake 'voluntary' peacekeeping and enforcement efforts, while strengthening its institutional links with the UN and recalibrating those with NATO. The reinvention of NATO as a military security organization as well as a defence alliance has occurred in parallel with these changes, and has also been a very uneasy process. The changes in relations between the EU, NATO, and UN are then described. However, despite these changes, there is no EU, NATO, or UN army as such, nor is there any automaticity between a desire to intervene and collective, institution-led action.[5] The chapter will conclude with some observations on the possible implications of this shift towards what has been called the militarization of the EU, and the interaction between this change and the new post-Cold War global discourse about the broadening of security.

## 1919–89

The Covenant of the League of Nations was underpinned by the new notion that the normal state of international relations had to be one of peace. The First World War was the war to end all wars, and now the peacemakers had to try to narrow the scope for the national use of force, and indeed to prevent wars from occurring in the first place by settling disputes peacefully with the use of arbitration and sanctions.[6] But the Covenant also included clauses stating that it was the duty of the League's Council to recommend 'what effective military, naval or air force the Members of the League shall severally contribute to the armed forces to be used to protect the covenants of the League' if other methods of dispute resolution failed, both in the case of members of the League and in disputes involving non-members.[7] It was the French, anxious about a revived German threat after the First World War, who had been most enthusiastic about the creation of an international army to enforce the League's provisions. In Britain, most still opposed a tougher League line to maintain collective security under the League with the use of force, but for different kinds of reasons. Those on the right favoured keeping the government's freedom of manoeuvre in national statecraft; and those leaning to the pacifist left sought more general disarmament and 'moral' sanctions, arguing that disarmament and peace could never anyway be found through multilateral institutions which themselves had provision to deploy military force.[8]

Very small groups of overseeing military officers were indeed used by the League in support of its initiatives in Vilna, Albania, Greece, and Colombia. A League Commission administered the Saar, with French troops based there until 1927, and with international forces used to monitor the 1935 plebiscite.[9] But these were minor operations, and the political will for more intense peace-enforcement did not exist in Europe. Article 16 became a dead letter. The League was burdened by the paradox that multilateral diplomacy and judicial mechanisms to prevent the outbreak of conflict lacked sufficiency, and it was not at all clear that institutions designed to sustain peace should have recourse to the use of force.

The story of the ignominious collapse of the League is well known. However, after the Second World War, the UN Charter went further than the League had gone: article 2(4) bans the use of force that is not consistent with UN purposes, but it was balanced by article 51 which preserves the 'inherent right of states to individual or collective self-defence'.[10] Ambitions to create a global collective security organization that could ensure that its wishes were carried out actually strengthened, and the UN Charter articles 43–47 provide for the creation of facilities to allow military forces to be used to maintain 'international peace and security'(article 43) and prevent war, including the establishment of an international Military Staff Committee which would be able to implement the decisions of the UN through the use of military force if this became necessary. Yet by the end of 1947, these articles had become a dead letter, as it became clear that Security Council members—including Britain and France—could not agree on how to set this up in a way that did not just become one more aspect of early Cold War competition.[11]

It is less often remembered that it was also the North Atlantic Treaty (NAT) in April 1949 that finally exposed the end of attempts to build a global collective security system within which a UN army could have played a role. There was considerable debate about the relationship between the UN and the NAT: although Western policymakers were anxious to present the latter as a new collective security instrument, it was at its core a Western defence alliance. The Soviets criticized it for exactly this reason, arguing that it breached the UN Charter. The effect of the creation of NATO was that most European troops, if they were ever to be used multilaterally at all, would be at the service of regional Cold War defence, rather than deployable for formal multilateral collective security operations through articles 43–47 of the UN.[12]

So the aspiration to create a UN army or police force has foundered, despite occasional attempts to reanimate it. UN peacekeeping—though the phrase is not found in the Charter—emerged as the more pragmatic option. Military forces were notionally impartial and were deployed in the expectation that fighting would not actually be necessary. They lacked longer term goals of state reconstruction, controlling political outcomes, or altering the balance of power within a state, although they were, for example in the case of the Congo, involved in a complex peacekeeping operation.[13] It is not without significance that those European countries most involved with peacekeeping during the period of the Cold War have been the Nordic countries, which include the neutrals, Finland and Sweden.[14]

## AFTER 1989

Europe's increasing willingness to use force through the EU and non-article five NATO actions was highly contested after 1989, as was the development of normative ideas about the use of force in this way.[15] It was also the case that change took place in the context of the most difficult international environment for Europeans since the 1940s. This was because of the end of the Cold War and the international turbulence generated by the collapse of Yugoslavia, the Iraqi wars, the invasion of Afghanistan, and a reconsideration of the colonial legacies of the European powers.

Europe's primary multilateral institution is obviously the EU. It was designed as a civilian institution that during the Cold War was almost completely under the protective umbrella of NATO.[16] Its slowly emerging foreign and external policies deployed civilian tools only, and did not encroach upon the national military capabilities of member states.[17] This in part reflected US power, but also increasingly it was a form of self-denying ordinance complementing the building of a postmodern, post-imperial European ethic in the wake of the two bloody world wars. After 1945, European states also had other and different reasons to be cautious about the collective use of force beyond defence. These included the experience of Nazism, fascism, and authoritarianism in Germany, Austria, Italy, Spain, Portugal, and beyond; the ending of European empires; the different complexes about hard power in France and Britain; the varieties of neutrality found across Europe; and then, for more recent EU members, the searing experiences of life under the Soviet Union for countries to the east of the continent.

The emergence of the EU as an actor with military capabilities deriving from the contributions of its member states was still a dramatic story, and it has been the most decisive cultural change the Union has experienced as an international actor. In 1992, the Western European Union (WEU) contributed decisively to the newer definitions relating to the military end of security delivery with the innovative Petersberg Tasks, although the WEU was not essentially an organization with active military capabilities. These new tasks of humanitarian and rescue missions, traditional peacekeeping, and 'tasks of military forces in crisis management' excluded defence proper, and so did not cut across NATO or WEU's broader mandate, and were therefore considered general enough to allow neutral members of the EC/EU to participate (as well as non-EU members if they wished). They also generated a hierarchy of optional military actions from keeping the peace to enforcing it, and to crisis management.[18] The Maastricht and Amsterdam treaties of the mid-1990s created an intergovernmental foreign and security (CFSP) administrative 'pillar' out of the earlier, very loose foreign policy cooperation procedures (European Political Cooperation), a 'High Representative' to manage the CFSP, and opened the way to a gradual incorporation of the Petersberg Tasks into the EU. The crucial Anglo-French meeting at St Malo in December 1998 was then to define the EU military-security diplomacy for the following decade. It stated that 'the Union must have the capacity for autonomous action, backed up by credible military forces, the means to decide to use them, and a readiness to do so, in order to respond to international crises'.[19] There was a fascinating and deeply contested story of treaties, summitry, institutional politics, and intense interstate and inter-institutional competition. By the time of the Nice Treaty of 2000, the EU had broken through the Cold War 'glass ceiling' of its civilian-only external policies and achieved, at least on paper, a commitment to the collective use of force for a normative, multilateral foreign policy, in support of the UN Charter, through its CSDP with the provision of a range of intergovernmental military and planning committees based in Brussels and serviced by staff from the national military headquarters.[20]

The American National Security Strategy of September 2002, with its chilling shift to national pre-emption, and the subsequent US-led invasion of Iraq in March 2003, however, provoked a major split on foreign policy between European member states. The European Security Strategy (ESS) document was then agreed by all EU member states in December 2003 as a diplomatic as well as a planning tool. It was in fact a form of first aid to help EU member states to cover up their own differences and find common ground in security policies during a particularly difficult moment in EU–US and internal EU relations. The ESS seeks to explain and contextualize developments since the end of the 1990s. It argues that the EU is a normative power, seeking foreign policy measures that are intended to instil confidence, partnership, and cooperation, and to prevent war. If all this sounds saccharine, the ESS also discussed the ways in which the use of military force could be more firmly embedded in these policies of the Union; and there is an echo in the Strategy that probably unintentionally harks back to the League as well as to the UN's quest to seek to prevent the outbreak of violence as its first priority, and frame peace not war as the 'natural' condition of international life. Although it is also ambiguous on the relation between the use of force and the role of the UN as the sole upholder of international law, it sets the EU firmly into 'an effective multilateral system' to include the UN, NATO, the OSCE, and economic bodies.[21] There have been over twenty operations since the launch of the ESDP, over half of which have been global, and nearly a dozen that are still active. The numbers involved in ESDP operations have been tiny compared with the forces deployed in major wars over the last century; seven have been police missions, and some missions have involved both military and policing (and rule of law) efforts. All have been linked to or at least sanctioned by the UN or NATO, and many have in practice been sequential post-conflict affairs following on from high-intensity US/NATO military operations.[22]

However, it has not just been the EU that has developed the capacity to use military force collectively. As the Cold War ended, it was NATO that was most challenged, as the Soviet Union—NATO's *raison d'être*—collapsed. Throughout the 1990s, NATO therefore sought to enter the same security arena into which the EU was also moving by reformulating its strategic concepts in 1990 and 1999, and by its first, tentative efforts in the field, when it tried to manage the unexpectedly brutal collapse of the former Yugoslavia. It is hardly surprising that, as it moved from territorial defence to 'voluntary' military operations in support of Western diplomacy, NATO—which had spent nearly fifty years planning, but which had never been to war—should find the experiences of intense international military cooperation in Bosnia and Kosovo bruising. In 1996, NATO devised a European Security and Defence Initiative, which was an attempt to build within NATO what was essentially a very similar intervention capability to that which the EU then came up with after 1999. While the details of the competing schemes need not trouble us, it remains startling that, within both the NATO and EU contexts, the European powers were trying (for different reasons) to find ways to back up foreign policy with the multilateral and collective use of force in ways that had not been considered before.

The third dimension to these post-Cold War changes was that both the EU and NATO sought to coordinate their activities with each other and to embed some of their actions into the UN as the apex of a wider multilateral system of international law, states, and institutions, which gave global legitimation to the use of force. As the ESS showed, the EU's global profile has been deliberately framed to be within the UN context, for UN peacekeeping is called 'the international community's principal form of collective military activity',[23] and the 2007 EU agreement with the UN, derived from one of 2003, built upon this. However, the agreement does not prevent the EU from acting alone, without a UNSC mandate (as happened in the Democratic Republic of Congo in 2003).

It has been far more complicated for European powers to redefine their relationship with(in) NATO since the end of the Cold War. This has been a competitive process, as many in the United States did not favour the St Malo process of 1998 onwards. The Europeans were all too aware of their relatively small actual military capabilities, and none wanted to create a situation either in which the existence of NATO itself would be threatened or in which other non-NATO or non-EU countries (Turkey is an example) could not involve themselves in military operations. By 2003, the Berlin Plus arrangements were found to deliver a more or less satisfactory set of agreements for the delivery of military security between the two. In practice, operations have proceeded more smoothly than the verbal diplomacy that surrounded the establishment of the relationship. There are now elaborate structures of double-hatting, of ad hoc agreements, and a developing convention that NATO operations are then taken over by the EU, especially in the former Yugoslavia. One of the consequences of these administrative changes was that the formal return of France to NATO's military command structure was less noticed than might have been expected.[24] It is arguable that, short of further major change, the EU/NATO relationship in this context has gone as far as it can.

The last part of this triangular relationship is that between the UN and NATO. As early as 1950, there was a brief offer to share resources in appropriate circumstances, but NATO remained a challenge to the one-world system envisaged by the creators of the UN, as it was an organization that both reflected and reinforced the bipolar divisions of the Cold War. Yet there was practical UN/NATO cooperation through UNPROFOR in 1994; in the 1995 Dayton Agreement (1031, IFOR and SFOR); in Afghanistan where ISAF is a UN-mandated NATO force; in Iraq where NATO is providing training under UNSC provisions; and, in Africa, where NATO has been working with the UN and the African Union (AU). Indeed, some of the most significant major military actions in which west European states have been involved since the end of the Cold War (the Gulf, Kosovo, Afghanistan, Iraq) can be characterized as a UN/NATO mixture of invasion and high-intensity war-fighting, counter-insurgency, and complex peacekeeping. However, NATO was prepared to undertake a major military mission over Kosovo that only retrospectively secured a UN mandate. Over the past ten years, there has also been a tentative debate about a more formalized UN/NATO arrangement.[25] From the UN perspective, the Capstone 'doctrinal framework' for those in the field in the widely defined area of global, multidimensional peacekeeping does not, however, refer to multilateralism, the EU, or NATO as such, but to stakeholders and partnerships with others, including regional actors and NGOs, and thus appears to be reasserting UN primacy in this policy area.[26] In September 2008, the UN and NATO established a framework for consultation over many areas including counterterrorism. It would seem that the initiative has come from NATO and is not universally popular within the UN: it covers areas in which NATO might help the UN with backroom support over issues relating to military operations, and at the same time improve its global public image by its closer association with the UN.[27]

## A NEW EUROPEAN SECURITY PROFILE?

This brief analysis reveals puzzling sets of priorities. It is clear that European powers have moved forward, using different national rationales, from resistance to the multilateral use of force across state borders as observed with regard to the League or UN, and away from the civilian ethos of the EU and its impotent WEU cousin, while retaining national military forces, the defence protection of NATO, and, in the case of Britain and France, 'independent' nuclear forces. There is general public support for UN peacekeeping and European CSDP efforts, yet considerable reluctance to generate capabilities that involve costs, not least while some states are mired in Iraq and Afghanistan in US-led efforts. There is a desire to end the spectre of failed states, brutal civil wars, the illegal drugs trade, and instances of unjust governance, but also a fear about overseas commitments and 'neo-imperialism'. The dilemma is between the desire for peace, which had animated the League of Nations, and the desire for justice across borders, and how this should be sustained.[28] Three observations follow.

First, there was an internal logic or a 'spillover' effect upon the organization of the EU that extended through the creation of common foreign policy instruments (through European Political Cooperation in the 1970s to the CFSP) to the use of force when necessary, when member states agreed that the external situation warranted it. The use of force was an extension of the development of the EU as a *sui generis*, quasi-federal, rather than confederal, actor. However, one problem with this is that the St Malo process was managed by the United Kingdom and France, the two states with the greatest reservations about a common European foreign policy and most protective of their national roles in international politics; so the process was not clear or straightforward. Nevertheless, such an explanation helps us to understand why it was that the expansion of NATO's role was contested in Europe after the Cold War, as the Atlanticist and European visions confronted each other in ways that were sometimes reduced to demeaning requests that, metaphorically, while the United States could do the cooking, the Europeans should do the dishes.[29]

Second, the shift of approach in the EU was also caused by external factors in the early 1990s, particularly those on its borders, and without which the Union might have been content to remain as a purely civilian actor, by and large nested within NATO. In this reading, the end of the Cold War meant that security—that is, protection of the bipolar status quo—was transformed into something far more amorphous and multifaceted, which transcended borders and was alarming to individual citizens, and that, while the EU was not a defence organization of any sort, it should now be prepared to take collective military action if needs be. In this context, the United States has clearly been pressurizing the European states to play a military role more commensurate with their economic strength and political weight in the world. Others look at the EU through a post-imperial lens, arguing that there is some kind of post-imperial reflex at work, reworking the EU as a new global power, as the great European states continue to make their imprint upon their former colonies. It is striking that some of the sites of military action—DRC and Sierra Leone—have a colonial history, and that the former colonial powers tend to be the lead states in collective military action.[30]

The third observation relates to the above and to the wider discourse about security and the nature of war in the post-Cold War period. This discourse has changed remarkably over the past twenty years, and this may explain the shift in Europeans' attitudes. Societal and human security are used to describe various aspects of policies relating to individuals, groups, health, environment, culture, and identity, while the use of the word security has itself implied that each policy area is one that nevertheless deserves priority treatment where action is imperative.[31] It has also become increasingly hard to identify the boundaries of security policies, especially those that relate, for example, to border regimes, trafficking, and environmental issues. Non-state actors, failed states, environmental and health scares, and migration and civil war have delivered a huge variety of challenges to the state (and to international institutions) that are not just within, or just beyond, its borders.[32] The extraordinary advance of technology and communications, and the sway of a globalized media have thus brought the 'foreign' further into the 'domestic', although many of these security issues, including intervention, terrorism, and environmental degradation, already had long pedigrees that had been masked by the Cold War structure and less sophisticated media delivery until the 1990s.[33]

'Security' in the context of complex peacekeeping operations has thus taken on new obligations beyond the Cold War characterization of security between states and peacekeeping through the UN. From primarily observing ceasefires and the separation of forces after interstate wars, the use of force by peacekeepers now means many elements—military, police, and civilian—collaborating to help lay the foundations for sustainable peace, more often than not in intra-state situations.[34] In the 1990s, international military coalitions were in enormous demand to sustain security, while post-conflict or state-building procedures were under way (e.g. Bosnia, Kosovo). As Paddy Ashdown put it when he started as High Representative to Bosnia Herzegovina, this was the beginning of 'a new world for international intervention—one designed not to pursue narrow national interests but to prevent conflict, to promote human rights and to rebuild war-torn societies'.[35] It was hardly surprising that debates about intervention and the responsibility to protect, what Nicholas Wheeler has called 'saving strangers', intensified in the 1990s. International priorities changed, humanitarian intervention across borders seemed morally urgent, although most states were not strong enough to inter-vene alone and multilateral groups anyway gave greater legitimacy. Security was seen as the prerequisite for development and stability, and therefore the ratio-nales for complex peacekeeping and development seemed to go righteously hand in hand.[36]

## CONCLUSION

What then are the consequences of this shift in thinking and practice about security and the use of force by Europeans? Giegerich and Wallace have shown the extent of Europeans' militarization, undertaken often in unrecorded ways, and usually without much serious discussion about the use of force, and they applaud this change.[37] However, this shift to solidarism, and the protection of the vulnerable across borders, has been contested on grounds varying between the poor outcomes for operations, to the loss of the EU's earlier characteristics, to EU-NATO tensions, to the resulting force-generation problems for the UN, and to the more general lack of public knowledge about the EU's activities. There are unpalatable, unintended (or unplanned) consequences of the use of force across borders, with slippage from intervention to complex peacekeep-ing, to state-building as in Bosnia, Kosovo, Afghanistan, and in Africa, where ambitions and end games are not clear (although this is not just an EU problem, but one that is of concern to the UN too). The invasion of Iraq and its consequences certainly gave all intervention a bad name, and the current reluctance of European powers to give greater resources to Afghanistan shows that there is still a genuine ambivalence about the ongoing use of force by

European powers for sustained non-defence military operations. The weakness of the ESS 2008 report reflects concerns that had been growing since 2003 about the costs of this more solidarist approach to intervention and complex peace-keeping, as well as anxieties that the practical outcomes of such operations had been less successful than was hoped. It is possible that the 1990s were just an exceptional, post-Cold War period, and that the CSDP and NATO are now both stuttering because of more fundamental reasons than a reluctance to spend cash. This raises questions both for the military input into voluntary actions by NATO and the EU, and raises issues about the ability of the UN itself to support its normative policies in a period when the costs of the activities of the 1990s and beyond are still being counted. Perhaps also, the use of the word security has been overdone, for 'when every human malady is construed as a security, nothing is a security threat'.[38]

There also remains the normative question about whether multilateral institutions intended to promote peace should themselves have recourse to the use of force. This difficulty underpinned the creation of the League, where the aspiration was that the norm of international life should be peace, although giving the League the capacity to bring force to bear to enforce its norms was rejected, leaving it with the paradox of virtue without capacity. Likewise, the UN failed to generate support for a UN army to enforce its norms. The fear expressed between the wars that to give an international institution the potential to use force would undermine its normative value was indeed later echoed about the UN, including by its Secretary-General Dag Hammarskjöld.[39] However, there have also been debates within the UN about the possibility of (re)creating a UN army, which could, of itself, undermine NATO and EU efforts—and generate a more genuinely global approach to the international system. European debates from the 1990s about what foreign policy tools the EU should allow itself to use clearly stem from this same ambivalence about the use of military force by states acting through multilateral institutions that are themselves promoting peace.[40] Those who approach contemporary security issues through very different lenses, including psychologists, also throw a new and very different kind of light upon the use of force and, with it, the possibility of overcoming very deep psychological traits relating to violence.[41] Is it possible that Europeans may be best-placed to play to their strengths through the EU as a more democratic institution than either NATO or the UN, and to stick to civilized and civilian rule-based, development, humanitarian, legal, and perhaps policing operations, as well as using their centuries of diplomatic skills in negotiating, monitoring, and arms-reduction initiatives?[42]

To complicate matters still further, the issue is different when we consider the European members within the context of NATO. The foundational rationale of NATO was as a defence organization. It means that territorial defence is still at its heart. This in turn still requires an existential 'other'—an enemy—to flourish.

Therefore, its role as an Atlantic security community exporting 'liberal' values remains a secondary one. This poses a challenge in consideration of any closer engagement between the UN and NATO (which was at its apogee in the Balkans in the mid-1990s). NATO's role in the international system as a major, multilateral provider of force in conjunction with the UN could make those closer security-policy relationships forged between the three problematic for the UN, and allow the image of the UN as driven by Western political considerations to flourish. The constant countervailing pressure from the United States to continue to manage its European allies through NATO adds even greater difficulty to the relationship between the three institutions as providers of security through the use of force, not least as the boundaries between NATO and the CSDP are often blurred for those outside the intricacies of their relations.

There is one other danger to the militarizing of the EU on the world stage, even within the framework of the UN, to which reference should briefly be made. Securitization of policy means that the rhetoric—and, indeed, often very real fear—relating to a specific threat can induce governments to work outside political norms and legal procedures. The assumption can be that security implies the need for priority action that may encourage the state to act outside the normal framework of politics and diplomacy.[43] It is a term that has been particularly widely applied since 9/11 to terrorism, and since the invasions of Afghanistan and Iraq, to imprisonment, rendition, as well as to the use of far greater powers of surveillance, detention, and police–military–intelligence cooperation. It can also be applied to other policy areas, including piracy and resource wars. The latter are a well-established phenomenon across the twentieth century, and the environmental challenges that present themselves are likewise vulnerable to securitization if core national interests appear threatened. There are other examples of securitization that could suffocate civil society, jeopardize democracy, and indeed perhaps create coercive states whose only legitimacy stems from countering increasing security threats.[44] These have been noteworthy over concerns to protect oil and energy supplies, and in consideration of environmental security challenges, including disputes over access to water and to sea lanes. To put this in the vernacular: we may be on a slippery slope in the ways we frame responses to a vast variety of security challenges. One does not have to take the bleak view that national and other security experts will always look for 'new missions' to perpetuate themselves, to see that the tidal wave of new security issues could become bolted onto a mindset of fear (of loss of basic resources, or of relative power, the control of putative terrorists, pre-emptive actions) that could lead to a bias towards military solutions.[45] The slippery slope of securitization may encourage fearful decision-makers to breach legal norms in the interests of 'security', while also being more readily prepared to use force to 'solve' frightening global challenges.

## NOTES

1. This chapter only refers to 'voluntary' operations, not military alliances or unilateral state actions that some—usually great powers—have deployed across borders over the past century, or non-European multilateral security institutions like the African Union. The right of individual sovereign European states to decide whether or not to participate in an action remains. The European Union (EU) dates from 1993; before this the Union was called the European Economic Community (EEC), and then European Communities (EC), although the acronym EU will be used throughout. It is not possible to generalize rigorously across Europe, as, for example, the Scandinavian experience is very different from that of Britain and France, many countries such as Spain, Italy, and Finland did not join the UN until 1955, and West Germany was not admitted until 1973. European countries have also joined the EU and/or NATO at very different times. I am grateful to Robert Ayson, Alyson Bailes, Martin Ceadel, Tom Davies, Sam Daws, Bethan Greener, Hanna Ojanen, Adam Roberts, and Sibylle Scheipers for comments and discussion.

2. The boundary between military actions and international police actions in which arms are carried is not developed in this chapter; for this see B.K.Greener, *The new international policing* (Basingstoke: Palgrave Macmillan, 2009).

3. Janne Haaland Matlary, *European Union security dynamics: In the new national interest* (Palgrave Macmillan, 2009), 3ff.

4. The Lisbon Treaty of 2009 renamed the European Security and Defence Policy as the CSDP, article 9E.2; section 2. It is noteworthy that European states still invoke a traditional national, rather than European interest, when they suffer losses on the battlefield.

5. Thomas G. Weiss and Sam Daws (eds.), *The Oxford Handbook on the United Nations* (Oxford: Oxford University Press, 2007), 4. Classic defence provision against territorial invasion has also been marginalized in Europe, where the sole defence alliance remains NATO for many states. Lisbon Treaty, article 28A, b)/i/2: 'The Common Security and Defence Policy shall include the progressive framing of a common Union defence policy. This will lead to a common defence, when the European Council, acting unanimously, so decides.'

6. Covenant of the League of Nations, articles 11–15; Stephen C. Neff, *War and the law of nations: A general history* (Cambridge: Cambridge University Press, 2005), 279; Lorna Lloyd, 'The League of Nations and the settlement of disputes', *World Affairs*, 157/4 (1995), 160–74.

7. Covenant of the League of Nations, article 16; Zara Steiner, *The lights that failed: European international history, 1919–1933* (Oxford: Oxford University Press, 2005), 42f., 582f.

8. Michael C. Pugh, 'An international police force: Lord Davies and the British debate in the 1930s', *International Relations*, 9/3 (1988), 335–50. See also Clement Attlee, 'Collective security under the United Nation', David Davis Memorial Institute lecture (1958); Andrew Webster, 'An argument without end: Britain, France and the disarmament process', in Martin S. Alexander and W. J. Philpott (eds.), *Anglo-French defence relations between the wars, 1919–1939* (London: Macmillan, 2001); Martin Ceadel, *Pacifism in Britain 1914–1945: The defining of a faith* (Oxford:

Clarendon Press, 1980), and Idem., *Thinking about peace and war* (Oxford: Oxford University Press, 1987), 105.

9. Alan James, 'The peacekeeping role of the League of Nations', *International Peacekeeping*, 6/1 (1999), 154–60.

10. For the interwar history to this particular clause, see Neff, *War and the law of nations*, 303–11.

11. Leland M. Goodrich and Edvard Hambro, *Charter of the United Nations: Commentary and documents* (Boston, MD: World Peace Foundation, 1946); Edward Johnson, 'British proposals for a UN force 1946–48', in Anne Deighton (ed.), *Britain and the first Cold War* (London: Macmillan, 1990).

12. US decision-makers prepared for a wave of opposition to NATO (which did not materialize), and in the United Kingdom, Whitehall took the exceptional decision to encourage the Foreign Office's legal officer to write a short book defending the legal position of NATO in the context of the UN Charter; W. Eric Beckett, *The North Atlantic Treaty, the Brussels Treaty and the Charter of the United Nations* (London: Stevens and Sons, 1950); see also Jack L. Granatstein, 'The United Nations and the North Atlantic Treaty Organization', in Gustav Schmidt (ed.), *A history of NATO—The first fifty years*, volume I (Basingstoke: Palgrave Macmillan, 2001), 29–40; E. Timothy Smith, *Opposition beyond the water's edge: Liberal internationalists, pacifist and containment, 1945–1953* (London: Greenwood Press, 1999), chapter 4; Anne Deighton, 'Three men and the world they made: Acheson, Bevin, Schuman and the creation of NATO in 1949', in Jussi Hanhimaki (ed.), *Transatlantic relations, 1949–2009* (London: Routledge, 2010).

13. Adam Roberts, 'From San Francisco to Sarajevo: The UN and the use of force', *Survival*, 37/4 (1995–6), 7–28, is the seminal article that covers different options available to the UN on the use of force. Evan Luard, 'Collective intervention', in Hedley Bull (ed.), *Intervention in world politics* (Oxford: Clarendon Press, 1984), 158. See also http://www.un.org/Depts/dpko/dpko/pastops.shtml for a list of past operations.

14. William J. Durch (ed.), *The evolution of peacekeeping* (New York: St Martin's Press, 1992). As far as I know, there has not been a study on the different attitudes of European powers towards UN peacekeeping, and how this affected their stances on European security policy since the end of the Cold War.

15. Alex J. Bellamy et al., *Understanding peacekeeping* (London: Polity, 2004), 5, 41–4.

16. Ireland, which joined the EC in 1973, is not a NATO member. After the Cold War, Austria, Finland, and Sweden joined the EU in 1995, and also retained their neutrality. Poland, Hungary, the Czech Republic, Slovakia, Slovenia, Estonia, Latvia, Lithuania, Bulgaria, and Romania are members of both. Cyprus and Malta are EU but not NATO members.

17. Daniel Moeckli, *European foreign policy during the Cold War: Heath, Brandt, Pompidou and the dream of European unity* (London: Tauris, 2009).

18. See also, 'European security: A common concept of the 27 WEU countries', WEU Council of Ministers, Madrid, 14 November 1995. WEU was almost completely disbanded by 2000, as most of its functions were taken over by the EU. For a

historical account of the WEU, see Anne Deighton (ed.), *Western European Union, 1954–1997: Defence, security, integration* (Oxford: European Interdependence Research Unit, 1997).

19. Joint Declaration at British–French summit, St Malo, 3–4 December 1998.

20. Cologne European Council, 3–4 June 1999, Annex III of Presidency conclusions. See also Anne Deighton and Gérard Bossuat (eds.), *The EC/EU: A world security actor?* (Paris: Soleb, 2007); Anne Deighton, 'The European security and defence policy', *Journal of Common Market Studies*, 40/4 (2002), 719–41; Jolyon Howorth, *Security and defence policy in the European Union* (Basingstoke: Palgrave Macmillan, 2007), especially chapter 3 for the nuts and bolts of decision-making. There was also an arcane discussion about the ESDP as a 'defence policy' but not a 'common defence', which was intended to forestall any impression that the EU was a challenge to NATO defence.

21. 'A secure Europe in a better world: The European Security Strategy, 2003', http:// ue.eu.int/uedocs/. Alyson Bailes, *The European Security Strategy: An evolutionary history* (Stockholm: SIPRI, 2005), has a very thorough analysis; Anne Deighton with Victor Mauer (eds.), *Securing Europe? Implementing the European Security Strategy* (Zurich: ETHZ, 2006). Lisa Martin, 'Multilateral organizations after the US–Iraq war of 2003', Harvard University, August 2003 refers to an 'ad hoc multilateralism'—what I have also called '*ad hocery*' in Deighton, 'European security and defence policy'. See also John G. Ruggie, 'Multilateralism: The anatomy of an institution', in Idem. (ed.), *Multilateralism matters: The theory and praxis of an institutional form* (New York: Columbia University Press, 1993); Lisa Martin, 'Interests, power and multilateralism', *International Organization*, 46/4 (1992), 765–92. The ESS 2008 update is at 'Report on the implementation of the European Security Strategy—Providing security in a changing world', 11 December 2008, EU, S407/08. It veers towards the banal: 'We need to continue mainstreaming human rights issues . . . faced with common problems, there is no substitute for common solutions'.

22. Anand Menon, 'Empowering paradise? The ESDP at ten', *International Affairs*, 85/2 (2009), 227–47.

23. Roberts, 'From San Francisco', 14.

24. In March 2009, http://www.rfi.fr/actuen/articles/111/article_3136.asp; I am grateful to conversations with Professor Maurice Vaisse on this issue.

25. Contacts have also extended into the policy areas of demining, civil emergency planning, terrorism, arms control.

26. *United Nations peacekeeping operations: Principles and guidelines* (2008), http:// www.peacekeepingbestpractices.unlb.org/Pbps/Library/Capstone_Doctrine_ENG. pdf

27. http://www.nato.int/issues/un/index.html. Private information. Adam Roberts and Dominic Zaum, *War and the United Nations Security Council since 1945* (London: IISS, Adelphi Paper 395, 2008), on the necessary selectivity of UN choice of operations; see also Michael F. Harsch and Johannes Varwick, 'NATO and the UN', *Survival*, 51/2, 2009, 5–12.

28. *The Responsibility to Protect* (2000), http://www.responsibilitytoprotect.org/index.php/publications/core-rtop-documents. I am grateful to Martin Ceadel for his comments on the peace and justice imperatives.
29. The question of whether how far these events were part of an electable integration process driven by spillover or a high-level governmental decision, an incremental and unplanned reaction to events, or in fact to do with bargaining that is primarily related to domestic politics is still open: see most recently, Christopher J. Bickerton, 'Functionality in EU foreign policy: Towards a new research agenda?', *Journal of European Integration*, 32/2 (2010), 213–27.
30. Kimberly Marten, *Enforcing the peace: Learning from the imperial past* (New York: Columbia University Press, 2004), 3. Marten uses the imperial analogy generally to help to explain the nature of contemporary, complex peacekeeping, for the 'tasks performed by imperial soldiers in many ways match what is being asked of today's peacekeepers', 17.
31. S. Neil Macfarlane and Yuen Foong Khong, *Human security and the UN: A critical history* (Bloomington, ID: Indiana University Press, 2006), esp. 238.
32. This definitional divide should not be exaggerated, given the drive in both capitalist and the communist countries to create 'national security' states and to control serious ideological opposition by citizens during the Cold War.
33. A cursory study of the Cold War numbers of *International Security* reveals that 'new' security issues were already on the radar of some writers.
34. *United Nations peacekeeping operations: Principles and guidelines.* 'While robust peacekeeping involves the use of force at the tactical level with the consent of the host authorities and/or the main parties to the conflict, peace enforcement may involve the use of force at the strategic or international level, which is normally prohibited for Member States under Article 2(4) of the Charter unless authorized by the Security Council.' Durch, *Evolution*, table 1.2, 10.
35. Quoted from the *New York Times*, 28 October 2002, in Marten, *Enforcing the peace*, 83.
36. For example, Alice E. Hills, *Policing post-conflict cities* (London: Zed, 2009); Nicholas Wheeler, *Saving strangers: Humanitarian intervention in international society* (Oxford: Oxford University Press, 2000).
37. Bastian Giegerich and William Wallace, 'Not such a soft power: The external deployment of European forces', *Survival*, 46/2 (2004), 163–82. They provide the most comprehensive statistical analysis of actual deployments.
38. Macfarlane and Khong, *Human security*, 264.
39. I owe this reference to Roberts, 'From San Francisco', 15.
40. There was a short debate amongst scholars and theorists of European integration about this shift. See, for example, the work of Christopher J. Hill, Karen Smith, Richard Whitman, Ian Manners, found in the extensive bibliography to Karen E. Smith, *European Union foreign policy in a changing world* (Cambridge: Polity, 2008), 73, who herself now seems to see the ESDP as a fait accompli.
41. See, recently, http://www.h-net.org/~diplo/ISSF and references therein.
42. Claudia Major, 'EU–UN cooperation in military crisis management: The experience of EUFOR RDCongo in 2006', Chaillot Paper No. 72 (Paris: EUISS, 2008). Geoffrey van Orden (member of EP Defence Sub-Committee), EU Observer.

com, 12 March 2009: 'The Chad mission would have been more successful and would have had continuity had the UN taken a role from the beginning, instead of acceding to the EU's politically-driven request for military involvement.' The ad hoccery of recent operations is best exemplified by the EU's contribution through Operation Atlanta to the issue of piracy.

43. A successful speech act 'through which an intersubjective understanding is constructed within a political community to treat something as an existential threat to a valued referent object, and to enable a call for urgent and exceptional measures to deal with the threat'. Barry Buzan and Ole Waever, *Regions and powers* (Cambridge: Cambridge University Press: 2003), 491. See also, Holger Stritzel, 'Towards a theory of securitization: Copenhagen and beyond', *European Journal of International Relations*, 13/3 (2007), 357–83.

44. Volker Franke, 'The Emperor needs new clothes: Securitizing threats in the twenty-first century', *Peace and Conflict Studies*, 9/1 (2002), 1–20.

45. Daniel Deudney, 'The case against linking environmental degradation and national security', *Millennium: Journal of International Studies*, 19/3 (1990), 461–76.

# 18

## Robots at War: The New Battlefield*

### P. W. Singer

There was little to warn of the danger ahead. The Iraqi insurgent had laid his ambush with great cunning. Hidden along the side of the road, the bomb looked like any other piece of trash. American soldiers had begun to call these jury-rigged bombs 'IEDs', official shorthand for improvised explosive devices.

The team hunting for the bomb was an explosive ordnance disposal (EOD) team, the pointy end of the spear in an effort to suppress roadside bombings. By 2006, there were 2,500 of these attacks a month and they were the leading cause of casualties among American troops, as well as Iraqi civilians. In a typical tour in Iraq, each EOD team would go on more than 600 calls, defusing or safely exploding about two devices a day. Perhaps the most telling sign of how critical the teams' work was to the American war effort was that the insurgents began offering a rumoured $50,000 bounty for killing an EOD soldier.

Unfortunately, this particular IED call would not end well. By the time the soldier had advanced close enough to see the telltale wires protruding from the bomb, it was too late. There was no time to defuse the bomb and no time to escape. The IED erupted in a wave of flame.

Depending on how much explosive has been packed into an IED, a soldier must be as far as 50 yards away to escape death and as far as a half a mile away to escape injury from the blast and bomb fragments. Even if you are not hit, the pressure from the blast by itself can break bones. This soldier, though, had been right on top of the bomb. Shards of metal shrapnel flew in every direction at bullet speed. As the flames and debris cleared, the rest of the team advanced. But they found little left of their teammate. Hearts in their throats, they loaded the remains onto a helicopter, which took them back to the team's base camp near Baghdad International Airport.

That night, the team's commander, a navy chief petty officer, did his sad duty and wrote home about the incident. The effect of this explosion had been particularly tough on his unit. They had lost their most fearless and technically savvy soldier. More important, they had also lost a valued member of the team, a soldier who had saved the others' lives many times over. The soldier had always taken the most dangerous roles, always willing to go first to scout for IEDs and ambushes. Yet the other soldiers in the unit had never once heard a complaint.

In his condolences, the chief noted the soldier's bravery and sacrifice. He apologized for his inability to change what had happened. But he also expressed his thanks and talked up the silver lining he took away from the loss. At least, he wrote, 'when a robot dies, you don't have to write a letter to its mother'.

The 'soldier' in this case was, in fact, a 42-pound robot called a PackBot. Just about the size of a lawnmower, the PackBot mounts all sorts of cameras and sensors, as well as a nimble arm with four joints. It moves using four 'flippers'. These are tiny tank treads that can also rotate on an axis, allowing the robot not only to roll forward and backward using the treads like a tank would but also to flip its tracks up and down (almost like a seal moving) to climb stairs, rumble over rocks, squeeze down twisting tunnels, and even swim underwater. The cost, to the United States, of 'death' was $150,000.

The destination of the chief's report was a two-story concrete office building, located across from a Macaroni Grill and Men's Wearhouse in a drab office park just outside Boston, Massachusetts. On the corner is a sign for a company called iRobot, the maker of the PackBot. The name is inspired by Isaac Asimov's 1950 science fiction classic *I, Robot*, in which robots of the future not only carry out mundane chores but make life and death decisions. It is at places like this that the future of war is being written.

The PackBot is only one of many new unmanned systems operating in the wars in Iraq and Afghanistan today. When US forces went into Iraq in 2003, they had zero robotic units on the ground. By the end of 2004, the number was up to 150. By the end of 2005, it was 2,400, and it more than doubled the next year. In 2006, it was projected to reach as high as 12,000 by the end of 2008. And these robots were just the first generation. Already in the prototype stage are varieties of unmanned weapons and exotic technologies, from automated machine guns and robotic stretcher-bearers to tiny but lethal robots the size of insects, which often look as though they are straight out of the wildest science fiction. As a result, Pentagon planners are having to figure out not only how to use such machines as the PackBot in the wars of today but also how they should plan for battlefields in the near future that will be, as one officer put it, 'largely robotic'.

The most apt historical parallel with the current period in the development of robotics may well turn out to be the First World War. Back then, strange, exciting new technologies that had been science fiction just years earlier were introduced and used in increasing numbers on the battlefield. Indeed, it was H.G. Wells' 1903 short story 'Land ironclads' that inspired Winston Churchill to champion the development of the tank. Another story, by A.A. Milne, creator of Winnie the Pooh, was among the first to raise the idea of using aeroplanes in war, while Arthur Conan Doyle (in 'Danger') and Jules Verne (*Twenty thousand leagues under the sea*) pioneered the notion of using submarines in war. These new technologies did not really change the fundamentals of war. But even their earliest models did quickly prove useful enough to make it clear that they were not going to be quickly relegated to the realm of fiction. And, more importantly, their effects began to ripple out, raising questions not only on how best to use them in battle, but also generating an array of new political, moral, and legal challenges. For instance, the US's and Germany's differing interpretations of how submarine warfare should be conducted helped draw America into the world war. Similarly, aeroplanes proved useful for spotting and attacking troops at greater distances, but also allowed for strategic bombing of cities and other sites, which extended the battlefield to the home front.

Much the same sort of recalibration of thinking about war is starting to happen as a result of robotics today. On the civilian side, experts such as Microsoft's Bill Gates describe robotics as being close to where computers were in the early 1980s—still rare, but poised for a breakout. On the military side, unmanned systems are rapidly coming into use in almost every realm of war, moving more and more soldiers out of danger and allowing their enemies to be targeted with increasing precision.

And they are changing the experience of war itself. This is leading some of the first generation of soldiers working with robots even to worry that war waged by remote control from distant locations will come to seem too easy, too tempting. More than a century ago, General Robert E. Lee famously observed, 'it is good that we find war so horrible, or else we would become fond of it'. He did not contemplate a time when a pilot could 'go to war' by commuting to work each morning in his Toyota to a cubicle where he could shoot missiles at an enemy thousands of miles away and then make it home in time for his kid's soccer practice.

As our weapons are designed to have ever more autonomy, deeper questions arise. Can the new armaments reliably separate friend from foe? What laws and ethical codes apply? What are we saying when we send out unmanned machines to fight for us? What is the 'message' that those on the other side receive? Ultimately, how will humans remain masters of weapons that are immeasurably faster and more 'intelligent' than they are?

## THE DEVELOPMENT OF ROBOT SYSTEMS

The unmanned systems that have already been deployed to Iraq today come in many shapes and sizes. All told, some twenty-two different robot systems are now operating on the ground. One retired army officer speaks of these new forces as 'the army of the Grand Robotic'.[1]

One of the PackBot's fellow robo-soldiers in Iraq is the TALON, made by Foster-Miller, Inc., whose offices are just a few miles away from iRobot's. Foster-Miller builds an EOD version of the TALON, but it has also remodelled the machine into a 'killer app', the special weapons observation reconnaissance detection system, or SWORDS. The new design allows users to mount different weapons onto the robot—including an M-16 rifle, a machine gun, and a grenade or rocket launcher—and easily swap them over. Another robo-soldier is the MARCBOT (multifunction agile remote-controlled robot). One of the smallest but most commonly used robots in Iraq, the MARCBOT looks like a toy truck with a video camera mounted on a tiny, antenna-like mast. Costing only $5,000, this minuscule bot is used to scout for enemies and to search under cars for hidden explosives. The MARCBOT is not just notable for its small size; it was the first ground robot to draw blood in Iraq. One unit of US soldiers jury-rigged their MARCBOTs to carry Claymore anti-personnel mines. If they thought an insurgent was hiding in an alley, they would send a MARCBOT down first and, if they found someone waiting in ambush, take him out with the Claymore. Of course, each insurgent killed in this fashion meant $5,000 worth of blown-up robot parts, but so far the army has not billed the soldiers.

The world of unmanned systems at war is not confined to the ground. One of the most familiar unmanned aerial vehicles (UAVs) is the Predator. At 27 feet in length, the propeller-powered drone is just a bit smaller than a Cessna plane. Perhaps its most useful feature is that it can spend up to twenty-four hours in the air, at heights of up to 26,000 feet. Predators are flown by what are called 'reach-back' or 'remote-split' operations. While the drone flies out of bases in the war zone, the human pilot and sensor operator are physically located 7,500 miles away, flying the planes via satellite from a set of converted single-wide trailers located mostly at Nellis and Creech Air Force bases in Nevada. Such operations have created the novel situation of pilots experiencing the psychological disconnect of being 'at war' while still dealing with the pressures of home. In the words of one Predator pilot, 'You see Americans killed in front of your eyes and then have to go to a PTA meeting.'[2] Says another, 'You are going to war for 12 hours, shooting weapons at targets, directing kills on enemy combatants and then you get in the car, drive home and within 20 minutes you are sitting at the dinner table talking to your kids about their homework.'[3]

Each Predator costs just under $4.5 million, which sounds like a lot until you compare it to the costs for other military aircraft. Indeed, for the price of one new F-35, the Pentagon's next-generation manned fighter jet (which has not even taken flight yet), you can buy thirty Predators. More important, the low price and lack of a human pilot mean that the Predator can be used for missions in which there is a high risk of being shot down, such as travelling low and slow over enemy territory. Predators originally were designed for reconnaissance and surveillance, but now some are armed with laser-guided Hellfire missiles. In addition to its deployments in Iraq and Afghanistan, the Predator, along with its larger, more heavily armed sibling, the Reaper, has been used with increasing frequency to attack suspected terrorists in Pakistan. According to news media reports in 2009, the drones were carrying out cross-border strikes at the rate of one every other day, operations which the Pakistani Prime Minister described as the biggest point of contention between his country and the United States.

In addition to the Predator and Reaper, a veritable menagerie of unmanned drones now circle in the skies over war zones. Small UAVs such as the Raven, which is just over three feet long, or the even smaller Wasp (which carries a camera the size of a peanut) are tossed into flight by individual soldiers and fly just above the rooftops, transmitting video images of what is down the street or on the other side of the hill. Medium-sized drones such as the Shadow circle over entire neighbourhoods, at heights above 1,500 feet, to monitor anything suspicious. The larger Predators and Reapers roam over entire cities at 5,000–15,000 feet, hunting for targets to strike. Finally, sight unseen, 40-feet-long jet-powered Global Hawks zoom across much larger landscapes at 60,000 feet, monitoring electronic signals and capturing reams of detailed imagery for intelligence teams to sift through. Each Global Hawk can stay in the air for as long as thirty-five hours. In other words, a Global Hawk can fly from San Francisco, spend a day hunting for any terrorists throughout the entire state of Maine, and then fly back to the west coast.

A massive change has thus occurred in the airspace above wars. Only a handful of drones were used in the 2003 invasion of Iraq, with just one supporting all of V Corps, the primary US army unit. In January 2009, there were more than 5,300 drones in the US military's total inventory, and today not a mission happens without them. One Air Force lieutenant general forecasts that 'given the growth trends, it is not unreasonable to postulate future conflicts involving tens of thousands'.[4]

## ROBOTIC ADVANTAGES

Between 2002 and 2008, the US defence budget rose by 74 per cent to $515 billion, not including the several hundred billions more spent on operations in Afghanistan and Iraq. With the defence budget at its highest level in real terms since 1946 (though it is still far lower as a percentage of gross domestic product), spending on military robotics research and development and subsequent procurement has boomed. The amounts spent on ground robots, for example, has roughly doubled each year since 2001. 'Make 'em as fast as you can' is what one robotics executive says he was told by his Pentagon buyers after 9/11.

The result is that a significant military robotics industry is beginning to emerge. The First World War parallel is again instructive. As a report by the Pentagon's Defense Advanced Research Projects Agency (DARPA) noted, only 239 Ford Model T cars were sold in 1908. Ten years later, more than a million were.

It is not hard to see the appeal of robots to the Pentagon. Above all, they save lives. And they also do not come with some of our human frailties and foibles. 'They don't get hungry,' says Gordon Johnson of the Pentagon's Joint Forces Command. 'They're not afraid. They don't forget their orders. They don't care if the guy next to them has just been shot. Will they do a better job than humans? Yes.'[5]

Robots are particularly attractive for roles dealing with what people in the field call the 'three D's'—tasks that are dull, dirty, or dangerous. Many military missions can be incredibly boring as well as physically taxing. Humans doing work that requires high levels of concentration need to take frequent breaks, for example, but robots do not. Using the very same mine detection gear as a human, today's robots can do the same task in about a fifth the time and with greater accuracy.

Unmanned systems can also operate in 'dirty' environments, such as battle zones beset by bad weather or filled with biological or chemical weapons. In the past, humans and machines often had comparable limits. When the early fighter planes made high-speed turns or accelerations, for example, the same gravitational pressures (g-forces) that knocked out the human pilot would also tear the plane apart. But now, as one study said of the F-16 fighter jet, the machines are pushing far ahead: 'the airplane was too good. In fact, it was better than its pilots in one crucial way: it could manoeuvre so fast and hard that its pilots blacked out.'[6] As a result of the new technologies, an official at DARPA observed, 'the human is becoming the weakest link in defense systems'.[7]

With continuing advances in artificial intelligence, machines may soon overcome humans' main comparative advantage today, the mushy grey blob inside our skull. This is not just a matter of raw computing power. A soldier who learns French or marksmanship cannot easily pass on that knowledge to other soldiers. Computers have faster learning curves. They not only speak the same language but can be connected directly to one another via a wire or network, which means they have shareable intelligence.

The ability to compute and then act at digital speed is another robotic advantage. Humans, for example, can only react to incoming artillery fire by taking cover at the last second. But the counter rocket artillery mortar (CRAM) system uses radar to detect incoming rockets and mortar rounds and automatically directs the rapid fire of its Phalanx 20 mm Gatling guns against them, achieving a 70 per cent shoot-down capability. More than twenty CRAMs—well known as R2-D2s, after the little robot in *Star Wars* they resemble—were in service in Iraq and Afghanistan by January 2009. Some think that the speed of such weapons means they are only the start. One army colonel said, 'the trend towards the future will be robots reacting to robot attack, especially when operating at technologic speed.... As the loop gets shorter and shorter, there won't be any time in it for humans.'[8]

Each branch of America's armed services has ambitious plans for robotic technologies. On the ground, the various army robotic programmes are supposed to come together in the $230 billion future combat systems (FCS) programme, which military robots expert Robert Finkelstein described as 'the largest weapons procurement in history . . . at least in this part of the galaxy'.[9] FCS involves everything from replacing tens of thousands of armoured vehicles with a new generation of manned and unmanned vehicles to writing some 34 million lines of software code for a new computer network that will link them all together. The army believes that by 2015 it will be in a position to reorganize many of its units into new FCS brigades. The brigades will present a revolutionary model of how military units are staffed and organized. Each is expected to have more unmanned vehicles than manned ones (a ratio of 330:300) and will come with its own unmanned air force, with more than 100 drones controlled by the brigade's soldiers. The aircraft will range in size from a 15 pounder that will fit in soldiers' backpacks to a 23-feet-long robotic helicopter.

At sea, the US navy is introducing or developing various exotic technologies, including new 'unmanned underwater vehicles' (UUV) that search for mines or function as mini-submarines launched from manned submarines in order to hunt down an enemy. The navy has tested machine gun-wielding robotic speedboats that can patrol harbours or chase down pirates (one has been used on patrols in the Persian Gulf, spooking local fishermen), as well as various robotic planes and helicopters designed to take off from surface ships or to be launched underwater from submarines.

In the air, this next generation of unmanned vehicles will likewise be a mix of upgraded current systems, convertible manned vehicles, and brand new designs. 'Unmanned combat aerial systems' (UCAS), such as the Boeing X-45 and the Northrop Grumman X-47, are the centrepiece of US military plans for drones. Described as looking most like 'a set piece from the television program *Battlestar Galactica*', this type of drone is designed to take over the ultimate human pilot role, fighter pilot.[10] Especially stealthy and thus suitable for the most dangerous roles, the unmanned fighter plane prototypes have already shown some impressive capabilities. They have launched precision-guided missiles, been 'passed off' between different remote human operators 900 miles apart, and, in one war game, autonomously detected unexpected threats (missiles that 'popped up' seemingly out of nowhere), engaged and destroyed them, then did their own battle damage assessment. The navy plans to test its drone on aircraft carriers within the next year, while the air force has taken its programme into the 'black' world of top-secret development.

As new prototypes of unmanned planes hit the battlefield, the trend will be for the size extremes to be pushed in two directions. Some drone prototypes have wings the length of football fields. Powered by solar energy and hydrogen, they are designed to stay in the air for days and weeks, acting as mobile spy satellites or even aerial refuelling stations. At the other size extreme are 'itty-bitty, teeny-weeny UAVs'.[11] The military's estimation of what is possible with micro air vehicles is illustrated by a contract let by the DARPA in 2006. It sought an insect-size drone that weighed under 10 grams, was less than 7.5 centimetres long, has a speed of 10 metres per second and a range of 1,000 metres, and could hover in place for at least a minute.

As our machines get smaller, they will move into the nanotechnology realm, once only theoretical. A major advance in the field occurred in 2007, when David Leigh, a researcher at the University of Edinburgh, revealed that he had built a 'nanomachine', whose parts consisted of single molecules. When asked to describe to a normal person the significance of his discovery, Leigh said it would be difficult to predict. 'It is a bit like when stone-age man made his wheel, asking him to predict the motorway,' he said.

## KEEPING HUMANS 'IN THE LOOP'?

Despite all the enthusiasm in military circles for the next generation of unmanned vehicles, ships, and planes, there is one question that people are generally reluctant to talk about. It is the equivalent of Lord Voldemort in *Harry Potter*, 'The Issue That Must Not Be Discussed'. What happens to the human role in war as we arm ever more intelligent, more capable, and more autonomous robots?

When this issue comes up, both specialists and military people tend either to change the subject or speak in absolutes. 'People will always want humans in the loop,' says Eliot Cohen, a noted military expert at Johns Hopkins who served in the State Department under George W. Bush.[12] An air force captain similarly writes in his service's professional journal, 'in some cases, the potential exists to remove the man from harm's way. Does this mean there will no longer be a man in the loop? No. Does this mean that brave men and women will no longer face death in combat? No. There will always be a need for the intrepid souls to fling their bodies across the sky.'[13]

All the rhetoric ignores the reality that humans started moving out of 'the loop' of war a long time before robots made their way onto battlefields. As far back as the Second World War, the Norden bombsight made calculations of height, speed, and trajectory too complex for a human alone when it came to decide when to drop a bomb. By the first Gulf War, Captain Doug Fries, a radar navigator, could write this description of what it was like to bomb Iraq in his B-52: 'The navigation computer opened the bomb bay doors and dropped the weapons into the dark.'[14]

In the navy, the trend towards computer autonomy has also been in place at sea since the Aegis computer system was introduced in the 1980s. Designed to defend navy ships against missile and plane attacks, the system operates in four modes, from 'semi-automatic', in which humans work with the system to judge when and at what to shoot, to 'casualty', in which the system operates as if all the humans are dead and just does what it calculates is best to keep the ship from being hit. Humans can override the Aegis system in any of its modes, but experience shows that this capability is often beside the point, since people hesitate to use this power. Sometimes the consequences are tragic.

The most dramatic instance of a failure to override occurred in the Persian Gulf on 3 July 1988, during a patrol mission of the U.S.S. *Vincennes*. The ship had been nicknamed 'Robo-cruiser', both because of the new Aegis radar system it was carrying and because its captain had a reputation for being overly aggressive. That day, the *Vincennes*'s radars spotted IranAir Flight 655, an Airbus passenger jet. The jet was on a consistent course and speed and was broadcasting a radar and radio signal that showed it to be civilian. The automated Aegis system, though, had been designed for managing battles against attacking Soviet bombers in the North Atlantic, not for dealing with skies crowded with civilian aircraft like those over the Gulf. The computer system registered the plane with an icon on the screen that made it seem to be an Iranian F-14 fighter (a plane half the size), and hence an 'assumed enemy'.

Though the hard data were telling the human crew that the plane was not a fighter jet, they trusted the computer more. Aegis was in semi-automatic mode, giving it the least amount of autonomy, but not one of the eighteen sailors and officers on the command crew challenged the computer's wisdom. They authorized it to fire. (That they even had the authority to do so without seeking permission from more senior officers in the fleet, which any other ship would have had to, was again only because the navy had greater confidence in Aegis than in a human-manned ship without it.) Only after the fact did the crew members realize that they had accidentally shot down an airliner, killing all 290 passengers and crew, including 66 children.

The tragedy of Flight 655 was no isolated incident. Indeed, much the same scenario was repeated just a few years ago, when US Patriot missile batteries accidentally shot down two allied planes during the Iraq invasion of 2003. The Patriot systems classified the craft as Iraqi rockets. There were only a few seconds to make a decision. So machine judgement trumped any human decisions. In both of these cases, the human power 'in the loop' was actually only veto power, and even that was a power that military personnel were unwilling to use against the quicker (and what they viewed as superior) judgement of a computer.

The point is not that machines are taking over, *Matrix*-style, but that what it means to have humans 'in the loop' of decision-making in war is being redefined, with the authority and autonomy of machines expanding. There are myriad pressures to give war-bots greater and greater autonomy. The first is simply the push to make more capable and more intelligent robots. But as psychologist and artificial intelligence expert Robert Epstein notes, this comes with a built-in paradox:

> The irony is that the military will want it [a robot] to be able to learn, react, etc., in order for it to do its mission well. But they won't want it to be too creative, just like with soldiers. But once you reach a space where it is really capable, how do you limit them? To be honest, I don't think we can.[15]

Simple military expediency also widens the loop. To achieve any sort of personnel savings from using unmanned systems, one human operator has to be able to 'supervise' (as opposed to control) a larger number of robots. For example, the army's long-term FCS plan calls for having two humans sit at identical consoles and jointly supervise a team of ten land robots. In this scenario, the humans would delegate tasks to increasingly autonomous robots, but the robots would still need human permission to fire weapons. There are many reasons, however, to believe this arrangement will not prove workable.

Researchers are finding that humans have a hard time controlling multiple units at once (imagine playing five different video games at the same time). Even having human operators control two UAVs at a time rather than one reduces performance levels by an average of 50 per cent. As a NATO study concluded, the goal of having one operator control multiple vehicles is 'currently, at best, very ambitious, and, at worst, improbable to achieve'.[16] And this is with systems that are not shooting or being shot at. As one Pentagon-funded report noted, 'even if the tactical commander is aware of the location of all his units, the combat is so fluid and fast-paced that it is very difficult to control them'.[17] So a push is made to give more autonomy to the machine.

And then there is the fact that an enemy is involved. If the robots are not going to fire unless a remote operator authorizes them to, then a foe needs only to disrupt that communication. Military officers counter that, while they do not like the idea of taking humans out of the loop, there has to be an exception, a back-up plan for when communications are cut and the robot is 'fighting blind'. So another exception is made.

Even if the communications link is not broken, there are combat situations in which there is not enough time for the human operator to react, even if the enemy is not operating at digital speed. For instance, a number of robot makers have added 'counter-sniper' capabilities to their machines, enabling them automatically to track down and target with a laser beam any enemy that shoots. But those precious seconds while the human decides whether or not to fire back could let the enemy get away. As one US military officer observes, there is nothing technical to prevent one from rigging the machine to shoot something more lethal than light. 'If you can automatically hit it with a laser range finder, you can hit it with a bullet.'[18]

This creates a powerful argument for another exception to the rule that humans must always be 'in the loop', giving robots in such settings the ability to fire back on their own. This kind of autonomy is generally seen as more palatable than other types. 'People tend to feel a little bit differently about the counterpunch than the punch,' notes Noah Shachtman. As Gordon Johnson of the army's Joint Forces Command explains, such autonomy soon comes to be viewed as not only logical but quite attractive. 'Anyone who would shoot at our forces would die. Before he can drop that weapon and run, he's probably already dead. Well now, these cowards in Baghdad would have to pay with blood and guts every time they shoot at one of our folks. The costs of poker went up significantly. The enemy, are they going to give up blood and guts to kill machines? I'm guessing not.'[19]

Each exception, however, pushes one further and further from the absolute of 'never' and instead down a slippery slope. And at each step, once robots 'establish a track record of reliability in finding the right targets and employing weapons properly', says John Tirpak, editor of *Air Force Magazine*, the 'machines will be trusted'.[20]

The reality is that the human location 'in the loop' is already becoming, as retired army colonel Thomas Adams notes, that of 'a supervisor who serves in a fail-safe capacity in the event of a system malfunction'. Even then, he thinks the speed, confusion, and information overload of modern-day war will soon move the whole process outside 'human space'. He describes how the coming weapons 'will be too fast, too small, too numerous, and will create an environment too complex for humans to direct'. As Adams concludes, the various new technologies 'are rapidly taking us to a place where we may not want to go, but probably are unable to avoid'.[21]

The irony is that for all the claims by military, political, and science leaders that 'humans will always be in the loop', as far back as 2004 the US army was carrying out research on armed ground robots that demonstrated the merits of armed ground robots equipped with a 'quick-draw response'. Similarly, a 2006 study by the Defense Safety Working Group, in the Office of the Secretary of Defense, discussed how the concerns over potential killer robots could be allayed by giving 'armed autonomous systems' permission to 'shoot to destroy hostile weapons systems but not suspected combatants'. That is, they could shoot at tanks and jeeps, just not the people in them. Perhaps most telling is a report that the Joint Forces Command drew up in 2005, which suggested that autonomous robots on the battlefield would be the norm within twenty years. Its title is somewhat amusing, given the official line that one usually hears: *Unmanned effects: Taking the human out of the loop.*

So, despite what one article called 'all the lip service paid to keeping a human in the loop', autonomous armed robots are coming to war. They simply make too much sense to the people that matter.

## RISK-FREE WARFARE

With robots taking on more and more roles, and humans ever further out of the loop, some wonder whether human warriors will eventually be rendered obsolete. Describing a visit he made to the 2007 graduating class at the Air Force Academy, a retired air force officer says, 'there is a lot of fear that they will never be able to fly in combat'.[22]

The most controversial role for robots in the future would be as replacements for the human grunt in the field. In 2004, DARPA researchers surveyed a group of US military officers and robotic scientists about the roles they thought robots would take over in the near future. The officers predicted that countermine operations would go first, followed by reconnaissance, forward observation, logistics, then infantry. Oddly, among the last roles they named were air defence, driving or piloting vehicles, and food service—each of which has already seen automation. Special Forces roles were felt, on average, to be least likely ever to be delegated to robots.

The average year the soldiers predicted that humanoid robots would start to be used in infantry combat roles was 2025. Their projection was not very different from that of the scientists, who gave 2020 as their prediction. To be clear, these numbers only reflect the opinions of those in the survey, and they could prove to be way off. Robert Finkelstein, a veteran engineer who now heads Robotic Technologies Inc. and who helped conduct the survey, thinks these projections are highly optimistic and that it will not be until '2035 [that] we will have robots as fully capable as human soldiers on the battlefield'. But the broader point is that many specialists are starting to contemplate a world where robots replace the grunt in the field, well before many of us will pay off our mortgages.

However, as H.R. 'Bart' Everett, a navy robotics pioneer, explains, the full-scale replacement of humans in battle is not likely to occur anytime soon. Instead, the human use of robots in war will evolve 'to more of a team approach'. His programme, the Space and Naval Warfare Systems Center, has joined with the Office of Naval Research (ONR) to support the activation of a 'warfighter's associate concept' within the next ten to twenty years.

Humans and robots would be integrated into a team that shares information and coordinates action towards a common goal. Says Everett, 'I firmly believe the intelligent mobile robot will ultimately achieve sufficient capability to be accepted by the warfighter as an equal partner in a human-robot team, much along the lines of a police dog and its handler.'[23]

A 2006 solicitation by the Pentagon to the robotics industry captures the vision: 'the challenge is to create a system demonstrating the use of multiple robots with one or more humans on a highly constrained tactical manoeuvre.... One example of such a manoeuvre is the through-the-door procedure often used by police and soldiers to enter an urban dwelling... [where] one kicks in the door then pulls back so another can enter low and move left, followed by another who enters high and moves right, etc. In this project the teams will consist of robot platforms working with one or more human teammates as a cohesive unit.'[24]

Another US military-funded project envisages the creation of 'playbooks' for tactical operations by a robot–human team. Much like a football quarterback, the human soldier would call the 'play' for robots to carry out, but like the players on the field, the robots would have the latitude to change what they did if the situation shifted.

The military, then, does not expect to replace all its soldiers with robots anytime soon, but rather sees a process of integration into a force that will become over time, as Joint Forces Command projected in its 2025 plans, 'largely robotic'. The individual robots will 'have some level of autonomy— adjustable autonomy or supervised autonomy or full autonomy within mission bounds', but it is important to note that the autonomy of any human soldiers within these units will be circumscribed by their orders and rules.

If the future is one of robot squad mates and robot wingmen, many scientists think it puts a premium on two things, both very human in nature. The first is good communication. In 2004, Lockheed tested an unmanned jet that responded to simple vocal commands. A pilot flying in another plane would give the drone some broad mission, such as to go to a certain area and photograph a specific building, and the plane would carry it out. As one report explains, 'the next war could be fought partly by unmanned aircraft that respond to spoken commands in plain English and then figure out on their own how to get the job done'.[25] The robot's response may even sound human. WT-6 is a robot in Japan that has a human-sounding vocal system, produced from an artificial tongue, lips, teeth, vocal cords, lungs, and soft palate made from polymers.

To work well together, robots and human soldiers will need to have confidence in each other. It sounds funny to say that about the relationship between a bucket of bolts and a human, but David Bruemmer, a scientist at the Idaho National Laboratory, actually specializes in how humans and robots work together. Without any irony, he says that 'trust is a huge issue for robot performance'.[26]

Trust is having a proper sense of what the other is capable of, as well as being correct in your expectations of what the other will do. One of Bruemmer's more interesting findings is that novices tend to make the best use of robotic systems. They 'trust' robot autonomy the most and 'let it do its job'. Over time, Bruemmer predicts robots will likely have 'dynamic autonomy' built in, where the amount of 'leash' robots are given is determined less by any principle of keeping humans 'in the loop' and more by their human team-mate's experience and trust level.

Lawrence J. Korb is one of the deans of Washington's defence policy establishment. A former navy flight officer, he served as assistant secretary of defense during the Reagan administration. Now he is a senior fellow at the Center for American Progress, a left-leaning think tank. Korb has seen presidential administrations, and their wars, come and go. And, as the author of twenty books and more than 100 articles, and a veteran of more than a thousand TV news-show appearances, Korb has also helped shape how the America media and public understand these wars. In 2007, I asked him what he thought was the most important overlooked issue in Washington defence circles. He answered, 'robotics and all this unmanned stuff. What are the effects? Will it make war more likely?'[27]

Korb is a great supporter of unmanned systems for a simple reason: 'they save lives'. But he worries about their effect on the perceptions and psychologies of war, not merely among foreign publics and media but also at home. As more and more unmanned systems are used, he sees change occurring in two ways, both of which he fears will make war more likely. Robotics 'will further disconnect the military from society. People are more likely to support the use of force as long as they view it as costless.' Even more worrisome, a new kind of voyeurism enabled by the new technologies will make the public more susceptible to attempts to sell the ease of a potential war. 'There will be more marketing of wars. More "shock and awe" talk to defray discussion of the costs.'

Korb is equally troubled by the effect that such technologies will have on how political leaders look at war and its costs. 'It will make people think "Gee, warfare is easy." Remember all the claims of a "cakewalk" in Iraq and how the Afghan model would apply? The whole idea that all it took to win a war was "three men and a satellite phone"? Well, their thinking is that if they can get the army to be as technologically dominant as the other services, we'll solve . . . these problems.'

Korb believes that political Washington has been 'chastened by Iraq'. But he worries about the next generation of policymakers. Technology such as unmanned systems can be seductive, feeding overconfidence that can lead nations into wars for which they are not ready. 'Leaders without experience tend to forget about the other side, that it can adapt. They tend to think of the other side as static and fall into a technology trap.'

'We'll have more Kosovos and fewer Iraqs' is how Korb sums up where he thinks we are headed. That is, he predicts more punitive interventions like the Kosovo strikes of 1999, launched without ground troops, and fewer operations like the invasion of Iraq. As unmanned systems become more prevalent, we will be likelier to use force, but also see the bar raised on anything that exposes human troops to dangers. Korb envisages a future in which the United States is willing to fight, but only from afar, in which it is more willing to punish via war, but less to face the costs of war.

Immanuel Kant's *Perpetual Peace* (1795) first expressed the idea that democracies are superior to all other forms of government because they are inherently more peaceful and less aggressive. This 'democratic peace' argument (cited by presidents across the partisan spectrum from Bill Clinton to George W. Bush) is founded on the belief that democracies have a built-in connection between their foreign policy and domestic politics that other systems of government lack. When the people share a voice in any decision, including whether to go to war, they are supposed to choose more wisely than an unchecked king or potentate.

Colonel R. D. Hooker Jr is an Iraq veteran and the commander of an army airborne brigade. As he explains, the people and their military in the field should be linked in two ways. The first is the direct stake that the public has in the government's policies. 'War is much more than strategy and policy because it is visceral and personal. . . . Its victories and defeats, joys and sorrows, highs and depressions are expressed fundamentally through a collective sense of exhilaration or despair. For the combatants, war means the prospect of death or wounds and a loss of friends and comrades that is scarcely less tragic.'[28] Because it is their blood personally invested, citizen-soldiers, as well as their fathers, mothers, uncles, and cousins who vote, combine to dissuade leaders from foreign misadventures and ill-planned aggression.

The second link is supposed to come indirectly, through a democracy's free media, which widen the impact of those investments of blood to the public at large. 'Society is an intimate participant [in war] too, through the bulletins and statements of political leaders, through the lens of an omnipresent media, and in the homes of the families and the communities where they live. Here, the safe return or death in action of a loved one, magnified thousands of times, resonates powerfully and far afield,' Hooker says.[29]

The news media's role in a free system, then, is not merely to report on a war's outcome, as if reporting on a sporting event. The public's perceptions of events on distant battlefields create pressures on elected leaders. Too much pressure can lead an elected leader to try to interfere in ongoing operations, as bad an idea in war as it is for the owner or fans to call in the plays for their favourite team. But, as Korb and Hooker explain, too little public pressure may even be worse. It is the equivalent of no one even caring about the game or its outcome.

Many worry that this democratic ideal is already under siege. The American military has been at war for the past eight years in places such as Afghanistan and Iraq, but other than suffering the indignity of smaller bottles of shampoo in their carry-on luggage, the American nation has not. Since the end of the draft, most Americans no longer have to think about whether their husband, wife, son, or daughter would be at risk if the military were sent to war. During the Second World War, by comparison, more than 16 million men and women, about 11 per cent of the American populace, served in the military—the equivalent of almost 30 million today.

By the start of the twenty-first century, even the financial costs on the home front had been displaced. After 11 September, industry did not need to retool its factories and families did not need to ration fuel or food, or even show their faith in the war effort by purchasing bonds. (Instead, a tax cut lightened the burden on Americans, especially the affluent.) When asked what citizens could do to share in the risks and sacrifices of soldiers in the field, the response from the commander-in-chief was 'go shopping'. The result is an American public that is less invested in and linked to its foreign policy than ever before in a democracy.

With this trend already in place, many worry that unmanned technologies will snip the last remaining threads of connection. Unmanned systems represent the ultimate break between the public and its military. With no draft, no need for congressional approval (the last formal declaration of war was in 1941), no tax or war bonds, and now the knowledge that the Americans at risk are mainly just American machines, the already falling bars to war may well hit the ground. A leader will not need to do the kind of consensus building that is normally required before a war, and will not even need to unite the country behind the effort. In turn, the public truly will become the equivalent of sports fans watching war, rather than citizens sharing in its importance.

But our new technologies do not merely remove human risk, they also record all they experience, and in so doing reshape the public's link to war. The Iraq war is literally the first conflict in which you could download video of combat from the Web. By the middle of 2007, there were more than 7,000 video clips of combat footage from Iraq on YouTube alone. Much of this footage was captured by drones and unmanned sensors and then posted online.

The trend towards video war could build connections between the war front and home front, allowing the public to see what is happening in actual battle as never before. But inevitably, the ability to download the latest snippets of robotic combat footage to home computers and iPhones turns war into a sort of entertainment. Soldiers call such clips 'war porn'. Particularly interesting or gruesome combat footage, such as an insurgent blown up by a UAV, is posted on blogs and forwarded to friends, family, and colleagues with subject lines like 'Watch this!' much the same way an amusing clip of a nerdy kid dancing in his basement is emailed around. A typical clip making the rounds showed people's bodies being blown into the air by a Predator strike, set to Sugar Ray's snappy pop song 'I Just Want to Fly'.

From this perspective, war becomes, as one security analyst put it, 'a global spectator sport for those not involved in it'. More broadly, while video images engage the public in a whole new way, they can fool many viewers into thinking they now have a true sense of what is happening in the conflict. The ability to watch more but experience less has a paradoxical effect. It widens the gap between our perceptions and war's realities. To make another sports parallel, it is the difference between watching a National Basketball Association (NBA) game on television, with the tiny figures on the screen, and knowing what it feels like to have a screaming Kevin Garnett knock you down and dunk over your head. Even worse, the clips of drone footage that people see do not show the whole gamut of war, but are merely the bastardized ESPN *SportsCenter* version of the game. The context, the strategy, the training, the tactics, and so on all just become slam dunks and smart bombs.

War porn also tends to hide another hard truth about battle. Most viewers have an instinctive aversion to watching a clip in which the target might be someone they know or a fellow American; such clips are usually banned from US-hosted websites. But many people are perfectly happy to watch video of a drone ending the life of some anonymous enemy, even if it is just to see if the machines fighting in Iraq are as 'sick' as those fighting in the *Transformers* movie—the motive one student gave me for why he downloaded the clips. To a public with so much less at risk, wars take on what analyst Christopher Coker called 'the pleasure of a spectacle with the added thrill that it is real for someone, but not the spectator'.[30]

Such changed connections do not just make a public less likely to wield its veto power over its elected leaders. As the former Pentagon official Korb observed, they also alter the calculations of the leaders themselves.

Nations often go to war because of overconfidence. This makes perfect sense; few leaders choose to start a conflict thinking they will lose. Historians have found that technology can play a big role in feeding overconfidence: new weapons and capabilities breed new perceptions, as well as misperceptions, about what might be possible in a war. Today's new technologies are particularly liable to feed overconfidence. They are perceived to help the offensive side in a war more than the defence, plus they are advancing at an exponential pace. The difference of just a few years of research and deployment can create vast differences in capabilities. But this can create a sort of 'use it or lose it' mentality, as even the best of technological advantages can prove quickly fleeting (a major concern for the United States, as forty-two countries are now working on military robotics, from Iran and China to Belarus and Pakistan). Finally, as one roboticist explains, a vicious circle is generated. Scientists and companies often overstate the value of new technologies in order to get governments to buy them, but if leaders believe the hype they may be more likely to feel adventurous.

James Der Derian is an expert at Brown University on new modes of war. He believes that the combination of these factors means that robotics will 'lower the threshold for violence'.[31] The result is a dangerous mixture: leaders unchecked by a public veto, combined with technologies that seem to offer spectacular results with few lives lost. It is a brew that could prove very seductive to decision-makers. 'If one can argue that such new technologies will offer less harm to us and them, then it is more likely that we'll reach for them early, rather than spending weeks and months slogging at diplomacy.'

When faced with a dispute or crisis, policymakers have typically regarded the use of force as the 'option of last resort'. Now unmanned systems might help that option move up the list, with each step up making war more likely. That returns us to Korb's scenario of 'more Kosovos, fewer Iraqs'.

While avoiding the mistakes of Iraq certainly sounds like a positive result, the other side of the trade-off would not be without problems. The 1990s were not the halcyon days some recall. Lowering the bar to allow for more unmanned strikes from afar would lead to an approach resembling the so-called 'cruise missile diplomacy' of that period. Such an approach may leave fewer troops stuck on the ground, but, as shown by the strikes against al-Qaeda camps in Sudan and Afghanistan in 1998, the Kosovo war in 1999, and perhaps now the drone strikes in Pakistan, they are military endeavours without any true sense of a commitment, lash-outs that yield incomplete victories at best. As one US army report notes, such operations 'feel good for a time, but accomplish little'.[32] They involve the country in a problem, but do not resolve it.

Even worse, Korb may be wrong and the dynamic may yield not fewer Iraqs but more of them. It was the lure of an easy preemptive action that helped get the United States into such trouble in Iraq in the first place. As one robotics scientist says of the new technology that he is building: 'the military thinks that it will allow them to nip things in the bud, deal with the bad guys earlier and easier, rather than having to get into a big ass war. But the most likely thing that will happen is that we'll be throwing a bunch of high tech against the usual urban guerillas. . . . It will stem the tide [of US casualties], but it won't give us some asymmetric advantage.'[33]

Thus, robots may entail a dark irony. By appearing to lower the human costs of war, they may seduce us into more wars.


## CONCLUSION

Whether it is watching wars from afar or sending robots instead of fellow citizens into harm's way, robotics offers the public and their leaders the lure of riskless warfare. All the potential gains of war would come without the costs, and even be mildly entertaining.

It is a heady enticement, and not just for evil warmongers. The world watched the horrors of Bosnia, Rwanda, and Congo, but did little, mainly because the public did not know or care enough and the perceived costs of doing something truly effective seemed too high. Substitute unmanned systems for troops and the calculus might be changed. Indeed, imagine all the genocides and crimes against humanity that could be ended, if only the human barriers to war were lowered. Getting tired of some dictator massacring his people? Send in your superior technology and watch on YouTube as his troops are taken down.

Yet wars never turn out to be that simple. They are by their very nature complex, messy, and unpredictable. And this will remain the case even as unmanned systems increasingly substitute for humans.

But let us imagine that such fantasies of cheap and costless unmanned wars were actually to come true, that we could use robots to stop bad things being done by bad people, with no blowback, no muss, and no fuss. Even such an outcome should give us pause. By cutting the already tenuous link between the public and its nation's foreign policy, pain-free war would pervert the whole idea of a democratic process and citizenship as they relate to war. When a citizenry has no sense of sacrifice or even the prospect of sacrifice, the decision to go to war becomes just like any other policy decisions, weighed by the same calculus used to determine whether or not to raise the bridge tolls. Instead of widespread engagement and debate over the most important decision a government can make, there will be popular indifference. When technology turns war into something merely to be watched, and not weighed with great seriousness, the checks and balances that undergird democracy go by the wayside. This could well mean the end of any idea of democratic peace that supposedly sets our foreign policy decision-making apart.

Such wars without costs could even undermine the morality of supposedly 'good' wars. When a nation decides to go to war, it is not just deciding to break stuff in some foreign land. As one philosopher put it, the very decision is 'a reflection of the moral character of the community who decides'. Without public debate and support and without risking troops, though, the decision to go to war only reflects a nation that does not give a damn.

Even if the nation sending in its robots acts in a just cause, such as stopping a genocide, war without risk or sacrifice becomes merely an act of somewhat selfish charity. One side has the wealth to afford high technologies and the other does not. The only message of 'moral character' a nation transmits is that it alone gets the right to stop bad things, but only at the time and place of its choosing, and most important, only if the costs are low enough. With robots, the human costs risked against those potentially saved become zero. It does not mean the nation should not act. But when it does, it must realize that even the just wars become exercises in playing God from afar, with unmanned weapons substituting for thunderbolts.

## NOTES

1. Charles Dean, 'Unmanned ground vehicles for armed reconnaissance', paper presented at the Military Robotics Conference, Institute for Defense and Government Advancement, Washington, DC, 10–12 April 2006. Charles Dean is a former Lieutenant Colonel with the Unites States Army, who now is project manager at Foster Miller.
2. Interview with Predator pilot, P. W. Singer, 28 August 2006.
3. Interview with Colonel Gary Fabricius USAF, Peter W. Singer, 29 August 2006.
4. Lieutenant General David Deptula, 'Unmanned aircraft systems', *Joint Forces Quarterly*, 49 (2008), 50.
5. Tim Weiner, 'Pentagon has sights on robot soldiers', *New York Times News Service*, 16 February 2005.
6. As quoted in George Friedman and Meredith Friedman, *The future of war: Power, technology, and American world dominance in the 21st century* (New York: St Martins, 1998), 296.
7. Cheryl Seal, 'Frankensteins in the Pentagon: DARPA's creepy bioengineering program', *Information Clearing House*, 25 August 2003, http://www.information-clearinghouse.info/article4572.htm
8. Thomas K. Adams, 'Future warfare and the decline of human decisionmaking', *Parameters*, 31/4 (2001), 57.
9. Interview with Ralph Peters, P. W. Singer, 7 July 2006.
10. Matthew Brzezinski, 'The unmanned army', *New York Times Magazine*, 29 April 2003.
11. Christian Lowe, 'High-flying, secret drone unveiled', defensetech.org, 24 July 2006, http://www.defensetech.org/archives/002598.html
12. Interview with Eliot Cohen, P. W. Singer, 15 November 2006.
13. Patrick Eberle, 'To UAV or not to UAV: That is the question; here is one answer', *Air & Space Power Journal – Chronicles Online Journal*, 9 October 2001, http://www.airpower.au.af.mil/airchronicles/cc/eberle.html
14. Ibid.
15. Interview with Robert Epstein, P. W. Singer, 25 October 2006.
16. Michael J. Barnes et al., 'Soldier interactions with aerial and ground robots in future military environments' (NATO, 2006).
17. Sean J. A. Edwards, 'Swarming and the future of warfare', Doctoral thesis, RAND Graduate School, 2005, 139.
18. Interview with US military officer, P. W. Singer, 17 October 2006.
19. Stephen Graham, 'America's robot army', *New Statesman*, 12 June 2006, http://www.newstatesman.com/200606120018
20. Ibid.
21. Adams, 'Future warfare', 58.
22. Interview with retired air force officer, P. W. Singer, 28 January 2007.
23. Interview with H.R. Everett, P. W. Singer, 20 October 2006.
24. Nick Turse, 'Baghdad 2025: The Pentagon solution to a planet of slums', *TomDispatch.com*, 7 January 2007, http://www.tomdispatch.com/post/155031/nick_turse_ pentagon_ to_global_cities_drop_dead

25. Lee Dye, 'New vehicles will make own decisions based on commands', *ABC News*, 17 November 2004, http://www.strategicstudiesinstitute.army.mil/about/contact-us.cfm
26. David Bruemmer, 'Intelligent autonomy for unmanned vehicles', unpublished manuscript.
27. Korb. Interview, 30 September 2006.
28. Richard D. Hooker, 'Beyond *Vom Kriege*: The character and conduct of modern war', *Parameters*, 3/2 (2005), 8.
29. Ibid.
30. Christopher Coker, *Humane warfare* (London: Routledge, 2001), 150.
31. Ibid.
32. Ibid.
33. Interview with Daniel Wilson, P. W. Singer, 19 October 2006.

\* An earlier version of this chapter was published in *The Wilson Quarterly* in Winter 2009.

# PART IV

# The Changing Identities of Non-combatants

# 19

# The Civilian in Modern War

*Adam Roberts*

There is a widespread view that civilians are worse off in today's wars than ever before. Civilians are often deliberately targeted by belligerents or are victims of 'collateral damage'. They form the majority of victims of landmines. They are used as human shields. They are displaced from their homes, even from their country. They are affected, often more than soldiers, by the pestilence, famine, and displacement that wars bring in their wake. They are often particularly vulnerable in the types of war that are most prevalent in the world today—including civil wars and asymmetric conflicts. Children are forced to become soldiers. How can it be that the lot of civilians in war remains so dire, when so much attention has been paid to the protection of civilians in war—not just in international treaties, but in the work of international organizations and also that of numerous humanitarian bodies?

This view, that in general civilians are vastly worse off than in earlier periods, is flawed. This survey explores changes in the past two centuries in the roles of civilians and in how they have been perceived. It questions the oft-repeated statistics purporting to show a general increase in the ratio of civilian to military casualties. It suggests that in the laws of war (also called international humanitarian law), there have been advances in internationally agreed standards of protection of civilians from the effects of war, and that in practice something has been achieved, including under the auspices of the United Nations and humanitarian relief bodies. Moreover, even though the protection of civilians has run into numerous problems, including some relating to the very definition and identity of the civilian, such protection is likely to remain an important aspect of international attempts to limit the effects of war. These matters are considered under the following headings:

- Changing roles and perceptions of the civilian
- The civilian in the laws of war
- The United Nations and the protection of civilians
- Conclusion: Survival of the concept of the civilian in today's wars

## CHANGING ROLES AND PERCEPTIONS
## OF THE CIVILIAN

The essence of the identity of civilians is that they are not members of the regularly constituted armed forces of a state. Further, in view of the centrality of civil war in the contemporary world, one can add that they are not members of armed groups of non-state parties. In theory this basic attribute—of not being part of any kind of army—might be thought to place them outside the realm of war, and to merit the fullest legal and physical protection from war's effects that can be obtained. Hence the 'ideal' form of war would be one where the soldiers fight and the civilians are left out of it. Yet war has not proved so straightforward in practice: the civilian has often been seen as part of the total war effort; as having a special role in conflicts; as being responsible for electing a belligerent government and therefore for its acts; and as the victim of deliberate assaults.

Many writers have perceived the role of the civilian as having changed fundamentally at one stage or another in the past few centuries. Raymond Aron, in the opening paragraph of his famous 1954 book, *The century of total war*, asserted that 'the soldier and citizen have become interchangeable'.[1] This view was no doubt based on the events of the Second World War, in which the public in many countries was deeply involved in war production, was often directly targeted by belligerents, and sometimes participated in armed resistance movements. It also reflected the fact that during the Cold War civilians on both sides of the Iron Curtain had the doubtful honour of being nuclear hostages—a fate that today no longer weighs so heavily on their shoulders. Yet Aron's proposition failed to gain traction. As will be seen, a different view of the citizen came to be widely accepted—at least in much official rhetoric, public discourse, and lawmaking.

Other writers have similarly grappled with the complexity of the role of citizens in relation to war. General Sir Rupert Smith, on the basis of much experience of command in post-Cold War crises, has advanced the proposition that the wars of the late twentieth and early twenty-first centuries are 'wars amongst the people'—in which the political effects of military actions may be more important than their immediate military effects.[2] He does not assume that the soldier and the citizen are indistinguishable: only that they are both acting in the same theatre, and that the ways in which their performances interact can determine the outcome. Is this state of affairs new? Arguably, war has always had an element of being 'amongst the people' in the sense in which Rupert Smith uses the term. Many aspects of modern war that are widely assumed to be wholly new turn out not to be so. However, it is not in dispute that most wars today do take place among the people—that is to say, they are fought in inhabited areas, with the citizen deeply involved, whether as audience, supporter, participant, or victim.

A number of factors connected to the changing character of war do explain the salience of civilians, and civilian casualties, in contemporary conflicts:

- *The civil war dimension of the majority of contemporary armed conflicts.* In civil wars, civilians are often, literally, what the war is about: for example, what the ethnic composition of the state is to be, and who is to govern. They are directly affected by the course and outcome of the war.

- *The developments in communications.* Information about casualties of war, including civilian casualties, sometimes reaches huge audiences in real time, and can lead to demands for action to prevent such tragedies.

- *The rise of doctrines and practices of humanitarian intervention and 'responsibility to protect'.* These are generally aimed at protection of civilians from violent oppression. Numerous military interventions—including in Northern Iraq in 1991, Somalia in 1992, Rwanda in 1994, Bosnia in 1995, Kosovo in 1999, and Côte d'Ivoire in 2003—have had, as one stated purpose, the protection of civilians. Although other purposes have been evident in particular cases, and ideas of humanitarian intervention have a long history, the fate of civilians has played an unusually central part in official decision-making about uses of force in the post-Cold War era.

- *The development of military technology.* In a number of wars in the post-Cold War era, it has been possible for US-led coalitions to conduct operations with considerable accuracy, and with no casualties among their own forces. The fact that modern precision-guided munitions are more accurate than their predecessors has resulted in a notable reduction in the number of civilian casualties of bombing campaigns compared to those in past eras.[3] However, the accuracy of weapons has also led to increased attention to civilian casualties, particularly as any deaths can easily appear to be deliberate and avoidable. There are inevitably questions about the morality of waging war from 10,000 feet or by robot. The shooting down of IranAir Flight 655 on 3 July 1988 is perhaps the most extreme example of civilians being killed by technological warfare—and poor decision-making.[4]

As a result of these and other factors, the conduct of combatant armed forces vis-à-vis the civilian is now widely seen as the litmus test of their role. In much public commentary and debate, failures to ensure the protection of civilians are taken as evidence not merely of the wrongfulness of a particular action but also of the unjustifiability of the overall cause of which it was part. The controversies over the Israel–Gaza War of December 2008–January 2009, alleging that there was unjustified shooting of civilians and destruction of property, are examples of the salience of the military treatment of civilians.

Despite the increased attention to the civilian, there is remarkably little writing on the concept, status, and treatment of civilians. Geoffrey Best casts a sceptical historian's eye on the subject, and expresses proper concern that the idea that civilians can be protected from the effects of war 'invites civilian war-lovers to imagine that they can have their belligerent cake and eat it'.[5] By contrast, some works published during the Cold War focus on the idea, and the actuality, of the civilian as victim.[6] So, too, do several subsequent works cited below. Hugo Slim's interesting book on the subject does look at the agency and activism of civilians in war, and he rightly emphasizes that civilians are not well served by a simplistic identity of innocence and victimhood. Yet he offers a grim view of the tragic position of the civilian in past as well as present wars:

> Attacks and atrocities against civilians are not a recent phenomenon as some people like to suggest. Armies, armed groups, political and religious movements have been killing civilians since time immemorial. Some commentators speak today as if civilian suffering or the intentional killing of civilian populations is a novelty. But this is very far from the truth. There may have been lulls when certain wars were fought more cleanly than others but these blips are tiny exceptions in humanity's long and bloody history of conquest, group rivalry, religious fanaticism, political extremism, empire building and modern state formation.[7]

Slim's analysis raises the question of whether civilians merit protection, not on the grounds that they are completely innocent of all involvement in war, but because the rule protecting civilians represents a practical approach to limiting the human costs of war. He argues that tolerance of civilian ambiguity makes more sense than simple denial, and the rule of civilian immunity, if it is to have any limiting effect on war, needs to be based on it.[8] This approach has the merit of taking account of the variety of the roles of civilians in war.

In some modern conflicts, civilians have even had a special role in constituting the spearhead of a territorial claim and even of a military attack. This phenomenon is not wholly new, but its widespread use reflects some unusual circumstances of the post-1945 era. Under the UN Charter it is unlawful for one state to use force against any other state, and at the same time the principle of 'self-determination of peoples' is upheld. Against this background it is not surprising that civilians have sometimes had a significant part in the making of territorial claims, even if their actions have been harbingers rather than substitutes for the use of armed force. A few examples:

- In November 1975, the Moroccan government organized the massive 'green march' of citizens to cross the border into the former Spanish colony of Western Sahara to claim the territory for Morocco. At the same time Moroccan armed forces entered Western Sahara clandestinely. The green march was called off after a few days, but not before it had strengthened Morocco's negotiating position against other claimants.

- On 19 March 1982, a group of Argentinians, posing as scrap metal merchants, occupied the abandoned whaling station at Leith Harbour on South Georgia, thus foreshadowing the war that began in earnest on 2 April 1982 with the Argentine invasion and occupation of the Falkland Islands and South Georgia.

- Since at least 1996, rival groups of civilians from Japan, Hong Kong, Taiwan, and China have played key parts in asserting the respective territorial claims of Japan, China, and Taiwan to the Senkaku Islands, which are located about 180 kilometres northeast of Taiwan.

In short, while the core definition of civilians remains—that they are not members of the armed forces—their role in relation to modern war is multi-faceted and complex: they are both agents and victims; both co-players in the theatre of war and objects of propaganda; both participants in the war economy and protected persons in the laws of war. The sheer variety of their roles in war is discussed further in the concluding section.

There is a widespread view that war has changed radically since the early twentieth century to the point where now, in the post-Cold War period, it has a more or less uniformly disastrous effect on civilians, whose lot is now much worse than a century ago. The European Union's European Security Strategy, proposed by Javier Solana, the EU's High Representative for Common Foreign and Security Policy, and adopted by the Heads of State and Government at the European Council in Brussels on 12 December 2003, stated: 'Since 1990, almost 4 million people have died in wars, 90% of them civilians.'[9] This view, frequently accompanied by unsubstantiated claims that in earlier wars the ratio of civilian to military victims was the opposite, has been called an 'urban myth' of our times: it is based on shaky statistical foundations, which I have explored elsewhere.[10] It obscures the extraordinary variety of the roles of civilians in modern war.


## THE CIVILIAN IN THE LAWS OF WAR

The laws of war provide the most concise, but still problem-ridden, answers to the questions 'What is a civilian?' and 'How can civilians be protected in war?' In the history of the laws of war, the idea of the civilian emerged relatively late. In medieval Christendom, non-combatant immunity was a key principle, but it was expressed in the form of canonical lists of those who did not have the occupation or social function of making war, and should not have war made against them: monks, pilgrims, travellers, peasants cultivating the soil, women, children, the infirm and aged, and those of unsound mind.[11] Thus the idea of a single category of civilians was far from self-evident.

A key intellectual foundation of the modern laws of war is Jean-Jacques Rousseau's view of the soldier. His statement on this begins with the famous words often cited by ICRC as a basis for the subsequent development of International Humanitarian Law:

> War is then not a relationship between one man and another, but *a relationship between one State and another*, in which individuals are enemies only by accident, not as men, nor even as citizens, but as soldiers; not as members of the fatherland, but as its defenders. *Finally, any State can only have other States, and not men, as enemies, inasmuch as it is impossible to fix a true relation between things of different natures....*
>
> Since the aim of war is the destruction of the enemy State, one has the right to kill its defenders as long as they bear arms; but as soon as they lay down their arms and surrender they cease to be enemies or the enemy's instruments, and become simply men once more, and one no longer has a right over their life. It is sometimes possible to kill the State without killing a single one of its members; and war confers no right that is not necessary to its end. These principles are not those of Grotius; they are not founded on the authority of poets, but follow from the nature of things, and are founded on reason.[12]

Rousseau's view of war has many problematic aspects. His principle for protecting civilians looks very frail in wars of the people, in which groupings of people who do not constitute a state are fighting on one and perhaps both sides in a conflict. In any case his implication that all those not in the armed forces should be spared from being killed in war was far from being universally accepted.

For example, in the Lieber Instructions issued in 1863 to the Union forces in the American Civil War there was profound ambiguity about the position of the citizen. On the one hand, Lieber stated that 'war is a state of armed hostility between sovereign nations or governments' and that 'the citizen or native of a hostile country is thus an enemy . . . and as such is subjected to the hardships of the war'. Nevertheless, 'the principle has been more and more acknowledged that the unarmed citizen is to be spared in person, property, and honor as much as the exigencies of war will admit'.[13] Protection was afforded to 'the inoffensive individual' or 'the inoffensive citizen'—the terms were interchangeable.[14] To this day we have not completely escaped from this ambiguity about whether the civilian is an enemy or a subject of protection; and whether, to merit protection, the civilian needs to be 'inoffensive', perhaps indeed entirely innocent of all entanglement in the ongoing conflict.

Most of the early codifications of the laws of war in the form of multilateral treaties were primarily concerned with the treatment of combatants rather than civilians. The term 'civilian' emerged only slowly. The first Geneva Convention, drawn up in 1864 and focusing specifically on the wounded, did not use the word 'civilians', and linked the immunity of 'inhabitants' (and of medical personnel) to their humane conduct. The 1868 St Petersburg

Declaration on explosive projectiles implicitly supported the idea that most members of society can be left out of war when it stated: 'That the only legitimate object which States should endeavour to accomplish during war is to weaken the military forces of the enemy.' The 1880 Oxford Manual—a document of the Institute of International Law that was not adopted in treaty form—was characteristic of its period when it stated: 'It is forbidden to maltreat inoffensive populations.' Other statements of that period similarly stressed that 'the peaceable inhabitants' should not be attacked, confirming the close link between the entitlement of citizens to protection and their peaceful behaviour.

The ICRC has noted that in the period 1874–1907 the term 'civilian' entered the laws of war in contradistinction to 'soldier'.[15] However, the civilian hardly entered with an intact identity and clear protection. In early codifications the actual term 'civilian' was used only in an article about spies: '. . . the following are not considered spies: Soldiers and civilians, intrusted with the delivery of despatches intended either for their own army or for the enemy's army.'[16] Thus the civilian makes an appearance as a person who may be involved in actions in support of one army or another, rather than being simply a peaceable inhabitant. Ambiguity was built in from the start, and legal protection remained sparse. The 1907 Hague Regulations made reference to 'inhabitants' primarily in respect of the occupation of territory by enemy armed forces, and even these relatively few provisions are fairly basic. Siege warfare was subject to only minimal restrictions.

The experience of the First World War showed the inadequacy of the various provisions for the protection of inhabitants. The mass internments of civilians upon the outbreak of hostilities, the treatment of inhabitants of occupied countries, and the technological development of weapons resulting in an enlarged field of military action were among the developments demonstrating that civilians were exposed to dangers as serious as those faced by combatants and needed more specific legal protection than they had hitherto been accorded. As Amanda Alexander has stated in an article on 'The Genesis of the Civilian':

> Governments and population alike acknowledged the vital role of non-combatants in the modern, industrialized war machine, while military strategists described them as a key military target. It was this paradoxical reconstruction of non-combatants as both weak and critically important, as both pitiful victims and primary targets, that constituted the new idea of the civilian population.[17]

After the First World War, the reluctance of states to envisage the possibility of a major war made them particularly unwilling to conclude regulations governing the status and protection of civilians in war. Although various international conferences considered these topics, the resulting texts were never formally adopted as treaties. For example, the matter was addressed in the 1923 Hague Draft Rules of Aerial Warfare. Article 22 introduced the term 'civilian' in its one-sentence text: 'Aerial bombardment for the purpose of terrorizing the civilian population, of destroying or damaging private property not of military character, or of injuring non-combatants is prohibited.' Although the Hague Air Rules were never ratified, on 21 June 1938, the British Prime Minister, Neville Chamberlain, drew on their contents when he enunciated in the House of Commons three fundamental principles of international law applicable to warfare from the air:

> In the first place, it is against international law to bomb civilians as such and to make deliberate attacks upon civilian populations. . . . In the second place, targets which are aimed at from the air must be legitimate military objectives and must be capable of identification. In the third place, reasonable care must be taken in attacking those military objectives so that by carelessness a civilian population in the neighbourhood is not bombed.[18]

These principles were embodied in a resolution which the League of Nations Assembly unanimously adopted on 30 September 1938. In addition, the 40th Conference of the International Law Association, held in Amsterdam in August–September 1938, approved in principle a Draft Convention for the Protection of Civilian Populations Against New Engines of War, a principal focus of which was the establishment of safety zones for certain classes of non-combatants.

In the interwar years, as part of an extensive discussion under the auspices of the Red Cross movement, the ICRC prepared a preliminary draft convention on the protection of civilians in war. However, the 1929 Geneva diplomatic conference, which revised the 1906 Geneva Convention on wounded and sick armed forces in land warfare and also adopted the convention on prisoners of war, failed to take this project further: it merely recommended that a study be made with a view to the conclusion of a convention on the protection of civilians.

The ICRC then prepared a new and more complete 'Draft International Convention on the Condition and Protection of Civilians of Enemy Nationality who are on Territory Belonging to or Occupied by a Belligerent', which was approved at the 15th International Conference of the Red Cross held in Tokyo in 1934. In January 1939, the Swiss government transmitted the ICRC draft convention, along with certain other texts including a 'Draft Convention for the Establishment of Hospital and Safety Zones in Time of War', to states as a basis for a diplomatic conference which the Swiss government planned to convene in Geneva in early 1940. However, the outbreak of the Second World War intervened before a new binding agreement could be reached. The few provisions on 'inhabitants' in the 1907 Hague Regulations remained the main treaty-based rules in force.

The Second World War was catastrophic for many civilian populations, especially those in besieged and bombarded cities and in occupied territories. The mass slaughter of Jews and gypsies showed that the killing of civilians could be, not just a side effect, but a major aim of some belligerents. Such rules as existed, for example, those outlined by Neville Chamberlain in June 1938, proved ineffective in face of the strategic requirements and extreme ideologies of belligerents. After the war, there was broad international acceptance of the need to adopt a new and stronger international agreement for the protection of civilians in time of war.

The 1949 Geneva Convention IV is the first treaty devoted exclusively to the protection of civilians in time of war. The 'Civilians Convention' is mainly confined to the treatment of civilians in the hands of the adversary, whether in occupied territory or in internment. It deals much less extensively with the protection of civilians from the effects of hostilities—a topic which has been addressed further in certain later agreements. Its notably indirect definition of the civilian reflects this narrow scope: 'Persons protected by the Convention are those who, at a given moment and in any manner whatsoever, find themselves, in case of a conflict or occupation, in the hands of a Party to the conflict or Occupying Power of which they are not nationals.' The same article adds that those protected by the other 1949 Geneva Conventions (wounded and sick, shipwrecked, and prisoners of war) would not be considered to be civilians.[19]

Despite the restrictive definition of civilians—essentially as people in the hands of the adversary—the extent to which the regime protecting them was elaborated by the Civilians Convention (the longest of the 1949 Geneva Conventions) was substantial. For example, it established the legal principle, which would be elaborated in subsequent agreements, that children should be protected from the effects of war. Its adoption led to an optimistic view that the laws of war now provided protection for every person in enemy hands. Jean Pictet, in his ICRC Commentary on the convention, referred to:

> a general principle which is embodied in all four Geneva Conventions of 1949. Every person in enemy hands must have some status under international law: he is either a prisoner of war and, as such, covered by the Third Convention, a civilian covered by the Fourth Convention, or again, a member of the medical personnel of the armed forces who is covered by the First Convention. There is no 'intermediate status'; nobody in enemy hands can be outside the law.[20]

This is a fine principle, but the Convention's limitations should be noted. It deals with one critically important situation—that which arises when people fall into enemy hands in the course of an international war. It does not deal extensively with situations in which citizens are exposed to other hazards of war, nor does it (except in common Article 3) address problems arising in non-international armed conflict, still less the protection of individuals abused by their own government.

As far as the protection of civilians from the effects of hostilities is concerned, the Civilians Convention's provisions have been extensively supplemented by subsequent agreements. The first of these is the 1977 Geneva Protocol I. By omitting the 1949 condition of being 'in the hands of' a belligerent, it revises the definition of the civilian to include anyone who is not eligible to be a prisoner of war. 'In case of doubt about whether a person is a civilian, that person shall be considered to be a civilian.'[21] This definition, as will be seen, is not problem-free.

Articles 48–78 of Protocol I spell out in unprecedented detail a series of rules on protection of civilians against the effects of hostilities, and on relief in favour of the civilian population, as well as on treatment of persons in the power of a party to the conflict. Its 'Basic Rule' is crucial:

> In order to ensure respect for and protection of the civilian population and civilian objects, the Parties to the conflict shall at all times distinguish between the civilian population and combatants and between civilian objects and military objectives and accordingly shall direct their operations only against military objectives.[22]

The protection of civilians in Protocol I is not absolute: a civilian taking part in hostilities can undoubtedly be targeted, even though there remains room for debate about the meaning and scope of such participation.[23] Moreover, Articles 48–78 have long been recognized as posing a range of problems. That is why numerous states made declarations indicating how they understood the meaning of particular provisions. They notably emphasized that the prohibition of attacks on civilians and civilian objects had to be interpreted in the light of the information available to the commander at the time; and that if civilian objects are used unlawfully for military purposes they will lose their protection.[24]

In the 1977 Geneva Protocol II, which applies to non-international armed conflicts in which the armed forces of a state are fighting dissident armed forces, the principle of general protection of civilians is again expressed strongly.[25] This is remarkable granted the difficulties of applying the principle in civil wars. That the principle survived so strongly is even more remarkable in view of the way in which, in the final negotiating session, in order to meet the concerns of states, this Protocol was severely reduced from 48 to 28 articles.

Despite the progress made in 1949 and 1977 in providing a legal basis for the protection of civilians, a central problem remained, and no amount of lawmaking could resolve it convincingly. This was the problem of the involvement of civilians—or, to put it differently, of individuals who were not members of the armed forces of a state or of a *levée en masse*—in acts of hostility. Did not the very existence of people who were farmers by day and guerrillas by night, or who appeared to be ordinary civilians but engaged in terrorist attacks, call into question the validity of the category of civilian? The prevalence of such forms of combat in the whole period since 1945 has certainly challenged the principle, which had been so eloquently advanced by Pictet, that every person in enemy hands is either a prisoner of war or a civilian. Indeed, even before the ink was dry on the 1949 Geneva Conventions, some had seen that there might need to be a third category of person— variously called 'unlawful combatant' or 'unprivileged belligerent'—this last term having the advantage that it does not imply an a priori judgement that every guerrilla was completely outside the framework of international law. Richard Baxter wrote in a memorable article in 1951:

> A category of persons who are not entitled to treatment either as peaceful civilians or as prisoners of war by reason of the fact that they have engaged in hostile conduct without meeting the qualifications established by Article 4 of the Geneva Prisoners of War Convention of 1949 thus continues to exist and to be subject to the maximum penalty which the detaining belligerent desires to impose.[26]

This approach recognizes a real problem—the existence of certain types of combatants who do not easily fit into the categories of the Geneva Conventions. However, to the extent that it might imply that there is no legal framework governing their treatment upon capture and detention, it is deeply problematic.

In 2009, the ICRC addressed the problem of the status of guerrillas and other unconventional combatants in its interpretive guidance on *Direct Participation in Hostilities*. Although the word 'civilian' does not appear in the title of this document, its central question is when civilian immunity does or does not apply to those who may at some point have taken, or be about to take, a direct part in hostilities. So far as international armed conflict is concerned, the ICRC's answer is:

> For the purposes of the principle of distinction in international armed conflict, all persons who are neither members of the armed forces of a party to the conflict nor participants in a *levée en masse* are civilians and, therefore, entitled to protection against direct attack unless and for such time as they take a direct part in hostilities.[27]

The report also states:

> International humanitarian law neither prohibits nor privileges civilian direct participation in hostilities. When civilians cease to directly participate in hostilities, or when members of organized armed groups belonging to a non-State party to an armed conflict cease to assume their continuous combat function, they regain full civilian protection against direct attack, but are not exempted from prosecution for violations of domestic and international law they may have committed.[28]

This approach is clear but also problematical. Many of the experts consulted in the process in 2004–9 were unhappy with the outcome, to the point of requesting that their names not appear in the published version.

(In the end, none of them was so named.) One of their concerns was the temporal reach of the concept of 'civilian'. They were unconvinced by the proposition that members of an armed group could be attacked only during periods of direct participation in hostilities. It was feared that the ICRC's approach would create a 'revolving door' effect, by which an individual becomes immune from attack once he or she returns safely home and until he or she commences another operation; and that if that was the outcome, it would mean that there was a dual standard, whereby the regular soldiers of a country's armed forces may be attacked at any time, whereas many of their guerrilla colleagues may not. Another concern of many of the experts related to the ICRC report's coverage of the rules on the kind and degree of military force permissible in attacks against legitimate military targets.

Whether or not the question of civilian participation in hostilities has been resolved by the lawmaking process since 1949 and the ICRC's interpretation thereof, the framework of law aimed at the protection of civilians has addressed, with some good effects, a number of more specific questions. Most notably it has addressed particular conventional weapons that have had lethal consequences for inhabitants of conflict zones, even long after the end of a given war. Treaties relating to this matter include:

- *The 1980 Convention on certain conventional weapons.* Note in particular its 1980 Protocol III on incendiary weapons, its 1996 Amended Protocol II on mines, and its 2003 Protocol V on explosive remnants of war. The latter two agreements place restrictions on the use of the wide range of mines and other unexploded and abandoned ordnance that regularly threaten civilians, peacekeepers, and humanitarian workers after the end of an armed conflict. By an amendment agreed on 21 December 2001, this Convention and its protocols also apply to non-international armed conflicts.

- *The 1997 Ottawa Convention on anti-personnel mines.* This prohibits possession of these weapons, as distinct from merely placing certain restrictions on their use.

- *The 2008 Convention on cluster munitions.* This too prohibits possession. It enters into force for participating states on 1 August 2010.[29]

The protection of civilians has other legal dimensions. For example, the statutes of the major international criminal tribunals (the International Military Tribunals at Nuremberg and Tokyo, the International Criminal Tribunals for Yugoslavia and Rwanda, and the International Criminal Court) all address crimes against the civilian population. In all of them the category of 'war crimes' encompasses a range of crimes against civilians, and the category of 'crimes against humanity' refers exclusively to crimes directed against any civilian population. In addition, human rights law and international refugee law aim at protection of all humans, including civilians, and have some application in armed conflicts and occupations.

Thus in formal legal terms not only is the civilian defined more broadly than before to encompass all who are not members of the armed forces, but the civilian is also the subject of a wider range of legal protections. These have practical consequences. This is only partly because attacks on civilians have led to prosecutions: these have in fact been few.[30] There are other ways in which the legal protection of civilians can have an effect. Some military campaigns—including NATO action in Bosnia in 1995 and Serbia in 1999—have been launched following shocking attacks on civilians. There have been sustained efforts by certain belligerents to reduce the impact of war on civilians, including enemy civilians. Many non-governmental organizations (NGOs) active in conflict zones have worked to protect civilians. In addition, the United Nations has not only passed resolutions regarding civilians and established tribunals but has also, at least sometimes, achieved results through other approaches.

## THE UNITED NATIONS AND
## THE PROTECTION OF CIVILIANS

In the post-Cold War era, the United Nations has been increasingly involved in a wide range of attempts to protect civilians from the effects of war. The General Assembly and the Security Council have sought to promote the development and implementation of international humanitarian law, and in particular to condemn, and take action against, violence against civilians. They have also developed ideas and doctrines in this area, especially through the adoption in 2005 of the concept of 'responsibility to protect'.[31] Moreover, certain UN specialized agencies, especially the UN High Commissioner for Refugees (UNHCR), have become deeply involved in the protection of civilians in armed conflict.

This UN involvement in civilian protection has been the result of tough circumstances: international public concern about the fate of civilians, including in areas where UN peacekeeping forces were operating, was far too great for inaction to be a viable option. NGOs operating in unstable situations shared the concern that providing material assistance was not enough: there was a need also to offer protection. The problem was, how?

The main, and the most controversial, form of UN involvement in civilian protection has been through UN peacekeeping.[32] Certain failures of the UN to take immediate action against mass killings of civilians, even in circumstances where there were UN peacekeeping forces in the area of the killings, are well known. The events in Rwanda in April–July 1994 and in the Bosnian town of Srebrenica in July 1995 are the clearest examples. Both caused serious harm to the UN's reputation. Both were the subject of detailed UN reports, the one on Srebrenica being particularly impressive.[33] In addition, there has been a major problem of sexual abuse and exploitation by UN peacekeepers.[34]

Despite these failures, there have been some significant UN achievements regarding the protection of civilians in the midst of war. The embattled capital of Bosnia and Herzegovina, Sarajevo, had a population of well over 350,000 that was at extreme risk during the siege of 1992–5. The city, and notably its civilian population, was saved from some of the worst consequences of siege warfare by two parallel but separate approaches. The first was a purely Bosnian construction: the very narrow tunnel, theoretically secret, that was built to connect Sarajevo to Bosnian government territory, enabling arms and other supplies to be brought in.[35] The second was the airlift and land convoy links with the outside world managed by UNHCR under the authority of the UN Security Council. The result of this action spearheaded by UNHCR was that, despite the many failures and interruptions, supplies of gas, water, electricity, food, and medicines were maintained. The figures for supplies brought in by the airlift are impressive. The longest running humanitarian air bridge in history, it lasted from 30 June 1992 to 5 January 1996. Although there were periods when, due to various factors including Serb threats, it was not possible for aircraft to make the journey to Sarajevo at all, during the three-and-a-half years of the airlift there were 12,951 sorties delivering 160,677 tonnes, of which 144,827 were food and the rest non-food items (such as shelter materials and medical supplies).[36] During many months of the war the airlift was believed to have provided more than 85 per cent of all assistance reaching Sarajevo. In addition, over 1,000 patients were medically evacuated by air, plus over 1,400 relatives.[37]

Action under UN auspices not only mitigated the effects of the siege of Sarajevo but also helped to end it. In summer 1995, as part of the UN Protection Force (UNPROFOR) in Bosnia, a 'rapid-reaction force' was created.[38] Comprising troops from France, the Netherlands, and the United Kingdom, and equipped with heavy artillery, it was deployed close to Sarajevo. Used in August–September 1995 in conjunction with NATO air operations, this 'rapid-reaction force' provided much stronger physical protection for the capital than had been available up to that time, and was a serious threat to the Serb forces besieging the city. It was a significant factor in the Bosnian Serb decision to end the siege, and in the events leading to the end of the Bosnian war later that year.

In the course of the 1990s, the UN Security Council became increasingly involved in civilian protection. The matter simply had to be addressed in the mandates of UN peacekeeping forces, most obviously in the case of UNPRO-FOR, the very name of which referred to civilian protection. Then in 1999, the

Council initiated a series of formal meetings and general reports on the protection of civilians, which became a major thematic issue.[39] In the UN Secretariat there was concern that the Council's involvement in civilian protection would be just one more impossible task which would result in failure.

How coherent is the UN Security Council's approach to the protection of civilians in war? The Secretary-General's September 1999 report on Protection of Civilians in Armed Conflict—the first major statement of the Council's involvement in civilian protection as a thematic issue—is vulnerable to criticism on several counts. For example, it presented a completely negative view of the implementation of the law of war in contemporary conflicts, stating in a typical passage:

> International humanitarian and human rights law set out the rights of civilians and the obligations of combatants during time of conflict. Yet, belligerents throughout the world refuse to respect these statutes, relying instead on terror as a means of control over populations.[40]

There was no recognition in this report that in some conflicts there had been serious attempts, at least by some parties, to observe certain basic norms; nor that the UN had at least some achievements to its credit in the protection of civilians. Nor did the report point out that some of those who had committed the most egregious violations of humanitarian norms (the Rwandan regime in 1994, and the Serbs at Srebrenica in 1995) had subsequently suffered serious military reverses.

The report made some worthwhile proposals regarding ratification of existing treaties, further development of the law, conflict prevention, and other matters. However, it merely reiterated certain proposals without discussing the tragedies ensuing from their application in practice in the 1990s. Thus it advocated arms embargoes in respect of situations where parties to the conflict target civilians, but failed to show any awareness of why particular forms of arms embargo came to be seen as deeply unsatisfactory in the former Yugoslavia in 1991–6 and in Sierra Leone from 1997. Likewise it failed to offer any detailed analysis of the Security Council's actual efforts in the preceding decade to act in various conflicts to secure physical protection of vulnerable populations. On this subject, the report made an apparently robust statement with a distinctly less-than-robust finale when it recommended that the Security Council

> [e]stablish, as a measure of last resort, temporary security zones and safe corridors for the protection of civilians and the delivery of assistance in situations characterized by the threat of genocide, crimes against humanity and war crimes against the civilian population, subject to the clear understanding that such arrangements require the availability, prior to their establishment, of sufficient and credible force to guarantee the safety of civilian populations making use of

them, and ensure the demilitarization of these zones and the availability of a safe-exit option.[41]

There is a case for the demilitarization of certain security zones—at least if it can be achieved with the agreement and ongoing consent of parties to a conflict. However, the apparent assumption here that any and every security zone should be demilitarized runs into an objection that needs to be recognized bluntly. There is an obvious risk in demilitarizing a zone and then putting all reliance for defence on outside forces, especially if those forces are imbued with the mentality of the 'safe-exit option' and fail to provide any defence when faced with serious attack. The risk is not theoretical. It was precisely those 'safe areas' in Bosnia that were subject to demilitarization agreements (albeit imperfect) that were conquered by Bosnian Serb forces in summer 1995. Those that had maintained their own defence system under the Bosnian government survived. In short, the report's coverage of the core issue it is supposed to address—the protection of civilians in armed conflict—is not serious.

In the same part of the report the Secretary-General also recommended, in more robust mode, that the Security Council,

[i]n the face of massive and ongoing abuses, consider the imposition of appropriate enforcement action. Before acting in such cases, either with a United Nations, regional or multinational arrangement, and in order to reinforce political support for such efforts, enhance confidence in their legitimacy and deter perceptions of selectivity or bias towards one region or another, the Council should consider the following factors:

1. The scope of the breaches of human rights and international humanitarian law including the numbers of people affected and the nature of the violations;

2. The inability of local authorities to uphold legal order, or identification of a pattern of complicity by local authorities;

3. The exhaustion of peaceful or consent-based efforts to address the situation;

4. The ability of the Security Council to monitor actions that are undertaken;

5. The limited and proportionate use of force, with attention to repercussions upon civilian populations and the environment.[42]

In the report, the greatest omission—not easy to remedy—was the failure to discuss the capacity and will of states to act. Proposals such as the one above depend crucially upon major regional or global powers, equipped with intervention forces, being willing to commit their military assets over a substantial period, and to accept the possibility of casualties. Such willingness is in limited supply. Hence the protection of civilians has sometimes assumed perverse or paradoxical forms, as it had in the empty promises to protect the 'safe areas' in Bosnia in 1992–5, and the bombing from a safe height as a response to ongoing killings and expulsions in Kosovo in 1999.

The Council's consideration in 1999 of the protection of civilians led to a resolution on the subject containing some useful proposals (e.g. regarding the disarmament, demobilization and reintegration of ex-combatants) and some necessary reaffirmation of basic principles of humanitarian law, but could not resolve the harder aspects of civilian protection.[43] The subsequent Security Council reports and resolutions on the same topic have shown continuing involvement with the problem of protecting civilians, but are hardly a chronicle of achievement. A 2009 report of the Secretary-General commented bleakly:

> Significant though they are, for all the reports, resolutions and actions of the last decade, the situation that confronts civilians in current conflicts is depressingly similar to that which prevailed in 1999. Civilians still account for the vast majority of casualties and continue to be targeted and subjected to indiscriminate attacks and other violations by parties to conflict.[44]

Despite the continuing problems, the Protection of Civilians (by now given its own acronym, POC) has increasingly been mandated as a core function of UN peacekeeping operations. A major report in November 2009 outlined the problems bluntly:

> Today eight UN peacekeeping missions are explicitly mandated to protect civilians under imminent threat of physical violence, as well as to uphold other protection measures, ranging from ensuring security for vulnerable groups to supporting IDP returns. Yet the UN Secretariat, troop- and police-contributing countries, host states, humanitarian actors, human rights professionals, and the missions themselves continue to struggle over what it means for a peacekeeping operation to protect civilians, in definition and in practice.[45]

Protection of civilians from the effects of armed conflicts—to which the UN Security Council has committed itself—is proving to be a particularly difficult and demanding task. Sometimes—as with the relatively weak hybrid peacekeeping force in Darfur since 2007—the efforts made seem incommensurate with the challenge faced. Sometimes protection involves taking sides against particular belligerents, which is by nature difficult for a wide range of international actors. There is a high risk of failure, which, when it happens, has damaging effects on the UN itself. Yet the work of the Council and UN peacekeepers has arguably had some positive results, including by providing conditions in which humanitarian organizations are able to act and journalists to report; and it may have contributed to a decline in deaths from war-exacerbated disease and malnutrition.[46] The final section of this survey glances briefly at some of the reasons why the protection of civilians has proved so problematical not only for the UN but also for states and other actors.

## CONCLUSION: SURVIVAL OF THE CONCEPT
## OF THE CIVILIAN IN TODAY'S WARS

Is the category of the civilian still relevant in the actual wars of the twenty-first century, and is the protection of civilians still a key principle by which the actions of belligerents, third parties, and international organizations are judged? It would be easy to say that the category of civilian risks getting lost in a general blurring of the distinction between civilian and combatant. There have always been difficulties in deciding whether or not certain individuals were combatants whom it was legitimate to attack in war, and those difficulties continue in the present era.

The reason why the critical distinction between soldier and civilian sometimes gets blurred lies in the very nature of those many wars, both past and present, which do not conform to the vision of war as a clash between national armies in which the civilians are essentially passive bystanders. That vision of war may be true of some, but by no means all, international wars. However, it does not reflect the developments in warfare in an era of largely non-international wars. In particular, it is difficult to reconcile with certain types of armed activity which, though not new, are undoubtedly prevalent today in both civil wars and international wars.

- *Campaigns of ethnic cleansing or of political/religious fanaticism.* Where a war aim is to kill or drive from their homes people of a particular ethnic group, class, or religious identity, the inevitable result is the direct targeting of civilians.

- *Guerrilla warfare.* This has always blurred the distinction between civilian and combatant.

- *Terrorist campaigns.* These overlap with guerrilla warfare and involve the same problems plus some others. Many contemporary definitions of terrorism assume that it is always aimed at civilians. While this is a historical oversimplification, it does highlight the challenge that contemporary terrorism poses to the idea of the civilian. Osama bin Laden has stated that 'it is a fundamental principle of any democracy that the people choose their leaders and, as such, approve and are party to the actions of their elected leaders. . . . This is why the American people are not innocent.'[47] Suicide bombing, extensively used by al-Qaeda, has particularly grave effects on civilians, not only because in many cases it is directed against them but also because it makes troops and police fear civilians and treat them as hostile, thus exacerbating the conflict between them. A further challenge to the category of civilian arises from the problem of how captured terrorist suspects are to be classified in laws of war. If they cannot be classified as prisoners of war, should they therefore, as some advocate, be classified as civilians? In order to preserve 'the civilian' as a meaningful category, it is necessary to accept that there is a third category, distinct both from the soldier and the civilian: the category variously called 'unlawful combatant' or 'unprivileged belligerent'. The category of civilian, in any case riddled with complexity and paradox, cannot reasonably be stretched to encompass every guerrilla and terrorist who fails to meet the well-known criteria for combatant status.

- *Use of civilian contractors.* Certain armed forces, including those of the United States, have increasingly used civilian contractors to perform a range of specialist tasks previously carried out by the military. These can include managing and servicing battle-related equipment; protecting particular places, people, or projects; and assisting an occupation administration in various ways. There is an emerging view that the concept of 'direct participation in hostilities' should encompass at least some contractor activity associated with the military effort, and that following this course would 'infuse the Law of Armed Conflict with much-needed pragmatism thus ensuring its longer-term integrity and compliance'.[48]

- *Involvement of armed forces in humanitarian activities.* In modern conflicts, armed forces—whether of belligerents, or of outside parties acting in peacekeeping or other modes—are frequently involved in civilian support activities of various kinds: protecting civilians from persecution, aiding civilian reconstruction, assisting refugee returns, and so on. Such activities, while they may appear favourable to civilians, can pose a problem for independent humanitarian organizations, which risk being seen as the humanitarian wing of particular armed forces rather than as having their own independent identity. The ICRC is among the humanitarian organizations that have expressed concern about the implications of this confusion of identities, and in particular the blurring of the civil and the military.[49]

- *Effects-based war.* The increased accuracy of US bombing could have been seen as leading to a form of warfare in which the 1868 St Petersburg principle, of limiting attacks to the armed forces of the adversary, was at long last capable of being applied. However, US doctrine has been moving in a different direction. Particularly in the campaigns in Kosovo in 1999, Afghanistan in 2001, and Iraq in 2003, there was a focus, not on slaughtering the adversary government's troops, but rather on undermining its sources of power directly. This involved, for example, attacks on dual-use targets, such as electrical power generation and distribution systems, and also on such targets as radio stations controlled by the adversary regime. In parallel with this change in practice, wording in certain US military handbooks was modified in such a way as to weaken, but not completely abolish, the prohibition of attacks on civilian objects.[50]

- *'Lawfare'*. This term has been invented by a US general, Charles Dunlap, to describe activities that seek to discredit the adversary by making its forces appear to be acting in violation of the laws of war. Dunlap attributes this mode of action primarily to the US's enemies: 'As more and more adversaries learn they cannot go up against our coalition forces on the battlefield, they have moved to attack us through the law to achieve their operational objectives.'[51] Typical acts of lawfare include using civilians as human shields for insurgent forces and military equipment, thereby inducing the adversary to attack civilians and civilian objects. The insurgent calculation is that such coalition acts, and the public fuss to which they give rise, will lead to public disillusion with the coalition cause. In other words, the political importance of the distinction between the civilian and the soldier is being recognized and exploited. While Dunlap's take on 'lawfare' identifies real issues, it is vulnerable to two criticisms. First, it is too US-centric: the use of some of the tactics he described is not confined to conflicts in which the United States is directly involved, and has occurred in other situations such as the civil war in Sri Lanka. Second, it is too fixed on the idea that the various activities subsumed under the heading of 'lawfare' are centrally orchestrated: in some cases human shields may be spontaneous and voluntary, rather than part of a campaign of 'lawfare'.

- *Active role of civilians vis-à-vis hostilities*. Civilians sometimes have an active, independent role in relation to hostilities. Possible examples are the movement to protect bridges in Belgrade from NATO bombing in 1999;[52] and cases of civil resistance aimed, as in Portugal in 1974, at supporting moves to end a war.[53]

- *Reluctance of some military occupants to accept full legal obligations*. Occupation law covers an important interface between armed forces and civilian populations. A problem in the implementation of 1949 Geneva Convention IV has been that states have only rarely been willing to view themselves as having the status of an occupying power. At various times, certain states have put forward arguments purporting to show that the situations in which their forces are involved differ in significant respects from the understanding of occupation in the laws of war. As in the case of the Israeli-occupied territories after 1967, this meant that civilian populations had reduced protection from such hazards as land seizures and the influx of settlers from the occupying country.

These developments suggest that the situation of the civilian in today's armed conflicts and occupations is hugely problematical. In particular, civilian protection cannot be absolute where civilians participate actively in hostilities. Yet the position of the civilian is not uniformly bleak. Assertions that 80 or 90 per cent of all victims of wars in the post-Cold War period are civilians are based on notably weak statistical foundations. The principle that civilians should not be attacked is widely accepted in international discourse and has found reflection in numerous legal procedures and military actions. The entitlement of civilians to protection is not based on a requirement that they be absolutely innocent of all connection with the armed conflict. The many efforts to protect civilians—both in lawmaking and in the work of states, international organizations, and NGOs—have achieved some significant results. Despite its problematic basis, the distinction between combatant and civilian, which emerged at the same time as civilians were increasingly seen as involved in various ways in war, is likely not just to endure, but to retain its political, legal, and moral salience.

## NOTES

1. Raymond Aron, *The century of total war*, translated by E.W. Dickes and O.S. Griffiths (London: Derek Verschoyle, 1954), 9.
2. General Sir Rupert Smith, *The utility of force: The art of war in the modern world* (London: Allen Lane, 2005), xiii. On p. 17, he lists six major trends that characterize war amongst the people.
3. In the NATO air campaign against Yugoslavia in the 1999 Kosovo War, approximately 500 civilians were killed, and probably over 820 were wounded, according to information in 'Final report to the Prosecutor by the committee established to review the NATO bombing campaign against the Federal Republic of Yugoslavia' (The Hague: International Criminal Tribunal for the Former Yugoslavia, June 2000), para. 53. Available at http://www.icty.org/x/file/About/OTP/otp_report_nato_bombing_en.pdf.
4. For an excellent account of the development of robotic warfare and its moral consequences, see Peter Singer's chapter in this book.
5. Geoffrey Best, *War & law since 1945* (Oxford: Clarendon Press, 1994), 45. See also the equally extensive and sceptical view of civilian immunity in earlier periods in his *Humanity in warfare: The modern history of the international law of armed conflicts* (London: Weidenfeld & Nicolson, 1980).
6. See, for example, Richard Shelly Hartigan, *The forgotten victim: A history of the civilian* (Chicago, IL: Precedent, 1982).
7. Hugo Slim, *Killing civilians: Method, madness and morality in war* (London: Hurst, 2008), 3.
8. See Slim's useful discussion of civilian ambiguity in *Killing civilians*, 181–211.
9. Javier Solana, *A secure Europe in a better world: European security strategy* (Paris: European Union Institute for Security Studies, 2003), 5. Available at http://www.iss.europa.eu/uploads/media/solanae.pdf.
10. Adam Roberts, 'Lives and statistics: Are 90% of war victims civilians?', *Survival*, 52/3 (2010). See also Mats Berdal's chapter in this volume.

11. James Turner Johnson, *Just war tradition and the restraint of war: A moral and historical inquiry* (Princeton, NJ: Princeton University Press, 1981), 131–2.

12. Jean-Jacques Rousseau, *Du contrat social* (1762), I. iv, in Victor Gourevitch (ed. & trans.), *Rousseau: The social contract and other later political writings* (Cambridge: Cambridge University Press, 1997), 46–7.

13. 'Instructions for the government of armies of the United States in the field' (the Lieber Code), promulgated as General Orders no. 100 by President Lincoln, 24 April 1863, Articles 20–22. Dietrich Schindler and Jiri Toman (eds.), *The laws of armed conflicts* (Dordrecht: Martinus Nijhoff, 1988), 6–7.

14. Lieber Code, articles 23 and 25.

15. International Committee of the Red Cross, *Interpretive guidance on the notion of direct participation in hostilities under international humanitarian law* (Geneva: ICRC, 2009), 20, n. 11.

16. 1907 Hague Regulations, article 29, para. 2. Similar wording had appeared in the 1874 Brussels Declaration, article 22, para. 2; and in the 1899 Hague Regulations, article 29. Schindler and Toman (eds.), *Laws of armed conflicts*, 30 and 85.

17. Amanda Alexander, 'The genesis of the civilian', *Leiden Journal of International Law*, 20/2 (2007), 360.

18. *Hansard, Commons*, 21 June 1938, cols. 937–8.

19. 1949 Geneva Convention IV on Protection of Civilians in Time of War, article 4, paras. 1 and 4.

20. Jean S. Pictet (ed.), *Commentary on Geneva Convention IV* (Geneva: ICRC, 1958), 51.

21. 1977 Geneva Protocol I on Protection of Victims of International Armed Conflicts, article 50, para. 1.

22. 1977 Geneva Protocol I, article 48.

23. Yoram Dinstein, 'Distinction and loss of civilian protection in international armed conflicts', in Michael D. Carsten (ed.), *International law and military operations* (Newport, RI: US Naval War College, 2008), 188–91.

24. See, for example, declarations of Australia, Belgium, Canada, Germany, Ireland, Italy, the Netherlands, New Zealand, Switzerland, and the United Kingdom. Texts available in Adam Roberts and Richard Guelff (eds.), *Documents on the laws of war* (Oxford: Oxford University Press, 2000), 500–12.

25. 1977 Geneva Protocol II on Protection of Victims of Non-International Armed Conflicts, articles 13–18.

26. Richard R. Baxter, 'So-called "unprivileged belligerency": Spies, guerrillas and saboteurs', *British Year Book of International Law 1951*, 28 (Oxford University Press, London, 1952), 328.

27. International Committee of the Red Cross, *Interpretive guidance on the notion of direct participation in hostilities*, 16, 20.

28. ICRC, *Interpretive guidance on the notion of direct participation in hostilities*, 17, repeated on p. 83. However, note the examples on pp. 36 and 81–2 of circumstances in which civilian protection might legitimately be viewed as suspended.

29. The Cluster Munitions Convention enters into force six months after the receipt of the thirtieth instrument of ratification or accession. By February 2010, thirty

states had deposited such instruments. Information from ICRC website http://www.icrc.org/ihl.

30. Carolin Wuerzner, 'Mission impossible? Bringing charges for the crime of attacking civilians or civilian objects before international criminal tribunals', *International Review of the Red Cross*, 90/872 (2008), http://www.icrc.org/Web/Eng/siteeng0.nsf/htmlall/review.

31. The 2005 UN World Summit Outcome Document, General Assembly resolution 60/1 of 16 September 2005, paras 58 and 134, called generally for the protection of civilians in armed conflict; and paras 138 and 139 spelt out the responsibility to protect populations from genocide, war crimes, ethnic cleansing, and crimes against humanity. All official UN documents cited here are available at http://www.un.org/en/documents/index.shtml.

32. For a detailed study of the extent to which the mandates of UN peacekeeping forces have, or have not, included explicit authorizations to protect civilians, see Siobhán Wills, *Protecting civilians: The obligations of peacekeepers* (Oxford: Oxford University Press, 2009), 1–87.

33. 'Report of the Secretary-General pursuant to General Assembly resolution 53/35: The fall of Srebrenica', UN doc. A/54/549 of 15 November 1999; and 'Report of the independent inquiry into the actions of the United Nations during the 1994 genocide in Rwanda', UN doc. S/1999/1257 of 16 December 1999.

34. See, for example, Nicola Dahrendorf, 'Addressing sexual exploitation and abuse in MONUC', a UN 'Lessons learned study', UN Department of Peacekeeping Operations, New York, March 2006, http://www.peacekeepingbestpractices.unlb.org/PBPS/Pages/Public/Home.aspx.

35. I visited this tunnel on 7 October 2002.

36. Figures supplied to the author by UNHCR, Geneva, 12 February 1996.

37. UNHCR, *The state of the world's refugees 1995* (Oxford: Oxford University Press, 1995), 126.

38. This rapid-reaction capability for UNPROFOR was authorized in Security Council resolution 998 of 16 June 1995.

39. 'Statement by the President of the Security Council', UN doc. S/PRST/1999/6 of 12 February 1999.

40. Report of the Secretary-General to the Security Council on the protection of civilians in armed conflict, UN doc. S/1999/957 (8 September 1999), para. 3. There are similarly negative views of implementation in paras 2, 7, 12, 13, and 21.

41. Ibid., recommendation 39.

42. Ibid., recommendation 40.

43. Security Council resolution 1265 of 17 September 1999. See also SC Res. 1674 of 28 April 2006, and Security Council resolution 1738 of 23 December 2006.

44. Report of the Secretary-General to the Security Council on the protection of civilians in armed conflict, UN doc. S/2009/277 (29 May 2009), para. 23.

45. Victoria Holt and Glyn Taylor, *Protecting civilians in the context of UN peacekeeping operations: Successes, setbacks and remaining challenges*, independent study jointly commissioned by the Department of Peacekeeping Operations and the Office for the Coordination of Humanitarian Affairs (New York: United

Nations, November 2009), 4, http://www.peacekeepingbestpractices.unlb.org/pbps/Pages/Public/Home.aspx.

46. Human security report project at Simon Fraser University, Canada, *Human security report 2009: The shrinking costs of war*, 17–35 and 44, http://www.humansecurityreport.org.

47. Osama Bin Laden, statement on Al Qal'ah (Internet), 14 October 2002, cited in Christopher M. Blanchard, *Al Qaeda: Statements and evolving ideology—CRS report for Congress* (Washington, DC: Congressional Research Service, 16 November 2004), 4n. The assumption that a person has to be innocent in order to be entitled to protection from murder is a questionable interpretation of the Qur'an.

48. Dale Stephens and Angeline Lewis, 'The targeting of civilian contractors in armed conflict', *Yearbook of International Humanitarian Law*, 9 (2006), 63.

49. Meinrad Studer, 'The ICRC and civil-military relations in armed conflict', *International Review of the Red Cross*, 83/842 (2001), 367–9, http://www.icrc.org/Web/Eng/siteeng0.nsf/htmlall/review. The author is a diplomatic adviser to and member of the ICRC's International Organizations Division.

50. See also Henry Shue's chapter in this volume.

51. Charles Dunlap, 'Legal issues in coalition warfare: A US perspective', in Anthony M. Helm (ed.), *The law of war in the 21st Century: Weaponry and the use of force* (Newport, RI: US Naval War College, 2006), 227.

52. Stéphanie Bouchié de Belle, 'Chained to cannons or wearing targets on their t-shirts: Human shields in international humanitarian law', *International Review of the Red Cross*, 90/872 (2008), available at http://www.icrc.org/Web/Eng/siteeng0.nsf/htmlall/review

53. Kenneth Maxwell, 'Portugal: "The revolution of the carnations," 1974–75', in Adam Roberts and Timothy Garton Ash (eds.), *Civil resistance and power politics: The experience of non-violent action from Gandhi to the present* (Oxford: Oxford University Press, 2009), 144–61.

# 20

# Killing Civilians

*Uwe Steinhoff*

According to international law and to most interpretations of just war theory, it is permissible to kill civilians in war or armed campaigns. However, civilians allegedly deserve a more protected status than combatants, at least as long as they do not themselves take part in the hostilities. For example, they are not to be targeted, it is claimed, or to be killed or maimed intentionally.

This chapter begins by discussing the distinction between civilians and combatants from a moral point of view, and argues that none of the available theories motivating this distinction can support the idea that soldiers are inherently more legitimate targets of attack than civilians. It then briefly discusses whether the foreseen killing of someone is, all else being equal, morally less bad than their intentional killing. This chapter argues that it is not, and that therefore the idea that concomitant slaughter (my term of choice for what others euphemistically call 'collateral damage') is not, all else being equal, as bad as terrorism is mistaken.

There are four serious approaches one might use in distinguishing the 'innocent' (those who cannot be justly killed, maimed, or injured) from the 'non-innocent' (those who can be justly thus treated); or, in other words, those who have a right not to be killed, maimed, or otherwise subjected to severe violence from those who do not have this right. These approaches are: the *moral guilt theory*, the *convention theory*, the *self-defence theory*, and the *justifying emergency theory*. The question, however, is whether the demarcations provided by these approaches coincide with the distinction between combatants and civilians.[1]

The *moral guilt theory*, which dominated just war theory for at least a thousand years after the church father Augustine,[2] claims, roughly, that those who bear responsibility for an unjust war are liable to attack. Augustine and his followers assumed such attacks to be punitive in nature. However, against Augustine—and certain critics of the guilt theory—it has to be pointed out that the *reasons* or *purposes* or the *cause* for which one fights have to be distinguished from the *criteria* by which one chooses legitimate targets.

For example, there can be moral guilt theories of forced indemnification: these theories might claim that someone who has culpably caused some unjust harm (e.g. by stealing something) can then be forced to redress it, whereas non-causers or non-culpable causers should not be forced to help the victim of the harm. However, most people think that indemnification and punishment are different things. By making amends (e.g. by giving back the stolen goods or paying for the damage), the culpable causer of the harm has only reinstated, as it were, the situation before his culpable act. *Punishing* him for this act requires more than just making him undo the harm he has inflicted. Perhaps he has to pay additional punitive fees or go to jail. In our context this means that the moral guilt theory of the distinction between those one can justly subject to violence and those one cannot neither depends on nor implies the idea that just wars have to be punitive in nature. The theory is, rather, entirely compatible with the idea that just wars are purely defensive in nature. (I will not go into the question here whether just wars *have* to be purely defensive.) Even when the reasons one fights are defensive, the criterion one uses to determine legitimate targets can still be moral responsibility for the unjust war. But since it is entirely clear that civilians can bear responsibility for unjust wars, the moral guilt theory cannot exclude civilians as legitimate targets of attack.

According to the *self-defence theory* of the distinction between legitimate and illegitimate targets, immediate aggressors would be legitimate targets of violent countermeasures (and thus, in the technical sense of the principle of self-defence, 'non-innocent', i.e. *harming*, from the Latin verb *nocere*), irrespective of whether one could morally blame them for their aggression. Conversely, individuals who are not immediate aggressors would even then be illegitimate targets if they were morally (co-)responsible for the aggression, for example, by supporting, or goading on, the immediate aggressor. Thus Robert K. Fullinwider, who has given this theory its perhaps paradigmatic expression, claims that if mobsters coerce Smith (for instance, with terrible threats against his family) into unjustly trying to kill Jones, the mobsters are not legitimate targets of the defender Jones, since they do not pose the immediate threat, while Smith, who has started shooting, is. The problem with this approach, however, is, first, that it is entirely unappealing from a moral point of view and, secondly, that it seems not even to be true that the principle of self-defence allows defensive measures only against the immediate threats or aggressors. As Lawrence A. Alexander remarks:

> May Jones invoke the Principle of Self-Defense to kill the mobsters instead of Smith if by doing so he will cause Smith to relent? Of course he may.... Jones not only could, but should, kill the mobsters rather than Smith if killing them would be no riskier than killing Smith and would remove the threat to Jones by removing Smith's motive for killing him.[3]

This is directly applicable to war. If the civilian cabinet of Aggressor Nation issues military orders to conscript by force children between 8 and 14 years of age and to send them off to invade Defender Nation, and Defender Nation could as easily end the invasion by mowing down the children (who pose the immediate threat) as by blowing up the civilian cabinet of Aggressor Nation, it seems morally outrageous to opt for the former strategy instead of the latter. The situation is not much different if we are talking not about politicians but about, say, an enormously influential group of clergy or tycoons who stand to profit from the invasion. If the conscription of the children and the unjust invasion are due to the unholy doings of these groups behind the scenes and could be stopped by giving *them* a taste of war instead of giving it to the innocent children, one could and should, all else being equal, do exactly that.

While the self-defence theory, narrowly interpreted, focuses on immediate or imminent threats or attacks, it makes sense to take into account less immediate threats and dangers as well. This is done by what I call the *justifying emergency theory*. For example, a sleeping soldier does not pose an immediate threat and of course is not currently attacking anyone; thus, on a narrow interpretation of self-defence (which is in fact suggested by the wording of some domestic jurisdictions and by some pacifists[4]), he cannot be liable to defensive countermeasures. However, it seems intuitively clear that one can also be justified in using violence against a danger that does not express itself in an *immediate* attack or threat. For instance, if a small woman has been kidnapped by a huge muscular man and chained in his cellar, and the kidnapper lies down to take a nap, after credibly assuring his victim that he will rape and kill her when he wakes up, then the woman, if she can free herself from the chains but not escape from the house or call the police, is entirely justified in attacking the kidnapper in his sleep, incapacitating or even killing him if necessary.[5]

This theory, in contrast to the self-defence theory (narrowly construed), can explain why sleeping soldiers can be liable to attack. But of course, like self-defence theory it does not exclude attacks on civilians. On the contrary, in the case of the evil clergy or tycoons, it allows attacks on these people even when the invading child army is not currently attacking but sleeping.

The *convention theory*, as formulated by George I. Mavrodes, argues that non-combatant immunity must be interpreted as a useful convention.[6] The convention restricts the brutality of war in the interests of the warring parties. As another author, Michael Green, formulates it:

> nations will wish to limit war so that the possibility of their nation being totally destroyed is minimised, or at least significantly reduced. Most will wish that enough of their country remains so that their country can be rebuilt and their way of life continued after hostilities. A nation will wish to preserve its cultural,

educational, and religious sites, its reproductive capacity (traditionally represented by women and children), and its non-military economic assets.[7]

But if the goal is to limit destruction, would not a single-combat convention, according to which, for example, the leaders or two other representatives of the warring nations should settle their differences in single combat, be much more useful?[8] The answer is 'no'. One must not forget that war damage is not to be avoided *at any price*. Many find at least some things valuable enough to risk some degree of destruction. Mavrodes himself does not see this point clearly enough, since he finds the single-combat convention attractive (though utopian). Yet the idea that, in a clash that would normally have led to war, 'whatever territory, influence, or other price would have been sought in the war'[9] should instead simply be handed over to the winner of individual combat is not as appealing as it might at first look. If the winning nation is out to rape, enslave, or murder the population of the other country, one can hardly expect—whether psychologically or morally—the threatened side to be willing to settle the matter by arm wrestling. This is also true if 'only' its freedom and self-determination are threatened. Thus, the single-combat convention is actually not preferable to the civilian-immunity convention.

However, it is worth noting that the civilian-immunity convention cannot be seen merely as a contract whose binding force rests on reciprocity. That would imply that as soon as one side in a conflict starts to disregard it, the other side is entitled to do the same. A stronger interpretation of the convention theory bases it rather on the rule-utilitarian principle, which states roughly that those rules should be adopted and followed that maximize human happiness. If this principle or something similar is accepted, a state is not allowed to break the convention merely because the enemy state has done so. Instead, it has to take into account the wider implications of still further violations of the principle. For instance, retaliation in kind might in the long run make the situation of human beings worse. However, it has to be noted that this will not always be so. There can be specific situations where adopting a rule that identifies precisely these situations as exceptions to the convention of civilian immunity might in the long run produce more good than bad. Sometimes situations are so specific or so extreme that the expected benefit of violating the convention in these situations in pursuit of certain valuable goals is not outweighed by the expected disadvantages of violating the convention. To give a hypothetical example: if by intentionally killing one innocent person one averts the destruction of the whole of humanity, one should kill the innocent person. Less extreme examples are readily available. Thus, the convention theory cannot uphold an absolute immunity of civilians either.

So far this chapter has discussed four approaches to distinguishing the 'innocent' from the 'non-innocent', that is, distinguishing those who have a right not to be killed or maimed or otherwise subjected to severe violence from those who do not have this right. *Each* of these approaches is centred on its own morally valid principle, namely the principle of moral guilt, the principle of self-defence, the principle of justifying emergency and the rule-utilitarian principle. The theories differ from the principles they are based on in that each theory raises its respective principle to an absolute status, and uses it as the one and only measure for distinguishing between legitimate and illegitimate targets and acts. Using more than one principle would lead to new and different approaches. In fact, all four principles need to be applied and weighed against each other.

Where does this leave civilians? Well, neither alone nor in concert can the four theories or principles explain or justify an absolute immunity of civilians. Of course, if one takes into account the epistemic restrictions, that is, the uncertainty and lack of knowledge under which combatants must often act in war, then in many situations the guilt theory, the self-defence theory and the justifying emergency theory go a long way towards establishing at least a *presumption* of innocence (whether 'innocence' is understood in the sense of the first of these theories or of the two latter ones), but this presumption is not defeasible. Sometimes combatants *know* or are at least reasonably certain that certain civilians are non-innocent with regard to the unjust war effort, and the combatants are also quite capable of targeting those civilians. This still leaves the rule-utilitarian principle as a last moral defence of even non-innocent civilians. However, in certain situations not only will it be outweighed by other principles but it will itself justify or even require attack on civilians.

Thus, there is no plausible theory that could explain why civilians should be absolutely immune from being subjected to violence. And in fact, both traditional just war theory and the laws of armed conflict have no particular qualms about allowing civilians to be subjected to violence, killed or maimed, and burned or blown into small pieces. Instead, both normative traditions are much more concerned about *targeting* civilians or *intentionally* killing them (by the way, one can intentionally kill civilians without targeting them, even if one allows for a distinction between intentional and foreseen killing). Both traditions accommodate concomitant slaughter, to the extent that it abides by certain restrictions.

The question is, how is this purported difference between intentional killing and foreseen to be explained? To be sure, one can further distinguish between different kinds of concomitant slaughter. It makes a difference whether one clearly foresees that innocent bystanders will be killed in an attack on a military target or whether one knows only that there is a certain risk that bystanders will be killed. Thus, there is a difference between killing one innocent person knowingly and killing one innocent person accidentally. On the other hand, it is anything but clear that attempting to kill one innocent person intentionally is worse than attacking a rather insignificant military target knowing that there is a 99 per cent risk that the 100 children in the adjacent nursery school will be killed. Indeed, if one could clearly achieve the same military advantage with either method, one should, from a moral point of view, use the former method instead of the latter.

Thus, the intentional killing of innocent persons is not necessarily worse than the accidental killing of innocent persons. This also means that concomitant slaughter, even where it abides by certain proportionality constraints, is not necessarily better than terrorism. If, moreover, we are talking not about the accidental but about the *foreseen* killing of innocents, it becomes even more mysterious why this should supposedly be so different from the intentional killing of innocents.

After all, none of the theories set out above can explain such a difference. As a matter of fact, *nothing* can explain this difference. Of course, the so-called doctrine of double effect is often adduced in defence of the claim that terrorism is worse than concomitant slaughter. Unfortunately, however, the doctrine of double effect explains absolutely nothing. It only *states* the conditions under which concomitant slaughter is (supposedly) justified, and simply *assumes* that the intentional killing of innocents is not justified.

Thus, according to this doctrine, an act with certain predictable negative consequences is allowed when the following conditions are met:

1. The agent acts with a good intention, and attempts to bring about a good effect (or at least a morally permissible one).

2. The agent does not want to bring about the predicted negative consequences or side effects, and attempts to avoid or mitigate them as much as possible.

3. The agent treats the negative repercussions or side effects neither as ends in themselves nor as means to another end.

4. There is an acceptable proportion between the predicted negative consequences and the positive effect.[10]

Yet the question is precisely why one should accept this or a similar doctrine. After all, the doctrine of double effect has suffered devastating criticisms in recent years,[11] and no convincing reply to those criticisms has been offered. Of course, some of the examples that have been adduced to show that the doctrine leads to absurd results do not actually work. However, most others work just fine, even where adherents of the doctrine might be tempted to deny that. Tony Coady, for example, tries to defend the doctrine with the following remarks:

> The DDE [doctrine of double effect] requires that we think in commonsense ways about what people intend and foresee. This means that there are various disentanglements of the parts of an action that we cannot really allow. Consider someone who has a great hatred of flies. To his horror, he finds a fly in his

apartment, and the only swatting implement to hand is a big, heavy hammer. The fly is very hard to keep up with, but it eventually settles on the bald head of his best friend, where it is clearly visible against the bald surface. If he smashes the hammer down upon the fly and the head it rests on, fully aware that he will thereby kill or severely injure his friend, it would surely be absurd for him to plead that he did not intend his friend's death or injury. The remark, 'I only intended to kill the fly, my friend's death was a foreseen but unintended side effect of my action,' just doesn't make sense. (Of course, if it did make sense, it would still be no excuse under the DDE because of the proportionality requirement, but the important point here is that we cannot take apart the smashing of the fly and the smashing of the head.)[12]

Actually, however, it is irrelevant for the doctrine whether one can take apart the act of smashing the fly and the act of smashing the head—one obviously cannot, because it is one and the same act. Instead, the important thing, according to the doctrine, is that one can distinguish between what is intended and what is merely foreseen, or between means, ends, and side effects. But, contrary to what Coady suggests, this is perfectly possible in his example. Moreover, if we slightly vary the example, the proportionality requirement can actually be satisfied. To wit, suppose the man with the hammer smashes the fly on his friend's head because that is the last chance to keep it from escaping from the lab with the doomsday virus it happens to be carrying, which would exterminate humanity. In this instance, what is supposed to be strange about saying, 'I did not *intend* to smash that person's head, in the sense that smashing his head was the end or purpose of my action or a means to the end of my action'? Besides, given what was at stake, this action actually also satisfies the other criteria laid down by the doctrine. And I do not have any problem with that. Where the silliness of the doctrine is evident, however, is when it claims that smashing with a hammer the fly sitting on the person's forehead is permissible given the proportionality considerations, while, in an alternative scenario, smashing the forehead of the person with a hammer in such a way that the fly sitting on the back of the head is squashed between the head and the wall is not, since in the former case smashing the innocent person's head is just an unintended side effect of the attack on the fly, while in the latter case it is a means of attacking the fly. The innocent person in the second case will certainly not think that his situation is dramatically improved if he swaps places with the innocent person in the first case, and it is certainly unclear why there should be something more fishy about the first kind of attack than about the second one.

Incidentally, if Coady's interpretation of the hammer example were correct, the absurdity he talks about would also be present in the case where some pilot drops a lot of bombs on a target, knowing full well that these bombs will kill both enemy soldiers and innocent bystanders. What is the normatively relevant difference supposed to be between, on the one hand, dropping cluster bombs on an area populated by both enemy soldiers and innocent civilians and, on the other hand, smashing with a hammer a locale populated by both a dangerous fly and an innocent person's head? If one cannot disentangle the parts of the latter act, one cannot disentangle the parts of the former.

Not only does the doctrine of double effect attribute normative relevance to distinctions that simply have no such relevance, it also sometimes prescribes the wrong course of action. The doctrine of double effect takes itself more seriously than the lives of innocent human beings. It is morally corrupt. This can be shown by the fact that in cases where the concomitant slaughter of 100 civilians would still be a proportionate side effect of the attack on a military target, the doctrine of double effect prefers this concomitant slaughter of 100 civilians to the intentional killing of just one innocent civilian *even where this latter course of action would clearly and demonstrably secure the same military advantage.* In light of this consideration, the terrorist who prefers the latter method has to be congratulated for his enlightened human-ism, while the concomitant slaughterer preferring the former method has to be reprimanded for his inhumane dogmatism.[13]

Often it is said that terrorists are intent on killing as many innocent people as possible,[14] while concomitant slaughterers are not. This, however, is empir-ically simply wrong. The three organizations, al-Qaeda, the United States of America, and the United Kingdom (all three organizations—and states cer-tainly are organizations—have engaged in terrorist activities and deliberately targeted innocent people, a business in which the first entity has still much to learn from the other two), do not try to kill as many innocent persons as possible. The United States actually could blow up the whole planet, but does not choose to. And whoever assumes that al-Qaeda wants to kill as many people as possible shows little acquaintance with its actual interests and concerns. Similar things can be said about all other so-called terrorist organi-zations, with the possible exception of one or two apocalyptic sects.

Moreover, it is anything but clear why someone who in the course of his struggle attempts to increase the number of civilians killed from 1 to 100 *because otherwise he cannot achieve his goal* should be morally inferior to someone who tries to decrease the number of civilians killed—on purpose or as a side effect—from 300,000 to 100,000 *because he does not need to kill more.* The fact is that a terrorist does not need to be more indifferent to the deaths of deliberately targeted civilians than a bomber pilot to the deaths of civilians he kills as a side effect of an attack. That one of them might want to increase the number of civilians killed while the other might want to decrease it does not reflect a contrast between indifference on the one hand and concern on the other, but only a difference in the means the two parties employ. Without information about what other options, if any, a party in a conflict has, the means the party uses in pursuit of its ends does not necessarily say very much about its attitudes.

Other generalizations critical of terrorism do not fare any better. Asa Kasher and Amos Yadlin, for example, offer the following argument:

> acts of terror . . . involve premeditated killing or otherwise injuring persons *qua* members of a population for the purpose of terrorizing that population, in order to serve their given goals. Clearly, an act of killing persons or otherwise injuring them is morally justified only if it is an act of self-defense, used as a last resort, against perpetrating persons. However, in the first place, an act of killing or injuring persons *qua* members of a population is not an act performed against perpetrators. Secondly, an act intended to terrorize a population by killing or otherwise injuring members of it is never an act genuinely used as a last resort. Thirdly and most importantly, killing or injuring persons in order to terrorize a population is using persons merely as means. Hence, acts of terror and activities of terror are always morally unjustified.[15]

One cannot help wondering why Kasher and Yadlin begin the second sentence of this quote with 'clearly', given that they do not rule out counterterrorist actions that involve the killing of innocent bystanders, and innocent bystanders are *clearly* not perpetrators. Of course, Kasher and Yadlin appeal dogmatically to the doctrine of double effect, but that doctrine is, as already argued, simply wrong. In addition, their claim that an action intended to terrorize a population by killing or otherwise injuring its members is never an act genuinely used as a last resort is entirely unwarranted. Even if it were not, terrorist campaigns that cost significantly fewer innocent human lives than non-terrorist military action accompanied by concomitant slaughter would cost need not really be a last resort in order to be preferable to concomitant slaughter. Besides, most wars are also intended to terrorize a population by killing or otherwise injuring members of it, whether or not these members are soldiers.

There is, however, something more going on in Kasher and Yadlin's criticism of terrorism. They suggest that the terrorist attacks persons '*qua* members of a population'. This talk about attacking persons '*qua* members of a population' is, to be sure, a clever and in certain circles very popular move to associate terrorism with genocide.[16] It is not a very convincing move, though. As Kasher and Yadlin themselves say, the terrorist kills members of a population in order to 'terrorise' that population. However, this is something very different from killing them *only because* they are members of the population. They do not kill them *qua* members of the population, they kill them because their death is a means to influence the rest of the population. Their *deaths* are the means to achieve this end, not the killed people themselves. The killed people are not used at all, they are simply killed. I use a waiter in order to get coffee; if I kill him, this means that I apparently have no further use for him. Of course, some would be inclined to say that using a person's death as a means to one's end is worse than accepting the person's death as a side effect of the pursuit of one's end. That, however, is again nothing more than an appeal to the mistaken doctrine of double effect.

Not only is there no convincing argument in sight which would show that the intentional killing of innocent people or terrorism is worse than concomitant slaughter; the fact of the matter is also that much slaughter in war that is officially justified by the doctrine of double effect might actually amount to terrorism itself. Michael Neumann aptly describes the attitudes and thought processes leading to this situation:

> Strategic bombing aims at military installations, factories important to the war effort, or vital infrastructure. It is often impossible to mount such attacks without inflicting civilian casualties....
>
> One might suppose that, before undertaking acts that we know with moral certainty will kill innocent civilians, we would require a very high degree of certainty that the act were truly necessary. Not at all. For one thing, as a matter of fact, military men rarely if ever claim anything like such certainty: of course there might be yet-unconceived strategies and tactics that would work as well or better. Besides, the strategic bombing strategy could fail, or prove far less effective than supposed. Usually the proponents of a particular strategic bombing campaign claim only that it would confer an important local advantage, not make the difference between victory and defeat.[17]
>
> In practice, military men use air power largely because they fear that otherwise they'll take considerably more casualties, and because they'd rather not test unproven alternatives.[18]

Neumann concludes from this that the 'doctrine of the double effect has questionable authority, but even unquestioned it does little to raise expected collateral damage above terror'.[19]

Even more, one might add, much of what is officially sold as 'collateral damage' or as the bombing of dual purpose facilities is in fact dual purpose bombing: the terrorizing effect on the population is actually intended. Sometimes politicians and the military accidentally let this slip. Admiral Sir Michael Boyce, for example, explained during the Afghanistan war that bombing would continue 'until the people of the country themselves recognise that this is going to go on until they get the leadership changed'.[20] Thus, the same logic of terror was at play here—harming the civilian population in order to make them put pressure on their government—that also inspired Churchill's bombing of German civilians, or for that matter the anti-civilian campaigns of certain subnational terrorist groups. Francis Boyle, a professor of international law and a member of the Commission of Inquiry into US war crimes during the first Allied war against Iraq, describes the bombing campaign that began on 17 January 1991 as follows:

> Most of the targets were civilian facilities. The United States intentionally bombed and destroyed centers of civilian life, commercial and business districts, schools,

hospitals, mosques, churches, shelters, residential areas, historical sites, private vehicles and civilian government offices. In aerial attack, including strafing over cities, town, the countryside and highways, the United States aircraft bombed and strafed indiscriminately. The purpose of these attacks was to destroy life and property, and generally to terrorize the civilian population in Iraq.[21]

The mentality behind such state terrorism is nicely captured by US military boot camp training chants like this one:

> Rape the town and kill the people.
> That's the thing we love to do.
> Throw some napalm on the schoolhouse.
> Watch the kiddies scream and shout.
> Rape the town and kill the people.
> That's the thing we love to do.[22]

Terrorism kills, mutilates, and wrongs innocent people. Concomitant slaughter also kills, mutilates, and wrongs innocent people. But sometimes there are moral dilemmas, and one has to face the possibility that in certain extreme circumstances, terrorist acts or acts of concomitant slaughter can be justified. Nevertheless, the justification must follow very strict standards. As regards the proportionality requirement, it is not sufficient, either in the case of terrorism or in the case of concomitant slaughter, to show that the harm inflicted upon innocent people within the theatre and time frame of the concrete war or conflict is not disproportionate in light of the military advantage. In addition, account has to be taken of the possibility that relaxed standards for the protection of innocents in one conflict might spill over to conflicts elsewhere and to future conflicts. A consideration of this will show that most, but not all, actual terrorism and concomitant slaughter are unjustified. The hypocrisy that goes into all the exaggerations and pejoratives when talking about the former but suddenly finds the sweetest and most soothing euphemisms for the latter is also unjustified.

## NOTES

1. For a detailed discussion of these issues, see Uwe Steinhoff, *On the ethics of war and terrorism* (Oxford: Oxford University Press, 2007), chapter 4.
2. Colm McKeogh, 'Civilian immunity in war: From Augustine to Vattel', in Igor Primoratz (ed.), *Civilian immunity in war* (Oxford: Oxford University Press, 2007), 66.
3. Lawrence A. Alexander, 'Self-defense and the killing of noncombatants: A reply to Fullinwider', in Charles Beitz et al. (eds.), *International ethics: A philosophy & public affairs reader* (Princeton, NJ: Princeton University Press, 1990), 99f.

4. See for instance David Carroll Cochran, 'War-pacifism', *Social Theory and Practice*, 22/1 (1996), 169.
5. Some (few) people actually deny this; and it seems some domestic jurisdictions do so too. German jurisdiction does not. In fact, it uses a wide definition of attack: the woman is under attack as long as she is deprived of her freedom by the kidnapper, and not only in the moment he grabbed her and chained her. In any case, whether one accepts a wide or a narrow definition of attack, German law is definitely to be commended for not asking the woman to wait until the kidnapper awakes in order to then fight him without any prospects of success. To do otherwise is not only inhumane, it seems absurd.
6. George I. Mavrodes, 'Conventions and the morality of war', in Beitz et al. (eds.), *International ethics*, 75–89.
7. Michael Green, 'War, innocence, and theories of sovereignty', *Social Theory and Practice*, 18/1 (1992), 57.
8. This is a question posed by Richard Norman, *Ethics, killing and war* (Cambridge: Cambridge University Press 1995), 164f.
9. Mavrodes, 'Conventions and the morality of war', 82f.
10. Cf. Nancy Davis, 'The doctrine of double effect: Problems of interpretation', *Pacific Philosophical Quarterly*, 65/1 (1984), 108.
11. Among many, see in particular Davis, 'The doctrine of double effect'; Frances M. Kamm, 'Failures of just war theory: Terror, harm, and justice', *Ethics*, 114/4 (2004), 650–92; Alasdair McIntyre, 'Doing away with double effect', *Ethics*, 111/2 (2001), 219–55; Steinhoff, *On the ethics of war and terrorism*, 33–52; and Judith Jarvis Thomson, 'Self-defense', *Philosophy & Public Affairs*, 20/2 (1991), 290–6.
12. Tony Coady, *Morality and political violence* (Cambridge: Cambridge University Press, 2008), 139.
13. Stephen Nathanson, 'Prerequisites for morally credible condemnations of terrorism', in William Crotty (ed.), *The politics of terror: The U.S. response to 9/11* (Boston: Northeastern University Press, 2004), 31, claims: 'Terrorist actions fail to be morally justified because *intentional* targeting of civilians is the most obvious form of failure with the "bend over backward" rule [which requires one to "bend over backward" to save civilians].' As my example shows, this is simply wrong.
14. I have heard this charge made quite often at terrorism and counterterrorism conferences—and of course it is made on the Web. That terrorists at least try to kill as many members as possible of certain ethnic groups is also implicit in the genocide charge—made by certain academics—to be discussed below.
15. Asa Kasher and Amos Yadlin, 'Military ethics of fighting terror: An Israeli perspective', *Journal of Military Ethics*, 4/1 (2005), 6.
16. Michael Walzer makes the same move. He claims that terrorists 'devalue not only the individuals they kill but also the group to which the individuals belong. They signal a political intention to destroy or remove or radically subordinate these people individually and this "people" collectively.' See Michael Walzer, 'Terrorism and just war', *Philosophia*, 34/1 (2006), 5. Yet, while he considers the bombing of German civilians in the Second World War as an instance of terrorism, he never suspects Churchill and Bomber Command or the pilots of the bombers of not wanting to accommodate the Germans or of radically

devaluing them, and does not seem to think that the Germans felt that Churchill or the bomber pilots were unwilling to accommodate them. Although Walzer usually makes sweeping statements about terrorism, he has on one occasion acknowledged that he 'should have written with more qualifiers'. See his 'Response to Jeff McMahan', *Philosophia*, 34/1 (2006), 19. Yet, after perfunctorily acknowledging this, he goes on to write without them anyway. He calls this strategy 'political' (Ibid., 20f.). I call it propagandistic. (Incidentally, when he mentions that the victims of terrorism experience terrorism as devaluation, he might perhaps, for a change, want to inquire how concomitant slaughter is experienced by its victims.) A note aside: An anonymous referee claimed that Walzer allows terrorist tactics only against threats of Nazi-like proportions. However, even if that were true, it would not undermine the point I was just making. Moreover, it is not true. See on this Steinhoff, *On the ethics of war and terrorism*, 132f.

17. Michael Neumann, 'Terror and expected collateral damage: the case for moral equivalence', http://www.law.ox.ac.uk./jurisprudence/colloquium/neumann.pdf, 3.
18. Ibid., 4f.
19. Ibid., 5.
20. Quoted from Milan Rai, *War plan Iraq: Ten reasons against war on Iraq* (London: Verso, 2002), 32.
21. Quoted from Beau Grosscup, *Strategic terror: The politics and ethics of aerial bombardment* (London: Zed Books, 2006), 112. Similar descriptions would aptly capture Israel's June 1982 bombing of Beirut and its 2008–9 bombing and invasion of the Gaza Strip.
22. Quoted from Ibid., 120.

# 21

## The Status and Protections of Prisoners of War and Detainees

*Sibylle Scheipers*

Prisoners of war (POWs) and their protections are a central part of the law of armed conflict, in particular since its legal codification began at the end of the nineteenth century. Yet the legal efforts to grant POWs protections are far from being a sweeping success story. One of the reasons for this is that protections for POWs are as much about protecting specific individuals—members of regular armed forces and militias—as they are about excluding others such as irregular fighters, guerrillas, and rebels. The question of who actually qualifies for the privileges and protections of POW status and how individuals who do not qualify should be treated lies at the heart of many shortfalls in the prisoner regime.

Legal provisions about the status and the treatment of POWs are geared towards protecting not only POWs themselves but also two other groups. First, they are intended to protect regular soldiers who have not (yet) been captured. By excluding irregular fighters from the privileges of POW status, the legal POW regime, it is often argued, aims at discouraging these irregular fighters from participating in armed conflict. Thus, it aims to eliminate a challenge that regular armies usually find very difficult to deal with: guerrilla wars and insurgencies. Secondly, the POW regime also indirectly aims to protect civilians. The pre-1977 regime in particular stipulates that only members of regular armed forces or militias who clearly distinguish themselves from civilians and who comply with the law of armed conflict qualify for POW status. Irregular fighters, who often blend in with the civilian population, by contrast, are excluded from the protections of POW status. Although it is questionable whether the exclusion of irregular fighters from the privileges of POW status has actually ever enhanced the protection of civilians, this argument is often used to justify this exclusion.[1] In addition, it is important to note that this argument only gained greater purchase after the Second World War, when the protection of civilians became the centrepiece of the law of armed conflict, whereas before the protection of combatants was the main concern.[2]

The intellectual history of the concept of prisoners of war reflects or, rather, *is* a debate over legitimate forms of warfare in the Western world.[3] It reached a critical juncture during the Revolutionary and Napoleonic Wars (1792–1815). At all times, the treatment of prisoners in war was linked to perceptions about the legitimacy of the captured fighter. Atrocities were often committed against captured rebels and guerrillas, and also against prisoners in wars, such as the crusades, which involved perceived religious or cultural differences. The French Revolutionary and Napoleonic Wars did not change this: the flipside of protections for prisoners in war was still the exclusion of some 'other'. However, the foundations of this exclusionary mechanism were narrowed down to two competing options: exclusion on the basis of national identity or exclusion on the basis of irregularity. These two options have continued to structure the debate over privileges and protections for prisoners in war during the subsequent two centuries. Moreover, the intellectual changes which occurred during the French Revolutionary and Napoleonic Wars also led to the breakdown of established practices regarding prisoners, such as exchange cartels, release on parole, and impressment into the captor's armed forces. As options to exchange, release or absorb captives were no longer viable, it became necessary to hold prisoners for longer periods of time. The breakdown of established practices led to the need to regulate long-term captivity. This had a vital impact on efforts to codify the constraints and rules applying to the treatment of prisoners in war, which began in the second half of the nineteenth century.

## BEFORE THE FRENCH REVOLUTIONARY AND NAPOLEONIC WARS

Contrary to the common misconception that war was a lawless and unrestrained enterprise before the explicit codification of the Lieber Code (1863) and the Hague Rules (1899 and 1907), war has always been subject to certain rules and constraints. These rules also applied to the issue of prisoners. The rules and customs of war in early classical Greece, for instance, envisaged that prisoners were offered for ransom to the opponent after the battle.[4] However, this rule apparently did not apply to all prisoners. There seemed to be an assumption that prisoners in wars between Greeks and non-Greeks were not necessarily protected by it.[5] Others caution that the distinction between Greek and non-Greek captives was not that clear-cut and that the actual treatment depended largely on the political and strategic purposes of the captor.[6]

War in medieval Europe was characterized by an evolving quasi-legal code of conduct restraining violence in warfare. This development was tied to the emergence of a warrior elite. The chivalric code stipulated that captured knights should be neither massacred nor enslaved. Rather, they were to be released for ransom.[7] However, these constraints applied neither to peasants nor to non-Christian prisoners. They were more likely to be executed or, in the case of non-Christian prisoners, enslaved.[8]

Early modern Europe was a period of transition regarding rules and constraints on warfare. On the one hand, massive changes in the structure of European societies led to the dissolution of the chivalric code. On the other hand, in the sixteenth and seventeenth centuries, states increasingly asserted control over their armed forces, which resulted in a trend towards greater restraint in warfare.[9] Massacres of prisoners were rare in early modern European wars. If they happened they usually involved some element of religious or ethnic difference between the opponents.[10] Sieges were also characterized by a high degree of violence, and the chances of survival for the inhabitants of a captured town were relatively low, in particular if their resistance prior to capture had been fierce. Prominent examples in this respect were the sack of Magdeburg in 1631 during the Thirty Years War and the sieges of Wexford and Drogheda in 1649 during the British Civil Wars. The treatment of prisoners in siege warfare seems to be one of the areas in the history of war that is characterized by continuity rather than change. The trend continued in the nineteenth century with the siege of Saragossa (1809) during the Peninsular War, and manifested itself even in the sieges of the First World War, for instance, in the siege of Liège in 1914. In the twenty-first century, siege warfare continues to be more brutal than other forms of military confrontations, with the siege of Fallujah in 2004 as the most vivid example.

Early modern Europe also saw the emergence of the distinction between legitimate combatants and illegitimate fighters. Rebels belonged to the latter category. In the sixteenth century, the Spanish legal thinker Baltasar Ayala argued that rebels were to be denied the right to make war and could not enjoy the protections of the laws of war if captured.[11] It should come as no surprise that this first mention of the difference between rebels and 'regular' fighters coincides with the emergence of the European state system. At the same time, earlier medieval distinctions overlapped with newly emerging ones, as noble rebels stood a greater chance of being recognized as legitimate belligerents and of being treated well upon their capture than revolting peasants.[12]

Apart from the exceptional cases of siege warfare and armed rebellion, the prisoner regime in early modern Europe envisaged three options for the treatment of captured members of the enemy armed forces: release for ransom, release on parole, and impressment into the captor's armed forces. While the latter was a common fate for ordinary soldiers, release for ransom and release on parole applied mainly to captured officers. Release on parole meant that the captive gave his word of honour not to return to the battle after he had been released to his home country. This practice reflects the social inequalities between officers and soldiers: only a gentleman's word could be trusted. Before the seventeenth century, the payment of ransom was arranged on an individual basis, which excluded ordinary soldiers since they were unlikely to muster the required resources to pay the ransom. During the seventeenth century, the cartel system developed. Ransom was no longer paid on an individual basis; rather, states now organized prisoner exchanges on a bilateral basis. Prisoners were exchanged either man-by-man or for ransom. Ordinary soldiers profited from the emergence of exchange cartels because their chances of being exchanged increased insofar as the sending state had an interest in their return. Social differences between soldiers and officers continued to manifest themselves in the cartel system, though, to the extent that officers were more 'expensive' than soldiers.[13] The cartel system survived into the second half of the nineteenth century and even the Lieber Code of 1863, which is often perceived as the first step in the legal codification of the law of armed conflict, still devotes considerable attention to exchange cartels (articles 105–110).[14] Yet the cartel system's slow death had already begun at the end of the eighteenth century with the French Revolutionary Wars, and despite several attempts to revive it, it was almost obsolete at the time of Lieber's writings.

## THE FRENCH REVOLUTIONARY AND NAPOLEONIC WARS

On 26 May 1794, the French National Convention passed a decree stipulating that the French Revolutionary Army was prohibited from taking prisoners among the British and Hanoverian troops they encountered on the battlefield.[15] This 'no quarter' policy was later extended to the Hessian and to the Spanish armed forces. Bertrand Barère, member of the National Convention, was one of the driving forces behind the decree and justified its harsh measures by pointing out that Britain in particular was guilty of committing crimes against universal human rights and human liberty. It attacked the very ideals that the French Republic claimed to champion: 'Soldiers of freedom, Britain is guilty of all attacks against humanity and all crimes against the Republic. She assaults the law of peoples and threatens to annihilate freedom.'[16] According to the decree, British, Hanoverian, Hessian, and Spanish captives were to be shot as an 'example of vengeance of an outraged nation'.[17] The 'no quarter' policy was a crucial part of the efforts to indoctrinate the revolutionary army and to nationalize war. The Manichean and annihilationist rhetoric evolved paradoxically from the ideational background of pacifism that had first been endorsed by the French revolutionaries. In this perspective, revolutionary war was a defensive war against the enemies of peace. In addition, the British constitutional tradition seemed paradoxically similar to what the French revolutionaries aspired to. The British 'revolutionary heritage made their enmity look like betrayal'.[18]

However, the decree was never implemented on the battlefield. Officers and soldiers preferred to stick to the traditional rules and constraints of the *ancien régime*, which formed an important part of their professional identity. The exigencies of the battlefield soon forced the French army, in particular the officer corps, to turn away from revolutionary principles and practices and to revert back to professional standards.[19] That nationalist ideologies had not taken hold among the French armed forces manifested itself in the fact that officers often negotiated bilateral arrangements with their opponents aiming at a better treatment of prisoners.[20] In addition, French generals in particular tried to keep as much control over the prisoner issue as possible.[21]

Despite the military's attempts at upholding their professional standards and at treating prisoners accordingly, nationalization left its mark on the issue of prisoners. It undermined or even eliminated the three core practices that had been the pivot of the pre-revolutionary prisoner regime in Europe: exchange cartels, release on parole, and impressment into the captor's armed forces. Regarding exchange cartels, policymakers in Paris found it unacceptable to exchange captured soldiers for money. On 19 September 1792, the National Convention passed a decree stipulating that soldiers could only be exchanged man-for-man and officer-for-officer, but not for money.[22] This decree reflects that the perception of soldiers had shifted from being a 'neutral' resource in the *ancien régime* to their being regarded as members of their own polities. Thus the value of the national soldier could no longer be expressed in monetary terms. The practical problem with this shift was that during the French Revolutionary and Napoleonic Wars there were many more French soldiers in British or Spanish captivity than vice versa. This forced the parties to the conflict to negotiate 'unequal' exchange rates. The unofficial exchange rate between Britain and France in the 1790s was three Frenchmen for one British soldier, but all attempts at formalizing this arrangement failed.

Release on parole was another practice that fell victim to the Jacobin phase of the French Revolution. On 22 June 1793, the National Convention passed a decree rejecting the release on parole for officers. French officers were encouraged to break their word of honour and to return to the fight upon their release. This rejection was based on two revolutionary principles: first, the perceived need to muster all available military resources, and, secondly, the fact that many Jacobins 'were deeply suspicious of "honour," viewing it as individualistic, aristocratic and threatening to republican virtue'.[23] Most officers would feel bound by their word of honour, but a substantial number violated their parole duties. This was sufficient to convince France's enemies, in particular Britain, that the French were actively undermining the prisoner regime. This sense of mistrust was a vital aspect in the final collapse of the *ancien régime* practices.

Finally, the common practice of inducing soldiers to swap sides and join the captor's armed forces was also prohibited by the National Convention decree of 25 May 1793.[24] As with the French view on exchange cartels, the idea was that soldiers who were fighting for 'their' nation and its cause ceased to be mere neutral 'manpower' that could be replaced by someone with similar qualifications. Arguably, Napoleon later replaced impressment with the absorption of large enemy armies into his forces, either by introducing conscription in areas over which he had assumed direct control or by forcing satellite states to raise armies for his wars.[25]

The collapse of the *ancien régime* practices of handling prisoners meant that prisoners had to be detained for longer periods. This presented all European states with a huge challenge. They often lacked the resources and infrastructure to run prison camps. This was the main reason why all major parties to the Napoleonic Wars tried to revert back to the old practices, in particular exchange cartels, throughout the conflict despite the fact that they kept breaking down and that every breakdown increased the mistrust among the opponents regarding the issue of prisoners. Breakdowns of exchange cartels were frequently blamed on Napoleon, but it should not be ignored that the Revolutionary Wars had already undermined the existing system regarding prisoners to such an extent that it was difficult to rebuild mutual trust.[26] Hence, in the absence of options to release prisoners, all parties to the conflict were forced to detain them for longer periods. The challenge was particularly huge for Britain, since it held comparatively high numbers of French prisoners. Britain struggled to create a sufficient number of prison camps, but the conditions in many of the makeshift detention facilities remained bleak throughout the Napoleonic Wars. Among the facilities with the worst conditions and the highest death rates were the infamous camp in Dartmoor and the prison hulks.[27]

While the French Revolutionary and Napoleonic Wars implied huge changes for the prisoner regime as far as the release and exchange arrangements were concerned, there was also continuity regarding some aspects. Legal thinking in early modern Europe had already provided arguments for the exclusion of rebels and irregular fighters from the protections granted to regular prisoners and this trend continued and was reaffirmed during the Revolutionary and Napoleonic Wars.

Not surprisingly, the earliest manifestation of this was a classic intra-state conflict, namely the war in the Vendée between French republicans and French royalists (1793–6). The war consisted of a series of revolts, the first of which broke out in 1793 when inhabitants of the Vendée resisted being drafted into the French revolutionary army. It was subsequently crushed with extreme violence by the republicans. It is estimated that during the first revolt alone (1793–4) the republicans killed up to 250,000 armed and unarmed civilians.[28] Republican tactics were particularly brutal in the Vendée, and included atrocities against prisoners. The most infamous incidents are the drownings of Nantes (November 1793–January 1794) in which thousands of suspected royalists, especially members of the clergy, were drowned in the Loire. The Vendée and the atrocities committed there are a particularly interesting case, because they seem to be located at the intersection of the 'nationalist' and the 'professional' paradigm: the royalist rebels fit into the nationalist pattern of exclusion insofar as they fought against nationalist, republican France, and in particular against one of the main symbols and means of nationalization: conscription. On the other hand, they matched the professional pattern of exclusion, since they were *rebels* and used irregular tactics. The coincidence of these two paradigms in the case of the Vendée might go some way to explain the particular brutality of this conflict.

However, there were more clear-cut cases confirming that the professional paradigm of protections and exclusion regarding prisoners survived during the Revolutionary and Napoleonic Wars and even grew stronger. All campaigns in which irregular fighters played a role were characterized by high degrees of violence in general and by atrocities towards prisoners in particular: the Peninsular War (1808–14), the Tyrol rebellion (1809–10), and Napoleon's invasion of Russia (1812). The Peninsular War acquired a particular status among those campaigns. Spanish guerrilla fighters in the Peninsular War were treated substantially worse than their regular counterparts. Executions of guerrilla forces were common. It is important to note, however, that the reverse was true as well: the guerrilla fighters were notorious for their massacres of soldiers of Napoleon's army. French generals tended to reply in kind, which sometimes led to a retaliatory dynamic that threatened to spiral out of control and only stopped once both sides had killed all prisoners they had held.[29] However, atrocities were not uniformly committed against all captured guerrillas. Sometimes the Napoleonic forces showed leniency.[30] On the other hand, some of the guerrilla forces themselves underwent a maturation process over the course of the conflict and regularized their tactics and behaviour, which included better treatment for prisoners.

## THE NINETEENTH CENTURY

The nineteenth century is particularly important with respect to the emergence of the modern prisoner regime because it was a transitory period between the breakdown of the *ancien régime* principles and practices during the French Revolutionary and Napoleonic Wars and the beginning of the codification of the law of armed conflict at the end of the nineteenth century. If it was largely understood that the old prisoner regime was about to be eroded at the beginning of the nineteenth century, the wars that were to follow, in particular the American Civil War (1861–5) and the Franco-Prussian War (1870–1), had a huge influence on the creation of the new regime. This is not to say that the nineteenth century demarcated a sharp break regarding the status and the protections of prisoners in war. On the contrary, in many of the conflicts following the French Revolutionary and Napoleonic Wars ancient practices were revived, and sometimes in a rather successful way: the Crimean War (1853–6), for instance, was the last war with a functioning prisoner exchange cartel. A large number of prisoners were also exchanged in the American Civil War, although cartels broke down repeatedly. In general, though, there was one major trend in the treatment of prisoners: the move away from the nationalist paradigm and the strengthening of the professional paradigm.

The issue of prisoners in the American Civil War was complicated by the difficult legal situation of the conflict. Initially, the Union did not recognize the Confederacy as a belligerent party and referred to the conflict as 'the rebellion' rather than the 'civil war'.[31] So theoretically, all Southern fighters could have been treated as traitors and punished by death upon their capture. However, this did not happen. Instead, in July 1861, Union General George McClellan agreed with representatives of the Confederacy to treat Confederate prisoners as prisoners of war and vice versa.[32] The agreement also envisaged prisoner exchanges between the Union and the Confederacy. However, it only applied to regular Confederate troops, whereas Southern irregulars were excluded from the protections. In 1862, General-in-Chief of the Union forces Henry Halleck ordered that captured irregulars were to be shot without trial upon their capture. This order extended to civilians who helped the irregulars.[33] Halleck also asked the legal scholar Francis Lieber to write a legal assessment of the status and treatment of guerrillas, which the latter produced in 1862. That Lieber produced the memorandum on guerrillas before he wrote the famous 'Lieber Code' in 1863 indicates the extent to which legal codification of the rules and customs of war was in fact influenced by the problems posed by irregular fighters.

In his 1862 memorandum, Lieber argued that the *levée en masse*, that is, a militia force raised to defend against an invasion, was the only form of 'irregular' fighter that can claim POW status. All other irregulars, such as brigands, partisans and free-corps, spies, rebels, and conspirators, should not enjoy POW protections and should be punished by death.[34] According to Lieber, their illegitimacy was based on the facts that, first, they did not fight on behalf of a proper authority; secondly, they were characterized by indiscipline and ignorance about the laws of war; thirdly, they posed a treacherous threat to the regular occupying army; and fourthly, they undermined the protections for civilians.[35] The third and fourth aspects were obviously related to the fact that irregular fighters did not distinguish themselves from the civilian population. In short, for Lieber and many of his contemporaries, irregulars were the counter-image of the regular forces. Moreover, the harsh approach proposed by Lieber seems to have been implemented on the ground.[36]

Compared with the fate of irregular fighters, regular POWs on both sides were slightly better off, although the conditions in many POW camps were dreadful. The Confederate camp in Andersonville was particularly notorious for its appalling conditions and high death rates, but the situation in Union camps was not substantially better. While in the South it was mainly a lack of resources that led to poor conditions, the North soon decided to retaliate by cutting rations for the prisoners in its camps.[37] The creation of prisoner camps had become necessary after the exchange cartel had broken down repeatedly. These breakdowns of prisoner exchanges were frequently caused by the Confederacy, as they tried to retain Union officers in order to blackmail the Union into granting POW status to Southern irregulars.[38] The South also refused to recognize black Union troops and their white officers as POWs, which infuriated the North. Many black troops were massacred by the Confederate armed forces, most infamously during the Fort Pillow massacre on 12 April 1864 in Henning, Tennessee.

What the American Civil War shows is once again, therefore, the tension between the exclusion of prisoners from privileges and protections on the basis of the regular–irregular pattern (Union) versus exclusion rooted in nationalist ideologies (Confederacy). *Opinio juris*, in the form of Lieber's early writings on the treatment of guerrillas, came down on the side of the former, and this trend would be reinforced over the following decades. However, there is a second trend that manifested itself during the American Civil War: once prisoners were held in prisoner camps for longer periods, the conditions of their captivity tended to become a central element in the war propaganda of their home states.[39] This trend builds upon the increased sense of national cohesion and belonging. It may be seen as the way in which nationalism continued to influence the issue of prisoners of war even after the legally codified prisoner regime had largely turned away from national allegiances as a factor in the status and treatment of prisoners.

The Franco-Prussian War (1870–1) reaffirmed the move towards making prisoners' protections and privileges dependent on whether they were regular or irregular fighters, at least as far as political rhetoric was concerned. After the defeat of the French army at Sedan on 1 September 1870, the French government decided to continue the fight against the German invasion with whatever forces it had left, including all troops that did not formally belong to the regular French army plus the infamous '*francs-tireurs*'. They were advised to wage a guerrilla campaign against the occupying German army by harassing the German forces and attacking their lines of communication rather than confronting them in open battle.[40] Although these irregular attacks did not inflict huge damage on the German forces and could not avoid France's eventual defeat, they forced the Germans to devote considerable resources to the protection of the rear areas.

German rhetoric towards the French *francs-tireurs* was fierce: according to Bismarck, they were murderers rather than soldiers.[41] They were to be shot or hanged if captured. The legal basis for this seems to be a Prussian decree of 21 July 1866, according to which civilian snipers were to be executed.[42] This approach was reiterated in an order issued on 22 August 1870 by the German high command.[43] After French criticism and insistence that the *francs-tireurs* were to be treated as legitimate combatants, Bismarck and General Albrecht von Roon issued a decree on 27 August 1870 stipulating that *francs-tireurs* should be sentenced to a minimum of ten years of forced labour if captured.[44] However, it is not clear to what extent these rules and orders were followed by troops on the ground. Executions of *francs-tireurs* and reprisals against the inhabitants of nearby villages did occur.[45] Whether this policy was implemented in a systematic way remains unclear, though. It seems that *francs-tireurs* who were captured and not executed were usually treated in the same way as regular prisoners of war. There is no evidence that they were formally tried for war crimes and sentenced to forced labour, as the 27 August 1870 decree envisaged.[46] Yet the fierce German rhetoric did not fail to leave an impression on the French government, which, by January 1871, succeeded in integrating the *francs-tireurs* into the French army.[47]

## LEGAL CODIFICATION

Both the American Civil War and the Franco-Prussian War resulted in legal reasoning and drafting—the Lieber Code and the Brussels Declaration. The Brussels Declaration was the outcome of a conference held in Brussels in 1874, which was intended to address the issues of occupation and the rights of resistance movements in occupied territory that had proven so difficult during the Franco-Prussian War.[48] In both the Lieber Code and the Brussels Declaration, the question of who is a legitimate belligerent and thus can claim the legal privileges of prisoner of war status were central to the emerging legal texts. In fact, the modern legal concept of 'prisoner of war' only evolved in demarcation against the irregular fighter.[49] The Brussels conference did not achieve a legally binding document, just a declaration. This showed that the issue of irregular fighters and their resistance to occupation was a politically highly divisive one: a law that was tough on resistance fighters would privilege great powers such as Germany and Russia and facilitate conquest. Lesser states such as Belgium and the Netherlands, supported by France and Britain, argued that they had to rely on militias and volunteer corps for the defence of their borders.[50]

Apart from this ideological conflict tied to a clash of national interests, the Lieber Code and the Brussels project partly also emerged from the necessity to create new rules after wars in the nineteenth century had repeatedly shown that the old practices of exchange cartels, parole, and impressment into the captor's armed forces had broken down for good. Long-term captivity of prisoners of war had to be regulated; questions of maintenance, treatment standards, labour, and release had to be addressed. Both the Lieber Code (article 49) and the Brussels declaration (articles 23–34) attempted to create standards in these areas.

More important for the further development of the modern law of armed conflict, however, was the explicit exclusion of irregular fighters (with the exception of militias and volunteer corps) from recognition as legitimate belligerents and thus as prisoners of war contained in the Lieber Code (articles 82–85) and the Brussels declaration (articles 9–11). The Brussels declaration laid the groundwork for what was to become the applicable law for the next century: legitimate belligerents were regular armies plus militias and volunteer corps provided they fulfilled four criteria:

1. That they be commanded by a person responsible for his subordinates;
2. That they have a fixed distinctive emblem recognizable at a distance;
3. That they carry arms openly; and
4. That they conduct their operations in accordance with the laws and customs of war.[51]

These criteria were reiterated in the 1907 Hague Rules on the Laws and Customs of War on Land, thus becoming internationally binding law.[52] Subsequent to the Hague Rules and the First World War, it seemed as if prisoners of war had all of a sudden developed into the lawmakers' most favoured war victim.[53] The 1929 Geneva Convention reiterated many of the protections that had already been included in the Hague Rules and added some new ones, such as the prohibition of reprisals against POWs. The 1949 Geneva Convention III on prisoners is the most comprehensive of the four Geneva Conventions and adds further detail to the standards of their treatment. Yet while these repeated efforts aimed at enhancing the protections of POWs, they did not change the definition of their status: the requirements for recognition as legitimate belligerents and the four criteria remained literally unchanged. Hence, the exclusion of irregular fighters became a pivot of the codified law of armed conflict that remained unchallenged for a long time. The law was modelled on and promoted the template of the modern regular army, and even militias and voluntary corps had to resemble this template as closely as possible regarding their organization, appearance, and tactics. Thus, the legal codification of rules pertaining to prisoners and detainees was as much about ordering the battlefield as it was about providing protections for captured combatants.

If anything had changed regarding the treatment of irregular and thus unprivileged combatants with the codification of the law, it was the introduction of minimum standards for their treatment in order to prevent mass executions and atrocities. Lawmakers were aware of the fact that the exclusion of irregular fighters had frequently led to massacres and felt compelled to provide at least minimum standards of humane treatment. The Martens Clause included in the Hague Rules was initially intended to provide residual humanitarian protections for the civilian population in occupied territories, especially armed resisters among them.[54] Common article 3 of the Geneva Convention fulfilled a similar function, and it also extended these minimal protections towards non-international armed conflict.

A real softening of the exclusionary mechanism along the regular–irregular cleavage line and a slight swing back towards the nationalism paradigm only occurred with the 1977 Additional Protocols. They emerged from the historical context of decolonization. The status and the treatment of prisoners in colonial wars and wars of national liberation had been precarious for a long time, but only the shift of power towards the legitimacy of the cause of national liberation movements made the creation of the Additional Protocols possible.[55]

Colonial warfare had always been a curious case, because here the older, less specific mechanism of exclusion along cultural and ethnic lines that often regarded the native inhabitants as 'uncivilized' coincided with the regular–irregular cleavage line. In fact, the two aspects often seemed to refer to each other in that native fighters were regarded as 'uncivilized' *because* their military organization and their way of fighting did not resemble regular armies.[56] Later, in the wars of decolonization the question of the treatment of prisoners was often entangled with the perceived legitimacy of their cause. For instance, in the 1950s and 1960s in Algeria the French army preferred to label the conflict as a 'domestic affair' rather than a war.[57] This meant that the Geneva Conventions did not apply and that the Algerian fighters would not be treated as prisoners of war. It followed quite logically from the legal rules that officially granting the Algerian fighters prisoner of war status would have amounted to recognizing them as legitimate belligerents. In this case, as in many other colonial wars and wars of decolonization, political and strategic considerations kept the conflict outside the remit of the law of armed conflict. Instead, these conflicts tended to be regulated by ever more extensive and elastic emergency laws.

Additional Protocol I and its lowering of the requirements for POW status were essentially a move back towards the nationalist cleavage line. Article 43 dropped the four criteria listed in the Hague Rules and the Geneva Conventions and replaced them with the requirement that combatants have to carry their arms openly during each military engagement and while they prepare to launch an attack. This move acknowledges the fact that in wars of decolonization, insurgents often cannot comply with the Geneva rules even if they wish to do so.[58] Their legitimacy, it seems, derives from the fact that their cause is, first, justified, and second, tends to put them into a situation that makes it difficult for them to resemble regular armed forces. It is important to keep in mind, however, that this line of thinking was not universally shared and that Additional Protocol I has not been universally ratified.


# CONCLUSION

The most recent developments regarding the question of who qualifies for POW status appear to indicate that the pendulum is currently swinging back towards the regular–irregular cleavage line. Despite all the criticism of the fundamentalist objectives and motivations of the irregular fighters captured in Iraq and Afghanistan, the main charge levelled against them concerns their irregular outlook and tactics. Indeed, some commentators have even gone as far as to criticize their irregular identity by equating it with barbarism and uncivilized behaviour.[59] This seems to indicate a movement back towards the arguments that surrounded colonial warfare.

The preceding sections have highlighted two aspects that should make us wary of such tendencies: first, that the boundaries and cleavage lines that exclude captives from POW status are man-made and neither 'objective' nor 'natural'; and second, that the way in which these boundaries are drawn largely reflects the distribution of social and political power at a particular point in time. Hence, chivalric privileges in the middle ages were a function of the power of the noble warrior elite over the peasants. Similarly, privileging regular armies over national resistance movements during occupations reflected the preponderance of great powers in nineteenth-century Europe. Finally, the exclusion of internal wars from the remit of the law of armed conflict was one way in which European dominance over the colonies manifested itself. Thus, being aware of the fact that many of the protections provided by the law of armed conflict emerged from such power struggles should guard against naively accepting that certain standards of treatment are justified because they are prescribed by the law. This is not to say that the law is necessarily meaningless or even illegitimate because it is infused with power political aspects. But it is important to consider the historical development that led to the exclusion of irregular fighters from the protections of POW status in order to assess what standards for the treatment of 'unlawful combatants' in current operations are justified and desirable. Admittedly, the argument that irregular fighters tend to put civilians at risk is to a certain extent persuasive. Yet the historical perspective indicates that the exclusion of irregulars has preceded the law of armed conflict's concern for civilians, and that repressive measures against irregulars have rarely actually enhanced the protection of civilians from the effects of war.

## NOTES

1. For example, John C. Yoo and James C. Ho 'The status of terrorists', University of California Berkeley, *Boalt Working Papers in Public Law*, 25 (2003), 14.
2. Cf. Amanda Alexander, 'The genesis of the civilian', *Leiden Journal of International Law*, 20/2 (2007), 359–76.
3. It was only with the 1977 Additional Protocols that this debate opened up to the non-Western world.
4. Josiah Ober, 'Classical Greek times', in Michael Howard, George J. Andreopoulos, and Mark R. Shulman (eds.), *The laws of war: Constraints on warfare in the Western world* (New Haven, CT: Yale University Press, 1994), 13.
5. Ibid.
6. Raoul Lonis, '*La guerre en Grèce. Quinze années de récherche, 1968–1983*', *Revue des études grecques*, 98/2 (1985), 366f.
7. Maurice Keen, *Chivalry* (New Haven, CT: Yale University Press, 1984), 221. Keen notes that there were exceptions, though, for instance, the Swiss were notorious for giving no quarter.
8. Robert C. Stacey, 'The age of chivalry', in Howard, Andreopoulos, and Shulman (eds.), *The laws of war*, 30.
9. Geoffrey Parker, *Success is never final: Empire, war, and faith in early modern Europe* (New York: Basic Books, 2002), 161.
10. Peter Wilson, 'Prisoners in early modern European warfare', in Sibylle Scheipers (ed.), *Prisoners in war* (Oxford: Oxford University Press, 2010), 39–56.
11. Parker, *Success is never final*, 149.
12. Wilson, 'Prisoners in early modern European warfare'.
13. Daniel Hohrath, '"*In Cartellen wird der Werth eines Gefangenen bestimmet.*" *Kriegsgefangenschaft als Teil der Kriegspraxis des Ancien Régime*', in Rüdiger Overmans (ed.), *In der Hand des Feindes: Kriegsgefangenschaft von der Antike bis zum Zweiten Weltkrieg* (Köln: Böhlau Verlag), 141–70.
14. Richard Shelly Hartigan (ed.), *Lieber's Code and the law of war* (New York: Legal Classics Library, 1995).
15. Erich Pelzer, '"*Il ne sera fait aucun prisonnier anglais ou hanovrien*": Zur Problematik der Kriegsgefangenen während der Revolutions- und Empirekriege (1792–1815)', in Rüdiger Overmans (ed.), *In der Hand des Feindes: Kriegsgefangenschaft von der Antike bis zum Zweiten Weltkrieg* (Köln: Böhlau Verlag), 189.
16. Quoted in Pelzer, '*Il ne sera fait aucun prisonnier anglais ou hanovrien*', 189.
17. Quoted in Gunther Rothenberg, 'The age of Napoleon', in Howard, Andreopoulos, and Shulman (eds.), *The laws of war*, 88.
18. David A. Bell, *The first total war: Napoleon's Europe and the birth of modern warfare* (London: Bloomsbury, 2007), 143.

19. Ibid., 88–9.
20. Ibid., 89.
21. Pelzer, '*Il ne sera fait aucun prisonnier anglais ou hanovrien*', 205.
22. Ibid., 204.
23. Gavin Daly, 'Napoleon's lost legions: French prisoners of war in Britain, 1803–1814', *History*, 89/295 (2004), 371.
24. Pelzer, '*Il ne sera fait aucun prisonnier anglais ou hanovrien*', 204.
25. Stuart Joseph Woolf, *Napoleon's integration of Europe* (London: Routledge, 1991), 162–4.
26. Daly, 'Napoleon's lost legions', 369, 373.
27. Ibid., 373ff.
28. Rothenberg, 'The age of Napoleon', 88.
29. René Chartrand, *Spanish guerrillas in the Peninsular War*, 1808–14 (Oxford: Osprey, 2004), 45–6.
30. Walter Laqueur, *Guerrilla warfare: A historical and critical study* (London: Transaction Publishers, 1998), 35ff.
31. In fact, the Union never explicitly recognized Confederate belligerency. However, the Supreme Court ruled in 1863 in the Prize Cases that the conflict between the Union and the Confederacy was a war. Stephen C. Neff, *War and the law of nations: A general history* (Cambridge: Cambridge University Press, 2005), 259.
32. Reid Mitchell, '"Our prison system, supposing we had any": The Confederate and Union prison systems', in Stig Förster and Jörg Nagler (eds.), *On the road to total war: The American Civil War and the German wars of unification* (Cambridge: Cambridge University Press, 1997), 567.
33. Michael Fellman, 'At the nihilist edge: Reflections on guerrilla warfare during the American Civil War', in Förster and Nagler (eds.), *On the road to total war*, 524.
34. Francis Lieber, *Guerilla parties considered with reference to the laws and usages of war* (New York: Department of War, 1862), 10ff.
35. Ibid.
36. Fellman, 'At the nihilist edge', 524ff.
37. Mitchell, 'Our prison system', 566f.
38. Ibid., 574.
39. Ibid., 566.
40. Michael Howard, *The Franco-Prussian War: The German invasion of France* (London: Methuen, 1981), 249.
41. Ibid., 251.
42. Isabel Hull, *Absolute destruction: Military culture and the practices of war in imperial Germany* (Ithaca, NY: Cornell University Press, 2005), 118.
43. Katja Mitze, '"Seit der babylonischen Gefangenschaft hat die Welt nichts derart erlebt": Französische Kriegsgefangene und Franctireurs im Deutsch-Französischen Krieg 1870/71', in Overmans (ed.), *In der Hand des Feindes*, 238.
44. Ibid., 239.
45. See, for instance, Mark R. Stoneman, 'The Bavarian army and French civilians during the war of 1870–1871: A cultural interpretation', *War in History*, 8/3 (2001), 271–93.

46. Mitze, '*Seit der babylonischen Gefangenschaft hat die Welt nichts derart erlebt*'; Manfred Botzenhart, 'French prisoners of war in Germany, 1870–71', in Förster and Nagler (eds.), *On the road to total war*, 588.
47. Ibid., 241.
48. Karma Nabulsi, *Traditions of war: Occupation, resistance, and the law* (Oxford: Oxford University Press, 1999), 5f.
49. Stefan Oeter, '*Die Entwicklung des Kriegsgefangenenrechts*', in Rüdiger Overmans (ed.), *In der Hand des Feindes*, 48.
50. Nabulsi, *Traditions of war*, 6.
51. 'Project of an international declaration concerning the laws and customs of war, 27 August 1874', 1 (Supp.) *American Journal of International Law*, 96 (1907).
52. *1907 Hague Convention IV respecting the laws and customs of war on land, annex to the convention: Regulations respecting the laws and customs of war on land*, article 1.
53. Geoffrey Best, *War and law since 1945* (Oxford: Clarendon Press, 1994), 135.
54. Theodor Merom, 'The Martens clause, principles of humanity, and dictates of public conscience', *American Journal of International Law*, 94/1 (2000), 79.
55. Best, *War and law since 1945*, 343ff.
56. Gerrit W. Gong, *The standard of 'civilisation' in international society* (Oxford: Clarendon, 1984), 15ff.
57. Raphaëlle Branche, 'The French in Algeria: Can there be prisoners of war in a "domestic" operation?', in Sibylle Scheipers (ed.), *Prisoners in war*, 173–86.
58. Best, *War and law since 1945*, 334.
59. Cf. Yoo and Ho, 'The status of terrorists', 10.

# 22

## The Challenge of the Child Soldier

*Guy S. Goodwin-Gill*

### BACKGROUND

In 1994, Ilene Cohn and I published *Child soldiers*, a study commissioned by the Swedish and Icelandic national Red Cross Societies and published under the auspices of the Institut Henry Dunant in Geneva.[1] The initiative for the study came from a conference, 'Children of War', which had been held in Stockholm in 1991. Here, a strong consensus had emerged that existing standards were inadequate and that the minimum age for recruitment into the armed forces and for participation in armed conflict should be an unconditional 18, and that the voluntary involvement of children under that age should not be permitted.

Although this particular initiative focused on the measures and means that might ensure the non-participation of children in armed conflict, the overall picture is clearly much bigger.[2] On the one hand stands what is *done by others* to children, which includes their forcible recruitment (whether into the ranks of national forces or of non-state armed groups), their 'induction' into the use of force, the steps taken to secure obedience, their direct participation in hostilities, their experience of combat and injury, and their treatment when captured. On the other hand, there are the things that children *do to others*, when provided with weapons and the opportunity and encouragement to use them. Criminal penalties are readily conceivable as a means to punish and deter those who recruit and use children, but they are not evidently so well suited for application to children alleged to have committed war crimes or other atrocities, and whose situation overall may place them rather in the category of victim.

In and among these contrasting aspects of the child soldier experience can be found a myriad other examples of abuse and deprivation—circumstances which allow the exploitation of children by reason of their vulnerability, and which add to the sum denial of childhood as a unique opportunity for growth and development, idealized though that often is. This chapter can only touch the surface, and its purpose is rather to identify present and emerging legal issues as opposed to the extensive non-legal dimensions to the phenomenon, to see just how far along the road we have come, and perhaps to see how far we have yet to go.[3]

The 1990s witnessed a plethora of initiatives, institutional and other, around the children and war issue. In 1996, Graça Machel published her report for the United Nations on the impact of armed conflict on children,[4] which led in turn to the establishment of the Office of the Special Representative of the Secretary-General for Children and Armed Conflict.[5] This contributed to collective efforts by United Nations Children's Fund (UNICEF), other UN agencies, and non-governmental organizations (NGOs) in the promotion of programmes and initiatives intended to deal with the various dimensions of children in armed conflict,[6] and to the now regular attention to the subject by the Security Council and the General Assembly.[7]

During the same period, the International Labour Organization (ILO)'s 1999 Convention on the Worst Forms of Child Labour identified 'forced or compulsory recruitment of children for use in armed conflict' as one such form.[8] The initiative started by national Red Cross societies also bore fruit. NGOs joined forces and states accepted the need in 2000 for two additional protocols to the 1989 Convention on the Rights of the Child: one on child prostitution and pornography, and the other on the involvement of children in armed conflict.[9]

## THE CHILD DEFINED AND PROTECTED

Who then is a child? According to article 1 of the Convention on the Rights of the Child, repeated in the 1999 ILO Convention, a child is any person under the age of 18, but the approach to the definition and description of childhood for international treaty purposes has varied over time and context. Efforts to protect children from the effect of armed conflict and from recruitment and participation have a long history, and being a 'protected person' within the scheme of international humanitarian law is particularly important. For example, protected persons such as civilians are not to be made the object of attack (article 52, Additional Protocol I),[10] and children are also entitled to 'special protection'. But just as a civilian who takes up arms and engages in hostilities loses his or her protected status, so too does the child; the child, however, does not lose that special protection which is due to all children.

The relevant provisions of the Fourth Geneva Convention mostly deal with children under 15. For example, article 23 requires free passage for 'essential foodstuffs, clothing and tonics' intended for such children; article 89 requires that they be given additional food, in proportion to their physiological needs; and article 70 of Additional Protocol I calls for priority to be given to children, among others, in the distribution of humanitarian aid. The parties to the conflict must take the 'necessary measures' to ensure that orphaned or separated children under 15 are 'not left to their own resources'; they should also facilitate their reception in a neutral country for the duration of the conflict, and endeavour to arrange for such children to be identified by the wearing of identity discs or other means (article 24; see also, article 50). As 'protected persons', they should benefit from any preferential treatment due to foreign nationals in the matter of repatriation (article 38). Those under 18 may not be subject to compulsory labour (article 51), or have the death penalty pronounced against them, and if they are detained special treatment is to be accorded to them as minors (articles 76, 119, 126).

Article 77 of Additional Protocol I deals specifically with the protection of children, declaring that they must be the object of special respect, protected against any form of indecent assault, and provided with the care and aid they require. Article 4 of Additional Protocol II on non-international armed conflicts endorses this approach, adding that children shall receive an education and that all appropriate steps shall be taken to facilitate family reunion (article 4(3)(a), (b)).

Article 77 of Additional Protocol I provides further in relation to the participation of children in armed conflict and its consequences:

2. The Parties to the conflict shall take all feasible measures in order that children who have not attained the age of fifteen years do not take a direct part in hostilities and, in particular, they shall refrain from recruiting them into their armed forces. In recruiting among those persons who have attained the age of fifteen years but who have not attained the age of eighteen years the Parties to the conflict shall endeavour to give priority to those who are oldest.

3. If, in exceptional cases, despite the provisions of paragraph 2, children who have not attained the age of fifteen years take a direct part in hostilities and fall into the power of an adverse Party, they shall continue to benefit from the special protection accorded by this Article, whether or not they are prisoners of war.

4. If arrested, detained or interned for reasons related to the armed conflict, children shall be held in quarters separate from the quarters of adults, except where families are accommodated as family units as provided in Article 75, paragraph 5.

5. The death penalty for an offence related to the armed conflict shall not be executed on persons who had not attained the age of eighteen years at the time the offence was committed.

In the case of non-international armed conflicts, however, states have gone further. Article 4(3)(c) of Additional Protocol II provides that 'children who have not attained the age of fifteen years shall *neither* be recruited in the armed forces or groups *nor* allowed to take part in hostilities'. Subparagraph (d) declares, moreover, that 'the special protection provided by this Article to children who have not attained the age of fifteen years shall remain applicable to them if they take a direct part in hostilities despite the provisions of subparagraph (c) and are captured....'

However, nothing in the Geneva Conventions provides that a child may never *become* a combatant. When the draft for Additional Protocol I was debated during the 1970s (dealing with international armed conflicts and assimilated conflicts, including national liberation struggles), it was clear that, while States were prepared to countenance limitations on the freedom to *recruit* children under 15, many governments wanted to avoid entering into any absolute obligation with regard to the *voluntary* participation of children. There was a sense that wars of national liberation, by definition perhaps, engaged all the people, and that children seeking to do their duty should not be obstructed, particularly if, from a cultural perspective, they were already regarded as adults.[11] The idea that children, and childhood, were deserving of protection, even from the consequences of their own actions, did not always carry weight. Even when the Convention on the Rights of the Child (CRC89) came to be adopted in 1989, the position on recruitment and participation in conflict adopted in the Additional Protocols was largely maintained, notwithstanding the fact that article 1 of the Convention itself opens with endorsement of the proposition that a child is any person below the age of 18.[12] A measure of qualified protection was nevertheless attempted, and Article 38 CRC89 provides:

1. States Parties undertake to respect and to ensure respect for rules of international humanitarian law applicable to them in armed conflicts which are relevant to the child.

2. States Parties shall take *all feasible measures* to ensure that persons who have not attained the age of fifteen years do not take *a direct part* in hostilities.

3. States Parties *shall refrain from recruiting any person who has not attained the age of fifteen years* into their armed forces. In recruiting among those persons who have attained the age of fifteen years but who have not attained the age of eighteen years, States Parties shall endeavour to give priority to those who are oldest.

4. In accordance with their obligations under international humanitarian law to protect the civilian population in armed conflicts, States Parties shall take all feasible measures to ensure protection and care of children who are affected by an armed conflict.[13]

Clearly, the words adopted allow room for manoeuvre, contrasting significantly with those agreed a year later in article 22 of the African Charter:

1. States Parties to this Charter shall undertake to respect and ensure respect for rules of international humanitarian law applicable in armed conflicts which affect the child.

2. States Parties to the present Charter shall take all necessary measures to ensure that no child shall take a direct part in hostilities and refrain in particular, from recruiting any child.

3. States Parties to the present Charter shall, in accordance with their obligations under international humanitarian law, protect the civilian population in armed conflicts and shall take all feasible measures to ensure the protection and care of children who are affected by armed conflicts. Such rules shall also apply to children in situations of internal armed conflicts, tension and strife.[14]

Why states did not take the opportunity to strengthen protection is unclear. The US representative argued that the standards set by international humanitarian law should not be altered by a human rights instrument, but it is difficult to accept that this alone was the reason, particularly given the African approach in 1990.[15]

## THE REASONS BEHIND CHILDREN'S INVOLVEMENT IN ARMED CONFLICT

This, then, was the situation at law in the first years of the 1990s. Children were being used in combat, then as now, in most continents and in conflicts, some of which continue to this day. The background and the conditions and reasons for the recruitment and use of child soldiers, and indeed for their uncoerced participation, certainly remain more or less the same, while the multidimensionality of causes presents its own challenges in the pursuit of protection.[16]

Although every situation of child recruitment and child participation will have its own peculiarities, children are commonly seen by military commanders as malleable, open to indoctrination, obedient, apparently fearless, and in these days of course able to carry powerful weapons without difficulty. Children can also be brutalized, which was the Mozambican National Resistance's (RENAMO) practice, and the road home was closed by forcing them to commit atrocities against family and village. In the course of conflict, children find themselves in conditions of extreme vulnerability which provide fertile ground, both for those who forcibly enlist, and for children themselves, isolated, lost, in need, and drawn into the ranks. They themselves may be victims of conflict, the orphans and the violated; they may be displaced and separated; they may come under peer pressure; they may be exposed to indoctrination in schools; or they may even be on the receiving end of common kindness, as happened in Uganda in the 1980s, when the National Resistance Army 'accommodated' many of the orphans and separated children as the lines of combat moved ahead.

Not all child combatants, as we found, are there against their will; and whatever the original circumstances and intent which led to inclusion in armed forces or groups, for many this was the better of bad alternatives, and they came to see the unit as their family; it provided them with security and food, and for that they became committed, and for that they would fight.

The very persistence of the problem presents its own challenges, of course, but some issues remain the same and abuse is generally the common denominator. In Sierra Leone during the late 1990s, as in Mozambique in the 1980s, children were abducted and brutalized, and forced or led, often drugged or drunk, to commit indescribable crimes—rape, mutilation, amputation, murder—sometimes even of their own family. The Secretary-General remarked:

> More than in any other conflict where children have been used as combatants, in Sierra Leone, child combatants were initially abducted, forcibly recruited, sexually abused, reduced to slavery of all kinds and trained, often under the influence of drugs, to kill, maim and burn. Though feared by many for their brutality, most if not all of these children have been subjected to a process of psychological and physical abuse and duress which has transformed them from victims into perpetrators.[17]

If many of the issues remain the same, there may yet be room, if not for questioning fundamental premises, then for considering whether some of the means chosen to address those issues need a more nuanced and sophisticated application. Already in 2000 and writing shortly after the adoption of the Optional Protocol to the Convention on the Rights of the Child on the Involvement of Children in Armed Conflict,[18] Matthew Happold queried whether new rules would have any effect on the behaviour of states, either in the developed or the developing world. In particular, he suggested, the Optional Protocol could be seen as failing still to deal with the root causes of child participation in conflict, while the principal issue was not so much the absence of rules, as their enforcement vis-à-vis non-state groups.[19]

## THE LEGAL FRAMEWORK *HAS* CHANGED

The last two decades or so have nevertheless witnessed consolidation and change in the legal framework governing the recruitment and use of children in armed conflict, as well as their protection in general. Besides the Optional

Protocol, the Statutes for the International Criminal Tribunals for the Former Yugoslavia (ICTY) and Rwanda (ICTR) and that for the International Criminal Court (ICC) have each emphasized the forcible transfer of children as an element in the crime of genocide.[20] In addition, the ICC Statute provides expressly that a 'war crime' shall include, 'conscripting or enlisting children under the age of fifteen into the national armed forces or using them to participate actively in hostilities'.[21] Finally, the ILO's 1999 Convention on the Worst Forms of Child Labour (C182), referred to above, obliges every ILO member state which ratifies the Convention to take 'immediate and effective measures to secure the prohibition and elimination of the worst forms of child labour as a matter of urgency' (article 1), including 'forced or compulsory recruitment of children for use in armed conflict' (article 3). For the purposes of this Convention, the term 'child' applies to all persons under the age of 18 (article 2).[22]

Lawyers and policymakers must still determine to what extent and how the recruitment and/or use of children in armed conflict, including their direct participation, can be prevented, and whether law can be effective in this context, for example, as a deterrent.[23] No less important is the question of what can and should be done with child soldiers who themselves have committed war crimes or other atrocities. To a certain degree, the law can provide the framework for demobilization, disarmament, and rehabilitation, and thereby also set out values and goals. But in particular instances, the application of the law may be challenged, for example, on the issue of age and criminal liability, in the matter of duress as a defence, or with regard to asylum, where it may be alleged that the child's own conduct is such as to warrant his or her exclusion from protection.[24] The cardinal principle set down in article 3 of the Convention on the Rights of the Child—that in every decision affecting a child, his or her best interests shall be a primary consideration— offers a particular approach or point of departure to these issues, but may not always determine the appropriate result.

Besides the above provisions, the 2000 Optional Protocol to the Convention on the Rights of the Child now requires states parties to take all feasible measures to ensure that members of their armed forces under 18 years of age do not take a direct part in hostilities,[25] and that those under 18 are not compulsorily recruited.[26] In principle, states are also required to raise from 15 to 18 the minimum age for voluntary recruitment,[27] and where under 18 recruitment continues to be permitted, it must be accompanied by certain safeguards to ensure that such recruitment is genuinely voluntary, that it is done with the informed consent of the individual's parents or legal guardians, that he or she is fully informed of the duties involved in military service, and that reliable proof of age is provided before acceptance for national military service.[28]

Non-state armed groups 'should not, under any circumstances, recruit or use in hostilities persons under the age of 18 years', and states are to take 'all feasible measures to prevent such recruitment and use, including the adoption of legal measures necessary to prohibit and criminalize such practices'.[29]

The threat of prosecution is thus more of a reality today than fifteen years ago, but whether this will deter the use of child combatants or help to shift community attitudes against their involvement remains to be seen. Some sixty states continue to permit the voluntary recruitment of under-18s, while forcible recruitment also continues, for example, in Somalia and the Sudan. Armed groups are especially resistant to change. In Afghanistan, Burundi, the Central African Republic, and Colombia, under-18s are used as combatants and for front-line duties. Girls are also inducted, raped, and subjected to sexual exploitation by the FARC in Colombia, in Cote d'Ivoire, the Democratic Republic of the Congo, and by the Lord's Resistance Army in Uganda.

Article 6 of the Optional Protocol goes on to require that states parties take all feasible measures to ensure that children recruited or used in hostilities are demobilized and, where necessary, that they are accorded all appropriate assistance for their physical and psychological recovery and their social reintegration. Save in the context of peace agreements, however-er, there is little progress to note in the way of demobilization or release.[30] Generally, non-state armed groups ignore international law, go back on commitments, resist pressure and persuasion, and are often out of reach. Even more challenging are the numerous irregular groups now in evidence, with obscure goals and shifting alliances; the changing character of conflict, including the use of children in terrorist activity, presents an ever-changing set of problems.[31]

## THE EXAMPLE OF SIERRA LEONE

In Sierra Leone, more than 10,000 children were involved on all sides in a particularly vicious conflict. In 2000, the Security Council authorized a Special Tribunal to prosecute those bearing the 'greatest responsibility' for violations of international humanitarian law, including specifically those who had con-scripted or enlisted children under 15 into armed forces or groups or used them to participate actively in hostilities.[32]

On 3 June 2004, Trial Chamber I began its hearing of the Civil Defense Forces (CDF) Trial.[33] The first of the three accused, Samuel Hinga Norman, had been called on by the government to organize resistance, and to conscript, initiate, and train traditional hunters—the Kamajors— into the CDF. But as the civil war progressed, the tactics of the CDF strongly resembled those of the rebels. Members of the militia, many of them children, routinely shot, hacked, or burned their victims to death. Norman objected that child recruitment was *not* a crime under international law during the relevant period (1996–2001). While Additional Protocol II and the Convention on the Rights of the Child may have *prohibited* recruitment, he argued, they had not criminalized the practice; so without a law, there was no crime.

The Trial Chamber determined that the motion raised a serious issue relating to jurisdiction and referred the matter to the Appeals Chambers which duly dismissed it, ruling that the offence of recruitment of child soldiers below the age of 15 did in fact constitute a crime under customary international law prior to the issue of the indictment.[34] The Trial Chamber in turn noted that there was widespread practice in support of criminalization and a discernible 'sense of pre-existing obligation', account being taken of the Additional Protocols, the Convention on the Rights of the Child, and the African Charter on the Rights and Welfare of the Child.

On 22 February 2007, the court was informed that Norman had died after undergoing medical treatment in Senegal,[35] and the proceedings against him were accordingly terminated. The trial continued against the co-defendants, one of whom, Kondewa, was found guilty of enlisting children under 15 into an armed group. However, his conviction was reversed on appeal, on the ground that the child in question had already been enlisted before Kondewa had initiated him into the Kamajor society.[36]

Meanwhile, on 20 June 2007, three members of the Armed Forces Revolutionary Council were convicted of, among others, the offence of enlisting children under 15, and on 2 August of the same year one member of the government-backed CDF was also convicted. These were the first convictions by an international tribunal relating to the conscription and use of children in armed conflict, and they were affirmed on appeal on 22 February 2008. More cases may follow.[37] These offences are included in the indictment of Charles Taylor, the former President of Liberia, who is also accused of backing the rebels in the Sierra Leone civil war. He was transferred for trial before the Special Court sitting in The Hague in 2006.[38]

Also on trial on similar charges in The Hague, but before the ICC, are Thomas Lubanga Djilo, who is accused of enlisting and conscripting children under the age of 15 years into the *Forces patriotiques pour la libération du Congo*/Patriotic Forces for the Liberation of Congo and using them to participate actively in hostilities in the context of both an international and a non-international armed conflict;[39] and Germain Katanga and Matieu Chiu, who face similar charges.[40] Offences involving children are also alleged against members of the Lord's Resistance Army.[41]

## The other side of the criminal coin

So prevalent were atrocities by child combatants in Sierra Leone that the Special Court's Statute provided for a juvenile chamber to try those aged between 15 and 18 at the time of the commission of their alleged offences. However, the Special Court's first chief prosecutor, David Crane, stated in 2002 that he would *not* use this procedure, and would only prosecute those aged 18 or over. It was also the Security Council's view that child soldiers were more appropriately dealt with through other accountability mechanisms, such as the Sierra Leone Truth and Reconciliation Commission.[42]

Other national and international tribunals have likewise stepped away from prosecution, supporting either in their practice or by the terms of their constitutions the view that child combatants should in principle be treated as victims, rather than as perpetrators.[43] The Statutes of the International Criminal Tribunals for the Former Yugoslavia and Rwanda, for example, contained no provisions governing the age of criminal responsibility, and recognizing perhaps that age might be a valid defence, no prosecutions of under-18s have taken place. The ICC Statute provides expressly that the court shall have no jurisdiction over anyone under 18 at the date of commission of alleged offences.[44] The State Court of Bosnia and Herzegovina[45] includes a Special Chamber for War Crimes, established in 2005, to prosecute those not dealt with by the ICTY. However, the Criminal Code contains an absolute prohibition on the prosecution of a child, defined as a person under 14. For those over 14 but under 16, only educational measures may be imposed, measures which in turn must be designed for rehabilitation and to avoid criminal procedures against juveniles.[46]

In most jurisdictions in fact, offences by children give rise to many and various problems, and there is no rule regarding their treatment which is sufficiently common as to justify being called a rule of international law.[47] Thus, the age of criminal liability varies considerably, as do notions of capacity to understand and/or to appreciate the difference between right and wrong. There is further uncertainty regarding the appropriate treatment for those children who may have committed war crimes or other atrocities, although there is substantial agreement that an approach going beyond punishment is called for.

Article 39 of the Convention on the Rights of the Child supports this trend—measures relating to children in armed conflict should be intended 'to promote physical and psychological recovery and social reintegration....' The 2007 Paris Principles, which are not blind to the duality of the child soldier as both victim and perpetrator, call for no prosecutions by international courts or tribunals, and that alternatives to judicial proceedings be sought for children at the national level.

So, even while, from an international law perspective, the option to prosecute child soldiers remains open,[48] countervailing principles such as the best interests principle—*a primary consideration in every decision affecting the child*—will need to be taken into account and minimum procedural safeguards laid down in a variety of international instruments will need to be observed, particularly if the goals of rehabilitation and reintegration are to be achieved. The Sierra Leone Truth and Reconciliation Commission was in fact the first with a clear mandate to pay special attention to the experiences of children in armed conflict, and in which children participated.[49]

## INSTITUTIONAL DEVELOPMENTS

### Involvement of the Security Council

In 1999, Security Council resolution 1261 affirmed that the protection of children was a peace and security concern, and in resolution 1379 (2001) it requested the Secretary-General to attach to his annual report on children and armed conflict a list of parties that recruit and use children in violation of their international obligations.[50] Perhaps the biggest step forward came with the adoption of resolution 1612 in 2005.[51] Here, the Security Council not only reaffirmed its strong condemnation of the recruitment and use of child soldiers and its conviction that the protection of children in armed conflict should be regarded as an important aspect of any comprehensive strategy to resolve conflict but it also approved the establishment of a monitoring and reporting mechanism and a working group on children and armed conflict. It requested the Secretary-General to implement the mechanism without delay and, in particular, to focus on those parties in situations of armed conflict which had been listed in the annexes to the Secretary-General's report.[52]

The Council welcomed the initiatives of UNICEF and other UN entities to gather information and, recalling resolution 1539 (2004), reaffirmed its intention to consider adopting country-specific resolutions and targeted and graduated measures against parties to armed conflict which were in violation of applicable international law relating to the rights and protection of children.[53]

No less important was the Security Council's endorsement of the Secretary-General's zero-tolerance policy on sexual exploitation and abuse by UN peacekeeping operations. It decided to continue the inclusion of specific provisions for the protection of children in UN peacekeeping mandates, including the deployment of child protection advisers on a case-by-case basis.[54] It called upon all parties concerned to ensure that the protection, rights, and well-being of children affected by armed conflict are specifically integrated into peace processes, and that relevant international obligations are met.[55]

The Working Group set up under Security Council resolution 1612 in July 2005 comprises the fifteen Council members. It meets in closed session to review the reports of the monitoring and reporting mechanism,[56] and progress in the development and implementation of the various action plans. A considerable number of country-specific reports have been considered, most recently on Afghanistan and the Central African Republic.[57] This has led to parties being listed when they engage in the recruitment and use of children in armed conflict, which in turn can be used as a basis for measures against offenders, including proceedings in national and international tribunals.

In resolution 1882, adopted on 4 August 2009, the Security Council reaffirmed its earlier resolutions and presidential statements, noting that they contributed to a comprehensive framework for addressing the protection of children affected by armed conflict. While remaining concerned at the lack of progress in some situations, where parties to conflict continued to violate relevant international law with impunity, the Security Council nevertheless acknowledged that the implementation of resolution 1612 had

> generated progress, resulting in the release and reintegration of children into their families and communities and in a more systematic dialogue between the United Nations country-level task forces and parties to the conflict on the implementation of time-bound action plans.

The Security Council decided that the monitoring and reporting mechanism would continue to be implemented in situations listed in the annexes to the report of the Secretary-General. It welcomed the activity and recommendations of the Working Group, reaffirmed its intention to take action against assistant perpetrators, and stressed that effective disarmament, demobilization, and reintegration programmes, 'building on best practices identified by UNICEF and other relevant child protection actors', are crucial to the well-being of all children who have been recruited or used by armed forces and groups.[58]

## UNICEF and the development of best practices

The law alone cannot solve the problems of recruitment and participation in conflict. For this reason, and in accordance with its mandate, UNICEF has long been engaged in providing assistance to children generally and specifically to those affected by conflict and other humanitarian emergencies.[59] It was closely involved in the preparation of the Machel Study in 1996, and has since actively promoted not only its own capacity but also the development and consolidation of international standards. For example, UNICEF and an NGO Working Group on the Convention on the Rights of the Child held a symposium in Cape Town, South Africa, in April 1997, the purpose of which was to develop strategies for preventing the recruitment of those under 18, and for effective demobilization and reintegration.

The Cape Town Principles and Best Practices on the Recruitment of Children into the Armed Forces and on Demobilization and Social Reintegration of Child Soldiers in Africa[60] were substantially developed and refined ten years later. A meeting organized jointly by the French Ministry of Foreign Affairs and UNICEF in February 2007 adopted two documents: the Paris Commitments to Protect Children Unlawfully Recruited or Used by Armed Forces or Armed Groups and the Paris Principles and Guidelines on Children associated with Armed Forces or Armed Groups. The 'Paris Commitments' are essentially about policy, and seek to strengthen political action to prevent children becoming associated with armed forces and armed groups and to ensure their successful reintegration. States commit themselves to make every effort to uphold and apply the 'Paris Principles', which in turn aim to guide action on the ground to prevent the involvement of children in armed conflict and to bring about their reintegration. Both documents adopt a rights-based approach, recognizing that child recruitment is a human rights violation requiring accountability, and also accepting children primarily as victims, not perpetrators, who deserve specific protection and treatment in accordance with international juvenile justice standards and on the basis of alternatives to judicial proceedings wherever possible. The child's human rights require that his or her release be actively pursued, including during conflict, and that reintegration into civilian life is the ultimate goal of securing release. Prevention, on the other hand, requires that the underlying causes of recruitment be dealt with, including economic and social factors, and that the special needs of girls receive special attention, for gender-based discrimination and violence are frequently exacerbated in times of armed conflict.[61]

## CONCLUSION

There is no conclusion, no end to the story of child recruitment and child participation in conflict; and if the *character* of war itself is changing, it would seem yet to show little desire for turning its effects away from those who ought to be protected.

But the last decade and a half has witnessed some very substantial legal and institutional progress. Similarly, a powerful civil society movement has consolidated and strengthened, and it shows no signs of losing its commitment and determination to bring to an end this irrecoverable waste of childhood. It may be that the rules now are sound enough, and that the problem remains one of application and enforcement. The law, however, can only play a small part in a whole picture which, of necessity, reflects deeply the very fabric of society and its economic, social, and political divisions. It is through grasping these nettles, as UNICEF and NGOs do at the field level, and in brokering peace at the political level, that concrete results such as demobilization are most likely to be secured. The law and the prospect of prosecution and punishment may be useful allies in the overall strategy to combat child recruitment and child participation in conflict, but there are likely to be other and more immediate, practical goals.

## NOTES

1. Irene Cohn and Guy S. Goodwin-Gill, *Child soldiers* (Oxford: Clarendon Press, 1994).
2. The BBC World Service report an estimated 300,000 child soldiers around the world: see www.bbc.co.uk/worldservice/people/features/childrensrights/children-ofconflict/soldier.shtml, which also carries audio accounts of children explaining how they became soldiers.
3. For links to relevant literature and action, see among others, Coalition to Stop the Use of Child Soldiers, *Child soldiers: Global report 2008* (London, 2008), www.child-soldiers.org; International Bureau for Children's Rights, *Children and armed conflict: A guide to International Humanitarian and human rights law* (Montréal, 2010), www.ibcr.org; UNICEF, *Machel study 10-year strategic review: Children and conflict in a changing world* (New York: UNICEF & Office of the Special Representative of the Secretary-General for Children and Armed Conflict, 2009); Watchlist on Children and Armed Conflict, 'UN Security Council resolution 1612 and beyond: Strengthening protection for children in armed conflict', www.watchlist.org; Children and Armed Conflict Unit, a joint project of the Children's Legal Centre and the Human Rights Centre at the University of Essex: www.essex.ac.uk/armedcon/default.htm; UNICEF, Factsheet: Child soldiers, www.unicef.org/emerg/index_childsoldiers.html
4. Graça Machel, 'Impact of armed conflict on children. Note by the Secretary-General', UN doc. A/51/306, 26 August 1996, www.un.org/children/conflict/english/themachelstudy.html
5. See Human Rights Council, 'Annual report of the Special Representative of the Secretary-General for Children and Armed Conflict, Radhika Coomaraswamy', UN doc. A/HRC/12/49, 30 July 2009; and for further information, see http://www.un.org/children/conflict/english/index.html
6. See UNICEF, Information: Impact of armed conflict on children: http://www.unicef.org/graca/

7. See, for example, Security Council resolution 1882 (2009), 4 August 2009; Security Council resolution 1612 (2005), 26 July 2005; General Assembly resolutions 64/146, 18 December 2009 and 62/241, 24 December 2008 on the 'Rights of the Child'. See also, Radhika Coomaraswamy, 'Machel study 10-year strategic review', Report of the Special Representative of the Secretary-General for Children and Armed Conflict, UN doc. A/62/228, 13 August 2007, http://www.un.org/children/conflict/english/machel10.html

8. Worst Forms of Child Labour Convention, 1999 (C182), http://www.ilo.org/ilolex/english/convdisp1.htm; text also in Ian Brownlie and Guy S. Goodwin-Gill (eds.), *Brownlie's documents on human rights* (Oxford: Oxford University Press, 2010).

9. 1989 Convention on the Rights of the Child: 1577 *UNTS* 3; Optional Protocol to the Convention on the Rights of the Child on the Involvement of Children in Armed Conflicts and Optional Protocol to the Convention on the Rights of the Child on the Sale of Children, Child Prostitution and Child Pornography, both annexed General Assembly Resolution 54/263, adopted without a vote on 25 May 2000. Texts also in Brownlie and Goodwin-Gill, *Brownlie's documents on human rights*, 458.

10. Of particular relevance to the present discussion are the 1949 Fourth Geneva Convention relative to the Protection of Civilian Persons in Time of War, 1977 Additional Protocol I (on international armed conflict), and 1977 Additional Protocol II (on non-international armed conflict). For texts, see www.icrc.org

11. This idea has certainly not disappeared. In 2009, a soldier in Chad was reported as remarking that 'there are children, but not just in the army, the rebels have them [too]. This is a war, we need everyone.' A UNICEF child protection specialist noted further that child recruitment is often the consequence of ignorance, with rebel leaders seeing those aged 14 as no longer children: 'Chad: Instability threatens demobilisation of child soldiers', 16 April 2009, www.irinnews.org/Report.aspx?ReportId=83963. An NGO worker in Yemen said similarly, 'We have a saying here: If you are old enough to carry the "jambiya" [a curved dagger traditionally worn in the belt of Yemeni men] then you are old enough to fight with your tribe. And children carry the "jambiya" from 12 years old': 'Yemen: Child soldiers used by both sides in northern conflict—NGOs', 10 December 2009, www.irinnews.org/Report.aspx?ReportId=87391

12. The threshold of 18 in Article 1 CRC89 is potentially qualified: 'unless, under the law applicable to the child, majority is attained earlier'. Article 2 of the African Charter on the Rights and Welfare of the Child, adopted a year later in 1990, adopts 18 years without qualification; for text, see www.africa-union.org/root/au/Documents/Treaties/treaties.htm; Brownlie and Goodwin-Gill, *Brownlie's documents on human rights*, 1067.

13. Emphasis supplied; the standard of protection is potentially less than that provided by Additional Protocol II in the case of non-international armed conflicts.

14. See above, note 12.

15. Cohn and Goodwin-Gill, *Child soldiers*, 69.

16. See generally Ibid., chapter 2; Rachel Brett and Margaret McCallin, *Children: The invisible soldiers* (Vaxjo, Sweden: Rädda Barnen, 1996); Rachel Brett and Irma

Specht, *Young soldiers: Why they choose to fight* (Boulder, CO: Lynne Rienner, 2004).

17. 'Report of the Secretary-General on the establishment of a Special Court for Sierra Leone', UN doc. S/2000/915, 4 October 2000, para. 32; also, Irene Cohn, 'The protection of children and the quest for truth and justice in Sierra Leone' *Journal of International Affairs* 55/1 (2001); 'The Special Court for Sierra Leone—*Amicus curiae* brief of University of Toronto International Human Rights Clinic and interested international human rights organizations', *San Diego International Law Journal*, 7 (2005–6).

18. On 30 April 2000, 132 States were party to the Optional Protocol. For text, see UN General Assembly resolution 54/263, 25 May 2000; Brownlie and Goodwin-Gill, *Brownlie's documents on human rights*, 475.

19. Matthew Happold, 'The Optional Protocol to the Convention on the Rights of the Child on the involvement of children in armed conflict', *Yearbook of International Humanitarian Law*, 3 (2000), 226–44.

20. Article 4, 1993 Statute of the International Criminal Tribunal for the Former Yugoslavia; article 2, 1994 Statute of the International Criminal Tribunal for Rwanda; article 6, 1998 Statute of the International Criminal Court.

21. Article 8(2)(b)(xxvi), article 8(2)(2)(e)(vii), 1998 Statute of the International Criminal Court.

22. See above, note 8. There were 172 States Parties on 30 April 2010.

23. See Kristin Barstad, 'Preventing the recruitment of child soldiers: The ICRC approach', *Refugee Survey Quarterly*, 27/4 (2009), 142–9.

24. According to article 1F(a) of the 1951 Convention relating to the Status of Refugees, the convention shall not apply to any person with regard to whom there are serious reasons to consider that he or she has committed a crime against peace, a war crime, or a crime against humanity. See further, Matthew Happold, *Child soldiers in international law* (Manchester: Manchester University Press, 2005), 141–69; Michael S. Gallagher, 'Soldier boy bad: Child soldiers, culture and bars to asylum', *International Journal of Refugee Law*, 13/3 (2001), 310–53; Mary-Hunter Morris, 'Babies and bathwater: Seeking an appropriate standard of review for the asylum applications of former child soldiers', *Harvard Human Rights Law Journal*, 21 (2008), 281–301.

25. Article 1, 2000 Optional Protocol to the Convention on the Rights of the Child on the Involvement of Children in Armed Conflict (hereafter 'Optional Protocol'). For a concise account of the background and negotiations of the Optional Protocol, see Happold, 'The Optional Protocol'.

26. Optional Protocol, article 2.

27. Ibid., article 3(1). On becoming a party to the Optional Protocol, States must deposit a binding declaration setting forth the minimum age at which they will permit voluntary enlistment (article 3(2)). The requirement to raise the minimum recruitment age does not apply to military academies (article 3(5)).

28. Ibid., article 3(3).

29. Ibid., article 4. Not surprisingly, this article provides that its application, 'shall not affect the legal status of any party to an armed conflict' (article 4(3)).

30. See, for example, 'Chad: Instability threatens demobilisation of child soldiers', 16 April 2009, www.irinnews.org/Report.aspx?ReportId=83963; 'Nepal: Reintegration challenges for Maoist female ex-combatants', 14 April 2010, www.irinnews.org/Report.aspx?ReportId=88806

31. Cf. 'Global: New threats to children in conflict need new responses, UN says', 18 June 2009, www.irinnews.org/Report.aspx?ReportId=84894

32. UNSC resolution 1315, 14 August 2000; also, Agreement between the United Nations and the Government of Sierra Leone on the Establishment of the Special Court for Sierra Leone, 16 January 2002, www.sc-sl.org/DOCUMENTS/tabid/176/Default.aspx

33. Documents, including the annual reports of the Special Court and the judgments of the Trials Chambers and the Appeals Chamber upon which this summary is based, are available at www.sc-sl.org/

34. Appeals Chamber, Decision on preliminary motion based on lack of jurisdiction (Child Recruitment), 31 May 2004, para. 53. The University of Toronto International Human Rights Clinic and UNICEF presented *amicus curiae* briefs; see 'The Special Court for Sierra Leone—*Amicus curiae* Brief of University of Toronto International Human Rights Clinic and interested international human rights organizations'.

35. The Court initiated an inquiry into Norman's death, and found that he had died of natural causes.

36. Trial Chamber I, Judgment of 2 August 2007; Appeals Chamber, Judgment of 28 May 2008. Michael Nesbitt, 'Lessons from the Sam Hinga Norman decision of the Special Court for Sierra Leone: How trials and truth commissions can co-exist', *German Law Journal*, 8/10 (2007), 977–1014.

37. Prosecutions may also occur at the national level. On 3 October 2008, President Bush signed into law the Child Soldiers Accountability Act (S. 2135), which will allow the United States to prosecute persons in the United States who have knowingly recruited or used children under 15 as soldiers, even if they were recruited or served outside the United States. It also allows for those who have knowingly recruited children as soldiers to be deported or refused admission: www.govtrack.us/congress/bill.xpd?bill=s110-2135

38. Cf. Cohn and Goodwin-Gill, *Child soldiers*, 29, 40, 112, 115 for references to forcible recruitment and use of children by Taylor's forces in Liberia during the early 1990s.

39. Democratic Republic of the Congo, ICC-01/04-01/06, *The Prosecutor v. Thomas Lubanga Dyilo*. The trial began on 26 January 2009: www.icc-cpi.int/Menus/ICC/Situations+and+Cases/Cases/

40. Democratic Republic of the Congo, ICC-01/04-01/07, *The Prosecutor v. Germain Katanga and Mathieu Ngudjolo Chui*. The trial began on 24 November 2009: www.icc-cpi.int/Menus/ICC/Situations+and+Cases/Cases/

41. See *The Prosecutor v. Joseph Kony, Vincent Otti, Okot Odhiambo and Dominic Ongwen*, ICC-02/04-01/05, http://www.icc-cpi.int/Menus/ICC/Situations+and+Cases/Cases/

42. See generally, William A. Schabas, 'The relationship between truth commissions and international courts: The case of Sierra Leone', *Human Rights Quarterly*, 25/4(2003), 1035–66.

43. Cf. Nienke Grossman, 'Rehabilitation or revenge: Prosecuting child soldiers for human rights violations', *Georgia Journal of International Law*, 38/2 (2007), 323–62; Chen Reis, 'Trying the future, avenging the past: The implications of prosecuting children for participation in internal armed conflict', *Columbia Human Rights Law Review*, 28 (1997), 629.
44. Article 26, Statute of the International Criminal Court.
45. For details and the work of the Court, see www.sudbih.gov.ba/?jezik=e
46. Articles 8, 9, and chapter X, 2003 Criminal Code of Bosnia and Herzegovina, www.iccnow.org/documents/criminal-code-of-bih.pdf
47. Cf. Karin Arts and Vesselin Popovski (eds.), *International criminal accountability and the rights of children* (Cambridge: Cambridge University Press, 2006).
48. See, for example, the continuing (May 2010) controversy surrounding the prosecution of Omar Khadr, a Guantanamo detainee, with regard to an offence allegedly committed in Afghanistan when he was aged 15: Peter Finn, 'Former boy soldier, youngest Guantanamo detainee, heads toward military tribunal', *Washington Post*, 10 February 2010, A01; Peter Finn, 'Military tribunal opens hearings on Guantanamo detainee Omar Khadr', *Washington Post*, 29 April 2010, A04; Human Rights First, 'The case of Omar Ahmed Khadr, Canada', www.humanrightsfirst.org/us_law/detainees/cases/khadr.aspx; also, www.omarkhadrproject.com/
49. The Final Report of the Sierra Leone Truth and Reconciliation Report, October 2004, is available at www.sierra-leone.org/TRCDocuments.html. See also Beth K. Dougherty, 'Searching for answers: Sierra Leone's truth and reconciliation commission', *African Studies Quarterly*, 8/1 (2004), 39–56.
50. UNSC resolution 1379 (2001), 20 November 2001, para. 16; see also UNSC resolution 1460 (2003), 30 January 2003.
51. UNSC resolution 1612 (2005), 26 July 2005.
52. The Security Council agenda has also been developed in a number of presidential statements; see, for example, those listed in the first preambular paragraph of UNSC resolution 1882 (2009), 4 August 2009.
53. Ibid., para. 9.
54. Ibid., paras 11, 12.
55. Ibid., paras 14, 15.
56. The 'mandate' of the monitoring mechanism is not limited to child soldiers, but focuses also on other grave abuses of children, including killing or maiming, attacks against schools or hospitals, rape and other grave sexual violence, abduction, and denial of humanitarian access for children.
57. In the period 1 January 2008–30 April 2010, the Secretary-General reported to the Security Council on children and armed conflict in, among others, Nepal, the Philippines, Uganda, Burundi, Colombia, Sri Lanka, Chad, Afghanistan, and Somalia. By September 2009, the Working Group had considered twenty-seven country reports; see www.un.org/children/conflict/english/securitycouncilwg.html
58. UNSC resolution 1882 (2009), 4 August 2009, paras 2, 7, 13. See also UNGA resolution 64/146, 'Rights of the Child', 18 December 2009, paras 19–21; UNGA res. 63/241, 'Rights of the Child', 24 December 2008, paras 51–63.
59. 'UNICEF in emergencies', www.unicef.org/emerg/

60. The Cape Town Principles are said to have led many practitioners to adopt the terminology of 'children associated with armed forces or armed groups' (CAA-FAG), rather than 'child soldiers'. For the purposes of disarmament, demobilization, and reintegration programmes, UNICEF itself defines a 'child soldier' as any child—boy or girl—under 18 years of age, who is part of any kind of regular or irregular armed force or armed group in any capacity, including, but not limited to: cooks, porters, messengers, and anyone accompanying such groups other than family members. It includes girls and boys recruited for forced sexual purposes and/or forced marriage. The definition, therefore, does not only refer to a child who is carrying, or has carried, weapons.

61. Follow-up meetings have brought to seventy-six the total number of Member State endorsements, http://www.un.org/children/conflict/english/parisprinciples.html

# PART V

# The Ideas which Enable us to Understand War

# 23

## American Strategic Culture: Problems and Prospects

*Antulio J. Echevarria II*

Since the 1970s, the term strategic culture has increased in currency. This rise in popularity has occurred despite the fact that the concept itself remains problematic, and its utility limited. Culture has always been difficult to define, and that task has not been made easier by appending the adjective 'strategic' to it. Depending on one's perspective and professional discipline, the concept of strategic culture might be used either to explain, as is the case with historians, or to predict, as is common among political scientists. Some early studies, in fact, attempted to use it to do both: to explain apparent patterns in Soviet decision-making and to predict Soviet biases, which were then to form the basis for certain Cold War policies.[1] Studies of strategic culture thus helped to define the search for distinct national approaches to strategy, without, however, sufficiently questioning whether such approaches actually existed. Nonetheless, they became a defensible, if not entirely compelling, alternative to the rational-actor model, and the belief that self-interest is the principal motive behind action.

However, the term's popularity does not eliminate the fact that it remains problematic, and that the first rule in applying it must be: 'let the buyer beware'. This chapter lays out some of the unresolved issues associated with using the concept of American strategic culture and what is assumed to be its 'subset and product'—the American way of war.[2] Prospects for continued use of the concept remain favourable so long as scholars and policymakers acknowledge its limitations, and refrain from asking it to do too much.

## STRATEGIC CULTURE

Literature reviews say that studies of strategic culture underwent three so-called generational shifts.[3] The first, which emerged in the 1970s–80s, looked for causal linkages between national cultures and strategic choices. It sought to be both descriptive and predictive.[4] The second generation, which appeared in the early to mid-1990s, attempted to provide more methodological rigour to strategic cultural studies.[5] In the process, strategic culture emerged as a legitimate focus of research in its own right, rather than merely as a means to discover causal linkages. The third generation, which emerged in the late 1990s, embraced constructivism, and explored the process and significance of identity formulation as part of the development of domestic and foreign policies.[6] Not surprisingly, this thirty-year migration of scholarly focus raised a number of issues that it then left unresolved.

The first and most obvious issue is that the term culture has been defined in many ways and none of them is authoritative. Likewise, no real consensus exists among scholars regarding the concept of strategic culture.[7] Such uncertainty is an acceptable state of affairs in academia, but it is undesirable and even risky in the realm of policy, where any course of action can have substantial consequences. Nonetheless, many scholars did not wait for an authoritative definition of culture before ascribing a positive importance to it. Instead, they applied the term directly to the practice of strategy formulation, maintaining that culture could capture 'the persistence of a distinctive strategic approach', one that endures despite fundamental changes.[8] Others defined strategic culture in an almost unwieldy manner as: 'a nation's traditions, values, attitudes, patterns of behaviour, habits, customs, achievements and particular ways of adapting to the environment and solving problems with respect to the threat or use of force'.[9] With such a range of factors it is difficult to see how anything could avoid falling into the category of strategic culture, albeit paradoxically undefined.

Added to this problem, there is no established list of sources of culture. Scholars can not only define the term almost as they wish, they can also pick and choose from a veritable menu of sources; these include—but are not limited to—geography, climate, resources, organization, traditions, historical practices, political structures, ideology, myths, symbols, generational change, and technology.[10] However, selecting from such a smorgasbord moves significance away from the concept of strategic culture and shifts it towards the sources themselves. Strategic culture thus quickly loses value as an overarching concept. Furthermore, case studies which focus on different sources cannot be compared, and thus lose their utility. It does not make much sense, for instance, to define American strategic culture by sources that differ from those used to define Japanese or Russian strategic culture. And, yet, that is quite often what we find.

Still other scholars contend that strategic culture should be thought of as the 'context' within which strategic debate and formulation take place.[11] While this argument is intuitively attractive, one must proceed with caution, since context itself has no objective end. One can point to any number of variables, whether geography or historical experience, which are said to constitute context. Where historians and other scholars draw the line in terms of relevant context—pertinent geographical features and historical experience—is, however, ultimately a matter of professional and personal judgement.

Another factor, as the late anthropologist Clifford Geertz cautioned, is that all interpretations of culture are 'fictions in the sense that they are "something made" or "something fashioned"'.[12] And, as historian Jeremy Black warned, any interpretation of a particular culture is likely to have an artificial coherence.[13] Put differently, the factors selected by historians or social and political scientists to define cultures will contribute to the creation of fictions that are themselves driven by, and part of, larger narratives, which are likely to be, at a minimum, political. American strategic culture can, thus, have many guises depending on who fashions it, and none of them may be particularly accurate or useful. Such limitations are all but expected in academia, but in the world of policymaking they are not. Hence, any fashioning of strategic culture, whether one's own or that of another, can lead to wishful thinking about likely reactions to any desired course of action.

Another obvious problem is that the same culture can appear quite different at various times, depending upon the time frames selected for study, even if the variables selected are the same. It would be unwise to argue that American strategic culture at the end of the nineteenth century contrasts little with what it was perceived to be at the end of the twentieth century. In fact, one can already see another change taking place—the strategic culture that is emerging in the United States now differs substantially in terms of its values and priorities from the one it is replacing, though the extent of that change may not be known for a few years. Another problem is distinguishing between cultures and subcultures, and the extent to which one subculture might achieve only limited or temporal dominance. Studies of strategic culture tend to suppress change in favour of continuity; tensions and uncertainties are overlooked. The result is a static picture with each of its various elements portrayed as discrete and established.

## AMERICAN STRATEGIC CULTURE

It is perhaps because of these problems that scholars have not achieved any real consensus on a set of characteristics that define American strategic culture, despite numerous efforts. One can, nonetheless, find traits repeated in the literature. The first is a preference for fighting wars as battles. The second is a fascination with technology, also known as technological romanticism. The third is casualty aversion.[14] However, one must keep a number of issues in mind. First, all of these traits pertain to the waging of war. They, thus, describe a 'way of war' more than a strategic culture, per se, which by definition should also encompass a 'way of peace', which as a term is not meant to be entirely glib. Strategic cultures, if one decides to use the term, should describe approaches for achieving peacetime objectives as well as wartime ones. Second, none of these traits appears uniquely American: all can be said to belong to a larger Western way of war, of which there are again different interpretations. Third, none appears to have the quality of permanence or semi-permanence about it; instead, they seem contingent on political objectives and conditions rather than enduring or established biases. They might, however, qualify as a snapshot of current or recent American strategic culture, as far as that pertains to war.

In fact, one could well argue that American strategic culture and its attendant way of war, as they have been fashioned, appear to have more coherence in retrospect than they warrant. Two such tensions not captured by contemporary studies, for instance, include: that the US military itself is neither wholly transformed, nor fully transitioned; it is not only divided by service cultures, as many militaries are, but also by conflicting generational cultures.[15] It is not clear, therefore, in which direction American strategic culture might evolve. Estimates of what it is fail to capture that uncertainty.

## Fighting wars as battles

Although this trait is typically defined as a reliance on force-oriented strategies, that is, either the annihilation or attrition of the foe, it is perhaps more accurate to say that American strategic leaders are somewhat preoccupied with the 'grammar' of war. In short, this means that they tend to reduce the winning of wars to the winning of battles.[16] A number of historians have essentially confirmed, whether directly or indirectly, that the American way of war has long been in reality a 'way of battle'.[17] Recent events in Afghanistan and Iraq reveal just how important it is to develop a genuine way of war, one that can readily make linkages from tactical to strategic successes, rather than merely win battles. Americans have clearly demonstrated that they can close with and destroy any enemy, regular or irregular. However, the mere winning of battles, important as it is, rarely proves sufficient for advancing one's strategic aims. In truth, the US military has begun thinking more seriously in terms of wars rather than battles, but it still has some way to go.

To the extent that American strategic culture exists, and is preoccupied with the grammar of war, it must also be said that this preoccupation is subject to a great deal of political influence in practice. This is not to say that this influence has been either logical or rational, that is, capable of maintaining a suitable balance among ends, ways, and means. Instead, political processes appear to follow more the logic of convenience, or to have a very near-term focus. For all the recorded complaints of military professionals with regard to political indecision or 'war by committee', the American war machine has generally been made to submit to the logic of politics.[18] Some examples are the relief of General Douglas MacArthur during the Korean War; the overall conduct of the Vietnam conflict, calling a halt to the advance of coalition forces during Desert Storm; and the overall design and execution of Operation Iraqi Freedom. All of these instances demonstrate the degree to which political concerns drive and shape the grammar of war in practice, for better or worse.

## Technological romanticism

This trait is somewhat curious, for no reputable scholar would maintain that technological romanticism was a particularly American characteristic one hundred years ago. Western Europe was keenly engaged in the technological revolution that grew out of the industrial revolution. A general arms race was also underway that benefited in no small way from this technological revolution. In fact, the naval arms race, perhaps the most visible and expansive of its day, did not involve the United States directly, but Great Britain and Germany. It also encompassed many qualitative and quantitative dimensions. While technological preoccupation could be found in various forms in Britain, France, Germany, and the United States, it was also attended by a certain dread or anxiety about how technology itself was changing society in dramatic and apparently irreversible ways.[19] This fear carried over into the conduct of war, as military theorists and war planners attempted to comprehend the effects that submarines, aeroplanes, machine guns, and quick-firing and heavy artillery would have on offensive and defensive operations.

Even fifty years ago, American military hardware was arguably only marginally better than that of its Soviet counterparts. During the Cold War, both sides competed aggressively in terms of quantity and quality of conventional as well as nuclear weapons. The recent enthusiasm for technological innovation appears to have been an outgrowth of the so-called revolution in military affairs that began in the 1990s, and its successor, defence transformation, which took hold about a decade later. Certainly, those combined endeavours have involved dabbling in all sorts of 'high' technology. Nonetheless, that does not diminish the fact that technology as such—a tool—is an indispensable dimension of war, and that the United States has taken the opportunity of late to indulge itself by vigorously exploring that dimension. Yet, no quality of permanence or semi-permanence is to be found here.

## Casualty aversion

The characteristic of casualty aversion cannot be considered to be a unique or enduring part of American strategic culture. It was not, for instance, a factor in any of America's wars of necessity, such as the Civil War of the nineteenth century, or the First and Second World Wars, or the Korean conflict. Reported casualties (dead and wounded) in those wars numbered 646,000; 320,000; 1,100,000; and 140,000, respectively, which are extremely high by any measure.[20] It is accurate to say, nonetheless, that casualty aversion is a critical element in any war of choice; in the Vietnam conflict, for instance, casualties numbered 214,000, which is somewhat lower than the Second World War when seen as a percentage of troops in service, but it is about the same percentage as in the Korean conflict.[21] In wars of choice, the political opposition can make bold and deliberate use of casualty figures to build a case against the 'unwise' policies of the incumbent administration. Casualty figures, thus, quickly become powerful political weapons in such wars, since they have to be repeatedly 'sold' to the public. That casualties can become political tools only underscores just how genuinely political the grammar of war has become in the American example.

In sum, none of the traits discussed above appears uniquely American: each could be found in some significant degree in the strategic culture of any Western nation.

## KEY OMISSIONS IN THE 'AMERICAN WAY OF WAR'

Scholars have recently linked strategic cultures to ways of war, calling the latter both a product and subset of the former.[22] If that is true, then the American way of war is likely to suffer from some of the same kinds of limitations as the concept of American strategic culture. That has not prevented scholars from maintaining that there is, in fact, a unique and discernible American way of war—a view which this author supports. Not surprisingly, what scholars have produced is not one American way of war, but several. Russell Weigley, Max Boot, and Colin Gray are just a few who have contributed separate, and not entirely incompatible, versions of it.[23]

Although the late Russell Weigley published the first study of this topic in the 1970s, Colin Gray has made a more recent, and eminently detailed, contribution, which is noteworthy for these reasons.[24] Gray argues that the American way of war has twelve distinctive characteristics.[25] First, it is apolitical: it pays little heed to how military operations will affect the peace that follows. Second, it is astrategic: it rarely concerns itself with strategy. Third, it is ahistorical, learning little from history. Fourth, it is underpinned by faith in the idea that all conditions or crises are problems to be solved, and that all such problems *can* be solved. Fifth, it is culturally ignorant: it lacks genuine knowledge of other cultures and is insufficiently self-critical. Sixth, it is technologically dependent, seeking technology-based solutions. Seventh, it relies more on firepower than manoeuvre or other techniques. Eighth, it believes in fighting wars in a 'big way'. Ninth, it is too focused on regular as opposed to irregular warfare. Tenth, it is impatient, wanting results in record time. Eleventh, it is 'logistically excellent', in that American troops have generally been well supplied wherever they have gone. Last, it is sensitive to casualties, perhaps too much so.

These characteristics are as defensible as they are contestable. One might question, for instance, how many might also be found in European styles of warfare, and to what degree. Certainly, one can make a case for all of them, with perhaps the penultimate being the most difficult to prove, but clearly not impossible. To use the fifth characteristic as an illustration, one should not forget just how profound and pervasive the effects were of the technological revolution that gripped Western society during the quarter-century or so before the Great War. The British, in fact, are credited with having invented the tank, and of course all the major powers searched earnestly for technological (and other) solutions to the deadlock of trench warfare. Plus, strategic bombing theory, which is indisputably technologically based, had its roots in Europe, as did modern mechanized warfare. What is more, one should not forget that throughout the twentieth century much of Western popular literature portrayed technology as something that had the potential either to help or harm humanity; this tendency in turn suggests that Western culture in general has something closer to a love–hate relationship with technology.

One would also do well to ask where, or not just when, the American way of war began. Since the 1980s, historians have given more attention to the period before the Revolutionary War, that is, the period before Weigley's survey. In the process, they discovered some interesting things about 'early American ways of war'.[26] For one, it is clear that Native American ways of fighting influenced the American way of war, though just how much is uncertain. The early colonists apparently did not adopt Indian fighting methods as readily as once believed; however, they did change their ways of fighting over time, and for different enemies, which was also the case before the settlers left Europe. Second, Native American fighting was not always just a ritualized affair with few casualties, but was at times quite bloody and 'extirpative'. Third, early Americans apparently had few qualms about fighting an 'unlimited and irregular' form of warfare that involved attacking and killing non-combatants, and laying waste to villages and crops.[27] In many respects, this practice seems to have been a carry-over from Europe's Thirty Years War and other such devastating conflicts of the seventeenth century. The upshot of all this is that there may well have been several American 'ways' of war in evidence at any one time, and Weigley's seminal analysis, while thorough in some respects, may not adequately account for them. It is even less clear, as one moves through the decades, which traits have survived.

Just recently, in fact, the American way of war appeared to embrace a new model or way of fighting based on a combination of 'precision firepower, special forces, psychological operations, and jointness'.[28] These characteristics contrasted dramatically with those associated with the so-called traditional model, the principal trait of which was reliance on the use of overwhelming force. The characteristics of 'speed, jointness, knowledge, and precision' were publicly briefed by former Secretary of Defense Donald Rumsfeld in the summer of 2003, which further defined the 'new' identity.[29] The quick collapse of the Taliban in Afghanistan and the dramatic successes in the initial phases of Operation Iraqi Freedom, which featured the fall of Baghdad in record time and with remarkably low casualties on both sides, seemed to validate this new way of war.

However, as the conflict in Iraq developed into a complex form of insurgency, the flaws of this model were exposed. In short, the model did not have, nor did it ever apparently intend to emphasize, the appropriate capabilities or doctrine for conducting counter-insurgency operations. The US military ultimately adjusted to the demands of fighting an insurgency, and to date has made substantial progress in addressing what it sees as a second grammar of war.[30] However, the result for the military itself is that its identity is divided along at least three pathways: it is in part still that of a legacy or industrial-age force; in part a small, fast-moving, information-centred force; and in part a tool for countering insurgencies. It is not clear yet which of these identities will emerge as dominant, if any will, or whether one might see a hybrid of the three, or something entirely different.

## AN OVERLOOKED CHARACTERISTIC: THEORY

Curiously, among the various characteristics scholars have postulated as belonging to American strategic culture or way of war, one in particular has been overlooked, the American penchant for theorizing when it comes to military affairs. That penchant has long been overlooked because the prevailing assumption has been that Americans tend to emphasize practice over theory: that they have a preference for pragmatism and that this preference is purportedly part of their national character. While early in their history, Americans copied a great deal from their European counterparts, by the Cold War, American military theories, proffered by civilians and military professionals alike, came into their own.

Perhaps not surprisingly, these theories range from the ridiculous to the sublime. On the side of the latter, we have the naval theories of Alfred Thayer Mahan, the 'limited' war theories advanced by Robert Osgood and others, the fundamentals of coercive diplomacy put forth by Thomas Schelling, and the theories of military professionalism developed by Samuel Huntington and Morris Janowitz, among others.

On the opposite side, we have the escalation ladder of Herman Kahn, the ring theory of John Warden, the facile precepts of 'shock and awe' and some of the failed schemes generated during the so-called revolution in military affairs, such as effects-based operations. There are also a number of poorly grounded theories appending themselves to the idea that warfare is transitioning through a series of generations, and that it is already in its fifth or sixth generation. In all, the penchant for theorizing about war and warfare is relatively consistent in American military history. The number of sound theories may, however, be a minority compared to those which are not.

Mahan's theories of sea power, though effectively criticized later by Julian Corbett, provided an enduring rationale for the expansion of the US Navy, and have remained foundational to its doctrine into the twentieth century.[31] The following principles can be traced back to Mahan's theories: the safeguarding of sea lines of communication for maritime commerce will remain critical; a large navy of 'capital' ships is the best tool for protecting sea lines of communication; and the principal task of any modern naval force is to destroy the opposing navy in a decisive battle at sea. Carrier battle groups have now replaced battleships, and it is not clear what the next stage in the evolution of naval vessels will be. The US Navy's force structure and doctrine still reflect a big-ship mentality, even though debates rage every few years between those who advocate winning decisively at sea, in the tradition of Mahan, and those who prefer power projection, in the spirit of Corbett. The persistence of Mahan's theories also reveals that the American way of war is as battle-focused at sea as it was on land.

William (Billy) Mitchell's theories about the importance of airpower in warfare differed little in substance from those of the Italian air theorist Giulio Douhet.[32] Both believed the bombing of vital population and industrial areas would bring wars to an end more quickly, obviating the need for costly surface campaigns. Mitchell's theories, if lacking in originality, were, however, enough to spark debates over the roles and missions of the air service, which later became the US Air Force. Disputes over how to prioritize air support to surface commanders, which included establishing air superiority and interdiction missions vis-à-vis strategic bombing, have continued to the present. Airpower theories were recently given a new twist by former Colonel John A. Warden III, and others who sought to take advantage of the greater precision of long-range strike capabilities.[33] The aim was to cause 'decapitation', or strategic paralysis, by striking certain communications and infrastructural (and even cultural) targets, and thus cause enemy resistance to collapse.

Although limited war was hardly new in the 1950s, either in concept or in practice, particularly in the American context, it gained greater value and increased attention as an important alternative to general conflict. The concept lacked theoretical definition until Robert Osgood provided it. His seminal work, *Limited war*, which appeared in 1957, set down the basic principles of the theory.[34] The most important of these was the need to consider armed conflict in terms of a broader range of policy objectives, rather than simply a decisive military victory. As Osgood explained: the 'purpose of war is to employ force skilfully in order to exert the desired effect on the adversary's will along a continuous spectrum from diplomacy, to crises short of war, to an overt clash of arms'.[35] Accepting the idea that there were legitimate military objectives short of destroying a 'decisive' portion of an opponent's armed forces seemed to open up new roles for military power, while also underscoring the fact that escalation was not necessarily automatic. Similarly, while the concept of using force to coerce an adversary into taking a particular course of action was not new in the 1960s, it received renewed significance when Thomas Schelling gave the concept some much needed clarity. He further developed the idea of limited war by arguing that military force could be applied to coerce, intimidate, or deter an adversary, all of which were both less and more than decisive victory.[36] Both Osgood and Schelling thus promoted the idea that the use of military force could still be a rational extension of policy even in the nuclear age.

In certain respects, however, such theories stood in stark contrast to those advanced by the so-called nuclear strategists. The physicist Herman Kahn was perhaps the most well known among them; he argued that there were a number of scenarios in which 'limited' nuclear exchanges could take place between states without necessarily ending in global destruction.[37] In 1965, Kahn published *On Escalation*, in which he delivered the first systematic analysis of the concept, and developed a detailed, forty-four-step escalation ladder, which laid out six psychological thresholds covering the entire spectrum of war.[38] The thrust of Kahn's theories, in short, was that nuclear escalation could proceed in a controlled manner and thus serve as a means of coercion, just like more conventional weapons.

Aside from addressing war's grammar and its complex relationship to war's logic, American theorists also explored the nature of military professions and civil–military relations. The undisputed leader in these fields, the political and social scientist Samuel P. Huntington, argued that the optimum way to maintain civilian authority over the military was through 'objective control', that is, by establishing norms of professional conduct for the military and by allowing it to operate with autonomy within a clearly defined sphere.[39] In theory, the military would not step outside this sphere for fear it would compromise its professional standing. This theory was subsequently challenged by prominent sociologists, such as Morris Janowitz, who maintained that military professionalism has evolved into a more 'constabulary' model, and that this is desirable as militaries are more likely to protect societies in which they are stakeholders.[40] Both models have become foundational to the Western understanding of the military as a profession, and to the importance of professionalism as a channelling influence in modern society; both models are cornerstones in the field of civil–military relations internationally. The American military sees itself as a blend of the two models with a certain resident tension between them that leaves neither one predominant.

The theories of Osgood and Schelling were as much about war's grammar, which they tried to expand, as its logic, which they attempted to redefine. However, they ran into direct conflict with the prevailing view of military professionals, who believed that war's logic typically failed to acknowledge the constraints imposed by its grammar.[41] American military theorists hotly debated these and other theories in US professional journals even as they endeavoured to restore the 'art' to the art of war.[42] Americans also borrowed heavily from Soviet doctrine, particularly the idea of the deep attack.[43] The culmination of these theories was AirLand Battle doctrine, which appeared in the 1980s and was the governing doctrine for Desert Storm. With the essence of the operational art defined as the 'identification of the enemy's operational center of gravity and the concentration of superior combat power against that point to achieve decisive success', the American way of war remained, at root, a way of battle.[44]

Each thus began to explore ways to incorporate information technology into existing ways of fighting, and thereby transform them. The theories that came out of the 'revolution in military affairs', or RMA, claimed that information was the key to lifting the 'fog of war'.[45] Pioneers of this approach, such as Admiral Arthur K. Cebrowski, advanced the idea of linking all military platforms and command structures together through an information infrastructure, which would permit rapid information-sharing and greater efficiency and flexibility in mission execution. This idea came to be called network-centric warfare, or NCW.[46]

The information supplied by such a network was to enable a new concept called effects-based operations, or EBO. In short, EBO was supposed to achieve a 'desired strategic outcome or "effect" on the enemy through the synergistic, multiplicative, and cumulative application of the full range of military and other national capabilities at the tactical, operational, and strategic levels'.[47] Its supporters presume that it is possible to predict, and thus achieve, first, second, third, and fourth-order effects.[48] This presumption provided the basis for a brief experiment in Operation Iraqi Freedom with a concept known as 'shock and awe', the essence of which is to launch an optimum combination of area and precision munitions against key targets so as to decapitate or demoralize an opponent into compliance.[49] Unsurprisingly, the theory failed to pan out in practice.

## CONCLUSIONS

Although studies of strategic culture failed to provide any reliable descriptive or predictive models, they did heighten awareness of the dangers of mirror-imaging with regard to strategic decision-making. While such studies can provide frameworks of understanding for scholars, the artificialities and limitations of such frameworks must be acknowledged in advance. In the realm of policymaking, where some degree of uncertainty is unavoidable, studies of strategic culture do not appear to reduce it in any appreciable way.

Studies of strategic culture can, however, help indirectly by offering conclusions that can be challenged and critically examined. It is worth identifying what items such studies might have overlooked. It is also worthwhile to see merit not only in enduring themes or tendencies but also in the frictions and tensions that such studies tend to suppress. Along the same lines, it is certainly not inaccurate to say that American strategic culture itself is in a state of becoming, defined as much by its continuities as its discontinuities. This is true not only because its underlying tensions remain powerful and unresolved but also because scholars continue to debate and revise what they suppose American strategic culture is.

## NOTES

1. Jack Snyder, *The Soviet strategic culture: Implications for nuclear options* (Santa Monica, CA: RAND, 1977), 8; cited from Jeffrey S. Lantis, 'Strategic culture and national security policy', *International Studies Review*, 4/3 (2002), 87–113, esp. 94.
2. The concepts of strategic culture and ways of war are linked in Lawrence Sondhaus, *Strategic culture and ways of war* (London: Routledge, 2006), 1.
3. For a summary, see: Dima P. Adamsky, *American strategic culture and the US revolution in military affairs* (Oslo: Norwegian Institute for Defence Studies, 2008), 8–12; also Sondhaus, *Ways of war*; and Jeffrey S. Lantis, 'Strategic culture: From Clausewitz to constructivism', *Strategic Insights*, IV/10 (2005), http://www.ccc.nps.navy.mil/si/2005/Oct/lantisOct05.pdf
4. Examples include: Snyder, *Soviet strategic culture*; Ken Booth, *Strategy and ethnocentrism* (New York: Holmes and Meier, 1981); Colin Gray, 'National style in strategy: The American example', *International Security*, 6/2 (1981), 35–7.
5. Examples include: Yitzak Klein, 'A theory of strategic culture', *Comparative Strategy*, 10/1 (1991), 3; Alastair Iain Johnston, 'Thinking about strategic culture', *International Security*, 19/4 (1995), 32–64; Colin Gray, 'Strategic culture as context: The first generation of theory strikes back', *Review of International Studies*, 25/1 (1999), 49–69.

6. Examples include: Ted Hopf, 'The promise of constructivism in International Relations', *International Security*, 23/1 (1998), 914; Peter Katzenstein (ed.), *The culture of national security: Norms and identity in world politics* (Columbia, NY: Columbia University, 1996); Colin Gray, *Out of the wilderness: Prime time for strategic culture* (Washington, DC: Defense Threat Reduction Agency, 2006); Theo Farrell, *The norms of war: Cultural beliefs and modern conflict* (London: Lynne Rienner, 2005).

7. Stuart Poore, 'What is the context? A reply to the Gray-Johnston debate on strategic culture', *Review of International Studies*, 29/2 (2003): 279–84.

8. Jack Snyder, 'The concept of strategic culture: Caveat emptor', in C.G. Jacobsen (ed.), *Strategic power: USA/USSR* (New York: St Martin's, 1990); cited from Sondhaus, *Strategic culture*, 4.

9. Ken Booth, 'The concept of strategic culture affirmed', in Jacobsen (ed.), *Strategic power*; cited from Sondhaus, *Strategic culture*, 5.

10. Darryl Howlett, 'Strategic culture: Reviewing recent literature', *Strategic Insights*, IV/10 (2005); http://www.ccc.nps.navy.mil/si/2005/Oct/howlettOct05.pdf

11. Colin S. Gray, *Nuclear strategy and national style* (Lanham, MD: Hamilton, 1986); cited from Lantis, 'Strategic Culture', 94.

12. Clifford Geertz, *The interpretation of cultures: Selected essays* (New York: Basic Books, 1973), 15. Of course, Geertz, who defined culture as a 'historically transmitted pattern of meanings', represented only one school of thought among cultural anthropologists.

13. Jeremy Black, *Rethinking military history* (London: Routledge, 2004), 142.

14. Cf. Adamsky, *American strategic culture*; Thomas Mahnken, *United States strategic culture* (Defense Threat Reduction Agency: SAIC, 2006); Theo Farrell, 'Strategic culture and American empire', *SAIS Review*, 25/2 (2005), 3–18; Jeffrey Record, 'Collapsed countries, casualty dread, and the new American way of war', *Parameters* (Summer 2002), 4–23; James Burk, 'Public support for peacekeeping in Lebanon and Somalia: Assessing the casualties hypothesis', *Political Science Quarterly*, 144 (1999), 53–78; Carnes Lord, 'American strategic culture', *Comparative Strategy*, 5/3 (1985), 289–90.

15. Leonard Wong, *Generations apart: Xers and boomers in the officer corps* (Carlisle, PA: U.S. Army War College, 2000).

16. Antulio J. Echevarria II, *Toward an American way of war* (Carlisle, PA: U.S. Army War College, 2004).

17. Cf. Russell F. Weigley, *The American way of war: A history of U.S. military strategy and policy* (Bloomington, IN: Indiana University Press, 1973); and Max Boot, *Savage wars of peace: Small wars and the rise of American power* (New York: Basic Books, 2002).

18. Wesley K. Clark, *Waging modern war: Bosnia, Kosovo, and the future of combat* (New York: Public Affairs, 2001), 451.

19. Antulio J. Echevarria II, *Imagining future war: The West's technological revolution and visions of wars to come, 1880–1914* (Westport, CT: Praeger, 2007).

20. Hannah Fischer, Kim Klarman, and Mari-Jana Oboroceanu, 'American war and military operations casualties: Lists and statistics', updated 14 May 2008 (Washington, DC: Congressional Research Service Report for Congress).

21. Fischer, Klarman, Oboroceanu, 'Casualties', CRS-3.

22. Sondhaus, *Strategic culture and ways of war*, 1.

23. Antulio J. Echevarria II, 'The American way of war', in James C. Bradford (ed.), *A companion to American military history* (2 vols, Singapore: Blackwell, 2010), II, 843–55.

24. Russell F. Weigley, *The American way of war: A history of U.S. military strategy and policy* (Bloomington, ID: Indiana University Press, 1973).

25. Colin S. Gray, 'The American way of war: Critique and implications', in Anthony D. McIvor (ed.), *Rethinking the principles of war* (Annapolis: Naval Institute Press, 2005), 13–40.

26. Wayne E. Lee, 'Early American ways of war: A new reconnaissance, 1600–1815', *The Historical Journal*, 44/1 (2001), 269–89.

27. John Grenier, *The first way of war: American war making on the frontier, 1607–1814* (New York: Cambridge University Press, 2005).

28. Max Boot, 'The new American way of war', *Foreign Affairs*, 82/4 (2003), 41–58.

29. Summary of Lessons learned, prepared testimony by Secretary of Defense Donald H. Rumsfeld and General Tommy R. Franks, presented to the Senate Armed Services Committee, 9 July 2003; see also the remarks by Vice President Dick Cheney, 'A new American way of war', to the Heritage Foundation, 1 May 2003.

30. Published jointly in 2006 by the US Army and US Marine Corps, FM 3–24 *Counterinsurgency* and MCWP 3–33.5 constitute a baseline doctrine: Department of the Army, *FM 3–24 Counterinsurgency*, 15 December 2006 (Washington, DC: GPO, 2006); it has been much criticized for addressing only the Maoist model, which it does, and for not providing specific guidelines for how to win in Iraq; see Michelle Gordon, 'Army, Marine Corps Unveil Counterinsurgency Field Manual', *Army News Service*, 15 December 2006.

31. Philip A. Crowl, 'Alfred Thayer Mahan: The naval historian', in Peter Paret (ed.), *Makers of modern strategy from Machiavelli to the nuclear age* (Princeton: Princeton University Press, 1986), 444–80.

32. William Mitchell, *Winged defense: The development and possibilities of modern air power—Economic and military* (Dover, 2006); Phillip S. Meilinger, *Paths of heaven: The evolution of airpower theory* (Maxwell AFB, AL: Air University, 1997).

33. John A. Warden III, *Air campaign: planning for combat* (Washington, DC: National Defense University, 1988); see John Andreas Olsen, *John Warden and the renaissance of American air power* (Washington, DC: Potomac, 2007).

34. Robert E. Osgood, *Limited war: The challenge to American strategy* (Chicago, IL: University of Chicago Press, 1957); and *Limited war revisited* (Boulder, CO: Westview, 1979).

35. Robert E. Osgood, 'The post-war strategy of limited war: Before, during, and after Vietnam', in Anthony W. Gray, Jr and Eston T. White (eds.), *National security management: Military strategy* (Washington, DC: National Defense University, 1983), 179–218.

36. Thomas C. Schelling, *Arms and influence* (New Haven, CT: Yale University Press, 1966), 16, 34.

37. Herman Kahn, *On thermonuclear war* (Princeton, NJ: Princeton University Press, 1960).

38. Herman Kahn, *On escalation* (New York: Praeger, 1965).
39. Samuel P. Huntington, *The soldier and the state: The theory and politics of civil–military relations* (Cambridge, MA: Harvard University Press, 1957).
40. Morris Janowitz, *The professional soldier: A social and political portrait* (New York: Free Press, 1960).
41. Harry G. Summers Jr, *On strategy: A critical analysis of the Vietnam War* (Novato, CA: Presidio, 1982).
42. Shimon Naveh, *In pursuit of military excellence: The evolution of operational theory* (London: Frank Cass, 1997).
43. Naveh, *Pursuit of military excellence*, 292–5.
44. Department of the Army, *FM 100–5 Operations*, 20 August 1982 (Washington, DC: GPO, 1982), 2-1, 2-2; see also Swain, 'Filling the void', 159, and Allan English, 'The operational art', in Allan English, Daniel Gosselin, Howard Coombs, and Laurence M. Hickey (eds.), *The operational art: Canadian perspectives, context and concepts* (Kingston, Ontario: Canadian Defence Academy, 2005), 16.
45. Bill Owens, *Lifting the fog of war* (New York: Farrar, Strauss, and Giroux, 2000).
46. Arthur K. Cebrowski, 'Network-centric warfare: An emerging military response to the information age', Paper presented at the 1999 Command and Control Research and Technology Symposium, 29 June 1999; see also David S. Alberts, John J. Gartska, and Frederick P. Stein, *Network centric warfare: Developing and leveraging information superiority* (Washington, DC: C4ISR Cooperative Research Program, 1999), 2, for the accepted definition: 'an information superiority-enabled concept of operations that generates increased combat power by networking sensors, decision makers, and shooters to achieve shared awareness, increased speed of command, higher tempo of operations, greater lethality, increased survivability, and a degree of self-synchronization'.
47. Rapid Decisive Operations White Paper, January 2002, 20.
48. General Mattis rejected EBO because the predictability it promised ran counter to his own personal experiences in war, and the history of warfare itself; see General J.N. Mattis, USMC, Commander US Joint Forces Command, 'Commander's guidance regarding effects-based operations', Memorandum, 14 August 2008; and 'USJFCOM Commander's Guidance for Effects-based Operations', *Parameters*, 38/3 (2008), 18–25.
49. Harlan Ullman and James P. Wade, *Shock and awe: Achieving rapid dominance* (Washington, DC: Center for Advanced Concepts and Technology, 1996); for counterpoints, see Eric L. Haney, *Beyond shock and awe: Warfare in the 21st century* (New York: Berkley Caliber, 2006).

# 24

## Morality and Law in War

### David Rodin

Considered from a moral point of view, war presents two basic problems. The first is to explain why certain forms of harmful behaviour—killing, maiming, destroying property—are permitted in war, when they would in other contexts be prohibited in the strongest terms. The second is to explain why the liberty to harm in war is nonetheless not unlimited; why certain forms of harm and certain potential objects of harm are morally excluded. Any ethics of war, therefore, must articulate and sustain a morally intelligible configuration of permissions and restrictions—rights, liberties, and duties.[1]

The just war theory provides just such an account of rights and duties in war. At its heart lies a distinction between two sets of rules. The *jus ad bellum* provides a set of conditions under which going to war is deemed just. Classically, these include the possession of a just cause (most notably self-defence against aggression), proper authority, right intention, last resort, reasonable prospects of success, and proportionality. The *jus in bello* provides a set of conditions for just conduct in war. The most important *jus in bello* provision is the principle of distinction or discrimination which states that soldiers are entitled to attack enemy combatants, but are always prohibited from intentionally attacking non-combatants including civilians, the sick and wounded, chaplains, medical staff, and prisoners of war.

According to the dominant modern interpretation of just war theory, the *in bello* rights and obligations of combatants are both *symmetrical* (they are possessed equally by combatants on both sides of any war) and they are *independent* (the *in bello* rights and obligations possessed by combatants are in no way dependent on the *ad bellum* status of the operation in which they are participating). This entails that combatants—ordinary soldiers, seaman, and airmen—are not required to concern themselves with the justice of their war as a whole. As long as they abide by the provisions of *jus in bello*, they are deemed to do no wrong by fighting in a war, even if that war is unjust. So familiar are these ideas that they may seem barely worth interrogating or defending.

Yet both assumptions about the rights and duties of soldiers in war have been subject to sustained philosophical criticism in recent years.[2] These criticisms generate a fundamental challenge to the just war theory. The critical arguments against a symmetrical and independent interpretation of *jus in bello* are powerful in part because they begin from an extremely minimal starting point that is correspondingly difficult to contest. This is the assumption that humans have rights, and that among the most important of these is the right not to be killed or subject to attack. It follows that any moral view that attributes to soldiers an entitlement to kill—as just war theory does— must explain why this entitlement is consistent with the human right to life. If such an explanation cannot be provided then it is difficult to see how the killing of enemy combatants in war can be morally differentiated from murder, and how war itself can be sustained as a minimally acceptable activity.

The just war theory does indeed contain an explanation of this kind. According to classical formulations of just war theory, one's right against being attacked and killed is only effective so long as one is not posing a threat to another. The right not to be killed is possessed only by the 'innocent', where this term is understood in the context of its Latin root to mean those who are not 'nocentes' or threatening harm to others.[3] This criterion for forfeiture of the right against attack explains the traditional just war theory specification that all combatants are liable to attack, whereas non-combatants are not. For non-combatants (even if they are uniformed soldiers *hors de combat*) do not pose a threat to anybody.

The problem with this traditional explanation is that it seems straightfor-wardly false, at least when considered in any context outside war. One does not become liable to be killed simply by posing a threat (even a lethal threat) to another. Consider a police officer using reasonable force to prevent a serious crime, or a rape victim using defensive force against her assailant. It would be absurd to suggest that such persons lose their right against being killed or attacked simply because they are *posing* a threat to another. The crucial point omitted from the traditional just war explanation is that one becomes liable to harm only by threatening harm to others that is itself *unjust*, where unjust means in contravention of that person's rights.[4] If a person has no right against force being used against him, then he has no right to use force to avert or ward off that threat. The same holds true also for third party defence.

Even this specification may be too narrow. There are circumstances in which a person can pose an unjust threat to another for which he is in no way responsible. For example a person may pose an unjust threat to you because he was pushed by a third party and is now falling towards you. Is such an 'innocent threat' liable to defensive force given that he is in no way responsible for the threat he is posing? This question is contested in the literature, but many feel that while it may be excusable to inflict harm on the innocent threat if it were necessary to ward him off, this is not harm to which he would *liable* in the sense that it would violate none of his rights. After all, he has done nothing to facilitate or contribute to the harm he currently poses, and it is a distinctive feature of rights that they can be lost or forfeited only on the basis of some responsible action of the right holder himself—they cannot simply be stripped from us independently of our action for which we are responsible. If this is correct then it suggests that contributing to an unjust threat is not sufficient; it is also a necessary condition that one be *responsible* to some degree for the contribution.

To recapitulate: humans have the right to life. This right can be forfeited in certain circumstances, rendering a person liable to be killed. But one can be liable to defensive force only if one is at the minimum morally responsible for an unjust threat to another. All this seems clearly correct, yet it raises three profound challenges for the traditional interpretation of the just war theory.

First, it challenges the idea that all combatants possess a symmetrical and independent liberty intentionally to attack enemy combatants. If one loses one's right against being attacked and killed only by being responsible for an unjust threat, then it seems that combatants who are fighting in a just war and acting in conformity to the *jus in bello*, must retain their rights against being killed. For though they are posing a threat to the lives of enemy combatants, the threat they are posing is not *unjust*. This in turn implies that combatants who fight against just combatants in an unjust war are doing wrong, even if they scrupulously and exclusively use force against enemy combatants. Such a conclusion is striking and disturbing. Many people, including a number of soldiers on active service, believed that the 2003 invasion of Iraq was unjustified. But if the possession of *in bello* combatant rights are dependent on the *ad bellum* status of the operation of which they are a part, as this argument suggests, then it seems to follow that the soldiers who served there committed a profound wrong simply by fighting.

The first challenge questions the permissive aspect of the principle of discrimination, that which permits intentional attacks on enemy combatants. The second challenge questions the restrictive aspect of discrimination: the principle of non-combatant immunity. There are reasons to think that it is a necessary condition for losing one's right against attack that one be morally responsible for a threat that is itself unjust. But if responsibility for an unjust threat is a necessary condition for being liable to attack, then perhaps it is also a *sufficient* condition, even if the person responsible is not the one posing the threat, or is not currently posing the threat. There do seem to be cases in which individuals may forfeit their right against attack even though they are not currently themselves posing a threat. For example, if you hire a hitman to hunt me down and kill me and I can stop the hitman only by using lethal force against you, it seems that I would be permitted to do so even though you are not personally posing the threat to me. Some authors have argued on the basis of similar examples that some non-combatants may be liable to be harmed in war, even though they are not posing a threat to anyone, because they are responsible for the unjust threat posed by military personnel (perhaps by voting for the policies that send them to war, funding them through taxation, etc.).[5]

This challenge is less persuasive than the first. Although as I have suggested, there are some cases that suggest the liability in the absence of directly posing a threat, other cases suggest the opposite. Suppose you are the care-provider for a criminally insane psychopath and you negligently fail to give him his medication, as a result of which he engages in an unprovoked attack on my life. It does not follow that you would be liable to be killed, or that you should be killed in preference to the psychopath, if either course of action would be equally effective in preserving my life. This is the case even if we accept that you have a higher degree of moral responsibility for the threat to my life than the psychopath. This, and other cases like it, suggests that mere responsibility for an unjust attack in the absence of other conditions is not always sufficient for liability.[6] On the other hand, the examples we have already discussed show that currently posing a threat is not always necessary for liability. The clarification of this issue is clearly critical to the ethics of war. Its resolution touches complex and highly contested issues in the theory of self-defence that will require substantial further research. However, one observation that does seem relevant is that the cases in which we are tempted to believe that the responsible party can be liable to attack even though he is not currently posing a threat, all seem to be cases in which there exists a strong 'unity of intent' between the responsible party and the threatening party. Either they are cases of criminal conspiracy, as in the hitman case, or they are cases of institutionalized chain of command, as in the case of military organizations (clearly, commanding officers and rear serving combatants may be liable to attack, though they may personally pose a direct threat to no one). Most civilians clearly do not possess an analogous kind of 'unity of intent' with the military who conduct operations, and this may form part of the resolution of this puzzle.[7]

The third challenge to just war theory is potentially the most disruptive of all. It claims that reflecting on the conditions under which persons can lose the right to life will push us inexorably towards a position of contingent pacifism. Contingent pacifism is the view that it is in principle possible for war to be morally justified, but that in reality the conditions for war's justification will never actually be met. The contingent pacifist challenge emerges out of the last two challenges. If morality does not permit soldiers simply to target enemy combatants, but rather requires them to distinguish combatants (and potentially also non-combatants) who are morally liable to be targeted from those who are not, then it is difficult to see how combatants at war could do what morality requires. For it seems highly unlikely that soldiers would ever be able to make such fine-grained distinctions about individual liability in the heat of battle. This is especially the case since, as we have seen, judgements about liability depend upon prior determinations about the justice of the threat they are posing and their responsibility for it. If combatants in war cannot appropriately distinguish between those who are, and those who are not, liable to be attacked, then it seems that they are not able to participate in war without violating centrally important rights and that the only morally prudent decision would therefore be not to fight at all.

## SEPARATING LAW AND MORALITY

The three challenges to just war theory that we have surveyed derive from an extremely minimal assumption about the human right to life and plausible interpretations of the conditions under which that right can be lost or forfeit. Yet they generate conclusions profoundly at odds with traditional just war theory. They entail, for example, that a soldier fighting in an unjust war at the behest of a legitimate state authority, commits a grave crime simply by fighting, even if he adheres scrupulously to the law of armed conflict.

There are two important possible responses to these challenges. In two highly penetrating papers, Jeff McMahan and Henry Shue propose that the solution lies in articulating an important (though for each quite different) separation in the normative grounds for regulating violence. McMahan draws a distinction between the laws of war on the one hand and the morality of war (what in a previous chapter he called the 'deep morality of war') on the other.[8] Shue suggests that the morality of war is distinct from and should not be judged on the basis of ordinary interpersonal morality. I believe that neither solution can be successful, and that the attempt to establish a two-tiered morality, which divides either ethics from law or the ethics of war from the ethics of ordinary life, is mistaken. The remainder of this chapter explores issues raised by these two responses.

Jeff McMahan is one of the most original and subtle critics of the traditional symmetrical interpretation of just war theory. He believes not only that unjust combatants act impermissibly if they use force against just combatants but also that non-combatants can sometimes be liable to intentional attack in war if they are morally responsible for an unjust war. However, he takes his position to have surprisingly few implications for the way that the laws of war should be formulated. Although he believes that the *morality* of war (which ought to govern the conscience and actions of individuals) prohibits attacks on unjust combatants, he says:

> The formulation of the laws of war is a wholly different task, one that has to be carried out with a view to the consequences of the adoption and enforcement of the laws or conventions. It is, indeed, entirely clear that the laws of war must diverge

significantly from the deep morality of war as I have presented it. Perhaps most obviously . . . the laws of war must be neutral between just and unjust combatants, as the traditional theory insists that the requirements of *jus in bello* are.[9]

The laws of war cannot have the same content as the underlying morality of war for McMahan, because institutionalizing the content of morality into a legal system would have highly damaging consequences.[10] There are a number of reasons why this might be so. First, it might be thought that holding soldiers responsible for participating in an unjust war would adversely affect the ability of states to organize and maintain effective military defence forces. Rejecting the moral equality of combatants may thus carry the risk of making just states vulnerable to aggression.

Second, rejecting the moral equality of combatants might reduce the likelihood that unjust combatants would comply with other important *in bello* prohibitions such as the norms of non-combatant immunity, necessity, and proportionality. This may be because unjust combatants will lack an incentive to comply with currently accepted *in bello* prohibitions if they are not granted equal war privileges. If there is no moral distinction between attacking just combatants and attacking non-combatants, then there is little incentive for unjust combatants to abstain from the latter given that they are already committed to attacking the former.

Henry Shue argues that an interpretation of *jus in bello* that was non-neutral, in the sense that it distinguished between the rights of just and unjust combatants, would be largely useless as an action-guiding principle for soldiers at war. He reasons that, if soldiers have decided to participate in a war, then they presumably believe that their cause is just. Therefore, a rule which prohibited soldiers from killing the enemy, if (counter to what the soldiers actually believe) the enemy is fighting justly, would be irrelevant to the deliberation of those soldiers. For if they already believe that their war is just, then there is no useful way that they could apply the rule to regulate their conduct in war.[11]

A final and important area of concern with the proposal that combatants be held responsible for participating in unjust war is the issue of victor's justice. We may expect that any victors in war will declare themselves just and their enemy unjust. In such a context, victor's justice would in many circumstances become a euphemism for revenge and retaliation, with little meaningful correspondence between the 'punishments' inflicted on soldiers and their individual or even collective liability.

Now there are a number of potential responses to the claim that withholding combatant rights from unjust combatants would have harmful consequences in these ways. Most obviously, any harmful consequences that arise from such causes would need to be balanced against the potential benefits that may arise from providing a sanction for participation in unjust war. If this sanction were effective, it could reduce the total incidence of war with commensurate benefits of justice and security. Moreover, Shue's worry—that non-neutral rules could not deter participation in unjust war because they could not guide the actions of soldiers who mistakenly believe their cause to be just—seems to be misplaced. Those who favour an asymmetric interpretation of *jus in bello* do not propose rules of war that are non-neutral in the sense that they have the form 'if you are a just combatant do x'; 'if you are an unjust combatant do y'. The point is rather about the scope of application of the *ad bellum* rules. According to the traditional symmetrical interpretation of just war, the scope of application of the *ad bellum* rules is restricted so that combatants enjoy a general exemption from the rules. For proponents of asymmetry, there is no special exemption from *ad bellum* rules for ordinary soldiers so that compliance with the *ad bellum* rules is a precondition for compliance with the *in bello* rules. The *in bello* rules themselves are perfectly neutral and address just and unjust combatants in precisely the same way. It is simply that unjust combatants cannot be in compliance with them (as the rules specifying lawful force in self-defence cannot be satisfied by an aggressor). Note also that an asymmetric interpretation of *jus in bello* is not committed to holding that there is no moral distinction between harming just combatants and harming non-combatants. The correct interpretation of asymmetry is that while harming just combatants in an unjust war is wrong, harming non-combatants is *worse*. Regulation of a prohibited activity such as participation in an unjust war can therefore be achieved through norms specifying aggravating conditions of offences.

Moreover, it is possible for systems of rules to regulate the behaviour of mistaken actors who believe they are in compliance with the rules. This is precisely what legal rules covering negligent or reckless mistaken actors do by imposing a penalty on those who mistakenly believed that they are in compliance with the law, but who should have known better. Rules, both legal and moral, perform many important regulatory functions beyond their role in guiding the immediate deliberations of those addressed by the norms. Most obviously they help to inform the response of others. Thus, when an agent violates a rule based on a mistaken belief, this may be excusable or it may be culpable. It may merit forgiveness, moral condemnation, or legal sanction on the part of others. Each of these reactions plays an important part in the behaviour regulating function of rules by creating incentives and disincentives for forming beliefs in morally appropriate ways.

We should also be highly sceptical of arguments about the likely effects of differing configurations of rules, especially when, as is almost always the case in international relations, it is difficult to support such arguments with solid empirical evidence. Take for example the claim that holding soldiers responsible for participating in an unjust war would reduce the security of just states. Empirical evidence linking the attribution of individual responsibility to reduced military effectiveness is lacking.[12] Moreover, even if there is such an empirical link, the security of a just state clearly depends on two factors: its ability to organize and maintain effective defence forces and, second, the ability of any potential aggressor to organize and maintain effective offensive forces. Given that the norm prohibiting offensive war is tolerably (though by no means perfectly) clear, it is not unlikely that the corrosive effects of personal responsibility on military effectiveness would be felt more strongly by a potential aggressor than a defender. If this were the case then an asymmetric law of war might *increase* the net security of just states, even if it does reduce the effectiveness of individual fighting forces. This argument about the likely beneficial consequences of asymmetric *in bello* rules seems as intuitively plausible as the argument about its likely harmful consequences. We seem to have two independently plausible, but contradictory, interpretations of the likely effect of asymmetric *in bello* rules. The correct conclusion is that speculating about the potential harmful or beneficial consequence of complex matters of rule formulation is usually a futile exercise and a poor guide to ethics or to the configuration of international law.[13]

So there are some specific reasons to be doubtful of the arguments typically given as to why an asymmetric *jus in bello* would have bad consequences if instituted in law. But a deeper question is why McMahan thinks that the consequences of applying and enforcing a rule play a role in determining the content of the *legal rules*, which they do not play in determining the content of *moral rules*. McMahan's position articulates a striking distinction between two forms of norms. The first is the moral code which directly informs the action of individuals. He takes this to be predominantly deontological in character, being centrally concerned with the rights and duties of individual persons. The second is the moral considerations which guide the appropriate formulation of public law.[14] He takes this second tier of morality, which we might call 'the morality of public rule formation', to be predominantly consequentialist in character, taking into account compliance costs, opportunity costs, perverse incentives, moral hazard, and the like. But this distinction can seem quite ad hoc, why should there be these two distinct tiers of moral norms? If the consequences of applying a rule can decisively determine the appropriate content of legal norms, why should they not play an analogous role in determining the content of underlying moral rules?[15] His answer is illuminating:

> The morality of war is not a product of our devising. It is not manipulable; it is what it is. And the rights and immunities it assigns to unjust combatants are quite different from those it assigns to just combatants. But the laws of war are conventions that we design for the purposes of limiting and repairing the breakdown of morality that has led to war, and of mitigating the savagery of war, seeking to bring about outcomes that are more rather than less just or morally desirable. For the reasons given ... the laws of war must be mostly or entirely neutral between just and unjust combatants.[16]

The laws of war, on this view, are simply a form of useful convention. They are a product of human devising, designed to perform an instrumental role in achieving a certain set of goods, in this case ameliorating the harms of war. It follows from this view that the form and content of the law should be assessed, so far as possible, by its effectiveness in achieving these goods.

Now some forms of law clearly do have a status of this kind. Consider laws that establish what lawyers call *mala prohibita* offences.[17] These are laws, such as parking regulations, that introduce a prohibition into what was previously a realm of complete liberty. In the absence of regulation, there would be no requirement to park in one way rather than another. The prohibitions fulfil a socially useful function by coordinating behaviour, and the design and content of the prohibition is entirely subordinated to the contribution they make to social utility. There is no underlying 'morality of parking' to which one might expect or require the law to conform.

But other aspects of law are clearly not like this. *Mala in se* offences, such as most aspects of criminal law, provide for the legal regulation of action that is already wrong, independently of the law. In such cases the law does not simply introduce a socially useful prohibition or coordinating function where previously there was a liberty. Rather the law articulates and makes administrable an underlying moral norm. It follows that the law is not free to assume any configuration that may be maximally useful; it is substantially constrained by the content of the underlying norms.

To see the way that the content of such law is morally constrained by the content of underlying moral norms, consider the following example. Imagine a society in which an ethnic minority is despised and subject to persistent abuse and harassment. This abuse culminates in a macabre tradition on the national anniversary in which a single man from the community is captured and ritually hanged in the central square of the capital city. In the years in which the scapegoat ritual is prevented or fails, the general violence and abuse against the minority increase dramatically resulting in several dozen additional deaths. Suppose now that a proposal is put forward to formalize a set of legal rules regarding the treatment of the minority in this society. The lawmakers are humanely motivated and they have good reason to believe that the optimal law for securing the rights of the ethnic minority as a whole would be one which permitted the hanging of the ritual scapegoat under strictly controlled conditions and provided robust legal protection to members of the community outside this unique context.

Would such a law be morally permissible? It seems clear that it would not, and the reason is that such a law conflicts with the underlying moral rights of members of the ethnic minority. It is important to be clear about what is the nature of this conflict. It is not that the proposed law is failing to *secure* or *protect* the rights of the minority, at least on one understanding of what it means to secure rights. We may accept, for the sake of argument, that the scapegoating law will yield the smallest possible number of rights violations across the society as a whole. The decisive moral objection consists rather in the way that the law instrumentalizes the violation of the scapegoat victim's moral rights. It is true that the law has not mandated the death of the scapegoat victim. But the law has created a legal liberty right to violate the moral right to life of the scapegoat victim, and it has created this right *as a means* to securing some further good. As such the law is itself in violation of the underlying rights of potential victims.

The analogy with McMahan's proposal for the laws of war is obvious. On McMahan's view, the laws of war establish a legal privilege for unjust combatants to kill morally innocent just combatants, as a means to securing overall compliance with the laws of war and hence to maximizing overall welfare. Moreover, the killing of just combatants by unjust combatants is not simply a matter about which the law passes over or remains silent. The legal privilege functions as a positive right to kill, much in the way that the liberty to kill in self-defence functions as a right within domestic criminal law.[18] It functions as a codified exception to an established prohibition that may itself be relied upon in normative and legal argumentation. As the UK *Manual of the Law of Armed Conflict* says in summary of the Law of Armed Conflict: 'Combatants have *the right* to attack and to resist the enemy by all the methods not forbidden by the law of armed conflict.'[19] If the asymmetry thesis is true, then such a configuration of the law of war is inconsistent with morality for precisely the same reason that the scapegoat law would be inconsistent with it—it creates a legal right for certain people to violate the moral rights of others, as a means to achieving a broader desirable end. Laws that have this form are themselves clearly rights violating.

Now to say that such a configuration of the law would constitute a violation of underlying rights is not the same as saying that it would be, all things considered, morally wrong. It is conceivable that if the consequences of any alternative configuration of the law would be sufficiently bad, then that configuration of the law (though admittedly rights violating) could be justified as the lesser evil. However, once we see that rights are in play—it is not simply a matter of balancing overall good and evil consequences of rules, as with *mala prohibita* offences—it becomes clear that the threshold for justification of such a law is very substantially higher. Are there any cases in which *mala in se* offences are justifiably constructed so as to deviate substantially from their underlying moral norms?

McMahan considers as an example the penalty for rape in domestic criminal law. He argues that, even if it were true that rapists deserve (morally speaking) to be punished with death, it would be wrong to institute death as the legal penalty for rape, because rapists would then have an incentive to kill their victims, thus minimizing the chance of prosecution with no risk of additional punishment. The example clearly presupposes many assumptions that may be questioned.[20] But even if the assumptions of the example are accepted, the case does not constitute an analogy to McMahan's proposed separation between morality and law in the regulation of war. McMahan proposes that the laws of war should, for consequentialist reasons, create a legal right (liberty) to do something which is morally prohibited (killing just combatants who are not liable to be killed). In the rape case there is no suggestion that rapists should be granted a legal right to rape. Any morally acceptable criminal justice system must criminalize and punish rape; it is simply that (accepting the example's assumptions) we ought not to punish the convicted rapists to the full extent of their desert. This is clearly a very different matter.

A better example is the legal immunity from prosecution enjoyed by serving diplomats and their staff. The justification for this immunity is clearly of the consequentialist lesser-evil form. Given the importance of maintaining open diplomatic relations between states, it would be too dangerous to allow states to prosecute diplomats under local jurisdiction, since there would be a temptation to engage in tit-for-tat legal harassment that could quickly lead to the wholesale break down of diplomatic relations. Yet even the exemption from prosecution contained within the norm of diplomatic immunity stops short of attributing a *right* to break domestic law. The Vienna Convention on Consular Relations which establishes the modern norm is explicit on this point: 'Without prejudice to their privileges and immunities, it is the duty of all persons enjoying such privileges and immunities to respect the laws and regulations of the receiving State.'[21]

Furthermore, because we are discussing a potential lesser evil justification, the numbers really matter. Diplomatic staff globally number in the tens or hundreds of thousands, whereas members of the armed forces number in the millions. Moreover, it is no part of the task of diplomats to use force or engage in other activities that characteristically violate domestic law. I know of only one modern example of a murder committed by a person enjoying the privileges of diplomatic immunity.[22] Soldiers on the other hand use lethal force as part of their stock in trade and, given the traditional precept that a war cannot be just on both sides, a significant proportion of the military action undertaken by soldiers is within the context of wars that are unjust. If, as McMahan believes, the killing and destruction inflicted by unjust soldiers on just combatants is a grave moral crime, then the law is creating a liberty right to engage in rights violations on a massive scale, as a means (and a means of unproven effectiveness at that) to achieve other goods. It is hard to imagine how such a configuration of the law could be acceptable as a matter of basic morality.

## SEPARATING THE MORALITY OF WAR FROM
## THE MORALITY OF ORDINARY LIFE

The second potential response to the three challenges proceeds differently. Henry Shue proposes that we respond to the argument for an asymmetric *jus in bello* by recognizing a separation, not between law and morality, but between two distinct kinds of moral code: that appropriate to war and that appropriate to ordinary life.[23] Shue argues that McMahan and other proponents of asymmetry in the rules of war systematically beg the question by drawing a false continuity between the rules appropriate to war and the rules appropriate to other aspects of ordinary life. War is fundamentally different from ordinary life. So much so, that the practice of war is necessarily incompatible with many of the rules of ordinary morality. Shue quotes with approval Michael Walzer's assessment of McMahan's position:

> What Jeff McMahan means to provide . . . is a careful and precise account of individual responsibility in time of war. What he actually provides, I think, is a careful and precise account of what individual responsibility in war would be like if war were a peacetime activity.[24]

Shue believes that the basic problem with the asymmetry argument is its insistence that the criterion for liability to attack in war is *individual* moral liability. However desirable it might be to align liability to attack in war with individual moral liability, this is simply not possible. Given the kind of activity war is, no combatant at war could determine whether the enemy combatant he is aiming at fulfils the conditions for moral liability (that they are at the minimum morally responsible for an unjust threat that constitutes a sufficient just cause for war). 'This is not an appeal to consequences,' says Shue, 'it is an observation about what is possible.'[25]

Therefore, if we are to have a morality of war—a moral code for regulating the conduct of war—it must presuppose a criterion for liability that is very different from that appropriate in contexts outside war. In particular, liability for intentional harm in war cannot be individual moral liability to harm, as it is in ordinary life. To criticize the morality (or laws) of war, on the basis that they diverge from the moral requirements of ordinary life is simply to beg the question. For one would first need to demonstrate that there is a meaningful continuity between the morality of ordinary life and war, and that the morality of war should conform to the morality of everyday life.

In one sense this is just the argument for contingent pacifism turned on its head. That argument claimed that human rights impose requirements on combatants that cannot be fulfilled in war, and therefore the moral possibility of war should be rejected. Shue's argument begins from the same premise, but concludes that the moral rules properly applicable to war cannot fundamentally be structured around human rights. This is why Shue is careful throughout to couch his argument in conditional terms: a separate morality of war is viable only 'if war can be tolerated',[26] and later 'unless we can eliminate war'.[27]

One important question here is clearly whether the contingent pacifist argument and Shue's related argument for a separate morality of war are correct in their assessment that the criteria of individual liability to harm are impossible to apply to the circumstance of war, thereby forcing us to reject either the permissibility of war or the overriding relevance of human rights to war. McMahan certainly does not see his argument as leading to a pacifist conclusion, but rather as suggesting a wholesale reinterpretation of the conditions for using force in war. Much will depend therefore on the crucial and still unresolved question about the grounds of liability to force that we touched upon earlier. If it were possible to demonstrate that minimal responsibility for an unjust threat is a necessary but not sufficient condition for liability to force, but that it can become sufficient in the context of present aggression, then it may be possible to arrive at plausible criteria that both allow the targeting of all combatants engaged in an unjust war, but prohibit the targeting of all or almost all non-combatants. However, it is very far from clear that it is possible to defend such criteria.[28]

Let us accept for the moment that this task cannot be achieved and that the 'impossible to apply to war' charge is a sound one. Would Shue's proposal to acknowledge a separate ethics of war (one that permitted the killing of those not individually morally liable to be killed) be an acceptable response? To see what is at stake here, consider how we might think of an advocate of slavery in 1806 who made the following response to prohibitionist critics:

> You tell me that slavery is morally impermissible because it is inconsistent with the dignity of persons and the fundamental precept that no human should be the chattel property of another. But this simply begs the question by applying the moral rules appropriate to ordinary life to the quite different activity of slave-holding. Nowhere have you demonstrated that there is a meaningful continuity between the moral rules appropriate to ordinary life and the moral rules appropriate to slave-holding. Indeed slave-holding is so different from ordinary life that the practice would be utterly impossible if one had to abide by ordinary moral rules such as the prohibition on owning another person—this is indeed one of the tragic things about slavery. But if we are to regulate the practice of slavery we must recognise that the content of those regulations must be very different from the content of ordinary morality and must allow the owning of other persons.

Clearly, we ought not to be very impressed with this line of thought.

The point, of course, is that from the fact that a particular practice or form of conduct requires its own divergent moral or legal rules, it follows neither that the rules nor that the activity itself are morally acceptable. Any practice that requires separate moral rules, divergent from the moral rules of everyday life, must itself be interrogated and assessed in moral terms. We cannot simply assume that the underlying activity and its special code are morally acceptable; in many cases—as with the slavery example—they will not be.

So how are we to assess the moral acceptability of practices that would require divergent moral codes? Two points are critical. The first is that we start with a defeasible presumption against such deviation. The fact that a practice requires a moral code inconsistent with the morality of ordinary life is a consideration that stands against it, and in need of some substantive justification. The second point is that this justification can only be achieved by reference to the values and principles of ordinary morality itself.

Consider for example, the separate and divergent sets of rules that allow prosecuting barristers to engage in aggressive questioning of witnesses, or allow psychiatrists not to disclose potentially incriminating information about their clients (within reason). In each of these cases, we ask whether permitting a localized deviation from ordinary moral rules by these special codes is justifiable in terms of the broader contribution they make to those same underlying ordinary moral values. In both cases the answer is yes, though it is equally apparent that the burden of proof is held by those who propose and maintain the separate moral code.

Shue complains that defenders of asymmetry are begging a question by assuming that moral norms from everyday life apply also to war. But it is only by reference to ordinary norms—the ordinary morality of everyday life—that we can establish whether a proposed practice and its divergent norms pass the minimum threshold of moral acceptability at all. Clearly, it would be entirely circular and question-begging to assess the morality of a practice like war, slave-holding, or cross-examination by barristers by the lights of special moral codes that already assumed the special rights and liberties in question. Ordinary everyday morality is thus inescapable.

But, it may be argued, war is equally inescapable. We shall never eliminate war, and precisely because it is a serious matter we must try to regulate it as best we can, moderating its evils to the extent that this is possible. This will necessarily require a permissive regulatory regime that recognizes, at some level, the legitimacy of unjust combatants engaging in war. We have no other choice, since we do not have the luxury of eliminating war by fiat of moral will.

This reasoning is certainly tempting, but it cannot be right. For consider: 200 years after the abolition of the UK slave trade, it is estimated that there are more slaves in servitude today in absolute terms than before prohibition. Slave-holding, like war, is a practice with deep societal and behavioural roots. In all likelihood, slavery, like war, will never be eradicated from the face of the earth. Similarly with theft, rape, murder, and most other criminal practices: though outlawed and morally prohibited, such practices will never be eliminated. Yet nobody supposes that the inescapable nature of these practices provides any reason to implement a permissive regulatory regime that implicitly recognizes their legitimacy.

But perhaps the difference is this. Even though slave-holding, rape, murder, and the like cannot be eradicated, they can be substantially controlled through prohibitionary norms. Prohibition of these practices protects the rights of potential victims more effectively than a regime of permissive regulation. It is this fact that explains why we prohibit rather than legitimize and regulate such practices. Moreover, it is precisely this expectation that we do not have in the case of warfare. If an outright prohibition of war could be expected to yield better protection than its permissive regulation, then participation in war (or at least participation in unjust war) should be prohibited, but until such time we must endorse a special 'morality of war' with its uncomfortable deviations from ordinary morality.

But this response, which turns on the consequences of prohibition compared with permissive regulation, entirely misrepresents the moral objection to a regulatory regime for slavery or most criminal practices. Suppose there had been good evidence in 1806 that a regime of strict regulation of the slave trade would yield better protection for the victims of slavery than its outright prohibition.[29] Would this be a good reason for implementing a 'humanitarian' regulatory regime for slavery and recognizing a special 'morality of slave-holding' (sadly at odds with the 'morality of everyday life')? It would not. This is essentially the same point as was made above against a consequentialist approach to the content of *mala in se* offences. When rights of fundamental importance are at stake—rights like the right against rape, the right against torture, the right not to be killed unless liable—then the content of moral and legal norms cannot be simply determined by consequences. The content of the rights sets basic constraints on what the content of the law can be, and whether it is morally intelligible to engage regulation (rather than prohibition) of the practice at all.

It is the nature of the right to life that is the fundamental sticking point. Shue characterizes the requirement never to kill intentionally those who are not morally liable as a requirement of 'the morality of ordinary life', implying thereby that it is a moral rule for civilian life; life excluding war. But this is misleading. The requirement is not a feature of the morality of 'ordinary life' understood as excluding the practice of warfare (anymore than the prohibition on ownership of another person is a requirement of the morality of 'ordinary life' excluding the practice of slave-holding). It is rather a central feature of the ordinary morality of human life—a form of life that includes practices as diverse as slavery, murder, self-defence, aggression, warfare, and so forth.

In 1939, G. E. Moore famously held up his hands before an audience at the British Academy and purported thereby to prove the existence of the external world.[30] Moore's common-sense 'proof' never persuaded committed philosophical sceptics, but the demonstration had a serious and persuasive point.

Propositions about the existence of ordinary objects like Moore's hands can be known with greater certainty than the premises of all the fancy sceptical arguments. Arguably, a similar point is true of the status of certain kinds of moral fact. That one ought never to kill a person who has done nothing to make themselves liable to be killed has a kind of elementary status in our morality (similar to the status possessed by the proposition one ought never to rape or hold another person as chattel property). Like the existence of Moore's hands in epistemology, it seems that *whatever* else we can know about morality, we can know *these things*. We can be more certain of these propositions than we could ever be of the largely consequentialist premises of arguments that seek to establish the viability of divergent legal or moral systems. The supposition of a viable, separate, and divergent morality of war or law of war may feel reassuring, but it is ultimately not sustainable.

# NOTES

1. The task is considerably complicated by the fact that the very possibility of justifying the permission to engage in war is challenged by the moral argument of pacifism, and the possibility of justifying restrictions in war is challenged by certain forms of realism.

2. These criticisms and the issues raised by them were the subject of a major Changing Character of War research project resulting in the book: David Rodin and Henry Shue (eds.), *Just and unjust warriors: The moral and legal status of soldiers* (Oxford: Oxford University Press, 2008).

3. See G.E.M. Anscombe, 'War and murder', in G.E.M. Anscombe, *Ethics, religion and politics*, volume 3 of *The collected philosophical papers of G. E. M. Anscombe* (Oxford: Basil Blackwell, 1981), 51–61 (essay first published in 1961).

4. There are further complex questions that need not detain us here about whether one can become liable to defensive harm for infringing a person's rights in a way that is all things considered justified because it is the lesser evil (e.g. a farmer who burns a neighbours field to stop a wild fire engulfing the town).

5. See in particular Jeff McMahan, *Killing in war* (Oxford: Oxford University Press, 2009), chapter 5; Jeff McMahan, 'The ethics of killing in war', *Ethics*, 114/1 (2004), 718ff.

6. I discuss this issue in David Rodin, 'The moral inequality of soldiers: Why *jus in bello* asymmetry is half right', in Rodin and Shue (eds.), *Just and unjust warriors*, 44–68.

7. Some civilians, of course, *do* possess this form of unity of intent because they are formal parts of the chain of command. A possible implication of this thought is that civilian leaders who are part of the formal chain of command should be considered as potentially liable to direct attack in war.

8. See Jeff McMahan, 'The morality of war and the laws of war', in Rodin and Shue (eds.), *Just and unjust warriors*, 19–43, and 'The ethics of killing in war', 729ff.

9. Ibid., 730.

10. He is not alone in thinking this. Commensurate arguments are presented in our volume by Adam Roberts and Judith Lichtenberg (see *Just and unjust warriors*, 'The principle of the equal application of the laws of war' and 'How to judge soldiers whose cause is unjust').

11. See Henry Shue, 'Do we need a "morality of war"?', in Rodin and Shue (eds.), *Just and unjust warriors*, 108ff.

12. It is often said, for example, that if soldiers were to be held responsible for *ad bellum* offences, then armies would presumably be required to grant them at least a *de facto* right of conscientious objection for wars which they believed to be unjust. Soldiers would be required to choose which wars and campaigns they participate in, and such a practice, it is assumed, would destroy the effective fighting discipline of a military force. But this assumption is not borne out by the experience of mercenaries or private military companies who only have a contractual relationship with their personnel. They are not able to coerce obedience through court martial, and yet they appear able to field effective and disciplined fighting units.

13. I call this 'the impasse problem' and explore it in detail in David Rodin, 'The problem with prevention', in Henry Shue and David Rodin (eds.), *Preemption: Military action and moral justification* (Oxford: Oxford University Press, 2007), 143–71.

14. McMahan himself articulates his view somewhat differently as positing a distinction between the morality of war and the law of war. But the real distinction underlying his position seems to be better articulated as a distinction between the morality of personal action and the morality of public rule formation. See McMahan, 'The morality of war', 33ff.

15. Compare Henry Shue, 'Do we need a "morality of war"?', 111.

16. McMahan, 'The morality of war', 35.

17. On the distinction between *malum prohibitum* and *malum in se*, see Jeremy Waldron, 'Torture and positive law: Jurisprudence for the Whitehouse', *Columbia Law Review*, 105/6 (2005), 1691f.

18. See on this David Rodin, *War and self-defense* (Oxford: Oxford University Press, 2002), 30f.

19. UK Ministry of Defence, *The manual of the law of armed conflict* (Oxford: Oxford University Press, 2004), 38 (emphasis added).

20. One such assumption is that equivalent punishments for rape and murder will incentivize murder (in many jurisdictions the maximum penalty for both rape and murder is life imprisonment). Moreover, the example will only be relevant if one assumes that criminal penalties are a matter of desert, rather than liability. A punitive sanction is deserved if the infliction of the sanction is morally mandated or good in itself, independently of the good consequences it may bring about. But to say that a person is liable to punishment is to say only that they would not be wronged in applying the punishment as a means to (or in the course of) bringing about some further good. If punishment is a matter of

liability rather than desert, then a law would be violating no underlying moral norm by failing to apply punishment to the full potential liability when doing so would be counterproductive.

21. Vienna Convention on Consular Relations, 1963, art 55.1.
22. In 1984, policewoman Yvonne Fletcher was killed by a person shooting from inside the Libyan embassy in London.
23. Shue, 'Do we need a "morality of war"?'.
24. Michael Walzer, 'Response to McMahan's Paper', *Philosophia*, 34/1 (2006), 43.
25. Shue, 'Do we need a "morality of war"?', 99.
26. Ibid., 95.
27. Ibid., 96.
28. For reasons to be sceptical, see McMahan, 'The morality of war', 30–3; Seth Lazar, 'Responsibility, risk, and killing in self-defense', *Ethics*, 119/2 (2009), 699–728; Idem., 'The responsibility dilemma for killing in war', *Philosophy and Public Affairs*, 38/2 (2010), 180–213.
29. This is not entirely implausible: the practice of slavery is deeply engrained—and profitable. Would prohibition be enforcible? Would it ever be effective? Would the trade simply move to other states with even less concern for the welfare of the 'cargo'?
30. G.E. Moore, 'Proof of an external world', *Proceedings of the British Academy*, 25 (1939), 273–300.

# 25

## Target-Selection Norms, Torture Norms, and Growing US Permissiveness

*Henry Shue*

### TWO CHALLENGES TO DEEP NORMS

'Here are soldiers moving away from the scene of a battle, marching over the same ground they marched over yesterday, but fewer now, less eager, many without weapons, many wounded: we call this a retreat. Here are soldiers lining up the inhabitants of a peasant village, men, women, and children, and shooting them down: we call this a massacre.'[1] In order to understand the movements of persons as human actions, we cannot simply describe them as physical behaviour, but we must credit them with meaning; and the meaning is often normatively charged. It is not often the case that there is a descriptive account of what a human action is, and then separately there is a normative assessment of the action. The normative assessment is ordinarily an essential part of the account of what the action is. We are often attempting to accomplish something and succeeding or failing to do so. Michael Walzer's plainly powerful prose reflects the facts that a movement is not a retreat unless it is a strategic failure, and an activity is not a massacre unless it is a moral failure. Civilized war, if there be such a thing, is a phenomenon that is centrally defined by what is permitted and what is not permitted within it. Military actions are described in part by whether they comply or fail to comply with permissions and prohibitions.

Setting out to kill people is not generally permitted. Neither is setting out to wound them, take them prisoner, or destroy their shelters and vehicles. But these and other normally prohibited displays of violence are permitted within even what is usually considered to be civilized war. Someone who does not understand that kinds of violent activities that are almost universally prohibited outside war are selectively permitted inside war would not understand what civilized war is. A civilized war is not a war in which no one gets hurt—it is a war in which only certain types of people get hurt. It is utterly fundamental to the nature of war both that it is an enterprise that permits certain selective uses of violence that are completely forbidden in any other circumstances and that this permission has distinct limits.

Of course people regularly challenge particular formulations of the rules specifying which uses of violence are permitted. Two such ongoing challenges, which I believe are misguided, are summarized here. Proposing to change the fundamental norms of war is not fiddling around the edges of war, but attempting to change the very essence of what civilized war is. This is not intended to be a general objection against change in fundamental norms or in favour of only incremental change rather than radical change. Deep norms can change, and change radically, as, for instance, happened when humanity concluded that one state might not own and rule another one. The limits on civilized war may change, but these changes must themselves be limited— without limits, we are into total war, not restrained or 'civilized' war.

The moral so far is simply that the stakes are high when we re-examine central, basic norms. Change in such norms not simply can be radical but is guaranteed to be radical, because it changes the nature of the enterprise and changes it specifically by redrawing the line between the permissible and the impermissible. What the norms are, then, matters profoundly. Debates about them are not like debates about whether to require the wearing of white clothes when one plays tennis but like a debate about whether to give points for how far one hits the tennis ball rather than whether it lands inside the lines on the other side of the net. Norms determine who and what may permissibly be attacked, and what may and may not be done to people who are captured. Ruling people in and out as permissible targets for various activities is a matter of life and death, and of sanity and trauma, insofar as the norms in question do in fact come to be accepted as guides for behaviour by people with weapons and power. The battles over norms are a crucial part of the overall war between civilization and savagery. How are we to understand contemporary war? One important way is to see what is permitted and what is not permitted by what people want to call 'civilized war'.

Recent years have seen powerful assaults on some of the fundamental norms of war by elements within the current military superpower, most famously perhaps the challenges in theory and practice to the prohibition on preventive war.[2] Here I shall very briefly summarize two other challenges; first, the challenge by the US military to the internationally accepted norm specifying legitimate targets or, in the terms of international law, 'military objectives'; and, second, the challenge by US political leaders to the internationally accepted definition of torture.[3] Efforts are underway to broaden the definition of military objective, so that attacks on a wider range of targets are permitted, at the same time as efforts to narrow the definition of torture, so that fewer forms of interrogation are prohibited. In both cases the changes are in the direction of extreme permissiveness and away from moderating limits.[4]

## WIDENING 'MILITARY OBJECTIVE'

The militaries with the largest budgets have in recent years greatly increased their stocks of precision-guided munitions (PGMs). The conclusion is sometimes drawn that war must therefore be becoming more restrained, but precision-guidance technology is only as good or bad as the strategies it serves and the rules that control its use. Many other things being equal, PGMs are more likely to hit their targets than the so-called 'dumb' munitions. Common sense might suggest, then, that in an era with increasing numbers of PGMs, the wealthiest militaries would find it, if anything, easier than ever to accept the standard understanding in international law of a military objective, or legitimate target. If one was able to live with the standard understanding while employing 'dumb' munitions, it should be increasingly easier to live with it as one acquired more PGMs. In any case, one might think, there would be no reason to push for looser, more permissive understandings of what counts as a military objective. So says common sense, but so much the worse for common sense, because just the opposite has been happening among the theorists of the US military.

Why, if one has more accurate weapons, would one want greater latitude about what to strike? The short answer is that PGMs have encouraged the rebirth of a fantasy that one can have bombing both ways: kill fewer civilians but simultaneously put more pressure on civilians nevertheless—Douhet without as many deaths. The US military is only a single case, but it is the most important one because of the extent of its air power; and it provides a provocative case study of the relation between changing technology and changing norms, including, sadly, retrogressive change in norms. What we will see is a new technology that one might have expected to take pressure off a norm—the norm governing acceptable targets—providing instead a rationale for putting more pressure on the norm in order to try to loosen it up. PGMs have given the targeteers the confidence to be more ambitious.

In 1998, the US air force issued Doctrine Document 2–1.2, *Strategic attack* (1998), which expressed decided and well-founded ambivalence about the ability of air power to achieve military results by the old means of breaking civilian morale: 'Despite attempts to achieve psychological collapse of an adversary through population attack—most notably by the German and British strategic air campaigns of World War II—*the ability of airpower to achieve victory through direct psychological impact alone (without resort to WMD) has not been substantiated.* A prolonged strategic air campaign against morale targets, on the contrary, may serve to stiffen national resolve and neutralize the desired psychological impact as occurred during the Battle of Britain during World War II and Operation Rolling Thunder in Vietnam. Thus, a *demoralizing* psychological impact can be an elusive objective.'[5] This is all perfectly true, and quite wise, but when Doctrine Document 2–1.2 was reprinted in 2003, the entire passage I have just quoted had disappeared from it. Why?

One significant factor that had intervened prior to the 2003 printing of *Strategic attack* was the appearance of *The commander's handbook on the law of naval operations* (1995),[6] along with its *Annotated supplement* (1999),[7] which reaffirm without qualification the permissive language about 'military objective' that has in recent years become habitual in US military publications.[8] In 2006, Michael N. Schmitt still described *The commander's handbook* and its *Annotated supplement* as 'the most recent and authoritative American LOIAC [Law of International Armed Conflict] manual'.[9] The *Annotated supplement to the commander's handbook on the law of naval operations* has the apparent merit of offering citations in support of its language, although on the question at hand they turn out to involve doubled misreadings of the sources invoked.

Paragraph 8.1.1 defining military objectives says: 'Military objectives are combatants and those objects which, by their nature, location, purpose, or use, effectively contribute to *the enemy's war-fighting or war-sustaining capability* and whose total or partial destruction...'[10] But this is not in fact the definition of military objective found in international law or in, notably, US Army Field Manual 27–10, *The law of land warfare*, in effect since 1956. The analogous portion of the standard definition says: 'Military objectives are limited to those objects which by their nature, location, purpose or use make an effective contribution to military action and whose total or partial destruction...'[11] The version of the definition of 'military objective' from the *Annotated supplement* (1999) contains two enormous departures from international law that expansively loosen the definition. First, 'contribution to...action' has been replaced by 'contribute to...capability'. Far more objects contribute to a nation's *capability* for military action than are contributing during any given period to *action*. So what the *Annotated supplement* (1999) claims may be bombed is not only what is effectively contributing to military action but also anything that could contribute effectively to sustaining a military action, which looks as if it includes most of any society's economy and certainly all its essential infrastructure, including most of what punishment bombing intended to break civilian morale would want to target, apart from civilians themselves. As distinguished legal authority Frits Kalshoven pointed out as early as 1991, 'to add "war-sustaining effort" is going too far, however, as this might easily be interpreted to encompass virtually every activity in the enemy country'.[12]

Nevertheless, the note to the sentence quoted from para. 8.1.1 declares that 'this definition is accepted by the United States as declarative of the customary rule',[13] and refers forward to a note accompanying the following even more permissive statement: 'Economic targets of the enemy that indirectly but effectively support and sustain the enemy's war-fighting capability may also be attacked.'[14] The note accompanying the last sentence quoted also begins with the declaration that 'the United States considers this a statement of customary law' and cites as its primary authority a letter written by the General Counsel of the Department of Defense on 22 September 1972.[15] In flat contradiction to the *Annotated supplement*, the most authoritative statement of customary law available today uses precisely the terms of 1977 Geneva Protocol I, Art. 52:2: 'Rule 8. Insofar as objects are concerned, military objectives are limited to those objects which by their nature, location, purpose or use make an effective contribution to military action and whose total or partial destruction . . .'[16]

In fact, the *Annotated supplement* misreads the 1972 Pentagon General Counsel's letter, and the 1972 letter, in turn, had misread one of its own primary sources, the 1954 Hague Convention.[17] It is worth noting each of these doubling errors. The 1972 letter does indeed advocate, in an entirely negatively phrased sentence, some understanding of military objectives that would be more permissive than the definition that was actually five years later incorporated into the 1977 Geneva Protocol I: 'Attempts to limit the effects of attacks in an unrealistic manner, by definition or otherwise, solely to the essential war making potential of enemy States have not been successful [in the sense of being adopted as State practice].'[18] Although it was somewhat confusing to write of 'effects of attacks' rather than of attacks and their objectives, the Pentagon Counsel's 1972 letter clearly intended, by declaring it to be unrealistic to attempt to limit the effects of attacks 'solely to the essential war making potential of enemy States', to embrace as acceptable targets objects beyond what the 1977 Geneva Protocol I would later describe as 'objects which . . . make an effective contribution to military action'. In this very general sense, the letter supports the proposal of the *Annotated supplement* to allow a wider range of objects to be targeted. But because of the letter's negative phrasing—attempts to limit solely to the essential war-making potential are unrealistic—nothing in particular follows about what would be 'realistic'. And certainly there is no specific support for the extremely wide range of objects that the *Annotated supplement* proposes classifying as military objectives when it advocates including 'economic targets . . . that indirectly . . . support and sustain . . . capability'. The specific proposal in the *Annotated supplement* goes well beyond anything explicit or implied in the Counsel's letter, which never mentioned objects only indirectly contributing to war-making.

The Counsel's letter, in its turn, misread the 1954 Hague Convention, which was supposed to be one of its main sources. The letter claimed that customary international law has what sounds like some kind of balancing test for what counts as a military objective: 'The test applicable from the customary international law, restated in the Hague Cultural Property Convention, is that the war making potential of such facilities to a party to the conflict may outweigh their importance to the civilian economy and deny them immunity from attack.'[19] The 1954 Hague Convention, however, was not discussing how to decide when an object deserved immunity as a civilian object and when it might instead be considered a military objective. It was discussing when cultural property of great value might be granted special protection if it was situated near an admitted 'important military objective'.[20] No discussion was offered about how to decide what was an important military objective; that question was treated as settled. The question is: given an important military objective, what can be done about protecting cultural objects of great value nearby? The basic answer in 1954 Hague Convention, Art. 8, para. 1, was that the objects might be placed under special protection, 'provided that they (a) are situated at an adequate distance from any large industrial centre or from any important military objective'. Para. 5 then goes on to discuss how even cultural property that 'is situated near an important military objective . . . may nevertheless be placed under special protection'. All this is completely irrelevant to the issue on which the Pentagon Legal Counsel cites it, namely how to determine whether an object should count as military when it might be considered civilian or might be considered military.

Something else that appeared in 2003 besides the next printing of *Strategic attack*, but in this case not from a single service or even from all services jointly, but from the General Counsel in the Office of the Secretary in the Department of Defense, that is, from the top civilians, were the *Military Commission Instructions*. These were the rules to govern the Guantanamo prison camps; the 'military commissions' were to be the administration's way of avoiding the holding of proper *courts martial*, in which evidence obtained through the torture also being authorized at that same time, from the top down, by the Secretary of Defense Donald Rumsfeld and the Department of Defense Legal Counsel Jim Haynes, would have been disallowed.[21] Somewhat oddly, given that the *Instructions* were mainly for dealing with prisoners, *Instruction* No. 2, para. 5D (30 April 2003), volunteered a definition of a military objective, specifically, the new permissive definition earlier proposed in *Annotated Supplement 1999*: '"Military objectives" are those potential targets during an armed conflict which, by their nature, location, purpose, or use, effectively contribute to the opposing force's war-fighting or war-sustaining capability.'[22] Thus, the 2003 version of the definition of 'military objective' from the Office of General Counsel in the Defense Department contained precisely the same two enormous departures from international law as the *Annotated supplement* (1999).

Already in 2002 in Joint Publication 3–60, *Joint doctrine for targeting* (17 January 2002), had come the following: 'Civilian populations and objects as such may not be intentionally targeted for attack. Civilian objects consist of all civilian property and activities other than those used to support or sustain the adversary's war-fighting capability.'[23] So, exactly as claimed in the *Military commission instructions* a year later, anything that sustained or supported the capability of fighting a war failed to be a civilian object and thereby came to be a military objective; again, this sounds like most of the economy. And all recent editions of the Army Judge Advocate General's School's *Operational law handbook*—2006, 2007, and 2008—give the following capaciously liberal account of economic objects that qualify as military objectives:

Economic

1. Power
2. Industry (war supporting manufacturing/export/import)
3. Transportation (equipment/LOC/POL)[24]

If one can attack export industry, import industry, and other manufacturing that 'supports' war, it is difficult to think of much that is left other than the corner convenience store.

Space does not allow me to pursue this in detail. It is already clear, however, that US accounts of what qualifies as a military objective are becoming looser and departing further from international law. These permissive revisions are emerging from the top civilians in the Pentagon, the air force, the navy, the army Judge Advocate General's School in Charlottesville, and the services jointly. Although one might have thought that this rewriting of international law was aimed at making the law more congenial to an 'effects-based' under-standing of denial, including notions about infrastructure constituting critical nodes of a system and so on, a truly remarkable passage in the 2007 edition of Joint Publication 3–60, *Joint Targeting*, made it clear that this is at least in part a daring attempt to return to morale-bombing: 'Civilian populations and civilian/protected objects, *as a rule*, may not be intentionally targeted, although *there are exceptions to this rule*. Civilian objects consist of all civilian property and activities other than those used to support or sustain the adversary's war-fighting capability. Acts of violence *solely* intended to spread terror among the civilian population are prohibited.'[25] This chilling passage not only twice emphasizes that there are allegedly exceptions to the prohibi-tion on intentionally targeting civilian objects even so narrowly defined as the United States has been proposing for over a decade, but it also went out of its way to volunteer that targeting 'solely' for the purpose of terror is prohibited, implicitly but unmistakably inviting the thought that, if you can find some other pretext, you may engage in targeting that has the possibly beneficial side effect of terrorizing the civilian population.

The 2007 edition of *Strategic attack* was released only two months later by the US air force. It supplies precisely the pretext wanted in order, as *Joint Targeting* suggests, to 'spread terror among the civilian population': 'Strikes against dual-use assets like electrical power, in addition to having system-wide denial effects, may prove effective in coercing regimes in which popular unrest is an issue.'[26] By treating 'dual-use' infrastructure as a military objective,

*Strategic attack* provided a pretext for depriving civilians of essential services where civilian deprivation is the primary purpose. We saw in the cruel US management of the UN sanctions against Iraq in the 1990s what a loosely undisciplined interpretation the US government is prepared to give to 'dual-use': 'Invoking "dual-use", the United States unilaterally blocked goods including child vaccines, water tankers during a period of drought, cloth, the generator needed to run a sewage treatment plant, radios for ambulances— any goods that could even conceivably be used by the military, for any possible purpose.'[27] The old dream of provoking popular uprisings by causing civilian misery survives at least among the theorists of the air force.[28]

Sole intention is a red herring: 'Acts or threats of violence the primary purpose of which is to spread terror among the civilian population are prohibited.'[29] The fact that such a purpose was not the 'sole' intention would by no means show that it was not the primary purpose. Terror can be the primary purpose without being the sole intention when the other intention is a secondary pretext intended to comply with the letter of the law. A mere pretext is precisely not a primary purpose.

At least some in the US military now seem to think that the trick is to terrorize civilians indirectly, not directly, by using precision-guided munitions (PGMs). One does not kill civilians with 'dumb' munitions, as in the Second World War and the Korean War; instead, one makes them miserable with PGMs that destroy their infrastructure. *Strategic attack* (2007) explains the logic with astounding explicitness:

> SA [Strategic attack] of valid military objectives can have the coercive effect of creating unrest among an enemy population and/or weakening the enemy's infrastructure. These mechanisms are aimed at impacting the enemy's popular will or perception.[30] In the past, these mechanisms have involved directly targeting civilian populations to increase disaffection and pressure the adversary leadership to accept the demands of the coercer. However, the legality and morality of directly attacking an enemy's civilian populace is against international law concerning the conduct of war. The US remains committed to these laws and principles that support them. Additionally, historical evidence suggests that strategies directed against an enemy's population seldom succeed. Now, however, with the advent of precision weaponry, the US is capable of carefully regulating the destructive effects of SA [strategic attack] thereby minimizing collateral damage. This capability enables the US to use these coercive mechanisms in a way that complies with the laws of armed conflict.[31]

One main target, then, is what is referred to as 'the enemy's popular will', that is, the morale of the civilian population. But it is against international law, and historically has not been effective, to target civilians directly, which was the old-fashioned way to try to break morale. So one targets, not the civilians themselves, but military objectives like electrical power, using PGMs, but this is nevertheless partly 'aimed at impacting the enemy's popular will or perception'. In other words, one can, without intentionally killing civilians, intentionally make them miserable enough to generate 'unrest'.

One causes the civilians misery indirectly—indirection is the key. Therefore, to follow this reasoning through, since one must operate indirectly, the more civilian objects that can count as military objectives the better. Hence, the decade-long campaign to make the understanding of military objectives more permissive.

So, a power with weapons that are more and more accurate can nevertheless campaign to make the targeting norm more permissive. Common sense might have thought that, with the introduction of PGMs, it would not be necessary to loosen the definition of military objective, but that rests on the assumption that the PGMs are to be used strictly for military denial. Their other, more ambitious, purpose is civilian punishment: some of this is 'morale' bombing for bonus terror beyond any denial effects, if the air force's *Strategic attack* (2007) is to be followed. In order to inflict enough punishment on civilians to make a military difference, it seems to be thought that the more of the social infrastructure one can destroy, the better. For that purpose, one wants as much of the social infrastructure as possible to count as military objectives. So one needs to loosen up the norm currently embodied in international law so that one can target infrastructure well beyond what would now be considered under generally shared interpretations of international law to count as military objectives. Making the law more permissive and making the munitions more precise go hand-in-hand because the aims now include not only denial but punishment indirectly achieved.

This encounters two problems: one factual and one normative. The factual problem, as already indicated, is that the entire strategy rests on the discredited myth that miserable civilians will become less loyal to their own government and troops. The most ludicrous element of the passage quoted above from *Strategic attack* (2007) is the repeated vague references to 'mechanisms'. But there are no mechanisms! This was Robert Pape's main finding in *Bombing to win*: 'The supposed causal chain—civilian hardship produces public anger which forms political opposition against the government—does not stand up. One reason it does not is that a key assumption behind this argument—that economic deprivation causes popular unrest—is false.'[32] No mechanism connects civilian misery to civilian disloyalty, because they are not connected in reality, only in the fantasies of air power advocates. Bomb-inflicted misery does not lead to war-ending disloyalty. The terrorists have not figured this out, and the air-power fanatics have not figured it out. So, civilians on all sides continue to suffer pointlessly.

The normative problem is that once 'the enemy's popular will', meaning civilian morale, becomes a military objective, much of the purpose of distinguishing military objectives from civilian objects has been defeated. The purpose of separating civilian objects from military objectives is to shelter civilian life to some degree from the fighting, to allow some vestiges of normal civil society to continue through the war, and to be available at the other end of the conflict, so that the combatants, victorious or defeated, can come home and make a life again. But even if civilians themselves may not be targeted, targeting the 'popular will' means adding to the deprivations and misery of civilians as much as one can in the hope that 'popular unrest' will speed the end of the war. But one of the unchallenged principles of legal interpretation is that any interpretation of a law that blocks the fulfilment of the purpose of the law is a mistaken interpretation. So, any interpretation of the distinction between military objective and civilian object that permits the unrestrained creation of civilian misery in the vain hope of civilian disaffection is a patently mistaken interpretation and ought to be removed from US military manuals.

## NARROWING 'TORTURE'

In the nineteenth century, Illinois lawyer Abraham Lincoln, serving as President, banned torture from a war that was undeniably an existential threat to the United States, when on 24 April 1863 he issued General Order No. 100, since best known as the Lieber Code, a landmark catalogue of the customary law of war, which contained the following: '16. Military necessity does not admit of cruelty—that is, the infliction of suffering for the sake of suffering or for revenge, nor of maiming or wounding except in fight, nor of torture to extort confessions'.[33] What passed for legal analysis concerning torture by the lawyers who were political appointees in the US executive branch during the first eight years of the twenty-first century has now been thoroughly exposed as disgraceful 'definitional shenanigans',[34] unworthy of a professional lawyer, much less of a public servant. Seasoned observer Anthony Lewis has described the collection of legal memoranda about torture as 'an extraordinary paper trail to mortal and political disaster: to an episode that will soil the image of the United States in the eyes of the world for years to come. They also provide a painful insight into how the skills of the lawyer—skills that have done so much to protect Americans in this most legalized of countries—can be misused in the cause of evil.'[35] In Senate testimony, the then-Dean of Yale Law School, Harold Hongju Koh, described one of the foundational August 2002 memos, known as either 'the Bybee memorandum' or the 'Bybee/Yoo memorandum',[36] as 'perhaps the most clearly erroneous legal opinion I have ever read', and noted that its discussion of the definition of torture yielded 'a definition of torture so narrow that it would have exculpated Saddam Hussein'.[37]

Although additional memoranda concerning torture from the Bush administration continue to be wrenched loose by freedom-of-information lawsuits, their authors have been pushed out of the government, which might appear to show that the battle against American torture is being won. Unfortunately, however, the problem is much deeper than the crimes of a single US administration, and its origins go back decades. Some of the worst reasoning has continued for twenty years, since the time of President Reagan's submission of the Convention Against Torture and Other Cruel, Inhuman and Degrading Treatment or Punishment (hereinafter Convention against Torture) for Senate ratification in 1988 and its actual ratification six years later in the first term of the Clinton administration, in what were fundamentally the same terms as those initially proposed by the Reagan State Department.[38] The Convention against Torture was embodied into US federal statutes by the Torture Statute of 1994 (18 *U.S.C.* 2340 and 2340A) and the War Crimes Act of 1996 (18 *U.S.C.* 2441), both signed into law by President Bill Clinton. The latest 'definitional shenanigans' are embodied in the Military Commissions Act of 2006 (hereinafter, MCA), which made profoundly misguided insertions into the War Crimes statute. Thus, much of the worst thinking about torture was accepted by the US Congress and written into the laws of the land signed by Presidents Bill Clinton and George W. Bush. Aberrant thinking, then, did not begin in the Bush administration. It has been the US government line for two decades, through four presidencies including the eight years of a Democratic government. This thinking is, nevertheless, such a distortion of the general understanding of torture that it strongly suggests that ulterior motives have been, and still are, at work in US policy.

From the time when the Convention against Torture was adopted internationally in 1984, elements in the US government have attempted to evade of the definition of torture at its heart. Article 1 makes it unmistakably clear that either physical torture or psychological torture counts as torture prohibited by the Convention against Torture: 'For the purposes of this Convention, the term "torture" means any act by which severe pain or suffering, whether physical or mental, is intentionally inflicted on a person' (Convention against Torture, 1984, art. 1). From the beginning, the US government has made persistent efforts to deny or dilute the second half of the definition of torture, which covers mental pain and suffering, or psychological torture.

One of the most recent attempts to obscure mental pain and suffering is President George W. Bush's Executive Order of 20 July 2007, based on the MCA. But the sustained campaign to erase or minimize psychological torture began with the understandings submitted to the US Senate in 1988 by the Reagan White House, when the Convention against Torture was submitted for treaty ratification.[39] The specific language of those understandings has echoed through US federal statutes ever since and is today in force domestically. Recently, scores of commentators have remarked on the preposterously arbitrary definitions of psychological torture proposed by government lawyers, Jay Bybee and John Yoo, in the secret memoranda provided to the White House and Central Intelligence Agency (CIA) by the Department of Justice's Office of Legal Counsel during the Bush administration. It is vital to understand, however, that the manoeuvres by Bybee, Yoo, and their collaborators were merely especially inept and recent attempts in a long series that preceded and succeeded their years in the Office of Legal Counsel. Indeed, the same evasions of international law against psychological torture were slipped through the US Congress in 2006 in the MCA, which attempted to shore up the defences of current interrogation practices against the Supreme Court's ruling in *Hamdan v. Rumsfeld [548 U.S. 557 (2006)].*

The core definition of torture as 'severe pain or suffering, whether physical or mental' was directly challenged by an understanding advanced by the US executive branch in 1988 concerning its obligations under the Convention against Torture and adopted by the US legislative branch when the Senate ratified the treaty in 1994:

> II. The Senate's advice and consent is subject to the following understandings, which shall apply to the obligations of the United States under this Convention: (1) (a) That with reference to article 1, the United States understands that, in order to constitute torture, an act must be specifically intended to inflict severe physical or mental pain or suffering and that mental pain or suffering refers to prolonged mental harm caused by or resulting from (1) the intentional infliction or threatened infliction of severe physical pain or suffering; (2) the administration or application, or threatened administration or application, of mind altering substances or other procedures calculated to disrupt profoundly the senses or the personality; (3) the threat of imminent death; or (4) the threat that another person will imminently be subjected to death, severe physical pain or suffering, or the administration or application of mind altering substances or other procedures calculated to disrupt profoundly the senses or personality.[40]

Now, the United States, like any sovereign state, can issue any understandings of a treaty it wishes. Such understandings have no effect, however, on the content of international treaty law like the Convention against Torture, as a number of US allies pointed out shortly afterwards. For example, on 26 February 1996, the Netherlands entered the following formal objection to the US understanding:

> The Government of the Kingdom of the Netherlands considers the following understandings to have no impact on the obligations of the United States of America under the Convention: II. 1a This understanding appears to restrict the scope of the definition of torture under article 1 of the Convention.[41]

And on 27 February 1996, Sweden similarly objected: 'It is the view of the Government of Sweden that the understandings expressed by the United States of America do not relieve the United States of America as a party to the Convention from the responsibility to fulfil the obligations undertaken therein.'[42]

The Dutch have turned out to be exactly right that the intention of the US declaration was 'to restrict the scope of the definition of torture', and what has mattered is, not the lack of legal force of the initial treaty understanding as such, but the repeated reassertion of the same language in binding US federal laws. Apart from the arbitrary injection of a general requirement for all torture of specific intent, which is an extremely important means of narrowing the scope of the behaviour that counts as torture, the US understanding of II(1) (a) directed its fire specifically at 'mental pain or suffering', or psychological torture. Two further means were employed in order to try to weaken the prohibition on psychological torture in particular by shrinking the scope of what counts: one arbitrarily imposed an allegedly necessary effect and the other imposed the very short list of four allegedly necessary causes that were listed in the treaty reservation. Unless both the effect and one of the four specified causes were present in addition to specific intent, there was no torture, irrespective of how much severe mental pain or suffering someone underwent.

Although the definition of torture in the War Crimes statute says that torture is 'an act specifically intended to inflict severe physical or mental pain or suffering' (*United States Code*, 2008, Title 18, sec. 2441 (d)(1)(A)), 'severe . . . mental pain or suffering' 'means the prolonged mental harm caused by or resulting from . . .' (*United States Code*, 2008, Title 18, sec. 2340 (2)). So, despite the Congressional drafters doing their utmost to obscure matters from citizens without law degrees, the operative definition of torture in the War Crimes statute now is an act specifically intended to inflict prolonged mental harm (but only from one of the arbitrary four specifically listed sources). The mental pain or suffering itself has completely disappeared, having been redefined as the harm that sometimes results from mental pain or suffering. This is the *substitution trick*: the trick of substituting a possible effect for its cause at the core of the definition so that the cause itself ceases to constitute torture. As a result, the US Congress has continued to participate in the attempted erasure of any infliction of mental pain or suffering that does not leave behind prolonged harm, in defiance of the fact that what the Convention against Torture prohibits is severe mental pain or suffering itself. Further, the arbitrary insistence on effects being prolonged, going back to 1988, while lifted by the MCA from cruel and inhuman treatment (*United States Code*, 2008, Title 18, sec. 2441 (d) (2) (E) (ii)), has been kept for the crucial category of psychological torture.[43]

Sadly, psychological torture can in fact be counted on to cause harm, which is often severe and prolonged. Even worse, substantial research suggests that psychological torture, as well as some cruel and inhuman treatment that might not qualify as torture at all, can cause more severe long-term damage than some physical torture.[44] The objections to the statutory insistence on resultant prolonged harm are: the intellectual dishonesty about an extremely well-established and understood concept (namely, torture); the political trickery involved in

Congress's deceptive manipulations of language; and the unilateralist arrogance of the insistence that one need not mean what the rest of the world means by a perfectly plain, familiar, and centuries-old term.[45]

Yet the strongest objection to insistence on resultant prolonged harm is its contribution, as one of three steps, to the creation of an impossibly high threshold for any action to quality as torture. Besides the insistence on harm being prolonged and the substitution trick, performed in section 2340 and incorporated by reference into section 2441, insistence also continues in the third claim, mentioned much earlier, that, only if the torturer specifically intends the prolonged harm, does his act constitute torture. The torturer must specifically intend to inflict 'severe physical or mental pain or suffering', but since the quoted phrase has been arbitrarily redefined to mean 'prolonged mental harm' [2340 (2), incorporated by 2441 (d)(2)(A)], he must actually (1) intend to produce and (2) produce prolonged mental harm. Only a sadist would inflict severe mental pain or suffering *with the intention* of inflicting prolonged mental harm. A 'normal', that is, non-sadistic, torturer whose goal was, for example, to extract information that would prevent a terrorist attack, might not really care what became of his victim after the information was obtained. He would generally have no particular reason specifically to intend to leave the source of the information with prolonged mental harm unless he genuinely was sadistic or had some special hatred for his victim. But to require sadism or hatred as a necessary condition of counting the infliction of severe mental pain or suffering as torture is a ridiculously narrow definition of psychological torture, excluding most of what would be included in the category either on any common-sense understanding or on the international legal understanding.

All this definitional legerdemain has the result that a torturer who specifically intends to inflict severe mental pain or suffering, as a means, but does not further intend as a goal that the severe pain or suffering should result in prolonged mental harm is not committing torture as defined under the US law governing war crimes. The law has defined away all psychological torture that is not truly sadistic or hateful towards its victims, which presumably is practically all the psychological torture employed by remotely professional interrogators. A torturer whose only purpose for intentionally inflicting severe mental pain or suffering is to extract information in order to prevent a terrorist incident does not count as a 'torturer' under US law as long as he does not specifically intend prolonged mental harm in addition to intending to extract the information. US law is obviously formulated in order to permit the intentional infliction of severe mental pain or suffering, which is the kind of torture that CIA has come to prefer. US law tells us that torture is not what we think it is: not pain, but prolonged results of pain.[46] And torturers are not people who inflict severe pain for the sake of, say, extracting information: someone is a torturer only if he specifically intended the pain to result in prolonged harm. As the Dean of Yale Law School said of the Bybee memorandum, this is 'a definition of torture so narrow that it would have exculpated Saddam Hussein'. These laws are disgracefully devious and utterly untrue to the nature of torture. Congress ought to repeal these absurdly narrow characterizations of psychological torture before many more torturers stride through the gate that the US Congress has flung wide open.

## CONCLUSION: NORMATIVE RETROGRESSION

Change in norms can go either way. Here we have seen two especially worrying cases: the norms of target-selection and the norms of torture, in which the recent conduct of the most powerful state in the world seems to be propelling us backwards away from moderation and restraint. The two cases of attempted norm change are not entirely similar. The proposals to broaden the understanding of 'military objective' have been relatively honest and straightforward, while the narrowing distortions concerning torture were secret or secretive and intended to deceive; and the former proposals seem to have emerged from theorists in various branches of the military services while the latter were a carefully coordinated and centralized campaign.[47] The attempt to practise torture, while keeping it hidden and protecting its perpetrators from punishment, has clearly been shamefully evil, while the attempt to allow the bombing of more kinds of targets may represent an honest disagreement among honourable people about how to conduct war. But in both instances the proposed departures from established international meanings are long-standing, have endured through several political administrations, and involve high stakes in that the mistaken normative judgements embodied in the proposals will cost lives and spread terror.[48]

## NOTES

1. Michael Walzer, *Just and unjust wars: A moral argument with historical illustrations* (New York: Basic Books, 2006), 14. I am grateful to Janina Dill for comments on earlier versions and for access to her research on targeting, which will appear as *The definition of a legitimate target in US air warfare: A normative enquiry into the effectiveness of international law in regulating combat operations* (D.Phil., Oxon). All assertions and judgements here are of course my own responsibility.
2. I have assessed this elsewhere: Henry Shue and David Rodin (eds.), *Preemption: Military action and moral justification* (Oxford: Oxford University Press, 2007).
3. Other attacks on established limits are underway from other militaries, of course. For a sustained critique of the normal understanding of the principle of distinction, see Asa Kasher and [Major General] Amos Yadlin, 'Military ethics of fighting terror: An Israeli perspective', *Journal of Military Ethics*, 4/1 (2005), 3–32; Asa Kasher and Amos Yadlin, 'Assassination and preventive killing', *SAIS Review of International Affairs*, XXV/1 (2005), 41–57; and Asa Kasher, 'The principle of distinction', *Journal*

*of Military Ethics*, 6/2 (2007), 152–67. For a reasoned re-affirmation of the generally accepted interpretation, see Avishai Margalit and Michael Walzer, 'Israel: Civilians & combatants', *New York Review of Books*, 56/8 (14 May 2009). And for further debate, see 'Israel & the rules of war: An exchange' by Asa Kasher and Amos Yadlin; and Avishai Margalit and Michael Walzer, *New York Review of Books*, 56/10 (11 June–1 July 2009).

4. Another example of US permissiveness is the ongoing effort to 'make the rules "as flexible as possible"' regarding the employment of drones for targeted killings by non-military agencies like CIA. See Charlie Savage, 'U.N. Report Highly Critical of U.S. Drone Attacks', *New York Times*, 2 June 2010; also see United Nations, Human Rights Council, 14th Session, 'Report of the Special Rapporteur on extrajudicial, summary or arbitrary executions', 28 May 2010, A/HRC/14/24/Add.6.

5. Ward Thomas, 'Victory by duress: Civilian infrastructure as a target in air campaigns', *Security Studies*, 15/1 (2006), 14, n. 57 (emphasis in original). The 2007 edition of Air Force Doctrine Document 2-1.2, *Strategic Attack* (12 June 2007), which we examine further below, now blames the failure of Rolling Thunder on its restricted and graduated nature and praises Linebacker II for 'sufficient scope and intensity to coerce a limited settlement from North Vietnam', 34. http://www. dtic.mil/doctrine/jel/service_pubs/afdd2_1_2.pdf (accessed 17 March 2009).

6. United States, Navy/Marine Corps/Coast Guard, *The commander's handbook on the law of naval operations*, NWP 1–14M, MCWP 5-2.1, COMDTPUB P5800.7 (1995).

7. 73 International Law Studies, A.R. Thomas and James C. Duncan (eds.), *Annotated supplement to The commander's handbook on the law of naval operations* (Newport, RI: Naval War College, 1999).

8. The permissive language, which replaces 'make an effective contribution to military action' with 'effectively contribute to the enemy's war-fighting or war-sustaining capability'—a change discussed in the text following—had already appeared a decade earlier in the previous edition of *The commander's handbook* and its *Annotated supplement* (1989), but it was accompanied by a strong qualification: 'This variation of the definition contained in Protocol Additional I, Article 52(2) is not intended to alter its meaning'—see [Rear Admiral] Horace B. Robertson, Jr, 'The principle of the military objective in the law of armed conflict', *US Air Force Academy Journal of Legal Studies*, 8 (1997–1998), 46. The *Annotated supplement* (1999) drops this qualification that was in the 1989 edition. As Admiral Robertson proceeds to argue, 'the inference that one may draw from this change in wording is that the United States (at least its naval arm) has rejected the presumptively narrower definition contained in Article 52 of Protocol Additional I in favor of one that, at least arguably, encompasses a broader range of objects and products'.

9. Michael N. Schmitt, 'Fault lines in the law of attack', in Susan Breau and Agnieszka Jachec-Neale (eds.), *Testing the boundaries of international humanitarian law* (London: British Institute of International and Comparative Law, 2006), 281.

10. *Annotated supplement*, 402 (emphasis added).

11. *1977 Geneva Protocol I*, article 52:2.

12. Frits Kalshoven, 'Noncombatant persons: A comment to chapter 11 of *The commander's handbook on the law of naval operations*' in Horace B. Robertson, Jr (ed.), *The law of naval operations* (Newport, RI: Naval War College, 1991), 310. For a recent powerful critique of the insertion of what this distinguished

authority on international humanitarian law dubs 'the slippery slope concept of "war-sustaining capability"', see Yoram Dinstein, 'Legitimate military objectives under the current *jus in bello*' in Andru E. Wall (ed.), *Legal and ethical lessons of NATO's Kosovo campaign* (Newport, RI: Naval War College, 2002), 145–6.

13. Ibid., note 9. The note continues: '*Compare* GP I [1977 Geneva Protocol I], art. 52(2) and San Remo Manual, para. 40, which utilize the term [*sic*] "make an effective contribution to enemy action"'. No comment is offered on the significance of the supposed difference in 'terminology' between 'war-fighting or war-sustaining capability' and 'enemy action', which actually is in any case a misquotation for 'military action'. US military publications tend to prefer the adjective 'enemy'.

14. Ibid., 403.

15. Ibid., note 11. The date of this then-twenty-seven-year-old letter is significant both in that it is prior to the adoption of the 1977 Geneva Protocol I and in that it was written by the Pentagon in defence of the widely criticized US bombing of Vietnam.

16. Jean-Marie Henckaerts and Louise Doswald-Beck, *Customary international humanitarian law*, vol. I: *Rules* (Cambridge: Cambridge University Press for the ICRC, 2005), 29.

17. Dinstein also explains why the attempt by the *Annotated supplement* to invoke the destruction of raw cotton in the Confederacy by Union forces during the US Civil War is a dangerous analogy, see Dinstein, 'Legitimate military objectives under the current *jus in bello*', 145–6. The cotton analogy is also rejected by Major-General Rogers; see A.P.V. Rogers, *Law on the battlefield* (2nd ed., Manchester: Manchester University Press, 2004), 70–1.

18. 'Excerpts from a letter dated 22 September 1972 from J. Fred Buzhardt, General Counsel of the Department of Defense, to Senator Edward Kennedy', *American Journal of International Law*, 67 (1973), 123.

19. Ibid., 123–4.

20. 1954 Hague Convention for the Protection of Cultural Property in the Event of Armed Conflict, art. 8. This is the article of the convention cited by the Counsel's letter. The United States is not party to the 1954 Hague Convention. For another mistaken assumption about 1954 Hague made by the Pentagon Legal Counsel, see Marco Sassoli, 'Targeting: The scope and utility of the concept of "military objectives" for the protection of civilians in contemporary armed conflicts', in David Wippman and Matthew Evangelista (eds.), *New wars, new laws? Applying the laws of war in 21st century conflicts* (Ardsley, NY: Transnational Publishers, 2005), 199.

21. The recent US adoption of torture is the second case summarized below, but specifically on the roles of Rumsfeld and Haynes in promoting torture, see Philippe Sands, *Torture team: Deception, cruelty and the compromise of law* (London: Allen Lane, 2008).

22. United States, Department of Defense, Military Commission Instruction No. 2, 'Crimes and elements for trials by military commission' (30 April 2003), para. 5D. http://www.defenselink.mil/news/May2003/d20030430milcominstno2.pdf

23. United States, Department of Defense, JP 3–60 (17 January 2002), Appendix A, 'International law and legal considerations in targeting', p. A-2. I am grateful to Janina Dill for this reference.

24. United States Army Judge Advocate General's Legal Center & School, International and Operational Law Department, *Operational law handbook* (Charlottesville, VA). 2006 edition, 20; 2007 edition, 21; and 2008 edition, 19.

25. United States Air Force, JP 3–60 (13 April 2007), *Joint targeting*, Appendix E, 'Legal considerations in targeting', E-2 (emphasis added). http://www.dtic.mil/doctrine/jel/new_pubs/jp3_60.pdf (accessed 17/3/2009).

26. *Strategic attack* (2007), 34.

27. Joy Gordon, *Invisible war: The United States and the Iraq sanctions* (Cambridge, MA: Harvard University Press, 2010), 4. *Invisible war* is the definitive account, devastating and meticulous, of how the US government, under Republican and Democratic administrations, manipulated the UN sanctions for its own purposes, which included blocking Iraq's restoration of its industrial capabilities— see especially 231–45. This is another case in which focusing on extremely broad capabilities rather than specific threats led to inhumane policies.

28. The dream is recurrent. In the Korean war, for example, 'to hide the true nature of the attacks from public scrutiny, FEAF [Far East Air Force]'s Deputy for Operations, General Jacob E. Smart, planned that "whenever possible attacks will be scheduled against targets of military significance so situated that their destruction will have a deleterious effect upon the morale of the civilian population"'; see Robert A. Pape, *Bombing to win: Air power and coercion in war* (Ithaca, NY: Cornell University Press, 1996), 160. Sahr Conway-Lanz observes in his careful historical study: 'The objects of attack were still "military targets," but the implicit definition of the term "military target" had grown to include virtually every human-made structure in enemy-occupied territory'; Sahr Conway-Lanz, *Collateral damage: Americans, noncombatant immunity, and atrocity after World War II* (London: Routledge, 2006), 103.

29. Henckaerts and Beck, *Customary international humanitarian law*, I, 8 [Rule 2]; *1977 Geneva Protocol* I, art. 51:2. I am grateful to Janina Dill for noting that 'primary', not 'sole', is the issue. The US air force had retained the correct category of 'primarily' at least through 1998; see United States Air Force, *Intelligence targeting guide*, Air Force Pamphlet 14–210 (1 February 1998), para. A4.2. www.fas.org/irp/doddir/usaf/afpam14-210/part17.htm

30. This shows undeniably what the primary aim is and what the pretext is.

31. *Strategic attack* (2007), 32–3.

32. *Bombing to win*, 24.

33. General Orders No. 100, *Instructions for the government of armies of the United States in the field*; Richard Shelly Hartigan, *Lieber's Code and the law of war* (South Holland, IL: Precedent Publishing, 1983), 48; and Leon Friedman (ed.), *The law of war: A documentary history*, vol. I (New York: Random House, 1972), 161. Hartigan contains commentary and other useful documents, including correspondence with Lieber, not available in other sources. See also http://www.icrc.org/ihl.nsf/FULL/110?OpenDocument

34. Jeremy Waldron, 'Torture and positive law: Jurisprudence for the White House', *Columbia Law Review*, 105 (2005), 1709; reprinted in Jeremy Waldron, *Torture, terror, and trade-offs: Philosophy for the White House* (Oxford: Oxford University Press, 2010) as chapter 7, 'Torture and positive law'.

35. Anthony Lewis, 'Introduction', in Karen J. Greenberg and Joshua L. Dratel (eds.), *The torture papers: The road to Abu Ghraib* (Cambridge: Cambridge University Press, 2005), xiii.

36. Greenberg and Dratel, (eds.), *The torture papers*, 172–217.

37. Harold H. Koh, Confirmation hearing on the nomination of Alberto R. Gonzales to be Attorney General of the United States: Hearing before the Senate Committee on the Judiciary, 109th Congress (2005), 534–7.

38. Alfred W. McCoy, *A question of torture: CIA interrogation from the Cold War to the war on terror*. (New York: Metropolitan Books, 2006), 100–2.

39. United States Senate. Message from the President of the United States transmitting the Convention Against Torture and Other Cruel, Inhuman or Degrading Treatment or Punishment, 100th Congress, 2d session, Treaty Doc. 100–20 (Washington, DC: Government Printing Office, 1988), iii–iv.

40. Office of the United Nations High Commissioner for Human Rights, *Convention Against Torture and Other Cruel, Inhuman or Degrading Treatment: Declarations and Reservations* (2008), 11. http://www2.ohchr.org/english/bodies/ratification/9.htm.

    McCoy mistakenly describes this as a reservation; it actually has the legally much weaker status of an understanding, which in itself has no legally binding effect internationally or domestically. However, this language was imported wholesale into federal law, which is of course domestically binding.

41. Office of the United Nations High Commissioner for Human Rights, 14. I am grateful to Guy Goodwin-Gill for pointing out the prompt Dutch and Swedish objections to the US understanding.

42. Office of the United Nations High Commissioner for Human Rights, 16.

43. Another change here would be hilarious in its brazenly ad hoc character if its consequences for the rule of law were not so serious. The progressive change from prolonged to not-necessarily-prolonged for cruel or inhuman treatment (as distinguished from torture) is subject to a bizarre dating procedure applied only to it. This change alone applies only from the date of the enactment of the Military Commissions Act, which happens to have been 17 October 2006 (*United States Code*, 2008, Title 18, section 2441 (d) (2) (E) (ii)). It is difficult to imagine any other reason for this provision than to shield from criminal prosecution people who acted under the authority of the Bush Administration prior to October 2006 to inflict cruel and inhuman treatment. This is a kind of bill of attainder in reverse: a declaration that the otherwise guilty are automatically innocent of everything cruel or inhuman they did before 17 October 2006.

44. See Metin Basoglu, Maria Livanou, and Cvetana Crnobaric, 'Torture vs other cruel, inhuman, and degrading treatment', *Archives of General Psychiatry*, 64/3 (2007), 277–85; and Metin Basoglu, 'A multivariate contextual analysis of torture and cruel, inhuman, and degrading treatments: Implications for an evidence-

based definition of torture', *American Journal of Orthopsychiatry*, 79/2 (2009), 135–45. I do not, however, accept the implication of the latter that the established international definitions, as distinguished from the arbitrary US definitions, require change. See also Almerindo E. Ojeda (ed.), *The trauma of psychological torture* (London and Westport, CT: Praeger, 2008).

45. Calling extreme psychological torture 'enhanced interrogation' and calling water torture 'water-boarding' are similarly Orwellian bits of euphemistic double-speak designed to confuse ordinary decent people about what is being done in their name and with their tax funds.

46. See McCoy, *A question of torture*.

47. See Sands, *Torture team*; Jane Mayer, *The dark side: The inside story of how the war on terror turned into a war on American ideals* (New York: Doubleday, 2008); and Jameel Jaffer and Amrit Singh, *Administration of torture: A documentary record from Washington to Abu Ghraib and beyond* (New York: Columbia University Press, 2007).

48. Further analysis of the misinterpretations of international law embodied in US domestic statutes will appear in David Luban and Henry Shue, 'Mental torture', under review.

# 26

## The Return of Realism? War and Changing Concepts of the Political

*Patricia Owens*

In the wake of the many and grave foreign policy errors of George W. Bush and Dick Cheney, there has been a revival in the fortunes of realism in international political thought. Realism has returned, we are told, in characteristic fashion to restrain the imperial hubris of the last superpower. As an attitude towards the human condition that is sceptical of claims about world transformation and universal morality, that sees the group as the central political unit, and the ever-present possibility of violence and tragedy, classical realism has indeed re-emerged largely intact after the 9/11 theory wars.[1] Neoconservative ideas, widely seen as the ideological underpinning of much that went wrong under Cheney and Bush, have—for now at least—been widely discredited. This reckoning, however, had more to do with the ideology's clash with facts and events on the ground in Iraq than with the genuine triumph of a competing theory. War cannot be left to ideological amateurs.[2] But which version of realism can be said to have returned after the neoconservative retreat? United States' foreign policy has reverted to its conventional realist posture under the administration of Barack Obama, but what of realism in international political theory more broadly, and hopefully more deeply?

There is another form of political realism whose intellectual standing greatly improved under the administration of George W. Bush, the strand associated with the authoritarian German jurist, Carl Schmitt (1888–1985). In both international and political theory, a cottage industry of scholarship has sought to expose the correspondence between Schmitt's legal and political thought and the Bush administration's conduct and justification of its wars. Schmitt's version of political 'decisionism' (defined below) is said to correlate with the Bush administration's claims about executive authority and state sovereignty. It has been argued that Schmitt's prioritization of the 'exception' over the 'norm' explains the power of the legal arguments deployed by administration officials in defence of torture at Guantanamo Bay and other emergency laws. Moreover, Schmitt's account of the fundamental political relation as expressed in the antimony of friend and foe has been read alongside Bush's pronouncements on the nature of the United States' existential enemies.[3] According to two of Schmitt's most perceptive readers in International Relations (IR), this infamous and disgraced legal scholar provides us with 'a deeper understanding of the present international crisis and epoch-making change';[4] at first glance—it would seem—we can learn much about the changing character of war through the international thought of Carl Schmitt.

Contemporary and conventional realists within the field of IR have largely ignored, if not explicitly marginalized, Schmitt's founding contribution to the realist tradition.[5] 'Carl Schmitt', as William Rasch has aptly put it, 'is an acquired taste'.[6] His role as the self-styled 'crown jurist' of the Third Reich will forever bring shame on one of twentieth-century Europe's greatest legal and political thinkers. For despite his well-documented moral failings and analytical sleights of hand, Schmitt has done much to unsettle complacency around the idea of the constitutional state bound by the rule of law and the normative authority of liberal democracy more broadly. Moreover, in terms of intellectual history, Schmitt reveals some important overlap between realist and neoconservative thought at the level of philosophical foundation.[7] Although polemicists define the neoconservative worldview in opposition to classical realism,[8] the 'founding fathers' of both schools were deeply influenced by Schmitt.[9] It was Schmitt, perhaps even more than Leo Strauss, whose thought expresses the logic behind the serious legal, political, and military crises that have beset the United States—and international thought—after the 9/11 attacks. However, while Schmitt's 'ingenious theories about the end of democracy and legal government', as Hannah Arendt once remarked, 'still make arresting reading',[10] it is sometimes forgotten that to elevate his thought in this manner is a condemnation, not a compliment.

In the wake of the catastrophe of the Bush years, the most important task of international political theory should be to dismantle rather than valorize Schmitt's conception of politics, war, and their philosophical presuppositions. While especially illuminating of the legal strategies adopted by the Bush administration, there are severe weaknesses to Schmitt's account of politics, war, and the law. Few, if any, contemporary commentators have offered a normative endorsement of Schmitt's political views. But too many have failed to distinguish properly between his role in revealing what exactly has been at stake in the conduct and justification of the so-called 'war on terror' and the normative, historical, and analytical flaws of Schmitt's thought. Above all, these failures stem from his absolutist account of state power, the concept of the political that underpins it, and his idealizations of Europe's political and military history abstracted from class and other social conflict. Schmitt's rewriting of Europe's political and military history was a wholly unpersuasive attempt to add an aura of legitimacy to Hitler's military conquests. It does not form the basis of a convincing international theory today.

The chapter is divided into two parts. The first section sets out what many have described as the 'decisionist' basis of the Bush administration's legal revisionism and its interpretation of the normative order more generally. The coincidence between the administration's neoconservative attack on the rule of law and Schmitt's similar assault on the possibility of legal regulation of unconventional combatants suggests that we either revise our assumptions regarding the validity of liberal constitutionalism or replace it with something that is more robust. It is argued that we need not accept that irregular combatants are forever outside the laws of armed conflict; nor should we take the correspondence between the political and legal strategies of the Bush administration and Schmitt's thought as the final evidence for abandoning the task of rethinking constitutional politics. The second section draws attention to German-American political theorist Hannah Arendt's (1906–75) rejection of both Schmitt's 'decisionism' and liberal constitutional rationalism in favour of a different understanding of law. For Arendt, law was the element of stability in the always-unpredictable worlds of military and political affairs.[11] While Schmitt's thought was motivated by an effort to rescue 'the political' from liberalism, her writing also points to his failure to distinguish adequately between politics and war. The recent turn to Schmitt has been ill judged. Nonetheless, it has been a useful and timely reminder of what happens when political and military theory is reduced to ideology in the service of state power.

## CARL SCHMITT AND THE CHANGING CHARACTER OF WAR

Not long after beginning the war to topple the Taliban in Afghanistan and disrupt the al-Qaeda network, the Bush administration stated that those accused of involvement in terrorist actions against US interests would not be recognized as regular combatants with protection under the conventional laws of war. The conduct and organization of al-Qaeda, it was argued, was fundamentally different from those of belligerents addressed in the 1949 Third Geneva Convention and Protocol I of the Geneva Convention of 1977. These agreements were designed to protect prisoners in conventional armed forces and (later) of militias and military volunteers who are commanded by a person responsible for their subordinates, wear a fixed distinctive sign recognizable at a distance, carry their arms openly, and conduct their operations in accordance with the laws and customs of war. The Bush administration consistently maintained that none of these criteria applied to large numbers of those it captured, detained, and/or rendered into others' custody. Al-Qaeda terrorists were mere killers. Under such circumstances, there were no existing laws able to regulate effectively the manner of detaining, interrogating, and prosecuting the accused.

What then was the legal and political basis of the detention of those accused of being members of al-Qaeda? It was argued that the decision regarding how to treat those detained was at the absolute discretion of the President. Instead of seeking to apply and/or adapt existing rules, the administration established detention camps at Guantanamo Bay and other 'black sites' and military tribunals. Based on a claim of extraordinary executive power and the changed character of war, the President's advisors argued that the executive branch could sidestep both international and domestic law to claim the most far-reaching use of detention and interrogation powers in the republic's history. The President could order torture and face no criminal liability. This was both quite an effective and a radical legal strategy, designed to ensure for as long as possible that international and domestic law could impose no constraint on what US officials could do in relation to the detained. At the President's discretion, torture was defined so narrowly as virtually to conflate it with murder. The minimum provisions of Common Article 3 of the Geneva Convention which bans outrages 'against personal dignity, in particular humiliating and degrading treatment' was set aside. Often modelled on Soviet and Chinese programmes, torture was what the executive—based on memoranda written by political appointees in the Departments of Justice and Defence—said it was.[12] At the time of writing, it appears that no lawyer who participated in writing the 'torture memos' will face any professional or criminal sanction.

In effect the Bush administration claimed the imperial principle that 'everything is permitted' in pursuit of its foreign policy goals and seizure of executive power.[13] It deliberately sought to dehumanize those detained by removing all legal rights, a method Hannah Arendt associated with the early stages of totalitarian rule. 'The first essential step on the road to total domination,' she wrote, 'is to kill the juridical person in man.'[14] The destruction of legal protection, which Arendt included under the category of the rights of man, is accomplished in two ways. First, it is achieved 'by putting certain categories of people outside the protection of the law' and by seeking others to recognize this 'lawlessness'. Second, after the establishment of a system of imperial camps, it is realized through locating the camps 'outside the normal penal system, and by selecting its inmates outside the normal judicial procedure in which a definite crime entails a predictable penalty'.[15] As a matter of both legal interpretation and national security, the strategic and normative grounds for arguing for the irrelevance of existing conventions—in favour of protecting all combatants and against 'preventive' (aggressive) war—were highly questionable. However, in a context in which the United States takes great pains to be seen to abide by the laws protecting civilians, something other than a clash of legal and strategic interpretations is at work here.

Helen M. Kinsella has persuasively argued that the disjuncture between the United States' apparent compliance with the laws of war protecting combatants and those protecting civilians cannot be understood in terms of straightforward military necessity. If military necessity were the sole criterion for determining degrees of compliance, then the United States should be expected to afford *greater* protection to enemy combatants given the threat non-compliance poses to US military personnel. In fact, the apparent protection of civilians—but abuse of prisoners—produces 'a hierarchy of practices', Kinsella writes, 'that distinguish the "civilised" from the "barbarians"'; the United States fights to protect civilians, Al Qaeda does not—the central claim persistently evoked to justify the war on terror as a war on behalf of civilization.[16] Similarly, neoconservative calls for 'war powers for a new world'[17] ought not to be viewed in merely instrumental terms, an obvious move given the limitations of law in relation to overwhelming military power. Rather we can consider law—and non-compliance with the law—as productive of US military and political subjectivity.

The two themes most relevant for our discussion concern the meaning of 'sovereignty' and executive authority in circumstances deemed to be exceptional and the capacity of law to regulate different military and political actors. Carl Schmitt has done a great deal to bring together these themes even though we may disagree with much of his argument. Any effort to use conventional law to regulate unconventional combatants, he argued, is incoherent and illogical given the nature of politics itself. Such a claim would appear to suggest, if not the validity, then the way to *understand* Bush administration claims regarding the applicability of the Geneva Conventions to al-Qaeda and the possibility of legal and political regulation of the United States.[18] We will take each theme in turn before offering some criticism of both the Bush administration and of Schmitt.

Carl Schmitt's claims about the relationship between war, law, and politics were made in the context of German history in the twentieth century, including the criminalization of the German state after the First World War. They are a product of a deep hostility towards liberal theory and practice, which he simultaneously presented as both devoid of meaningful politics and seeking to conceal its politics. The liberal constitutionalism on display in the Weimar period, especially the notion that state power could be limited by legal norms, produced a dangerous delusion about the real character of politics. Legitimacy, Schmitt argued, could not be reduced to 'legality'.[19] Taking aim at all forms of legal positivism, scientific theories of law, and all efforts to subordinate legal judgement to general norms, Schmitt claimed that in a moment of crisis unconstrained political sovereignty would always triumph. Legal and political theory needed to be rescued from 'normativism' and liberalism's dangerous inability to think adequately about politics beyond the law.[20] The state—if it is sovereign—*decides* what it wants and claims legitimacy with reference to the rule of law. Sovereignty is legally independent of all law and its power is not derived from anything other than the decision. All legal norms are always already based on a prior political act, a 'pure decision not based on reason and discussion'.[21] 'I'm the decider,' as George W. Bush put it, 'and I decide what is best.'[22]

This logic of sovereignty, Schmitt argued, is captured in the idea of the exception in which the normal rule of law is suspended. 'Sovereign is he who decides the exception.'[23] Legal and political order is defined by what is deemed exceptional to it and only the 'sovereign' can decide when the law can be suspended because the sovereign is already the lawgiver, deciding the space in which the rule of law has validity. Indeed, all legal order is based on concrete, territorial order that is itself founded on a violent act of land appropriation, the 'nomos of the earth'.[24] On this view, suspensions of the law, declarations of emergency, or the establishment of detention centres where the Geneva Conventions do not apply are not rare or marginal phenomen.[25] States of emergency reveal the fundamental structure of the rule of law and the real character of juridical and political order. The exceptional situation calls forth the potentially all-powerful sovereign. All legal choices (normal and exceptional) are predicated on an irrational 'decisionist' moment whose trajectory cannot be determined in advance. The concrete moment of decision carries more legal weight than any abstract legal 'norm'; the norm-governed order of technical and mechanical constitutional procedures cannot capture the exception. The exception cannot be suppressed by the 'negative constraints' of liberal constitutionalism.

Schmitt was obsessed by political authenticity and actors who sought—inauthentically—to depoliticize essentially political and violent antagonism by turning conflict into a question of law, the 'old liberal negation of the state vis-à-vis the law'.[26] Liberalism conceals political domination with the fiction of formal equality and replaces properly political relations with economic and moral laws. Schmitt pointed to US domination over Europe after the Second World War in which surplus value was abstracted through the seemingly non-political means of private exchange in the capitalist market supported by the rule of law.[27] Against liberalism, Schmitt sought to recover what he took to be the true meaning of politics, and provide its basic definition, which he argued 'can be obtained only by discovering and defining the specifically political categories . . . to which all action with a specifically political meaning can be traced'.[28] For Schmitt, the political is defined and structured by the distinction between friend and enemy and always involves the potential of physical killing and destruction. The clearest manifestation of the difference between enemy and friend is war, the concrete and real possibility of killing. The most authentically political conflicts are between political entities that are existentially different. The enemy must be truly 'the other', he wrote, 'the stranger; and it is sufficient for his nature that he is, in a specially intense way, existentially something different and alien, so that in the extreme case conflicts with him are possible'.[29] These potential and real physical battles are not merely the continuation of politics by other means, a mere instrument to achieve a preconceived end, as in the crude rendition of Clausewitz. War is also an existential mode of being, the ultimate expression and foundation of the political.

The ever-present possibility of war is necessary for basic political tensions and 'antithesis', in Schmitt's words, 'whereby men could be required to sacrifice life, authorised to shed blood, and kill other human beings'.[30] Any world without the friend–enemy distinction, the fundamental political relation, would be tantamount to the end of politics. At the same time, political founding and constitution making are only possible through the prior identification of a political enemy against whom the group may go to war. For Schmitt, the fundamental law of any successful polity presupposes the existence of an ethnically or racially homogenous nation able to define itself against the 'other', the 'foe'. This identification of a foreign enemy is constitutive of the identity and strength of the national people. This is the full force of the constituent power produced by the sovereign out of a normative vacuum, not the totting up of individuals with pre-political rights. In other words, Schmitt adopted Thomas Hobbes's absolutism without Hobbes's individualism; the independent and self-reliant individuals found in Hobbes's (bourgeois) commonwealth would make it harder for the sovereign to distinguish friend from foe.[31] The ability to make such distinctions structures the political space by creating bounded homogenous communities.[32] All communal identity depends on the irreducibly political decision that distinguishes enemy from friend. State and civil society are fundamentally distinct; social conflict had to be neutralized; ultimately, government is the rulership of the masses by decree.[33]

The political retains existential primacy over the moral, aesthetic, economic, and legal spheres because, Schmitt claimed, it 'is the strongest and most intense of the distinctions and categorizations'.[34] The juridification of politics—and war—does nothing to resolve the 'irreducible antagonism' between political entities. That such agonistic conflict can never be escaped is at the core of Schmitt's much-cited objection to the idea of a 'just war'; killing can only be politically, not morally, justified. 'The justification of war does not reside in its being fought for ideals or norms of justice, but in its being fought against a real enemy.'[35] To repeat, the real enemy is an existential adversary who threatens the way of life of the community. This potential for violence is obscured by the liberal fetishization of a narrow conception of law and refusal to accept the essentially irrational basis of all order. The mythological and theological substance of politics is suppressed in favour of only apparently rational procedure. This is the theological, as well as authoritarian, basis of

Schmitt's argument—the decision of who is the enemy in concrete circumstances is an irrational act of faith. This is not to deny the existence of real conflicts of interests, for example, between an occupying power and armed resistance. Indeed, if war is determinative of political action and thought, then it is not difficult to understand why such partisan warfare reveals the primary political distinction and, in later Cold War writing, was taken by Schmitt to be 'the key to recognizing political reality'.[36]

There are at least two reasons why the history and theory of partisan warfare are significant to Schmitt: one positive and one negative. The negative reason is that revolutionary partisan fighters (seeking to overthrow the norms of the state system) challenge the legal grounds for regulating war. War between existential enemies, or any form of authentic politics, cannot be regulated because the whole political and social order is brought into question. In particular, revolutionary partisans adopt new methods and means of combat that disrupt the existing military and political order. If the ultimate expression of politics is a struggle to the death between enemies, then the intensity of political commitment in revolutionary partisan war reveals a deeper source of enmity than conventional war between states.[37] In *Der Nomos der Erde*, Schmitt mythologized war between European states in the so-called Westphalian era up to the First World War, whose system of public interstate law, he alleged, was contained by more or less limited goals and the political–legal distinctions 'between', in his words, 'war and peace, combatants and non-combatants, enemy and criminal', and, we should add, public and private.[38] Schmitt imagined this system to have limited, or 'bracketed', war on the European continent while allowing the great powers to engage in land appropriation in the rest of the world, 'zones designated for agonal tests of strength'.[39] If the power that emerges between partisans cannot be so channelled into a nation-state and the interstate system—if the resumption of 'peace' is not possible after a limited victory—then we are describing a fundamentally different form of warfare and participant in war. Just such claims about the radicalism of al-Qaeda—that it would be impossible to live in peace with such barbarians—sustained the Bush administration's effort to abandon the Geneva Conventions.

The second, more positive reason for the centrality of partisan warfare for Schmitt is that it challenged the effort of the victorious liberal democracies after the Second World War to universalize their values. With the total defeat of the German state in 1945 the way was open for the United States to pursue its legal and seemingly apolitical form of economic domination, only tempered by the equally universalistic drive of Soviet ideology. In *The Theory of the Partisan*, Schmitt identified the activities of Mao Zedong in China, Che Guevara in Cuba, and Ho Chi Minh in Vietnam as the most effective resistance to the United States' effort to monopolize the 'political' by depoliticizing it into a 'spaceless universalism'. In the face of the ideological and material challenges emanating from the superpowers, but especially the United States, what Schmitt imagined as the classical Westphalian system was wearing down. Schmitt lamented the decline of the *jus publicum Europaeum* and wrote in nostalgic praise of what he presented as its 'non-discriminatory concept of war' in which Europeans states had equal rights in international law. He feared that any transformation of the normative foundation of world politics towards a 'spaceless universalism' would radically transform the purpose of war and ultimately lead to a domestication of world politics. If the right to wage war was no longer exclusively a fundamental sovereign right but an act whose object was an abstract concept such as humanity, then war itself becomes something akin to global law enforcement. About this, of course, Schmitt was right.[40] He was correct to condemn the false universalisms and hypocrisy of the liberal democratic states. But we do not need to engage in historical mythology to make such an argument. As the next section will argue, neither Schmitt's nor the Bush administration's grandiose and ideologically motivated agenda of violent political change reveals any deeper political meaning. They are both anti-political, representing, as Hannah Arendt might put it, a 'conspicuous disdain of the whole texture of reality'.[41]

## AUTHORITARIANISM, ABSTRACTION, AND INDISTINCTION

The Bush administration approach to international law is usually understood in terms of a defence of sovereignty and perhaps even an attempt to have an exceptional status for the United States codified in international law.[42] The wider and longer term neoconservative goal is to place the political and military conduct of the United States beyond the reach of any form of global governance. Moves towards the constitutionalization of international law are viewed with hostility by neoconservatives keen to present any emerging global political or legal culture as equally hostile to the values of the United States.[43] In any case, they argue, all such claims on behalf of the civilizing effect of international law, including the requirement to recognize the Geneva Conventions, are a mere façade over which real political conflict is fought. Europeans who complain about the treatment of those detained and interrogated at Guantanamo Bay and elsewhere are decadent hypocrites.[44] In addition to the requirements of an unfettered pursuit of the national interest, this apparently statist defence of United States' values against creeping transnational norms is bolstered by appeals to popular sovereignty and democratic procedure as the true basis of legitimacy. The 'new sovereigntists'[45] reject what is derisively presented as European and therefore somehow non-American—the view that some issues transcend the law established among states of sovereign equality which, in Jürgen Habermas's even more expansive formulation, should be codified in terms of a law of world citizens.[46] That international law, let alone cosmopolitan law, might prevail over domestic law is presented as unconstitutional and a threat to the founding principles of the republic.

If we are to take seriously the coincidence between Carl Schmitt's thought and Bush administration policy, then we have to think beyond the conventional idea of state sovereignty described above, which is also the purview of narrow realism. The 'new sovereigntists' are interested in more than state sovereignty vis-à-vis the international system, or even the fictional 'sovereignty of a body of people bound and kept together . . . by an identical will which', Arendt mocked, 'somehow magically inspires them all'.[47] The gravest challenge to the republican constitutional order and the so-called society of states is not from international or cosmopolitan law but from the neoconservatives themselves. Recall that in Schmitt's narrative of the Westphalian spatial order, states were sovereign in a very particular way. Absolutism, as much as state-centrism, made the *jus publicum Europaeum* possible on Schmitt's account.[48] Neoconservatives are better characterized as defenders of an *authoritarian* state-centrism than defenders of sovereignty; they are the greatest threat to the existence of republican government in the United States and any system of international law. In seeking to replace the rule *of* law with rule *by* law, or, as Cheney continues to propose, turn a republic governed by laws into a mere country ruled by men,[49] they have gravely damaged the Constitution, the separation of powers, and basic civil liberties in the United States and beyond.[50]

We do not need Carl Schmitt to explain or understand the dangers to republican government under the Bush administration.[51] Nor does he illuminate much about European political and military history or about how the character of war has changed. Consider his claim that 'sovereignty' derived from the ability of a people—a homogenous unified *Volk*—to express its identity through collective wilful action. This is the meaning of 'democracy', for Schmitt—the more homogenous a people the greater its capacity for political strength. 'That these various forms of domain came to be labelled "states"', Martti Koskenniemi writes of Schmitt's view, 'did not result from their attainment of some determinate form of social power or territorial control . . . but of the development of authoritarian political theory that secularised monotheism into the theory of the single sovereign'.[52] There was far greater diversity of state form and levels of state control over both populations and the use of force during the period of the *jus publicum Europaeum* than accounted for in *Der Nomos der Erde*.[53] Schmitt's account of the unitary and absolutist state and the 'Westphalian' spatial order are as much idealizations of history as those found in the legal positivism he rightly criticized, but these mythologies are required for Schmitt's 'concept of the political' to make any sense. The result, as Benno Teschke has persuasively argued, is a socially de-contextualized account of European history that obscures, among other things, the centrality of social property relations, including geopolitical accumulation, as the basis of European state-formation.[54] Moreover, contra Schmitt, US-led global capitalism was not a 'spaceless univeralism'. His turn to political economy to account for the peculiarities of US world-order building in the twentieth-century—the simultaneous presence of economic accumulation and 'political' absence—contradicts Schmitt's claim that all legal orders are territorial, 'concrete' orders.[55]

The idealizations and assumptions of liberal thought do not accurately reflect the relationship between politics, war, and the law.[56] However, Schmitt's polemical approach to this relationship is also unconvincing both historically—in terms of abstracting away from societal conflict in favour of a depersonalized and autonomous sovereign state—and conceptually. There is a clear circularity to his theoretical argument; the concept of the political is already defined in a way to ensure that law can never be more than a disciplining façade under which domination lurks. Moreover, while Schmitt criticized the invocation of 'just war' by the liberal powers, his own writing was a justification of war, Nazi war. Though captured and detained in 1945 and interrogated at Nuremberg, Schmitt was never prosecuted for his role in justifying Nazi crimes. These 'crimes . . .' Arendt wrote in 1946, 'explode the limits of the law; and that is precisely what constitutes their monstrousness'. Nazi guilt, she maintained, 'overstep[ed] and shatter[ed] all legal systems'.[57] But the choice in responding to such authentically unprecedented events is not between liberal constitutional rationalism and Schmitt's repulsive vision, or even between these accounts and the realism of mainstream international thought.[58] Conventional realist theory, and indeed much post-Marxist scholarship, rightly argues that law alone can never be a match for political and military power. But, to date, these approaches have tended to under-theorize law, paying too little attention to the constitutive character of law, what law can do.

To be sure, the classical system of the laws of war emerged at a time when territorial state control of the organization and use of armed force was at its greatest. But, as the Bush administration chose to forget, there has *always* been a disjuncture between the use of force and the laws of armed conflict. This disjuncture certainly grows when the character of war rapidly changes. Fragile laws can never be stable given what Clausewitz described as war's variable 'pulsations of violence' and its generative character. War, he wrote, can surpass 'all conventional limits'.[59] There is little intrinsic to military action that is stabilizing and limiting. But, as Hannah Arendt argued, law does provide an element of stability and regulation to the unpredictable character of military and political affairs. New laws were indeed established to punish the Nazis' *genuinely* extraordinary crimes. An international criminal court exists to punish crimes against humanity even though some crimes are so great that no legal system can ever mete out appropriate justice. This development does not imply the emergence of a republic of world citizens as Habermas hopes and neoconservatives allegedly fear. The purpose of a trial, Arendt argued, could only be 'to render justice, and nothing else; even the noblest of ulterior purposes . . . can only detract from the law's main business'.[60] We should not expect or even wish for an institutionalized global public realm to emerge from the International Criminal Court. Punishing crimes against humanity is not a question of enforcing the will of an imaginary world citizenry, but of indicating that genocidal violence is the worst political sin as it seeks to destroy the very basis of politics, which is human plurality.

So conceived by Arendt, laws are 'stabilizing forces', the only check on the inherent unpredictability of political and military affairs and could be theorized not simply as a system of regulations but as that which establishes a relationship between people.[61] She contrasted the Greek word *nomos*, indicating a system of commandments to be obeyed, and the Roman term *lex*, which 'indicates a formal relationship between people rather than the wall that separates them'.[62] For the Greeks, law established the boundary between political communities and political relations were deemed to end at the border. The law was both this wall-like structure and a system of 'precepts and prohibitions whose sole purpose is to demand obedience'.[63] The Romans, in contrast, understood law as relational, not just a boundary or a system of rules. Treaties and laws instituted a relationship, including between enemies that were first encountered in battle. This different spatial significance of law had enormous implications for the conduct of war and its relationship to politics, Arendt argued, first and foremost its role in reducing (though not eliminating) the possibility of annihilatory war.

Arendt's *Origins of totalitarianism*, published one year after *Nomos*, suggested that without such conventions military and political worlds would be little more than a Hobbesian state of nature, or more accurately a desert, a 'lawless, fenceless wilderness of fear and suspicion'.[64] Schmitt's '*nomos* of the earth' was, for Arendt, the territorial principle established by the European comity of nations. Like Schmitt, Arendt never identified this system as embodying potentially universal and abstract norms that could be divorced from force and imperial power, far from it. Such an order was only praiseworthy to the extent that it reflected, in her words, that 'the earth is inhabited by many peoples and that these peoples are ruled by many different laws'.[65] Rather than Schmitt's idealization of the territorial national state, Arendt viewed all nationalism as obsolete: useful for military mobilization in the specific context of the nineteenth century, but in the twentieth century it 'could no longer either guarantee the true sovereignty of the people within or establish a just relationship among different peoples beyond the national borders'.[66] Human dignity, she argued, needed a 'new guarantee ... whose validity ... must comprehend the whole of humanity while its power must remain strictly limited, rooted in, and controlled by *newly defined* territorial entities'.[67] In other words, Arendt also rejected Schmitt's assertion that all political and legal orders were founded on a violent act of land appropriation and the absolute domination of a homogenous group. In *Eichmann in Jerusalem*, she divorced the concepts of 'territory' and land. As she put it,

> 'territory', as the law understands it, is a political and a legal concept, and not merely a geographical term. It relates not so much, and not primarily, to a piece of land as to the space between individuals in a group, whose members are bound to, and at the same time separated and protected from, each other by all kinds of relationships. ... Such relationships become spatially manifest insofar as they themselves constitute the space wherein the different members of a group relate to and have intercourse with each other.[68]

Laws and boundaries serve a limiting function to the extent—and only to the extent—that each member of the group respects plurality. Not enmity but plurality is the condition of politics if the concept of the political is to possess a distinctive meaning at all.

Much of Schmitt's writing is a series of assertions about the boundaries, nature, and distinctiveness of politics. Yet given the *lack of distinction* between war and politics in his account—these activities exist on a mere continuum of degrees of violence—there can be no politics and indeed no meaningful distinction between politics and war in his political thought. Schmitt's model for politics, like much of the Western tradition of political thought, is borrowed from the realm of organized violence. Arendt argued that political action, though sometimes occurring during wartime, is fundamentally different from the act of waging war. The meaning of war is coercion and being coerced. The meaning of politics is the freedom to act in concert with plural equals. Politics is full of conflict and disagreement. But it is also limited by the condition of plurality, that there are many and not one of us. Plurality, not homogeneity, makes politics possible. Schmitt's concept of the political and the sovereign decision is the very antithesis of the real experience of politics. Its ultimate expression is not Schmitt's struggle to the death between enemies. It is the ability to appear before plural equals and to debate, and to act to build a common public world. Arendt agreed with Schmitt that there was a need to reassert the distinctiveness and autonomy of the political against liberalism and the modern bureaucratic state. But as a defender of the absolutist concept of state power—as a fascist— Schmitt mistook the attractions of agonistic political action for the existential glory of war.

## CONCLUSION

First and foremost, the changing character of war must be understood in historical and empirical terms. But at some point is also has to be conceived in terms of political definition and even foundation, that is a terrain on which political and international order is made and remade. This is not only in the sense of political actors making rhetorical claims regarding the 'new-ness' of various forms of warfare, a point which applies to Mary Kaldor's liberal cosmopolitanism in *New and Old Wars* as much as the Bush administration's more overtly imperial and neoconservative agenda.[69] It is tempting, even easy, to make exaggerated claims regarding the unprecedented and extraordinary in military affairs because the claim itself is a form of political action. Carl Schmitt saw this clearly and tried to match his polemical formation of political and legal concepts to the political conflicts in which he was engaged. To that extent, Schmitt is useful because he reminds us of the grave dangers of too readily accepting governments' claims regarding the unprecedented and extraordinary in military affairs, a special danger in a field of inquiry occupied by defence intellectuals and others happy to adopt the language of the regime of the day. In such circumstances, political theory is reduced to political ideology and itself can become a motor for military change. The wide acceptance in recent years of politically and historically contestable claims regarding war and change has done much to raise the spectre of Carl Schmitt. His rage against liberal hypocrisy turned into a nihilistic glorification of violence. His righteous anger and then delight in unmasking this hypocrisy, to borrow Arendt's words, 'could not even be spoiled by Hitler's very real persecution of the Jews'.[70] There is a similar danger today. Some of his most recent defenders suggest Schmitt would have been among the first to condemn the neoconservative language of good versus evil, but it is difficult to see the genuine grounds for such a position.[71] There is no criterion for political legitimacy in Schmitt's work, as David Dyzenhaus has pointed out, 'other than those that are existentially determined by the participants in the battle'.[72] The danger of relying on Schmitt to illuminate the legal and political strategies of the Bush administration is that it becomes harder to think of a politics beyond Schmitt. Arendt's unusual realism is far better placed to support the institutions necessary to restrain imperial hubris.

## NOTES

1. Duncan Bell (ed.), *Political thought and international relations: Variations on a realist theme* (Oxford: Oxford University Press, 2008).
2. Robert Gilpin, 'War is too important to be left to ideological amateurs', *International Relations*, 19/1 (2005), 5–18.

3. For a wide selection of such arguments, see Louiza Odysseos and Fabio Petito (eds.), *The international political thought of Carl Schmitt: Terror, liberal war and the crisis of global order* (London: Routledge, 2007); Chantal Mouffe (ed.), *The challenge of Carl Schmitt* (London: Verso, 1999); also see William E. Scheuerman, 'Carl Schmitt and the road to Abu Ghraib' *Constellations*, 13/1 (2006), 108–24; William Hooker, *Carl Schmitt's international thought: Order and orientation* (Cambridge: Cambridge University Press, 2009).

4. Odysseos and Petito, 'Introduction', in *International political thought of Carl Schmitt*, 3.

5. Eckard Bolsinger, *The autonomy of the political: Carl Schmitt's and Lenin's political realism* (Westport, CT: Greenwood Press, 2001); Alessandro Colombo, 'The "realist institutionalism" of Carl Schmitt', in Odysseos and Petito (eds.), *International political thought of Carl Schmitt*, 21–35.

6. William Rasch, 'Carl Schmitt and the new world order', *South Atlantic Quarterly*, 104/2 (2005), 182.

7. Hans Morgenthau claimed Schmitt plagiarized the main arguments of his 1929 dissertation. William E. Scheuerman, *Morgenthau* (Cambridge: Polity Press, 2009).

8. See, for example, Lawrence F. Kaplan and William Kristol, *The war over Iraq: Saddam's tyranny and America's mission* (San Francisco, CA: Encounter Books, 2003), chapter 4.

9. Heinrich Meier, *Carl Schmitt and Leo Strauss: The hidden dialogue* (trans. J. Harvey Lomax; foreword by Joseph Cropsey) (Chicago: University of Chicago Press, 1995); William E. Scheuerman, 'Carl Schmitt and Hans Morgenthau: Realism and beyond', in Michael C. Williams (ed.), *Realism reconsidered: The legacy of Hans J. Morgenthau in international relations* (Oxford: Oxford University Press), 62–92.

10. Arendt, *The origins of totalitarianism* (new edition with added prefaces) (New York: Harcourt Brace Jovanovich, 1966), 339. Elsewhere Arendt described Schmitt as one of a number of 'outstanding scholars' who nonetheless 'did their utmost to supply the Nazis with ideas and techniques'. Arendt, 'The image of hell', in *Essays in understanding, 1930–1954* (edited and with an introduction by Jerome Kohn) (New York: Schoken Books, 1994), 201.

11. On Arendt's complicated relation to realism, see Owens 'The ethic of reality in Hannah Arendt', in Bell (ed.), *Political thought and international relations*, 105–21. For other writing on Arendt contra Schmitt, see William E. Scheuerman, 'Revolutions and constitutions: Hannah Arendt's challenge to Carl Schmitt', in David Dyzenhaus (ed.), *Law as politics: Carl Schmitt's critique of liberalism* (forward by Ronald Beiner) (Durham, NC: Duke University Press, 1998), 252–80; and Andreas Kalyvas, *Democracy and the politics of the extraordinary: Max Weber, Carl Schmitt and Hannah Arendt* (Cambridge: Cambridge University Press, 2008).

12. Jane Mayer, 'The hard cases', *The New Yorker*, 23 February 2009. In 2006, the Supreme Court ruled against the Bush administration's claim that the Geneva Conventions did not apply to the 'war on terror'.

13. On the distinction between the imperial principle 'everything in permitted' and the totalitarian principle 'everything is possible', see Arendt, *Origins of totalitarianism*, 440–4.
14. Arendt, *Origins of totalitarianism*, 447.
15. Ibid.
16. Helen M. Kinsella, 'Discourses of difference: Civilians, combatants, and compliance with the laws of war', *Review of International Studies*, 31 (2005), 180.
17. John Yoo, *The powers of war and peace: The constitution and foreign affairs after 9/11* (Chicago: University of Chicago Press, 2006).
18. Gabriella Slomp, 'The theory of the partisan: Carl Schmitt's neglected legacy', *History of Political Thought*, 26/3 (2005), 502–19; Tarik Kochi, 'The partisan: Carl Schmitt and terrorism', *Law and Critique*, 17/3 (2006), 267–95.
19. Carl Schmitt, *Legality and legitimacy* (translated and edited by Jeffrey Seitzer; introduction by John P. McCormick) (Durham, NC: Duke University Press, 2004).
20. Carl Schmitt, *The crisis of parliamentary democracy* (translated by Ellen Kennedy) (Cambridge, MA: MIT Press, 1985).
21. Carl Schmitt, *Political theology: Four chapters on the concept of sovereignty* (translated and with introduction by George Schwab; new foreword by Tracy B. Strong) (Chicago: Chicago University Press, 2005), 66.
22. Sheryl Gay Stolberg, 'The decider', *The New York Times*, 24 December 2006.
23. Schmitt, *Political theology*, 5.
24. '*Nomos* is the immediate form in which the political and social order of a people becomes spatially visible—the initial measure and division of pasture-land, i.e. the land-appropriation as well as the concrete order contained in it and following from it.' Carl Schmitt, *The nomos of the earth in the international law of the Jus Publicum Europaeum* (New York: Telos Press, 2006), 70.
25. For a discussion and critique of Giorgio Agamben's extension of Schmitt's argument to refugee camps, see Owens, 'Reclaiming "bare life"? Against Agamben on refugees', *International Relations*, 23/4 (2009), 567–82.
26. Schmitt, *Political theology*, 21.
27. Schmitt, *The nomos of the earth*, chapter 5.
28. Schmitt, *The concept of the political* (translated and with introduction by George Schwab; new foreword by Tracy B. Strong) (Chicago: University of Chicago Press, 1996), 25f.
29. Schmitt, *Concept of the political*, 27.
30. Schmitt, *Concept of the political*, 35.
31. David Dyzenhaus, *Legality and legitimacy: Carl Schmitt, Hans Kelsen, and Hermann Heller in Weimar* (Oxford: Clarendon Press, 1997), 93.
32. William Rasch, 'Lines in the sand: Enmity as a structuring principle', *South Atlantic Quarterly*, 104/2 (2005), 253–62.
33. For Arendt, what was so original about totalitarian government was, quoting Schmitt's 1934 book, *Staat, Bewegung, Volk*, 'The Movement ... is States as well as People, and neither the present state ... nor the present German people can even be conceived without the Movement.' In Arendt's words, 'The Movement

by now is above the state and people, ready to sacrifice both for the sake of its ideology.' Arendt, *Origins of totalitarianism*, 266.

34. Schmitt, *Concept of the political*, 27.
35. Schmitt, *Concept of the political*, 49.
36. Schmitt, *The theory of the partisan: A commentary/remark on the concept of the political* (translated by A. C. Goodson) (East Lansing, MI: Michigan State University Press, 2004), 431.
37. Schmitt, *Theory of the partisan*, 35, 20.
38. Schmitt, *Theory of the partisan*, 6. Too much is made of this in Odysseos and Petito where Schmitt's historical accuracy is taken for granted. It is no longer possible, if it ever was, to suggest that *Der Nomos der Erde* is 'the most compelling history of the development of international law' after the appearance of Koskenniemi's *From apology to utopia* and *The gentle civilizer of nations*. For such a claim, see Odysseos and Petito, 'Introduction', 1. Martti Koskenniemi, *The gentle civilizer of nations: The rise and fall of international law 1870–1960* (Cambridge: Cambridge University Press, 2001) and *From apology to utopia: The structure of international legal argument* (Cambridge: Cambridge University Press, 2006).
39. Schmitt, *The nomos of the earth*, 99. For an entirely persuasive dismantling of Schmitt's account of early modern warfare, and much else, see Benno Teschke, 'Fatal attraction: Re-reading the international thought of Carl Schmitt', Paper presented at Queen Mary, University of London, 7 October 2009.
40. 'Legal wars thereby take on the significance of global police operations.' Jürgen Habermas, *The divided West* (edited and translated by Ciaran Cronin) (Cambridge: Polity Press, 2006), 189. At grave risk of stating the obvious, to be sceptical of the moral claims of warmongering states and the self-appointed representatives of civilization, is *not*, as Richard Devetak suggests, to endorse the state as the highest moral authority, dogmatically reject all forms of cosmopolitanism, or posit 'non-intervention as good and intervention as evil'. See Devetak, 'Between Kant and Pufendorf: Humanitarian intervention, statist anti-cosmopolitanism and critical international theory', *Review of International Studies*, 33 (2007), 169. Devetak makes the bizarre claim because he wants critical international theorists to believe that the theoretical choice is between Schmitt and Habermas (a variation on Pufendorf and Kant). Unsurprisingly, this mirrors Habermas's presentation of the choice as (his version of) 'Kant or Schmitt'. From a totally distinct perspective, Arendt's work is significantly more cognizant of the difficult relationship between politics and organized violence than either Schmitt's or Habermas'. See Owens, *Between war and politics: International relations and the thought of Hannah Arendt* (Oxford: Oxford University Press, 2007).
41. Arendt, *Origins of totalitarianism*, viii. For a fuller discussion, see Owens, 'Beyond Strauss, lies and the war in Iraq: Hannah Arendt's critique of neoconservatism', *Review of International Studies*, 33/2 (2007) 265–83.
42. Michael Byers, 'Preemptive self-defense: Hegemony, equality and strategies of legal change', *Journal of Political Philosophy*, 11/2 (2003), 171–90.

43. For an excellent discussion, see Jean-Francois Drolet, 'Containing the Kantian revolutions: A theoretical analysis of the neoconservative critique of global liberal governance', *Review of International Studies*, 36/3 (2010), 533–60.

44. John Bolton, *Surrender is not an option: Defending America at the United Nations and abroad* (New York: Threshold, 2007).

45. Peter J. Spiro, 'The new sovereigntists: American exceptionalism and its false prophets', *Foreign Affairs*, 79/6 (2000), 9–15.

46. Jürgen Habermas, *The post-national constellation: Political essays* (Cambridge: Polity Press, 2001).

47. Hannah Arendt, *The human condition* (Chicago, IL: University of Chicago Press, 1958), 245. 'Among modern political theorists', Hannah Arendt recognized Schmitt as 'the most able defender of the notion of sovereignty. He recognises clearly that the root of sovereignty is the will: Sovereign is he who wills and commands.' Arendt, *Between past and future: Eight exercises in political thought* (New York: Viking, 1961), 296n. C.f. 'Where men wish to be sovereign . . . they must submit to the oppression of the will . . . If men wish to be free, it is precisely sovereignty they must renounce.' Arendt, 'What is freedom?', in *Between past and future*, 164–5.

48. Martti Koskenniemi, 'International law as political theology: How to read *Nomos der Erde*', *Constellations*, 11/4 (2004), 500.

49. Transcript of PBS Frontline's 'Cheney's Law', http://www.pbs.org/wgbh/pages/frontline/cheney/etc/script.html (accessed 11 March 2010).

50. William E. Scheuerman, 'Emergency powers and the rule of law after 9/11', *The Journal of Political Philosophy*, 14/1 (2006), 61–84.

51. Arendt more persuasively observed the dangers during the American war in Vietnam, the effort to establish unrestrained and unitary emergency executive authority in a war potentially without end. See *Crises of the republic* (New York: Harcourt Brace Jovanovich, 1972).

52. Koskenniemi, 'International law', 498.

53. Janice E. Thompson, *Mercenaries, pirates, and sovereigns: State-building and extraterritorial violence in early modern Europe* (Princeton: Princeton University Press, 1994).

54. Benno Teschke, *The myth of 1648: Class, geopolitics and the making of modern international relations* (London: Verso, 2003).

55. Teschke, 'Fatal attraction'.

56. Allen Buchanan, for example, argues that multilateral institutional safeguards could reduce the chances of powerful states abusing 'preventive self-defence' to pursue other (imperial) interests. Buchanan, 'Justifying preventive war', in Henry Shue and David Rodin (eds.), *Preemption: Military action and moral justification* (Oxford: Oxford University Press, 2007), 126–42. But, as usual with liberal thought, there is no account of the extent to which international institutions are also disciplinary apparatuses that help produce what current world power demands—obedient, productive, and loyal client states in the global South.

57. Arendt and Karl Jaspers, *Correspondence, 1926–1969* (edited by Lotte Kohler and Hans Saner; translated by Robert and Rita Kimber) (New York: Harcourt Brace Jovanovich, 1992), 54.

58. John Mearsheimer, 'A case study of Iraq—Analogies to Vietnam?', in Christian Hacke, Gottfried-Karl Kindermann, and Kai M. Schellhorn (eds.), *The heritage, challenge, and future of realism* (Göttingen: V&R University Press, 2005), 139–48.

59. Carl von Clausewitz, *On war* (edited and translated by Michael Howard and Peter Paret) (Princeton: Princeton University Press, 1976), 87, 592.

60. Hannah Arendt, *Eichmann in Jerusalem: A report on the banality of evil* (New York: Viking, 1963), 253.

61. Hannah Arendt, *The promise of politics* (New York: Schocken, 2005), 186; Arendt, *Origins of totalitarianism*, 467.

62. Arendt, *The human condition*, 63f.

63. Arendt, *Promise of politics*, 189.

64. Arendt, *Origins of totalitarianism*, 466.

65. Arendt, *Eichmann in Jerusalem*, 264.

66. Hannah Arendt, *The Jew as pariah: Jewish identity and politics in the modern age* (edited and introduction by Ron H. Feldman) (New York: Grove Press, 1978), 141.

67. Arendt, *Origins of totalitarianism*, ix. Emphasis added.

68. Arendt, *Eichmann in Jerusalem*, 262f.

69. Mary Kaldor, *New and old wars: Organized violence in a global era* (2nd ed.) (Cambridge: Polity Press, 2006). For an analysis of the overlap between these two otherwise conflicting positions, see Louiza Odysseos, 'Crossing the line? Carl Schmitt on the "spaceless universalism" of cosmopolitanism and the war on terror', in Odysseos and Petito (eds.), *International political thought of Carl Schmitt*, 124–43.

70. Arendt, *Origins of totalitarianism*, 335.

71. Chantal Mouffe, 'Schmitt's vision of a multipolar world order', *The South Atlantic Quarterly*, 104/2 (2005), 245–51. Schmitt opposed any idea of the potential unity of the world favouring a multipolar configuration of different regions, led by a dominant imperial power, balancing against each other.

72. Dyzenhaus, *Legality and legitimacy*, 95.

# 27

# Strategy in the Twenty-First Century

## Hew Strachan

For the historian, strategic studies today present an interesting paradox. Thirty years ago, strategic studies was a hybrid, a disciplinary mix of history, politics, law, some economics, and even a little mathematics. Today the subject has been increasingly appropriated by departments of political science, its identity often subsumed under the amorphous title of 'security studies'. As a result the study of strategy has been largely divorced from the historical roots in which it first flourished. This is not to say that history has no value for political scientists. They use case studies all the time, but they tend to choose those topics which prove or disprove a thesis, not subjects which are to be studied in their own historical contexts. Stories told without context obliterate the woof and warp of history, the sense of what is really new and changing as opposed to what is not.

This is not a historian's diatribe against a discipline other than his own. Historians can be just as guilty of tunnel vision, too readily feeding the caricatures of themselves painted by political scientists. They are the party poopers who respond to claims that all is new and different by saying the reverse (and the perverse), claiming precedents which stress continuity, not change. So, for example, if the character of war is changing in the twenty-first century, those changes can be associated with non-state actors and private military companies, both of which are familiar to early modern historians, or with terrorists and insurgents, also equally well known to historians, in this case of Napoleonic Europe or of nineteenth-century imperialism.[1] If this difference in disciplinary approach were uniformly true, what follows should be entirely predictable. Written by a historian, it should stress continuity, saying that not much that is really new is likely to appear in the twenty-first century (and in some respects it will do that). Following the same logic, if the chapter had been written by a political scientist, it would have predicted dramatic changes, presenting major threats in that recurrent cliché, 'an increasingly globalized world'.

The challenge for the historian is much harder than the identification of continuity. That is the easy bit. The next stage is to use that as the bedrock from which to identify what is really new, as opposed to what merely seems to be new, to distinguish the revolutionary and the evolutionary from the evanescent and ephemeral.[2] For the historian who looks at current strategic studies, what is striking is the apparent loss of this capacity within political science. Empiricism seems to be out of fashion. Theory, having been granted primacy, creates expectations of reality and so prevents the hard-headed interpretations of events, blocking rather than refracting the light shed on theory by change. The result, paradoxically, is that historians can be readier to identify change than are students of strategy.

Most inimical to the idea of change in strategy is a relatively new idea (another paradox), the concept of 'strategic culture', which—in the words of one historian—'has gradually gained support within the ranks of political scientists studying international relations', but 'has attracted few followers outside of political science'.[3] Jack Snyder, whose report on Soviet strategic culture in 1977 for the RAND Corporation is credited with launching the concept within the political science community, defined strategic culture as 'the sum total of ideas, conditioned emotional responses, and patterns of habitual behaviour that members of a national strategic community have acquired through instruction or imitation and share with each other with regard to nuclear strategy'. Although Snyder acknowledged strategic culture could develop and adapt, he argued that it would so only slowly: 'we also assume a large residual degree of continuity', he wrote. 'Culture is perpetuated not only by individuals but also by organizations. . . . Rationales can outlive the conditions under which they were developed and to which they were most appropriate.'[4]

Although Snyder has since distanced himself from the body of ideas to which he gave birth, two things are noteworthy about his original formulation. The first is its association with nuclear weapons, and the second is the presumption that strategic culture inhibits change.[5] These two themes are linked. In 1982, Laurence Martin, the BBC's Reith Lecturer in 1981, and professor of war studies at King's College, London, between 1968 and 1977, attributed to nuclear weapons what he called 'the deceleration of history'.[6] The Cold War both created strategic studies and then imposed on it a sort of stasis through its stress on the use of nuclear deterrence to prevent major war. The inner certainties of the strategic studies community between the 1960s and 1980s provide a healthy reminder of the dangers of hubris, especially when contrasted with the uncertainty (but also volatility and hence creativity) surrounding the subject at the start of the twenty-first century.

Since the end of the Cold War, nuclear deterrence has lost its state of semi-permanence, at least in its more evident forms, and as a result strategic culture too, at least in the formulation originally offered by Snyder, has lost some of its explicatory power—not entirely, not as an interpretative tool for the past, but in terms of its predictive value. Military historians have long been familiar with the idea that nations have particular 'ways of warfare'. Gil-li Vardi, in her contribution to this book, uses culture to explain the continuities in German military thought between the First World War and the interwar period, despite the massive discontinuity of defeat in 1918. But after 1945, Germany (albeit not the same Germany or the same army) was able to initiate such massive cultural change that the reluctance of the Bundeswehr to wage war in Afghanistan since 2006 has provoked frustration on the part of the very powers which imposed the cultural change in the first place.[7]

The father of national ways of war is Basil Liddell Hart's 'British way in warfare', first articulated in 1927 and itself a product of the marriage of history to politics. Liddell Hart linked maritime power, economic strength, and expeditionary capability to argue both that Britain possessed a distinctive national strategy and that that strategy possessed the force of continuity. What his theory could not cope with was reality. British strategic practice throughout the first half of the twentieth century and beyond defied Liddell Hart's model, despite that fact that it was precisely because of its prescriptive value that he had formulated it in the first place. Britain created a mass continental army for use in Europe in the First World War. The principal point in the 'British way in warfare' was that Liddell Hart thought that had been a mistake. He was not heeded: Britain repeated the trick in the Second World War (in defiance of fiscal and economic sense), and left the British Army on the Rhine after the war was over. Its remnants are still there.

Strategic culture may (like many theories) raise important questions about strategy for the twenty-first century, but its lack of predictive power suggests that it will leave us short of answers. This is not the view of Colin Gray, who has argued vehemently for the links between strategic behaviour and strategic culture. Gray sees strategic culture as nationally and geographically determined, the product of history and place, and therefore internalized 'within us'.[8] Gray, a student of politics, uses history to argue that not much changes. 'There is an essential unity to all strategic experience in all periods of history,' he asserted (in 1999 and in italics) on the opening page of *Modern strategy*, 'because nothing vital to the nature and function of war and strategy changes.'[9]

One thing that has changed a great deal over the last two centuries is what we understand by the word strategy. Coined in the late eighteenth century, it was barely used by Napoleon, who spoke either of grand tactics or of policy, with nothing in between. And yet it was his practice in war which inspired the writings of Carl von Clausewitz and Antoine-Henri Jomini, the first theorists to give currency and even primacy to strategy in military thought. Clausewitz's definition of strategy, 'the use of the engagement for the purposes of the war', was sufficiently close to what became the orthodoxy in the nineteenth century to be the sort of definition used by the generals of the First World War.

They saw the goal of strategy as the achievement of the decisive battle, but like Clausewitz and Jomini they located it in its relationship with tactics. However, the definition of strategy which gained currency in the light of that war, and with increasing force as the twentieth century proceeded, was very different. Its focus was not on the relationship between tactics and strategy, but on that between strategy and policy. Liddell Hart, in this respect at least, reflected what has been a common assumption since 1945 when he defined strategy as 'the art of distributing and applying military means to fulfil the ends of policy'.[10] So at the start of the twenty-first century the word 'strategy' has come to carry very different connotations from those with which it was associated at the end of the eighteenth. Gray rides roughshod over change across time and assumes that there can be a concept of strategy, and a practice derived from it, for epochs and civilizations which had no word for it. His hero, Clausewitz, knowing that strategy was a recent phenomenon, did not. Nor is Gray alone: Edward Luttwak, the author of *Strategy: The logic of war and peace* (1987), one of the most influential works on the subject of recent times, went on to write *The grand strategy of the Byzantine empire* (2009), a book which argued that the Byzantines, like the Romans before them, knew what they were doing even if they did not speak of what they knew.[11]

Implicit in this reading of strategy, and therefore in its application to our expectations for the twenty-first century, is the idea of continuity, the expectation that strategy, not least because it enshrines eternal verities, has a predictive and prudential quality. It may not enable us see to the end of the century, but it should at least help us along its next three decades or so. This is the sort of time frame set by current procurement cycles and—probably for related reasons—embraced by official think tanks, like the British Ministry of Defence's Development, Concepts and Doctrine Centre. But for the military historian, inherently reluctant to leave the past for the present and certainly not ready to embrace the future, there is a worrying naivety here, a rejection of contingency and of the role of surprise and shock. Particularly striking is an inherent contradiction between two recurrent claims of strategic studies, that strategy possesses an underlying continuity and that strategy is the use of war for the purposes of policy.

Policy occupies the domain of contingency. Of course, nations have policies which aspire to be long term and generic, but they are subject to the competing dynamics of politics. For democratic states in particular, policy has to be adaptive and reactive as well as purposeful and deliberative. If strategy is today defined as operating on the boundary between war and policy, then it is being expected to be prudent and far-seeing while also being contingent and adaptive. To that extent, strategy as it is understood by purists has a paradoxical tendency to become a peacetime business: the result of the efforts of one polity to shape international affairs, including through the threatened and actual use of armed force, in its own national interest. In the competitive and fast-moving environment of war, where neither side can monopolize control, however much each struggles to do so, the dynamic and reciprocal nature of war shapes strategy more than strategy shapes war. The 1997–8 process in Britain, which led to the Strategic Defence Review, was much trumpeted for being 'strategy-led', as though that quality gave it an underlying consistency and coherence. Over the medium term, it did no such thing. Its assumptions were completely wrong-footed by the political decisions, incapable of adequate prediction before the 9/11 attacks in 2001, to invade Iraq and then to deploy British forces to Helmand in 2006.

To square this circle, to reconcile the contrast between strategy's long-term aspirations and its need for flexibility, we need to distinguish between strategic theory on the one hand and strategy in practice on the other. Nineteenth-century strategic thinkers were better at this than those of the twenty-first century. Clausewitz sought systems which would enable him to understand war as a general phenomenon. His self-education in philosophy as an adolescent officer left its mark, prodding him to seek an explanatory theoretical framework which would be constant across time. He was constantly frustrated by his own intellectual and historical rigour: hence practice intruded, resulting in his recognition of exceptions to his own rules and producing the slipshod conclusion by lazy readers of *On war* that he rejected systems, despite that being his ultimate goal.

By following Jomini, other nineteenth-century strategic thinkers adopted a different tack when addressing the same set of problems. They stressed the principles of war, ten or so leading ideas to be used as an interrogative basis for looking at the character and conduct of individual wars. In 1909, the British army published its first ever official manual on war, the *Field service regulations*. Confronted with the imminence of colonial war, which meant fighting on the north-west frontier of India or in Afghanistan, while preparing for the more remote (but in practice not very distant) contingency of major war against Germany in Europe, it responded with a set of generic principles of war. This first edition of the *Field service regulations*, unlike those published after the First World War, has been attacked for not actually spelling out what those individual principles were. But this misses the most important principle of all: that all wars, whatever the geographical conditions and the identity of the enemy, required the application of similar considerations—whether it be that of economy of force or concentration of mass on the decisive point.

These Clausewitzian and Jominian solutions grew out of the need for strategic theory to generate precepts that were of practical application, that were of use to soldiers. However, the outcomes were very different when strategy proceeded from practice, not from abstract conceptions. Strategic theory, beginning in Clausewitz's and Jomini's day, and continuing right up until the mid-twentieth century, remained much more interested in the relationship between strategy and tactics, what would now be called the operational level of war: herein, it seemed, lay consistency across time, despite the impact of industrialization on war. It required the experience of the First World War to highlight the relationship between strategy and policy, and to spawn the terms 'grand strategy' or 'national strategy'. Both phrases were legitimated by the conduct of the Second World War and the advent of the Cold War. In the years between 1914 and 1945, strategy in practice was therefore much more concerned with the relationship between strategy and policy than with that between strategy and tactics.

That is the departure point for any analysis of strategy in the twenty-first century: the need to differentiate not only between the longer term aspirations of strategic theory and the more immediate and contingent preoccupations of strategy in practice but also to recognize that the normative statement that war is a continuation of policy is in fact an acknowledgement that strategy in practice must always struggle to possess consistency and longevity. The statement that war is a continuation of policy, however helpful to our ability to understand and define strategy, creates an entirely false sense of stability. The very use of the word 'continuation' implies a persistence and endurance which works against the recognition of change.

When Clausewitz discussed the relationship between war and policy (which in fact he did not do very much), he did so to understand better the phenomenon of war, and in particular to understand wars which did not obey what he saw as war's inherent logic, its drive towards absolutes, its escalatory dynamic. In the wars he had experienced, the wars of the French Revolution and of Napoleon, the role of policy, although obviously present, was less evident in the conduct of war than it had been in the more limited wars of the eighteenth century. His interest was in war itself and its conduct; he did not write about the causes of war. What led him to stress the role of policy in relation to war was that for Frederick the Great policy had prompted restraint in the conduct of the war, whereas for those who followed the French Revolution policy removed limitations: as he put it, 'we might doubt whether our notion of its absolute nature had any reality, if we had not seen real warfare make its appearance in this absolute completeness right in our own times'.[12] Today we too often use his normative statement about war's relationship to policy as though it applied to the causes of the war, and so fail to recognize how often states go to war not to continue policy but to change it. The declaration of war, and more immediately the use of violence, alters everything. From that point on, the demands of war tend to shape policy, more than the direction of policy shapes war. This volatility in the relationship between war and policy is what deprives strategy in practice of its consistency.

During the Cold War, the relationship between war and policy lost its dynamic quality precisely because it was used to prevent war, not to wage it. The Clausewitzian norm became a statement about war's causes, and because there was no war it became an argument that underpinned the stable balance of terror created by the threat of mutually assured destruction. By the same token, strategy became applicable to situations without war, a virtual synonym of foreign policy, and its most obvious focus was deterrence. Deterrence conflated strategic theory, with its aspirations to continuity and unchanging principles, with strategy in practice, and so that distinction too became forfeit. Strategic culture was one product of this hybridization. Half a century or so is long enough for such approaches to be deemed normal, for the distinction between strategy in theory and strategy in practice, and for the awareness of war's discontinuous effects on policy, to be forgotten or neglected—particularly in a strategic studies community less disposed to think historically.

The effect of policy is what creates uncertainty for states in relation to the use of war. Armed forces and their capabilities crave and create long lead-times. Hierarchies establish stable organizations, their more ambitious members are encouraged to plan careers in phases of twenty years or more, and procurement cycles for the technologies that shape those careers last even longer. So armed forces demand an element of certainty from strategy in practice, which strategy in practice cannot provide. Policy generates decisions to go to war over much shorter lead-times. 'While policy can turn on a dime, as the old saying goes', Colin Gray wrote in 2009 (and to quote him with approbation), 'the major capabilities available to strategy to advance policy will have lead-times that typically are measured in several years'.[13]

The spread of democratic government (if that remains a long-term object for the west and if the project is itself successful) is more likely to increase this unpredictability than reduce it. In democracies, domestic political imperatives to act can exercise greater leverage on decision-makers than may be the case in totalitarian regimes. Mrs Thatcher's decision to retake the Falkland Islands in 1982 is a case in point. Would another Conservative leader have made the same decision, given the views of senior cabinet ministers, the absence of the Chief of Defence Staff in New Zealand, and the hesitations not only of many senior civil and armed servants but also of her own defence minister? Her action, which proved to be right after the event but seemed deeply hazardous and even counter-intuitive at the time, turned her premiership round, giving her a domestic authority which she had hitherto lacked and which was not exhausted for nearly a decade.[14] George W. Bush's decision to invade Iraq in March 2003, not least while the war in Afghanistan had still not delivered on its initial objective, the capture or elimination of Osama bin-Laden, prompts similar questions. Political pressures, albeit in this case applied by close governmental associates from the Vice-President down, trumped strategic sense. Would a Democrat president have been more resistant or less to such pressures? In this case the political calculation proved wrong, and the United States was saddled with a lame-duck leader (albeit one it re-elected) for almost six years. In both cases the armed forces found that the strategies to which they had bought in were trumped by what civil–military relations theorists call 'objective' political control. Having committed themselves to a coalition within Europe, in 1982 the British mounted a major expeditionary campaign on the other side of the Atlantic. In Washington, in 2001–2, the Joint Chiefs of Staff, having similarly planned for a different sort of war, found themselves cut out of the decision-making loop by the Vice-President and the Secretary for Defense,[15] and, while the initial invasion of Iraq was brilliantly executed at the operational level, plans for the subsequent phases of the war were deliberately stifled for political reasons.[16]

Empowerment through the media is a second way in which democracy has added to unpredictability in political decision-making in the use of war. The comparative silence of political opposition in the mainstream democracies in time of war is not new; nor is the press's assumption of the role of critic and chorus-leader in its stead. Both were phenomena evident in Britain in the First World War. Without a free(ish) press many wartime leaders would have had a comparatively easy ride, however incompetent their administrations. What is newer is the role of the media, and especially the visual media, in creating a public appetite for and acceptance of the decision to use military force in wars unlike the First World War: wars of intervention, wars of choice, and wars fought at a considerable distance in areas of the world largely unknown to the public. Wars that are the product of the 'responsibility to protect' or of humanitarian need rely on television pictures to legitimate the determination to intervene. National self-interest at the governmental level can be fused with humanitarianism, so uniting right and left. The notion that human rights can trump the sovereign rights of the state, articulated by Tony Blair in his Chicago speech on 24 April 1999, was the justification of the Kosovo campaign then under way. Increasingly, and retrospectively, the same argument has been used to legitimate the wars in Afghanistan and Iraq. Commenced as campaigns intended to remove specific threats, they became struggles to create economic and human security through the establishment of good governance (so showing once again how war changes policy). The challenge which confronted President Obama in March 2009, when he announced his strategies for both conflicts, and indeed the challenge for any Democrat in the United States and all liberal interventionists everywhere, was how to limit them by redefining their objectives in terms of national self-interest without robbing them of their rationale in the courts of liberal and international public opinion.

So, if policy's part in the formulation of strategy in practice generates change and unpredictability, what can give continuity to strategy—and particularly the sort of continuity that makes it even worth talking about future strategy— particularly over as long a time frame as the course of the twenty-first century? One answer is to turn back to strategic theory, and to acknowledge that what lies at the heart of strategic theory is not policy but war itself.

War's character changes, and it does so for reasons that are social and political as often as they are technological, but war's nature still provides sufficient fixed points to make the study of war as a discrete historical phenomenon a legitimate activity. The differences between the historian's approach to war and the political scientist's can be recast to clarify the point. War shows both change and continuity, reflected in the distinction between its character and its nature. The forms of individual wars are of course profoundly affected by the circumstances of their own times, but the dynamic generated by the decisions of two sides to use armed force against each other generates recurrent features—many of them too easily forgotten because they have become clichés: the fog of war, the play of friction, the role of chance, the importance of will, the function of courage and fear. Most important of all is the reciprocity in war created by the clash of wills. War cannot be the unilateral continuation of policy by other means because both sides are using war to thwart, subvert, or change each other's policies. The clash of wills creates a clash of policies, which themselves become subject both to the requirements of waging war and to what the military is actually capable of delivering.

Strategic theory sets out to put shape on what can be inchoate and unpredictable, to apply rationality to what is disordered. But it can only do that effectively if it proceeds from an appreciation of war's nature, a point which the emphasis on war as a continuation of policy tends to downplay. The cry during the wars in Iraq and Afghanistan that strategy—both strategic theory and strategic practice—had been neglected, not only by governments, particularly those of the United States and the United Kingdom, but also by multilateral organizations, such as NATO, is a reflection of the fact that strategy has submerged itself within policy; in the process it has failed to recognize the nature of war, which lies at the heart of strategy in both its forms. By stressing the apparent rationality and logic of policy, strategy has downplayed the irrationality and different logic of war. During the Cold War, strategy too often left the business of actually conducting war to one side, and it has still not recovered.

A clear indication of this last point is the fact that by 2008–9 the challenge confronting the state in relation to the making of strategy was not normally seen in these terms. Strategy was required to predict the future. The tendency, at least in government, was to regard the failure of strategy since 1990, or even more since 2001, in terms of its failure to respond to new threats. The real issue was the lack of flexibility, and the problem was pragmatic and methodological; strategy needed to become better at asking questions, and also at responding to answers which were different from those that were expected. But the actual response veered towards futurology. A succession of high-level documents, beginning with the *European security strategy* in 2003, spoke of 'global challenges', rolling unverified statistics into a mix of issues predicated on the catchphrase that 'security is a precondition of development'.[17] In the United Kingdom, the *National security strategy*, published in March 2008, said little about war or the use of armed force but a great deal more about climate change, migration, disease, and other long-term threats to security broadly defined. The British had taken their concerns about climate change to the United Nations in March and April 2007 (although it was not always clear whether countering climate change was waging a global war or not countering it would result in global war).[18] At the beginning of 2009, James Jones, on his appointment as Obama's National Security Advisor, announced that he planned to widen the role of the United States's National Security Council from its traditional areas of responsibility in defence and foreign policy to embrace over-reliance on fossil fuels, poverty, disease, corruption, and the global economic crisis.[19] In other words the Western world, and especially Britain and America, seemed bent on reconfiguring strategy to deal with most of the globe's long-term ills as well as many of the responsibilities already entrusted to other government departments.

Such statements represent either a utopianism, which smacks of hubris and borders on unreality, or paranoia. Governments have imported into policy the academic world's determination to redefine strategic studies as security studies, have consequently confused national security with human security, and are in danger of disregarding one of the more obvious truisms of the early deterrence theorists that security can only ever be relative, never absolute.[20] Creating litanies of threats that lack specificity makes it inherently difficult to produce operational solutions. In other words there can be no national strategy—no means for action—contained in statements about global security.

However, what was also striking about Britain's *National security strategy* of 2008, especially given the date of its composition, was its pragmatism and good sense on terrorism and its implicit rejection of the so-called 'global war on terror'.[21] One of the merits of listing so many other dangers, therefore, was the consequent ability to put into perspective those to which the press headlines and the government's own actions had given greater urgency. After all, David Milliband, the then British Foreign Secretary, did not get round to renouncing the phrase for another ten months,[22] and in 2009 his government continued to justify Britain's involvement in the war in Afghanistan in terms of countering terrorism at home. By then, the British scepticism about the 'global war on terror' was also mirrored across the Atlantic.[23] In the United States, the Obama administration sought to distance itself from the phrase; the important and much more difficult question is whether it has rid itself of the thinking which underpinned it. To do that effectively it will have to go back to the drawing board of strategy.

The 'global war on terror' was simultaneously symptomatic of a lack of strategic rigour in the opening decade of the twenty-first century and a principal driver in the desire to produce 'security strategies'. Because so little strategic thinking went into counterterrorism, the threat from terrorism failed to produce adequate strategies to counter it.[24] Instead the problem was 'securitized', and so was linked to economic backwardness, governmental weakness, and religious fundamentalism, all of them bigger and more amorphous challenges which are not themselves terrorism. The effect was further to empty out the strategy from the statements on security, since without terrorism the principal threats to security came less from conflict than from natural disasters and man-made environmental mismanagement. The security strategies tended to be blithely dismissive about the danger of interstate war, and thus they lacked scenarios for war traditionally defined sufficiently credible to underpin defence budgets, many of which were still often shaped by Cold War assumptions.

So the most striking feature about statements on strategy at the outset of the twenty-first century is less their predilection for terrorism and more their near certainty that certain sorts of war belong to the past. The hypothesis is very hard to test as it is not clear exactly which sort of war is being considered: is it a war defined by its aims, in other words a war between states, or is it a war defined by its conduct, a so-called 'regular' war? Or is it a regional issue? It is true that certain neighbours who were at one point ready to fight each other— the United States and Canada, or France and Germany—seem increasingly unlikely to do so. But to extrapolate such pregnant examples from either an American context or a European one to the rest of the world, to Asia and Africa in particular, seems fanciful. The threat of interstate war remains latent between Russia and its neighbours, and Israel and its, not to mention between India and Pakistan and between North and South Korea. Moreover, those whose thinking is shaped by the Western tradition have almost no historical evidence to support a belief in the obsolescence of certain sorts of war, despite its near orthodoxy. Europe enjoyed relative peace between the end of the Napoleonic Wars in 1815 and 1848 or 1914, according to one's taste on what is a major war, but the peacemakers of 1815 were never guilty of believing that they had put the problem of war behind them. It was their very lack of hubris that made them particularly vigilant for the first thirty years of what some have seen as a century of European peace, and, as we now know, they were right to be so. True, interstate war has declined in frequency and in intensity since 1945, and the United Nations Security Council can probably take some credit for this.[25] But it has not entirely disappeared: with the exception of a couple of years in the early 1990s, it has continued at a constant, even if low, level ever since 1945. For a time, civil wars (which are of course frequently about statehood and nationality) took their place, but that surge was above all generated by the aftermath of colonial withdrawal and the end of the Cold War, and it abated during the 1990s as the newly formed states established their monopoly of armed force.[26] The evidence for such optimism with regard to the likely incidence of 'traditional' or modern (as opposed to 'postmodern') war in the future seems to derive largely from another hypothesis developed by political scientists but about which historians are deeply sceptical—that of the 'democratic peace'. The thesis that democracies do not fight each other either rides roughshod over differences between types of democracy or has to operate with so many exceptions that it is really unsustainable. But, instead of being thrown out, it has been widened into more general norms, including the self-evidently bogus notion that democracies are inherently reluctant to wage war.

There is a paradox locked in the heart of the national security strategies. Before the 9/11 attacks, when defence departments engaged in scenario building designed to imagine where wars might occur in twenty or thirty years time, and over what (themselves classic illustrations of the use of strategy for predictive purposes), they focused on the possibilities of conflict generated by scarcities of resources. The twin phenomena of climate change and urbanization seemed likely to create competition for water, fuel, and food. The presumption was that if assets such as health, wealth, and nutrition were in short supply, we would fight for them rather than distribute what we have through multinational organizations or by some form of global government. But, if this scenario building is followed through to its logical conclusion, it suggests that free trade will be abandoned and economic autarchy will be prevalent: the haves will hold on to what they have, and the have-nots will have to fight to get what they need. Control of territory will be an important indicator of relative wealth and will also be a crucial ingredient in economic capacity. The so-called 'resource wars' were remarkably familiar before the stabilization of national frontiers, and if they recur a likely consequence will be battles between neighbours along and across their mutual borders. This is a reasonably immediate issue not just for states in areas becoming subject to desertification but also for more northerly (and highly sophisticated) states which abut the Arctic. The need to control sea lanes and natural resources is producing competing claims to the land mass under the melting ice cap and has already led to the assumption that the region will be 'militarized'.[27] If these issues are not resolved without war (and of course they may be: so far the states irrigated by the Nile have managed to agree on the use of its water without conflict), then the wars that follow seem likely to be remarkably traditional—wars fought between states for control of territory.

The biggest challenge that confronts strategy today and tomorrow is not terrorism; it is, as it always has been, war, and possibly even war in its more traditional form, interstate war. Strategy is the only tool we have for conceptualizing armed conflict and—if war breaks out—for directing it, but strategy in the absence of actual war cannot be certain of where such a war will occur, between whom, and for what ends. So, if strategy is a science, it is a very imprecise one—and, in the vocabulary of the physicist or chemist, the matter with which it deals is both very volatile and unpredictable in its effects. Strategy aspires to control and direct war, but will always struggle to do so, because war has its own dynamic, which is independent of the rational calculations of any one actor. True, from the perspective of western Europe and even of North America, as well as of the Antipodes and of some other places in the world, interstate war appears to be the least of our worries. But that is precisely the challenge. Can we in the West therefore go one stage further and consign more traditional definitions of war to the rubbish bin of history? The focus on terrorism, which may be a more immediate and recurrent problem, obscures the fact that, were an interstate war to occur, it would be a far more serious issue. Strategy therefore matters: however imperfect it is as an intellectual tool, it is the best we have for the task available.

States—or, rather, some states—remain the most powerful military actors in the world, and the issues surrounding statehood still generate more wars than the issues surrounding resource availability or climate change. Britain's insouciance about interstate war is remarkable given that it has fought against another state four times in the last quarter century—to retake the Falklands in 1982, to drive Iraq out of Kuwait in 1990–1, to protect the Kosovars in 1999, and to topple Saddam Hussein in 2003. Moreover, the deployment of British troops to Sierra Leone and to Afghanistan was an example of armed conflict where the issues were ones of governance and state formation. If Britain is an example, states have not abandoned using war as a continuation of policy. The growth of private military companies has been the consequence, above all, of the state's continued desire to employ armed forces, and is therefore a product of the state's economic muscle as much as of the post-heroic societies on which those states rest.[28]

All this does not mean there has not been change in the state's use of war. States have stopped using total war or major war as an instrument of policy. This is where strategic theory has been slow to adapt to the tenets of strategic practice. The doctrines of the armed forces of NATO rest on the idea of the 'spectrum of conflict', and at one end of the spectrum is 'general war' or all-out nuclear exchange. Strategic theory has still not adequately responded to the absence of 'general war', not just since 1990 and the end of the Cold War, but since 1945 and the end of the Second World War.[29] The world has suffered only one total war, defined as such while it was being waged by those who fought it, and that was the Second World War after both the Soviet Union and the United States entered it in 1941. The First World War was not generally identified as a total war until after it was over.[30] The theoretical force of the Second World War has been with us ever since, partly because the idea of total war was present in the literature of warning produced in the 1930s, partly because the total war of 1941–5 was then found to have precedents, and partly because the conclusion to the war—the dropping of the atom bombs on Hiroshima and Nagasaki—carried its own warnings. As a result total war became the foundation stone for strategic theory in the second half of the twentieth century, and its contribution to that theory was deterrence.

Nor was it just the advent of nuclear weapons that confronted major wars with redundancy after 1945. Many states, both in Europe and Asia, remain reluctant to use military force because of the memory of the Second World War and its horrors; it may be the 'good' war for the countries that fought fascism, but for those they defeated (and even for some of those that did the defeating) the scale of the war has become an argument for preventing wars, not waging them. Self-deterrence, although often not declared, is crucially important to the more general success of deterrence. For central Europe, and for Japan, war lacks political utility: they have, in some senses, become profoundly un-Clausewitzian.

Like most of the basic nostrums of deterrence, this one is absurdly simple. The fact that deterrence became a driver in the design and procurement of nuclear weapons in the Cold War resulted in a determination to over-theorize, and the additional and frequently unnecessary intellectual baggage of deterrence may have been one reason why it was too readily ditched from the vocabulary of strategy after 1990, especially on the Atlantic's eastern seaboard. But deterrence is still in play, albeit in ways that are largely unrecognized and therefore unsung. The principal function of deterrence is to prevent total or major war, not to provide the excuse for lesser wars. This is not to say that deterrence cannot operate to prevent lesser wars or that deterrence cannot operate within war. But wars initiated in order to 'restore deterrence', an argument used in the United States to justify pre-emption and in Israel to explain the use of force against its neighbours, represent a failure of deterrence. One reason why so much attention has shifted to terrorism and to non-state actors in the discourse on war is that deterrence is one of the factors that has made major war between states an ineffective tool of policy.

The success of deterrence since 1990, however unacknowledged, has not in fact denied military force its utility. Some states remain robustly ready to use military force in the pursuit of policy goals. To name only the most obvious and immediate, Russia did so in south Ossetia in 2008, Israel in Gaza in 2008–9, and the United States in Iraq and Afghanistan in 2002 and 2003. But all these states have used military force within constraints. Geographically, wars have remained more regionally focused than the rhetoric of globalization and especially of the 'global war on terror' suggest. Temporally, despite the prolongation of many wars, the timetable for withdrawal frames strategy. Militarily, major states do not bring their full resources to bear and do not mobilize either their economies or their peoples for war. Most significantly of all, nuclear powers treat each other with restraint: neither India nor Pakistan used the Mumbai terrorist attacks of November 2008 as an excuse to expand the latent hostility between them.

Therefore, as well as deterrence, there is another concept which has also gone out of fashion but which needs rethinking, and that is limited war.[31] During the Cold War, the wars in Korea and Vietnam and the proxy wars fought in Africa or Latin America, which melded colonial withdrawal with Communist-inspired revolutionary warfare, had at their roots ideas which were capable of expanding wars, not contracting them. But the participants often had an interest in curbing the effects of these ideas. Global revolutionary war, however beloved in the 1960s by communist theorists and by the writers of counter-insurgency textbooks, was trumped by those who waged it. For the belligerents themselves, the objective was national independence. For their sponsors, the superpowers, the balance of terror created by the possession of nuclear weapons provided an incentive for containment, not expansion. Future wars, if fought over resources between neighbours, could be limited not only geographically but also ideologically. Here, as elsewhere, the character of war changes through reversion to older forms as well as through genuine innovation.

Like the limited conflicts within the Cold War, the wars of the early twenty-first century are not ideologically constrained. The objectives for which wars are waged—for the advancement of democracy, for the furtherance of Islam, or for the protection and promotion of human rights—are remarkably grandiose and open ended. In the wars waged since the 9/11 attacks, both sides have actively pursued the globalization of their causes, so that the issues at stake are at odds with the means employed. If states are genuinely engaged in a 'long war', as Philip Bobbitt has argued,[32] or a 'global insurgency', the term which David Kilcullen has used,[33] or even the war of the twenty-first century or the 'global war on terror', the two phrases employed by George W. Bush, then they are setting about it in a very strange way. The mismatch between ends and means suggests that strategy in practice is flawed.

In the first decade of the twenty-first century, policy and the use of war have been at odds with each other. The United States fought its wars in Afghanistan and Iraq under the banner, first, of the 'global war on terror' and, then, of 'the long war'. Broadly speaking, the United States's allies, despite declaring their solidarity with America after the 9/11 attacks, did not follow its lead. They even rejected the use of the word 'war' in relation to countering international terrorism. In Britain, in early 2009, both the Prime Minister, Gordon Brown, and the Secretary of State for Defence, John Hutton, stressed that British troops were fighting in Helmand in the national interest, but at the same time the Ministry of Defence refused to say that Britain was at war.[34] From the public's perspective, the evidence of killed and wounded soldiers, brought to them by the media and also by charities like 'Help for Heroes', implied the opposite, that Britain was indeed at war. The same discontinuities between thought and action, between policies and within policy, were played out across other states in Europe, in different ways and at different tempos.

Some of these differences have been evident in the differences between politicians and their senior service advisors. Our image of strategy is that it is formed at the interface of the civil–military relationship, whose weight in most democratic strategic theory rests on the relationship between the governments and their armed forces. But absent from the theory, certainly as it was developed in the Cold War and particularly in the work of Samuel Huntington, is the role of what Huntington called 'subjective control'.[35] In one of his most important passages, Clausewitz used the metaphor of the Christian trinity to capture the nature of war, the three elements being passion, the play of probability and chance, and logic or reason. From this he derived a secondary trinity, the actors in a nation at war, more than the characteristics of war itself—the people, the armed forces, and the government. Western norms concerning the formation of strategy at the beginning of the twenty-first century focus on the armed forces and the government but neglect the people.[36]

Where are the people in strategy today? Counter-insurgency strategy, as expressed for example in the US Army Field Manual 3–24, published in December 2006, is well aware of the people as the object in war, of the need to gain the support of the population in the country where insurgents are active.[37] The United States armed forces are also determined to ensure the support of the American people for the war, having concluded after the Vietnam War that it had lost the war on the television screens of American citizens. However mistaken that is as diagnosis of the reasons for America's defeat, its legacy was evident in the determination to have retired officers appear on television as pundits during the war in Iraq.[38] Also influential here is the phrase used by General Sir Rupert Smith in *The utility of force*, published in 2005, that wars today are 'wars among the people'. That particular insight is not as new as the frequency with which it is cited, especially in relation to the sorts of counter-insurgency campaigns and peacekeeping operations of which Smith and other British soldiers have so much experience. Both Northern Ireland and Bosnia taught that lesson. Much more challenging for strategy is another of his insights, that contemporary warfare is a form of theatre, played out by a small, separate group (i.e. a professional and not a conscript army), orchestrated by a team of unseen directors, stage managers, and lighting engineers, but watched by many more.[39]

The people are the audience for war. Colin McInnes has used the analogy not of theatre but of 'spectator-sport warfare'.[40] Sporting events, for example a World Cup football match played out by two teams of eleven players, command global television audiences of millions. Similarly, the limited wars of today are rendered unlimited by the mechanisms of their reporting. Moreover, the technologies now employed—blogs, websites, mobile telephone images— mean that the distinction between combatant and reporter is removed. The combatant is his own reporter, and because the reporter interprets the events which he or she observes, almost in real time, the reporter is no longer a neutral but a participant.[41]

The newness of the challenge posed by non-state actors in war to our understanding of strategy is less the fact that they do not belong to states than the fact that they have displayed a better understanding of the 'trinity' of strategy. Like Maoist guerrillas, at least in Maoist theory, they recognize that the people must be participants, even if only passive and secondary ones, not neutral onlookers. One of the most enduring criticisms of NATO strategy in Afghanistan has related to its public communications, where the Taliban has enjoyed the advantage of tempo and also, at times, of content. But the means by which propaganda (the word is not pejorative, but accurate: another example of how Western states loosen their grip on ideas by relaxing their use of language) is disseminated ensures that the message to the people of Afghanistan is also potentially the same message to the people of the United States, however different their economic circumstances or their religious or political beliefs. Thus the people in the audience are not just the people in the war zone, nor even the populations of all the belligerent states, but the court of world opinion. It really is like a World Cup match. What has perplexed Western governments is less the fact that they have struggled to win over the other side's potential supporters, which is always going to be a struggle, and more that they have not got their own crowd cheering them on. The populations of NATO states can support the players, that is, the armed forces, but they withhold support for the team managers and for the war itself.

There may be a danger here of mistaking the specific for the general: reluctance to support an unpopular war may not be the same as a refusal to support all wars waged in the name of the nation. But there is still a general observation to be made, which is that—paradoxically—democratic states seem to be frightened by the democratization of war reporting. If democratic states believe that their armed forces are fighting for democratic objectives, then the democratization of the popular battle space should in the long run produce better coordinated strategy: people, armed forces, and government should really become three in one.

So far strategic theory has yet to get its head round this aspect of twenty-first century strategic practice. This is potentially a classic illustration of how strategic theory is developed. Experience, and the experience of failure, is fed back into theory in order to give it purchase on the future by its incorporation of the lessons of the past. Above all, strategy provides the strategic narrative (and there can be no such narrative without strategy in the first place), within which government and army can understand what is going on and communicate that understanding to the people. That narrative then gives the context into which specific episodes in a war can be placed. When the Western, democratic state can do that better than it was doing it in 2009, it will have reconsolidated its position in the strategic firmament.

For a historian to argue, as this essay has done, in terms that combine change and continuity is no more than a matter of sticking to his last. Much of the change suggested here is a change backwards, a reversion to the ideas of deterrence and limited war, and such changes—particularly when they refer to ideas which were current in strategic theory until comparatively recently, can therefore also be seen as forms of continuity. The wars waged at the start of the twenty-first century were still predominantly the products of national, religious, and ethnic identity; their aims remained governance and state formation. Paradoxically, however, they have been seen as wars of a new variety, principally because we have mistaken the character of individual wars for war's normative nature. The wars of the later twenty-first century may well be waged for assets, to which we feel in theory all humanity should have equal access but for which in practice we compete. But if we cannot share resources without war, then we are most likely to fight for them as members of states or multinational alliances, since only thus will we have the leverage to use war effectively. But, if what therefore happens is indeed another change backwards, a reversion to the sorts of wars waged in Europe at least until 1648, and in some respects to 1789, and to the sorts of wars waged outside Europe until the end of empire, then there is hope that they can also be limited. If wars for resources replace wars of ideologies, if the notion of the 'global war on terror' and the 'long war' prove as locked in the circumstances and timing of their coining as this essay thinks likely, then the wars of the later twenty-first century have a chance of being ideologically empty and geographically contained. For that optimism to be also realism (and so to mix schools of international relations theory), then the strength of the state remains not only a sine qua non but also central to the coherence of deterrence. Deterrence is not just about nuclear weapons, but short of an effective non-proliferation regime it remains the most effective envelope within which their possession can not only be contained but also contribute to world security. But that thought, like everything else written here, assumes that security is relative, not absolute.

## NOTES

1. See, for example, the chapters by David Parrott and Michael Broers in this book.
2. See the quotation from Marc Bloch, *Strange defeat*, cited in the introduction, p. 13.
3. Lawrence Sondhaus, *Strategic culture and ways of war* (London: Routledge, 2006), vi. It is noticeable that the first edition of the textbook, *Strategy in the contemporary world: An introduction to strategic studies*, edited by John Baylis, James Wirtz, Eliot Cohen, and Colin Gray (Oxford: Oxford University Press, 2002), contained no chapter on strategic culture; that was only added in 2007, to the second edition.
4. Jack Snyder, *The Soviet strategic culture: Implications for limited nuclear operations* (Santa Monica, CA: RAND, 1977), 8f.

5. See the comparative definitions given by Sondhaus, especially under the heading of 'durability/changeability', *Strategic culture*, 124f.; for the development of Snyder's own thinking, 3–6.

6. Laurence Martin, 'Security in an insecure age', *Naval War College Review*, 35/5 (1982), 1. For an earlier attack on deterrence theory and its problems with identifying change by the present author, see Hew Strachan, 'Deterrence theory: the problems of continuity', *Journal of Strategic Studies*, 7/4 (1984), 394–404.

7. A point made at the Changing Character of War conference by Sibylle Scheipers.

8. Sondhaus, *Strategic culture*, 126; see Colin Gray, *Strategy and history: Essays on theory and practice* (Abingdon: Routledge, 2006), 151–69.

9. Colin Gray, *Modern strategy* (Oxford: Oxford University Press, 1999), 1.

10. Quoted, significantly enough, by John Baylis, James Wirtz, Eliot Cohen, and Colin S. Gray (eds.), *Strategy in the contemporary world: An introduction to strategic studies* (Oxford: Oxford University Press, 2002), 4.

11. Edward Luttwak, *Strategy: The logic of war and peace* (Cambridge, MA: Harvard University Press, 1987), 62–5, 138; contrast 239f.; the relevant books by Luttwak are *The grand strategy of the Roman empire from the first century A.D. to the third* (Baltimore, MD: Johns Hopkins University Press, 1979), and *The grand strategy of the Byzantine empire* (Cambridge, MA: Harvard University Press, 2009). For a recent assertion of similar points, see Beatrice Heuser, 'Strategy before the word: ancient wisdom for the modern world', *Journal of the Royal United Services Institute*, 155/1 (2010), 36–43.

12. Carl von Clausewitz, *On war*, translated by O.J. Matthijs Jolles (Washington, DC: Infantry Journal Press, 1950), book 8, chapter 2, 570.

13. Colin Gray, *After Iraq: The search for a sustainable national security strategy* (Carlisle, PA: Strategic Studies Institute, US Army War College, 2009), 38.

14. Lawrence Freedman, *The official history of the Falklands campaign*, volume I (Abingdon: Routledge, 2005), 208–11.

15. Bob Woodward, *Bush at war* (New York: Simon & Schuster, 2002), 24, 44, 61, 99, 128f., 174f.; Seymour Hersh, *Chain of command: The road from 9/11 to Abu Ghraib* (London: Harper Collins, 2005), 176; Frederick W. Kagan, *Finding the target: The transformation of American military policy* (New York: Encounter Books, 2006), 289–300, 326–8; Michael Gordon and Bernard Trainor, *Cobra II: The inside story of the invasion and occupation of Iraq* (New York: Vintage, 2006), 38–47; Steven Metz, *Iraq and the evolution of American strategy* (Washington, DC: Potomac Books, 2008), 120f., Thomas E. Ricks, *Fiasco: The American military adventure in Iraq* (London: Penguin, 2006), 37, 40f., 66f., 89f.

16. James Fallows, 'Blind into Baghdad', *Atlantic Monthly*, Jan/Feb 2004, 53–74; Anthony H. Cordesman, *The Iraq War: Strategy, tactics and military lessons* (Washington, DC: Greenwood, 2003), 153–71, 496–509; Kagan, *Finding the target*, 333–45; Metz, *Iraq and the evolution of American strategy*, 130–44; Ricks, *Fiasco*, 78–81.

17. *A secure Europe in a better world: European security strategy*, 12 December 2003; see also Anne Deighton's chapter in this book.

18. Andrew Clark, 'Climate change threatens security, UK tells UN', *Guardian*, 18 April 2007.

19. *Economist*, 12 February 2009.

20. Janne Haaland Matlary, 'Much ado about little: The EU and human security', *International Affairs*, 84/1 (2008), 131–43; see also Mary Kaldor, 'Human security: A new strategic narrative for Europe', *International Affairs*, 83/2 (2007), 273–88.

21. Cabinet Office, *The national security strategy of the United Kingdom: Security in an interdependent world*, Cm 7291 (March 2008), 4, 10 (para 2:1), 11 (para 2.9), 28 (para 4.15).

22. *Guardian*, 15 January 2009.

23. Oliver Burkeman, 'War on terror is over, overseas contingency operations begin', *Guardian*, 26 March 2009.

24. See Audrey Kurth Cronin's contribution to this volume.

25. Vaughan Lowe, Adam Roberts, Jennifer Welsh, and Dominik Zaum (eds.), *The United Nations Security Council and war: The evolution of thought and practice since 1945* (Oxford: Oxford University Press, 2008), 44–58.

26. Ibid, 47, albeit followed by less optimistic comments on 49; Jean-Pierre Derriennic, *Les guerres civiles* (Paris: Presses de Science Po, 2001), 261–70 is cautiously positive; but see especially the contribution of Stathis Kalyvas to this book.

27. Tom Parfitt, 'Russia plans military force to patrol Arctic as "cold rush" intensifies', *Guardian*, 28 March 2009; 'Russia won't bully Canada in Arctic', *Globe and Mail* (Toronto), 27 March 2009; see also Jeffrey Mazo, *Climate conflict: How global warming threatens security and what to do about it*, Adelphi paper 409 (London: Routledge for the International Institute for Strategic Studies, 2010).

28. See Sarah Percy's chapter in this book.

29. John Mueller, *Retreat from doomsday: The obsolescence of major war* (New York: Basic Books, 1989); Idem., *The remnants of war* (Ithaca, NY: Cornell University Press, 2004).

30. Hew Strachan, 'On total war and modern war', *International History Review*, XXII/2 (2000), 341–70.

31. Hew Strachan, 'Strategy and the limitation of war', *Survival*, 50/1 (2008), 31–53.

32. Philip Bobbitt, *Terror and consent: The wars for the twenty-first century* (London: Penguin, 2008); self-evidently, this chapter profoundly disagrees with Bobbitt's use of history, and his attempt to build a structure on false foundations. For a critical (and in this writer's opinion well-founded) criticism, see Adam Roberts, 'Limits of a new-age worldview', *Survival*, 51/2 (2009), 183–90.

33. David Kilcullen, 'Counterinsurgency *redux*', *Survival*, 48/4 (2005), 111–30; David Kilcullen, *The accidental guerrilla* (Oxford: Oxford University Press, 2009), 12–16; see also John Mackinlay, *The insurgent archipelago from Mao to bin Laden* (New York: Columbia University Pres, 2009); for a critique of 'global insurgency', see David Martin Jones and M.L.R. Smith, 'Whose hearts and whose minds? The curious case of global counter-insurgency', and a riposte by John Nagl and Brian M. Burton, 'Thinking globally and acting locally: Counter-insurgency lessons from modern wars—A reply to Jones and Smith', *Journal of Strategic Studies*, 33/1 (2010), 81–121 and 123–38.

34. Gordon Brown, 'We are about to take the war against terror to a new level', *Observer*, 22 March 2009; Richard Norton-Taylor, 'Hutton tells allies to "step up to the plate" over Afghanistan', *Guardian*, 16 January 2009.

35. Samuel P. Huntington, *The soldier and the state: The theory and practice of civil-military relations* (Cambridge, MA: Harvard University Press, 1957), 80–5.

36. See also Pascal Vennesson's chapter in this book.

37. *The U.S. Army \* Marine Corps counterinsurgency field manual: U.S. Army field manual No. 3–24: Marine Corps warfighting publication No. 3–33.5* (Chicago, 2007; first issued 15 December 2006), passim, but for example 5–4, 5–60 to 5–80, 7–8.

38. 'Behind TV analysts: Pentagon's hidden hand', *New York Times*, 20 April 2008.

39. Rupert Smith, *The utility of force: The art of war in the modern world* (London: Penguin, 2005), 284–5.

40. Colin McInnes, *Spectator sport war: The west and contemporary conflict* (Boulder, CO: Lynne Rienner, 2002).

41. Nik Gowing, *'Skyful of lies' and black swans: The new tyranny of shifting information power in crises*, RISJ Challenges (Oxford: Reuters Institute for the Study of Journalism, University of Oxford, 2009).

# Conclusion

## Absent War Studies? War, Knowledge, and Critique

*Tarak Barkawi and Shane Brighton*

War, as father
of all things, and king,
names few
to serve as gods,
and of the rest makes
these men slaves,
those free.

Heraclitus, Fragment 44[1]

### INTRODUCTION

While destructive, war is a generative force like no other. Little in human existence goes untouched by it. As a maker, breaker, and transformer of politics, society, economy, and culture, it is almost beyond comparison: occupying historic junctures and switchpoints to an extent and in ways quite unlike any other social activity. Accordingly, the changing character of war concerns relations between the transformation of polities and societies through war and the effects of those transformations on war itself. In this chapter, we begin with the observation that knowledge about war is caught up in these transformations, in this field of relations between war, politics, and society. We focus on the relationship between war and knowledge about war, and offer a view of the impact of the changing character of war on war studies.

We begin with a question: why, despite its historical omnipresence and vital importance in processes of historical change, has war never become the primary subject of an academic discipline? Why does the Anglo-American academy lack a discipline of 'war studies'? This is not, of course, to suggest that nobody studies war. Neither is it to suggest that much current and past study of war is 'undisciplined' or lacking in quality, insight, or rigour: the reader need look no further than the other chapters of this volume to dispel such a view.

Nor are we suggesting there are no university programmes or departments where such work is done. 'War studies' does occasionally crop up in university prospectuses, albeit mostly in the United Kingdom. Rather, we note that other fundamental dimensions of human existence—society, economy, and politics, for example—have become the subject of dedicated academic disciplines found in any university worth the name and supported by national academic professional associations and an array of journals and other attributes of disciplinarity. We ask: why not war?

For us, it is especially significant that much work that might be considered 'war studies' rarely centres war as the object of analysis. The question of what war *is* rarely receives sustained attention. Further, with the partial exception of strategic studies (which we consider below), inquiry tends to apprehend war through other domains of life, be it economy, society, culture, ethics, law, or what not. This observation—what we term the *decentring* of war—is a starting point for our critique of the heralded 'interdisciplinarity' of war studies. Below, after some discussion of the absence of war studies, we argue that the nature of war poses special epistemological difficulties that, among other effects, deprive war studies of the kinds of foundational problematics and objects of inquiry around which scholarly disciplines and projects develop. We attend also to the power/knowledge dynamics set in train by the tensions between war and knowledge about war, and by their mutual implication in politics. In doing so, we offer a framework of 'War/Truth' which extends well beyond academic knowledge about war but nonetheless impacts upon its possibilities in fundamental ways.

Like many writers in this volume then, we situate the changing character of war within its myriad relations with politics and society. In their introduction to this volume, Sibylle Scheipers and Hew Strachan draw a sharp distinction between the 'empirical manifestations' of change and continuity and the 'conceptual fabrications' of scholars. We foreground, first, the not always obvious mutual relations between these and, second, the need to position scholarly 'fabrications' in relation to those operationalized within governments, militaries, and the wider public discourse through which war is conducted. At the centre of these relations between concepts and reality is knowledge about war. The plurality of views on this subject—attested to by the impossibility of a single, unifying academic discipline—tells us much of the character of war itself, albeit obliquely and in a manner requiring a reflective, critical approach. Through describing how war disrupts knowledge (and thereby generates the need for new knowledge) and how this process of disruption and generation has direct consequence for political authority, we address the third aspect of change and continuity Scheipers and Strachan identify: politics. The legitimation of political authority, we conclude, is constituted in no small measure through authoritative narratives about the relation between war and truth about war. Focusing on uncertainty and the disruption of knowledge in war—the impossibility of any final authoritative War/Truth narrative—also provides us with an account of continuity in warfare and its wider social and political implications.

## KNOWLEDGE, DISCIPLINARITY, AND THE ABSENCE OF 'WAR STUDIES'

The study of war has a rich classical heritage. From Herodotus, Thucydides, and Xenophon, through to Caesar, Josephus, Polybius, Marcellinus, and Vegetius, over to Sun Tzu and Ibn Khaldun, up to Machiavelli and Edward Gibbon, and crowned by a philosopher-soldier, Carl von Clausewitz, there is a tradition more than sufficient to get a modern intellectual enterprise off the ground. The reason for this heritage is obvious: war's ubiquity in human history. 'Peace', the idea of a social order from which war is abolished, is a relatively recent invention.[2] Even so, 'peace' managed to more or less banish war from social and political thought. As Michael Mann observes, 'from the Enlightenment to Durkheim most major sociologists omitted war from their central problematic' believing 'future society would be pacific and transnational'.[3] Proceeding in this manner was possible even as wars raged inside and outside Europe because many Enlightenment thinkers understood civilization as a teleological process through which violence—barbarous, rude, uncivil— was being removed from society.[4] Alternatively, as for some eighteenth-century theorists, war was a pathology generated by the politics of commercial competition between states, to be avoided by restructuring commerce.[5] More generally, rational inquiry and debate, embodied in the academy, were conceived as the very antithesis of force and as chief instruments in the progress of civility, a view elegantly recapitulated by Jürgen Habermas as the 'forceless force of the better argument'.[6] Today, this othering of violence from inquiry is registered institutionally in the scarcity of university departments and scholarly associations principally devoted to war.[7]

Even so, aspects of war are studied in disciplinary subfields, most extensively military history and military sociology, and also in literature, anthropology, psychology, and psychiatry. Scholars of international relations widely study war and it plays a significant role in the study of culture and memory broadly conceived, as well as in public opinion research. Not least, war has its own policy science, strategic studies, found in military history, political science, and international relations, and practised in staff colleges, national security planning staffs, and think tanks. What, then, is missing?

Scholarly disciplines and their institutional apparatuses presuppose some core object of inquiry, such as society or economy. They divide on how to understand and approach this object and significantly, if not frequently, dispute just what this object *is*, how best to characterize it. In the absence of a discipline, war itself is not centred as the object of analysis and debate in this way, as itself the focus of a continuing scholarly conversation. At issue are the concerns of *some other* scholarly conversation, such as the relationship between war and state building, the effects of war on public opinion and elections, the war proneness of the international system, the legality of war, or war's consequences for society. Whatever insights may be derived about these subject matters, they do not centrally concern war per se. Of course we learn much of war through studies of these and other kinds. But all too frequently what war consists of is taken for granted, usually as only the clash of arms.

We are highlighting here in an initial kind of way how it is that war is strangely decentred and fragmented as an object of inquiry, a problem intensified by the institutional diversity of the sites where war is studied. As H.A. Durfee comments, 'since Heraclitus proclaimed that "war is the king of all" the ontological foundations of war and peace have been seriously neglected, even though war and peace as social phenomena have been a daily concern'.[8] Broadly speaking, attention has been fixed on particular *wars* rather than *war* as a general force. The historiography concerning various wars is extensive, but there is remarkably little in the way of thought on war as such. John Keane understates, 'political reflection has lagged far behind empirical events'.[9] Set against the staggering totality of armed conflict and its consequences in modern history, the social and political theory of war is remarkably thin, amounting to a handful of major works and essays.[10] An instance of war may command extraordinary political and popular attention, yet scholars and thinkers neglect the problem of war.

In sum, studies of 'war and *x*'—as in 'war and society' or 'war and the state'—involve a decentring of war as well as its apprehension through, and reduction to, other domains. We offer in the conclusion of this chapter the formulation 'war *in* society' as a corrective. Underlying this decentring is the more fundamental problem of the conceptual black hole surrounding the notion of war itself. What is it? How ought we to think about it, inquire into it, and situate it in relation to other social phenomena? Questions of this sort require collective and sustained scholarly endeavour and debate. What is missing is a scholarly project that takes war as its central object of analysis and is adequate to it. Below we illustrate and develop some of these points and in doing so, critique the 'interdisciplinarity' of actually existing war studies.

## WRITING ABOUT WAR

It is worth beginning with strategic studies, seemingly an exception to the argument that inquiry is not centred on war. In fact, we suggest, strategy is not about war per se, but about how to prevail in it, or more broadly, how to use military and other instrumentalities to attain or secure interests and other valued ends. Clausewitz's 'definition' of war as the continuation of politics with the addition of other means is in fact a strategic appropriation of war, a plea for the rational direction of war from the standpoint of policy. In contemporary terms, strategic studies is primarily an instrumental science concerned with how to survive and flourish in a world of competing armed powers. The domain of inquiry is limited to what is useful and relevant to strategy, with consideration of historical cases usually designed to extract general lessons or principles.[11] This domain may be conceived narrowly or broadly but the overall direction is to conceive war in strategic terms, from the standpoint of rationality and interest.

Strategic studies is located amid what we term 'the War/Truth nexus', that is, caught up in the politics of knowledge surrounding war. While there are scholars in university posts who study strategy and write strategic analyses, by far the greatest producers of strategic discourse are states, particularly foreign policy and 'defence' bureaucracies. Additionally, in the Western democracies this field is populated by political parties, legislators and their staffs, think tanks, interested corporations, the media, retired generals and officials, and so on. Questions of strategy more or less directly concern the ultimate values and purposes of a polity, not to mention the more material interests at stake in arms procurement and foreign policy. A host of political investments, commitments, and powers are regularly at stake in a way that is only exceptionally the case in most other fields of inquiry in the social sciences and humanities.

As a field of inquiry, strategic studies has an 'axis of cohesion' in its instrumental standpoint towards war.[12] Its frequently impressive analytical coherence derives directly from this focus. Elsewhere, under the banner of 'interdisciplinarity', the lack of such an axis hobbles actually existing war studies. In practice it becomes a series of diverse topics from different disciplinary perspectives. A sense of the difficulties involved can be gleaned from a representative text, *War*, edited by Lawrence Freedman and published in Oxford University Press's 'Oxford Readers' series. Used in the flagship undergraduate and master's degrees in the world's leading department of war studies at King's College, London, it is organized in sections of readings with the following titles: 'The experience of war'; 'The causes of war'; 'War and the military establishment'; 'The ethics of war'; 'Strategy, total war and the great powers'; 'Limited war and developing countries'. As a set of descriptive categories, these capture a great deal of writing in strategic and war studies. But the volume leaves unanswered a core question: how are these categories justified conceptually or theoretically? What unifies this field of inquiry other than an unexamined use of the word 'war'? Although it would seem an essential, even elementary, task, the editor of *War* is able to provide almost nothing in the way of either definitions or theories of war.[13] Freedman's introduction argues that an important reason for studying war 'is that very little else in human affairs can be understood without reference to it'. But the closest he comes to a definition or theory is 'war is a function of ambiguities in the state system', vaguely reducing war to an epiphenomenon of international politics.[14] If something is so important that we cannot understand anything in human affairs without it, either there should be a battery of theoretic approaches, as in any other serious field of social and political inquiry, or developing such approaches should be the first order of business.

The failure to realize the inadequacies of studying war only as a collection of disparate topics from various disciplines and perspectives is a significant one. When the Department of War Studies was refounded at King's College, London, in 1962, the idea of studying war 'in the round', through the lenses of different disciplines, was a progressive move that helped lift the study of war out of staff colleges and the narrower pursuits of military history. Reflecting back on that period in his autobiography, the department's founder, Michael Howard, wrote:

> The history of war, I came to realise, was more than the operational history of armed forces. It was the study of entire societies. Only by studying their cultures could one come to understand what it was that they fought about and why they fought in the way they did. Further, the fact that they did so fight had a reciprocal impact on their social structure.[15]

Howard's conceptual categories—'cultures', 'societies'—are somewhat basic and reified. His core insight, however, is that war is shaped by and shapes its social context, with the clear implication that war cannot be studied merely as the conduct of military operations, much less as the history of decisive battles. Rather, it demands a mastery of phenomena covered by a variety of disciplines. Howard's *The Franco-Prussian War* sought to make good on this promise, centring the war but situating it and the militaries that fought it amid political and social context as well as their respective cultural dispositions. Key to this model of the history of a war is Howard's own polymathic scholarship, combining political, military, and social history, and bringing them to bear on the origins, course, and consequences of the Franco-Prussian War. Howard provided here a solid beginning for war studies, but not one without problems. He made no effort to theorize his approach, either in terms of method or a substantive theory of war. Moreover, political, social, and cultural phenomena are all dealt with historically; there is no effort to critique, revise, and incorporate theoretic traditions from the social sciences. However limited in these respects, Howard's model of interdisciplinarity was to bring to bear insights and approaches from a variety of scholarly viewpoints *in one study*. This was a war and society approach that sought to keep war centred while also placing it in broader context.

These fragile beginnings ran into the 'virtually unbreakable' structure of the established disciplines.[16] Other historians, such as Brian Bond, did much to replicate and advance Howard's achievement in respect of the histories of other wars and periods. But even at its best, 'interdisciplinarity' in war studies departments and programmes came to mean having scholars from a few disciplines who worked on their separate projects related to wars and militaries. This is *multidisciplinarity*, where scholars retain their separate disciplinary identities and practices. Unsurprisingly, departments of this sort have not advanced the project of war studies adequate to its object, nor have they begun to address the conceptual difficulties associated with such a project raised in this paper. Rather, as in Freedman's *War*, war studies amounts to collecting together the work of scholars from different disciplines, as well as other writers, on subjects related to war. There is no cumulative, interactive scholarly project centred on war.

## THE ONTOLOGY OF WAR

This absence is in no straightforward sense an outcome of intellectual failure. For us, it stands as evidence of a wider set of dynamics in the study of war that become apparent only when war itself is analysed anew. We do this by offering some propositions about the ontology of war. These centre upon those elements of war that shape it as a knowledge problem, but they are not reducible to epistemology. We seek to say something fundamental about what war *is*, not simply about the challenges of knowing about it, although the two are importantly linked. In addition, we approach war as a question for ontology because—through the functioning of 'War/Truth'—we take it to be an event of ontological significance for politics and society as such.

So, what can be said of the ontology of war, of that fundamental character which manifests itself in each instance of war and is true of war in general? As we suggest above, given the vital centrality of war in the making and unmaking of politics and society, this is a question posed with extraordinary infrequency. It is the absent centre of a dissipated body of inquiry concerned almost exclusively with war in the particular. War presents itself in historically specific ways and most writing about it reflects this. Analysis of war beyond the specific manifestation of a particular war tends to arise only as a consequence of analytical failure. Strategists and policymakers alike, when faced with apparently insuperable problems in their own time, seek to recover eternal verities from the disparate narratives of past campaigns.

A proper approach to the ontology of war does not seek to resolve this discomforting tension, as though some decision were possible between 'war' and 'wars' as the proper object of analysis. Rather, we propose to take it as a basic framework from which to proceed. We are not the first to do so. Clausewitz, who has been described tellingly as both historically specific to the point of irrelevance and a source of timeless insight,[17] also grapples with the universal and the historically contingent character of war, what we would call its *historicity*, in Book I of *On war*. We consider this effort shortly. For now though, we note a difference between perspectives produced by strategists, commanders, staff officers, soldier poets and memorialists, and academic literature such as the 'war and society' tradition. These participant perspectives, with varying degrees of directness, centre on *fighting*—the reciprocal, organized use of armed force whether past, current, or potential. Fighting is that which thematically unifies war in general and the particular—'war' with 'wars'—and no ontology of war can exclude it. However, what fighting *is*, how its effects might be understood, and how they should be positioned within a fundamental theory of war cannot be taken for granted. From the perspective of an ontology of war that might find a social scientific approach to it, to focus on fighting simply as the Clausewitzian duel and the efforts of combatants misses its wider implication and importance.

That analysis of fighting tends to be limited to the 'kinetic exchange' between combatants and the immediate problems of managing and sustaining it is, we suggest, an outcome of the historicity of war. War's reality as an actual and potential threat is such that it compels an instrumental relation to it, such that knowledge about war is never fully outside an order of necessity war itself creates. Fighting always entails the problem of how to survive and prevail, and the question of the appropriate instruments and means by which to do so occupies the minds of soldiers, strategists, and political leaders who embark on war. The question is what is occluded by such instrumentalization—by the order war creates—and what might be said of the wider ontological significance of fighting? Before approaching this question we offer a first observation on the ontology of war and war as a knowledge problem: war is defined by fighting or its immanent possibility and, as an historical presence in the lives of those who seek to understand it, this definitive element resists disinterested analysis, while tending to instrumentalize perspectives on war.

One work that describes the powerful grasp of war on thought, notable even though its comments on war are almost incidental to its philosophical objectives, is Emmanuel Levinas's *Totality and infinity*. An extended essay on the relationship between ontology and ethics, Levinas's work begins from the proposition that the proximity between war and knowing is fundamental, asking rhetorically whether or not '...lucidity, the mind's openness on the true consist[s] in catching sight of the permanent possibility of war?'[18] His point is the pervasive, if not always recognized or acknowledged, influence of war on knowledge, the 'truths' of which are understood here as a function of public rationality and institutions, oriented towards the flourishing and survival of the polity. Examples include the notion of the military—and therefore political—indispensability of the Prussian Junkers, or that of the technological supremacy of the United States, or its self-conception as an 'exceptional nation' greeted everywhere as a liberator. War for such ideas and the institutions based on them serves as a reality against which their truths are tested. Despite dissimulations by political figures and official organs, 'the trial by force is the test of the real', a point of vindication or failure for those who might speak truth about political reality.[19]

So far, this orientation appears to offer an imperative for instrumentalized strategic thought, for getting it right or facing ruin on the battlefield. But where Clausewitz identifies war as a political instrument, Levinas goes further to suggest there can be no rational comprehension of politics, no political calculation without understanding how 'in advance [war's] shadow falls over the actions of men'. Vitally, this imbrication of war and truth goes beyond the narrow framework of strategic thought and public rationality. That it does so is revealed in the reality of war itself, the violence of which: 'does not consist so much in injuring and annihilating persons as in interrupting their continuity, making them play roles in which they no longer recognize themselves' in an 'order from which no one can keep his distance'. While fighting remains a kinetic exchange, the Clausewitzian *Schlacht*, and the most fundamental element of war, it is also an event or process with the ability to draw in and disrupt wider certitudes and coordinates of human life, to shape and accelerate the transitory and mutable in human affairs: a 'casting into movement of beings hitherto anchored in their identity . . . by an objective order from which there is no escape'.[20]

This transformative power, the capacity to rework the reality of social and political existence is, of course, the objective of waging war. War drives change and strategy is both the science of its management and the means to a 'superior peace'. But Levinas's point (and the basis of his ethical intervention) is that, irrespective of their being rendered such in strategic calculus and destroyed as such in fighting, people and things are not only, or even primarily, brute facts, strategic datum. Rather, while never completely reducible to such, they are bearers of meaning: manifestations of contemporary truth. They are by extension, products, outcomes, and authors of social, political, economic, and technical processes. Reinvested with full meaning, fighting marks the disruption of this wider order—the unmaking and remaking of certainties, of meaning and potentially, the coordinates of social and political life.

As the basic element of the ontology of war then, fighting drives the intellectual instrumentality of truth about war through its historicity and immediacy, but always exceeds the terms of that immediacy. This 'excess', the capacity of organized violence to be more than kinetic exchange, to be generative—to 'cast into motion' subjects who are then alienated from themselves and come to know themselves and the world in new ways—is, we claim, the centre of the ontology of war, that which gives war its status as an ontological event. From this critical standpoint we hold on to the ontological primacy of fighting, but wrest it from the instrumentality its historicity demands. We note that in doing so the material and intellectual importance of this historicity: how war has the power to draw in contemporary resources—technical, social, political, and intellectual—unmake and rework them in ways that cannot be foreseen. This disordering and reordering shapes both the problematics of strategic thought and the subjective violence, the violence to meaning, to which Levinas testifies. We note also that this violence exceeds the standard 'conservative' and 'liberal' enframements of war: in its contingency and destruction it exceeds the strategic calculi of war as an instrument of policy; in its generative power of remaking it exceeds reduction to its destructive consequences alone.

It is not simply troops who are required to 'march towards the sound of the guns' to meet an uncertain fate, but social and political orders, and they do so in ways that far exceed the formal duration of hostilities. The potential of fighting to unmake fundamental aspects of the polities and societies engaged in it also imposes within them a burden of remaking: a generative necessity in which power and order are at stake and for which comprehension of war itself, its institutions, technologies, and their social and political significance is implicated. Consider the long process by which the American polity recovered and reordered itself from the shock of Vietnam, a process that involved everything from the attitudes of university students (from protest to careerism) to the future wars the military planned to fight (from the political mire of 'small war' to the operational elegances of the 'AirLand battle'). We return to these generative properties of war below.

## KNOWING WAR: CLAUSEWITZ'S 'SPECIAL PROBLEM'

We noted with approval Clausewitz's effort to describe and theorize on the basis of the historicity of war. Returning to his analysis allows us to further illustrate and deepen some of these points concerning the ontology of war. In book I of *On war*, he expresses the tension between war in the universal and particular through the metaphor of the 'true chameleon that slightly adapts its characteristics to a given case', going on to argue that as a 'total phenomenon' war is *'more* than' this true chameleon.[21] This 'more than' we take to be fundamental and, to some degree at odds with Clausewitz's refusal to consider war as an object of analysis in itself. More than a true chameleon, war's adaptation across time is not superficial, but more radical altogether—something he suggests can be only fully captured within the encompassing socio-political ontology of the trinity: the historically contingent and constantly transforming structure of people, government, and military. Preceded by the primary trinity of passion, reason, and contingency, relations between each of these societal elements, 'deep-rooted in their subject and yet variable in their relationship to one another', are liable to change such that pursuit of a fixed, transhistorical account is 'totally useless'.[22]

As a comment on the ontology of war, this statement might be taken to confirm the intimate link between fighting, polity, and society. As a statement of uncertainty and an expression of the limits of knowledge about war, it might superficially be taken as secondary to the neater, more famous dicta that precede it: war as 'the pursuit of policy with the admixture of other means', as 'duel', as 'wrestling match'. These after all, are taken to define his position, have attracted the approval of 'Clausewitzians' and provoked his critics to suggest Clausewitz's analytical utility has ceased.[23] From the perspective of the ontology of war, however, are his remarks on uncertainty not also the points at which Clausewitz tells us what war 'is'?

Answering this question properly requires us to return to the duality of fighting identified above and recognize that *On war* proceeds along two separate but intimately linked analytical axes: that Clausewitz sought to write both as a staff officer offering guidance on strategy to his colleagues and policymakers, and as philosopher of war whose primary concern was less instruction than interpretative, descriptive analysis. *On war* rests then, on a tension between the need to write of war both strategically and descriptively. On the one hand, to write in a way that produces certainties through identifying and methodically limiting uncertainties, in which uncertainty is viewed above all instrumentally and as a problem for the conduct of operations; and on the other hand, in a register that recognizes uncertainty *itself* is that which is most enduring, most *certain* in war.[24] Viewed from the first perspective, war cannot stand alone as an object of analysis, since strategy and policy must frame inquiry. From the second perspective though, war emerges differently.

Again, we would suggest that a 'decision' between these two analytical registers is not necessary or desirable: offering an ontology of war requires that both be grasped and their relationship accounted for. For now though, we suggest that uncertainty in war needs to be analysed not in the first instance as a practical problem but as a defining characteristic, as part of that which provides the unity of war in general and particular, as that which is inescapably and centrally part of the ontology of war. So how might 'uncertainty'—a nebulous and unhelpful concept to be sure—provide a foundational element for the study of war?

Clausewitz consistently accompanies his positive dicta about war with qualifying comments about the role and centrality of uncertainty, the absence of knowledge and, correspondingly, the importance of chance and luck. This extends from the conceptual problem of theorizing war in general, to a proper understanding of the qualities required for command, to the challenge of providing advice on the actuality of the battlefield. (Indeed, he suggests uncertainty on the battlefield is the main barrier to offering a positive theory of the conduct of war.) This is the context in which Clausewitz's account of 'friction' and danger in battle are to be understood since here, in fighting and the potential for fighting, the essential activity of war, we find the point at which uncertainty is generated. This is the point also at which the presence of uncertainty is generalized as a knowledge problem, wherein *'the light of reason is refracted in a manner quite different from that which is normal in academic speculation'*.[25] In battle and on campaign, the only certainty is uncertainty and 'the general unreliability of all information' must be taken for granted. A recurrent theme in his efforts to describe war's basic nature, perhaps more definitive and certainly more recurrent in his analysis even than *die Schlacht* is its resistance to and potential to disrupt certainties. This presents 'a special problem in war' in that 'for lack of objective knowledge one has to trust to talent or to luck'.[26]

We mark in particular Clausewitz's use of the term 'special' to describe the problem of knowledge both in and about war—the continuity of the knowledge problem between his theorization of war and his comments on its conduct. It is a special problem first because it is unique: it pertains to war in ways and to an extent that has no direct parallel elsewhere, although, we will suggest, its significance goes well beyond war alone. Second, it is special because it is consistent. All who experience war can be certain of encountering uncertainty. The 'special problem' of knowledge is common to war as a protean phenomenon across ages immemorial; it is that which always in part occludes war—'more than a true chameleon'—from those who would seek to know it. Even 'the face of battle', seemingly the most direct source of knowledge of fighting, is, as John Keegan reminds us, only ever partially glimpsed by those who participate and perhaps the hardest of analytical objects for those who would study it.[27] Searching for the ontology of war leads to a basic paradox: that which is most continuous is the absence of continuity, that most certain the absence of certainty.

## WAR/TRUTH

Fighting then, presents itself superficially as the duration of the clash of arms. But this duration is equally an always contingent, yet potentially decisive, switchpoint, or emergent event in which both strategic instrumentality and the order of public reason which permits and contextualizes it are stretched, distorted, and potentially unmade. In fighting, reason and knowing are, to use Clausewitz's term, 'refracted', like light projected through an irredeemably distorted optic beyond which no one can expect to see with clarity (although some might compensate more skillfully for its effects). In this way, an initial sense of war's wider importance as an ontological *event* for politics and society becomes apparent. The enframing certainties of pacific order, of identity, continuity, and certainty always exist subject to war's undoing, to the threat that the composition of our objective order of social and political truth might be unmade in ways that cannot be fully seen in advance, or necessarily understood afterwards. The duration of fighting is a time of contingency with the power to draw in and disrupt previous continuities and certainties. The essential nature of war is thus the actual and potential undoing of all that stands as essential: both its ontological structure and its ontological status as an event centred on the undoing of certitudes. As an event then, it is always in excess of the formal or juridical duration of fighting. This excess places war beyond the discrete ontology that fighting evidences to take on an elemental function within 'peace', such that orders of peace consist in significant measure of veiled traces and effects of fighting.[28]

Clausewitz's emphasis on war as uncertainty and correspondingly the importance of critique, judgement, and 'genius' in military command were of a piece with the post-Kantian idealism of his day—a conceptual framework he mobilized to good effect against writers such as Bülow, Jomini, and other rationalists whose excessive Cartesianism he considered dangerous.[29] But there is a far more important dimension to the relation between his circumstances and his position in *On war*. His emphasis on the chaotic and unpredictable unmaking of certainties reflected both his military experience and the violent social and political transformation to which he was witness: the impact of the Napoleonic way of war on a profoundly conservative military and society still enthralled by the campaigns of Frederick the Great. Clausewitz was a member of a small group of military intellectuals who struggled to reform the Prussian service against a monarchy that resisted change and proclaimed its command of war with reference to an authoritative Frederician legacy.[30] This past record of military supremacy not only determined the training of troops and the conduct of war on the battlefield but also legitimated the social order around which the Prussian army was formed and in which it found expression. Clausewitz spent a substantial part of his career seeking change in a deeply conjoined social, political, and military regime that brooked no revision until its humiliation by Napoleon at Jena and Auerstadt and which, after Napoleon's final defeat, set about undoing the work of the reform movement.[31]

The ontology of war then, was not simply a conceptual problem: it was political. Mastery of the means of war and who spoke authoritative truth about war were inseparable from the regime of truth and power to which he was subject. In prizing hereditary social status above dangerously French notions such as meritocracy, this regime determined his own chances of advancement and command just as it limited his soldiers' capacity to manoeuvre effectively against their enemy. In Clausewitz's thought and writings, the separation of strategy from policy and the trinitarian separation of the executive from military and population, were calculated interventions that would bolster the function of the nascent Prussian general staff in military matters and limit the power of what Clausewitz and his fellow reformers saw as an ineffectual, strategically inept hereditary monarchy.

It is this dimension of Clausewitz's account, one that situates him historically and his writing politically, that we foreground and which we take to be most significant. The power to speak truth about war, to embody the Prussian tradition, was central to a social order and the legitimation of political authority. This linkage between authoritative knowledge about war and the legitimation of power—the need to exercise power from within a collective narrative of which the event of war is a fundamental element—is, we suggest, a consistent and fundamental character of politics as such. The intimate relation between authoritative knowledge about war, symbolic proximity to martial tradition, and the legitimation of power we bring together under the term 'War/Truth'.

While the power of War/Truth is clearly apparent in the political context of Prussian military reform, a cursory glance at recent events shows its operation no less. The Blair and Bush administrations that initiated military action in Iraq both invoked the need to act against Saddam's regime as an extension of armed struggle against tyranny, for which the defeat of Nazi Germany stood as an exemplary precedent.[32] This narrative of emancipatory violence was one in which they positioned their own actions—one which Blair had not only invoked previously to justify action against the Serbs over Kosovo but had situated within a doctrine of 'international community' that he saw as inseparable from the civil order of world politics.[33] Both leaders suffered serious loss of legitimacy as their strategic project foundered. Their discourse about the war lost authority, while their ability to sustain authoritative power as executives declined. Later, for Bush at least, the apparent success of the 'surge' partially recast his fate as far as Iraq was concerned. The strenuous efforts of war leaders generally to shape public discourse and perception is further indication of War/Truth's powers: powers extending well beyond the reputation of leaders to shape entire social and political orders.

## CONCLUSION: WAR STUDIES AND 'WAR IN SOCIETY'

We alluded earlier to the generative power of war, something that with more space than that available here we might have illustrated in reference to the 'gunpowder revolution' in early-modern Europe and its determinacy for the centralization of state power, bureaucracy, and the European diplomatic system.[34] We might add the vital role of war in the consolidation of state education and the production of other powerful 'civil' systems of expertise such as town planning, medicine, and engineering. Here though, we have made an additional claim regarding the generative power of war: the centrality of War/Truth in the production and sustaining of political order—something that both makes other civil practices possible and provides their context. Such orders and the practices they enable exist in a plural world in which other powers wield the threat of war. A consequence is an intimate interarticulation between political authority and knowledge about war. This fundamental function of War/Truth in the determination of social and political orders sets war apart within the sociology of knowledge. War's very proximity to power and the possibility of control delimits and defines the status of knowledge about war in distinct ways, which allows us to return to our opening observation about the absence of war studies in a new way.

The relation between political power and knowledge about war means that the academic study of war finds itself uniquely constrained and in continual competition with state institutions and their civilian advocates in ways that are unique. Discourse about war, in scholarly and public spheres, is shaped by military staffs, defence ministries, state executives, their combined public relations operations, the media, and civilian defence intellectuals who set university research and curriculum agendas. Social and political orders have enormous and varied investments in War/Truth. In this context, critical perspectives—to say nothing of an entire discipline, if such a thing were possible—beginning from the uncertainty of war present a challenge to the vital foundation of political authority itself, since such authority rests in part in its own authoritative claim to knowledge in a manner that stresses the conjoined certitudes of its own political tradition and powers of command. To analyse the nature of war and trace its effects in reference to an unknowable, never quite controllable field of contingency is to question the basic presumptions of competence on which political authority rests.

This challenge becomes clearer yet when we recognize that the nature of War/Truth is inherently creative, less a product of the generative powers of war than a primary site for their realization. To function, War/Truth requires the imposition of retrospective certitudes on the contingency of war. Thus, war as an historical event, a site of contingency and uncertainty in its own time and a complex, contested interpretative challenge subsequently, must be tamed into a discursive element of contemporary power. To play its role in the legitimation of a political order, the uncertain, contingent, and disruptive historical event of war must be reduced to a securing, normative certainty. Thus, the final element of war's ontology is its power to remake what is unmade. War drives the remaking of social and political certitudes, not least authoritative certainties about war itself.

The absent centre of war studies then, stands as a direct expression of the relation between war and knowledge about war. The historicity of war as we have described shapes the institutionalization of its study: dissipating it across disciplines while rendering it effectively beyond disciplinization. The institutional manifestation of 'actually existing war studies' thus remains disjointed, itself a contingent combination of forces in which the instrumental logics of strategic studies—the policy science of armed force—inevitably pass for a central axis of cohesion. Our intent here is not to suggest that, somehow, our argument takes us beyond 'War/Truth' and the historicity of war, as though some position outside history were possible. Nor by extension, do we place our own scholarship beyond the ontology of war. Rather, we have indicated how, as a consequence of War/Truth, there is little in the social order that is not in some way related to war. There is little exterior to the orders war creates. But scholars in the social sciences and humanities operate in a mostly pacific universe. The result is that we misname and misconceive that around us as belonging to the order of peace and not that of war. By implication, in writing war back into the polity—in engaging war *in* society—we make a potentially democratizing move, wresting war and authority over knowledge of it from the exclusive control of any central political authority and the knowledge complex around it. To those who study war, we propose War/Truth as an object worthy of research, albeit one from which objective distance stands as a methodological aspiration rather than a given. This worth lies not least in its potential for conceptualizing the wider social and political impact of change and continuity in war.

## NOTES

1. Heraclitus, *Fragments* (New York: Penguin, 2003), 29.
2. Michael Howard, *The invention of peace* (London: Profile, 2000), 1, 6.
3. Michael Mann, *States, war and capitalism* (Oxford: Blackwell, 1988), 147.
4. John Keane, *Reflections on violence* (London: Verso, 1996), 14ff.
5. Istvan Hont, *Jealousy of trade* (Cambridge, MA: Harvard University Press, 2005).
6. Jürgen Habermas, *Moral consciousness and communicative action* (Cambridge MA: MIT Press, 1990), 23.
7. Potential exceptions include the Society for Military History and The Inter-University Seminar on Armed Forces and Society. However, neither 'military history' nor 'armed forces and society' are the same objects as 'war'. See the argument about the 'decentring' of war below.
8. H. A. Durfee, 'War, politics, and radical pluralism', *Philosophy and Phenomenological Research*, 35/4 (1975), 549.

9. Keane, *Reflections on violence*, 6–7.

10. Setting aside Clausewitz and the tradition of strategic thought, the list of important theoretic works more or less directly concerned with war includes: Hannah Arendt, *On violence* and *The origins of totalitarianism*; Frantz Fanon, *The wretched of the earth*; Michel Foucault, *Society must be defended*; Keane, *Reflections on violence*; Vladimir Ilyich Lenin, *Imperialism*; Machiavelli, *The art of war*; Mao, *On guerrilla warfare*; Lewis Fry Richardson, *Arms and Insecurity*; Carl Schmitt, *Theory of the partisan*; Martin Shaw, *Dialectics of war*; Paul Virilio and Sylvère Lotringer, *Pure war*; Kenneth Waltz, *Man, the state, and war*; Michael Walzer, *Just and unjust wars*; Quincy Wright, *A study of war*.

11. Historical survey is frequently the methodological basis for strategic analysis. To cite two major examples, Clausewitz studied hundreds of campaigns as the basis of his theoretical work and Liddell Hart's most important work *Strategy: The indirect approach* (London: Faber, 1954) began as *The decisive wars of history* (London: Faber, 1929).

12. Andrew Abbott, *Chaos of disciplines* (Chicago: University of Chicago Press, 2001), 140.

13. The sole exception is two pages by Quincy Wright on definitions of war. Wright, 'Definitions of war', in Lawrence Freedman (ed.), *War* (Oxford: Oxford University Press, 1994), 69f.

14. Freedman, 'General introduction', in Freedman (ed.), *War*, 3, 5.

15. Michael Howard, *Captain Professor* (London: Continuum, 2006), 145.

16. Abbott, *Chaos of disciplines*, 149.

17. Cf. Martin van Creveld, *The transformation of war* (New York: Free Press, 1991); Mary Kaldor *New and old wars* (Cambridge: Polity, 1991); Colin Gray, *Modern strategy* (Oxford: Oxford University Press, 1999).

18. Emmanuel Levinas, *Totality and infinity: An essay on exteriority* (Pittsburgh: Duquesne University Press, 1969), 21.

19. Ibid.

20. Ibid.

21. Clausewitz, *On war* (London: Everyman, 1993), 101. Italics added. While Howard and Paret's translation is a less than literal rendition of Clausewitz's '*Der Krieg ist also nicht nur ein wahres Chamaeleon . . .*', it does convey the sense of his argument.

22. Ibid.

23. There have been various 'post-Clausewitzian' theories of war that begin with critical departure from his work, most offering critiques of Clausewitz's state-centrism and his insistence on the primacy of politics. Kaldor, for example, explicitly distanced what she termed the 'new wars' of the post-Cold War period from 'old wars' of the sort Clausewitz described. In his *History of warfare*, John Keegan describes war as 'cultural' rather than 'political'. Van Creveld argues that the 'asymmetric' character of much contemporary conflict places it outside the military activity described in *On war*. For a useful collection of essays, see Gert de Nooy, ed., *The Clausewitzian dictum and the future of western military strategy* (The Hague: Kluwer, 1997).

24. For an overview of Clausewitz's account of chance and uncertainty, see Katherine Herbig, 'Chance and uncertainty in *On war*', in Michael Handel (ed.), *Clausewitz and modern strategy* (London: Frank Cass 1989), 95–116.

25. Clausewitz, *On war: a biography*, 133. Italics added.

26. Ibid., 161.

27. John Keegan, *The face of battle* (London: Penguin, 1978), chapter 1.

28. For a sustained analysis of the civil order as an 'order of battle', see Michael Foucault, *Society must be defended* (London: Allen Lane, 2003), esp. 14–17, 50–2.

29. See Azar Gat, *A history of military thought* (Oxford: Oxford University Press, 2001), 141–51.

30. For biographical detail on Clausewitz's role in Prussian military reform, see Hew Strachan, *Clausewitz's On war* (New York: Grove, 2007), chapter 1.

31. For broader historical analysis of the Prussian military reformers, see Karl Demeter, *The German officer-corps in society and state 1650–1945* (London: Weidenfeld & Nicolson, 1965); Peter Paret, *Yorck and the era of Prussian reform* (Princeton, NJ: Princeton University Press, 1966); and *Clausewitz and the state* (Oxford: Clarendon Press, 1976); William Shanahan, *Prussian military reforms 1786–1813* (New York: Columbia University Press, 1945); Walter Simon, *The failure of the Prussian reform movement* (New York: Cornell University Press, 1955).

32. For media discussion of the politics of this analogy, see: http://www.guardian.co.uk/world/2003/feb/19/iraq.artsandhumanities, accessed 2 May 2009. There are numerous sources that testify to the moralization of the 'Iraq issue' in neoconservative thinking and the explicit comparison between Iraq under Saddam and Germany under Hitler. See for example, Paul Wolfowitz's comments to the *New York Times*, reproduced in Thomas Ricks, *Fiasco: The American military adventure in Iraq* (London: Penguin, 2006), 16.

33. Prime Minister Tony Blair, speech on 'Doctrine of the international community', 24 April 1999, http:///www.number-10.gov.uk/output/Page1297.asp

34. See Clifford Rogers (ed.), *The military revolution debate* (Boulder, CO: Westview, 1995).

# Index

# DATE DUE

| | |
|---|---|
| 10/05/11 | |
| MAY 2 2 2012 | |
| MAY 2 4 2012 | |
| SEP 1 0 2014 | |
| | |
| | |
| | |
| | |
| | |
| | |
| | |
| | |